MANAGEMENT

SECOND EDITION

THE WEST SERIES IN MANAGEMENT

CONSULTING EDITORS
DON HELLRIEGEL Texas A & M
JOHN W. SLOCUM, JR. Southern Methodist University

ALDAG AND BRIEF Managing Organizational Behavior
BURACK Personnel Management: Cases and Exercises
BURACK AND SMITH Personnel Management: A Human Resource Systems Approach
COSTLEY AND TODD Human Relations in Organizations
DOWNEY, HELLRIEGEL, AND SLOCUM Organizational Behavior: A Reader
HELLRIEGEL AND SLOCUM Organizational Behavior, 2d Ed.
HITT, MIDDLEMIST, AND MATHIS Effective Management
HREBINIAK Complex Organizations
HUSE Organization Development and Change, 2d Ed.
HUSE Management, 2d Ed.
IVANCEVICH, LYON, AND ADAMS Business in a Dynamic Environment
KELLEY AND WHATLEY Personnel Management in Action: Skill Building Experiences, 2d Ed.
MATHIS AND JACKSON Personnel: Contemporary Perspectives and Applications, 3d Ed.
MORRIS AND SASHKIN Organization Behavior in Action: Skill Building Experiences
NEWPORT Supervisory Management: Tools and Techniques
RITCHIE AND THOMPSON Organization and People: Readings, Cases, and Exercises in Organizational Behavior, 2d Ed.
SCHULER Personnel and Human Resource Management
SCHULER AND HUSE Case Problems in Management
SCHULER, McFILLEN, AND DALTON Applied Readings in Personnel and Human Resource Management
VEIGA AND YANOUZAS The Dynamics of Organization Theory: Gaining a Macro Perspective

WEST PUBLISHING COMPANY
St. Paul   New York   Los Angeles   San Francisco

MANAGEMENT

SECOND EDITION

EDGAR F. HUSE

Completed with the assistance of

Randall S. Schuler
University of Maryland

A study guide with self-correcting exercises has been developed to assist you in mastering important concepts that you will encounter in this text. It is available from your local bookstore under the name *Study Guide* to accompany Huse's *Management, Second Edition,* prepared by Pat Long and David Gray.

Illustrations: Brenda Booth
Design and art direction: Janet Bollow
Copy editing: Margaret Jarpey, Naples Editing Services
Indexing: Sheila Ary, Naples Editing Services
Composition: York Graphic Services, Inc.

COPYRIGHT © 1982 By WEST PUBLISHING CO.
　　　　　　　　50 West Kellogg Boulevard
　　　　　　　　P. O. Box 3526
　　　　　　　　St. Paul, Minnesota 55165

Library of Congress Cataloging in Publication Data

Huse, Edgar F.
　　Management.

　　(West series in management)
　　Rev. ed. of: The modern manager. c1979.
　　Includes bibliographical references and indexes.
　　1. Management. I. Title. II. Series.
HD31.H825　　1982　　　658.4　　　81–16204
ISBN 0–314–63256–5　　　AACR2
1st Reprint 1982

INTL. ED. ISBN 0–314–68190–6
1st Reprint 1982

CONTENTS

CHAPTER 2
THE EMERGENCE OF MANAGERIAL THOUGHT   29

CHAPTER 3
SYSTEMS—DIAGNOSING THE ORGANIZATION
57

CHAPTER 4
MANAGERIAL DECISION MAKING
79

PART II   PLANNING

CHAPTER 5
ESTABLISHING OBJECTIVES

CHAPTER 6
THE PLANNING PROCESS   139

CHAPTER 7
STRATEGIC PLANNING   163

PART III   ORGANIZING

CHAPTER 8
STAFFING AND MANAGING
HUMAN RESOURCES

CHAPTER 9
ORGANIZATIONAL DESIGN— BASIC PRINCIPLES

223

CHAPTER 10
ORGANIZING EFFECTIVELY   249

PART IV   CONTROLLING   279

CHAPTER 11
FUNDAMENTALS OF CONTROL   281

CHAPTER 12
SELECTED CONTROL TECHNIQUES   305

CHAPTER 13
DESIGNING EFFECTIVE
CONTROL SYSTEMS   329

PART VI MANAGEMENT AND THE ENVIRONMENT   495

CHAPTER 23
SOCIAL RESPONSIBILITY AND
THE ENVIRONMENT   573

CHAPTER 24
THE INTERNATIONAL ENVIRONMENT   595

PART VII   A CONCLUSION AND A BEGINNING   615

CHAPTER 25
EFFECTIVE MANAGING—A COMPARISON
AND A SUMMARY   617

FOREWORD

Edgar Huse was nearing completion of this revision of *The Modern Manager* when he died on January 31, 1981. He had suffered a heart attack in June of 1980, but despite the urging of his family to work less, he felt there were important changes he wanted to include in this revision. So, it is with a mixture of sadness and pride his children and I view this edition: sadness, that he will not enjoy the publication of the book on which he worked so hard; and pride, that we have his books as a memorial to him and his work.

Ed began his study of workers and organizations shortly after we were married in 1950. I feel privileged that he shared with me his ideas and insights as they evolved from his early work in efficiency studies and the selection process to encompass the complex science of organizational behavior. Throughout his career, Ed was committed to the principle that the basis of good management is respect for the integrity of the individual employee, and his or her willingness to be an effective worker if the organizational climate supports this. This principle was the basis of his work and his life.

I am especially grateful to Ed's colleagues at Boston College, who were of tremendous support to him during his teaching career. In particular, they gave generously of their time and ideas for this book. They include: Jean Bartunek, James Bowditch, Thomas Dunn, Dalmar Fisher, Judith Gordon, Walter Klein, John Lewis, David Murphy, C. Peter Olivieri, and Alan Thayer; Pearl Alberts, reference librarian, who always found whatever references Ed needed; graduate assistant Barbara Haroz, and student assistant Grace O'Donnell, for their assistance with the details of the book; and Kumiko Di Salvo, for her fine secretarial help. I am also indebted for the support and encouragement Ed received from the administration of Boston College: to John Neuhauser, Dean of School of Management; the Reverends J. Donald Monan, S.J., President, Charles Donovan, S.J., former Dean of Faculties; and J. Allen Panuska, Dean of Faculties.

Finally, I am indebted to Randy Schuler, who put aside much of his own work to finish the revision of this book. His tremendous investment of time and energy has enabled the publication of the book as Ed had planned.

MARY LOU HUSE

PREFACE

The Purposes of the Book The challenges of managing have never been greater, especially with current attention focused on such issues as international competition, inflation, product quality, productivity, and quality of work life. Yet these challenges must be met for organizations to address successfully all of the issues which dominate the business climate today. A major purpose of this book is to help meet these challenges by providing you with a thorough understanding of how to manage organizations effectively. The book stresses the nature, function, and process of management and management skills that are applicable in a wide variety of organizations, including private, governmental, and not-for-profit, as well as very large to very small organizations.

Another purpose of the book is to provide you with an enjoyable reading and learning experience. Although the book draws upon the most current and useful research in management, it presents and summarizes the material in an easily understandable way. Numerous real-life examples and cases highlight the applicability of the text material.

The Plan of the Book The book is divided into seven major parts. The theme that follows through and ties these parts together is that effective management requires an understanding of what managers do and how what they do works the way it does. In essence, management is a set of functions and processes. Effective management is knowing about these functions and processes and knowing when and how to implement them. As the functions and processes are presented, suggestions are made to help you know when and how to implement them.

Part I describes what management is, what managers do, and in what types of settings managers manage. It concludes with a discussion of how managers make decisions. Since a sense of the past aids appreciation for the present and future, Part I also includes a chapter on the history of management.

Part II is devoted to planning. Whereas the first edition of this book had only one chapter on planning, this edition has two. This reflects the growing importance of planning in organizations today. Since an important part of planning is knowing where to go, there is a chapter on establishing goals and objectives.

Part III presents the issues related to designing and then staffing an organization. Basic guidelines are given for organizing and improving organizational structure. Legal and technical aspects of staffing an organization with the right people are discussed in detail.

Part IV then addresses the concerns for controlling the organization and people that are a product of Part III. Because controlling is such a vital management activity, three chapters on controlling are presented, as opposed to one chapter in the first edition. Part IV then concludes with a chapter on analytical aids which can be used in planning and decision making, as well as in controlling.

Part V describes how managers lead individuals and groups and how they communicate with others. The final chapter will help managers to help others manage their careers. It also provides important and useful information to aid students planning their own careers.

Organizations cannot remain static. Part VI therefore describes how stress and conflict can be handled productively, and how organizational change and development can be brought about.

Organizations do not exist in isolation. Rather, they affect, and are affected by, their environment. The first chapter in Part VI examines the crucial issues of ethics, power, and politics. A later chapter provides suggestions for the effective manager to understand and work with the environment outside the organization, and treats the growing importance of social responsibility. The final chapter in Part VI shows how the organization affects, and is affected by, the international environment.

Part VII compares and contrasts management and managers in a wide variety of organizations and provides students with suggestions for personal career planning and development.

The Teaching Approach of the Book   To provide you with an enjoyable reading and learning experience, each chapter contains many features, several of which are new to this second edition. New features include cartoons, marginal art and marginal notes, "For Your Career" suggestions, and extensive examples from real life called "On the Job." The marginal art and notes highlight, summarize, and outline the text material. The "On the Job" features are meant to aid your career success. These features come from sources such as *Business Week* and *Wall Street Journal*. Past experience indicates that students particularly enjoy these articles. "For Your Career" suggestions, at the end of each chapter, are also intended to help you to achieve successful careers. These suggestions relate directly to the material in each chapter, and are derived from the careers of many successful managers.

Features retained from the first edition include: chapter outlines, cases at the beginning and end of each chapter, figures, tables, chapter summaries, study questions, and a thorough set of up-to-date references.

Many of the opening cases and cases for discussion are new to this edition. The cases are all based on real events. This complements the same emphasis in the "On the Job" feature. Finally, there is an extensive glossary at the end of the book. This glossary defines the important terms that appear in boldface type throughout the text. Many of the terms are new to this edition.

Ancillary Materials   In addition to the text itself, there are a number of items available as aids to you and your instructors:

1. *Study Guide.* This supplement, written by Pat Long and David Gray, outlines the key sections of *Management,* provides students with self-testing questions for each chapter, and includes cases and experimental exercises.
2. *Casebook.* The book, *Case Problems in Management,* was prepared by Randall S. Schuler and Edgar F. Huse to accompany the text. It contains cases that reflect real management problems in a wide variety of settings from public to private and large to small organizations. The casebook is accompanied by an excellent instructor's manual.
3. *Instructor's Manual.* The instructor's manual for *Management* is very extensive and thorough. It outlines each chapter, provides many teaching suggestions, discusses the cases, and provides essay questions. In addition, there is a comprehensive series of objective questions. The questions have been classroom-tested. For each chapter there are between 25 and 30 multiple-choice questions and 20 to 30 true-false questions.
4. *Transparency Masters.* Transparency masters are available for many figures and tables in the text. Additional masters are also included.

ACKNOWLEDGMENTS

Many fine people provided invaluable contributions in the review and preparation of this textbook. We extend our thanks to those people, who include:

Sexton Adams

Charles Beavin

Nicholas Beltsos

Richard Chase

Richard Cosier

Charles R. Crain

Dan Dalton

Cathy Enz

Steve Fitch

Jeffrey D. Ford

David Gray

David Gustafson

Douglas T. Hall

Francine S. Hall

Ed Harrick

Jane Hass

Don Hellriegel

Carol A. Hughes

Jerry Jurwitz

Richard E. Kopelman

Alan H. Leader

Cynthia Lee

Mary Lippitt

Kenneth M. Long

Pat Long

Vincent Luchsinger

Arlyn H. Melcher

J. Stan Mendenhall

Jack L. Mendleson

Gail Miller

James H. Morris

Edward A. Nicholson

Joseph Nowlin

Eugene Owens

Chad Pierson

James E. Post

Paul Preston

Karl G. Rahdert

Robert Rosen

Vijay Sathe

John Slocum

Charles Thomas

Leete Thompson

Paul Thompson

Warren A. Thrasher

David D. VanFleet

Jim Ware

Daniel A. Wren

Special thanks go to Richard T. Fenton, sponsoring editor, and Sherry H. Romig, production editor, who have been an integral part of this book from the very beginning. Without their dedication, persistence, and professional competence, this book would not have been possible.

RANDALL S. SCHULER

MANAGEMENT

SECOND EDITION

The Managerial Function

PART I

The Importance and Activities of the Manager

CHAPTER 1

CONTENTS

A DAY IN THE LIFE OF A MANAGER

Located in Denver is a large warehouse cluttered with various types of trash as well as used tables, chairs, and couches. A woman in blue jeans fills a trash barrel and maneuvers her way through the clutter, dragging the barrel outside for later pickup. "Trash collection," she pants, "is one of the many 'joys' of owning a corporation."

As president of David's Moving & Storage, Del Goetz has many similar "joys." These include dealing with unhappy customers, unloading trucks, and even using a plunger on a stopped toilet.

Goetz and her partner took over a failing used furniture and moving company in 1974. Within a year they doubled sales and cut costs considerably. Goetz and her partner had each put in approximately sixty hours per week that year, and the pace continues.

The business became profitable in late 1975 as the result of a number of steps by Goetz. She established good relationships with local real estate firms to get referrals. She contacted larger trucking firms in order to pick up their overflow business. She became expert at negotiating prices for packing furniture prior to moving. By frequently checking the prices at other used furniture stores she made certain hers were competitive. She developed good sources for the furniture. She centralized the used furniture business at the front of the warehouse and installed a twelve-by-twelve-foot door that opens onto the sidewalk. Shoppers now find it easy to come in and browse.

Goetz and her partner employ four furniture movers and a part-time clerk. In the peak season the payroll may swell to thirteen movers—college students and others willing to work part time.

On the day of Goetz's "trash collection," she arrived at the warehouse about 8 A.M. Technically, Goetz runs the moving operation, and her partner manages the furniture store. But her partner frequently has to leave the warehouse for another building, where she inventories and prices furniture. As a result, Goetz often has to take over both jobs, answering the telephone and spending time with actual or potential customers, the lifeblood of the business.

Today, in the course of an hour, Goetz gave specific instructions to a moving crew about a special customer and informed them of the moving schedules for the next two days. She also called a florist to order flowers for the birthday of a local real estate agent, supervised the loading of two used chairs for delivery to a customer, helped one of the workers move a dresser to make room for a couch, and answered questions from several customers.

Later in the afternoon Goetz began making out the payroll. This work was interrupted by customers and phone calls. She left the warehouse about 6:30 P.M.

Goetz is pleased with the volume of the moving business and the profitability of furniture sales. Still, she knows that the hectic pace is not likely to let up.

Besides her business, a number of organizations claim Goetz's time. They include an association that helps women get jobs and loans for starting businesses.[1]

This case raises several key questions about the job of being a manager, which you should be able to answer after reading this chapter. The questions include:

1. What tasks distinguish a managerial job from a nonmanagerial job?
2. What are the most important tasks a manager has to perform?
3. Is the day in the life of Del Goetz typical of managers?
4. What does it take to be a really good manager?

1

The Del Goetz case illustrates two basic concepts: organizations are everywhere, and managers influence them in important ways. Managers are important because they direct and coordinate the activities of the organization. They also make sure that tasks are accomplished and that the organization's goals and objectives are reached.

The rest of the chapter shows where managers are, what they do, and how they work. It then explores some basic characteristics of managerial work and describes some of its challenges and rewards.

DEFINING MANAGEMENT AND MANAGERS

Organizations are all around us. Consider how many organizations must function in order for the daily newspaper to be hand-delivered: the delivery service; the newspaper company and its associated wire services, correspondents, and bureaus; the organizations needed to procure and cut the logs and produce paper from the wood pulp; telephone and electric power companies; and manufacturers of various types of equipment and supplies, to name just a few. No single person or organization could provide the daily newspaper; a network, or system, of organizations is needed.

In this book **organization** is defined through the classic questions of who, what, when, why, and how.

Who: Individuals and groups.

What: Human, financial, and other resources.

When: Over a period of time.

Why: To achieve common objectives by operating as a complex whole or system.

How: Through a number of interpersonal, informational, and decision-making activities.

What Is a Manager?   Used collectively, *management* refers to individuals engaged in planning, organizing, controlling, and directing the efforts of members of an organization and using organizational resources in order to achieve stated goals. A **manager** is a person who plans, organizes, controls, and directly supervises one or more people in a formal organization.

A number of terms can be used for *manager;* they include *director, administrator, supervisor,* and *president.* The term *manager* is used more frequently in profit-making organizations, while the terms *administrator* and *director* are used more widely in government and nonprofit organizations such as universities, hospitals, and social work agencies. (Some of the similarities and differences among managerial jobs in different organizations are described in Chapter 25.) A manager can be a prime minister, the director of a symphony orchestra, or the owner of a local service station.

Where Do Managers Work? Many people think of managers of organizations as being involved in large manufacturing corporations such as General Motors, General Electric, and Westinghouse. When asked how many nonfarm U.S. businesses are in manufacturing, a number of people put the amount at greater than 50 percent; some said 80 percent. Yet government statistics tell a different story:

- About 5 percent of nonfarm companies are manufacturing firms; 16 percent are financial, real estate, and insurance firms; 29 percent are in wholesaling and retailing; and a whopping 34 percent are service organizations.
- Of all U.S. businesses, more than four-fifths percent had gross receipts of less than $100,000 per year, while only about 2 percent had gross receipts of more than $1 million.
- From 1970 to 1975 the number of laborers employed in manufacturing decreased by about 20 percent, the number of employees in service occupations increased by about 13 percent, and the number of professional and technical workers in health care increased by about 33 percent.
- Only about one-tenth of 1 percent of U.S. businesses employ 2,500 or more people.
- Approximately 90 percent of manufacturing firms employ 100 or fewer people.
- All but some 2 percent of U.S. firms employ fewer than 50 people.
- The federal government is the single largest employer in the United States, with about 2.7 million employees. State and local governments employ about 12.5 million employees.[2]

Table 1.1 shows the number and percent of professional, technical, and managerial employees by organizational category. Manufacturing organizations employ approximately 21 million people, 10.7 percent of whom are professional and technical workers and 7.1 percent of whom are managers and administrators. The category of services is not only the largest, but also the one with the greatest percentage of professional and technical employees (38.3 percent). The category of finance, insurance, and real estate has the largest percentage of managers and administrators.

There are slightly more than 1 million businesses in the United States. About 980,000 of them, including some of the largest, are family owned or dominated. For example, over 42 percent of the largest publicly held corporations are controlled by either one person or a family, and another 17 percent are possibly under family control. Another major category of large privately-owned companies includes organizations with fewer than five hundred shareholders. These companies (which are not required to disclose financial figures) include Hallmark Cards, the Hearst Corporation, Cargill, and the Bechtel Corporation.[3] Some well-known family-managed firms include the H. J. Heinz Company, which has over

TABLE 1.1. Location of Professional, Technical, and Managerial Employees by Organizational Category

ORGANIZATIONAL CATEGORY	NUMBER OF EMPLOYEES (IN THOUSANDS)	PERCENT OF PROFESSIONAL AND TECHNICAL EMPLOYEES AMONG TOTAL EMPLOYEES	PERCENT OF MANAGERS AND ADMINISTRATORS AMONG TOTAL EMPLOYEES
Services	28,110	38.3	7.6
Manufacturing	21,911	10.7	7.1
Wholesale and retail	19,507	2.0	19.1
Transportation and public utilities	6,274	8.9	9.8
Finance, insurance, and real estate	5,811	5.5	19.2
Construction	5,765	3.0	11.7
Public administration	5,142	19.6	12.8
Agriculture	2,836	2.2	1.0
Mining	907	14.8	7.9

Source: U.S. Department of Labor, Bureau of Labor Statistics, *Handbook of Labor Statistics,* Bulletin 2070 (Washington, D.C.: Government Printing Office, 1980).

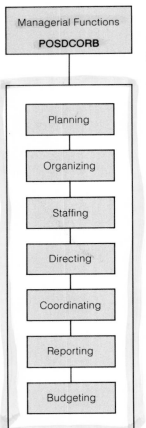

Managerial Functions

POSDCORB

- Planning
- Organizing
- Staffing
- Directing
- Coordinating
- Reporting
- Budgeting

$1 billion in sales; Triangle Publications, which owns the *Morning Telegraph, TV Guide,* and *Seventeen;* and Kaiser Industries.

These figures indicate that, statistically, a college graduate who obtains a job as a manager is likely to do so in a small firm rather than a big one; in a privately-owned or controlled organization rather than a publicly-owned or controlled one; and in government or wholesale, retail, or service firms rather than in manufacturing. The Del Goetz case illustrates this trend.

Common Functions of Management Earlier in this chapter managers were described as having four basic functions: planning, organizing, controlling, and directing. Some writers on the subject of management have identified more. In 1916 a French businessman named Henri Fayol listed five: planning, organizing, coordinating, commanding, and controlling.[4] In the 1930s, management author Luther Gulick expanded the list to seven:

Planning: Developing in broad outline the things that need to be done to accomplish the objectives of the organization and the most effective ways of doing them.

Organizing: The activities necessary to develop the formal structure of authority through which work is subdivided, defined, and coordinated to accomplish the organization's objectives.

Staffing: The personnel function of employing and training people and maintaining favorable work conditions.

Directing: The continuous process of making decisions and conveying them to subordinates, including both general and specific instructions.

Coordinating: The functional activity of interrelating the various parts of the work to be done so it will flow smoothly.

Reporting: Keeping supervisors, managers, and subordinates informed as to what is going on within the manager's area of responsibility through records, research, inspection, or other methods.

Budgeting: Handling budgets, fiscal planning, accounting, and control.[5]

POSDCORB, the acronym created from the names of the preceding seven functions, has been used to describe the work of managers at all levels. However, some writers do not agree that all these functions are common to all levels of management. Others believe that even more functions, such as communicating and motivating, are common to all levels. Despite areas of disagreement, some variation of POSDCORB is widely accepted as describing the basic framework of the manager's job.

Many managerial activities do not fit any of these basic categories, however. How does one classify Del Goetz's filling of a trash barrel and ordering of flowers for the birthday of a real estate agent? A manager may attend the funeral of a subordinate's mother. An executive may visit a customer because, as an executive, she has greater status than the more knowledgeable salesperson.

Although these activities are not covered by the POSDCORB framework, the seven functions identified therein are nevertheless useful as "ways of indicating what we need to explain."[6]

THE WORKING ROLES OF THE MANAGER

A number of studies have examined what managers do and how they allocate their time. A wide variety of managerial positions in countries such as the United States, Canada, Great Britain, and Sweden have been analyzed, sometimes from responses of managers to questionnaires, sometimes from diaries that they were asked to maintain.[7] The most productive information was obtained by observing managers at work.

Managerial Roles Henry Mintzberg, a management professor and analyzer of managerial behavior, has studied a variety of managerial roles and has synthesized the empirical studies of managerial work. He suggests that ten clusters of activities, or roles, can be used to describe the basic ways managers go about accomplishing the job. Much of the following discussion is based on his synthesis of the literature.[8]

A *role* is a set of systematically interrelated and observable behaviors that belong to an identifiable job or position. Management includes ten different but highly interrelated roles, or activities. Management roles can be separated into three different groups: those primarily concerned with personal relationships **(interpersonal roles),** those primarily con-

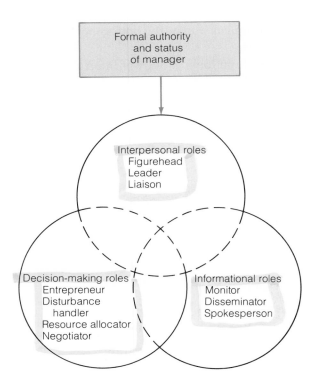

FIGURE 1.1 The interlocking and interrelated roles of the manager

cerned with the gathering and transfer of information **(informational roles),** and those essentially involving decision making **(decision-making roles).** Figure 1.1 shows all ten roles.

Several points will be made before these roles are discussed in more detail. First, every manager's job consists of some combination of these activities. Second, each activity can be observed. Third, the roles account for the variety of activities engaged in by different managers. Fourth, the roles can be described individually but cannot be isolated; they form an integrated whole. Finally, the roles to be emphasized depend on the job, the position of the manager, and similar considerations.

The Manager Has Authority and Status Formal authority and status allow the manager to act in the interpersonal roles of figurehead, leader, and liaison. By assuming these roles, the manager is able to move into the informational roles. The results of decisions provide the manager with the feedback needed for adjusting activities to changing conditions that may have resulted from the decisions.

THE INTERPERSONAL ROLES OF THE MANAGER

Interpersonal roles:

- Figurehead
- Leader
- Liaison

The Manager Is a Symbol or Figurehead The manager represents the organization or one of its units in formal matters, including ceremonial and symbolic activities; this is the **figurehead** role. Almost all managerial positions require some symbolic duties—duties that involve significant interpersonal activities but not significant information processing or decision making. The president of a university gives out the diplomas at commencement. The factory supervisor attends the wedding of one of the workers. The governor of the state cuts the ribbon signifying the opening of a new highway.

Symbolic activities are expected of managers. In some cases these activities are made necessary by internal or external rules or customs, as when a university president signs diplomas. Although relatively little attention has been paid to the figurehead role, it is an important one.

The Manager Is a Leader   **Leadership** involves responsibility for directing and coordinating the activities of subordinates to accomplish organizational goals. One part of the leadership role concerns staffing—making sure that hiring, training, promoting, dismissing, and related activities are performed properly. Another part concerns motivating subordinates in such a way that the needs of both the organization and the subordinates are met. Thus the manager may give special praise to one subordinate for a task well done, may reassure other subordinates who are unsure of their work, and may represent a group of subordinates in a battle with higher management. Sometimes the leadership role is unpleasant, as when firing or other disciplinary actions are required. Part 5 of this text covers this topic of directing in much more detail.

The Manager Is an Interpersonal Link   In the **liaison** role, the manager develops and maintains informational contacts outside the vertical chain of command in order to bring information into the unit and to gain favors from others. Knowing the proper people to contact is an essential part of the manager's job. These key people include those who send work into the unit, those to whom the unit or organization sends its goods and services, and others who can be of help to the unit. The role of liaison may involve selling, purchasing, innovating, lobbying, advising, and making informal contacts.

To be effective a manager needs to maintain a tremendous number of relationships with individuals and groups outside the organization or unit. This activity often consumes about half the manager's time. For example, a first-level supervisor may have contact with twenty-five or more people from outside the unit during a typical work day.

The interpersonal roles of figurehead, leader, and liaison are frequently combined in one task. For example, a manager may attend a ceremonial dinner in the figurehead role but, in the liaison role, may meet and start a relationship with someone who is important as a future contact.

THE INFORMATIONAL ROLES OF THE MANAGER

Receiving and communicating information are two of the most important aspects of a manager's job. In the interpersonal roles described

Informational roles:

- Monitor
- Disseminator
- Spokesperson

above, the manager builds a network of contacts. In the informational roles the manager uses these contacts to become the *nerve center* of the unit—the central focus for the receiving and sending of nonroutine information. Three roles characterize the manager as a nerve center: monitor, disseminator, and spokesperson.

The Manager Is a Monitor   In the **monitor** role the manager continually scans the environment to receive and collect information that can be used to the advantage of the unit. The effective manager designs a personal information system that is more informal than formal, more oral than written. The manager uses the formal and informal contacts developed in the liaison role as well as the reports generated by the organization, such as current sales and expense figures. The manager pieces together all incoming information into a mental image, or model, of the unit and its interaction with the external environment or with other units. (One such model is described in Chapter 3.) The model is used as a monitor of whether the unit is operating properly. Any digression from the model is noted and evaluated, which allows immediate detection of changes or problems or opportunities for improving the function of the unit. This monitoring system usually enables the manager to be the best-informed member of the unit.

Del Goetz's job exemplifies the need for continual monitoring. She had to know the status of sales, whether furniture was being packed properly, and whether moving schedules were being kept. Her information had to be current.

The Manager Is a Disseminator of Information   The **disseminator** role involves passing to subordinates special or privileged information that they would not otherwise obtain. For example, the president informs the vice-president that he has just heard that Company X, a supplier, is going bankrupt. The vice-president immediately informs the purchasing agent, since the situation may affect orders that have been placed with Company X. Del Goetz acted as a disseminator when she gave schedules to the movers.

A stumbling block for the disseminator is delegation. To use a computer analogy, the manager, as the nerve center for the unit, has much information stored in memory that is not easily passed on to subordinates. Much of it was received orally and never written down, so passing it along would be time-consuming. Yet the manager must continually see to it that the necessary pieces of this stored-memory information are passed on at the appropriate time.

The Manager Is a Representative and Spokesperson   In the **spokesperson** role, the manager speaks for the unit or for the entire organization and represents it to others. One part of this role is to represent subordinates to higher-level supervisors, as when a sales manager responds to complaints from salespeople about slow delivery time by asking the manufacturing supervisor for faster delivery or when a manager recommends pay increases for subordinates.

Another important part of the spokesperson role is communicating outside the organization or unit, as when the head of an oil company presents the organization's position to a congressional committee or when a first-line supervisor suggests to an engineer how a product can be better designed.

In summary, the informational roles involve the manager in gathering and receiving information (as a monitor) and transmitting that information to others (as a disseminator and spokesperson). The manager also uses this information in the decision-making roles, which are the subject of the next section.

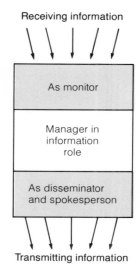

Receiving information

As monitor

Manager in information role

As disseminator and spokesperson

Transmitting information

THE DECISION-MAKING ROLES OF THE MANAGER

Developing a network of interpersonal relationships and gathering and disseminating information are not ends in themselves. They are important because they provide the basis for decision making. This is the third and perhaps most important category of the manager's roles. Decision making incorporates the roles of entrepreneur or planner, disturbance handler or controller, resource allocator, and negotiator. (Chapter 4 deals more specifically with the decision-making process itself.)

Decision-making roles:

- Entrepreneur
- Disturbance handler
- Resource allocator
- Negotiator

The Manager Plans for Needed Change   In the **entrepreneur** role the manager formulates plans to improve the unit, to implement beneficial changes. Some new ideas may be put into action immediately, as the Del Goetz case showed. Other ideas may require much more extensive planning and development as shown in the following case of two airlines.

A few years ago Eastern Airlines instituted a new shuttle service for the cities of Boston, New York, and Washington that was innovative in several respects. Planes left hourly, no reservation was required, and passengers could board directly and purchase tickets in flight. Every passenger was guaranteed a seat. If the airplane was filled, another was brought out—even for a single passenger. This operation resulted from a strategic planning project that took a number of years to implement, since capital had to be raised, operating procedures established, equipment purchased, and the approval of a number of regulatory agencies gained. The project was an instant success. Later New York Airlines entered the market with the fruit of its own strategic planning—a system even more successful than that of Eastern Airlines, in which reservations were required but fares were approximately half the price of Eastern's on many flights.

In both airlines somebody was acting in the entrepreneur role, putting new ideas into action. This story also shows the need for continuing innovative planning in that Eastern's success was eventually overshadowed by New York Air's newer idea.

The Manager Controls Disturbances   In the **disturbance-handler** role, the manager takes corrective action against unexpected pressure and change. There are many potential reasons for disturbances, including new legislation, wildcat strikes, machine breakdowns, storms, fires, and competing innovative products.

By their very nature, disturbances must be controlled quickly, so the manager must shift activities to find an immediate solution, even if it is only a short-term solution. The disturbance-handler role is highly significant, because decisions made under pressure may set precedents that affect longer-term strategy.

The Manager Allocates Resources   In the **resource allocator** role, the manager allocates both the resources of the unit and the manager's own time. Resources of the unit include time, money, material, equipment, people, and the unit's reputation. Since almost all organizations have limited resources, this allocation requires careful planning.

Decisions on resource allocation are not made completely on the basis of objective facts. On the basis of a thorough cost and feasibility analysis, a large multinational company approved the installation of a computer in the company's office in Switzerland. The company's well-respected and capable London manager strongly objected to the choice of Switzerland, feeling that this detracted from his own status and prestige. Because of his protest, the organization decided to install two computers, one in Switzerland as originally intended and one in London to assuage the feelings of this manager.

The Manager Negotiates   The final decision-making role is that of **negotiator.** Managers discuss and bargain with other units or organizations to obtain advantages for their own unit. Managers spend a large amount of time as negotiators, since only they have the authority and information that negotiating requires. The owner of a football team negotiates with a superstar who is holding out for more money; a first-line supervisor negotiates with the maintenance department to get machines repaired faster; the sales manager negotiates prices with a profitable customer.

As in other roles, the manager as negotiator is frequently dealing with uncertainty and change; yet this role cannot be shirked, since it cannot be performed by anyone else.

THE MANAGER'S ROLES— A CONTINGENCY APPROACH

Although the ten managerial roles have been described separately, they form an integrated whole. The manager needs *liaison* contacts in order to develop sufficient external information to *monitor* the situation, to do an adequate job of *planning* and *controlling,* and to *pass on* important information to others. Different managers give different emphasis to each of the roles, depending on the organizational level, the type of organization, and the function of the unit being managed. Much of the role variation also depends on the manager's personality and on the situations that arise.[9]

The organizational level appears to be more important than the type of organization.[10] Whatever the organization, the president and others at the top level are sure to spend more time in the figurehead role than will a manager who supervises janitors.

Levels in the Organization Every organization must function on at least three distinct but overlapping levels, with each level having a somewhat different managerial focus and emphasis.[11] The three levels—operating, managerial, and strategic—are depicted in Figure 1.2.

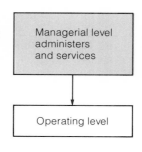

The Operating Level Every formal organization performs certain functions related to the actual production of goods and services. Thus the functions of the **operating level** are at the core of the organization, as Figure 1.2 suggests. This level concerns the development, use, and interaction of resources (people, facilities, information, materials, money, and ideas) to provide the goods, services, or ideas for which the organization was established. The operations manager is expected to develop the best allocation and combination of resources for producing a particular product, service, or idea in the proper amount, at the proper time, and at the desired level of quality. While the president of McDonald's is concerned with the strategic location of new stores, the local manager is performing at the operating level by ensuring that customers are served quickly and well.

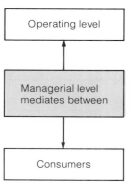

The Managerial-Administrative Level As organizations get bigger and more complex, so do their problems—especially those that arise in the attempt to coordinate the activities of the staff and to determine which products will be made or which services will be provided. In a school system, teachers must be selected, classes provided, courses scheduled for particular times, and maintenance and janitorial services

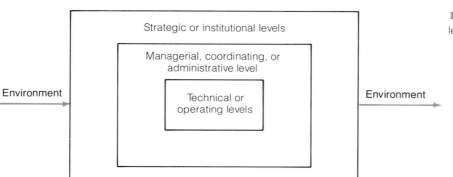

FIGURE 1.2 The three levels of management

organized. In a manufacturing organization, the plant must be run not just to produce a product but to produce a specific product for specific purposes at specific selling prices. These and other problem areas are handled by the **managerial level** (sometimes called the *administrative level*), which performs two basic functions: administering and servicing the operating level and mediating between this level and those who use the products or services.

This is a two-way process. For the operating level to do its work, the managerial-administrative level must satisfy the operating level's needs for the right materials and for whatever else is necessary to ensure that the product is sold as well as produced.

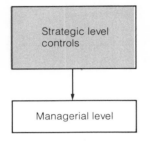

The Strategic Level   The **strategic level** controls the managerial level and mediates between the organization and the community served by the organization. Examples of this level are presidents or administrators of organizations (otherwise known as chief executive officers—CEOs), directors and boards of trustees of nonprofit organizations, and school superintendents and board members.

The strategic level is concerned with making certain that the managerial level operates properly within the broader social system. It also determines the long-range direction of the organization by its strategic planning, and it attempts to influence its external environment. An oil company may lobby to have laws changed in its favor, or a school board may impress on the public the need for a new school building.

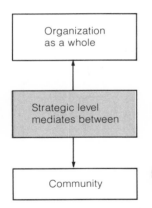

Distinguishing among the Levels   Distinguishing among these three levels can help in understanding how the manager's job differs at each level. Bear in mind, however, that the division of an organization into only three levels is arbitrary, and many managerial jobs cannot be neatly fitted into only one level, as the case of Del Goetz shows.

Another set of terms used widely in business and other types of organizations is top management, middle management, and first-level management. As Figure 1.3 shows, the term *top management* corresponds with the strategic, or third, level (executives). The term *middle management* corresponds with the coordinating, or second, level (managers).

FIGURE 1.3   The different levels of management

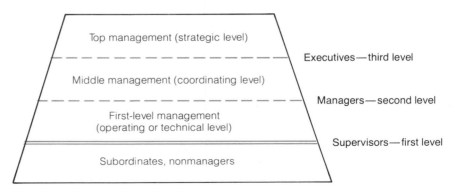

The term *first-level management* corresponds with the operating, or first, level (first-level supervisors). The line between each level is dotted to show that the distinction between each level is not always clear-cut. The double line separates managers from nonmanagers.

The word *manager* is used for a broad range of jobs, covering all levels from the strategic to the operating, from the president or chairperson to the first-level supervisor, from top management to lower management. Since many first-level supervisors are promoted from the ranks of workers, this book will concentrate more on the management jobs that ordinarily require a college degree.

Variation by Types of Jobs Jobs at the strategy level tend to be broader in scope than jobs at the coordinating or operating levels. The lower the level the narrower the scope. The president of Coca-Cola may deal with foreign countries regarding the import and manufacture of Coke, while assembly supervisors may negotiate with production engineers about redesigning a part to make the assembly process easier.

Managers at the same level but in different units tend to allocate their time differently. Manufacturing managers spend the majority of their time in the negotiator and disturbance-handler roles, and they spend more time with subordinates.[12] Sales managers spend more time in dealing with external contacts (the liaison and figurehead roles); some spend more time with customers than with people inside the company.

Managers of specialists such as accountants, computer programmers, and industrial engineers form another distinct group. They tend to work alone and to be heavily involved with paperwork, although they also advise others in peer and lateral relationships. These managers spend a great deal of time within the specialty function of their units. As a result, the monitor and spokesperson roles are most important for them.

In summary, each managerial job involves observable activities that can be classified into interpersonal, informational, and decision-making roles. The emphasis given each role differs according to individual managerial style, organizational level, type of job, and type of organization.[13] There are differences of scope as well as of emphasis. The chief executive is concerned about and responsible for the effectiveness of the entire organization and obtains a great deal of information from the external environment. In contrast, the first-level supervisor gathers and disseminates information of a more specific and concrete type, primarily from within the organization itself. The next section of the chapter covers some basic characteristics of managerial work common to all levels.

BASIC CHARACTERISTICS OF MANAGERIAL WORK

Studies of a variety of managers at all levels and in a number of different types of organizations indicate that four basic characteristics of managerial work are common.[14] They are demanding, taxing work required for a variety of activities rather than for a single activity, a large percentage of

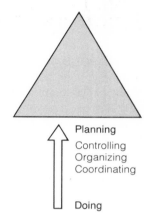

Planning
Controlling
Organizing
Coordinating

Doing

Activities by organizational level

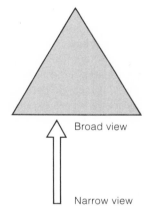

Broad view

Narrow view

Perspectives of concern by organizational level

Characteristics of managerial jobs:

- Variety of activity
- Active, nonroutine tasks
- Oral communications
- Communication networks

On the Job

IMAGES FOR RENT: WHEN RESPECTABILITY IS JUST A PINSTRIPE AWAY

MINNEAPOLIS—A lawyer appearing in court needs a "respectable" three-piece suit, grey or blue, conservative with natural shoulders, says John Meegan, tailor and lessor of suits.

The clothes worn by a banker ask for respect, authority and credibility. Muted glen plaids are fine, says Meegan. Also pinstripes.

The whole idea of suit leasing, Meegan says, is to help employers project the desired "corporate image" in the clothing worn by their representatives.

"A company may spend millions to create the proper image," he says. "Company people are expected to drive a certain year car. Sometimes the company leases expensive cars for their employees. The company spends huge amounts to have facilities that are impressive and build the proper image. And

then it finds that its people, those who are out representing the company, overlook personal image by not knowing how to dress."

Meegan, 27, and his partner, Suzanne Murphy, 25, employ 13 tailors and two salesmen in Top Shelf, their custom clothing firm here. Top Shelf deals in made-to-measure garments for men and women. Last year it got into suit leasing.

The company leases custom-made suits with a signed agreement and a down payment of 40 percent of the lease cost. The minimum two-year lease costs $5000, for which Top Shelf provides 12 to 15 suits costing around $420 apiece.

Top Shelf counsels the people who'll wear the suits, and the corporation writes off the down payment as a consulting fee— "education," Meegan calls it. The

balance is paid off in monthly payments made over two years.

The wearer must pay taxes on 60 percent of the suit's actual leasing cost because the garment amounts to an executive perk of sorts.

Meegan, and Top Shelf's advertising, stress that before entering the program, a company should check with its lawyers and tax accountants to determine whether the company would be entitled to deduct the consulting fee as a business expense.

Corporations which participate ask selected personnel to fill out a questionnaire. Questions include: Would you prefer to look older, younger or neither? Taller or shorter? Thinner or huskier? Do you judge your personality to be strong, moderate or mild? Would you prefer to be more liked, or respected? Are you

Source: Gale Tollin, "Images for Rent: When Respectability Is Just a Pinstripe Away," *Boston Globe,* March 1, 1981, pp. 64, 66. Reprinted by permission of Associated Press.

active and nonroutine tasks, many face-to-face oral communications, and involvement in a series of communication networks and contacts.

Variety of Activities A computer programmer may spend months designing a single program. A manager, on the other hand, is never preoccupied for long with a single project but usually addresses a variety of tasks in a single day. Some first-level supervisors average almost six hundred incidents each day, an average of one every forty-eight seconds.[15] Even for chief executives half of the typical day's activities are completed in fewer than nine minutes, and only a tenth take more than an hour. A study of 160 managers found that they had little time to

complimented on your appearance often, seldom or never? Are you interested in cultivating new markets? Is your country club conservative, moderate or liberal?

Top Shelf determines what image is appropriate for the company. Meegan meets with the participants and decides which of more than 4000 available materials go best with the person's physical characteristics. Next he submits recommendations for fabrics and styles to senior management for approval.

The suits are made by a Baltimore associate, and shipped to Top Shelf. The people who'll wear them get personal fittings.

At the end of the two-year lease period, the suits are returned to Top Shelf.

Meegan says suit leasing began about four years ago in England, where some companies were embarrassed by the tacky appearance of their executives. Because of Britain's lower wage rates and high taxes, some executives couldn't afford expensive clothes.

In the United States, the IRS is thought to be watching for potential abuses. Leased suits are intended for business, but who's going to make sure they're not worn at nonbusiness parties?

A "direct buy option" is offered. If interest rates or other factors make leasing unrealistic for a company, the suits can be purchased. Again, the consultation fee of about 40 percent can be deducted as a business expense.

Obsolescence isn't built into custom tailored suits, Meegan says. Quality fabrics don't go out of fashion, and styling stays near the middle-of-the-road. Meegan says the suits are "made to be worked on." His company assumes the wearer will change dimensions. The suits therefore are made so they can be altered to compensate for a 20 percent weight gain or loss.

It's a fact of corporate life, Meegan says, that some qualified people get passed over for promotions "because they don't look important." Also, he says, hirings frequently depend upon the reaction personnel managers get during interviews.

Meegan says most people don't care whether lapel stitching is one-sixteenth of an inch from the edge, or three-sixteenths. But something that subtle helps create an effect, a reaction. "An impression is felt, even though the reason for it isn't known," he says. It's his business, Meegan says, to know the subtleties of "subliminal engineering" in clothing.

---

spend on thinking. On the average, during the entire four weeks of the study, the managers spent only nine half-hour periods alone and without interruption. True breaks were seldom taken. Coffee and even lunch were consumed during meetings (formal or informal) while work was being accomplished.[16]

Managing an organization or unit is taxing. There is a lot to be done and relatively little time to do it. Faced with a variety of activities, the manager must be prepared to shift from one subject to another frequently and quickly. Managers handle many pressing problems quickly. Often they have little time to plan, and sometimes this lack of planning contributes to the frenetic pace.

One reason managers work hard is the challenge of the job. An engineer can finish a particular design on a particular day, and a lawyer can win or lose a case at a specific time. The manager's job, like "Old Man River," just keeps going. The manager can never be sure whether a little more effort might not contribute significantly to the success of the organization or unit.

Active and Nonroutine Tasks   The personality of most managers is such that they react first to whatever is definite and concrete. They seek out the more active, nonroutine elements of the job; and a management job provides a large percentage of such tasks. They give top priority to the current information they receive informally and frequently from unscheduled meetings, telephone conversations, and other sources. Because of this thirst for current information, managers may neglect mail and routine reports. Most reports deal mainly with the past, and managers are more concerned with the present.

When chief executives hear about a competitor's action, they respond immediately. When factory supervisors hear of a possible parts shortage, they respond just as quickly. Because managers want current information, they are willing to accept a high degree of uncertainty. Hearsay, gossip, and speculation are important ingredients in their information diet.

Oral Communications   Managers strongly prefer oral communications. An estimated 60 to 80 percent of the manager's time is spent in conversation. Figure 1.4 shows the distribution by the amount of time and the type of activity involving communications by top executives. Scheduled meetings take up a high percentage of time; they tend to occur when a large amount of information needs to be transmitted or when scheduling a meeting is the only way to bring a number of people together.

Unscheduled meetings and telephone calls tend to be relatively short. Meetings usually last about twelve minutes and phone calls about six. Although individually these forms of communication take little time, together they constitute about two-thirds of the manager's contacts. An important point is that, unlike other workers, the manager does not leave the meeting or the telephone to go back to work. These forms of communication *are* managerial work. The manager's productive output is measured primarily in terms of getting the job done by other people.

One middle-level manager commented after a long and busy day, "What we have around here is wall-to-wall meetings." During that particular day, the manager had been able to spend only about fifteen minutes at her desk. The rest of the day had been spent in meetings. On several occasions the manager had been called out of meetings for phone calls, and on the way to or from meetings she had spoken to several dozen other people. (The subject of communications is expanded on in Chapter 18.)

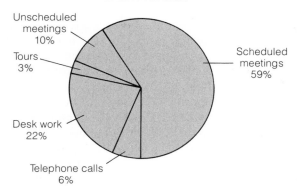

Distribution of hours

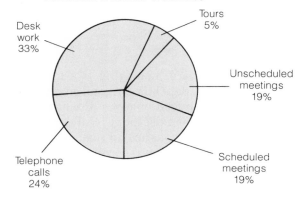

Distribution of number of activities

FIGURE 1.4 Distribution of managerial time and activities

Source: Fig. 4 (p. 39) from *The Nature of Managerial Work* by Henry Mintzberg. Copyright © 1973 by Henry Mintzberg. Used by permission of Harper & Row, Publishers, Inc.

Involvement in a Series of Communications Networks and Contacts The manager is the center of a series of communication networks involving superiors, subordinates, and people outside the work unit. One-third to one-half the manager's time is spent with subordinates, but much time is also spent with peers and others outside the actual work unit. The average supervisor may be in contact with twenty-five to fifty individuals a day, including a wide variety of persons in the operating and service departments.

By dealing with a large number and variety of outsiders, the manager serves as the hub of a series of communications networks. Conversations involve giving and receiving information as well as negotiating and bargaining with people over whom the manager has little or no direct authority.

The Personal Style of the Manager Managerial styles vary. Some are calm and reflective, others impulsive and fast-moving. Although most managers prefer direct oral communications with others, some prefer written communications. The personality of the manager greatly influences the way the job is done.

Sometimes the manager's personality and the job do not harmonize. In one case, a regional sales manager had been repeatedly passed over for promotion to marketing manager. The marketing manager in this organization handled strategic planning and the development of marketing strategy. The regional sales manager was impulsive and fast-moving and had been characterized as a person who was happiest when he had three phones on his desk, all ringing at the same time. Consequently, the company preferred a person who was good at long-range planning in the job of marketing manager. Eventually, the sales manager and the company were both satisfied when it was decided to promote the sales manager to the position of assistant to the marketing manager. In this job he had no direct supervisory responsibilities but handled all the emergency situations that would normally have required the marketing manager's attention. By splitting the original job of marketing manager into two parts, the company was able to ensure satisfactory function, since one person handled the long-range planning while the other received the excitement and variety he craved by dashing off to various cities, putting out figurative fires.

MANAGING—A REWARDING CAREER

Although managers work hard, managing is a rewarding career. The success of the organization depends on good management skills at all levels of the organization. Indeed, many of the organizations that were giants fifty years ago no longer exist today, while others have grown and prospered, mostly as a consequence of management. Penn Central, Rolls-Royce, and W. T. Grant suffered because of poor management and the inability to change with the times. IBM, Polaroid, and Xerox expanded far beyond anyone's expectations. (A less than astute manager once refused to rent an early Xerox copier, saying, "Nothing will ever replace carbon paper!")

Challenge and Meaningful Work Managing is an especially challenging job. Managers get a sense of accomplishment out of seeing the organization function well. This feeling is not limited to managers, of course, but managers gain special satisfaction from knowing that they are essential in putting all the complex pieces of an endeavor together.

Components of managerial careers:

- Challenge
- Meaningful work
- Power
- Prestige
- Self-esteem
- Opportunity for progress
- Financial reward

GOOSEMYER PARKER & WILDER

Source: GOOSEMYER by Parker & Wilder. Courtesy of Field Newspaper Syndicate.

On the Job

STUDY SAYS MANAGERS WASTE TIME

NEW YORK (UPI)—Business managers and professionals waste a lot of time by not being well enough trained in behavioral skills, a couple of recent research studies suggest.

One by Booz-Allen & Hamilton, Inc., concluded better use of automated office tools conceivably could eliminate $100 billion worth of wasted time by what the study called "knowledge workers" in the next five years.

The other study by Atlanta Consulting Group raised an interesting but unasked question: does a corporation president really have to know much about the business his company is engaged in?

The Atlanta study, based on replies by 60 corporation presidents, listed the main problems that occupy big company presidents.

Not a single one of these problems appeared to be derived from the nature of any particular business. All involved behavioral matters such as inability to get subordinates to carry out orders, or failure to get critical information. But all these behavioral anxieties had one result— they wasted a lot of the big man's time.

The Booz-Allen & Hamilton study said it appeared that, on

the average, about 15 percent of the time of managers and office professionals could be saved by better utilization of automation tools and that, for many companies, the investment in these tools would yield big returns.

For some manufacturers, perhaps the average large manufacturer, this saving could be translated into a gain of up to 15 percent in pre-tax operating income, Harvey L. Poppel, a senior vice president of Booz-Allen, said.

Popell said the study showed managers and professionals in many companies spend up to 40 percent of their time in wasteful, unproductive activities, plain clerical work, finding and screening information, traveling, scheduling and organizing and checking up on previously assigned work.

Poppel said the total compensation of these knowledge workers in American business will rise to $1.35 trillion by 1990. He said, however, at least $300 billion of this could be offset by office automation, the elimination of unnecessary travel and better use of time.

The Atlanta Consulting Group study said 54 of the 60 presidents quizzed listed formal training in behavioral management

skills as the big executive need in the coming decade. More than half the presidents said they have begun to get some such formal training from universities or by consulting professional experts.

Next to failure of subordinates to carry out orders and failure to get critical information, the presidents listed as their most serious behavioral problems the anxieties caused by having to fire people, incompetence of co-workers, the tendency of proprietors, board members and subordinates to challenge the president's decisions or recommendations and the personal difficulties in reviewing the performance of subordinates.

The needed behavioral management skills were listed in order as analytical ability, leadership, ability to communicate, ability to listen, ability to deal constructively with anger and ability to guide confrontations.

The way the questions were asked produced much duplication in the replies, but the answers nevertheless made it plain that knowing how to get people to do what has to be done seems to most presidents to be more important than knowing the nuts and bolts and machinery of the business.

Source: Leroy Pope, "Study Says Managers Waste Time," *Columbus Dispatch.* Reprinted by permission of United Press International.

Typically, people who become managers have a stronger than average need for challenge and accomplishment in meaningful work. Management jobs are well suited to satisfy this need.

Power   Managers enjoy seeing action result from their decisions. They acquire a sense of power from their authority to use human, financial, and other resources. As one manager reported, "I really get a kick out of making things happen." Moreover, managers have the opportunity of influencing people and events by their decisions and of helping to accomplish organizational goals. Capable managers gain increasingly more freedom and responsibility to exercise power and authority.

Prestige and Self-esteem   Self-confidence and the desire for the admiration of others are two other important motivating factors. To the effective manager, being well thought of by others is important, whether the others are subordinates or supervisors, insiders or outsiders. A certain amount of self-confidence is necessary for a manager to take the kinds of action that elicit the admiration of others, and the job of manager provides opportunities for these kinds of action.

A beginning manager in the lower levels does not have as much prestige as a company president but can still gain the admiration of others. In one situation, a young manager in a bank was asked by a vice-president to close out a bad debt from a company in bankruptcy. Rather than giving the folder to a clerk to follow the routine procedures for such cases, the manager read through the folder. She noticed that at the time of the loan application the company had listed a bank account in another state. She phoned the other bank, found that the account still existed, and was able to get the debt repaid. This independent action increased her own self-esteem and gained her the admiration of higher-level bank managers. A promotion soon followed.

Opportunity for a Progressive Career   No guaranteed methods exist for becoming the president of an organization (unless the organization is family-owned). There are many more college graduates in management than there are positions as chief executive officers. Only a few make it to the top. Nevertheless, an effective manager can expect opportunities for a progressive career in management that could lead to the top level.

In one situation a college graduate was placed in a training program that brought him into contact with capable senior-level executives. The opportunity to observe and learn from these executives influenced the young man greatly. He began to act and think like a top executive. When promotion did not come quickly in the original company, he applied for and got the job of executive vice-president in a smaller organization. When the president resigned to take over a larger company, the young man became president—seven years after graduation from college.

Financial Reward   Money is both essential to a comfortable life and a measure of one's success. The financial rewards for managers increase as their level of achievement and responsibility increases. In two-career families, competition sometimes develops between spouses over the money each is bringing home. Also, women in management have traditionally been paid less than men. This inequity is being reduced, though slowly. Recent equal opportunity laws and regulations are reducing the pay gap between male and female managers.

SUMMARY

Our society is composed of a variety of overlapping, interdependent organizations. We constantly come in contact with these organizations, directly or indirectly, through simple events such as receiving a daily newspaper at our homes or such complex events as undergoing surgery. We are members of many and varied organizations, even though we may work (and manage) in only one.

Many types of organizations exist, and all of them need to be managed. The basic task of the manager is to plan, organize, lead, and control the work of others to establish and maintain the conditions under which individuals and groups can work together to accomplish organizational goals. Managerial talent is necessary not only for existing organizations but to help evolve new programs to solve social, environmental, and other problems.

Managers have a variety of titles. Some are broad, such as supervisor, executive, administrator, director, and president; others are more specialized, such as dean, department head, chief librarian, marketing manager, personnel director, credit manager, and head nurse.

To accomplish the common managerial functions of planning, organizing, leading, and controlling, a manager engages in a variety of activities that can be grouped into three basic categories: interpersonal relationships, information processing, and decision making. The three categories can be further divided into ten observable working roles. These managerial roles form an interrelated, interdependent whole. Although they can be described individually, each depends on the others.

The manager occupies a unique position as a nerve center for information necessary to the organization. Contacts with subordinates and with those outside the unit yield a powerful data base of internal and external information. As a result, the manager possesses the best store of nonroutine information.

Much of the manager's information is tangible, current, and oral. It is used to detect changes, to inform outsiders and subordinates, to identify both problems and opportunities, and to build a base for decision-making, planning, and controlling.

The manager makes or approves the significant decisions for the unit. Some of the decisions bring about change and improvement; others handle unexpected problems. The manager also oversees the allocation of the unit's resources. In order to perform the decision-making and allocation activities, the manager must negotiate with other organizations or units.

To accomplish organizational goals, managers work hard at a variety of activities and are involved in a series of communication networks. Usually the type of personality that leads a person into a management job is one that prefers active and nonroutine tasks and enjoys direct personal relationships. How the specific work is done depends in part on the personal style of the manager.

Managing can be a rewarding career because of the challenge of meaningful work, the potential for increasing prestige and self-esteem, the opportunity for progressing, the power, and the money it offers. Not everyone is suited for a management job, however, and not every manager is motivated by the same needs. Equating movement into higher and higher ranks with success is sometimes a mistake. The regional sales manager described earlier in this chapter would have been unhappy if he had been promoted into the planning job. He was much happier and more effective as a high-level trouble shooter. (Ways of thinking about and planning for career development are described in more detail in Chapter 19.)

Although rewarding, the manager's job is also complex. The rest of this book further explores concepts and aspects of the managerial job that can help anyone become a better manager.

STUDY QUESTIONS

1. What is a manager?
2. Why are organizations needed?
3. After reading the chapter, do you think the organizations to which you belong are managed effectively? Explain.
4. Give examples of the three management levels.
5. Select a variety of managers to observe, such as the manager of a service station, the manager of a clothing store, a head nurse, and a manufacturing supervisor. What roles do they appear to emphasize?
6. Identify and discuss as many different roles as you can from the Del Goetz case.
7. Explain what is meant by the statement, "The basic managerial roles are observable."
9. Discuss the concept of nerve center. In what way is the idea important?
10. Can one be an effective manager without getting oral information? Explain.
11. From your own experience, give examples of the different roles of the manager. Does the emphasis seem to vary with the organization? Explain.
12. What roles does a department head emphasize? A college dean? An editor of a school newspaper? A football coach? Which roles does each seem to spend the most time on?
13. What would you find rewarding in being a manager? What aspects of being a manager might you dislike?
14. Read several issues of *Fortune* or *Business Week*. According to these magazines, what do managers do?

Case for Discussion

THE POWER OF SUBORDINATES

A small firm had about twelve secretaries reporting to managers. Working hours were 9 A.M. to 5 P.M. One morning the president of the company was looking out his office window, which was directly above the entrance to the building. He noticed that his own secretary was about ten minutes late to work and that the others were coming in as much as ten to fifteen minutes late. Angrily, he called in his secretary and dictated a memorandum to all the secretaries.

The memo stated essentially that working hours were from 9 to 5 and that each secretary was expected to arrive promptly or be docked pay for the lost time. The memo was hand-delivered to each secretary.

The next morning all the secretaries arrived at exactly 9 A.M. The president was pleased. His decision had been effective.

That afternoon he called in his secretary about 4:30 P.M., as was his custom, to begin dictating letters to be typed the next day. (Frequently the dictation would take about an hour.) The secretary arrived with her steno pad, and the president began dictating. Normally he would continue dictating until all the letters were finished. This particular day, however, his secretary stood up at 4:45 and closed her notebook even though a considerable amount of dictation remained.

She gently reminded the president that working hours were from 9 to 5 and that she would need the remaining time to clear up some unfinished business. Throughout the organization, all the other secretaries were doing much the same thing. Promptly at 5 P.M. every secretary left the building.

1. How effective was the president's decision?
2. What inferences had he made?
3. Had he considered all the alternatives? All the consequences?
4. What would you have done in his place?
5. What was the problem the president was trying to solve?
6. Did he properly evaluate the alternative he chose?

FOR YOUR CAREER

1. If you are looking for a peaceful, quiet, contemplative life, do not plan on being a manager.
2. If you like challenge, variety, hard work, and opportunities for achievement, then think seriously about a managerial career.
3. Most students are shocked by their first several jobs after college. They expect organizations to be neat, orderly, disciplined, and rational. Organizations are really rather messy and disorderly.
4. If you want to succeed, hard work is not the only ingredient, but it helps.
5. Look on problems as opportunities, not as headaches.
6. Be diligent in building good informational contacts throughout the organization in which you work. They will be invaluable to you.
7. Maintain good relationships with secretaries. They have far more power than you think.

FOOTNOTES

1. J. Libman, "Going It Alone, Female Entrepreneurs Like Del Goetz Make 'Man's Work' Pay Off," *Wall Street Journal,* August 22, 1975, p. 1. Reprinted with permission of The Wall Street Journal, © Dow Jones & Company, Inc., 1975. All rights reserved.
2. U.S. Department of Commerce, Bureau of the Census, *Statistical Abstract of the United States,* 97th ed. (Washington, D.C.: Government Printing Office, 1976); and U.S. Department of Labor, Bureau of Labor Statistics, *Handbook of Labor Statistics,* Bulletin 1905 (Washington, D.C.: Government Printing Office, 1976).
3. L. Barnes and S. Hershon, "Transferring Power in Nuclear Power Plants: The Family Business," *Harvard Business Review* 54 (July–August 1976): 105–114.
4. H. Fayol, *General and Industrial Management,* trans.
C. Storrs (London: Sir Isaac Pitman and Sons, 1949). Originally published in French in 1916.
5. L. Gulick, "Notes on the Theory of Organization," in *Papers on the Science of Administration,* ed. L. Gulick and L. Urwick (New York: Columbia University Press, 1937).
6. D. Braybrooke, "The Mystery of Executive Success Re-examined," *Administrative Science Quarterly* 8 (1964): 537.
7. R. Stewart, *Managers and Their Jobs* (London: Macmillan, 1967); R. Stewart, "The Jobs of the Manager," *Management Today,* July 1976, pp. 64–67; R. Stewart, "To Understand the Manager's Job: Consider Demands Constraints, Choices," *Organizational Dynamics* 4 (Spring 1976): 22–32; and W. Tornow and P. Pinto, "The Development of a Managerial Job

Taxonomy: A System for Describing, Classifying and Evaluating Executive Positions," *Journal of Applied Psychology* 61 (1976): 410–416.

8. H. Mintzberg, *The Nature of Managerial Work* (New York: Harper & Row, 1973); H. Mintzberg, "The Manager's Job, Folklore and Fact," *Harvard Business Review* 53 (July–August 1975); 49–61; and H. Mintzberg, "Managerial Work: Analysis from Observation," *Management Science* 18 (October 1971): B–97 to B–109.

9. F. Aguilar, *Scanning the Business Environment* (New York: Macmillan, 1967); R. Davis, *Performance and Development of Field Sales Managers* (Boston: Division of Research, Harvard Business School, 1957); and S. Nealey and F. Fiedler, "Leadership Functions of Middle Managers," *Psychological Bulletin* 70 (April 1968): 313–329.

10. C. Shartle, *Executive Performance and Leadership* (Englewood Cliffs, N.J.: Prentice-Hall, 1956).

11. T. Parsons, *Structure and Process in Modern Societies* (Glencoe, Ill.: Free Press, 1960); E. Lawler, III, and J. Rhode, *Information and Control in Organizations* (Pacific Palisades, Calif.: Goodyear Publishing, 1976).

12. Mintzberg, *Nature of Managerial Work;* Stewart, *Managers and Their Jobs;* Stewart, "To Understand the Manager's Job"; I. Choran, "The Manager of a Small Company" (MBA thesis, McGill University, 1969); and H. Stieglitz, "The Chief Executive's Job—and the Size of the Company," *Conference Board Record* 7 (September 1970): 38–40.

13. Mintzberg, *Nature of Managerial Work.*

14. J. Hemphill, *Dimensions of Executive Positions,* Research Monograph Number 98 (Columbus: Ohio State University, 1960); S. Carlson, *Executive Behavior* (Stockholm: Strongbergs, 1951); Stewart, *Managers and Their Jobs;* R. Guest, "Of Time and the Foreman," *Personnel* 32 (May 1956): 478–486; Q. Ponder, "The Effective Manufacturing Foreman," in *Industrial Relations Research Association Proceedings of the Tenth Annual Meeting,* ed. E. Young, Madison, Wisconsin, December 1957, pp. 41–54; Mintzberg, *The Nature of Managerial Work;* Mintzberg, "The Manager's Job: Folklore and Fact" L. Sayles, *Managerial Behavior: Administration in Complex Organizations* (New York: McGraw-Hill, 1964); J. Horne and T. Lupton, "The Work Activities of 'Middle' Managers—An Exploratory Study," *Journal of Management Studies,* February 1965, pp. 14–33; and Nealey and Fiedler, "Leadership Functions of Middle Managers."

15. Stewart, *Managers and Their Jobs.*

16. Ibid.

The Emergence of
Managerial Thought

CHAPTER 2

CONTENTS

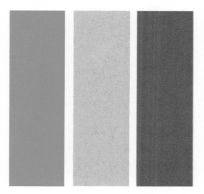

AN EARLY MANAGEMENT PROBLEM—THE GREAT PYRAMID

The Great Pyramid was built as a tomb for Cheops, a Pharaoh of Egypt, about 2000–3000 B.C. Extensive management skill was required to plan, schedule, and coordinate its building. Exactly how the construction was managed is still uncertain and subject to a great deal of debate.

Cheops commissioned the project. An architect selected the specific site and drew up the plans. Many problems had to be overcome. A schedule had to be developed and coordinated. Adjustments for design changes and construction problems had to be made, and the quality of the construction had to be closely overseen. The end result was a product so perfectly constructed that a knife cannot be inserted into the joints between the stones.

Scholars disagree on how the project was actually accomplished. Were ramps used? Did the builders have engineering skills the scholars know nothing about? Whatever the case, the building of the pyramid was a tremendous feat of planning and coordination.[1]

Were the Great Pyramid to be built today, the approach would undoubtedly be different, but many of the problems of planning, coordination, and decision making would be the same. This chapter examines the evolution of management thought over the centuries. There has been an explosion of management ideas in recent years. Nevertheless, the same basic management problem exists today as in Cheops's time: What is the best way to go about attaining the goals of the enterprise? History provides helpful clues toward solving this problem. By looking at the past, we can better see the future.

The story of the Great Pyramid raises several critical questions which you should be able to answer after reading this chapter. The questions include:

1. Has there always been a need for managers? Explain.
2. How do managers of today differ from those of years ago?
3. Is it easier to be a manager today than it was when the Great Pyramid was built? Explain.
4. Can an understanding of the history of management help the practice of management today? How?

2

Chapter 2 begins with some examples of management thought as it developed thousand of years ago. The Arsenal of Venice provides an excellent example of this development. A review of the impact of the Industrial Revolution and recent developments on modern society follows. The review includes a look at several of the more important management ideas that have been developed since the turn of the century. Several myths are debunked in the process.

ANCIENT EXAMPLES OF MANAGEMENT AND MANAGEMENT TECHNIQUES

Formal organizations consist of three levels: the strategic or institutional level, the managerial or coordinating level, and the technical, operating, or administrative level. Figure 2.1 illustrates the relationship of culture and society to the three levels by adding a fourth level—societal patterns.

Historically, organizations and management interact with and are interdependent on society and culture. **Society** is the totality of social relationships among human beings. **Culture** is the totality of socially transmitted ideas, beliefs, and values within a society.

The Egyptians who built the Great Pyramid firmly believed in a life after death. Their culture also encouraged belief in the Pharaoh as a deity who needed a suitable home after death. Society demanded the building of a suitable tomb. The size of the tomb in turn affected the strategic level

FIGURE 2.1 The interaction between society and organizational levels

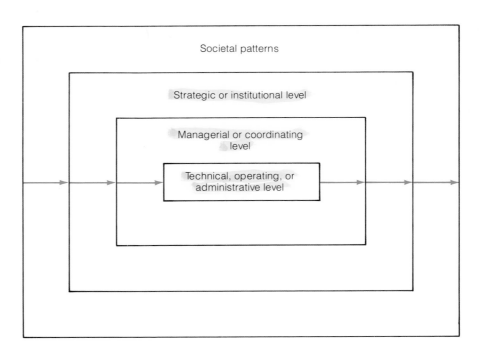

of organization. The best estimates of the adult male population of Egypt at the time are no more than half a million. Therefore, the organization for the actual construction required a high level of resource commitment. Without the cultural and societal pressure, such commitment would not have been possible.

The project also required that all three levels of the organization be well managed. In addition to managing the actual building of the tombs, the Egyptian managers kept meticulous documents. They knew exactly how much was received, from whom, when it arrived, and how it was used.

Written Management Tools Written accounting systems date back to earliest civilizations. For example, the temple records of the Sumerian civilization date back to about 3000 B.C.[2] The priests of the Sumerian temple collected and controlled a large fortune of worldly goods. The religious tax provided them with vast revenues, estates, flocks, and herds. Some Sumerians felt that individual priests might be lining their own pockets. As a result, an elaborate accounting system was developed. The chief priest got a regular accounting from the lesser priests of their income and expenses. This is one of the early instances of managerial control through organizational accounting as well as one of the earliest sets of written documents in the world. The five-thousand-year-old documents were used not for religious purposes but to meet managerial needs.

Managerial Laws, Rules, and Regulations About 2000 B.C., King Hammurabi united the cities along the Euphrates and Tigris rivers into one powerful nation, Babylon. At the same time, he developed the Code of Hammurabi, a set of laws covering trade, business, real estate, personal property, labor, and the family. Most of the laws dealt with partnerships, sales, loans, contracts, promissory notes, and other business agreements. The code described in specific detail the legal procedures to be followed in business transactions such as minimum wages, control, and responsibility.

About fifteen hundred years later, another strong manager came to the helm of Babylon. Nebuchadnezzar reunited the Babylonians and led them to new military and domestic heights. During his rule color-coding methods of production control were used in the textile mills and granaries. Incentive wage payments were also introduced; the wages paid women who were spinning and weaving were determined by their level of production.[3]

These examples show that civilizations established laws, regulations, production scheduling, and color coding long before the rise of capitalism as we know it.

Job Descriptions and Civil Service Exams The first known job descriptions for civil servants were written in China about 1100 B.C. Descriptions existed for all civil servants, from the prime minister down to the most humble household servant. The duties, responsibilities, and limitations of each job were spelled out in clear language.[4]

About 120 B.C., the Chinese developed the first civil service examination system. Many clerks and administrators could not read and thus were unable to fully understand government laws and regulations. Somewhat irked by this, Prime Minister Kin-Sun Hung established a system of examinations whereby those who scored highest were given government jobs. About three hundred years later, the system was expanded. Civil servants were classified into nine different grades, depending on such factors as knowledge, experience, ability, and character. The grading was performed by an impartial judge.[5]

MEDIEVAL MANAGEMENT

In the fifteenth century, Venice was a thriving mercantile city state, with a large private merchant fleet. For purposes of defense, the city opened its own shipyard, the Arsenal, in 1436.

As trade prospered, the need grew for a navy to defend the merchant fleet. As a result, the Arsenal grew also. By the sixteenth century, the Arsenal of Venice was probably the largest industrial plant in the world, employing almost two thousand workers and covering more than sixty acres of land and water.

Modern managerial techniques:

- Assembly line
- Personnel practices
- Standardization
- Control techniques
- Accounting
- Cost
- Inventory
- Warehouse

The Arsenal had a three-fold purpose: manufacturing and assembling war galleys, arms, and equipment; storing material and equipment until needed; and repairing and refitting ships already manufactured. To reduce costs and increase efficiency, the Venetians running the Arsenal developed and employed a number of the managerial techniques still in use today. These techniques included an assembly line, personnel training and reward systems, standardization, accounting control, inventory control, cost control, and warehouse control.[6]

The Assembly Line   Warehouses were arranged along a canal so that the galleys could be brought directly to the equipment, rather than bringing the equipment to the galleys. The warehouse arrangement allowed the galleys to be outfitted in the proper sequence. As the galley was towed past the appropriate warehouse, arms and equipment were passed through the windows of the warehouse onto the galley.

Personnel   Workers at the Arsenal were closely supervised, particularly with regard to working hours and output. The type of job determined whether workers were paid by the piece or on a daily basis. For example, oar makers were paid on a piecework basis while day wages were paid to those performing menial labor. Skilled artisans worked in separate craft shops. Merit-rating plans were developed, and employees, especially master craftsmen, were reviewed twice a year for pay purposes.

Standardization To allow the use of assembly line techniques, a certain amount of standardization was required. All rigging and deck equipment was uniform, and sternposts were identical in design so that rudders need not be specially fitted. Standardization was used in weaponry as well. All bows were made so that standard arrows would fit any of them.

Accounting Control One of the first control techniques used at the Armory was accounting. Complete and accurate accounts were kept of purchases, materials, and project times. Different accounting methods were tested in an attempt to find an accurate method of keeping track of all expenditures and disbursements, as well as effective ways of evaluating the expenditures.

Inventory Control Detailed records were kept of the quantities and destinations of outgoing munitions. Physical counts of materials leaving the Arsenal were kept by the doorkeepers of each warehouse. Special officials, called appraisers, kept track of goods bought by the Arsenal. The appraisers were responsible for inspecting incoming goods, especially timber, and reporting the value of goods received. They were also responsible for inspecting finished products, especially those done on piecework.

Warehousing It was necessary not only to furnish new ships but to repair and refit older ships. The Arsenal kept many items in storage for this purpose. All items were numbered and stocked in specific areas of different warehouses. This system helped implement both the assembly line procedure and ensure the accuracy of the inventory.

The inventory of finished products presented few problems; the products were neatly stacked and numbered and easy to locate. It took managers of the Arsenal a long time to develop a system for the orderly storage of unprocessed wood, however. Because this problem was expensive, a better form of cost control was eventually developed.

Cost Control For more than a hundred years after the Arsenal was opened, there was no regular system for the orderly arrangement of some of the goods received. The cost of a search for a particular piece of wood might run more than three times the original cost of the wood. By developing an efficient sorting system, management reduced costs by almost two thousand ducats per year and increased the accuracy of the inventory.

The Arsenal of Venice exemplifies the development of sophisticated management principles as early as the fifteenth century. The modern organization, however, did not begin to emerge until the Industrial Revolution.[7]

THE INITIAL IMPACT OF THE
INDUSTRIAL REVOLUTION

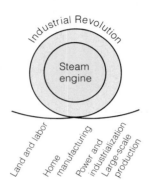

The development of the steam engine changed the economy of Western civilization and made the modern organization possible. The steam engine brought power for factories, ships, and trains. The economy began to shift its emphasis from land and labor to power and industrialization. The interactions among culture, organization, coordination, and administration in this new environment were particularly clear.

The cultural climate in England favored the growth of commerce and industry. The English government was more open and sensitive to the development of commerce than were the governments of many other European countries. The English social values favored achievement and profit making. In addition, England had ample supplies of coal and iron, essential ingredients for an industrialized society.

Before the development of the steam engine, England had had a number of small but thriving industries in such areas as textiles and iron products. The introduction of the steam engine made possible the vast expansion of these industries by lowering production costs, which increased markets. As the markets expanded, the need grew for more production, more machines, more workers, and more capital to finance the expansion. Division of labor became more common. These shifts in administrative practices required new and different management practices and new types of organizations. The expansion of the industries changed the culture that made the growth possible. These cultural changes came about as the mechanization of production forced shifts from home manufacturing to large-scale factory production—the Industrial Revolution.

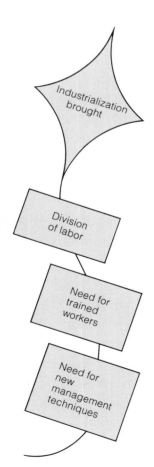

The Industrial Revolution destroyed *cottage industry*, work performed in the home by domestic artisans who generally owned all the tools of their trade. The new machines were much too expensive to be owned by individuals, so it became necessary to bring machines and workers together in large factories where the building, the machinery, and the materials were owned by a few people. In addition, as the work was simplified and the use of machinery grew, women and children began to be employed on a large scale. Thus the building of large factories, the use of expensive equipment, and the employment of large numbers of relatively unskilled people forced changes in work methods.

Unskilled workers unused to factory work required more discipline. Planning and coordination received more emphasis. Different methods of training and of wage payment were developed. There was a sharper distinction between the capitalist and the worker.

The Industrial Revolution emerged from a society and culture that encouraged business and commerce. In turn, the same society and culture were changed by the resulting new organizations and administrative practices. The increasing industrialization created the need for a higher and more capable level of managers. As manufacturing tech-

On the Job

THE ANALYTICAL ENGINE

I have sacrificed time, health, and fortune, in the desire to complete these Calculating Engines. I have also declined several offers of great personal advantage to myself. But, notwithstanding the sacrifice of these advantages for the purpose of maturing an engine of almost intellectual power, and after expending from my own private fortune a larger sum than the government of England has spent on that machine, the execution of which it only commenced, I have received neither an acknowledgment of my labors, nor even the offer of those honors or rewards which are allowed to fall within the reach of men who devote themselves to purely scientific investigations. . . .

If the work upon which I have bestowed so much time and thought were a mere triumph over mechanical difficulties, or simply curious, or if the execution of such engines were of doubtful practicability or utility, some justification might be found for the course which has been taken; but I venture to assert that no mathematician who has a reputation to lose will ever *publicly* express an opinion that such a machine would be useless if made, and that no man distinguished as a civil engineer will venture to declare the construction of such machinery impracticable. . . .

And at a period when the progress of physical science is obstructed by that exhausting intellectual and manual labor, indispensable for its advancement, which it is the object of the Analytical Engine to relieve, I think the application of machinery in aid of the most complicated and abstruse calculations can no longer be deemed unworthy of the attention of the country. In fact, there is no reason why mental as well as bodily labor should not be economized by the aid of machinery.

Source: Charles Babbage, *Passage from the Life of a Philosopher* (London: Longman, Green, Longman, Roberts, & Green, 1864), p. 97.

niques changed, the need for a trained, motivated work force increased. New operating techniques resulted. England shifted from an agricultural economy to an industrial one. The age of management emerged.

THE SECOND PHASE OF THE INDUSTRIAL REVOLUTION

Standardization in some form has been in use for a long time.[8] The early Egyptian army used standardized bows, arrows, and spears. For centuries, the Catholic Church had definite, worldwide specifications for the sizes, shapes, and properties of sacramental wines and for the sizes, shapes, and properties of candles. Henry I of England standardized the yard as a unit of measurement, proclaiming that it consisted of the distance from his armpit to his outermost finger tip. The Arsenal of Venice used standardized equipment such as stern posts and rudders.

Pressure for Standardization   The Industrial Revolution brought about mass production and mass distribution of goods. The need for more effective standardization became painfully clear. For example, the early railroads used many track gauges, shapes and sizes of rolling stock, and patterns for parts such as couplings. It was impossible to ship goods over more than one line without transferring them at every change of line, a costly and inconvenient process. The railroad companies agreed to make track gauges, boxcars, and couplings uniform and interchangeable in order to eliminate these problems.

The Development of Interchangeable Parts Use of uniform, interchangeable parts marked a major advance in standardization. Eli Whitney deserves primary credit for developing interchangeable manufacturing methods in the United States. After receiving a contract for the manufacture of muskets in 1789, Whitney ran into trouble getting good workmen. He solved the problem by developing a method of simplified production in which each part of a musket could be interchanged with a corresponding part. If a musket required repair, a new part exactly fitted the place of the old part, which eliminated the need for costly refitting and reforming.

The Colt Revolver The development of the Colt revolver is perhaps the best-known early case of standardization. The revolver, patented by Samuel Colt in 1836, was to be constructed of completely interchangeable parts. When Colt was unable to get financial backing in the United States, he took out patents in both England and France. He returned to the United States and opened a factory, which failed after six years.

Then came the Mexican war. Orders began to pour in for Colt's repeating firearm, which Texans wanted for fighting Mexicans and Indians. A weapon that fired six rounds as fast as the finger could pull the trigger would bring terror to the enemy. The Colt revolver eventually became known as the "weapon that won the West."[9]

The Significance of Standardization Standardization became fully effective during World War I, when it was promoted by the War Industries Board. The board used standardization to reduce the number of styles used by the military in products as varied as rubber footwear, tires, and washing machines. By the end of the war, standardization programs in the United States had created an estimated 15 percent annual saving in the quantity of material used. A tremendous increase in productive capacity was also observed.

The explosion in automobile sales following World War I was also made possible by standardization and interchangeability of parts. Without these techniques, the Model T Ford could not have existed.

The need for further standardization still exists today. For example, European and other countries continue to use the metric system, while the United States essentially does not. England continues to have automobiles with the steering wheel on the right; the rest of the world has the steering wheel on the left. Automobiles built in England and exported to countries such as the United States require costly redesign.

THE RISE OF SCIENTIFIC MANAGEMENT

As management became more important to industry, books on management techniques appeared. One of the books that had a tremendous impact on management thought was Frederick Taylor's *The Principles of Modern Management*, originally published in 1911.[10] Taylor suggested increasing productivity by using four basic scientific principles:

A principle of scientific management:

Work smarter, not harder

1. Developing a true **science of management** to determine the best and most efficient method for performing each specific task.
2. Selecting the workers carefully and scientifically so that workers would be given responsibility for performing the tasks for which they were best suited.
3. Educating and training workers scientifically to perform tasks in the best prescribed manner.
4. Arranging close cooperation between those who plan the work and those who do it to assure that all the work would be performed in strict accordance with the principles derived from scientific analysis.

Taylor believed that these principles would benefit both the organization and the worker—the organization through greater productivity and the worker through higher pay.

Taylor's Report on Bethlehem Steel   Much of Taylor's published work was based on his report on work improvement tests performed at Bethlehem Steel around the turn of the century. Taylor reported that the company had about seventy-five men employed to load pig iron into freight cars. He selected a Pennsylvania Dutchman named Schmidt and offered him an increase in pay from $1.15 per day to $1.85 per day if he would follow orders with no back talk. Taylor projected that following orders would increase Schmidt's productivity from about twelve tons a day to more than forty-seven tons. Schmidt agreed to the proposal. Taylor claimed to have trained the other workers until the entire crew had raised their productivity in this manner.

Later research into Bethlehem Steel's records, Taylor's published and unpublished revisions of his own work, and other sources indicated that this report was almost completely a lie. Since 1911, however, writers on management have accepted Taylor's account as true and have thereby continued the myth about his work.[11] Reports questioning Taylor's work in *The Principles of Scientific Management* have appeared. One of them suggests:

> The fact that an account of a happening was presented in three different ways by its instigator is enough to make one raise an eyebrow. That this was wittingly done by a man who could not abide liars and who insisted on the strict observance of even the slightest rule is a sign of aberrant behavior. That this man who behaved aberrantly was also the founder of a system of management which has deeply affected work relationships to this day requires investigation.[12]

Apparently, Taylor had a vivid imagination and relatively little regard for the truth. Through his writings and speeches, however, he did impress management with the need to study operating practices to increase worker efficiency. Thus, although Taylor's research at Bethlehem Steel was mostly myth, the fact that it was believed has produced some desirable results.

The Gilbreths   Many experimenters followed Taylor's example and tried using scientific methods to increase efficiency. Two of the most famous, Frank and Lillian Gilbreth, refined and advanced the scientific approaches made popular by Taylor. Frank Gilbreth identified seventeen basic motions or thought processes for analyzing a job. The motions included search, find, grasp, transport, and position. These basic units of behavior were called "therbligs," a slightly altered, backward spelling of Gilbreth. Identification of basic motions allowed jobs to be analyzed in finer detail.

Symbol	G
Therblig	Grasp
Color	Lake red
Symbol	A
Therblig	Assemble
Color	Blue
Symbol	TE
Therblig	Transport empty
Color	Olive green
Symbol	PN
Therblig	Plan
Color	Brown
Symbol	UD
Therblig	Unavailable delay
Color	Yellow ochre

Taylor had studied relatively gross body motions. Gilbreth developed more refined methods through the use of motion pictures. Each picture of an action included a large-faced clock with the hands moving through fractional parts of a minute. This and other techniques made it possible to determine more precisely the time and motion involved in the work itself, thus increasing the accuracy of the analysis.

The Gilbreths opposed Taylor's suggestion that a worker should follow orders with no back talk. They involved the workers in their studies. They inaugurated the scientific method of analyzing work and fatigue with the study of worker psychology and participation.

Time and motion studies are still used as a way of determining standard times and costs for making a product. In addition, the interest in worker psychology and participation is growing at an accelerating pace. Newspaper headlines such as "GM Finds Advantages in Giving Workers Decision-Making Role" reflect this growing interest.[13]

The Gilbreths are said to have applied scientific management not only to industry but also to their own household, including their twelve children. Taking a bath was seen as both a necessity and an unavoidable delay. As a result the Gilbreths installed a hand cranked record player in the bathroom so the family could listen to German and French language instruction while bathing.[14]

THE RISE OF HUMAN RELATIONS

Another myth was created in the 1920s by a series of scientific management experiments. This time the misconceptions involved human nature. Although false conclusions were reached, the experiments indicated the importance of group dynamics and humans as social beings. The series of experiments began as a competition between companies that sold industrial gas lighting fixtures and companies that sold electric fixtures for factories' business.

The Establishment of Comparative Studies Around the turn of the century, manufacturers of gas and electrical fixtures struggled for control of industrial and residential lighting markets. Industry tended to use gas, the cheaper lighting method until more modern tungsten filament lamps were developed. The new lamps made electricity more efficient and thus cheaper than gas lamps.

Since the new tungsten lamps were more efficient, the electric companies were afraid of a drop electrical current sales. Their advertising began to stress better illumination for increased productivity. From 1918 to 1923 a number of studies showed that better lighting (electricity) resulted in higher productivity. Because the tests were financed and frequently designed by the electrical industry, management remained skeptical.

To overcome the skepticism, several large electrical companies, including General Electric, decided to finance a series of additional studies. These studies would not appear to be connected in any way with the electrical industry. The Committee on Industrial Lighting, officially sponsored by the National Academy of Sciences, was established to conduct the studies. The chairman, an MIT professor, recommended that the studies be made at the Hawthorne plant of Western Electric.[15]

The Hawthorne Studies In all, seven studies took place at the Hawthorne plant between 1924 and 1932. The studies examined the effect of factors such as illumination, rest periods, piece work, shorter workdays and workweeks, and soup or coffee at breaks. Two of the best known studies took place in the relay assembly room and in the bank wiring room.

In the relay assembly room, the productivity of the six female employees systematically increased as the amount of illumination was increased. However, productivity also increased as the illumination was systematically decreased.

In the bank wiring room, no changes were made. Instead, the workers were systematically observed. There were fourteen employees in the department, divided into three semiautonomous, but interdependent, work groups. The study indicated that each group had a clear-cut standard for production, a standard established within the group, not by management. Men who exceeded the group's internal standards were called slaves or rate busters; those who fell below the groups standards were called chiselers. The workers had their own means of enforcing the standards. One conclusion of the study of this small group was that group production standards were more important than management or wage incentives in affecting output. Another finding, given little or no emphasis at the time, was that the workers did not increase productivity because of the interest of the observers.

Results of the Hawthorne Studies One of the major findings of the Hawthorne studies was the fact that the work group itself is important. The studies revealed that a group's production is better predicted by the

Hawthorne effect:

People respond because of the attention, not the technique } Myth

standards or norms of the group than by working conditions, incentive pay, or efforts by management.

The Hawthorne studies also gave rise to the myth of the **Hawthorne effect.** The myth suggests that special attention given to workers by management increases productivity regardless of actual changes in working conditions.

Criticisms of the Hawthorne Studies   There have been a number of major criticisms of the Hawthorne studies. They include charges of scientific illiteracy, promanagement bias, and unwarranted conclusions drawn from small samples. Outputs did not increase under all conditions. Productivity actually dropped when piecework was eliminated, when the workday was lengthened, and when rest periods were eliminated. In one of the studies, an increase in the use of piecework alone increased productivity by 12 percent. Interest in the worker did not directly increase productivity in every case; studies of the bank wiring observation room showed this.

The Importance of the Hawthorne Studies   The Hawthorne studies generated a great deal of interest in group behavior and its influence on the individual. The studies counterbalanced the ideas fostered by proponents of scientific management, particularly in the 1930s and beyond. Because of the Hawthorne studies, more attention began to be given to the noneconomic aspects of motivation, group dynamics, and the effect of group norms on the individual.

THE EMERGENCE OF STRUCTURAL THEORY

Organizational structure refers to the design and relationship of the parts of the organization. Structure has always been an important component of organizations. Two major influences on the modern organization were the Roman military and the Catholic Church. Modern interest in organizational design and structure started shortly after the beginning of the Industrial Revolution.

One chief component of organizational structure is division of labor. It was described by Adam Smith in 1776 in *The Wealth of Nations.* Smith noted that a single worker could make about 20 pins a day. By subdividing the task into a number of operations, Smith reported, ten workers could produce 48,000 pins a day—240 times what a single worker could produce alone. Division of labor remains a viable technique for use in production.

Some of the more influential works on organizational design appeared shortly after the turn of this century. These works indicated the international nature of the development of structural theory. Similar ideas were propounded simultaneously and independently in France, Germany, Great Britain, and the United States.

Imagine being in France about 1915, visiting a large coal mine. You might have had the opportunity to meet Henri Fayol, the president of the coal mine and one of the more modern writers on industry. Fayol's first book was published in a French journal in 1916 as *Administration industrielle et générale*. It received considerably more attention when printed in the United States under the title *General and Industrial Management*.[16]

Fayol developed six categories for business activities, as shown in Figure 2.2. *Technical activities* involve areas such as manufacture and production. *Commercial activities* include buying, selling, and exchange. *Financial activities* include the search for and best use of capital. Security activities include the protection of persons and property. *Accounting activities* include costs, balance sheets, and statistics. *Managerial activities* include planning, organization, command, coordination, and control. Fayol put primary emphasis on managerial functions. He believed that managerial skills had been the most neglected of the skills needed in business.

To emphasize the managerial function, Fayol developed the fourteen principles of management shown in Table 2.1. He was careful to use the term *principles* rather than *rules* or *laws* because he believed that organizations need to adapt to changing situations and that principles must be flexible. By drawing up these principles, Fayol paved the way for others to follow, change, and modify them as they learned more about management.[17]

An American author, Luther Gulick, expanded on Fayol's managerial functions and developed POSDCORB. Gulick defined the basic managerial functions as planning, organizing, staffing, directing, coordinating, reporting, and budgeting.[18] POSDCORB is an acronym for these functions.

Max Weber, a German sociologist, took a slightly different approach to organizational structure. He argued that bureaucracy represented the ideal organizational design. He believed that rules and regulations keep the organization functioning and protect its members from favoritism. Weber defined the bureaucratic organization as having certain basic characteristics: (1) a division or specialization of labor, (2) a well developed hierarchy, (3) a system of procedures that defines and protects the rights and duties of employees, (4) interpersonal relationships based on position rather than personality, and (5) promotion and selection based on technical competence. Weber stated that bureaucracy's well defined rules and expertise were effective ways of getting rid of organizational

Originally, bureaucracy was a favorable word.

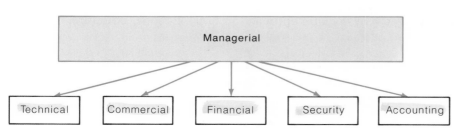

FIGURE 2.2 The activities of a business

TABLE 2.1 Fayol's Fourteen Principles of Management

1. *Division of work:* The specialization of workers, including management, to improve efficiency and increase output.
2. *Authority and responsibility:* The right to give orders and the power to exact obedience (p. 12). Authority leads to responsibility.
3. *Discipline:* Obedience, application, energy, and behavior (p. 22) given to the organization, depending on the leaders.
4. *Unity of command:* No person should have more than one boss.
5. *Unity of direction:* There should be only one plan for accomplishing goals (an extension of the unity of command principle).
6. *Subordination of individual to general interest:* The concerns of the organization placed ahead of individual concerns.
7. *Pay:* Arrangements for pay that are fair and satisfactory to all and competence rewarded but not overrewarded.
8. *Centralization:* The consolidation of the management function according to the circumstances surrounding the organization.
9. *Hierarchy:* The lines of authority should run clearly from the top of the organization to the lowest level.
10. *Order:* People and materials should be in the right place at the right time and people should be in the jobs most suited to them.
11. *Equity:* Loyalty should be encouraged by justice, kindliness, and fairness.
12. *Stability:* High employee turnover both causes and is the result of inefficiency and good organizations have stable managements.
13. *Initiative:* The necessity of "thinking out a plan and ensuring its success (p. 39)" and of giving subordinates the opportunity to perform.
14. *Esprit de corps:* Oral communications should be used to keep teams together.

Source: Henri Fayol, *General and Industrial Management,* trans. C. Storrs (London: Sir Isaac Pitman and Sons, 1949). Note that individual page numbers are given with the items in the table. *Administration industrielle et générale* first appeared in French in 1916 in the third issue for that year of the *Bulletin de la Société de l'Industrie Minerale.* It was published in book form in 1925 by Dunod Frères of Paris.

favoritism, arbitrary authority, payoffs, kickbacks, and incompetence. He believed that the resultant job security would promote innovation as well.[19] Today, unfortunately the term *bureaucracy* has become associated with red tape, inefficiency, slowness, and waste.

Fayol's, Gulick's, and Weber's approaches were similar. All three proposed an ideal way to design an organization, emphasized a single chain of command and clear lines of communication, and studied only organizations that produced a single, relatively simple product. For this reason, the three may not have been completely correct in their conclusions. Nevertheless, many of their ideas apply to modern business. They correctly pointed out the importance of the managerial job, and they encouraged a systematic approach to organizational structure.

THE GROWING IMPORTANCE OF TECHNOLOGY AND ENVIRONMENT

Early in the century, Taylor distinguished between the organization producing large quantities of the same product and the organization producing special products to customer order. He suggested that each case required different management approaches. Taylor's suggestion was largely ignored by both the classical writers on structure such as Fayol and Weber and the writers studying human relations.

Woodward's Findings   Eventually, Taylor's distinction was found to be valid. Joan Woodward, a British management professor and industrial researcher, studied a hundred firms in England to find out whether the classical structural principles of organization held true in all cases. In analyzing her data she found that the principles suggested by people like Fayol and Weber did not always hold up. She discovered unexplained organizational differences among successful firms. Puzzled, she reexamined her data and began to identify the importance of a new concept, *technology*. The differences among firms made sense when the organizations were classified by the technology used in their production processes.

Woodward distinguished three broad groupings representing three **types of technology.** She divided the technologies according to production techniques and the complexity of production: (1) unit and small-batch production, such as custom-tailored clothing, or products manufactured in small quantities such as machine parts; (2) mass or large-batch production, such as automobiles or large quantities of standard electronic components; and (3) continuous or process production, such as chemical and oil-refining.

Figure 2.3 shows unit and small-batch production as the least sophisticated technologically, large-batch or mass production as intermediate, and continuous process production as the most sophisticated.

In general, Woodward placed the firms on a scale according to the predictability of results and the degree of control over the production process. Unit production exhibited the lowest predictability, and continuous process production the highest predictability. The type of management used by the more successful firms varied along the scale of predictability. For example, the less predictable the technology the greater the number of managers and management levels, and the greater the technologial predictability the greater the number of clerical and managerial people involved. Firms that did not follow these and other principles were less successful. Woodward found that each of the three tech-

Fewer management levels		More management levels
Unit and small-batch production	Large-batch or mass production	Continuous process production

Low predictability of technology   High predictability of technology

FIGURE 2.3 The continuum of predictability of technology

nologies had specific types of organizational structures that were associated with success.[20]

Stable versus Turbulent Environments   Shortly after Woodward's studies, two other researchers came up with similar results. They found that successful firms had one of two basic types of organizational structures, depending on the nature of their operating environment. These environments of different organizations, or subunits of organizations, were placed at different points on a continuum, as shown in Figure 2.4.

Environment may influence the structure of organizations

A **stable environment** shows little or no unexpected or sudden change; the few product changes that do occur generally can be predicted well in advance. Organizations making cotton string, burlap, and manhole covers, for example, exist in a relatively stable environment. In a stable environment, successful organizations exhibit well-defined procedures, rules, and functional roles. These characteristics typify a *mechanistic organizational structure.* Mechanistic organizations follow a bureaucratic model of organization. They are characterized by a high degree of reliance on task specialization, clear rules, precise job descriptions, and an understanding of rights and responsibilities.

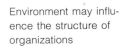

A **turbulent environment** has many sudden, rapid, and frequently unpredictable product changes. Organizations in the computer and medical instrument fields, for example, exist in a turbulent environment. In a turbulent environment, successful organizations use an *organic organizational structure.* This structure emphasizes taking and giving orders and places great value on the use of special knowledge from lower levels of the organization. In mechanistic organizations, leadership is centered at the top; in organic organizations, leadership and decision making are diffuse. The emphasis is on consultation and decision making by consensus.[21]

The classical approach to organizational structure emerged from a relatively stable society and culture. When Ford brought out the first mass-produced car, it was said, "You can have any color, so long as it is black." Today's culture is subject to rapid change. Organizations and administrative techniques also change. The abacus, a computing device has been used unchanged in Asia for hundreds of years. In today's Western culture, last year's pocket electronic calculator is obsolete this year. Further attention is paid to evolving organizational structure in Chapters 9 and 10.

FIGURE 2.4 The continuum from stable to turbulent environment

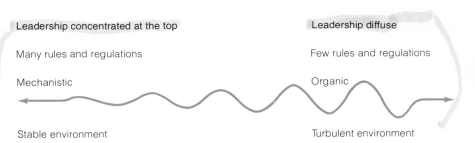

CURRENT INTEGRATIVE TRENDS

During the past thirty years a large body of knowledge dealing with management and organization has been built up. Research in the field is continually expanding. The large number of books, journals, and articles dealing with management attest to this. Growing interest in management and organization is due in part to the shift from a relatively unchanging society to a society undergoing constant change and becoming more interdependent. As a result of the research, three important integrative trends have developed: (1) the systems concept, (2) the contingency approach, and (3) the quality of work life (QWL) movement.

The Systems Concept The term *system* refers to a series of interrelated and interdependent parts. In a system the interaction or interplay of any of the parts affects the whole. In this book, **system** means the entire organization and **subsystem** applies to the different groups or units within the organization. Thus the organization as a system is composed of a number of interrelated and interdependent components, and each component affects the other components. Using this view, the organization can be considered a subsystem of the larger culture.

Inputs
(information, financial, and other resources)

Organization as an open system

Outputs
(goods and services)

The pressure exerted on industry by the public illustrates this point. The Civil Rights Act was passed in 1964. Between 1964 and 1970, American Airlines dismissed approximately three hundred stewardesses because they had become pregnant. In 1977, the airline settled with the fired stewardesses. American Airlines agreed to rehire the women, pay them for the time they had lost from work, and make Social Security back payments for the time the case was in the courts. The airline had previously considered the stewardesses only as a subsystem of the company. The airline failed to consider itself as a subsystem within the larger society. The societal suprasystem, at the stewardesses' request, decided the dismissals were not strictly an internal matter.

Although managers have always been aware that the organization is a unified, purposeful system composed of interrelated parts, they dealt with the various parts of the organization separately. The system approach gives managers a way of looking at the organization as a whole that is greater than the sum of its parts.

Engineers, for example, have known for years that automobile design affects roadability, handling, and gas consumption. At forty miles an hour an automobile uses as much power to overcome air resistance as it does to overcome mechanical friction. Even so, automobile manufacturers chose to consider design and performance as separate problems. In 1973, General Motors did only three hundred hours of testing in wind tunnels to examine overall design. By 1979, however, the figure had risen to twenty-five hundred hours, and it is increasing steadily each year.[22]

As in the automobile example, the systems approach provides a powerful tool for diagnosing organizational performance. Through this approach, managers can tell if the organization is operating well. When the

On the Job

PUTTING WORKERS INTO WORKMANSHIP

A big reason for the stunning invasion of the U.S. auto markets by the Japanese is that their cars have a better reputation for workmanship. Detroit admits the problem and blames much of it on a traditional style of labor relations that usually ignores worker suggestions and typically loads up production lines with as many as one-third more inspectors. General Motors Corp. began tackling the issue several years ago with a broad, Quality of Work Life program. Now Chrysler Corp. and Ford Motor Co. are trying a more focused approach: small groups of workers called "quality circles" that figure out ways to cut costs, improve quality, and in the process smooth out relations between labor and management.

The Ford and Chrysler programs got their start in the last round of contract talks in 1979, when the United Auto Workers and Ford agreed to a National Joint Committee on Employee Involvement. Chrysler followed last spring with an agreement to establish "action teams." The companies have set up dozens of quality circles, and in conjunction with other quality programs, these are already producing benefits. Peter J. Pestillo, Ford's vice-president of labor relations, says that about 95% of the cars made at Ford's Escort/Lynx plant in Wayne, Mich., are free of first-

run production defects—about 10 points above the company's average in 1979. "It's a question of trying to remain competitive," says Robert J. Jensen, an official of the UAW's Chrysler department.

Indeed, the success of quality circles will be instrumental in determining whether U.S. auto makers can regain sales—and jobs—that have been lost to the Japanese. In a survey taken last spring by the Motor & Equipment Manufacturers Assn., 51% of 10,000 consumers polled favored the engineering of Japanese cars, compared with 21% for small U.S. models. They favored Japanese durability by 44% to 25%. A survey of 450 consumers taken last March by Chicago-based Leo Shapiro & Associates showed that 75% of those who want a Japanese car prefer one made in Japan, while only 2% would want the same car if it were made in the U.S. Improved quality, says Donald F. Ephlin, director of the UAW's Ford department, "is good for the company, our members, and the consumer who buys the car."

Problem-solving Techniques

Ford and Chrysler's quality push is an attempt to catch up. Although the theories that sparked quality circles were conceived in this country, their widespread use began in Japan in the mid-

1960s. The idea began gaining attention in the U.S. in the mid-1970s, and consultants estimate that 1,000 U.S. companies will have some kind of quality circle program by the mid-1980s. General Motors and the UAW began a Quality of Work Life program in 1973 that incorporates quality improvement in a broader effort to make work more satisfying and productive, and GM has such programs in 84 plants. But U.S. auto makers have generally been slow to change because "workers and management assumed that consumers would accept anything we gave them," says Kenneth J. Kruickshank, assistant manager at Ford's Wayne plant. "Japan showed that consumers like its quality better. Our goal now is to be better than them."

Detroit's quality circles vary by plant, but generally they are comprised of 7 to 10 workers and a leader who is often from management. The number of circles in each plant depends on the number of problems and how many workers volunteer for the programs. Many circles get a two-day course on problem-solving techniques before meeting regularly, on company time but often off the plant floor, to discuss ways of producing more "perfect" cars and thus reducing in-plant repairs, plus warranty costs. For instance, one quality circle recently found that a vacuum tube on Escort/Lynx engines was being damaged as the engines were placed on material handling racks. It suggested that the supplier, also a Ford plant, send the pieces separately for assembly on-site. Ford says the change has saved money, but it will not say how much.

Cutting Costs At Chrysler's K-car plant in Newark, Del., action teams are working on emission systems, water leaks, hood fits, and door fits, among other problems. One team recently found that door leaks could be prevented by heating rubber gaskets before mounting them on the doors. This makes the gaskets more malleable and easier to install properly, and provides a better seal. The team used heat lamps until permanent equipment could be installed, and now it is working on leaks around the rear hatch of station wagons.

The quality circles are also cutting material costs, as at Ford's Sheffield casting plant in Sheffield, Ala. After consulting with the plant's maintenance, production, and quality control departments, one circle suggested a different production procedure that resulted in a 50% reduction in aluminum scrap generated during the making of engine parts. The team pre-

sented the plan to management, even though by then most of the circle's members had been laid off.

A side benefit of the circles is that they are improving relations between employees and supervisors. Workers like to apply their skills outside the assembly-line routine, says Robert L. Pierce, a UAW official at Chrysler's Delaware plant. "In the past, suggestions weren't listened to. Now at least they're heard and get results." The circles also increase the pride employees take in their work: "I now have people wanting to know how we did on the daily inspection audit," says Ford's Kruickshank. And at Ford, where the circles can address working conditions as long as they steer clear of contract questions, grievances are declining. Officials at Ford's Chesterfield II trim plant in Mt. Clemens, Mich., attribute much of a recent 80% decline in monthly grievances (in part caused by a 40% decline in the plant's work force) to the company's Employee Involvement program.

Despite these gains, many experts believe that Ford and Chrysler must improve their programs in order to make significant gains in quality. Robert E. Cole, director of the Center for Japanese Studies at the University of Michigan and an expert on worker relations in Japan,

argues that workers must become even more deeply involved.

Quality consciousness in Japan, Cole writes in a book published in 1979, begins when rank-and-file workers and top management attend study groups together. As a result, he writes, quality control has been "shifted from being the prerogative of the minority of engineers with limited shop experience to being the responsibility of each employee. Instead of adding layers of inspectors when quality problems arise, as is customary in many U.S. companies, each worker is expected to take responsibility for solving quality problems." Cole believes that this accounts for the high quality of Japanese cars and Toyota Motor Co.'s ratio of 1 inspector for 30 workers, vs. 1 for 20 at GM, while the traditional American approach implies "a basic lack of confidence and trust" in workers. He adds, in an interview, that too many inspectors make workers lax by creating the perception that workers have little responsibility for quality.

Promising Beginning Cole also believes that U. S. auto companies rely too heavily on new technology to enhance quality and productivity. "There is a stress on the big bang rather than on the small, sectoral increases the worker can make that in the aggregate can be enormous," he says. Cole adds that in 1980 each production worker at Toyota generated 17.8 suggestions and that 90% were adopted. By contrast, GM workers made an average of less than one suggestion each, and

only 31% were adopted.

But workers think that the Ford and Chrysler programs are a promising beginning. William G. Stevenson, UAW chairman at Ford's Sterling Van Dyke axle plant in Sterling Heights, Mich., concedes that some of his mem-

bers "think the company is using us now because it's in trouble." But he says that as many as 30 workers have applied for some of the plant's 10-member quality circles, and he adds: "You can't lose by having a say in what's going on."

parts of the organization are out of alignment, things do not go as well as they can. The next chapter describes the systems concept in more detail and examines its use in diagnosing the health of the organization.

The Contingency Approach According to the second integrative trend, the **contingency approach,** the best way to lead, plan, organize, and conduct managerial activities varies with the situation.[23] Highly effective techniques in one situation are less effective in other situations or cultures. The best way to organize a firm engaged in small-batch production is not the best way to organize a firm engaged in continuous process production. Managing unskilled workers is very different from managing highly trained professionals. In some situations the manager's best approach to a subordinate may be directive and authoritarian; in others, a considerate and appreciative approach may be more appropriate.

Therefore, a major managerial task involves choosing the best approach needed to reach the goals of the organization in each circumstance. The contingency approach applies to almost every managerial action. The effective manager must continually ask, "Which method will work best here? " A decisions helping an individual subunit of the organization may not be helpful in reaching the goals and objectives of the entire organization.

The Quality of Work Life The third and most recent integrative trend was first introduced in the late 1960s. It represents an attempt to improve the prevailing and needlessly poor quality of life at the work place.[24] A broad concept, **quality of work life** refers to the degree to which work "provides an opportunity for an individual to satisfy a wide variety of personal needs—from the need to survive with some security to the need to interact with others, to have a sense of personal usefulness, to be recognized for achievement, and to have an opportunity to improve one's skills and knowledge."[25]

The quality of work life process is an attempt to change the work place in order to increase productivity and to provide better opportunities for individuals and groups to develop on the job. A variety of organizations, including industrial, nonprofit, military, and public administration, use the QWL approach. Both General Motors and Procter and Gamble have built a number of new plants based on QWL principles.

Unions often participate in firms' QWL efforts. A prime example of a joint union-management project is the UAW-GM modification of the existing GM plant in North Tarrytown, New York. Over a number of years, the plant spent approximately $1.6 million on a QWL program. Both Irving Bluestone, then vice-president of the UAW, and Robert Guest, who has studied automobile plants for many years, consider the project a success.[26] Absenteeism dropped from 7.25 percent to about 2 percent. At the end of December 1978 only thirty-two grievances remained on the plant's docket, compared to two thousand earlier. The plant, once one of the poorest in quality performance, recently won an award from GM for its quality performance. No strikes or work stoppages have occurred for seven years. Due to these results and results from a number of other projects, General Motors is involved in work restructuring and QWL projects in a number of locations.

QWL
Union-management

Cooperation

Productivity in the United States has been dropping steadily. In 1980 more automobiles were produced in Japan than in the United States. Although technological innovations, such as automation, create some productivity increases, QWL represents a major attemp to further increase productivity. At the same time, QWL efforts provide greater opportunity for satisfaction of human needs in the workplace.

The need for the rapidly increasing concern with quality of work life is underscored by several recent studies. Nationwide surveys of this type were conducted by the Survey Research Center in 1969, 1973, and 1977.[27] The most recent survey reported substantial declines in overall job satisfaction, in desire to stay with the present employer, and in enjoyment of life in general. Some analysts believe these declines are due to workers' rising expectations and feelings of being underutilized in their jobs. Other studies, based on economics, show decreased job satisfaction as a major cause of lowered productivity and increased turnover.

All these results suggest a need to redesign jobs to provide not only for increased productivity but also for greater psychic rewards on the job.[28] Industry is developing methods for accomplishing these aims. The *quality circle,* a method of improving quality, is widespread in Japan but used in only a few companies in the United States. Ford and Chrysler in agreements with the UAW have recently instituted quality control procedures allowing production workers to stop assembly lines if they spot defective or shoddy work.

SUMMARY

Knowledge is steadily accumulating in both the hard sciences and in management science. More is known about organizations, management, and managers than was known even a few years ago. While building a pyramid was a complex task, it was not as complex as designing or managing many modern organizations. Building a supersonic jet or sending a probe to Mars requires even more planning, coordination, and attention to close tolerances than moving a stone block down the Nile. Of course, many organizations are not complex; some are relatively simple. However, all organizations must be managed.

Managing receives more systematic attention now than ever before. Yet the fundamental goal of management and managers—to plan, direct, and organize work activities to accomplish the goals of the organization—remains essentially unchanged.

This chapter contains only a few selected samples of management thought through the ages. These samples show how such thought has affected and been affected by society and culture. Without the cultural beliefs and the approval of society, the Great Pyramid could never have been built. The Arsenal of Venice grew out of the cultural need to protect the Venetian mercantile society.

Stress on factors stimulating productivity led to research on motivation, group dynamics, and the quality of work life. Major resulting movements promoting study of scientific management and human relations greatly influenced current management thought. Conclusions from Taylor's early work and the Hawthorne studies turned out to be based primarily on myth. However, both studies had, and still have, a profound impact on today's thinking. Taylor and the following efficiency experts placed too much emphasis on impersonal analysis; the Hawthorne studies suggested rehumanizing the workplace.

The growing complexity of organizations meant a greater need to examine them as a whole. Fayol, Weber, and others responded to the need to systematize organizations. They sought to provide managers with a way of guiding organizational structure. Although these early writers dealt with organizations having a relatively simple technology and stable environment, the principles they laid down provided the basis for management thought and practice today. Much of this early work has now been replaced or expanded. As Fayol knew, theorists propound principles and not laws.

Managers now understand that no single set of laws can be applied to all management problems. Using the systems approach management can diagnose situations and choose the proper fits between subsets of the organization. The contingency approach leads management to apply different basic guidelines, depending on the particular situation. Recent drops in productivity suggest that greater attention be paid to the quality of work life. The quality of work life approach promotes greater productivity through greater attention to the needs of both individual workers and groups. The effective manager, being a good diagnostician, selects the proper approach for the given situation.

STUDY QUESTIONS

1. Assume that you are in charge of building the Great Pyramid of Cheops. Knowing what you know today, how would you go about designing the organization structure; recruiting, training, and paying employees; and handling other details?

2. Explain how the myth of Taylor's work at Bethlehem Steel and the conclusions of the Haw-

thorne studies came to be so widely believed.

3. Why is it important for you to learn about and understand the development of different management theories?

4. What was Mayo's principal contribution to management knowledge?

5. Which of Fayol's principles and functions of management do you believe still apply today?

6. How much do you think writers such as Fayol and Weber were influenced by the culture in which they lived?

7. Do you think Fayol would describe organizations now as he did when his book was first published (in 1916)?

8. Does the systems approach seem more appropriate for our time and culture than for Fayol's? Explain.

9. According to the contingency approach, what is the major task of the manager?

10. Read about and report on the life and work of one of the following: Chester Barnard, Ralph C. Davis, Harrington Emerson, Mary Parker Follett, Luther Gulick, Hugo Munsterberg, Robert Owen, Fritz Roethlisberger, Herbert Simon, or Max Weber.

11. If you were able to have a conversation with any person from the past, whom would you pick? What would you choose as the subject of conversation?

Case for Discussion

REORGANIZING THE ROMAN ARMY

As a popular and successful general, Caius Marius had been elected Consul of the Roman republic five times. In 102 B.C., at the height of his popularity, he reorganized the Roman army—a reform that had been needed for about fifty years. The structural reorganization was relatively simple. The Roman legion consisted of about six thousand men. Marius divided them into sixty centuries (one hundred men), each under a centurian. He grouped each century into ten cohorts, and he had the heads of the cohorts report directly to the general of the legion. This division made the army more efficient, but the real reorganization was based on changes in society.

Before the reorganization, the army was based on the draft; and under the Roman constitution, the draft applied only to citizens who owned a certain amount of property. But over time, the rich landowners, merchants, and others who were eligible no longer had either the aptitude or the taste for military service. The draft was kept, but Marius allowed the poor and unemployed to volunteer. Soon the reluctant farmers and merchants disappeared from the army. The volunteers were those who saw service under a successful general as a prospect for adventure or escape from poverty.

Then, the army began to supply equipment to the soldiers, instead of having each individual furnish his own. This meant fewer distinctions based on wealth and ensured that both equipment and training were more standardized.

The bulk of the volunteers were farm laborers or small farmers so heavily in debt that they were in danger of losing their farms. In addition to the prospect of prizes from a successful campaign, a general in search of recruits could promise that, if the army were disbanded, the soldiers would be given an allotment of land. Thus the new Roman army gave more prominence to generals with established reputations whose names would bring in recruits.

The common soldier began to shift allegiance from the republic or the senate to the general. The senate might back down or delay on promises, but the soldiers could count on their generals to fight political battles for them. This made it almost impossible for one general to take an army from another or to remove another general from command.

Thus the army fell more and more under the control of the generals. In turn, the generals became servants of their own armies. They could not retire from public life if their own army were disbanded, since they had to fulfill the promises by which they had obtained volunteers.

Although the Roman soldier respected the constitution, the armies would not hesitate to support their generals against the government if the generals had good reason for attacking it. In 51 B.C., approximately fifty years later, Julius Caesar and Pompeius Magnus (Pompey) began a political struggle. In 50 B.C. Pompey violated the constitution, and Caesar's soldiers enthusiastically followed him. Caesar crossed the Rubicon and invaded Italy, and the civil war began. It ended in 44 B.C. with Caesar being voted a perpetual dictatorship. This was the beginning of the downfall of the Roman republic.

1. How do societal patterns, organizations, managing, and operating levels interact in this case? In the short run? In the long run?
2. Given hindsight, could the army have been reorganized differently?
3. What implications might this historical information have for the world we live in today?
4. What similarities and dissimilarities do you see in this case to such areas as scientific management, the emergence of human relations, and organizational structure?
5. What effect might systems thinking have had?

Sources: Guglielmo Ferrero, *The Greatness and Decline of Rome* (London: William Heinemann, 1909); and Frank Burr Marsh, *A History of the Roman World* (New York: Barnes & Noble, 1963).

FOR YOUR CAREER

1. The Arsenal of Venice illustrates the use of basic management principles developed in the fifteenth century. Knowledge of history can help you become a better manager.
2. This book can provide you with guidelines for good management. Of course, you will have to select the ones to use and apply them carefully.
3. Avoid the mistakes of the many large organizations that are now out of business. Keep an open mind and always be prepared to learn about new approaches to management.
4. Reading such journals as the *Harvard Business Review,* the *California Business Review,* the *Journal of the Academy of Management,* and specialized journals in your particular field will help you keep an open mind.
5. Whenever possible, diagnose the situation before taking action. There are many ways of examining the situation. The next chapter will provide guidelines for such examinations.
6. Repeated throughout the book will be the admonition to avoid the "not invented here," or NIH, factor. Many managers presented with a new idea respond, "That's all right for another situation (company), but it would not work in my situation (company)."

FOOTNOTES

1. A. Erman, *Life in Ancient Egypt,* trans. H. Tirard (London: Macmillan, 1894); and F. Bratton, *A History of Egyptian Archaeology* (New York: Crowell, 1968).
2. M. Childe, *Man Makes Himself* (New York: New American Library, 1951).
3. G. Contenau, *Everyday Life in Babylon* (London: Edward Arnold Publishers, 1954).
4. U. Kuo-Cheng, *Ancient Chinese Political Theories* (Shanghai: Commercial Press, 1928).
5. A. Lepawsky, *Administration* (New York: Knopf, 1949).
6. C. George, *The History of Management Thought* (Englewood Cliffs, N.J.: Prentice-Hall, 1968); and F. Lane, *Venetian Ships and Shipbuilders of the Renaissance* (Baltimore: John Hopkins Press, 1934).
7. G. Filipetti, *Industrial Management in Transition*

(Chicago: Richard D. Irwin, 1949); C. George, Jr., *History of Management Thought,* rev. ed. (Englewood Cliffs, N.J.: Prentice-Hall, 1972); and D. Wren, *The Evolution of Management Thought* (New York: Ronald Press, 1972).

8. *Industrial Standardization* (New York: National Industrial Conference Board, 1929); B. Melmitsky, *Profiting from Industrial Standardization* (New York: Conde-Nast Publications, 1953).

9. J. W. Oliver, *History of American Technology* (New York: Ronald Press, 1956), pp. 169–170; and C. Singer, E. J. Holmyard, A. R. Hall, and T. I. Williams, *The History of Technology, 1750–1850* (London: Oxford University Press, 1958).

10. F. Taylor, *The Principles of Modern Management* (New York: Harper & Bros., 1911).

11. C. Wrege and A. Perroni, "Taylor's Pig-Tale: A Historical Analysis of Frederick W. Taylor's Pig-Iron Experiments," *American Management Journal* 17 (March 1974): 6–27; C. Wrege, personal communication; J. Gillespie and H. Wolle, "Report on the Establishment of Piecework in Connection with the Loading of Pig-Iron at the Works of the Bethlehem Iron Co., South Bethlehem, Pennsylvania," in Wrege and Perroni, "Taylor's Pig-Tale," p. 17.

12. C. Wrege and A. Perroni, "Taylor's Pig-Tale," *Academy of Management Journal* 17 (March 1974): 11.

13. "GM Finds Advantages in Giving Workers Decision-Making Role," *Hartford Courant,* November 24, 1977, p. 1.

14. F. Gilbreth, Jr., and E. Carey, *Cheaper by the Dozen* (New York: Crowell, 1948).

15. C. Wrege, "Solving Mayo's Mystery: The First Complete Account of the Origin of the Hawthorne Studies—The Forgotten Contributions of C. E. Snow and H. Hilbarger," *Academy of Management Proceedings,* Kansas City, Missouri, August 11–14 1976; and C. Wrege, personal communication.

16. H. Fayol, *General and Industrial Management,* trans. C. Storrs (London: Sir Isaac Pitman and Sons, 1949).

17. Ibid.

18. L. Gulick, "Notes on the Theory of Organization," in *Papers on the Science of Administration,* ed. L. Gulick and L. Urwick (New York: Columbia University Press, 1937).

19. M. Weber, *The Theory of Social and Economic Organization* (New York: Oxford University Press, 1947).

20. J. Woodward, *Management and Technology* (London: Her Majesty's Printing Office, 1958).

21. T. Burns and G. Stalker, *The Management of Innovation* (New York: Barnes & Noble, Social Science Paperbacks, 1961).

22. M. Schuon, "Detroit's Engineers Hunt for Economy in Wind Tunnels," *New York Times,* July 8, 1980.

23. F. Luthans, "The Contingency Theory of Management: A Path out of the Jungle," *Business Horizons* 15 (June 1973): 447–465; and F. Kast and J. Rosenzweig, eds., *Contingency View of Organization and Management* (Chicago: Science Research Associates, 1973).

24. L. Davis, "Enhancing the Quality of Work Life: Developments in the United States," *International Labour Review* 116 (July–August 1977): 53–65; and E. Huse, *Organizational Development and Change,* 2d ed. (St. Paul, Minn.: West Publishing, 1980).

25. G. Lippitt and J. Rumley, "Living with Work—The Search for Quality in Work Life," *Optimum* 8 (January 1977): 38.

26. "United Auto Workers Vice President Bluestone on QWL with General Motors and Others," *Massachusetts Quality of Working Life Center* 3 (January 1979); and R. Guest, "The Quality of Work Life—Learning from Tarrytown," *Harvard Business Review* 57 (July–August 1979): 76–87.

27. G. Staines and R. Quinn, "American Workers Evaluate the Quality of Their Jobs," *Monthly Labor Review* (January 1979): 3–11.

28. R. Freeman, "Job Satisfaction as an Economic Variable," *American Economic Review* 68 (May 1978): 135–141; and L. Thurow, "Psychic Income: Useful or Useless?" *American Economic Review* 68 (May 1978): 142–148.

Systems—Diagnosing the Organization

CHAPTER 3

CONTENTS

THE MANAGEMENT INFORMATION SYSTEM

A large multinational organization decided to develop an integrated, computer-based management information system (MIS) to use in one of its plants. The plant employed approximately 7,000 people and manufactured seventeen models of complex equipment used for a variety of civilian and defense purposes and marketed in fourteen countries besides the United States.

The organization manufactured or bought more than 25,000 different parts each year to enable it to fill its approximately 3,200 original equipment orders and 25,000 spare parts orders. On an annual basis, it manufactured or processed almost 8 million parts. From the time an order was received, each piece of equipment required approximately twelve to fifteen months to build and ship.

Through a series of fifteen major computer programs, the proposed MIS was to provide assembly and manufacturing schedules, record customer orders, streamline inventory control, allow prediction of personnel and machine requirements, and provide information to assist in the control of the flow of work through the factory. Management expected the computer to provide the purchasing department with requirements for materials, supplies, and parts from outside vendors.

Through these services the MIS would replace or integrate a multitude of manual or partly computerized systems already existing at the plant.

Savings from the use of the new system were expected to be more than $1 million annually. Under the old approach, approximately 18,000 work hours (nine work years) were required to make the more than 3 million hand calculations needed to develop a comprehensive planning schedule for the plant. The frequent schedule changes required about forty working days to complete. The MIS was expected to reduce rescheduling time to four or five days, limit hand calculations to fewer than 100, and increase accuracy.

After three years of intense effort and the outlay of several million dollars, the MIS program faded away, although it was never officially abandoned. Before its demise, the director of the program resigned to take a better job elsewhere in the organization. The members of the MIS task force condemned middle managers for being uncooperative. The middle managers complained that the task force was not generating data suitable for their needs. Each time the programs cut across departmental boundaries, managers in one department refused to trust inputs from other departments and insisted on controlling their own information (data bases). Lower-level production schedulers and clerks complained about program errors. The task force maintained that program errors were due to a lack of sufficiently current information to put on the computer.[1]

This opening case of the multinational organization raises several critical questions about organizations which you should be able to answer after reading this chapter. The questions include:

1. What do house thermostats and General Motors have in common?
2. How do you interpret the phrase "The whole is greater than the sum of its parts"?
3. What are the major differences between a physical system and a social system?
4. Are organizations closed or open systems? Explain.

3

Why did the management information system fail in spite of three years of hard work and expenditures of several million dollars? The main reason was the failure of those involved to conduct a proper diagnostic analysis of the organization and the possible impact of the computer programs on the organization as a system.

Initially, the members of the task force demonstrated an awareness of the management information system as it related to the larger environment. They knew it would have a broad impact on the entire organization. In the pressure to get the MIS designed and implemented, however, they lost sight of this fact. Middle- and lower-level managers focused their efforts on the here and now, sacrificing the improved future MIS offered. Thus rather than diagnosing and understanding relationships of different elements and factors within the organization, those involved concentrated on their own operations and neglected the needs and demands of the larger organization.

Under the systems approach the manager's job is one of managing systems. The manager defines the organization or its unit as a system, establishes objectives, and creates, integrates, and coordinates necessary subsystems. The systems manager recognizes the contribution and interdependence of each part to the whole system. Failure to meet objectives usually reflects improper system design or misalignment of the components of the system rather than flaws in the system's components. Once a systems point of view prevails, instead of explaining the whole in terms of its parts, parts are explained in terms of the whole, as one manager has put it.[2]

Systems approach:

- Define organization or unit as a system
- Establish objectives for it
- Create, integrate, and coordinate necessary subsystems

WHY STUDY SYSTEMS?

General systems theory embraces a major, ongoing attempt to identify how certain general laws and concepts unify a number of different fields.[3] For the practicing manager, however, the ability to unify knowledge from different fields is not the most important reason for studying the systems approach. The manager who uses systems concepts tends to be less judgmental. The systems approach encourages managers to look beyond single-cause thinking. More importantly, knowledge of the interrelatedness and interdependence of the parts of a system aids the manager in diagnosing and identifying reasons for effectiveness or lack of effectiveness within an organization.

This chapter describes the basic characteristics of systems. It also presents methods for distinguishing between systems in general and organizations as social systems. It examines single-cause thinking and compares it to systems thinking as a diagnostic tool for managers. It then develops a diagnostic model to illustrate why the MIS in the case study was doomed to failure before it started.

BASIC CHARACTERISTICS OF SYSTEMS

Systems have:

- Subsystems
- Inputs
- Operations
- Outputs
- Boundaries
- Feedback
- Environment
- Function
- Synergism
- Equifinality

An organization is a system. A **system** is "a set of interdependent parts which together make up the whole because each contributes something and receives something from the whole, whch in turn is interdependent with the larger environment. Survival of the system is taken to be the goal."[4] Due to the interdependence and the interactions of the subsystems, they are as important to survival as the total system. A car will not start without a battery even if the rest of the parts are in good condition.

A basic outline of a system is given in Figure 3.1. This figure illustrates some of the basic characteristics of the organization as a system. It shows the relationship of an organization to the environment, to management, and to the system's inputs, operations, outputs, feedback, and boundaries.

The MIS program in the case study at the beginning of the chapter exemplifies a complex system. It existed within an even more complex system, the organization, which in turn existed within yet a larger system, society.

Subsystems, Total Systems, and Suprasystems **Subsystems** are the parts of a system. All the subsystems within a system constitute the total system. A series of interrelated and interdependent systems forms a **suprasystem.**

A change in any of the subsystems within a total system affects that system. The passenger transportation system of an airline is a complex system with subsystems. The system is designed to see that passengers are successfully loaded on planes for transport to another airport. Its subsystems include aircraft, ground support equipment, passenger and baggage loading systems, the passengers and their luggage, and the transportation system operators. If any of these subsystems fails to operate properly the impact on the other subsystems is immediate.

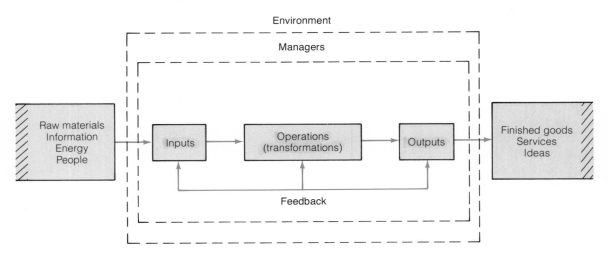

FIGURE 3.1 The organization as a system

The boundaries of a total system depend on the chosen definition. The University of California at Los Angeles represents a total system made up of academic and administrative departments, or subsystems. The university also functions as a subsystem of the State of California's total system of higher education. The California state government can be considered either a suprasystem or a total system. The state government can then be redefined as a subsystem of the United States government.

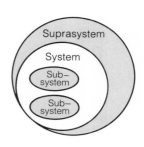

Thus the precise definition of a particular system depends on the purpose in studying or analyzing it. The freedom a manager possesses to define the system for analysis is one of the major advantages of the systems approach. The manager can choose the level of abstraction at which to analyze an organization without forgetting that the system is interacting on many levels with other systems.

Inputs, Operations, and Outputs Systems and subsystems contain a series of inputs, operations, and outputs, as shown in Figure 3.1. **Inputs** are resources such as labor, information, energy, and materials in the form that they enter the system or subsystem. They come from the environment or from one or more related subsystems. **Operations** transform inputs into other forms. They represent the process of converting resources into finished products or completed services. **Outputs** are inputs transformed through operations. The finished product or completed service is the output.

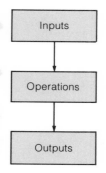

Air transportation systems receive inputs of arriving passengers. Operations check luggage and tickets; load planes with fuel, meals, and passengers; fly planes to their destination; and return luggage to departing passengers. When these operations are complete, the input to the system, arriving passengers at one terminal, has been transformed into the output of the system, departing passengers at another terminal.

Open and Closed Systems Systems can be viewed as either open or closed. A **closed system** does not receive inputs from outside the system; nor does it distribute output to the outside. **Open systems** do exchange input and output with the environment.

Few closed systems exist in real life. Instead, systems exhibit degrees of openness. They receive a certain amount of information, energy, or material from the environment. Completely closed systems suffer *entropy*; they run down. A mechanical alarm clock, a relatively closed system, needs to be wound periodically to prevent entropy. Organizations are open systems that are deeply imbedded in and responsive to the environment.

Nevertheless, the concept of the closed system proves useful when analyzing organizations. An analyst cannot study all aspects of an organization simultaneously. A manager who wants to analyze a specific department in an organization can treat that unit as a closed system. At the same time the manager must stay aware of the unit as a subsystem of the larger organization and realize that any changes in the subsystem have ramifications for the entire organization.

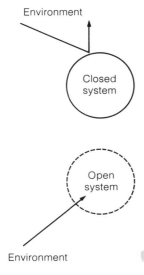

Environment

Environment

Boundaries **Boundaries** mark the borders or limits of the system. Few systems have impenetrable physical boundaries; almost all systems at least require outside energy to survive.

Defining the boundaries of social systems is difficult because of the continuous inflow and outflow of energy through them. In most cases, the definition of organizational and subsystem boundaries is somewhat arbitrary. In a social system with multiple subsystems, the characteristics chosen to define the boundary for one subsystem may not be the same characteristics chosen to determine the boundary of a different subsystem. How can a precise boundary be established for a company such as General Electric? Are subsidiaries and suppliers inside the boundaries of the total system? Arbitrary boundaries may have to be assigned according to the variable to be stressed. The boundaries used for analyzing leadership may be quite different from those used to study marketing strategy.

Just as systems vary from open to closed, the permeability of boundaries varies from fixed to diffuse. The boundaries of a prison are more fixed than those of a university; the boundaries of a family are less diffuse than those of a political party.

Feedback As used in the systems approach, **feedback** is information regarding the actual performance or the results of the activities of a system (see Figure 3.2). Not all such information is feedback, however. Only information used to control the future functioning of the system is generally considered feedback.

Managers use feedback on one hand to maintain the organization in a steady state and on a prescribed course and on the other hand to help the organization adapt to changing circumstances. The McDonald's management uses closely controlled feedback processes to assure that a meal in one outlet is as similar as possible to a meal in any other McDonald's outlet. A sales department uses feedback reflecting poor sales in the field as a sign indicating a need for organizational change. Feedback can provide information both to keep the organization on course and to change directions when necessary.

Function A **function** is the contribution made by a partial activity, a unit, or a subsystem to the total system. The function of a spark plug unit in an automobile engine system is to ignite the gasoline. In some organizations, informal groups serve the function of protecting workers from a hostile management.

FIGURE 3.2 The idea of feedback

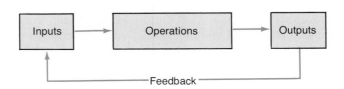

The concept of function plays an important role in understanding the operation of a system for several related reasons. An understanding of function is necessary to an understanding of any unit or subsystem as a part of the larger whole. The concept of function helps show how a subsystem is a product of multiple, interdependent, and interacting forces. Diagnosis of the relationship of the unit or subsystem to the operation of the larger whole also benefits from a knowledge of function. If a spark plug fails to ignite properly, more must be known before an accurate diagnoses of the problem results. Is the plug properly adjusted? Does the gasoline contain the proper mixture of oxygen? Is the engine properly timed? Failure in any or all areas relating to the function of the spark plug can reduce the effectiveness of the operation of the automobile. Describing the unit as good or bad serves little purpose. Analysts need to be able to diagnose and understand multiple causation in a complex system; they need to understand function.

Synergism **Synergism** describes the capability of the organization as a total system to accomplish more than any of its subsystems. A large secondary school system provides more educational variety for its students than several independent rural schools could. Alcohol and drugs taken together have more effect than the sum of the two alone.

Equifinality In closed mechanistic systems, a direct cause-and-effect relationship exists between the initial conditions and the final state of the system. Room temperature controlled by a thermostat illustrates this relationship. Biological and social systems operate quite differently. In both these systems equally satisfactory final results may be achieved beginning with somewhat different initial conditions and using different means. This concept is called **equifinality.** The term is meant to suggest that the manager can vary inputs and operations and still attain satisfactory outputs. Thus the management function involves more than a search for a single, rigid solution. It involves developing a variety of satisfactory alternatives. To increase sales of a particular product, a company can reduce the price, increase advertising, increase the number of salespersons, improve the quality of the product, or employ any combination of these factors. In systems theory, the statement that there is no single best way to design an organization is an expression of equifinality.

SOCIAL ORGANIZATIONS AS OPEN SYSTEMS

All open systems exhibit similarities. Some fundamental differences, however, do exist between social systems and physical or biological systems, even though they are all open systems. The most basic difference exists in the area of structure, the arrangement of the subsystems within the total system. The structure of a social system such as an organization can be planned, changed, or modified by forces within the system.

The overall structure of the lower-level physical and biological sys-

There are several equally good ways to reach the same end.

Equifinality:
Different inputs and different operations can be used for equally satisfactory outputs

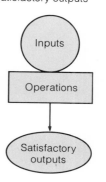

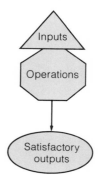

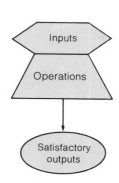

tems remains permanent unless it is changed or modified from the outside. Each part of a lower-level system usually has a definite function that does not change and thus is easily identified. An automobile cannot redesign itself to improve its functioning. Changes in an automobile's structure or function always come from outside.

A few social systems do exist in nature; ant colonies and bee hives are two examples. Because they are based primarily on instinct or early learning these systems change very little over time. Human social organizations are more open, more adaptive, and more easily restructured or redesigned from the inside. Organizations are structured by the members of the system and can be changed by these members. According to Fremont E. Kast and James E. Rosenzweig, "the fact that social organizations are contrived by human beings suggests that they can be established for an infinite variety of purposes and do not follow the same life-cycle patterns of birth, growth, maturity, and death as biological systems."[5]

Because openness provides the possibility of self-design and internal restructuring, the performance of individual parts of an organization are less vital than the performance of subsystems in physical or biological systems. If a person's heart stops beating, the individual dies. In contrast, if an industrial plant burns down, the organization can build a new one. Organizations change employees, buy or sell factories, and change products while still remaining the same organizations.

Primary responsibility for structuring the organization and its subsystems belongs to the systems manager, not to an outside force. Effective managers do not accept the design of the organization or its subsystems as givens. They continually obtain feedback from both inside and outside the organization and use the information to diagnose whether the structure of the organization is appropriate to present conditions. If feedback from sales shows poor results, the sales manager can rearrange the structure of the sales territories and the responsibilities of different salespeople.

SINGLE-CAUSE VERSUS SYSTEMS THINKING

Managers and management professors are well aware of the interdependence of an organization's subsystems and the interdependence of the entire organization and its environment. But they often lack full understanding of the systems concept. This leads to the use of the "single-cause habit of thinking."[6] Single-cause thinking is the human tendency to perceive problems in isolation and look for single causes of problems. People like to explain events that they observe with simply, usually in terms of right and wrong, good and evil. The tendency is to look for *the* reason for something happening. Managers find it easier to say that someone is lazy or lacks motivation, than to examine the deeper causes for the behavior.

Single-cause, or linear, thinking looks at a problem as having a single cause requiring a single solution. Single-cause thinkers evaluate the solution solely for its impact on the original problem.

Single-cause thinking occurs continuously in all sorts of situations. Think of the average person's response if unemployment appears, if a strike takes place, if a child is abused, or if a student gets a low grade. A great amount of energy goes into discussing the rights and wrongs of the situation, deciding who is to blame, and taking sides. Very little energy goes toward understanding the forces behind the situation and deciding how to control them. By looking for the villain instead of studying the events, both past and present, that have contributed to the situation, people end up judging what should be rather than what is.

A way out of the dilemma of single-cause thinking exists. Events need to be seen as the result of many forces acting on each other in complex relationships. This approach results in *systems thinking*, which implies thinking in terms of multiple causes and complex interrelationships of a large number of forces. In systems thinking, the problem is seen as being embedded in a situation. As in linear thinking, the problem requires a solution, but the solution, under systems thinking, has multiple components and may itself be a system (see Figure 3.3). Any solution creates both intended and unintended effects. These effects need to be identified and analyzed whenever possible. Once implemented, the solution is still not permanent; the situation may change, and a new solution may be required.

Planning Over the past few years, management literature has shifted emphasis from problem-solving techniques for individual problem situations to planning. **Planning** describes a technique for dealing with a *system* of problems. It represents the attempt to solve a set of problems as interdependent and interactive situations. Planning techniques are not yet well developed. Improved capabilities for dealing with interacting and interdependent problems are needed.

Efforts at urban renewal show one failure of planning to provide solutions for modern problems. When planners have isolated such areas as transportation, health, housing, or narcotics and tried to improve one particular area, the city as a whole has not improved. Approximately a quarter of a century of effort and billions of dollars have been expended in solving individual problems in particular cities. The sum of the solu-

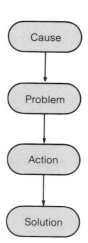

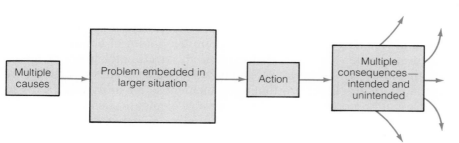

FIGURE 3.3 Systems thinking

tions of these problems has not solved the problems of the city. Experts in the planning field are just beginning to develop the technology to solve problems as interactive sets in a complex system.

A MODEL FOR DIAGNOSING THE SYSTEM

The manager's job within the system is influencing behavior in a desired direction. The need to accomplish specific tasks or organizational goals determines the direction. The manager needs to develop skills in diagnosing patterns of organizational behavior in order to influence behavior. What are these skills? First, the manager must understand observed patterns of behavior. Second, the manager must predict the direction behavior will move as a result of managerial action. Third, the manager must use this knowledge to control behavior. Understanding, predicting, and controlling require the manager to diagnose the system in terms of its effectiveness.

Organizations are too complex, however, for the manager to deal with all aspects of the system's effectiveness at once. By developing a model that reduces the complexity of organizational activities, the manager can limit confusion and simplify reality to a level where diagnosis becomes possible.

A diagnostic model for organizations provides a way of simplifying reality without losing sight of the dynamic nature of organizations as social systems. To be useful a model should focus on a set of key organizational concepts or components and their relationships with each other. The analysis and diagnosis of key components provides a concise overview or snapshot of the organization.

Among the many models of organizations, no model is accepted as being the single best way of representing organizations.[7] Indeed, everyone has his or her own mental image of an organization with a corresponding organizational model.

The following example is based on a model developed by management professor and consultant John Kotter.[8] Kotter suggests seven major elements for a model of organizational dynamics as an open system: (1) key organizational processes, (2) the external environment, (3) employees and other tangible assets, (4) formal organizational arrangements, (5) the internal social system, (6) the organization's technology, and (7) the dominant coalition of the organization.

The model, shown in Figure 3.4, presents a simple and workable approach. It leads the manager through a systematic diagnostic process without ignoring either the highly complex nature of organizations or the multiple dependencies within them. In selecting the major elements for the model, two criteria were considered: the existence of convincing evidence in the literature that each element is an important factor in understanding open system dynamics and elements chosen to meet the requirements of logic by being as mutually exclusive and collectively exhaustive as possible.

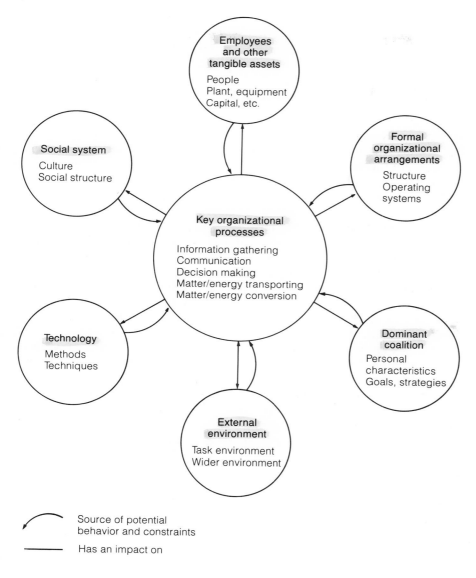

FIGURE 3.4 A model of organizational dynamics

Source: From John Kotter, *Organizational Dynamics: Diagnosis and Intervention,* © 1978, Addison-Wesley Publishing Company, Inc., Chapter 3, p. 24, Figure 3.1, "Short-run Dynamics." Reprinted with permission.

Key Organizational Processes   **Key organizational processes** form the central element in the chosen diagnostic model. This element focuses on two interdependent key processes: the processing of information and the transforming of matter and/or energy.[9] To diagnose these processes the manager asks, "What are the major information-gathering, communication, decision-making, matter/energy converting, and matter/energy actions of the organization?" The answers are found in specific areas such as purchasing, research and development, market planning, leadership, and production, in conjunction with other less specific processes describing the actual behavior of the formal organization.

These key processes vary with the type of organization, from simple

Key organizational processes:

- Information gathering
- Communicating
- Decision making
- Matter/energy transporting
- Matter/energy converting

and primitive to complex and elaborate. In organizations such as newspapers and school systems, information processes carry the most importance. In a bakery or restaurant, matter/energy processes are foremost.

To determine the state of the key processes in a specific organization, it is necessary to trace the flow of both matter/energy and information as it passes into, through, and out of the organization. Possible questions at this diagnostic stage are:

1. What supplies and resources does the organization import?
2. How are these materials or resources changed into goods or services?
3. How are the goods or services disposed of?
4. How efficient are the transformation processes?
5. Who makes the key decisions, and how are they made?

External environment:

- Task environment
- Wider environment

The External Environment The other six major elements form satellites around the key organizational processes. The external environment has two basic parts: the task environment and the wider environment. The **task environment** consists of all possible markets, suppliers, regulators, competitors, and associations relevant to the current products and services of the organization. The **wider environment** includes the economy, the social structure of society, the state of technological development, the political system, price levels, laws, and regulations.[10]

As with the key organizational processes, the task environment varies widely among different types of organizations. The plant manager of an organization making a simple product for a large number of similar customers has a different task environment than the head of a large urban teaching hospital who deals with a host of influences from accreditation agencies to local community groups.

The specific external environment of a particular organization is determined by identifying and describing actual or potentially relevant competitors, suppliers, and customers or clients and the current and projected relationships the organization has with them. Possible questions to help in this process are:

1. What are the most important organizations, groups, or people in the task environment? The wider environment?
2. Who are the more and less successful competitors?
3. Which external elements does the organization most depend on?
4. What legal, political, technological, social, and economic trends appear to be most important?

Tangible assets:

- Employees
- Cash
- Equipment
- Inventories

Employees and Other Tangible Assets The number of employees and the value of tangible assets, make up another major element in the diagnostic systems model. *Tangible assets* are the concrete possessions of the organization, such as buildings, tools, inventories and money. The resources of an organization and the condition of these resources affect not only the organization's key processes but also its future development.[11] The organization with more tangible assets and more positive, diverse, and skilled employees can take on greater volume and diversity of processes. An organization with an engineering department is more likely to develop new products than one without such a department. An organization of a hundred loyal employees and high morale is likely to perform better during a period of crisis than a competitor with a hundred dissatisfied employees.

Taking an inventory of the assets of an organization means cataloging the tangible assets and collecting pertinent facts about employees. Diagnostic questions might include:

1. What are the organization's owned or leased tangible assets, including cash, securities, inventories, equipment, supplies, land, and buildings?
2. What condition are they in? How have they been maintained?
3. What are the backgrounds, skills, knowledge, and abilities of the different employee groups? How do they feel about the organization and each other?

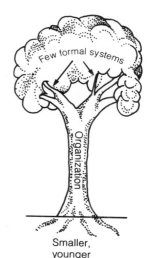

Smaller, younger organization

Formal Organizational Arrangements **Formal organizational arrangements** include all formal systems used to regulate the actions of employees and equipment. They are divided into structure (departmentalization, reporting hierarchy, policies, rules, plans, job design) and operating systems (allocation of resources; planning, hiring, training, and development systems; and performance appraisal, pay, and reward systems). Structure influences employee behavior and organizational processes by specifying where employees work, with whom, what they are responsible for, and how they go about performing their tasks. Measurement, pay, and reward systems influence people to join organizations and to work toward particular objectives.[12]

Younger and smaller organizations usually have fewer formal systems; older and larger organizations usually have many. Typical diagnostic questions for analyzing formal organizational arrangements include:

1. What does the organizational design look like? What are the main types and groupings of departments? What committees, teams, and task forces are in existence?
2. How are resources allocated and financial resources controlled?
3. What ways are used to measure individual, unit, or systems performance?
4. How are people recruited, selected, trained, and rewarded?

The Social System The internal **social system** is the fifth key element in this diagnostic model. It is composed of two main parts: culture and social structure. *Culture* includes the relevant norms and values shared by most employees or subgroups. *Social structure* consists of existing employee relationships and attitudes among employees concerning such areas as cooperation, affiliation, trust, and power. As opposed to the formal structure of the organization, the social system is the series of informal relationships, values, norms, and rules that emerge when peo-

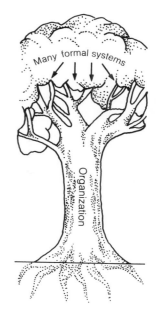

Formal organizational arrangements:

- Structure
- Operating system

Social system:

- Culture
- Social structure

Culture: Totality of socially transmitted ideas, beliefs, and values within a society

Social structure: Totality of social relationships among human beings

ple work together over a period of time. This informal structure is not usually written down but has a high degree of influence on the behavior of those in the organization.

Again, great variety exists among the social systems of different organizations. One system may emphasize cooperation, quality, and productivity; another system may have low norms of productivity and collaboration. Some organizations have highly egalitarian social systems. Others emphasize status and hierarchy making it difficult and costly to process large amounts of complex information. What possible consequences emerge from these differences? All things being equal, the organization with a higher norm of productivity produces more than organization with a lower norm of productivity.

Typical diagnostic questions include:

1. What norms or rules exist about how hard people should work? About how conflicts between people should be resolved?
2. How much cooperation is there among subgroups of employees? Is work generally coordinated voluntarily or through the use of power?
3. Do different groups or subgroups trust or mistrust each other?
4. Does the informal organization work toward organizational goals? Toward self-protection?

Technology:

• Methods
• Techniques

Technology   Kotter's sixth systems diagnostic element is the technology of the organization. **Technology** consists of the major methods (having to do with underlying assumptions about cause and effect) and techniques (actual processes) employees use while engaging in organizational activities. Methods and techniques are also programmed into the machines and other equipment.[13] Technology can vary from materials techniques, such as glass blowing and steel making, to informational techniques, such as market research; from highly automated approaches, such as methods of oil refining, to custom hand work, such as methods for repairing antique furniture.

As a later chapter will show, technology helps shape an organization's processes and its evolution over time. Technology influences organizational processes by making some things possible and others impossible. An organization without modern market research technology performs its market planning differently from a similar organization possessing that technology.

To understand an organization as a system, a manager must determine the state of the specific organization's technologies. An organization specializing in women's high fashion uses different key organizational processes from those used in an automobile service station.

Possible questions that might be asked in this stage of diagnosis include:

1. What is the core technology that the organization uses in creating its primary goods or services? Is it highly automated? Highly labor intensive? Does it require skilled or unskilled labor? Is it relatively complex or simple?
2. What other technologies does the organization use?

On the Job

NEAT, FAST BUT LACKING HUMANITY, PAINTERS JOIN GM'S ASSEMBLY LINE

DETROIT—Despite dismal automobile sales, three new guys have just gone to work for General Motors Corp. And eight more will be put to work soon. All 11 are called N. C. Painter.

The N.C.—for Numerically Controlled—Painters are robots. Like the cars they paint, the painters were designed and produced by GM. Until lately, GM has bought its automatons from a dozen or so small manufacturers. The painters, though, are the first of GM's own stamp, and the company is considering making many more, at first to use itself and later, possibly, to sell to other automobile makers.

GM has spent five years developing its own robot, says Thomas O. Mathues, vice president of manufacturing. Three painters are spraying cars in GM's Doraville, Ga., plant, the other eight are on the way, and GM expects eventually to employ many more. Mr. Mathues thinks

the company may turn out 400 or 500 painters a year by 1983 for internal production.

No Wasted Paint Although GM's robots don't demand salaries, much less raises, fringes and holidays, their initial cost is in the $200,000 neighborhood. Nonetheless, GM thinks they're more careful, thorough, and speedy than the occasionally imperfect humans who assemble GM cars. Because the painters don't breathe, they don't breathe paint. Nor do they waste it, as humans do, GM says.

Magnetic and optical sensors allow painters to "see" a car body entering the paint booth. Then a painter's eight-foot mechanical arm reaches over the car body, firing a spray gun back and forth evenly, and only in the right places. The painter has a hand to open and close doors to paint the inside of the car.

Rival Isn't Worried Mr. Mathues says that by April GM will decide whether to jump into robot manufacture all by itself, or form a joint venture with another company, or perhaps just contract outside for robot manufacture. In any case, Mr. Mathues says, he doubts that GM will tackle the entire manufacturing and assembly job alone. Unimation Inc., Danbury, Conn., the leading American robot-maker, isn't fearful of GM's potential competition. A spokesman for the subsidiary of Condec Corp. says Unimation has been "working with GM" on the painter and "from our experience with GM, it's highly unlikely that it will produce it by itself."

Robots can do welding and other jobs in automobile manufacture. GM already employs some 450 of them. The number is expected to rise to 5,000 by 1985 and 13,000 by 1990.

Source: Charles W. Stevens, "Neat, Fast but Lacking Humanity, Painters Join GM's Assembly Line," *Wall Street Journal,* February 10, 1981, p. 29. Reprinted by permission of The Wall Street Journal, © Dow Jones & Company, Inc. 1981. All rights reserved.

The Dominant Coalition The final diagnostic element in the model, the **dominant coalition,** is the minimum group of cooperating employees who control the basic policy making and oversee the organization, or subunit, as a whole. Elements of the dominant coalition include the personal characteristics of the members, internal relationships among those members, and the objectives they have and the strategies they use to accomplish the objectives.[14]

The dominant coalition usually consists of those people designated by the formal structure, such as the president and immediate subordinates. Because of the social system and informal arrangements the domi-

Dominant coalition:

- Personal characteristics
- Goals and strategies

nant coalition sometimes excludes some of these people and includes others. The number of employees in the coalition varies. If no one is in control, the dominant coalition has no members. In other situations the coalition could be comprised of twenty or more people.

Since, by definition, the dominant coalition occupies the top position of power in an organization's social system, its members usually have more impact on the organization than those employees who have positions of lesser power. In analyzing the dominant coalition, managers might ask:

1. Who are the members of the dominant coalition? What are their personal skills, abilities, attitudes, and motives about organizations?
2. What are the relationships among the coalition members? How cohesive are they as a group?
3. How powerful is this group?
4. What are its members' perceptions about technology? About the future of the company?
5. Are they conservative or risk-taking in their approach?

USING THE DIAGNOSTIC MODEL

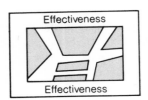

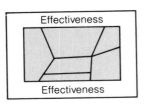

The tighter the fit among different parts of the system, the more effective it is.

A basic premise underlying the systems concept is that the parts of the system must fit or work together. Other things being equal, the greater amount of consistency or fit among the different elements of the system, the more effective the organization. An activity is effective if it leads to high levels of goal attainment, use of resources, and adaptation to changing circumstances.[15]

Successful use of the model requires that the manager properly diagnose the system, determine whether the fit between elements is consistent or inconsistent, and then take action to improve the nature of the fit. This must be accomplished without causing problems in the rest of the system.

Table 3.1 shows some suggested questions regarding the nature of the fit among major diagnostic elements of the model. They illustrate the type of questions that a manager might ask in analyzing the relationships of the major elements of the organization. The table shows only a small sample of both the possible combination of the elements and the potential questions to be asked. Nevertheless, the table provides a diagnostic guide for examining the overall health of a total system or of one of its subsystems. If the relationships among any of the six basic structural elements are not aligned, that is, they do not fit, the organization will not be as effective as it might be; problems will then develop.

In the case at the beginning of the chapter, the poor fit between the MIS and the existing organization doomed the effort to failure. The new computer programs were out of alignment with many, if not most, of the key organizational elements. The MIS constituted a major change in the key organizational processes, particularly information gathering, deci-

TABLE 3.1 Suggested Diagnostic Questions

FIT	QUESTIONS
Organizational processes—environment	Are the information-gathering processes consistent with the environment? Does the organization have adequate devices to scan the environment? Can the organization react to the environment? Influence it?
Environment—employees	What are the existing approaches for recruiting and training employees? Are the tangible assets modern and flexible enough to adapt to environmental change? Have they been properly maintained?
Employees—formal arrangement	Do the reward systems match present and future employee needs? Are tasks in the proper organizational groupings? Are organizational arrangements consistent with the demands of the task, and do these arrangements motivate employees?
Formal arrangement—social system	Does the informal organization work with or against the formal organization? How much conflict or cooperation exists between organizational subunits? Are there cliques or coalitions? What is the quality of intergroup relationships? How political is the social system?
Social system—technology	Does the informal organization structure facilitate proper use of the technology? Does the technology require the cooperation of the informal system? Do individuals have the skills and abilities to meet task demands?
Technology—dominant coalition	Does the dominant coalition understand the technology? Is the dominant coalition willing to change the technology to conform to environmental or employee needs? Does the planning process take into consideration the fit between employees and technology?

sion making, and communications. No efforts were made to alter the feelings of employees, a major part of the social system, to balance the change. Formal organizational arrangements were changed without sufficient preparation or necessary changes in the reward systems. The MIS violated many existing informal relationships and norms. The dominant coalition did not really understand the new technology and therefore gave it only partial support, particularly in the face of opposition from respected middle managers. Under these handicaps, the activities of those setting up the MIS could not be effective. Middle managers gained nothing from efforts to cooperate and saw nothing to lose by ignoring the new system.

SUMMARY

An organization is a social system. As such it has a number of major characteristics:

1. It is composed of a number of subsystems, all of which are interdependent and interrelated.
2. It is open and dynamic, having inputs, outputs, operations, and feedback.
3. It attempts to maintain a proper balance between status quo and change through the use of feedback.
4. Since its subsystems serve a number of purposes and have different functions and objectives, the potential exists for conflict between the subsystems.
5. Use of a systems approach can significantly reduce the human tendency toward single-cause thinking.
6. The manager can use models to diagnose and understand the degree of fit, or alignment, of the elements of the system. Lack of proper fit will cause difficulty.

Social organizations differ from lower-level systems in that they can be changed and modified from within. The effective manager must be aware of the range of possible approaches between closed system and open system thinking. While managers do not usually admit to using single-cause, or linear, thinking, many still look for and settle on a single cause for an event. From a systems point of view, most events have multiple causes and multiple consequences, some intended and others unintended. In the MIS case at the beginning of the chapter, everyone involved seemed to fall into the trap of closed-system thinking. As a result, the system failed even though a great deal of hard work, effort, and money had been poured into it.

The effective manager must choose the level of diagnosis and analysis for different problems or situations. For example, the manager may want to focus on an individual or on a small group as a system while still recognizing that this system interacts with larger systems. At broader and higher levels the manager may wish to diagnose and analyze how subsystems or departments interact. At the top, or strategic, level the manager may wish to focus on the interactions of the organization, as a system, with the outside community. Attention and concern must be directed to the present or future impact of changes on the national and international, as well as the local, scene. The assembly-line supervisor may need to pay little attention to the relationships among Israel, Egypt, Saudi Arabia, and Iran, but these relationships may be an important concern for the president of an oil company.

Because organizations can be modified, changed, and improved from within, the effective manager develops a comprehensive map or model of organizations. The model described in the chapter can be used to diagnose the degree of fit for the major elements of the system. Probably the most powerful use of the systems concept is in diagnosing the effectiveness of a system to determine if change is desirable. The better diagnostician tends to be the better manager. Good managers have and use good models.

STUDY QUESTIONS

1. What new meanings does the term *system* have for you after reading the chapter?
2. List at least five ways in which the systems approach and systems thinking can be helpful to the manager.
3. Describe, from a systems point of view, what would happen if a jumbo jet loaded with passengers had to be diverted to land at a tiny airfield generally used only for small, private airplanes.

4. Find a small organization or subsystem of a larger organization. Diagram the flow through the organization, using Figure 3.1 as a guide.

5. List the inputs, operations, and outputs for two organizations such as fast food outlets and service stations. What are the similarities between the organizations? What are the differences?

6. Interview several managers to develop a sytems model of their organizations. What do these managers see as key systems elements? Compare and contrast these models to Kotter's model, shown in Figure 3.3. What are the simi-

larities and differences?

7. Using Figure 3.3 as a model, diagnose an organization, or subsystem, with which you are familiar.

8. Observe yourself and others; look for specific examples of single-cause and systems thinking. Describe them.

9. Describe, in your own words, why this chapter emphasized the concept of diagnosis. Give examples from your own experience of the consequences of the failure to use such an approach.

Case for Discussion

ENERGY SYSTEMS DIVISION

The systems analysis group of Energy Systems Division consists of seven analytical engineers and their group leader. The engineers have worked at Energy Systems for one to twelve years. Because of the variable nature of the analytical problems to be solved, the organization of the group is flexible. In assigning a specific project the group leader usually selects the available senior engineer who is best suited for the project and outlines the objectives and ground rules to him. If the size and priority of the project warrant it, the senior engineer selects one or two junior engineers to work on it. This assignment technique has worked well for many years.

The newest of the seven engineers, Glenn Sawyer, has learned systems analysis very quickly and very well during his first year on the job. His per-

formance reviews indicate that he is thorough, fast, creative, and cooperative and that he takes the initiative on projects. In fact, by the time of his fourth review (at eighteen months) he was performing at a level equal to or greater than that of the senior members of his group. He had even received the company's "outstanding engineer" award.

A problem has been developing, though. The senior engineers are not choosing Sawyer for their projects even though they know that he would turn in a topnotch performance on them. At the same time, several of the junior engineers in the group have been complaining that Sawyer overshadows their efforts on all the projects on which they are coworkers. They say that he does not only his own assigned tasks but theirs as well.

1. Is Sawyer a good performer? To what extent does getting along with others count as good performance?

2. What would you do with Sawyer if you were his supervisor?

3. What would you do if you were Sawyer?

4. Organizations often require cooperation among their members and units. This being the case, is there any room in most organizations for someone like Sawyer? Explain.

FOR YOUR CAREER

1. It is human nature to look for the villain, to see things as right and wrong, good and bad. Watch this, since the tendency leads directly to single-cause thinking.
2. When you hear someone saying, "But the real reason is, . . ." you can bet that that person is using single-cause thinking.
3. When in doubt, spend more time in diagnosis.
4. You will hear people say, "But it takes too much time to do all that diagnosis." Many offices counter that argument with a sign that says, "Why is it that there is never time to do it right the first time but always time to do it over?"
5. By placing labels, for instance, by saying that younger workers are not motivated like they used to be, people feel absolved from further analysis. They stop looking for further, deeper causes. Avoid this error.
6. Keep refining your model. The one given in the text is only a guide. Build your own map—one you feel comfortable with.
7. Watch out for absolutes, such as the terms *always,* and *never.* These terms are usually a resort to single-cause thinking, not systems, diagnostic thinking.
8. The systems approach allows the manager to view problems as embedded in the larger situation. Even when you think you have solved a problem, do not be surprised if it pops up again in slightly different form.
9. Look beyond the obvious; keep asking the question, "What if . . ."
10. Remember the following adage: "When you are up to your neck in alligators, it is hard to remember that your original purpose was to drain the swamp."

FOOTNOTES

1. E. Huse, "The Impact of Computerized Programs on Managers and Organizations: A Case Study in an Integrated Manufacturing Company," in *The Impact of Computers on Management,* ed. C. Myers (Cambridge, Mass.: MIT Press, 1967), pp. 282–302; and E. Huse, unpublished report, 1966.
2. R. Ackoff, "A Note on Systems Science," *Interfaces* 2 (August 1972): 40.
3. C. Churchman, *The Systems Approach* (New York: Delta Books, Dell Publishing, 1968); F. Kast and J. Rosenzweig, *Organization and Management: A Systems Approach* (New York: McGraw-Hill, 1974); D. Katz and R. Kahn, *The Social Psychology of Organizations* (New York: Wiley, 1966); F. Luthans and T. Stewart, "A General Contingency Theory of Management," *Academy of Management Review* 2 (April 1977): 181–195; and J. Lorsch and J. Morse, *Organizations and Their Members: A Contingency Approach* (New York: Harper & Row, 1974).
4. J. Thompson, *Organizations in Action* (New York: McGraw-Hill, 1967), p. 6.
5. F. Kast and J. Rosenzweig, "General Systems The-
ory: Applications for Organization and Management," *Academy of Management Journal* 15 (December 1972): 455.
6. J. Seiler, *Systems Analysis in Organizational Behavior* (Homewood, Ill.: Dorsey Press, 1967), p. 11.
7. D. Nadler and M. Tushman, "A Diagnostic Model for Organizational Behavior," in *Perspectives on Behavior in Organizations* ed. J. Hackman (New York: McGraw-Hill, 1977), pp. 85–101; M. Weisbord, *Organizational Diagnosis* (Reading, Mass.: Addison-Wesley, 1978); Katz and Kahn, *The Social Psychology of Organizations;* P. Mills and N. Margulies, "Toward a Core Typology of Service Organizations," *Academy of Management Review* 5 (April 1980): 255–265; and B. Carper and W. Snizek, "The Nature and Types of Organizational Taxonomies: An Overview," *Academy of Management Review* 5 (January 1980): 65–75.
8. J. Kotter, *Organization Dynamics: Diagnosis and Intervention* (Reading, Mass.: Addison-Wesley, 1978).
9. P. Khandwalla, *The Design of Organizations* (New York: Harcourt Brace Jovanovich, 1977).

10. W. Starbuck, "Organizations and Their Environment," in *Handbook of Industrial Psychology,* ed. (Chicago: Rand McNally, 1976); and R. Hall, *Organizations* (Englewood Cliffs, N.J.: Prentice-Hall, 1972).

11. J. Ford and J. Slocum, Jr., "Size, Technology, Environment, and the Structure of Organizations," *Academy of Management Review* 2 (October 1977): 561–575.

12. J. Kotter, L. Schlesinger, and V. Sathe, *Organization* (Homewood, Ill.: Richard D. Irwin, 1979); J. Galbraith, *Organization Design* (Reading, Mass.: Addison-Wesley, 1977).

13. J. Thompson, *Organizations in Action* (New York: McGraw-Hill, 1967); and C. Perrow, *Organizational Analysis* (Belmont, Calif.: Wadsworth, 1970).

14. Kandwalla, *The Design of Organizations.*

15. Nadler and Tushman, "A Diagnostic Model for Organizational Behavior."

Managerial Decision Making

CHAPTER 4

CONTENTS

WHO MAKES THE DECISION?

Oil companies produce a large number of different products, including the familiar ones of gasoline, jet fuel, heating oil, and lubricants. In addition, each company makes a variety of specialty items, generally designed for industrial uses; some of these goods are made for only one industrial customer.

The finance manager of a relatively small company operating in only a few states found that the organization was producing an increasing number of specialty items on which it consistently lost money. For example, it manufactured one barrel of special lubricating oil per year for a single company. From a detailed study, the manager identified three hundred specialty items that cost the company the most and recommended that they be dropped. The study had shown that raising the price to cover costs on these items would upset custorners more than would dropping the items.

The sales manager and the salespeople insisted that they had to have all the specialty items in order to keep customers buying the larger items. They pointed out that the organization purchasing the single barrel of special lubricating oil, for example, also purchased large quantities of fuel oil, gasoline, and other standard products. What if refusal to make specialty items like the lubricating oil resulted in the loss of major accounts, they asked. (Their concern was heightened by the fact that they worked for commission as well as salary.)

At the annual sales meeting a number of alternatives were explored, among them: (1) to discontinue selling the large-loss products (the basic recommendation of the finance manager), and (2) to continue selling the products, since there seemed to be no way to tell if dropping them would substantially reduce sales on other products (the basic recommendation of the sales manager).

After considerable discussion the salespeople still felt strongly that most of the specialty items should continue to be sold, or loss of goodwill and other sales would be great. Management consequently decided to drop only about fifty of the items, having concluded that dropping more would cause hostility and resentment in the salespeople.

Still more discussion produced another decision: No commission would be paid on heavy-loss specialty items that were not dropped. The salespeople agreed that it was not fair for the organization to pay sales commissions for items on which it took substantial losses.

During the next two years the demand for specialty items dropped by almost 85 percent; more than half of those offered by the company were no longer requested. The reason? Salespeople were no longer "pushing" the products now that they were aware of the problem (and now that they received no commission from them). Frequently they suggested alternate standard products to their customers when a specialty item was requested. Although the company was relatively small as oil companies go, the reduction in the sale of speciality items saved it more than a million dollars per year.

This case raises several critical questions about decision making, which you should be able to answer after reading this chapter. The questions include:

1. Why is it important to consider decision making in the aggregate as well as in its separate stages?
2. How can resistance to change influence the effectiveness of decision making?
3. What is the relationship between decision making and organizational politics? Explain.
4. How can you tell a good decision from a bad decision?

This chapter examines the decision-making process and suggests how to make better decisions. Good decisions, which are forward-looking to achieve organizational goals, involve identifying problems, constructing alternatives, and choosing among them. They have both intended and unintended consequences. They can be relatively certain or can involve much risk and uncertainty. (Some of the more qualitative aids to decision making, planning, and controlling are discussed in detail in Chapter 14.) Poor decisions are frequently the result of (1) not thinking carefully enough about whether the decision actually furthers the organization's objectives, (2) the tendency to ignore problems in the hope they will go away, (3) insufficient examination of alternatives, and (4) the desire to avoid risk.

WHAT IS A DECISION?

A **decision** is a choice made among alternative courses of action. **Decision making** is the process involved in making the choice. The purpose of making a decision is to establish and achieve organizational objectives. The reason the decision is necessary is that a problem exists. Either organizational objectives are wrong, or something is standing in the way of accomplishing them.

Thus the decision-making process is fundamental to management. Almost eveything a manager does involves decisions; indeed, some suggest that the management process *is* decision making.[1] Herbert A. Simon, who won the Nobel Prize in 1978 for his work on administrative decision making, holds this view.

Although managers cannot predict the future, many of their decisions require that they consider possible future events. Often managers must make a best guess at what the future will be, trying to leave as little as possible to chance; but since uncertainty is always there, risk always accompanies these decisions. Sometimes the risk has substantial consequences, and sometimes it does not.

The process of decision making has been studied for many years. The more we understand the mental processes of human beings, the more we understand decision making. Four basic elements within the decision-making process can be identified: choice, alternatives, goals, and consequences.

Choice is the opportunity to select among alternatives; if there is no choice, there is no decision to be made. Decision making is the process of choosing, and many decisions involve a broad range of choices. For example, a student chooses among a number of different courses in order to implement the decision to obtain a college degree. For managers, every decision has constraints based on policies, procedures, laws, precedents, and the like. These constraints exist at all levels of the organization.

Alternatives are the possible courses of action among which choices are made. If there are no alternatives, there is no choice and therefore no

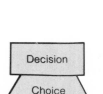

decision. If no alternatives are seen, the problem may not have been thoroughly examined. For example, managers sometimes treat problems in an either/or fashion; this is their way of simplifying complex problems. But the tendency to simplify blinds them to other alternatives, which never get formulated.

At the managerial level, decision making includes limiting alternatives as well as identifying them, and the range is from highly limited to practically unlimited. In the case at the beginning of the chapter, before the meeting with the salespeople the alternative of not paying commissions on the heavy-loss items had not been considered.

Decision makers must have some way of determining which of several alternatives is best—that is, which contributes most to the achievement of organizational goals. An **organizational goal** is an end or a state of affairs the organization seeks to reach. Because individuals and organizations frequently have different ideas about how to attain the goals, the best choice may depend on who makes the decision. Frequently, departments or units within an organization make decisions that are good for them individually but that are less than optimal for the larger organization. Called *suboptimization*, this is a tradeoff that increases the advantages to one unit or function but decreases the advantages to another unit or function. For example, the marketing manager may argue effectively for an increased advertising budget. In the larger scheme of things, however, increased funding for research to improve the product might be more beneficial to the organization.

These tradeoffs occur because there are many objectives that organizations wish to attain simultaneously. Some of these objectives are more important than others to the company overall, but the degree of importance of each objective may also vary from person to person and from department to department. Different managers define the same problem in different terms. When presented with a common case, sales managers see sales problems, production managers see production problems, and so on.[2]

The priorities of multiple objectives are also based, in part, on the values of the decision maker.[3] Such values are personal; even one's own values are hard to understand, because they are so dynamic and complex. Certainly, many value judgments were made in the Watergate cover-up leading to President Nixon's resignation. In many business situations different people's values about acceptable degrees of risk and profitability cause disagreement about the correctness of decisions.

People often assume that a decision is an isolated phenomenon. But from a systems viewpoint, problems have multiple causes, and decisions have intended and unintended consequences, as Figure 4.1 shows. Thus the skillful manager looks toward the future consequences of current decisions. In the specialty items case, to unilaterally reduce the manufacture and sale of all the heavy-loss specialty items could have alienated the sales force and reduced sales of other items. After three years the positive consequences of the group decision were still apparent; besides the achieved savings, the number of specialty items sold was still being gradually reduced.

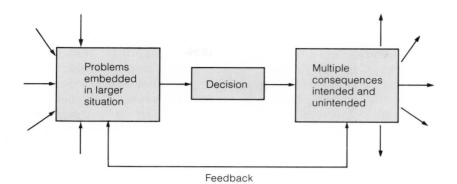

FIGURE 4.1 Multiple causes and consequences of decisions

Decisions made by a subunit of an organization frequently can have unforeseen effects on other parts of the organization. As a result, there are constant renegotiations and new decisions. For example, the number of specialty items manufactured by the company described earlier had slowly increased over the years as a result of decisions made by the sales force to respond to customer needs for special products. In the same way, the number of specialty items was reduced as a result of decisions made in the sales meeting.

CONDITIONS UNDER WHICH DECISIONS ARE MADE

Managers make many different kinds of decisions under different circumstances.[4] Decisions of such magnitude as building a new plant may require the approval of the board of directors as well as outside financing. Bringing out a new product may involve a great deal of uncertainty. In contrast, the decision of what to pay a new employee in an organization with a union may be highly certain, programmed in advance. This section will describe some of the conditions under which managers make decisions.

The Importance of the Decision Decisions for an organization range from relatively unimportant to crucial. The decision in one company to buy a different brand of ink for the mimeograph machine was relatively unimportant. But the decision by the R. J. Reynolds Tobacco Company to spend $40 million in six months to introduce a new cigarette was major. REAL cigarettes were introduced in June 1977. For almost four years, fewer than fifty people at Reynolds had been involved in the secret project to gather an additional 1 to 2 percent of the highly profitable $15 billion cigarette market. Even then the project failed.[5]

A manager can determine whether a decision is important by asking a series of questions:

1. What effect will the decision have on the goals of the organization?
2. How many people will be affected? A decision affecting ten people in a small organization will have a relatively greater effect than one involving the same number of people in a large organization.

3. How much money is involved? Again, the importance of this question is relative to the size of the organization. A $100,000 expenditure for a local grocery store might be crucially important, while the same amount of money for a supermarket chain might be unimportant.

4. What is the relative frequency of this type of decision? Decisions that are made frequently tend to be routine. For example, the decision to buy paper clips is made often and routinely in many organizations, but the decision to build a new plant is made infrequently and is very important.

5. What is the time pressure? Decisions made under conditions of urgency may be important, but the time allotted to them may be minimal. Frequently, deadlines are set by circumstance or by people other than the manager. A sudden breakdown of the assembly line, for example, will force quick decisions; later, there may be time to study the situation in more detail and determine ways to prevent further breakdowns.[6]

Programmable versus Unprogrammable Decisions A major part of decision making is to determine whether the decision can be programmed or whether it is unique and unprogrammable.[7] (These terms are borrowed from computer language, where a program is a series of steps for the automatic solution of a problem, such as a statistical analysis.)

Programmable decisions are repetitive and routine because definite systematic procedures have been established for making the choice. A high percentage of the decisions made in any organization are programmable in that they are determined by policies, procedures, and rules. There are standard methods for computing payrolls, for making out sales orders, for admitting patients to hospitals, for assembling instruments, and for registering students. The manager's chief action in these decisions is to judge whether they are routine enough to be programmed and then to ensure that the "programs" are running properly. (Aids to programmed decision making are discussed in Chapter 14.)

Unprogrammable decisions are less structured than programmable decisions. (Indeed, a completely unprogrammable decision is unique; it has no rules or guidelines.) Buying a car, purchasing stocks or bonds or a house, arranging a merger, developing a new product—all are examples of unprogrammable decisions. They are made on the basis of fewer rules, procedures, and guidelines; and they require more judgment on the part of the manager. Often the objectives are not clear.

Programs are constantly being developed for previously unprogrammable decisions. For example, investment decisions made by bank officers generally result from a mixture of the officers' experience, knowledge, influence from personal contacts, and intuition; over time, the officers develop rule-of-thumb guidelines for these decisions. In one study, a computer program was constructed to duplicate a bank officer's investment decisions. An investigator observed the decisions the officer made, interviewed him, and then developed a computer program to imi-

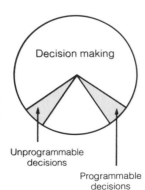

Decision making

Unprogrammable decisions

Programmable decisions

tate the decisions as closely as possible. The model was tested by comparing the computer selection with decisions made by the officer on four investment accounts. Although not identical, the two sets of decisions were very similar.[8]

Thus one part of the decision-making process is to seek ways of turning unprogrammable decisions into programmable ones. Programmable decisions require relatively little managerial time; thus more time can be spent on major, unprogrammable decisions.

Decisions under Conditions of Certainty, Risk, and Uncertainty

Managers make decisions to establish and accomplish desired future objectives. The objective may be immediate, such as having someone work overtime to complete a particular assembly. Or it may be long term, such as the decision of Freddy Laker to start his Skytrain service between the United States and England, which took a number of years and numerous court battles. These decisions require the manager to try to predict the future on the basis of available information. Depending on the amount and quality of information available, the decisions are made under one of three possible conditions: certainty, risk, and uncertainty.[9] Figure 4.2 shows the continuum from certainty to uncertainty.

Conditions of Certainty   Under **conditions of certainty,** the manager has enough information to be able to closely predict the outcome of various choices among alternatives. He or she makes the decision that will maximize the desired outcome. Some of these decisions are simple. If the manager decides to have a meeting with a subordinate in the afternoon, the chances are good that the subordinate will attend the meeting. If a first-line supervisor decides that certain parts should be assembled, that person can be reasonably sure that power failure will not interrupt the assembly operation. Of course, the future is never completely certain; the subordinate may become ill, or a power failure may stop the assembly operation. However, under conditions of certainty people behave as though such problems will not occur.

Sometimes decisions made under conditions of certainty are highly complex, such as the scheduling of a number of different machines and products to be manufactured and assembled. In those situations complex mathematical models, such as linear programming, can be used (see Chapter 14).

Conditions of Risk   Under **conditions of risk** the manager develops al-

FIGURE 4.2   The certainty-uncertainty continuum

ternatives and estimates the probability of each leading to the desired outcome. (*Probability* is the percentage of times a specific outcome would occur if an action were taken a large number of times.) Insurance companies, for example, charge different premiums for people of different ages. Frequently automobile insurance for men under twenty-five costs more than for men over twenty-five, since the probability of younger male drivers having accidents is greater than that for older male drivers, all other things being equal.

In some cases the probability can be estimated on the basis of past experience. Also, mathematical tools such as decision trees (graphic representations of decision-making models) can help reduce the risk in some decision making.

Conditions of Uncertainty   Predictions of the future are never infallible, but under **conditions of uncertainty** the probabilities attached to the available alternatives are even less well known than under conditions of risk. If there are a large number of factors to consider and if the factors are not similar to each other and are in a constant state of change, the manager must use judgment, experience, and intuition to assign approximate probabilities to the different alternative.

For example, it may be impossible to predict precisely how valuable a new piece of equipment will be before it is installed. One organization that purchased a number of computerized machines found that the productivity level was only about 25 percent of what had been estimated.

Under conditions of uncertainty the manager can use several group techniques to develop alternatives and to establish approximate probabilities. With the *Delphi method,* a technique for forecasting developments (especially technological ones), the members of the group do not meet face to face. With the *nominal group* method, another such technique, members of the group are physically together but do not directly interact. (Both techniques are discussed in more detail later in the chapter.)

Limits to rational decision making:

- Bounded rationality
- Satisficing

Limits to Rational Decision Making   In uncertain conditions the manager may finish working on a problem as soon as a satisfactory solution is found, even though all the alternatives may not have been identified or analyzed and the "satisfactory" solution may not be the best solution. This approach to decision making, called **satisficing,** is the practice of striving for a satisfactory rather than an optimum decision. Since the alternatives do not receive the most rational evaluation, it has also been called "the science of muddling through."[10]

With complex problems, alternatives may be so numerous that managers cannot evaluate them all, even using the most sophisticated computers. Therefore, they reduce the complexity of a problem to the level at which they can handle the possible alternatives. This technique is known as **bounded rationality.**

It is important to distinguish between satisficing and bounded rationality. Bounded rationality is a natural limit on the human ability to handle complex situations, but satisficing is a deliberate choice to limit the number of alternatives considered to reach a satisfactory solution. The first is naturally imposed; the second is purposefully selected.

If we were to look for the "optimum" decision in all situations, we would make far fewer decisions because each one would take so much time. Instead, we usually decide things quickly and then move on to the next problem. Value judgments also play a part in our decisions; often we don't like some alternatives and therefore don't consider them thoroughly.

The Politics of the Situation Decisions are not always made on the facts of the case, as a casual reading of any newspaper will show. Many decisions in the Arab-Israeli or the Southern Ireland–Northern Ireland conflicts are made on a political basis. Government officials frequently make decisions that are influenced by how the voters feel or by pressures from other sources. Generally, the more important the decision, the more politics is involved. Business organizations are also influenced by politics.[11]

Kermit Vandivier, a newspaper reporter, has described a major problem with politics at the B. F. Goodrich Company. In 1967 the company received a contract to build brakes for a new Air Force plane, the first contract from the Air Force in ten years. The original brake design was bad, but because of some intricate politics the design was never changed. Instead, the Air Force was given glowing reports of the success of the brake. More and more people became involved in the situation, and eventually the final qualifying reports contained inaccurate and misleading data. Vandivier was involved in writing the final report. When the brakes failed in the actual test flight, Vandivier went to his lawyer, who suggested that Vandivier was part of a conspiracy to defraud and strongly recommended that he report the details to the Federal Bureau of Investigation. Vandivier resigned his position and ten months later, in 1969, was the chief witness before a Senate subcommittee looking into the brake situation. Goodrich eventually redesigned the brake properly. But Vandivier reports that several of the involved parties have since been promoted.[12]

Granted this illustration is an extreme case. Yet it does point out that managerial decisions are affected by the politics of the situation. That politics is involved does not mean that managerial decisions are forced to be dishonest; it simply means that others' wishes must be taken into consideration in decision making.

STEPS IN THE RATIONAL DECISION-MAKING PROCESS

Particularly for important, unprogrammable decisions involving risk, the decision-making process can be complex. Managers have limited time and knowledge and frequently are under pressure to make decisions quickly. Some steps exist that keep the decision-making process rational and help the manager avoid some pitfalls.[13] These steps are shown in Figure 4.3.

Manager must distinguish problem from symptoms.

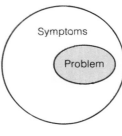

Identifying and Defining the Problem   What usually leads the manager to recognize that a problem exists? Frequently it is a symptom of the actual problem. For example, a manager may notice that many employees are quitting. Although this can be called a turnover problem, the turnover is probably a symptom of a more fundamental problem, which is the one that should be solved. Identification of this fundamental problem is critical.

Problem identification is a matter of locating deviations from objectives and then looking for the reasons behind them.[14] Relevant information includes *historical data,* which may show that the performance of the unit or organization is declining relative to past performance; *planning data,* which suggest that results are not meeting planned objectives; and *criticism* from outsiders, which may show poor organizational performance. Still another source of information is newspapers, which describe what the U.S. Congress is doing, what executive moves are being announced, and what competitors are doing.

Problem identification is hindered by people's reluctance to recognize that a problem exists, by their feeling that the cure may be worse than the disease, by their tendency to rationalize and to postpone decisions, and by their reluctance to make unpopular decisions. In Vandivier's organization, many executives simply did not want to admit that the original aircraft brake was poorly designed and would never work. Managers also tend to stick to tried and true methods of handling prob-

Sources of information:

- Historical data
- Planning data
- Criticism

FIGURE 4.3 Steps in the decision-making process—the rational approach

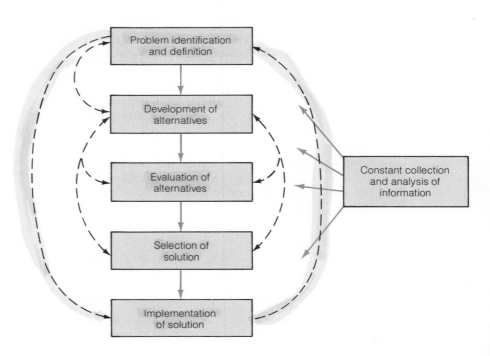

lems rather than collecting and analyzing information to make sure of identifying the underlying basic problem. The following example illustrates the importance of thorough data collection for accurate problem identification.

An organization was making an electrode used in medical instruments. Suddenly a leak was discovered in a piece of platinum tubing used to hold a fluid within the electrode. The tubing was crimp welded (that is, the end of the tubing was crushed together to seal it). For weeks attempts were made to improve the crimp welder, which had been identified as the problem. Some improvement occurred, but leakage continued. Finally, someone began asking questions that elicited information leading to the diagnosis of the underlying problem. A metallurgist who was finally consulted explained that a crimp weld could work only if the platinum was pure. Since the welding was done after the fluid was inserted, it would never work properly. A new method was found for welding the platinum tubing shut by heating it until it melted. Thus the real problem was not the crimp welder on which so much time had been spent.

Diagnosis requires complete evaluation of the symptoms. This means collecting and analyzing all relevant information rather than automatically responding in traditional fashion. It also means distinguishing clearly between problems and symptoms and identifying the reasons a decision is needed as well as the possible obstacles to reaching a satisfactory one.

Developing Alternative Solutions   Once we know what the problem is, we can look for solutions. The range of alternatives depends on a variety of related issues, among them: How important is the problem, and how expensive is it? The more important the problem, the more time the manager will spend developing alternatives.

Some managers prefer to use traditional methods to handle problems without looking for newer, more creative ways of doing things. Yet it is important that decision makers not skip this step of *developing* alternatives. Often groups are particularly helpful at this stage, since they offer a diversity of viewpoints and ideas. In a creative atmosphere they can develop novel ways of handling problems. (This is discussed further in Chapter 16 and at the end of this chapter.)

Evaluating the Relative Worth of Alternatives   The process of evaluating the relative worth of alternatives is closely related to that of developing the alternatives, since there is usually a tentative evaluation of alternatives as they are being developed. (However, a premature evaluation may reduce the number of alternatives generated.)

Two basic questions will reveal the effectiveness of each alternative: How realistic is the alternative in terms of the goals, objectives, and resources of the organization? How well will it help solve the identified problem?

An alternative may be logical, but if it is not feasible, it is not a useful

On the Job

WHAT IS A PROBLEM?

A problem may be defined as an identifiable situation which is perceived by the decision-maker as a potential source of dissatisfaction, and for which preferable alternatives may exist. These two aspects are integral to an understanding of the nature of problems, and are worth closer examination.

First, a problem should be viewed as "a potential source of dissatisfaction." It is not necessary for trouble to have actually occurred. As long as the potential for dissatisfaction is present, a problem exists. It should be noted that dissatisfaction should be viewed in the broadest possible context. For example, if an apparel manufacturer has failed to produce a new, fast-moving style of clothing and thus missed an opportunity to increase profit, this would constitute a cause for dissatisfaction, and hence, a problem.

Second, "preferable alternatives" to the factors giving rise to dissatisfaction must be available before a problem exists. If a decision-maker is faced with a number of unfavorable circumstances, but can do nothing to remedy the situation, *no problem*

exists. For example, for an individual textile firm, cheap imports, rising oil prices and government labeling regulations may not constitute problems because there is nothing the manager can do to alter these conditions. These factors compose part of the business environment within which the firm must operate. Little is to be gained by attacking environmental factors that are beyond the firm's control.

Managers should not waste time on factors they cannot influence. However, proper problem definition can show how factors that seem beyond control can be dealt with effectively.

There is an old saying, "a problem well-defined is half-solved." In spite of the validity of this statement, managers seldom devote enough time to defining a problem. All too frequently, the decision-maker assumes he or she knows the nature of the problem and starts looking for solutions. Good problem definition involves not only identifying the source of dissatisfaction, but also examining the factors contributing to its existence. A problem seldom has a single origin. Typi-

cally, it is composed of a group of interrelated factors. These interrelationships must be identified before a problem can be completely defined.

The way in which a source of dissatisfaction is defined can affect whether or not a problem exists. For example, a manufacturer is faced with rising oil prices. If he defines "oil prices" as the source of his dissatisfaction, no problem exists because there is nothing the firm can do to influence the international price of oil. However, if the source of dissatisfaction is defined as "rising cost of inputs," other favorable alternatives may exist. Perhaps cheaper inputs or conservation methods may improve the firm's profits. It is also possible that the problem exists throughout the industry level, rather than just for the individual firm. For example, it may be possible for an industry to influence government policy that will affect the price of oil.

Therefore, the manager's perception of a source of dissatisfaction can have a great influence on his or her ability to remove its effects.

Source: "What Is a Problem?" *Management World,* July 1980, p. 13. Reprinted by permission of Management World, Copyright 1980 by Administrative Management Society, Willow Grove, PA 19090, article by Wallace R. Johnston, Ph.D., and G. Creighton Frampton, July, 1980.

alternative. Suppose, for example, that a problem is identified as the failure to meet profit objectives. Several solutions immediately come to mind. One is to cut costs. But if costs have already been cut or if further cutting may reduce the quality of the product or service, then this alternative is not useful. Also, alternatives that are too costly or that strain other resources of the organization are not desirable. For the problem at hand a useful alternative may be to redesign the product to make it more attractive to the purchaser, thereby allowing the price to be raised.

Another pitfall is to use the wrong criteria or standards. Often decisions are based on an alternative's contribution to overall profit. But if return on investment is the ultimate goal of the organization, looking only at the profit contribution may lead to the selection of the wrong alternative. It is critical that the criteria used for evaluating be consistent with the goals the decision maker wishes to attain. When the alternatives have been evaluated, they should be ranked according to their practicality and effectiveness in solving the identified problem.

Selecting the Best Solution One could assume that if a good job has been done in constructing and evaluating alternatives, then selection of the best one should be fairly easy. However, managers know that they cannot always get all the facts. Thus decisions are made under circumstances of uncertainty and risk. The decision maker may not know, for example, how large a market will develop for a new product or if the competition will be heavy or light. To further compound the problem, it is often not known what impact a particular alternative will have.

As a result, the "best" alternative is based on the amount and degree of information available at the time the decision must be made. Frequently it is the result of compromising among a number of different factors, each with its own tradeoffs. Furthermore, since managers have a tendency to make use of bounded rationality and to satisfice, it is often impossible for them to reach the optimum solution.

Finally, managers may wish to try out the solution to determine how it works. For example, many organizations test-market new products in specific geographical areas before going ahead with national or international distribution. This tentative approach allows managers to anticipate problems that may occur when the decision is finally implemented.

Implementing the Decision On the one hand, implementing a decision is the easiest part, since the manager need only trigger the mechanism to get things going. On the other hand, the manager must be concerned with the effects of the decision, and these are not always predictable.

One area of potential trouble in decision making is the way others view the decision. What a manager thinks and believes and what subordinates or peers think and believe can be very different. Therefore, another decision to be made is whether to accept or reject change resulting from someone else's decision. The effective implementation of the first decision depends on whether it is accepted by the people involved. This acceptance in turn depends on agreement about problem identification and diagnosis, alternative solutions, and selection of the best alternative. When any of these steps are seen differently, there is danger of the results of the decision being rejected. Consequently, some managers keep appropriate people informed of the reasons for a decision in an effort to get them to accept it. Since decision making is a combination of both information and value judgments, people can disagree with either or both.

The best decision can sometimes be the wrong decision. Often people choose an alternative that cannot be implemented or that causes new problems. And, of course, since human nature is complex, there is seldom consensus among leaders and followers except on the simplest of decisions. Still, the job of the manager is to make decisions, however unpleasant the task may be.[15]

The rational decision-making steps explained here frequently are not followed in actual practice. To find out why, we will first look at several psychological factors and then examine a more descriptive approach.

SOME PSYCHOLOGICAL FACTORS IN THE DECISION-MAKING PROCESS

The chapter earlier mentioned that decisions have value judgments attached to them. There are also several other psychological factors to consider. Two such factors are the distinction between the decision and the person and the distinction between facts and emotions.[16]

The Person versus the Decision   Since decisions involve both facts and judgments, they tend to be personal in nature, even when they are made by a committee. Yet a distinction can be made between the decision and the decision maker. The decision is external to the individual; that is, others should be able to accept the decision maker while disagreeing with or rejecting the decision. Many people, however, are unable to make this distinction. It is therefore important that decision makers try to explain to others how they have arrived at their decisions; this can be done by telling others the value judgments, assumptions, and objectives entailed in their decisions.

Person | vs. | decision

Facts versus Emotions   One reason people do not always make the best decision is that value judgments and emotions enter into the decision-making process. Since people cannot eliminate them, they need to be aware of them—especially if they seem to be in opposition to the data. This is necessary because people need to be clear about their assumptions. The following example illustrates how emotional factors and values can enter into decision making. A large company maintained a fleet of cars for its employees. Whenever possible, people on company business were required to drive one of these cars rather than their personal cars in order to reduce insurance risks. The fleet manager wanted to

Fact | vs. | emotion

trade in the cars every two years. To make such a policy change he was required to use the company index, a mathematical formula for computing return on investment (ROI). Using the complete records that were kept on each automobile, the manager found that no matter how he looked at it, the index showed it was cheaper to maintain the same cars for several years than to trade them in every two years. One day, someone suggested that he had forgotten two essential variables—company image and employee morale. Driving a new car, the person said, would be better for both image and morale than driving a car six or seven years old. Several weeks later, the manager triumphantly reported, "The index shows that I should trade cars every two years." He had been able to insert new numbers to get the results he wanted.

Often we make stereotyped value judgments about managers, seeing them as emotionless machines. Many managers have even been told not to exhibit or to consider feelings; all their decisions are to be rational, impersonal, and controlled. This is nonsense. Humans are not computers; their feelings and emotions are important. Thus an important part of the decision-making process is recognition of the legitimate part that feelings and emotions play in decision making.

Figure 4.4 shows the continuum between emotional and rational decisions. A completely **rational** decision is based solely on objective facts, while a completely **emotional** decision is based solely on subjective feelings. At the far left are decisions resulting from emotion, such as fear, anger, or joy. Next on the continuum are decisions based primarily on intuition. Although not emotional, these decisions have little data to back them up. They are frequently made under conditions of uncertainty when the probabilities attached to the available alternatives are relatively unknown and the manager needs to rely on intuition and judgment. At the far right of the continuum are purely rational decisions based completely on fact. For example, a customer may enter a store and purchase a number of items. The sales clerk adds up the prices and announces, "That will be $25.42." This is a decision, but it is so closely

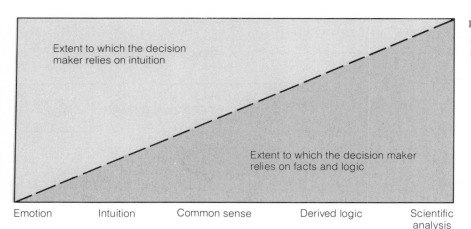

FIGURE 4.4 Approaches to decision making

bound by rules and regulations that the conclusion is inevitable. However, if the customer is a friend, the clerk may decide to give the person a discount, which involves judgment and emotionality.

THE DESCRIPTIVE APPROACH TO DECISION MAKING

Figure 4.3 showed five steps in the decision-making process—rational steps for coming up with an optimal solution. But people do not always decide by the rules. In fact, often they avoid the act of deciding when they see a problem. Instead they procrastinate (which is also a decision).

Even when people do attempt problem solving, they tend to take shortcuts. First, they think they see a problem. As soon as they tentatively identify it, they come up with a possible solution. If the solution does not work, or if somebody objects to it, they begin to redefine the problem, usually coming up with another possible solution. If that works, they stop. If it does not, they further redefine the problem, coming up almost immediately with another solution (as shown by Figure 4.5).

This figure illustrates several important points. First, it shows a process by which people finish working on a problem as soon as a satisfactory solution is found. Rather than seeking the optimum solution, the busy manager frequently wants one that is only good enough. (This is called satisficing, and it was described earlier in the chapter.) Second, because not all the alternatives can be identified particularly under conditions of uncertainty, the manager often reduces the complexity of the problem through bounded rationality (also described earlier in the chapter). Finally, managers are sometimes more concerned about avoiding risks or losses than about making gains, more concerned about the personal consequences of the decision than about the organization's goals.

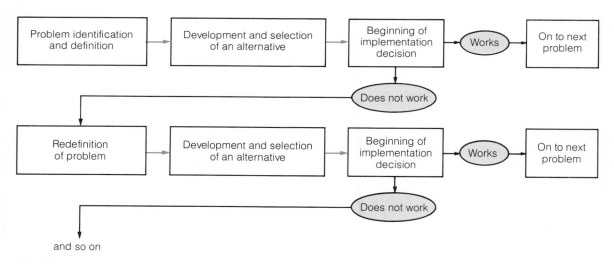

FIGURE 4.5 Steps in the decision-making process—the descriptive approach

As a result, decisions tend to be more conservative than they should be, as the following example shows.

A company president learned about a small company available for purchase that had a good chance to make a large profit. After considering the matter, she decided not to bring the decision up to the board of directors, who would have to approve the purchase. Her reasoning was that if her company bought the small company and the decision turned out well, she would be seen only as doing a good job as president. Although the odds were small, if the purchase did not turn out well, she might be seen as having made a highly visible mistake. Thus she herself had nothing to gain by recommending the purchase; and even though it probably would have helped the company, she chose not to take the risk. The board of directors never knew.

When one compares the descriptive model of decision making (Figure 4.5) with the rational model (Figure 4.3), the differences become apparent. The objective of the descriptive model is to explain how individuals and organizations make decisions. The objectives of the rational model are to prescribe techniques for accomplishing a specific end and to explain how managers should behave to maximize goal accomplishment.

Both approaches are important. The rational model gives managers guidelines for efficient action. However, it makes some unrealistic assumptions about the world. The descriptive model shows that the real world is far more complex than theory would suggest, and it helps managers learn to appreciate the usefulness of judgment. Thus both approaches help managers deal with the realities of organizational life.

The effective manager generally uses the rational approach in areas that are relatively programmable and simple and the descriptive approach in complex, unprogrammable situations. Of course, the decision-making process ideally should approach the rational model whenever possible, and the manager should be alert to any deviations from that ideal.

WAYS TO IMPROVE DECISION MAKING

There are many ways to improve the decision-making process. One is simply to gain knowledge of the different tools available, which involves an increase in one's vocabulary. For example, nomads living in the Middle East have many different words for sand but only one word to cover snow, slush, and ice. Conversely, Eskimos and skiers have many more words for snow than for sand. The greater the vocabulary for a given subject, the more easily a person can deal with that subject. The good skier, for example, uses different waxes for different weather conditions.

Another way to improve decision making is practice. Carrier pilots practice landings and takeoffs over and over again until they can make landings under a variety of different conditions. The astronauts for the Apollo missions practiced for countless hours in a simulator so they could make split-second decisions under a wide variety of different conditions.

Other ways of improving decision making are (1) education and training, (2) use of mathematical and similar aids, and (3) use of group techniques involving subordinates and others. These three areas will be explored in further detail in this section.

Education and Training   Training is a broad process that involves the learning of concepts, skills, rules, and attitudes. Education and training from classrooms and books can lead to more effective decision making if the decision maker applies the acquired knowledge. Thus book learning about decisions can increase the probability of reaching better decisions but does not guarantee that result. This book, for example, provides some managerial language, concepts, theories, and approaches that will serve as a foundation for further study and learning and for effective action only if the reader acts on the knowledge gained.

We cannot think productively about subjects we lack knowledge of. A prospective manager who knows little about such concepts as motivation, group dynamics, budgeting, return on investment, and linear programming is as hampered in effective decision making as a carpenter who knows little about the uses of hammers, screwdrivers, chisels, and planes. Through study and discussion with others, including instructors, one can learn material that will help develop a personal theory of managing. Although not everything learned from books and classes will be remembered, one should be better able to track down whatever knowledge is needed. A characteristic of the effective manager is the ability to learn from almost every life experience and from other people's expertise.

Learning on the job involves careful evaluations of the results of one's decisions. Some people have ten years of experience, while others can be better described as having one year of experience repeated ten times. The basic difference between them is that the first group of people have carefully reviewed what happened after decisions were made and used this information to improve future decisions.

Use of Mathematical and Similar Aids   Many different tools have been developed to help improve the decision-making process. Some of these tools are qualitative; others are numerical or mathematical. Qualitative tools consist of knowledge of individual motivation, of group dynamics, and of organizational structure. For example, knowledge of the proper way to design jobs enables one to make decisions that lead to improved quality and quantity of work. Knowledge of new types of organizational structure and the dynamics involved leads to creative decisions that can improve the organization.

Some mathematical tools that are of direct help in decision-making, planning, and controlling are presented in a discussion of analytical aids in Chapter 14. To illustrate, the chapter will describe how a major airline was able to effect substantial savings in fuel costs using a mathematical approach called linear programming. Chapters 12 and 13 also present a number of mathematical/numerical tools, including budgeting, break-even analysis, and performance ratios. These tools range from relatively simple to relatively complex in nature.

The more mathematically skilled the manager, the quicker he or she is to use mathematical tools, but less mathematically inclined managers should become aware of these tools and know where they are useful; managers who lack the ability to employ such tools should know where to seek help.

Many managers are reluctant to use all the tools available to them. For example, managers sometimes choose to use a sophisticated planning model not as the result of a cost benefit analysis but because they discover that a competitor or trusted acquaintance is using such a model.[17] To be effective managers need to be active in making decisions, and they should exert initiative in finding and using tools of all types to improve the decision-making process.

EFFECTIVE DECISION MAKING WITH SUBORDINATES AND OTHERS

Much of a manager's time is spent working with other people, and much of what a manager does is therefore influenced by others, as Chapter 1 shows. Most decisions involve others, and many are arrived at through some sort of group process. Frequently, even where an individual manager has the responsibility for solving a specific problem, getting the decision put into effect requires the involvement and participation—and therefore the commitment—of others. Thus the decision-making process may involve the manager making the decision alone, with selected subordinates, with subordinates as a group, or with groups composed of both immediate subordinates and others.[18]

This section provides guides as to when the manager should include others in the decision-making process. Different types of groups that may be included in the process are interacting, nominal, and Delphi groups; each one performs a different function. **Interacting groups** are groups in which people work and act together. Discussion groups are one example of them. **Nominal groups** are physically together, but the members do not directly interact. **Delphi groups** are composed of a panel of people who are not physically together but who interact through the use of questionnaires or other mechanisms.

Types of interacting groups:

- Discussion group
- Nominal group
- Delphi group

GUIDELINES TO DECISION MAKING WITH OTHERS

Guidelines on when and how to involve individual subordinates or groups in the decision-making process are based on three assumptions:

1. That the decision-making style should vary with the situation.
2. That the amount of participation by subordinates and others should vary with the situation.

3. That no single decision-making style is appropriate to all situations.[19]

The manager needs to pick the decision-making style that is most effective for a given situation. Table 4.1 lists five styles of decision making under different conditions.

The manager should then ask a number of questions to determine which decision-making style is most appropriate to the situation. The questions are listed below and are illustrated by a **decision tree,** a graphic representation of the decision-making process, in Figure 4.6. The questions, which can be answered on a yes-no basis, are arranged across the top of the figure. To use the model for any situation, one starts at the left side and works toward the right, asking the question immediately above any box in the figure. The basic questions are:

A. Is there a quality requirement that makes one solution more rational than another? If the answer is no, the manager can use decision style AI.

B. Is there sufficient information to make a good decision? If the answer is no, then decision style AI will probably not be appropriate.

C. Is the problem structured? Is it clear what information is needed and where it can be obtained? If the answer is no, then styles AII, CII, or GII may be appropriate, depending on the need for acceptance by subordinates.

D. Is acceptance of the decision by subordinates critical to its implementation? If the answer is yes, then styles AI and AII will not be appropriate and style GII may be the most appropriate.

E. If the manager makes the decision, is it reasonably certain to be accepted by subordinates? If the answer is yes, then style AI or AII may be appropriate, depending on the information available to the manager. If the answer is no, then styles CII or GII may be more appropriate, depending on the situation.

F. Can subordinates be trusted to base their solutions on the achieve-

---

TABLE 4.1 Decision-Making Styles[a]

AI. The manager makes the decision, using the information available at the time.

AII. The manager gets necessary information from subordinates and then makes the decision. Subordinates may or may not be told about the problem or the decision.

CI. The manager shares the problem with subordinates on an individual basis, requesting their suggestions and ideas without bringing them together as a group. The manager then makes the decision, which may or may not be influenced by the subordinates.

CII. The manager discusses the problem with a group of relevant subordinates, requesting their collective ideas and suggestions. The manager then makes the decision, which may or may not be influenced by the group of subordinates.

GII. The manager shares the problem with subordinates as a group. The group generates and evaluates alternatives and attempts to reach agreement on the proper solution by consensus. The manager accepts the decision that has the support of the entire group.

[a]The numbering in this table corresponds to the numbering used in Figure 4.6.

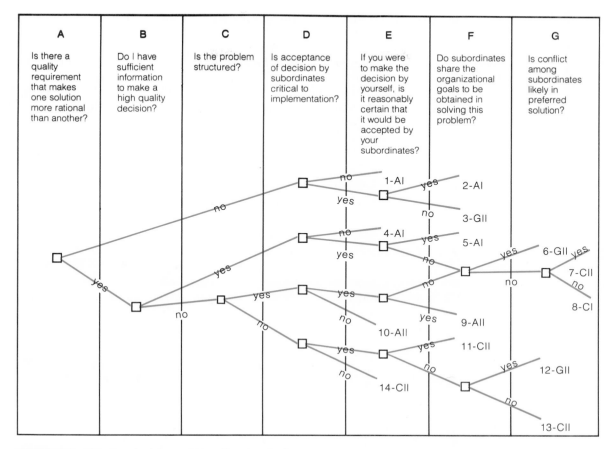

FIGURE 4.6 Effective decision making with subordinates

Source: Reprinted by permission of the publisher from "A New Look at Managerial Decision-Making," by V. Vroom, *Organizational Dynamics,* Spring 1973, p. 68, © 1973 by AMACOM, a division of American Management Associations. All rights reserved.

ment of organizational goals? If yes, decision style GII may be most appropriate.

G. Is conflict among subordinates likely to occur if the preferred solution is chosen? If the answer is yes and if a good decision needs to be reached, style GII will probably not be appropriate and styles CI or CII should probably be used.

This approach to decision making provides simple guidelines for when to involve subordinates. For example, if the problem is known and structured, if the manager has the necessary information, and if there is little or no problem with subordinate acceptance, decision style AI is probably most appropriate. On the other hand, if there is a variety of potentially good solutions, if subordinates can be trusted, and if the problem is complex (with no single person having all the information), decision style GII may be most appropriate. When different styles seem equally appropriate, the manager should select the one that is least costly in terms of time and resources.

Group decision making may be highly important when more than one organizational unit is involved. In such a case, a decision made by one unit is frequently resisted by another unit affected by the decision. Therefore, if a decision affects more than one organizational unit— particularly if the units are organized under different managers— representatives of all the units should help in the decision making. Failure to involve all units will almost automatically mean opposition.[20]

To avoid unnecessary complexity, the decision tree used in Figure 4.6 is limited to subordinates in interacting groups. But decision making can also be improved by the appropriate use of peers and of nominal and Delphi groups.

The Nominal Group   The nominal group consists of people knowledgeable on the issue to be decided who are in the same physical location and who are aware of each other but who do not directly interact while they are working together.[21] The specific techniques for using the nominal group in decision making vary with the situation, but usually the following steps are involved:

1. The manager brings the group together and outlines the problem.
2. Each member of the group generates a number of ideas in writing.
3. Each member then presents a single idea at a time to the entire group. The ideas are written on a blackboard or on large pieces of paper, and discussion of them is limited to clarification.
4. The round robin continues, with members adding to others' ideas.
5. When no further ideas emerge, or when the manager feels the process has gone far enough, each member votes on the ideas, again in writing.
6. The final decision is the summed outcome of the individual votes, but the manager is free to accept or reject it.

Although the research is not clear-cut, there is evidence that nominal groups are superior to interacting groups in fact-finding, idea-generating, avoidance of dominance, reduction of conformity, and prioritizing of objectives.[22]

The Delphi Technique   The Delphi technique, named after the oracle at Delphi in ancient Greece, involves using the creative ideas of a group of people knowledgeable about the issue at hand who work anonymously to solve the problems presented.[23] The general process follows:

1. A panel of people who are knowledgeable about a particular problem is selected. The members of the group never actually meet. The panel can have members both inside and outside the organization, and the individual members may or may not know who the other members are.

2. A questionnaire about the problem to be solved is sent to each member of the panel. Each person is asked to make anonymous suggestions. These suggestions are pooled, and a feedback report is developed.

3. The feedback report and a more advanced, second-stage questionnaire are sent back to the panel members.

4. Each panel member independently evaluates the feedback report, votes on the priority of the ideas contained in it, and generates new ideas based on it.

5. The process is repeated until a consensus is reached or until the manager feels that sufficient information has been received to make a decision.

6. A final summary feedback report is developed and sent back to the group members.

A major advantage of the Delphi approach is its anonymity. In groups that interact face-to-face, one person may dominate, or everyone may watch the manager for clues to what is wanted. Further, in interacting groups an individual may take a stand and not want to back down for fear of losing face. Frequently experts are more concerned with defending their position than with reaching a good decision.

Many large companies use the Delphi approach to identify and solve problems. For example, TRW, a highly diversified, technically oriented company, has a number of Delphi panels. These panels suggest services and products that will have marketing potential and predict significant social, political, and economic events that will affect the company. The

"Then it's agreed, gentlemen, that as soon as possible, we purchase a conference table."

Source: *Saturday Evening Post,* January–February 1981, p. 32. Reprinted from *The Saturday Evening Post,* © 1981 The Curtis Publishing Company.

approach has been used successfully in a variety of areas, including the military, government, health, and education. For example, the city of Norman, Oklahoma, successfully used the Delphi approach to revise the community's city plan. Members of the city government felt that the Delphi was successful not only in producing a satisfactory revision of the plan but also in precipitating a consensus on other issues among the city's leaders.[24] In another situation, a large industrial corporation was having difficulty in getting revised personnel policies accepted and implemented. The organization had six major divisions, each with an industrial relations director, and four to eight plants per division, each with a personnel director. A modified Delphi technique was suggested to help solve the problems involved, and the technique was used with resounding success.

Research suggests that nominal and Delphi groups differ little in the quantity of ideas generated and that both groups generate significantly more creative ideas than do interacting groups. Interestingly, members of nominal groups appear to be more satisfied with the results than are members of either Delphi or interacting groups.[25]

In selecting members for interacting, nominal, or Delphi groups, the manager must be sure to include representatives of each area of the organization that will be affected by the decision in order to ensure acceptance of the decision.[26]

SUMMARY

This chapter has examined the importance of the decision-making process in accomplishing the objectives of the organization. Managers may make hundreds of decisions a week. Some relatively certain and unimportant ones require only a few seconds to make. They are highly programmable and require little thought. Other, more important ones, especially those made under conditions of uncertainty, may require innovative approaches and, consequently, a great deal of time for data collection, analysis, and creative thinking. Deciding to purchase mimeograph ink is very different from deciding where, when, and how to build a new plant.

To help managers improve the decision-making process, a number of rational steps have been outlined. Unfortunately, many people are hindered from following these steps by their impatience and by their tendency to make value judgments that are not based on fact. When people cannot or choose not to take time to assimilate all the facts, they of

necessity elect not to try for the best solution. Instead they *satisfice*—that is, aim for a solution that is barely satisfactory. Some psychological reasons for satisficing also exist. One is the desire to minimize personal risk. (Seeking the optimal as opposed to the barely adequate solution often entails more risk of failure.) Another is the temptation to procrastinate in the hope that the problem will go away. (Witness the college student who writes a paper the night before it is due.)

Emotions have a great influence on decisions, although some people believe the myth that managers are like computers, making decisions solely on the basis of facts. Since, in truth, all people are affected by their own and by others' emotions, managers can benefit from being aware of these emotions.

There are a number of ways to improve decision making. The first is to become aware of one's own values. Another is to learn, through education and training, about the tools available to aid decision making, including mathematical and other tools. Many managers do not make enough use of such tools.

When the decision is complex, when the manager does not have all the information, and when the acceptance of the decision by others is important, the manager may wish to involve subordinates and others in the decision-making process. The decision tree can serve as a guide for when to involve subordinates. Many managers are not aware of the improved decision making that can be accomplished by the proper use of nominal and Delphi groups. These are tools that need to be used more frequently; yet often their existence is not known.[27]

STUDY QUESTIONS

1. Why is decision making considered the most important management function?
2. Should a manager make a decision differently under conditions of certainty, risk, and uncertainty? Explain.
3. In what ways do people's values and company politics affect decisions?
4. Explain the basic differences between satisficing and bounded rationality.
5. What are the steps in the rational decision-making process?
6. What are some of the reasons these steps are not always followed?
7. Do you follow the steps given in the chapter for making rational decisions, or do you tend to jump from problem identification to tentative solutions and back again?
8. What are the conditions under which managers should involve subordinates and others in the decision-making process?
9. What are the basic differences between interacting, nominal, and Delphi groups?
10. Observe the manager of a local business or organization. What kinds of decisions are made? How are they made? What suggestions can you offer to improve the decision-making process?
11. Think of the most effective and least effective decisions you have experienced or heard about. What seemed to make the difference?

Case for Discussion

THE THREE MILE ISLAND PLANT

Simply stated, a nuclear reactor is a sophisticated machine that produces the steam used to drive a turbine and produce electricity. It is comparable, mechanically, to the boiler in a coal- or oil-fired powerplant. The reactor at Three Mile Island is called a pressurized, light-water reactor because it uses light (ordinary) water held under extreme pressure to remove heat from the nuclear core. The high pressures, about 2,200 pounds per square inch, permit the water to be heated to about 600 degrees Fahrenheit without boiling. This superheated water moves from the core to a piece of equipment called a steam generator, where its heat is used to boil another supply of water. The steam generated by this second supply turns the turbine and produces electricity.

Two separate water supplies are used in this type of reactor because the water flowing through the nuclear core picks up some radioactivity and must be kept isolated from the environment. It is called the primary system water, while the supply that turns the turbines is called the secondary system.

In the early morning of March 28, 1979, the nuclear reactor at Three Mile Island was running at almost full power. At about 4:00 A.M. an event occurred that triggered the worst accident in the history of commercial nuclear power. A malfunction stopped the flow of secondary system water to the steam generator, causing the primary cooling water and the nuclear core to overheat. Although the reactor quickly shut itself down and safety functions automatically started to function, the operators misunderstood some instruments and turned off some of the automated safety systems. This caused the nuclear core to become short of cooling water and to overheat, and serious damage resulted.

Large amounts of radioactive materials and gases escaped from the core itself into the reactor system and subsequently into the massive concrete and steel containment building surrounding the reactor. Before the plant personnel realized what was happening to the reactor, this contaminated water was pumped into storage tanks outside the containment building. These tanks were the source of most of the radioactive releases at the plant. Unknown amounts of radioactivity escaped into the environment. Although the amount of radioactivity released was not believed to be significant, much confusion existed at the time of the accident.

During the first few days after the accident there was much concern about the hydrogen bubble that had formed inside the reactor system and about the potential for a complete core meltdown. The hydrogen had been formed as a result of a chemical reaction of the superheated water with the zirconium metal tubes used to encase the uranium fuel. There was tremendous fear that the hydrogen, which is a very unstable element, might explode and break open the reactor system, which would make it impossible to cool the nuclear core. If this had happened, the situation could have resulted in a complete core meltdown and a possible major release of radioactivity into the atmosphere.

The hydrogen explosion never occurred, however; and some experts now believe that such an explosion was not possible, since oxygen (necessary for an explosion) was not present with the hydrogen. For a while, however, the possibility of an explosion seemed real. Estimates are that the worst conceivable release of radioactivity from such a nuclear accident could involve the immediate death of 3,300 people, early illnesses in another 45,000, and contamination of several thousand square miles of land.

Immediately after the accident there was a great deal of confusion, and proposals to evacuate the surrounding area were made. It was clear that the plant operators and owners, the nuclear industry, and the state and federal governments did not fully understand and were not prepared to deal with the events as they happened. This event rekindled serious questions about the safety of nuclear power and threatened to further reduce the potential of nuclear power in the energy future of the United States.

1. What does this case say about the systems approach to decision making.
2. If you were the decision maker at Three Mile Island, what information would you need in order to identify and diagnose the problem?
3. What does this case say about the influence of values and politics on rational decision making?
4. The Three Mile Island accident greatly reduced public support for nuclear power; yet no one was killed. Why don't mine disasters which kill many workers, reduce public support for using coal as a power source?

Sources: "The Three Mile Island Nuclear Accident: GAO's Role," *GAO Review,* Winter 1980, pp. 26–28; and "TMI—One Year Later," *Progressive,* April 1980, pp. 7–8.

FOR YOUR CAREER

1. Keep an open mind. Beware of the seductive and deadly NIH (Not Invented Here) factor, manifested when a manager responds to something new with, "That may be very well for the X Company, but it won't work in my organization."
2. When the situation is clear and you know the answers, go ahead and make the decision. You would not call a group meeting to debate whether or not somebody should pull the fire alarm in case of fire.
3. Choose your method of decision making according to which people in the organization will be affected by the decision. Autocratic methods are more appropriate in situations where subordinates or peers are unaffected by the decision and participative methods when the cooperation of subordinates or peers is critical or when these people's information and expertise are required.
4. Avoid making important decisions under pressure.
5. Identifiable problems usually are connected to other, less noticeable problems, and whatever action is taken against them may have unforeseen consequences. Be prepared to look for and to deal with these unexpected problems.
6. If you are not mathematically inclined, get others to help you use mathematical models. If you are mathematically inclined, remember that many aspects of the decision situation cannot be quantified.
7. Try to learn from your decisions, but once a decision has been made, don't agonize over the results.
8. Most importantly, cultivate good sources of information both inside and outside the organization.

FOOTNOTES

1. P. Drucker, *The Practice of Management* (New York: Harper & Bros., 1954); J. Forrester, "Managerial Decision Making," in *Management and the Computer of the Future,* ed. M. Greenberger (New York: Wiley, 1962); H. Simon, *The Shape of Automation for Men and Management* (New York: Harper Torchbooks, 1965); and H. Simon, *Administrative Behavior,* 3d ed. (New York: Free Press, 1976).
2. D. Dearborn and H. Simon, "Selective Perception: A Note on the Departmental Identification of Executives," *Sociometry* 21 (January 1958): 140–144.
3. G. England, "Personal Value Systems of American Managers," *Journal of the Academy of Management* 10 (March 1967): 53–68; and W. Guth and R. Tagiuri, "Personal Values and Corporate Strategy," *Harvard Business Review* 43 (September–October 1965): 123–132.
4. R. Morrell, *Managerial Decision-Making: A Logical Approach* (Milwaukee: Bruce Publishing, 1960); C. Kepner and B. Trego, *The Rational Manager* (New York: McGraw-Hill, 1965); and C. Gremion, "Toward a New Theory of Decision Making," *International Studies of Management and Organization* 2 (Summer 1972): 125–141.
5. A. Crittenden, "$40 Million for a Real Smoke," *New York Times,* May 15, 1977, Sec. 3.
6. See F. Shull, A. Delbeque, and L. Cummings,

Organizational Decision Making (New York: McGraw-Hill, 1970); D. Miller and M. Starr, *Executive Decision and Operations Research* (Englewood Cliffs, N.J.: Prentice-Hall, 1960); and S. Beer, *Brain of the Firm* (London: Penguin Books, 1973).
7. H. Mintzberg, D. Raisinghani, and A. Theoret, "The Structure of Unstructured Decision Process," *Administrative Science Quarterly* 21 (June 1976): 246–265; T. Burns and G. Stalker, *The Management of Innovation* (London: Tavistock Publications, 1961); D. Heenan and R. Addleman, "Quantitative Techniques for Today's Decision-Makers," *Harvard Business Review* 54 (May–June 1976): 32–62; D. Rados, "Selection and Evaluation of Alternatives in Repetitive Decision Making," *Administrative Science Quarterly* 17 (June 1972): 196–206; and P. Soelberg, "Unprogrammed Decision-Making," *Proceedings of the 26th Annual Meeting of the Academy of Management,* December 27–29 1966, pp. 3–16.
8. G. Clarkson, "A Model of Trust Investment Behavior" in *A Behavioral Theory of the Firm,* ed. R. Cyert and J. March (Englewood Cliffs, N.J.: Prentice-Hall, 1963), pp. 265–266.
9. S. Archer, "The Structure of Management Decision Theory," *Academy of Management Journal* 7 (December 1964): 269–287; and K. MacCrimmon, "Managerial Decision-Making," in *Contemporary*

Management: Issues and Viewpoints, ed. J. McGuire (Englewood Cliffs, N.J.: Prentice-Hall, 1974), pp. 445–495.

10. H. Simon, *Administrative Behavior* (New York: Macmillan, 1957); C. Lindblom, "The Science of 'Muddling Through,'" *Public Administration Review* 19 (Spring 1959): 79–88; and J. Thompson and A. Truden, "Strategies, Structures and Processes of Organizational Decision," in *Readings in Managerial Psychology,* ed. H. Leavitt and R. Pondy (Chicago: University of Chicago Press, 1964).

11. R. Hall and J. Clark, "Problems in the Study of Interorganizational Relationships," *Organization and Administrative Sciences* 5 (January 1974): 45–65; S. P. Sethi, *Up Against the Corporate Wall* (Englewood Cliffs, N.J.: Prentice-Hall, 1974); and S. Midlin and H. Aldrich, "Interorganizational Dependence," *Administrative Science Quarterly* 20 (September 1975): 382–392.

12. K. Vandivier, "The Aircraft Brake Scandal," *Harper's Magazine,* April 1972, pp. 45–52; and K. Vandivier "Why Should My Conscience Bother Me?" in *In the Name of Profit,* ed. R. L. Heilbroner (New York: Doubleday, 1972), pp. 3–31.

13. C. Watson, "The Problems of Problem-Solving," *Business Horizons* 19 (August 1976): 88–94; and C. Kepner and B. Tregoe, *The Rational Manager: A Systematic Approach to Problem Solving and Decision Making* (New York: McGraw-Hill, 1965).

14. W. Pounds, "The Process of Problem Finding," *Industrial Management Review,* Fall 1969, pp. 1–19.

15. A. Elbing, *Behavioral Decisions in Organizations* (Glenview, Ill.: Scott, Foresman, 1970); and N. Maier, *Problem-Solving Discussions and Conferences: Leadership Methods and Skills* (New York: McGraw-Hill, 1963).

16. D. Emery and F. Tuggle, "On the Evaluation of Decisions," *SMU Business Topics* 24 (Spring 1976): 42–48; N. Hill, "Self-Esteem: The Key to Effective Leadership," *Administrative Management* 37 (August 1976): 24–36; J. Pfeffer, G. Salancik, and H. Leblebuci "The Effect of Uncertainty on the Use of Social Influence in Organizational Decision-Making," *Administrative Science Quarterly* 21 (June 1976): 227–246; R. Lauer and R. Thomas, "A Comparative Analysis of the Psychological Consequences of Change," *Human Relations* 29 (March 1976): 239–248; and J. Dickson, "The Adoption of Innovative Proposals as Risky Choice: A Model and Some Results," *Academy of Management Journal* 19 (June 1976): 291–303.

17. R. Blanning, "How Managers Decide to Use Planning Models," *Long Range Planning* 13 (April 1980): 32–35.

18. N. Maier, *Problem-Solving and Creativity in Individuals and Groups* (Belmont, Calif.: Brooks-Cole Publishing, 1970); C. Argyris, "Interpersonal Barriers to Decision-Making," *Harvard Business Review* 44 (March–April 1966): 84–97; J. Gibb, G. Platts, and L. Miller, *Dynamics of Participative Groups* (St. Louis, Mo.: Swift, 1959); M. Shaw, *Group Dynamics* (New York: McGraw-Hill, 1976); and B. Baker, D. Fisher, and D. Murphy, "Project Organization: Factors Affecting the Decision Environment," Paper Presented to the Midwest Conference, American Institute for Decision Sciences, Minneapolis, Minnesota, May 1974.

19. V. Vroom and P. Yetton, *Leadership and Decision Making* (Pittsburgh: University of Pittsburgh Press, 1973); V. Vroom, "A New Look at Managerial Decision-Making," *Organizational Dynamics* 1 (Spring 1973): 66–80; V. Vroom and P. Yetton, "A Normative Model of Leadership Style," *Readings in Managerial Psychology,* 2d ed, ed. H. Leavitt and L. Pondy (Chicago: University of Chicago Press, 1973); D. Field, "A Critique of the Vroom-Yetton Contingency Model of Leadership Behavior," *Academy of Management Review* 4 (April 1979): 249–257; and C. Margerison and R. Blube, "Leadership Decision-Making: An Empirical Test of the Vroom and Yetton Model," *Journal of Management Series* 16 (February 1979): 45–55.

20. E. Huse, "The Behavioral Scientist in the Shop," *Personnel* 42 (May–June 1965): 50–57.

21. D. Taylor, P. Berry, and C. Block, "Does Group Participation When Using Brainstorming Facilitate or Inhibit Creative Thinking?" *Administrative Science Quarterly* 3 (March 1958): 23–47; and A. Van de Ven, *Group Decision-Making Effectiveness* (Kent, Ohio: Kent State University Press, 1974).

22. T. Bouchard and M. Hare, "Size, Performance, and Potential in Brainstorming Groups," *Journal of Applied Psychology* 54 (February 1970): 51–55; G. Burton and D. Pathak, "Social Character and Group Decision Making," *Advanced Management Journal* 43 (Summer 1978): 12–20; J. Campbell, "Individual vs. Group Problem-Solving in an Industrial Sample," *Journal of Applied Psychology* 52 (June 1968): 205–210; and D. Gustafson, R. Shukla, A. Delbeca, and G. Walster, "A Comparative Study of Differences in Subjective Likelihood Estimates Made by Individuals, Interacting Groups, Delphi Groups, and Nominal Groups," *Organizational Behavior and Human Performance* 9 (April 1973): 280–291.

23. A. Delbecq, A. Van de Ven, and D. Gustafson, *Group Techniques for Program Planning* (Glenview, Ill.: Scott, Foresman, 1975), pp. 10–11; F. Luthans and T. Balke, "Delphi Technique Helps Set ASFSA Goals," *School Foodservice Journal* 20 (June 1974): pp. 40–41; "Forecasters Turn to Group Guesswork," *Business Week,* March 14, 1970, p. 10; and F. Luthans, *Organizational Behavior,* 2d ed. (New York: McGraw-Hill, 1977), pp. 198–199.

24. D. Morgan, J. Pelissero, and R. England, "Urban Planning: Using a Delphi as a Decision-Making Aid," *Public Administration Review* 39 (July–August 1979): 380–384.

25. A. Van de Ven and A. Delbecq, "The Effectiveness of Delphi and Interacting Group Decision Making Processes," *Academy of Management Journal* 17 (December 1974): 605–621; and T. Bouchard, Jr., J. Barsalous, and G. Drauden, "Brainstorming Procedure, Group Size and Sex as Determinants of the Problem-Solving Effectiveness of Groups and Individuals," *Journal of Applied Psychology* 59 (April 1974): 135–138.

26. F. Miner, Jr., "A Comparative Analysis of Three Diverse Group Decision Making Approaches," *Academy of Management Journal* 22 (March 1979): 81–93; and S. Stumpf, R. Freedman, and D. Zand, "Judgmental Decisions: A Study of Interactions among Group Membership, Group Functioning, and the Decision Situation," *Academy of Management Journal* (December 1979): 765–782.

27. G. P. Huber, *Managerial Decision Making* (Glenview, Ill.: Scott, Foresman, 1980); P. Herriot, "Decision Theory and Occupational Choice—Some Longitudinal Data," *Journal of Occupational Psychology* 53 (1980): 223–236; G. F. Pitz, "Procedures for Eliciting Choices in the Analysis of Individual Decisions," *Organizational Behavior and Human Performance* 26 (1980): 396–408; J. Wales, "A Four-Culture Model of Problem-Solving," *Management of International Review,* 20 (1980): 100–111; B. L. Maheshwari, "Participation in Organizational Decision-Making," *Indian Journal of Management* 9 (1980): 134–147; E. A. Locke and D. Schweiger, "Participation in Decision Making: One More Look," in *Research in Organizational Behavior,* Vol. 1, ed. B. M. Staw and L. L. Cummings (Greenwich, Conn.: JAI Press, 1979): 265–339; R. S. Schuler, "A Role and Expectancy Perception Model of Participation in Decision-Making," *Academy of Management Journal* 23 (1980): 331–340; and D. Tjosvold and D. K. Deemer, "Effects of Controversy within a Cooperative or Competititve Context on Organizational Decision Making," *Journal of Applied Psychology* 65 (1980): 590–595.

Planning

PART II

Establishing Objectives

CHAPTER 5

CONTENTS

HOSPITAL OBJECTIVES—HOW MUCH AGREEMENT?

A general hospital with about four hundred beds had four areas of general performance, which were broken down into twelve specific objectives for the hospital. The performance areas and objectives are shown in Table 5.1.

Nurses, senior physicians, and junior physicians were asked to rank the first eleven of the twelve objectives in terms of importance. The twelfth objective was not used in the rankings. Each of the three groups agreed among themselves as to the importance of different objectives but disagreed with the other two groups. For instance, nurses ranked "comfort level" and "considering both psychosocial and medical condition of the patient" as most important and "keeping high bed occupancy" as least important. These rankings suggest that the nurses were primarily concerned with creating an environment in which specialized health care could be carried out.

Senior physicians were oriented toward the patient in a different way. They gave greatest weight to such objectives as "providing full information to patient," "using hospital resources efficiently," and "not keeping patients waiting for admission."

Junior physicians took a position between the positions of the nurses and senior physicians. However, they also gave much more weight to "good training and teaching" than did the other two groups. The three groups agreed in placing least importance on "bed occupancy" and "length of hospital stay." However, these two items were considered the most important by an outside agency that rated the effectiveness of the hospital.[1]

TABLE 5.1 Performance Areas and Specific Objectives for a General Hospital

GENERAL PERFORMANCE AREAS	SPECIFIC OBJECTIVES
Resource utilization (efficiency)	1. Keeping stay of patient as short as possible. 2. Using time of senior medical staff efficiently. 3. Using all resources efficiently. 4. Keeping bed occupancy high.
Innovation and adaptiveness to environment	5. Preventing excessively long waits for patients before admission. 6. Keeping a good community reputation. 7. Providing a high comfort level for patients. 8. Maintaining high morale for staff. 9. Considering both psychosocial and medical conditions of patients. 10. Providing patients with full information about illness and treatment.
Goal achievement (effectiveness)	11. Providing good training and teaching. 12. Providing high-quality nursing and medical care.

This opening case raises several key questions which you should be able to answer after reading this chapter. The questions are:

1. Is it likely that all members of an organization will have the same objectives and goals? Explain.
2. How can you predict what objectives and goals members of an organization have?
3. Why are goals and objectives important for an organization?
4. Are goals and objectives the same concept? Explain.

5

It can be assumed that the people in the hospital's business office would view "keeping high bed occupancy" and "hospital stay" as more important than "providing good teaching and training." One of the reasons the business office might stress the importance of "hospital stay" is that many insurance plans, including Medicare, will not pay for a patient who does not medically need to remain in the hospital. At the same time, the hospital staff may be searching frantically for an available bed in a nursing home for a patient who needs nursing care rather than hospitalization. In one situation a patient remained in a hospital for almost forty days because a nursing home bed was not available. The hospital had to absorb the cost.[2]

Organizational objectives, or goals, are important as a guide for managerial action. If objectives are not clear, they may never be reached. Because of the complexity of many modern organizations, a hierarchy of objective exists. In this hierarchy, broad, strategic objectives, usually of a continuing nature, appear at the top management level; specific, short-term objectives appear at the lower level. The lower the level, the narrower the objectives.

Another characteristic of objectives in most organizations is that they consist of two types: official and actual. Sometimes actual objectives differ sharply from official ones, as will be explained later in the chapter.

Most objectives need occasional review, since organizations exist in a changing world and certain objectives may become inappropriate over time. The effective manager continually reassesses them to ensure that they are serving both organizational and individual needs.

ORGANIZATIONAL OBJECTIVES

All organizations and all individuals need a sense of direction. People who do not have a good idea of where they are going, will not know when they get there, and will not be able to plan effectively to get there. Plainly, good management requires clear organizational objectives. They provide the foundation for creating strategies, making plans, assigning priorities, allocating resources, and other managerial actions. The development and achievement of realistic goals is at the heart of good management.

> A few writers distinguish between objectives and goals, using goals to mean levels of aspiration that are relatively timeless and objectives to mean goals that are more specific and shorter-range. This book treats objectives, goals, targets, and similar terms as interchangeable.

What are organizational objectives? They can be defined as "desired states of affairs which the organization attempts to realize."[3] They are ideas or statements that help steer or direct the organization's activities. The organization may or may not reach the desired state, but the chances of doing so are greater if the objectives are understood. Failure here is one of the most common causes of organizational problems. Without clear objectives, intelligent planning is impossible. Objectives vary with the nature and type of the organization, of course. A profit-making organization probably has different objectives than a municipality or a university.

Avis, the international car rental firm, operated at a loss for many years despite a number of different actions by management, including some acquisitions, until Robert Townsend took over as president and set the objectives that gave Avis a new sense of direction. In three years Avis was number two in its field.

Townsend's first step was to define the basic purpose of the company as the "renting and leasing of vehicles without drivers." Focusing attention on this main purpose immediately reduced the number of less purposeful activities. In Townsend's words, defining the basic objective allowed Avis to "stop considering the acquisition of related businesses like motels, hotels, airlines, and travel agencies. It also showed us we had to get rid of some limousine and sightseeing companies we already had."

After establishing the basic purpose of the organization, Townsend formulated more specific long-range objectives. He said, "It took us six months to define one objective: 'We want to become the fastest-growing company with the highest profit margins in the business of renting and leasing vehicles without drivers.' . . . I used to keep a sign where I couldn't miss it: 'Is what I'm doing or about to be doing getting us closer to our objective?'" He believes that the sign kept him from getting caught in a lot of useless activity.[4]

HOW DO OBJECTIVES GET ESTABLISHED?

As indicated earlier, organizational objectives are desired states of affairs that the organization attempts to realize. Some are broad, overall objectives that are relatively unchanging, and others are specific objectives that are, or should be, subject to frequent change if changing circumstances so warrant. Figure 5.1 shows the complex interplay of internal and external forces on objectives, plans, and controls.

External and Internal Environment   Organizational objectives affect and are affected by the environment, which includes competitive issues, suppliers, customers, stockholders, special interest groups, and economic, technical, and other factors. For example, quickly changing computer technology strongly affects not only computer manufacturers but also organizations that use computers. Recent legislation and changes in public attitudes have brought more emphasis to the social responsibility of businesses than in the past.

Within the organization objectives are affected by such factors as the

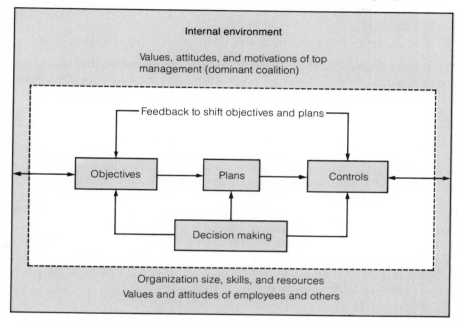

External environment

Competitive issues
Suppliers
Economic, social, political, and technological factors
Other factors

Customers
Stockholders
Special interest groups
Other groups

Internal environment

Values, attitudes, and motivations of top
management (dominant coalition)

Feedback to shift objectives and plans

Objectives   Plans   Controls

Decision making

Organization size, skills, and resources
Values and attitudes of employees and others

FIGURE 5.1 Some factors influencing organizational objectives

size, skills, and resources of the organization, the values and attitudes of the dominant coalition, and the values and attitudes of employees and others. As objectives change, the planning and control processes that exist to ensure accomplishment of objectives also change. The process of decision making is involved both in the determination of the objectives and in the planning and control that issue from them.[5]

The response of U.S. auto makers to the dramatic rise in imports of small cars (particularly Japanese cars) from 1973 to 1980 and to the more stringent demands on automobiles manufactured in the United States is an example of how changes in the external environment can cause changes in the objectives of an organization. Internally, the attitudes and values of the dominant coalition of the U.S. automobile companies appeared to shift. Small automobiles rather than large ones were stressed, and corresponding design changes, such as diesel engines and front wheel drive, were highlighted. By 1985 major U.S. auto makers are expected to spend $80 billion to improve automobiles to the point where they will average 27.5 miles a gallon, twice the 1975 average.[6]

Influences on Objectives As these illustrations suggest, specific objectives in an organization are changed when top management (the dom-

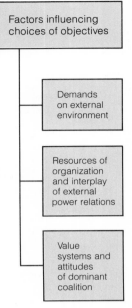

Factors influencing choices of objectives

Demands on external environment

Resources of organization and interplay of external power relations

Value systems and attitudes of dominant coalition

inant coalition) reacts to the complex interplay of forces from the external environment and from within the organization. Three basic factors influence these changes:

1. The demands of the external environment, including external power relationships.
2. The resources of the organization and the interplay of internal power relationships.
3. The value systems and attitudes of the dominant coalition.

The next section will show some of the specific pressures that the dominant coalition must balance in establishing and maintaining objectives.

ORGANIZATIONS NEED MULTIPLE OBJECTIVES

Most managers and management writers agree that organizations are a part of society and require society's approval. Therefore, organizations must both serve society and make a contribution to it. Making a profit cannot be an organization's only goal. Besides, in the long run, profits will remain high only if sufficient consideration is given to such areas as good citizenship, employee welfare, and management development. Furthermore, lower-level managers in most organizations cannot measure the impact of their decisions on even short-run profits, so they need other, more specific objectives.

Objectives for All Organizations   Specific objectives beyond profits that are important to managers fall into two basic categories: those that pertain to organizations in general and those that pertain to profit-making organizations. Some broad and **continuing objectives** that apply to all organizations are:

Organizational objectives

Identification

Integration

Collaboration

Adaptation

Revitalization

1. *Identification*. The organization should be clear about its identity and committed to its organizational objectives.
2. *Integration*. The needs of the individual and the organization should be integrated.
3. *Collaboration*. The organization should have mechanisms for the productive use and control of conflict.
4. *Adaptation*. The organization should be able to respond quickly and appropriately to changes in the environment.
5. *Revitalization*. The organization should be able to continually renew itself so as to be able to deal with problems of both growth and decay.[7]

Objectives for Business Organizations   These five primary objectives help steer the activities of any organization toward the attainment of its goals. Of course, objectives that are specifically for business organizations tend to be more result-oriented. Most people think that profit is a primary business objective. As management consultant Peter Drucker points out, however, this is an oversimplification. Drucker suggests that an organization needs to have result-oriented objectives in at least eight key areas.[8] Although these eight areas were originally identified for use in profit-making organizations, many of them can also apply to public sector and service organizations.[9]

1. *Market standing*—the market share held by the organization versus the market share held by competitors. One organization may want to increase its share of the market by 5 percent each year. An organization with a large market share may decide that increasing its market share could bring about an antitrust action. In the public sector clients frequently have no choice. There is relatively little competition for Medicare, the post office, or police and fire departments. In such circumstances the concern for market standing may be translated into a concern for how well the client is being served. AT&T, for instance, has elaborate indexes to determine this.

2. *Productivity*—the amount of input to output necessary to produce a given amount of goods or services. Organizations of all types need to be continually concerned about productivity. Two of the continuing objectives of the hospital discussed at the beginning of the chapter were using time of senior medical staff efficiently and using all resources efficiently.

3. *Profitability*—the ratio of outputs to inputs. A major objective for organizations in the private sector is profits. The counterpart to this objective for nonprofit organizations or organizations in the public sector keeping costs down and balancing funds for the greater public good. For example, the Secretary of Health and Human Services (HHS) is responsible for balancing such programs as hot meals for the elderly, Medicaid, cancer research, and supporting the development of elementary school curriculums.

4. *Physical and financial resources.* Organizations need adequate financial reserves. They also need to protect and maintain equipment, buildings, and inventory. A hospital must maintain enough cash on hand to pay its bills and to meet the payroll. After an automobile is built and sold, the manufacturer must maintain an inventory of parts so the car can be repaired.

5. *Innovation.* For an organization to stay in operation, it must bring out new products and services or improve existing ones. Serious questions are always arising in this area. In cancer research, for example, should the innovation be aimed at funding research into the causes of the disease or at treating those who already have the disease?[10] Given limited resources, should a hospital try for improved teaching or the purchase of specialized new equipment? How can different but equally important objectives be balanced?

6. *Manager performance and development.* The organization, public or private, that does not develop its management will not exist long. To develop this resource the organization must provide the tools and the opportunities that allow its managers to do a good job.

Performance areas in profit-making organizations:

- Market standing
- Productivity
- Profitability
- Physical and financial resources
- Innovation
- Manager performance and development
- Worker performance and attitudes
- Public and social responsibility

7. *Worker performance and attitudes.* The organization must be continually concerned about worker performance and attitudes, since it is through people that the work gets done.
8. *Public and social responsibility.* More and more organizations in the private sector must accept some social and public responsibility and concern themselves with the improvement of the deteriorating environment and its effect on the quality of life.[11] Indeed, one of the primary purposes today of organizations in the public sector is the fulfillment of public and social responsibility goals. Thus public health is a continuing, long-term goal.

Drucker developed the eight key performance areas as a result of his consulting work with General Electric. At that time GE was measuring managerial success primarily on the basis of a single objective—the rate of return on investment. A clever manager could make high profits by neglecting long-term considerations, such as innovation, equipment maintenance, and employee attitude. Because of the apparent success, the manager might be quickly promoted, but the next manager would be faced with major problems. To avoid this situation Drucker recommended that return on investment be expanded to the eight key areas listed above. As he reported, "Objectives are needed in every area where performance and results directly and vitally affect the survival and prosperity of the business."[12]

OBJECTIVES IN A CHANGING WORLD

Increasingly, managers face the task of developing overall objectives that satisfy a number of "influence" groups. An **influence group** is any group that exerts pressure on an organization.[13]

Balancing Objectives As Figure 5.2 shows, before taking action, managers must deal with a multitude of influence groups. These groups include employees, creditors, customers, suppliers, the public at large, special interest groups, and stockholders. All of them may have valid, though conflicting, claims. For example, managers who are concerned with the organization's future may feel they must satisfy the desires of public interest groups concerned about pollution. Shareholders, on the other hand, may worry more about the impact of pollution control on current dividends and the stock prices. Furthermore, if suppliers raise prices sharply, managers may choose to absorb some of the direct costs rather than raise their company's prices, since price increases may send customers to competing products. The managers may then have to defend their action to bankers when it is time to negotiate new loans.

Government regulations often have a profound impact on organizations. In 1977 the concept of equal employment opportunity was broadened when the Department of Health, Education and Welfare (now the Department of Health and Human Services) announced regulations for-

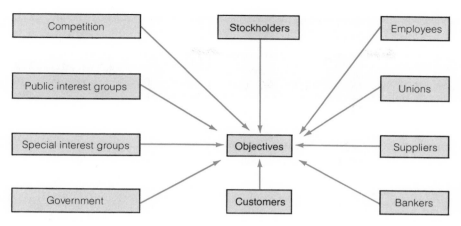

FIGURE 5.2 The many influences on the organization

bidding employment discrimination against handicapped people. The change in mandatory retirement from sixty-five to seventy also had far-reaching consequences for organizations as well as individuals.

These are only a few examples of how influence groups affect organizations. Managers must be alert to the politics of any situation and be ready to implement quick and unexpected changes in specific objectives. Although the organization's broad, overall goals may not change, a shift in priorities may be appropriate. A good manager anticipates the need for such a shift by interpreting events in the external and internal environments.

A recent study shows that managers feel strongly that the interests of such groups as consumers, stockholders, and labor need to be fairly balanced in formulating objectives. According to this study most modern managers desire to earn only a reasonable or fair profit for stockholders and are highly conscious of the social responsibilities of business.[14]

Some organizations are better able than others to adapt and shift objectives and priorities. For example, Du Pont makes fluorocarbons, which include substances trademarked as Freons, the principal gases used as aerosol propellants. There is some evidence that Freons affect the ozone layer that shields the earth from dangerous ultraviolet radiation. When the federal government recommended a gradual phaseout of aerosol sprays propelled by fluorocarbons, Du Pont agreed to cooperate.

Changes in Organizational Objectives over Time To show the kinds of changes that can occur in objectives over time, the chapter will review three studies conducted over a period of about twenty years, one in 1959, one in 1967, and one in 1979. The studies involved different types of organizations and different approaches, so they are not directly comparable; but they should give an idea of what objectives are important to organization in general and how the objectives have changed over the years.

The 1959 study reported the three most important organizational ob-

On the Job

GM's AMBITIOUS PLANS TO EMPLOY ROBOTS

General Motors Corp. will spend more than $200 million by mid-1983 in the auto industry's most massive conversion to high-technology automation. The project will convert 14 GM assembly lines in seven plants to sophisticated systems developed in Italy. About 800 robots will weld the bodies of virtually every new car the company introduces over the next three model years. GM is expected to invest almost $1 billion by 1990 to add 13,000 more robots of varying sophistication and size to paint, load and unload machines, and assemble components.

GM already uses about 150 large welding robots, mainly to assemble the body of its popular X-car compacts. The new systems, which are considerably more complicated, will be used to produce front-wheel-drive versions of the auto maker's subcompact, intermediate, and full-size cars. Says Stanley J. Polcyn, senior vice-president of Unimation Inc., which will supply the robot welders: "They [GM] have really committed themselves to the technology."

The equipment GM will install in seven of its 19 final assembly plants will be used to turn stamped steel panels into complete auto bodies. Normally, that process is done in 40 to 50 steps by workers using handheld welding guns. The new method replaces human welders with robots and assembles the entire car body in two or three steps with the help of a computerized clamping system called Robogate, which was developed by Italy's Comau, a Fiat affiliate. GM worked with Robogate Systems Inc., Comau's Detroit licensee, in designing its systems.

Industry sources say the GM system will slash the auto maker's labor costs for that portion of auto production by as much as $14 per hour, or about 70%. The highly mechanized equipment will also improve the consistency of welds and, according to Frank A. DiPietro, production engineering director for GM's Fisher Body Div., reduce body rattles and vibration.

Pioneered by Chrysler Robogate systems are relatively new to Detroit. Chrysler Corp. installed the first Robogate three years ago to produce subcompact Omni and Horizon bodies. Similar systems are used to produce the company's K-car, and Chrysler is installing another Robogate this year. Ford Motor Co. uses some welding robots but has not switched to the Robogate system.

GM sees its welding program as only the start of a much more sweeping switch to robotics. "We see the largest use of robots by 1990 in assembly of things smaller than a bread box," says Richard C. Beecher, a GM specialist in robotics. Most of that work will probably be done by small Puma robots developed by GM and Unimation (BW—June 9). GM predicts that by 1990 it will use 5,000 Puma robot arms in assembly and another 4,000 to load and unload machines. GM has developed another robot arm, this one for painting, and plans to manufacture them itself. The auto maker is expected to begin factory tests within a month. GM's Beecher predicts that his company will be using 1,500 robot painters by 1990.

The United Auto Workers estimates that assembly line labor could be cut by as much as 50% over the next nine years because of robots and other automation projects. But the UAW believes there is little it can do to stop the process. Says UAW researcher Daniel Luria: "We have bigger worries than robotics," particularly the surge in imported cars and components.

Controlling Quality Besides the labor savings from automating production lines, the use of robots offers vastly improved quality control. In manual assembly, tolerances can stray as the auto body moves from one step to the next. The result: poorly fitting doors, missing welds, rattles, and leaks. Robogate eliminates most of the variations. Says GM's DiPietro: "We have a plan for the implementation of robots to improve quality throughout all our operations."

jectives as making a profit (first choice of 36 percent), providing a good product (first choice of 21 percent); and growth (first choice of 12 percent). The subject of community relations was not chosen as an objective; only 5 percent gave weight to employee welfare, and another 5 percent chose keeping pace with or staying ahead of competitors.[15]

In the 1967 study, responses from more than a thousand managers were little different from those in the 1959 study. The three goals viewed as most important in terms of influencing managerial behavior were organizational efficiency (first choice of 60 percent), high productivity (first choice of 60 percent), and profit maximization (first choice of 56 percent). Social welfare was seen as having relatively little impact on managerial behavior (only 4 percent said it was a goal), and employee welfare had only slightly more (17 percent saw it as important).[16]

These two studies suggest that, up to 1967 at least, managers saw high profits and productivity as the most important goals and social responsibility and employee welfare (or quality of work life) as much less important. By 1979, however, emphasis had shifted to other organizational objectives. Table 5.2 shows the major objectives reported by eighty-two organizations from four industrial groups—food processing, chemicals and drugs, packaging, and electrical and electronics organizations—in 1979.[17] The number of goals reported by individual organizations ranged from one to eighteen, with an average of five to six. Research suggests that having too few organizational objectives can give disproportionate importance to a single objective, such as profit, while too many specific objectives impairs economic performance.[18]

As Table 5.2 shows, the top three goals in 1979—profitability, growth, and market share—were still primarily economic. Profitability must be viewed as important if the organization is to survive. Growth is important if it is to maintain or improve its position in the field. Market share— the percent of total industry sales attributed to one company—is important because of its influence on profitability. Large-volume production can help the organization achieve lower unit production costs and can

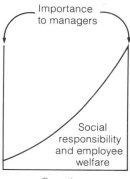

Importance to managers

Social responsibility and employee welfare

Over time

TABLE 5.2   Range of Corporate Goals in 1979

CATEGORY	NUMBER[a]	PERCENT[b]
Profitability	73	89
Growth	67	82
Market share	54	66
Social responsibility	53	65
Employee welfare	51	62
Product quality and service	49	60
Research and development	44	54
Diversification	42	51
Efficiency	41	50
Financial stability	40	49
Resource conservation	32	39
Management development	29	35
Multinational enterprise	24	29
Consolidation	14	17
Miscellaneous other goals	15	18

[a] Total number is 82.
[b] Adds to more than 100 percent because most companies have more than one goal.

Source: From Y. Shetty, "New Look at Corporate Goals," *California Management Review* 22 (Winter 1979): 73. © 1979 by the Regents of the University of California. Reprinted from *California Management Review*, Volume XXII, No. 2, p. 73 by permission of the Regents.

spread expenses for areas such as product development, marketing, and advertising over a larger sales volume.

Two critical noneconomic goals:

- Social responsibility
- Employee welfare

The next two goals in priority, however, contrast sharply with results of the earlier studies. Corporate social responsibility and employee welfare were ranked high despite their noneconomic nature. As society's expectations of organizations have changed, these noneconomic goals have received more attention from the organizations themselves. The concept of employee welfare has been broadened to mean quality of working life. The objective of social responsibility has become strong enough to involve organizations in social problems such as environmental pollution and discrimination against minorities.

As Table 5.2 shows, organizations have also given themselves some new goals: resource conservation, financial stability, multinational expansion, and consolidation. These goals reflect changes in the external environment of the organization. Resource conservation arises, at least in part, from energy shortages, the rising cost of nonrenewable resources, and the growing belief that today's lack of planning could have disastrous consequences for the organization in the future.

In conclusion, at least some of the objectives of an organization change with the passage of time, in response to problems that arise in the industry of that organization, and through changes in the country's economic situation, the degree of uncertainty in the environment, the relative size of the organization, and the shifting values and attitudes of top management, the work force, and the country at large.

CHARACTERISTICS OF GOOD OBJECTIVES

The objectives for the entire organization are necessarily broader than the objectives for one department or work group. Nevertheless, good objectives in either case have certain characteristics in common, as shown in Table 5.3.[19]

Hierarchy of Objectives To make certain that objectives are accomplished it is important to distinguish among the levels of management. The three main levels—strategic, managerial, and operating—were described in detail in Chapter 1 and will be briefly reviewed here. The strategic level of management mediates between the organization and the wider social environment. It determines the strategy and overall direction of the organization. The managerial, or administrative, level coordinates activities within the organization. The operating level is concerned with the production of goods and services.

Thus there is a hierarchy of objectives that corresponds to the three broad managerial levels, as demonstrated in Figure 5.3. The **hierarchy of objectives** is a graded series in which the organization's objectives are supported by each succeeding managerial level down to the level of the individual. The example used in the figure is that of market standing. The strategic marketing decision is to increase the market share of widgets by 10 percent during the year. The managerial objective is to produce and sell 2,775,610 of all types of widgets. In order for this number of widgets to be manufactured and sold, the purchasing department must develop a comprehensive parts list. The list must include the time of ordering and the time needed for the order to be processed and shipped, since manufacturing will have certain essential items earlier than less essential ones. Finally, the buyer who specializes in purchasing electronic parts must make certain that the specific parts are inside the factory ten working days before needed. (Previous study has shown that inventory costs are greatly increased if the material arrives more than ten days in advance.)

TABLE 5.3 Characteristics of Good Objectives

1. They form a hierarchy.
2. They are specific and well understood.
3. They are balanced.
4. They identify expected results.
5. They consider internal and external constraints.
6. They are measurable and quantitative in nature.
7. They are within the power of the individual manager or work unit.
8. They are acceptable to everyone in the organization.

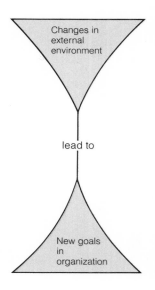

Changes in external environment

lead to

New goals in organization

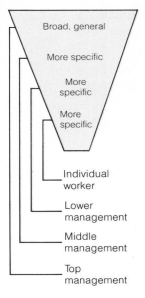

Hierarchy of objectives

Broad, general

More specific

More specific

More specific

Individual worker

Lower management

Middle management

Top management

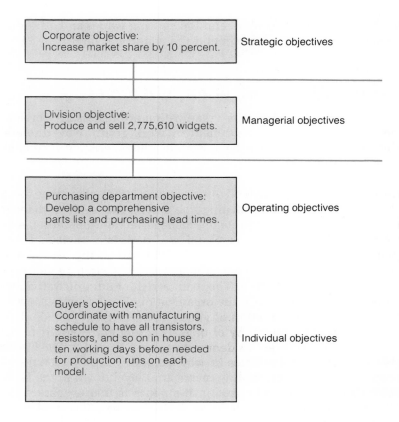

FIGURE 5.3 The hierarchy of objectives

Specific and Well Understood   Objectives must be specific and well understood. The organization must be clear about its identity; only in this way can objectives be understood by those who are part of it. The objectives at the top of large organizations are broader and more strategic than those lower in the organization, which tend to be more specific, tangible, and technical in nature. Nevertheless, the objectives of the individual unit need to be understood and tied in to the objectives of the larger organization.

Balanced   Objectives must be balanced. Clarity and understanding are not enough; objectives must also be balanced. Since objectives are used as guides to action, they help integrate the activities of the different units, functions, and departments. Many organizations run into trouble because their customer service objectives are not properly related to their profit objectives. Other organizations employ too many college graduates to be consistent with the organizations objectives. Since there is no opportunity to use all these high-potential individuals, the result is high turnover. As one noted writer put it, "Every organization and every part of every organization must be an expression of the purpose of the undertaking concerned or it is meaningless and therefore redundant."[20]

Expected Results Identified   Objectives must identify results. In the case at the beginning of the chapter, high quality medical care is a broad organizational goal. As such it is difficult to measure. Objectives must clearly identify the results expected if they are to commit individuals to action. High quality medical care and making profits are not meaningful guides to action. Keeping the bed occupancy rate at or above 85 percent and making a 10 percent profit after taxes are such guides.

Internal and External Constraints Considered   Most organizations operate within a framework of external constraints, including legal, environmental, and competitive restrictions. They also have internal constraints, such as limits on financial and other resources. As the environment changes, some of the more specific objectives need to change. General Motor's overall objectives may not have changed over the years, but more stringent laws regarding automobile exhaust systems have caused many specific objectives within the organization to change.

Measurable and Quantitative in Nature   Objectives should be measurable if expected results are to be identified and determined. Many objectives can be stated in terms of quantity, quality, cost, and time. However, a danger of overmeasurement also exist. When managers are faced with two objectives, one easily measurable and the other not, they tend to focus more sharply on the measurable one.

Within the Power of the Individual Manager or Work Unit   Objectives should be attainable; yet, for an organization to grow and prosper, they should also contain a certain amount of stretch. If they are too low, there is little challenge. If they are too high, people may not attempt to achieve them or may become frustrated by failing to achieve them.[21]

Acceptable to People in the Organization   An objective that is not accepted by people in the organization will not be put into action. To gain this acceptance, objectives should integrate the needs of individuals with those of the organization. Furthermore, the organization should have ways to use and control conflict productively. Involving employees in deciding how to achieve objectives is one way of encouraging them to accept the objectives.

A manufacturing plant manager received orders from corporate headquarters to reduce the work force by 20 percent because of a drop in sales. He believed that the reduction would be temporary, but he could not be sure. He and his immediate subordinates discussed a number of approaches to the problem. Finally, he decided to give the workers the facts and some alternative approaches. After considerable discussion, the 20 percent reduction was achieved. Some workers began four-day workweeks. Some took unpaid vacations. Others asked for official layoff notices so they could collect unemployment. There was never any question about the reduction itself, since it had been decided by corporate management. However, the workers themselves decided how the objective was to be achieved. Both managers and workers felt positive about the way the objective was implemented.

OFFICIAL VERSUS ACTUAL OBJECTIVES

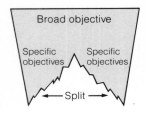

Official   Actual

Broad objective

Specific objectives Specific objectives

←— Split —→

Almost all organizations have both official and actual objectives.[22] **Official objectives** express the general purpose of the organization. They are used in annual reports and other authoritative pronouncements. Although they are called objectives, they could more properly be termed philosophical statements. "To provide high quality medical care to the patient," "to promote employee welfare and morale," and "to fulfill the organization's social responsibility to the community" are all official objectives. These objectives are often drawn up for public consumption by special committees, signed by the president or the chairperson of the board of directors, and hung in executive offices and lobbies. They are seldom reexamined or changed. Usually they are so general as to be of little practical use and so innocuous that nobody can be against them.

Actual objectives, on the other hand, guide the activities of the organization, "regardless of what the official goals say are the aims."[23] Several years ago, the manufacturing plant of an organization with an official objective of social responsibility to the community received complaints about its pollution of a small river. A waste by-product was turning the water red. Although the dominant coalition of the organization subscribed to the objective of social responsibility, the plant manager saw profit maximization as the primary objective by which he was rewarded. To remove the noxious waste would have been expensive, so the manager solved the problem by putting in a storage tank and dumping the waste only at night, when the color would not be seen. The manager was proud of his solution to the problem; top management was unaware of it.

Goal Conflict Although official objectives rarely inspire conflict, operating objectives frequently do. For example, a university school of management may have an overall goal of providing quality education to the student. Yet conflict may occur over which courses should be required for students. Departments may compete in order to maintain their own power bases and to attract the better students to major in their areas.

Although little actual research has been done on disagreements among individuals or units of the organization concerning objectives, it is obvious that different interpretations of objectives can create conflict. So can an organizational unit's desire to gain resources or to preserve its power and freedom of action. Conflict over interpretation of objectives, however, may raise the quality of decisions, while conflict over resources may lower it.[25]

People, Not Organizations, Have Objectives In truth, organizations do not have objectives; people in organizations have objectives stemming from their own views and motivations. Thus organizational objec-

On the Job

THE PRESIDENT FIRED AT JOHNS-MANVILLE

Conflict can come about when one member of the dominant coalition is perceived by the others as being unusual. During the time that Richard Goodwin was president and chief executive officer of Johns-Manville Corporation sales rose 91 percent (from $578 million in 1970 to $1.1 billion in 1975). Net profit went up 115 percent. Goodwin also shifted the corporate headquarters from New York City to a 10,000-acre ranch sixteen miles from Denver—a ranch that customers, suppliers, and others were asking to visit.

On September 1, 1976, Goodwin was to attend a board of directors meeting. He felt justifiably proud of his accomplishments. The evening before the meeting, however, he met with three board members, who told him that the majority of the board wanted him to resign. At the board meeting his resignation was announced, and a new president was appointed.

What happened? All the facts may never be known, but the most likely explanation is that Goodwin was too flamboyant for the conservative members of the board. Although he had followed their instruction to get the company moving, he was never a trusted member of the dominant coalition. The first reason given for Goodwin's dismissal was "irreconcilable policy differences." When asked to explain what that meant, one of the board members said, "Personality conflict was the key to the whole situation."[24]

Source: Adapted from Herbert Meyer, "Shootout at the Johns-Manville Corral," *Fortune,* October 1976, pp. 146–154.

tives are really shifting and uneasy compromises among the individuals within the organization and the changing demands made by the outside environment. As social psychologist Robert Katz says: "Every strategic action must strike a balance between so many conflicting values, objectives and criteria that it will always be suboptimal from any single viewpoint. Every decision or choice affecting the whole enterprise has negative consequences for some of the parts."[26]

It is commonly assumed that objectives are developed at the top and then passed down and accepted by each of the lower levels. However, forceful arguments against this assumption exist. Some individuals within any organization may be unconcerned about profits. The research and development department may focus on elegant designs. Marketing may want a variety of products to attract the customer. Manufacturing may want fewer and simpler high-volume products to reduce costs. The president may want to minimize risks. The research director may want to develop an esoteric new product or write articles. Certainly none of these conflicting desires shows any development of organizational objectives from the top down.

Nonindustrial organizations have the same types of conflicts. University administrators may seek to reduce costs by having each faculty member carry a heavy teaching load. Individual faculty members may prefer to spend more time on their own consulting, research, or writing. Thus the **actual objectives** of the organization are the result of a continuing series of compromises and negotiations among constituencies. In the hospital case at the beginning of this chapter, some objectives of importance to hospital administrators and insurance agencies were given little weight by nurses, senior physicians, and junior staff, each of whom stressed other objectives.

Multiple and conflicting objectives emerge from bargaining among the organization's personnel, and the bargaining occurs because people are not satisfied. (A satisfied need is not a motivator.) Each person has needs or demands that may pop up at different times. Thus many organizations have objectives that are contradictory but that are not so recognized because they are held by different members or groups and are rarely considered simultaneously.

As Chapter 1 described, many managers do not have the time to fully inform their subordinates. In addition, as situations change, managers keep general objectives in mind but constantly shift priorities.

Perceptual Differences Regarding Objectives As a result of changing and shifting objectives, personal needs, and many other factors, a surprising amount of disagreement can exist between supervisor and subordinate on what the subordinate's job is. The results of one widely known study are shown in Table 5.4. The supervisor-subordinate pairs in the study were surprised at the results. Of particular significance is the amount of their disagreement in rating job performance. Although both supervisor and subordinate believed that they understood what was required in the subordinate's job, each was perceiving it differently. The same kind of perceptual disagreement can be found in a classroom when a student feels prepared for a test after studying hard, only to find a series of unexpected questions.

MANAGEMENT BY OBJECTIVES

Suppose that the actual objectives of an organization are the result of a series of compromises, that objectives are multiple and conflicting, that

TABLE 5.4 Perceptual Differences of Supervisor-subordinate Pairs Regarding Subordinate's Job and Performance

	AGREEMENT ON HALF OR LESS THAN HALF OF THE ELEMENTS	AGREEMENT ON MORE THAN HALF OF THE ELEMENTS
Job duties	54%	46%
Job qualifications	67	33
Performance	92	8

Source: Adapted and modified from Norman Maier et al., *Superior-Subordinate Communication in Management,* AMA Research Study #52 (New York: American Management Association, Inc., 1961), p. 10.

objectives and priorities change over time, and that there is honest perceptual disagreement between manager and subordinate pairs. In this situation managers and subordinates may need help in communicating about objectives and agreeing on actions to take.

One approach to setting objectives that provides this kind of help is **management by objectives (MBO),** a philosophy of management that has been gaining popularity in recent years. MBO is based on the assumption that encouraging employees to establish personal objectives in their jobs facilitates communication and results in greater employee commitment, which leads to improved performance. It aspires to bring organizational objectives together with employees' personal objectives, so that people at the lower levels of management will understand, accept, and work toward both organizational and personal goals. Through the use of a hierarchy of objectives, all levels of management, from the strategic to the operating, are involved in some common goals.

An effective MBO program employs periodic manager-subordinate meetings for mutual planning of the work, review of accomplishments, and mutual solving of problems that arise in the course of getting the job done.[27] There are three basic steps in this process:

1. The manager and the subordinate jointly determine the subordinate's specific areas of responsibility. An essential part of this process is mutual agreement about the tasks to be accomplished.
2. The manager and the subordinate agree on the priorities and standards of performance for each area of responsibility.
3. The manager and the subordinate agree on a general work plan for achieving the desired results in each broad area of responsibility—the results tying in with the overall objectives of the organization or unit.

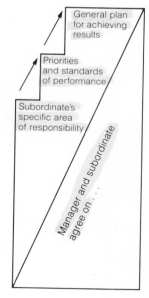

The Steps Are Important Failure to go through all the steps can cause problems. In one instance, the president and vice-president of a company had agreed on a major task for the vice-president—to find a company that their firm could either purchase or merge with. The vice-president worked on the problem for about six months, with little success. Although he located several companies, he and the president did not agree on the choices; and they were not clear about why they disagreed.

At this point the company began to consider installing an MBO program. In the process, the president and vice-president were asked independently to write down the vice-president's major activities. They disagreed on some major issues (step 1); but after discussing them, they reached agreement. The two were then asked, again independently, to write down the performance standards of the purchase or merger (step 2). They did so and again found areas of disagreement. The president, for example, expected the vice-president to locate an organization relatively close to a major airport. The vice-president, on the other hand, was examining only organizations within a two-hour driving radius of the

On the Job

PITFALLS OF MANAGING BY OBJECTIVES

Management by objectives programs have received a great deal of publicity, most of it good, within the last several years. MBO is especially attractive because it serves many purposes. It provides a basis for evaluating a person's performance, since goals are set jointly by subordinate and supervisor, and when they are reached they point clearly to promotions and salary increases. If the MBO program is designed so that goals reached do represent performance, there is little objection to its use as a criterion for employee advancement.

Unfortunately, however, MBO is almost inevitably used as a program to rate individual improvement rather than quality of performance. Certainly it is rea-sonable to expect people to improve at their jobs as time goes by. They are, after all, more experienced. The problem is that many MBO programs discriminate against superior performers. Consider the sales performance of the people below:

	SALES BEFORE MBO	SALES AFTER MBO
Joan A.	400 units	360 units
Jim B.	100 units	150 units

Clearly, Jim B. has improved. By percentage, he has improved markedly. Joan A's sales, conversely, are down 10 percent. Surely, however, we cannot conclude that Jim B. should receive a higher raise than Joan A. or be promoted over her. Yet by many MBO standards, Joan A. has not done as well as Jim B. even though she has sold more than twice as many units.

As a manager implementing an MBO improvement-type program, how would you answer your best salesperson, your "superstar," when she says: "By what percentage will my sales increase next year? Are you kidding? You're damn lucky to be getting what you're getting." How do you ask for improvement from someone who dramatically outperforms other employees?

What is said here is not intended to demean MBO programs. The intent is only to warn against using MBO to indiscriminately force improvement on all employees, which could penalize the very people who are most productive in the organization.

company. This major area of disagreement did not emerge until the two actually went through the steps outlined above, even though they had been discussing the project for six months.

The MBO Process The MBO process is a cyclical one of work planning, review, and new planning. It is based on three psychological principles, shown in Figure 5.4. These principles indicate that subordinates can best improve their performance on the job when they:

Employees perform better when they:

- Know what's expected
- Receive feedback
- Get coaching and assistance

1. *Know what is expected of them.* The planning process gives subordinates better information than they would otherwise have about priorities, expected results, methods by which results will be measured, and resources available to do the job.
2. *Receive feedback about how they are doing.* Knowledge of results is the basic principle. Appropriate and timely feedback is essential for improving job performance.

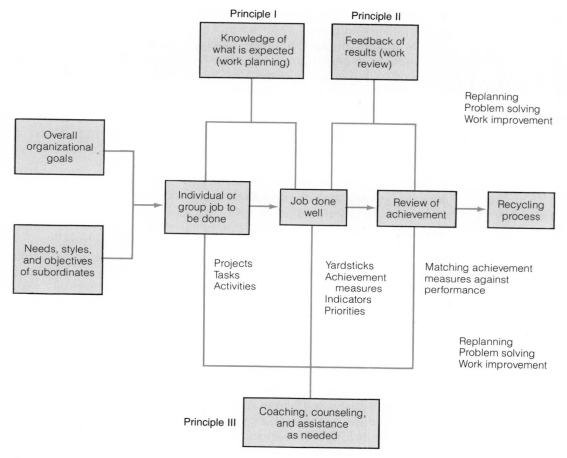

FIGURE 5.4 Work planning and review
Source: Adapted with permission from Edgar F. Huse and Emanuel Kay, "Improving Employee Productivity through Work Planning," in *The Personnel Job in a Changing World,* ed. J. Blood (New York: American Management Association, 1964), p. 305.

3. *Can obtain coaching and assistance as needed.* The process must be changed from management by crisis to planning ahead, so the manager can act as a helper rather than a judge.

When properly installed, MBO can positively affect goal achievement and subordinate development. One research project compared managerial groups using MBO with control groups not using it. Subordinates of the managers using MBO reported greater goal involvement, achievement, and accomplishment, together with greater agreement with supervisors about the jobs to be done and ways of improving job performance.[28] A number of studies in a variety of organizations report similar findings.[29]

Two forms of MBO

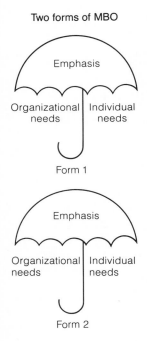

Emphasis

Organizational needs | Individual needs

Form 1

Emphasis

Organizational needs | Individual needs

Form 2

Criteria for a successful MBO program:

• Fits the needs of each organization
• Gives equal attention to training processes and training content
• Avoids destructive competitiveness
• Is implemented slowly and involves all departments

Two Backgrounds of MBO   Not all MBO programs are successful in their implementation and application. One of the problems is that MBO has two historically and philosophically different forms. One form is based almost completely on the organization, stressing the need for highly quantitative measurement to reach organizational objectives.[30] Little attention is paid to the individual or to individual differences, and a great amount of attention is directed toward specific techniques such as using proper forms, having specific times for discussions, and following certain prescribed approaches. This form usually has a great deal of top management support, but little opportunity exists for lower-level subordinates to modify the process.

The second form is concerned with organizational goals but emphasizes the growth and development of subordinates.[31] It ties organizational goals to individual goals, strengths, and growth potential. Supervisors and subordinates work together in a freer and more open fashion, discussing and ultimately agreeing on broad job responsibilities. Subordinates are free to develop short-term performance goals, specific action plans, and criteria for self-appraisal, all subject to the approval of the immediate supervisor. Subordinates discuss their self-appraisals with supervisors, and both develop a mutually agreed upon set of new performance goals and plans. The second form of MBO appears to be the more successful of the two in terms of both individual and company goals.

MBO Motivates   A properly installed MBO program motivates subordinates for three main reasons:

1. It allows satisfaction of the need for achievement and accomplishment—a need that is more often unsatisfied in lower-level managing jobs than in higher-level managing jobs.
2. It allows managers to clarify for subordinates the path to personal rewards.
3. It allows managers increased opportunities to provide subordinates with a better fix on the job and on the relationship of performance to goal attainment.[32]

Unsuccessful MBO Programs   Not all MBO programs are successful. An incorrectly applied MBO program can have unintended, negative results.[33] If it is based on a power-backed, reward-punishment psychology, it can damage employee self-esteem. If subordinates' goals are established so as to make the manager or unit look good rather than to contribute to the overall objectives, it will not benefit the organization. One supervisor said: "Just tell me what you want my boss to look good on, and I'll make it happen, even if I have to cheat on something else." Following are some major reasons that MBO programs fail:

1. *Inadequate top-management support.* Frequently, top management is led to believe that MBO is a panacea for every organizational problem. In a number of instances, MBO was installed for everybody but top management and their immediate subordinates—a sure tip-off to failure.

2. *Inadequate explanation and training.* MBO requires a new kind of superior-subordinate interaction. Too often, MBO is introduced across the organization with little explanation, training, or assistance. The program cannot work if supervisors and subordinates do not understand it.

3. *Setting arbitrary goals.* MBO calls for joint action from supervisors and subordinates in setting goals. A sure cause of failue is for the supervisor to be authoritarian and to set arbitrary goals for subordinates.

4. *Failure to limit objectives.* Stating too many objectives obscures priorities and leads to a sense of failure, since not all the objectives can be accomplished. The number of objectives should be limited to those that are most relevant to the particular job. Priorities should be established to distinguish between critical objectives, necessary objectives, and desirable objectives.

5. *Failure to insist on verifiability.* To provide knowledge of a job well done, each objective must have measures of how well the objective was achieved. Vague objectives like "improve the effectiveness of the personnel department" are impossible to verify. What is meant by "improve"? By "effectiveness"? With a little effort, such broad objectives can be restated so that they are verifiable, as in "reduce the turnover in department X by 10 percent."

6. *Overinsistence on numbers.* Insisting that every objective be reduced to a set of numbers is as much a problem as vagueness. Many important objectives cannot be meaningfully expressed in numbers. Research and development projects, and sales and advertising projects often require less tangible measures than do number of units produced.

7. *Overemphasis on paperwork.* The thrust of MBO is to bring supervisors and subordinates together to discuss objectives and determine when they have been reached. If too much paperwork is required, especially in the form of reports sent to personnel offices, the technique rather than the process of MBO is emphasized.

The successful MBO program should meet four major criteria:

1. It should be individually designed to fit the needs of each organization.

2. It should give equal attention to training processes and training content.

3. It should avoid destructive competitiveness.

4. It should be implemented slowly and should involve all departments.[34]

SUMMARY

Objectives are necessary for any organization. They determine the direction in which the organization will go, and they point to a desired state of affairs that the organization is attempting to realize. As a result, they form the basis for planning, organizing, and controlling the nature and future of the organization.

Frequently those who are not familiar with organizations assume that objectives are set at the top, are relatively unchangeable, and are agreed on by all members of the organization. As the hospital case at the beginning of the chapter showed, these assumptions are misleading. Effective managers know that objectives are often slippery concepts. In any fast-moving society, the manager must be able to keep the overall objectives in mind even as specific objectives change in emphasis and nature.

Managers must also be politicians. Operating or actual objectives come about from a constant series of negotiations among both internal and external groups. Effective managers are therefore adept at partly satisfying each of the groups. No influence group is ever fully satisfied; thus managers can only strike a balance among the groups' conflicting demands.

Effective managers are also aware that peo-ple, not organizations, have objectives. As a result, managers do not expect the various individuals or groups within the organization to subscribe fully to all the organization's objectives. For example, the manager of the hospital in the case at the beginning of the chapter should be aware of and accept the differing perceptions of the nurses, the senior physicians, and the junior physicians.

Management by objectives is one important way of bringing together organizational, individual, and group objectives. When properly used, MBO provides a method for transmitting objectives throughout the hierarchy while allowing for individual differences. Some individuals follow orders almost blindly; others need latitude in carrying out their jobs. MBO makes certain that managers and their subordinates agree in advance on what is expected and what criteria they will use to determine how well a job has been done. Properly used, MBO can be a most effective tool.

STUDY QUESTIONS

1. What is an organizational goal or objective?
2. Explain the importance of objectives.
3. What are the characteristics of good objectives?
4. In what way are broad objectives, specific objectives, plans, and decision making interrelated in an organization?
5. What is meant by *hierarchy of objectives?*
6. What are the differences between official and actual objectives?
7. Why is it sometimes necessary to change objectives?
8. What is meant by the term *management by objectives?*
9. What are some reasons for the success and failure of MBO programs?
10. Do the objectives at the beginning of this

chapter agree with your personal objectives? How might they be changed if you were to discuss them with your instructor? With the author?

11. Are there any similarities between those objectives and MBO programs?
12. Select organizations of different sizes and interview several members of these organizations. What is their perception of the organizational objectives? How much agreement is there? Does the size of the organization affect people's responses?
13. In the case at the beginning of the chapter, different groups placed different importance on specific objectives. Is it a good idea to try to get everyone to place equal importance on each objective? Explain.

Case for Discussion

THE MARSHALL COMPANY

The Marshall Company manufactured automobile shock absorbers that were sold as replacement parts by dealers, service stations, auto repair shops, and other retailers. Competition was growing intense, and the Marshall Company was losing some of its share of the market. After extensive discussion and analysis, the president and the board of directors decided to reduce the price of the shock absorbers by 5 percent to keep up with the competition. Since the profit margin was small, a corresponding increase in productivity would be necessary. The manufacturing manager explained the situation to his subordinates.

After about two weeks, productivity had gone down by 7 percent. The manufacturing manager met with the unit manager of fabrication, the unit manager of assembly, and the unit manager of quality control. (Quality control ensured that parts passed inspection before being assembled and that the assembled shock absorbers met established standards before being shipped.)

Manufacturing Manager: I've called you together because we have a serious problem. As you know, two weeks ago we agreed to raise productivity by 5 percent because of increased competition and the need to lower prices. Since then, productivity has *decreased* by 7 percent.

Unit Manager of Fabrication: I can tell you what the problem is, and it's a simple one. Pat [the unit manager of assembly] is sending back more parts than ever before to be reworked. We are making the parts to the same tolerance that we always have; yet about two out of five parts are coming back.

Unit Manager of Assembly: Unless we get better quality parts, we can't maintain our present production level, much less increase by 5 percent. We don't mind taking time to try to get the parts to fit together when we're not under pressure. If we're going to increase productivity, we have to have parts that fit like they're supposed to. That's why we're sending them back.

Unit Manager of Quality Control: I can tell you one thing. My inspection foreman and inspectors are under more pressure from Chris's [unit manager of fabrication] and Pat's people than ever before. They are trying to get substandard parts and shocks approved. If we're going to continue to put out a quality product, we have to hold to the standards. My people are not going to give in under pressure. We have to maintain high quality standards.

Just then the telephone rang. The manufacturing manager answered it. The secretary said: "The union business agent is on the telephone. He wants to see you right away. Something about a union problem with a speedup."

1. What is happening in this case? Why has people's behavior changed?
2. Is the objective clear and measurable? Has everyone agreed to it? Explain.
3. What should the manufacturing manager do? What should he tell the other managers? The union agent?
4. Could the situation have been avoided?

FOR YOUR CAREER

1. A major objective can be one of discovering what objectives are supported by the dominant coalition that most affects you. Disagreeing with the objectives does not necessarily cause problems as long as you are aware of the disagreement.

2. Usually an objective is not ongoing unless someone is willing to put time, money, or other resources into achieving it.

3. Anyone who makes the solemn pronouncement that the only purpose of the enterprise is to make a profit is probably using linear rather than systems thinking.

4. Objectives do change over time. Don't stick with making buggy whips in the age of automobiles.

5. Watch out for packaged programs that are touted as the answer to all the organization's ills. They are not necessarily solutions to any problems.

6. When in doubt, think small and keep things simple. The organization that thinks it can install an MBO or similar program overnight is headed for trouble.

7. A program unsupported by top management is likely to fail.

FOOTNOTES

1. Adapted by permission of the publisher from "The Many Dimensions of Performance Measurement" by C. Davies and A. Francis, *Organizational Dynamics,* Winter 1975, ⓒ 1975 by AMACOM, a division of American Management Associations. All rights reserved.

2. Ibid.

3. A. Etzioni, *Modern Organizations* (Englewood Cliffs, N.J.: Prentice-Hall, 1954), p. 6.

4. R. Townsend, *Up the Organization* (Greenwich, Conn.: Fawcett, 1971), pp. 111–112.

5. J. Carrington and L. Aurelio, "Survival Tactics for Small Business," *Business Horizons* 19 (February 1976): 13–24; T. Leavitt, *The Third Sector* (New York: AMACOM, 1973); and A. Frank, "Goal Ambiguity and Conflicting Standards: An Approach to the Study of Organization," *Human Organization* 17 (Winter 1958–1959): 8–13.

6. I. Peterson, "Loss of $468 Million, a Company Record, Reported by Ford," *New York Times,* July 30, 1980, p. 1.

7. W. Bennis, *Organizational Development* (Reading, Mass.: Addison–Wesley, 1969).

8. P. Drucker, *The Practice of Management* (New York: Harper & Bros., 1954), p. 62.

9. M. Murray, "Comparing Public and Private Management: An Exploratory Essay," *Public Administration Review* 35 (July–August 1975): 371–374; N. Long, "Public Policy and Administration: The Goals of Rationality and Responsibility," *Public Administration Review* 14 (Winter 1954): 18–34; and L. Lynn, Jr., and J. Siedl, "'Bottom-Line' Management for Public Agencies," *Harvard Business Review* 55 (January–February 1955): 145–153.

10. F. Greve, "The Big Cancer Oversell," *Boston Globe,* April 25, 1978.

11. Drucker, *The Practice of Management,* p. 62.

12. Ibid., p. 63.

13. S. Hunt, "Conducting a Social Inventory," *Management Accounting* 55 (October 1974): 15–22; M. Anshen, ed., *Managing the Socially Responsible Corporation* (New York: Macmillan, 1974); J. Paluszek, *Business and Society: 1976–2000* (New York: American Management Association, 1976); and D. Aaker and G. Day, "Corporate Responses to Consumerism Pressures," *Harvard Business Review* 50 (November–December 1972): 114–124.

14. C. Edmonds III and J. Hand, "What Are the Real Long-Run Objectives of Business?" *Business Horizons* 19 (December 1967): 75–81.

15. J. Dent, "Organizational Correlates of the Goals of Business Managements," *Personnel Psychology* 12 (Autumn 1959): 365–393.

16. G. England, "Organizational Goals and Expected Behavior of American Managers," *Academy of Management Journal* 10 (June 1967): 107–117.

17. Y. Shetty, "New Look at Corporate Goals," *California Management Review* 22 (Winter 1979): 71–78.

18. J. Child, "What Determines Organizational Performance? The Universals vs. the It-All-Depends," *Organizational Dynamics* 3 (Summer 1974): 1–15.

19. C. Granger, "The Hierarchy of Objectives," *Harvard Business Review,* 42 (May–June 1964): 63–74; S. Elion, "Goals and Constraints," *Journal of Management Studies* 8 (October 1971): 292–303; G. Latham and G. Yukl, "A Review of Research on the Application of Goal Setting in Organizations," *Academy of Management Review* 18 (April 1975): 824–845; and G. England, "Organizational Goals and Expected Behavior of American Managers," *Academy of Management Journal* 11 (June 1967): 107–111.

20. L. Urwick, *Notes on the Theory of Organization* (New York: American Management Association, 1952), p. 19.

21. V. Vroom, *Work and Motivation* (New York: Wiley, 1964).

22. L. Barnes and S. Hershon, "Transferring Power in the Family Business," *Harvard Business Review* 54 (July–August 1976): 105–114; W. Turcotte, "Control Systems, Performance and Satisfaction in Two State Agencies," *Administrative Science Quarterly* 19 (March 1974): 60–73; B. Buchanan II, "Government Managers, Business Executives and Organizational Commitment," *Public Administration Review* 34 (July–August 1974): 339–347; and Frank, "Goal Ambiguity and Conflicting Standards."

23. C. Perrow, "The Analysis of Goals in Complex Organizations," *American Sociological Review* 26 (December 1961): 854–866.

24. H. Meyer, "Shootout at the Johns-Manville Corral," *Fortune,* October 1976, p. 154.

25. T. Kochan, L. Cummings, and G. Huber, "Operationalizing the Concepts of Goals and Goal Incompatabilities in Organizational Behavior Research," *Human Relations* 29 (June 1976): 527–544; and R. Cosier and G. Rose, "Cognitive Conflict and Goal Conflict Effects on Task Performance," *Organizational Behavior and Human Performance* 19 (August 1977): 378–391.

26. Robert L. Katz, *Management of the Total Enterprise* (Englewood Cliffs, N.J.: Prentice-Hall, 1970), p. 13.

27. E. Huse, *Organization Development and Change* (St. Paul: West Publishing, 1975); E. Huse and E. Kay, "Improving Employee Productivity through Work Planning," in *The Personnel Job in the Changing World,* ed. J. Blood (New York: American Management Association, 1964), pp. 300–330; D. DeFee. "Management by Objectives: When and How Does It Work?" *Personnel Journal* 56 (January 1977): 32–38; and H. Weihrich, "Management by Objectives: Does It Really Work?" *University of Michigan Business Review* 28 (July 1976): 27–35.

28. Huse and Kay, "Improving Employee Productivity."

29. A. Raia, "Goal Setting and Self-Control," *Journal of Management Studies* 2 (February 1965): 34–58; H. Torsi and S. Carroll, "Management Reaction to Management by Objectives," *Academy of Management Journal* 11 (December 1968): 415–426; and J. Ivancevich, "Changes in Performance in a Management by Objectives Program," *Administrative Science Quarterly* 19 (December 1974): 574–593.

30. Huse, *Organization Development and Change.*

31. H. Levinson, "Management by Whose Objectives?" *Harvard Business Review* 48 (July–August 1970): 125–134; V. Ridgway, "Dysfunctional Consequences of Performance Measurements," *Administrative Science Quarterly* 1 (June 1956): 240–247; G. Morrisey, "Without Control, MBO Is a Waste of Time," *Management Review* 64 (February 1975): 11–17; J. Bucalo, "Personnel Directors. . . . What You Should Know before Recommending MBO," *Personnel Journal* 56 (April 1977): 176–178; and H. Weihrich, "An Uneasy Look at the MBO Jungle: Toward a Contingency Approach to MBO," *Management International Review* 16 (September 1976): 103–109.

32. D. McClelland, *The Achieving Society* (Princeton, N.J.: Van Nostrand, 1961), pp. 36–62; E. Huse, "Putting in a Management Development Program That Works," *California Business Review* 8 (Winter 1966): 73–80; and R. House, "A Path Goal Theory of Leader Effectiveness," *Administrative Science Quarterly* 16 (September 1971): 321–338.

33. W. Mahler, "A Systems Approach to Managing by Objectives," *Systems and Procedures Journal* 17 (October 1966): 1; and S. Kerr, "Some Modifications in MBO as an OD Strategy," *Academy of Management Proceedings,* August 13–16, 1972, p. 40.

34. R. Byrd and J. Cowan, "MBO: A Behavioral Science Approach," *Personnel* 51 (March–April 1974): 42–50.

The Planning Process CHAPTER 6

CONTENTS

THE BEST LAID PLANS . . .

Sears, Roebuck is a giant among retailers. Its 1977 sales were over $17 billion, an increase of 16 percent over the previous year. The $2.3 billion increase was greater than the total sales of many large retail firms, including the R. H. Macy Co.[1]

Although Sears was profitable over all, its profits from retailing dropped off substantially as compared to profits from such organizations as Allstate, Sears's insurance subsidiary (which has a reputation for excellent long-range planning). In fact, Sears did not make a penny on the extra $2.3 billion in retail sales. Instead, its overall profit from retailing dropped by about 13 percent. This drop can be compared to J. C. Penney's profit increase of about 28 percent and Montgomery Ward's increase of 17 percent in the same year. Needless to say, Sears's stockholders were not happy.

Sears has consistently been one of the most successful retailing organizations in the world, primarily because of the foresight and planning of its early leaders. Around the turn of the century, the company created the first honest mail-order catalogue. In the 1920s it recognized the growing importance of the automobile and pioneered in the building of shopping malls. At that point it became a leader in retail sales. Sears's early success was based on its image as a low-cost merchandiser.

In 1967 Sears changed its approach and began to sell higher-priced merchandise in order to attract more affluent shoppers. It increased its advertising budget and directed much of its effort toward bringing in middle- and upper-class customers. The strategy had only limited success. Over time, Sears's image as a merchandiser of low-priced goods was severely eroded. Competitors such as K mart and Penney began taking the lead in this market.

Belatedly recognizing the trend, Sears reorganized in 1975, centralizing more decisions at its corporate headquarters in Chicago. In 1976, it developed a strategic plan for increasing sales the following year. The plan contained several approaches: (1) many more promotional sales than usual, (2) price slashes on many items, (3) longer sales (as long as three to four weeks instead of the usual three to nine days), (4) more money spent on advertising (approximately $1 million more than the previous year), and (5) increased bonuses for store managers, based primarily on sales volume.

One of the purposes of the strategic plan was to get customers into the store. Sears's management assumed that once people entered the store, they would buy more than just the promotional items. For the first nine months, the strategy seemed to work. About a quarter of new business came from the marked down merchandise. But in November and December 1977 and January 1978 more than 40 percent of the new business came from markdowns. Sears began to suspect that store managers, given bonuses for increased volume only, were ignoring profit. Whatever the reason, during those three months, Sears's profits declined by 30 percent.

As a result, Sears reorganized once again; 1978 may have marked a turning point for the company. It hired a new vice-president in charge of logistics to keep inventory levels down and a new vice-president of planning. It also formulated a five-year merchandising plan, the first in its history. The 1979–1983 plan was intended to firmly reestablish Sears as a family store for middle-class, home-owning Americans. It set long-term goals for each merchandising group and spelled out the means for accomplishing these goals. The plan called for increases over 1977 sales within each group of 71 percent to 95 percent by 1983. Sears also changed the bonus plan for executives, placing much less emphasis on volume.

This case presents several questions which you should be able to answer after reading this chapter. The questions include:

1. Did Sears do an effective job of planning? How could it have been better?
2. How is planning related to decision making? To goals and objectives?
3. How do long-term plans affect an organization? In what ways can they be good and in what ways can they be bad?
4. How effective are you at planning your own life?

With this case as a base, Chapter 6 will examine the importance and nature of planning, the hierarchy of planning, major dimensions of planning, stages in effective planning, and roadblocks to effective planning. Strategic, or long-range, planning is so important that the following chapter will be devoted to it.

Planning is an essential activity for organizations. Only after direction has been established can managers decide "what is to be done, when it is to be done, how it is to be done, and who has to do it."[2]

All managers plan. At the top level they determine strategic goals and continuing objectives. At the lower levels they determine how to accomplish the goals set at the top.

WHAT IS PLANNING?

Planning:

One of the most critical managerial functions

Planning asks:

- Where are we?
- Where do we want to be?
- What is the gap?
- How do we reduce the gap?

In the simplest sense, a **plan** is anything that involves selecting in the present a course of action for the future. A football team plans for the season by observing how opposing teams play and then mapping out strategies and specific plays. During a game the quarterback or coach plans the next play. The choice of plays depends on what has happened during the game, the team's position on the field, the score, the time remaining, and a multitude of other variables.

Planning is perhaps the most important managerial function. Before managers can perform any other function, they must have plans that offer purpose and direction. Planning is the function that answers four basic questions:

1. Where are we now? This question is concerned with assessing the present situation and forecasting how the situation may change in the future.
2. Where do we want to be? Answers to this question involve determining the desired objectives in terms of the present and the future.
3. What is the difference between where we are now and where we want to be?
4. How can we get there from here? This question requires an outline of actions and a careful analysis of future implications of present decisions.

Planning looks to the future to determine the direction in which an organization or its units should be going. As Figure 6.1 shows, it helps bridge the gap from where we are to where we want to be. Decision making occurs at each of three levels from the present to the future: continuous monitoring and forecasting, developing plans, and developing controls to ensure that the plans are implemented. In the case of Sears, monitoring the environment caused major changes over the years. In 1977 monitoring showed that Sears's image as a low-cost merchandiser was being eroded. Plans were developed to increase the volume of sales, but the controls showed that the volume increase was also causing reduced profits. As a result, new plans had to be made. Each step, of course, involved decision making.

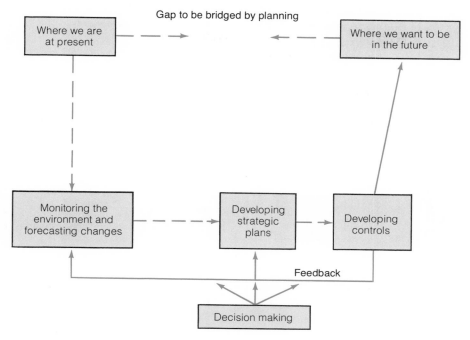

Gap to be bridged by planning

FIGURE 6.1 The strategic planning process

THE HIERARCHY OF PLANNING

Chapter 5 described organizational goals as desired states of affairs that the organization attempts to realize. They are ideas or statements that help to steer or direct the activities of the organization. That chapter also described a hierarchy of objectives that exists to support overall organizational goals.

In the same way, as Figure 6.2 shows, goals are the end points of planning; their establishment provides the basic direction for more specific planning (such as strategies, policies, detailed plans, and controls). Strategic planning assists in bridging the gap between the present and the future. Specific plans help identify and activate the organizational behavior needed for attainment of the ends. Leadership, communications, and control assure that the planned behavior becomes reality.

To illustrate, one objective of an electronics firm may be to grow and achieve leadership in its field. An accompanying objective may be to achieve a 15 percent compound rate of growth in sales over the next ten years to place its performance in the top 4 percent of the industry. To accomplish these objectives requires a hierarchy of strategic, cooperative, and operational planning.

Like organizations, plans have hierarchies.

Strategic Planning **Strategic planning** is "the process of determining the major objectives of an organization and the policies and strategies that will govern the acquisition, use, and disposition of resources to achieve these objectives."[3] In this context, policies are broad guides to

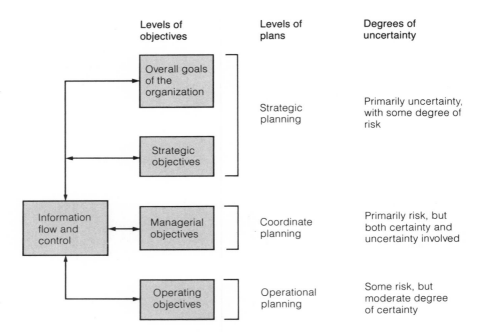

FIGURE 6.2 The hierarchy of planning

The three levels of plans:

- Strategic
- Tactical
- Operational

action, and strategies are the means to deploy resources. Although all managers plan, strategic planning takes place primarily at the top level of management and is directed toward attaining a desired position for the organization in the environment. Such planning determines what should be the overall and continuing objectives of the organization. A greater degree of uncertainty exists in this planning than in planning at lower levels, since the probable outcomes of alternate plans are harder to predict. The relevant environment is generally external to the organization and includes political, social, legal, and financial issues. As a result, the criteria for making decisions are mainly subjective. Top management must rely more heavily on qualitative standards for determining the effectiveness of plans than do those lower in the management hierarchy.[4]

Coordinative or Tactical Planning At the middle, or coordinating, level of management, planning is directed toward implementing strategic plans by coordinating the work of different organizational units. Planning at this level, sometimes called **coordinative planning,** or tactical planning, involves determining how certain areas of a business will deploy resources to reach objectives by following the policies and strategies that have been established in the strategic planning process.

A major characteristic of tactical planning is the coordination of the most important functions of the organization in the service of the strategic plans. Managers develop alternatives and estimate the probability of the alternatives leading to desired outcomes. Various degrees of uncertainty are involved in their decisions; for some they can rely in part on the past performance of the organization, but other decisions cover entirely new ground. The influencing environment at the middle level is more internal than that at the top, and the manager is constrained by top-level decisions about continuing objectives and the implementation of strategy and policy. The degree of risk can be reduced at this level by using techniques that quantify, such as market research and forecasting.

Detailed tactical plans are usually made for such major functional areas as manufacturing, marketing, personnel, research and development, finance, and capital expenditures. The major thrust is toward specific and detailed coordination of the various parts of the organization.[5]

Operational Planning At the lowest, or operating, level of management, the managers need to follow the tactical plans established by the middle level of management to achieve the strategic plans formulated for the entire organization. **Operational planning** is short term, detailed, and concentrated primarily on the functional aspects of the production of goods and services. It involves, for example, the production scheduling of goods and services, the purchase of materials for inventory, and the development of course outlines by classroom teachers. Since operational plans are generally specific and tangible, they involve risk. Usually, however, enough information is at hand for the manager to closely predict the outcome of decisions. Environmental constraints are primarily internal, consisting of policies, budgets, procedures, and rules. Thus plans at this level can be more automatic than plans at higher levels, and decisions can be quantitative (as in creating production schedules and adhering to costs and budgets).

As pictured in Figure 6.2, activities in the three managerial levels often overlap in the everyday functioning of an organization. Information is continually flowing both up and down. (Strategic planning is also called top-down planning because it provides the middle and lower levels with information they need to use in developing operational, or bottom-up, plans.) It is through the interchanging, reviewing, and recycling of top-down and bottom-up plans that the planning activity in general is coordinated and the plans themselves sorted into long-range and short-range categories. In the Sears case, information from the lower levels indicated that the strategic plan to increase the volume of sales also needed to take into account the amount of profit that would be generated.

Ideal Time Allotments for Plans Another way to distinguish strategic, tactical, and operational planning is to examine the time span of planning. Figure 6.3 shows ideal time allocations for managers at different levels in the organization. They are, of course, relatively arbitrary and are best only for certain medium-sized companies under ideal conditions, but they provide rough guidelines that can be applied with modifications to any organization. For very large organizations, such as aerospace companies, public utilities, steel companies, airlines, and companies involved in advanced technology, more emphasis would be

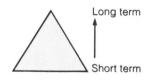

Planning horizons by organizational level

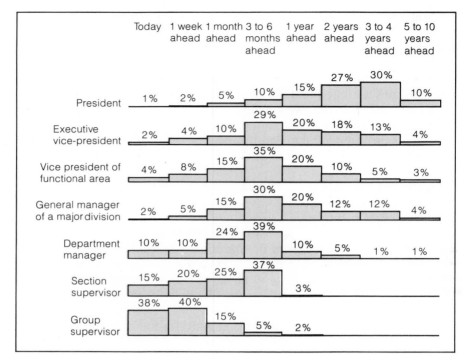

FIGURE 6.3 Ideal allocations of time for planning in the average company

Source: Reprinted with permission of Macmillan Publishing Co., Inc. from *Top Management Planning* by George A. Steiner. Copyright © 1969, The Trustees of Columbia University in the City of New York.

appropriate for the period beyond five years. For small organizations, such as a restaurant owned and operated by one person, planning would be concentrated in a shorter time span.

Seldom does the reality of daily life in an organization fit any ideal presented by a theory. Most managers are active, dynamic people, and the role of handling disturbances frequently takes precedence for them over the entrepreneurial (planning) role. The percentages of time allocated for short-term planning would be much higher for most managers than what is shown in Figure 6.3. The average president would find it hard to limit time spent on today's problems to less than a quarter of total time spent planning (the ideal presented in the figure), and first-level supervisors frequently spend 75 percent or more of their time on today's problems.

Top management at Sears (in contrast to its subsidiary, Allstate) apparently did not spend enough time in recent years planning beyond the immediate future of one to two years.

DOES PLANNING PAY?

It pays to plan.

Planning does not guarantee success, but studies have consistently shown that those who plan outperform those who do not. These studies have covered hundreds of different types of organizations, and some have spanned more than twenty years. In each case, such measures of performance as sales, earnings, growth rate, stock price, and profit demonstrated the value of formal planning.[6]

One such study was conducted in two stages.[7] First, thirty-six organizations were selected from six industries: drugs, chemicals, food, steel, oil, and machinery. Organizations were classified as formal planners if they determined corporate goals and strategy for at least three years ahead and if they established specific projects, procedures, and action plans for achieving the goals. Others were classified as informal planners and were viewed as being, essentially, nonplanners. From the thirty-six organizations, seventeen formal and nineteen informal planners were selected because they offered comparisons over periods extending from seven to fifteen years.

As shown in Figure 6.4, the planners significantly outperformed the informal planners on three of the five measures used: earnings per share (44 percent higher for formal planners), earnings on common equity (38 percent higher), and earnings on total capital employed (32 percent higher). The comparisons for average sales and stock prices were greatly influenced by a single company, so statistical averages could not be used.

The second phase of the study compared the performance of the formal planners after planning against their own performance before planning. Only three measures of economic performance were available, but

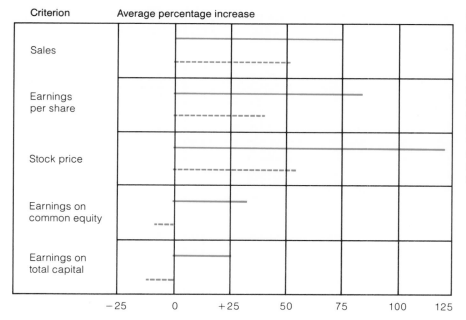

FIGURE 6.4 Performances of formal and informal planning during planning period

Source: Stanley S. Thune and Robert J. House, "Where Long-Range Planning Pays Off," *Business Horizons* 13 (August 1970): 83. Copyright, 1970, by the Foundation for the School of Business at Indiana University. Reprinted by permission.

the increases were impressive, as shown in Figure 6.5. Sales increased 38 percent, earnings per share increased 64 percent, and stock prices rose 56 percent. In both phases, adjustments were made to ensure that other factors than planning were not involved in the success of the formal planners.

A second study sought to extend the findings to see whether they would hold up over a longer period of time.[8] The same sample of firms would have been used, but mergers, acquisitions, and other events made this impossible. Three of the original formal-versus-informal pairs in the drug industry and two pairs in the chemical industry were available for a seven-year comparison. The formal planners significantly outperformed the informal planners in both sales and profits.

As Figure 6.6 indicates, formal planners increased their profits by 139 percent, as opposed to only 59 percent for informal planners, and increased their sales by 150 percent, as opposed to 89 percent for the informal planners. Perhaps more importantly, the formal planners not only outperformed the informal planners but also widened the margin of their success; that is, they improved faster than the informal planners.

These and other studies indicate that, all other things being equal, planning does pay. Although most studies with clear-cut results have been from the profit-making sector of the economy, planning has been shown to pay in other sectors as well.

Allstate, the subsidiary of Sears discussed earlier, is an example of a successful formal planner. Since the early 1960s it has been doing long-range planning, which could be one reason why it contributed so heavily to the profit of its parent company in recent years. In 1978 Sears,

FIGURE 6.5 Performances of companies before and after formal planning

Source: Stanley S. Thune and Robert J. House, "Where Long-Range Planning Pays Off," *Business Horizons* 13 (August 1970): 83. Copyright, 1970, by the Foundation for the School of Business at Indiana University. Reprinted by permission.

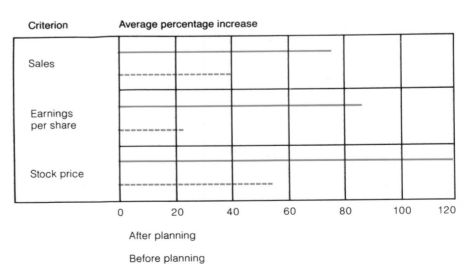

Data used for five industries. Steel was excluded because the preplanning period for this industry was atypical. Data on earnings on common equity and total capital were not available for the preplanning period.

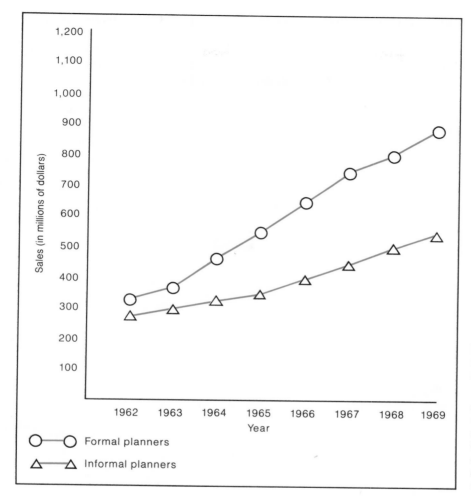

FIGURE 6.6 Increases in sales for formal versus informal planners

Source: Reprinted by permission of the publisher from David Herold, "Long-Range Planning and Organizational Performance: A Cross-Validation Study," *Academy of Management Journal* 15 (March 1972): 95.

perhaps influenced by the success of its subsidiary, developed its first five-year merchandising plan.

MAJOR DIMENSIONS OF PLANNING

Most of the research on planning suggests that it must be tailored to the particular organization. A planning approach that works in one organization will not necessarily work in another. Government agencies have different problems, which require different approaches to planning, than schools, hospitals, or profit-making organizations. The time horizon for steel companies is much different from the time horizon for manufacturers of high-fashion women's clothing. Moreover, even within a single organization different types of planning may be needed at different

Planning is influenced by the type of organization and its environment.

times. Finally, different managers have different approaches to planning.

Despite the variety possible in types of planning, some basic types can be classified by means of a relatively sophisticated system demonstrated in Figure 6.7. Five **dimensions of planning** are shown: organization (meaning the type of organization for which planning is done), subject, elements, time, and characteristics.[9] Although the model focuses primarily on planning for businesses, these dimensions are valid for planning for schools, hospitals, government agencies, and other organizational types.

Organization Plans vary according to the size and type of the organizational unit involved. Planning for an entire organization, such as a

FIGURE 6.7 Dimensions of planning

Source: Reprinted with permission of Macmillan Publishing Co., Inc. from *Top Management Planning* by George A. Steiner. Copyright © 1969, The Trustees of Columbia University in the City of New York.

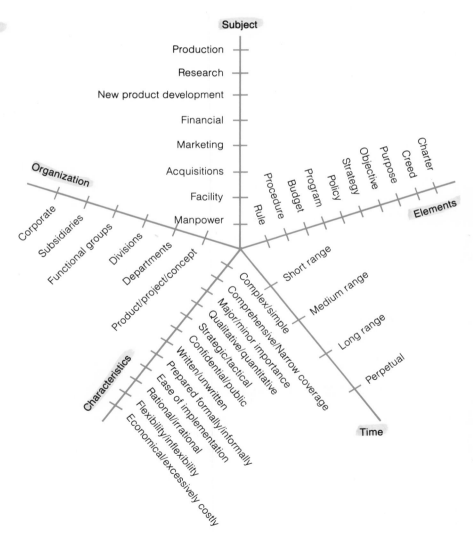

On the Job

PRACTICAL MODELING FOR RESOURCE MANAGEMENT

Managers of manufacturing companies face a major challenge during the next decade. In a business environment increasingly dominated by scarcities and uncertainties, managers will begin to encounter, if they haven't already, several complex problems in the allocation of resources and the balancing of corporate activities:

☐ Existing levels of demand will often strain available production capacity, and the capital for capacity expansion will become increasingly more expensive.

☐ Physical and political factors will limit supplies of raw materials and fuels and, what is worse for the purposes of planning, may subject them to unpredictable interruptions.

☐ The costs of energy, transport, materials, labor, and other factors will continue to rise, often precipitously and without warning, so that accepted trade-offs between operating activities may be cancelled almost overnight.

No longer will it be possible to plan production along the straightforward, linear sequence that has worked in the past—the sequence in which, broadly speaking, demand determines desired production and desired production determines investment. Instead, managers of manufacturing companies will have to adapt to changing circumstances by selecting the constellation of products, markets, and strategies that will yield the best overall return on company resources. Flexible, innovative planning techniques will be required to aid the managers in making this selection. Applying these techniques will often make the difference between a good competitive position and stagnation. For many companies, it will be a matter of survival.

Source: Excerpted from Paul S. Bender, William D. Northrup, and Jeremy F. Shapiro, "Practical Modeling for Resource Management," *Harvard Business Review* 59(2) (March–April 1981): 163–173.

large university, is more complex and difficult than planning for a sub-unit of the organization, such as the university bookstore. Furthermore, different subunits of the organization will have different purposes and so require different types of plans.

Subject Plans also vary according to their subject matter. Planning for production, for example, may entail decisions on investing capital in order to set up production facilities, whereas planning for product marketing may require decisions regarding advertising and choice of markets. Planning for worker development involves still different considerations, since the feelings and attitudes of managers must be weighed. In each case the subject matter of the plan dictates how the manager should proceed with the process of planning. A sampling process may be essential to marketing plans but irrelevant for worker development.

Elements As Figure 6.7 shows, plan elements vary from extremely broad to highly specific. At the strategic level managers are concerned with the broad charter, the overall purpose of the organization. At the supervisory or operating level they are concerned with specific operating rules and procedures. The broader the effect of a plan, the more comprehensive it must be. From these broad, general plans the more specific plans are derived, and each type is appropriate for a certain level of management. Top management may be deeply, and appropriately, involved in developing a complex corporate plan for an acquisition or a merger but should not be involved in developing a procedure for ordering stamps and envelopes.

Time   In many discussions of planning, five years is considered long range, one to five years medium, and less than one year, short range. A better way to discuss the time horizon may be to consider the factors that management can affect. In long-range planning management can affect the strategy and structure of the organization. Thus long-range planning may include a fundamental redirection of the organization. In medium-range planning management may have to accept the general structure and strategy of the organization but can have an immediate impact in determining which people and materials are involved in implementing a given plan. In short-range planning, again, strategy may be fixed, but specific activities can be scheduled or changed. In other words, long-range plans determine the strategy and mission of the organization, medium-range plans determine the quantity and quality of input, and short-range plans determine day-to-day scheduling activities.

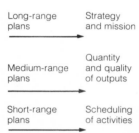

Time span
of planning

Long-range   Strategy
plans   and mission

Medium-range   Quantity
plans   and quality
               of outputs

Short-range   Scheduling
plans   of activities

The time horizon is also affected by the nature of the industry. Long-range plans in the automobile industry may cover ten or more years. Long-range plans for a small, struggling garment manufacturer may extend no more than six months to a year because of fashion and style changes.

Characteristics   In one sense each of the dimensions named in Figure 6.7, except possibly those listed as characteristics, is, or can be, a plan. Characteristics are, in fact, the plans' traits or qualities. Plans range from highly complex to very simple, from qualitative in nature to quantitative (an example of quantitative being a plan for reordering parts or supplies), and from confidential to public (some government plans, for example, are known to those outside the government while others are not).

To some extent the policies of the organization and the styles of its managers will affect the characteristics of plans. The environment of the organization also has an effect. Thus a cigarette company can keep its plans to bring out a new cigarette confidential, while a utility company planning to build a nuclear power plant has to be publicly involved with a number of federal, state, and other agencies.

STAGES IN AN EFFECTIVE PLANNING SYSTEM

There are broad, general steps to planning, but each organization needs to develop its own tailored planning procedures. This section will briefly describe a tactical and operational planning system used by a successful manufacturer of products for a variety of geographical markets.[10] In each of the last five years the company grew more than 15 percent. Its planning system is revised and improved each year. (Steps in strategic planning will be described in more detail in the following chapter.)

Figure 6.8 shows outlines the planning system, which is divided into four basic stages: analysis, development of alternatives, evaluation and choice, and production of a written plan.

For these stages to progress satisfactorily, managers should be trained in the concepts and techniques of planning. Furthermore, all the managers of areas relevant to the plan should be invited to provide information and participate in the planning process.

Analysis The first step in the analysis stage is to examine the environment and the competition. A qualitative and quantitative review of the environment should include economic, social, political, and technological areas. The assessment of the organization's strengths and weaknesses for the future, should take into consideration the organization's position among competitors.

Forecasts should then be made for each of the areas named. In the area of technology a forecast would address the questions: What is the current state of the art? What research are competitors involved in? What innovations might be produced? Written estimates should show in what way each forecast constitutes a threat or an opportunity. For example, a forecast that oil prices will continue to rise may be a threat to organizations that depend on oil for a source of energy but an opportunity for organizations that develop alternative energy sources.

Organizational policies and limits should then be reviewed in light of the forecasts. Are there policies that should be changed or modified? What possible targets may be established for the future?

Alternatives In the alternatives stage each division of the company is asked to develop contingency plans for a number of different environments or alternative futures. These alternative futures, called scenarios,[11] are based on the forecasts made in the analysis stage. Multiple scenarios are necessary because there is no sure way of predicting the future accurately. Three or four descriptions of possible futures should be developed to cover a range of behaviors for the important variables identified in examining the environment and the competition.

For each scenario a plan can be developed to tentatively identify the most likely targets and actions from the wider range of possibilities delineated in the analysis stage.

Evaluation and Choice In the evaluation and choice stage the following factors are evaluated in each tentative plan: objectives and targets, potential actions, investments, profits, risks, and crucial factors for success.

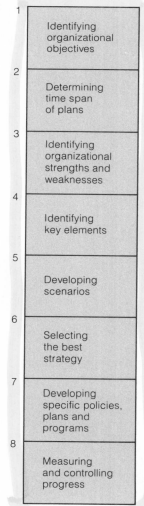

Long-range planning steps

1. Identifying organizational objectives
2. Determining time span of plans
3. Identifying organizational strengths and weaknesses
4. Identifying key elements
5. Developing scenarios
6. Selecting the best strategy
7. Developing specific policies, plans and programs
8. Measuring and controlling progress

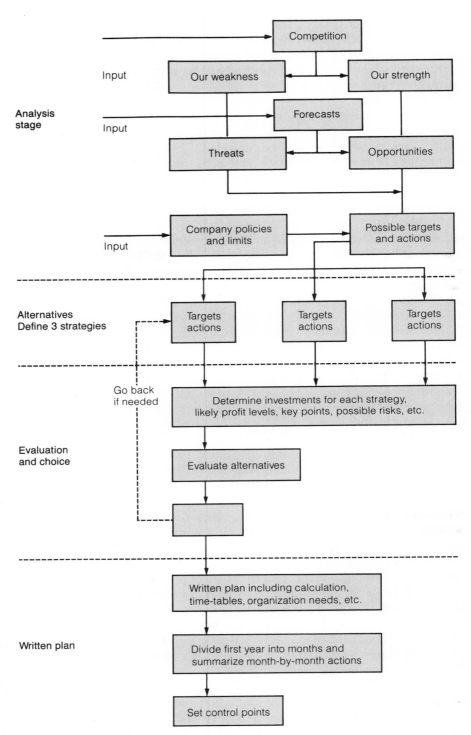

FIGURE 6.8 Outline of a planning system

Source: Reprinted with permission from *Long Range Planning,* 12, 6, J. Martin, "Business Planning: The Gap between Theory and Practice," Copyright 1979, Pergamon Press, Ltd.

Since plans for the future influence decisions for the present, an organization should choose a plan that is not only based on the most probable scenario but is also flexible enough to shift as contingent factors shift. In today's rapidly changing state of social, economic, and political affairs, any plan over a year old could be dangerously wrong. Management should review all tentative plans at least annually and preferably more often than that. Frequently the event least expected comes to pass, and the plan is rendered invalid. What management strategist would have predicted, for example, the Russian incursion into Afghanistan and the resulting U.S. boycott of the 1980 Summer Olympics in Moscow?

Evaluation and choice stage:

- Objectives and targets
- Potential actions
- Investments
- Profits
- Risks
- Crucial factors for success

Written Plan   In the final stage the information collected and analyzed earlier is incorporated in a written plan that describes strengths and weakness in the present position of the organization; prescribes actions to capitalize on opportunities and avoid threats; and includes forecasts, timetables, and detailed operational plans that answer the questions of who, what, when, and how. In addition, at the time the plan is written a timetable should be established for its periodic review.

If the stages described are followed, a plan will be finalized only after a variety of alternate plans have been developed and thoroughly analyzed. Otherwise, a tentative plan is likely to become definite despite charges indicated by the active thinking of all relevant managers. In other words, the planning process may play second fiddle to the plan rather than being essential to it.

Management by objectives was described in Chapter 5 as a way of linking organizational objectives to individual managers, enabling the lower levels of management to understand, accept, and work toward the attainment of those objectives. MBO is actually a planning and review process that is a good way of making certain that plans are achieved. Plans should lead to specific action statements that can be explicitly or implicitly made known to and acted upon by specific individuals or work groups.

ROADBLOCKS TO EFFECTIVE PLANNING

Roadblocks to effective planning occur in three major areas: attitudes and values of management, design of the planning systems, and implementation of plans.[12]

Attitudes and Values of Management   Almost every thoughtful study on planning stresses that effective planning depends heavily on the attitude of managers at all levels of the organization, but especially top management. Some roadblocks that can occur here follow.

Planning Seen as Unimportant   If top management views systematic, long-range planning as unimportant, lower-level managers will exert minimal effort and thought. The message that planning is unimportant

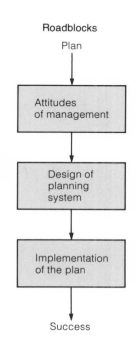

Roadblocks

Plan

Attitudes of management

Design of planning system

Implementation of the plan

Success

can be conveyed in many ways. In one instance, a company president hired a professional planner and then subtly indicated that he, the president, had now done his job and deemed further effort on planning unnecessary. Sometimes, too, managers are comfortable with what they see as the direction of the organization as it is and do not recognize a need for planning. For a long time, movie makers saw no need to consider television in their plans, because they viewed themselves as being in the movie business rather than in the entertainment business.

Design of the Planning System.   The design of the planning system can constitute a roadblock in several following ways.

Lack of Rewards   Managers are active, busy people who tend to address their attention to immediate, tangible problems; and often the appraisals of their performance, their compensation, and their promotions are based strictly on the short-term results of their performance (profits). If systematic planning for long-term results is not rewarded by top management, it will receive little attention.

Lack of Participation   Although planning needs to be initiated, directed, and influenced by top management, it also needs to be carried out at all levels in the organization. People who are involved in making plans effective need to play a major role in developing them. People who are not involved in planning tend to resist both the planning process and the resulting plans.

Lack of Specific Objectives   Instead of stating specific objectives which are to be attained upon completion of a plan, many managers often state only broad generalized objectives such as management development, quality of work life, public responsibility, and the like. Those few who do rarely go beyond generalizations, as in, "We will provide a good environment for our staff to work in."[13] Qualitative objectives are not easy to measure; evaluation is subjective and difficult to justify. Thus such objectives tend to be ignored, particularly if they conflict with more quantifiable ones, such as profit.

Lacking in Proper Balance between Formality and Informality   In some cases a planning system is too informal. Without clear-cut and well understood responsibility assignments (who does what), effective planning is not likely. Both duplication of effort and gaps in performing vital activities can occur.

In contrast, some planning systems are too formal, requiring thick planning manuals, extensive and excessive documentation, and extensive number crunching. In such cases, more attention may be given to the form than the substance. Managers who follow the procedures can be viewed as competent, even though effective planning is not getting done. To avoid this problem an organization should review the planning process at least annually to update and improve it.

The Plan   Four major obstacles to the implementation of effective plans are confusion between planning and reality, lack of motivation to implement plans; lack of an action orientation, and lack of training for managers.

Confusion between Planning and Reality   The value of plans lies in their effect, not in the process of creating them. Yet all too often plans become an end in themselves. Of particular importance in this context is the concept of time. Most reporting systems, especially financial ones, are tied to time. Organizations have annual, semiannual, quarterly, monthly, and sometimes weekly reports—the results of which may be evaluated against the goals outlined in the plan. The key elements of the plan, however, may not lend themselves to a rigid timetable, and operating managers may receive an inflexible set of responsibilities that are impossible to dispatch. Events may change while the budget remains fixed. As a result, managers are forced to take short-range actions to deal with unexpected events that result in long-run harm.

Lack of Motivation to Implement Plans   Planning must be rewarded through such means as performance appraisals, recognition, bonuses, and promotions, or it will cease. The reward and punishment system of most organizations is not tied to planning, particularly strategic, long-range planning.[14] In a majority of organizations managers are rewarded or punished on their short-term performance in meeting budget targets. They frequently receive no reward or penalty for their performance in meeting long-range targets (plans beyond one budget year).

Obstacles to implementation of plans:

- Confusion between planning and reality
- Lack of motivation to implement plans
- Lack of action orientation
- Lack of training for managers

Lack of an Action Orientation   Many formal planning systems do not involve managerial participation or even consider the way today's managerial actions or decisions influence tomorrow's performance and results. "Rather, the technicians take over and emphasize scientific forecasts, overly sophisticated analytical techniques, and other analytical tools that have no real meaning to the action-oriented manager."[15]

One city engaged an expensive consulting firm to develop a master plan for its orderly growth and development. There was little involvement of managers or citizens. In due course, thick sets of documents were delivered to the mayor, the city council, and key municipal departments. The firm received its fee, and the plans were ignored by all concerned.

Lack of Training for Managers   Managers are active people, strongly oriented toward achieving short-term results with daily, immediate, operational problems. When they are suddenly asked to think about what the world will be like in the distant future, the transition can be difficult. Although the analogy is not exact, it is something like asking a college junior, in the middle of finals, to predict what he or she will be doing in five or ten years and to spell out the exact strategies for accom-

On the Job

PERSONAL PLANNING CAN GO ASTRAY

I'm quitting! I can't stand this job. Every morning I drag myself out of bed and force myself to drive to work. It's hard to believe that nine months ago I thought taking this job was the smartest move I'd ever made.

Last May, when I was a month away from graduation, I narrowed my choices down to three companies. I knew exactly what I was looking for. The ideal company had to be a small division of a national organization, had to provide good advancement opportunities, and had to offer a high salary. I even had the interviewing process down to a science. My philosophy was to have a good résumé and to tell the company what it wanted to hear. Salesmanship was my key to interviewing. After weeks of interviews and a second visit with Electronics, Inc., I knew

what job to take. I was wined and dined at the corporate headquarters in New York for three days, during which the company recruiters told me about the management training program and about the successful young managers. The company met all of my criteria, and the people were professional and friendly. I felt I would fit in.

I had no way of knowing at the time that the person who previously had my job resigned after three months and that the position had been left vacant for six months. Mary Alcott, one of the nonmanagerial workers, had been trying to handle the job in the interim. Another bit of information no one gave me at headquarters was that my future boss, Sam Durbin, was not meeting his profit plan and would be fired one month after I started

the job. It wasn't until I had moved from the West to the Midwest and had settled into the regional office that I got my first insight into a job that wasn't even close to what had been described in New York. My job was to manage inventory, which required more paperwork and knowledge of rules and procedures than it did intelligence. I was to supervise a staff of twelve clerical employees, all of whom had college degrees. My scheduled training was canceled because the company needed a manager in my position immediately.

During the short time I spent with Mr. Durbin I was given a project that was not related to my job responsibilities. On the arrival of Cheryl Kent, my new boss, I had yet to be exposed to the functions of my job.

Source: Prepared by Cathy Enz; adapted from Randall S. Schuler, *Personnel and Human Resource Management* (St. Paul, Minn.: West Publishing, 1980), pp. 374–75. Used with permission.

plishing this goal. A planning system that asks managers to suddenly become long-range thinkers without participation and without training is not likely to succeed.

SUMMARY

This chapter examined the nature of planning in general. In the simplest sense, a plan is anything that involves selecting a course of action for the future. Planning extends

throughout the organization in the form of a hierarchy. Strategic planning determines the major objectives of the organization and the ways of achieving them. Tactical planning is

My relationship with Ms. Kent has probably been the single most frustrating aspect of this job. She expected me to know my job when she arrived, and my explanation of the situation didn't matter. She recommended that I have Mary train me, a suggestion I found uncomfortable to implement since I was her boss and in theory supposed to evaluate her on her performance. How could I manage her and still rely heavily on her advice and instruction? Furthermore, Mary is reluctant to train me for a position she thinks she should occupy. Because Ms. Kent tends to go directly to Mary for information, Mary has become a key informal leader of the office staff. The other workers won't cooperate with me unless Mary gives them the go-ahead. So here I am,

watching my boss bypass me to conduct business with one of my subordinates. The other workers don't follow me, and Ms. Kent yells at me for lacking leadership ability. Mary really should have been given this job, but I can't help that.

Last week I got so fed up I marched into Ms. Kent's office and explained my frustration with the situation. She agreed that the lack of training was unfortunate and that she had frequently violated the line of authority, but she said that she was under constraints to make the regional office profitable. She went on to say that she had had to work her way up the ladder from a clerical position with little guidance and that I shouldn't need handholding. I told her I was working from 7:30 A.M. to 9:00 P.M. and

was trying hard to learn on my own. She just smiled and shrugged her shoulders.

At this point I see few alternatives to the existing situation. Mary is still reluctant to provide me with information. Ms. Kent doesn't have time to help me. There isn't another person in the region with a job similar to mine. I'm losing my self-confidence, my subordinates have little respect for me, and I don't even like the kind of work I'm doing.

My problem is that I can't quit. I'm two thousand miles from my family and friends, I just bought a car, and I really need the money. Besides, Ms. Kent probably wouldn't give me a good reference anyway. I thought I knew what I was doing when I took this job; all I know now is that I want out.

---

directed toward implementing strategic plans by coordinating the different functions of the organization to that end. Operational planning focuses on the production of goods and services.

Studies show conclusively that organizations that engage in formal planning are more successful than those that plan informally or not at all. Although planning should be tailored to the particular organization, major dimensions of it apply to all organizations.

They are the type of organization, the different elements of plans, the subject of planning, the time span of planning, and the characteristics of different plans.

The basic stages in an effective planning system include careful analysis of the organization and its environment, development of alternatives, evaluation of the alternatives and choice of a tentative plan, and development of a written plan.

Many roadblocks to planning exist. Some

of them stem from the attitudes and values of management. Planning may be seen as unimportant, may not be rewarded, and may fail to involve the participation of managers. The design of planning systems may lack focus, confuse forecasting with planning, overemphasize numbers and planning models, incorporate conflicting objectives, and be either too formal or too informal. The plan itself may confuse planning and reality, may fail to pro-vide motivation for implementing plans, may not allow for the impact of managerial action, and may overlook a need to train managers in various aspects of the plan.

Planning is one of the most important managerial functions. Managers at every level of the organization must plan. The better the planning, the more successful the organization.

STUDY QUESTIONS

1. Do you think the planning done by Sears was realistic? From a systems point of view, would you have done anything differently?
2. Are plans that are best for one unit or department always best for the entire organization? Explain.
3. What are the four basic questions that planning answers?
4. At what levels of the organization should planning take place? Explain.
5. List some ideal time allocations for plans.
6. Present evidence from this chapter and elsewhere that planning pays.
7. What are the five key dimensions of planning?
8. What are the major roadblocks to planning? From your learning to date, how would you anticipate and reduce them?
9. Interview members of large and small organizations. Do the people you have talked to know or agree on the objectives of their organizations? How much planning is done in each organization? Are the people you talked to involved in the planning process? Describe their involvement.

Case for Discussion

RADIO SHACK INTERNATIONAL

In 1973 Radio Shack opened its first European store, in Belgium. In 1977 the organization had 459 overseas outlets but had not added a new store in eighteen months. In addition, it had lost $21 million from its European operations in the previous three years.

Charles D. Tandy had spent thirteen years building Radio Shack into the leading merchandiser of amateur electronic gear in the United States. He bought Radio Shack Corporation in 1963, when it was in trouble. In the first nine months of fiscal 1977, the six-thousand-store chain had earnings of $56.2 million on revenues of $732.6 million—respective increases of 14 percent and 32 percent. Retail stores accounted for 95 percent of the company's earnings and revenues.

Radio Shack's success in the United States appears to be a combination of well located stores, discount prices, a wide product mix, and heavy advertising. Tandy believes that this approach will work in Europe and that the four years of heavy losses are only temporary. He says, "I see nothing different about the people in Europe from the people in the U.S." As a result, he plans to continue with the same strategies. Others suggest that the problem is more fundamental—that discounting methods that work in the United States will not attract Europeans, who are highly brand- and quality-conscious.

In a blitz operation the European market was blanketed with hundreds of stores, many in poor locations. In many cases local laws and customs were overlooked or disregarded. When the first store was opened in Belgium, for example, Tandy overlooked a law that requires a government tax stamp on window signs. In Holland the first Christmas promotion was geared to December 25, since the company was unaware that the Dutch exchange holiday gifts on St. Nicholas Day, celebrated on December 6. In Germany one of the biggest losses occurred when Radio Shack gave away flashlights to promote its stores and was served with an injunction for violating German sales laws.

In the United States, citizens band radios are Radio Shack's best-selling item, accounting for 22 percent of sales. Belgium, Britain, and Holland bar citizens band radios. Various laws have curbed the sale of other items as well.

European competitors suggest that Europeans are willing to pay premium prices for top quality items and that Radio Shack's image as a discount house keeps customers away. The quality image is especially strong in France, where Radio Shack has only eight stores, none of which is in Paris.

Despite the losses, sales are slowly increasing, and Tandy is optimistic that his basic strategy will work. In fact, he predicts that the foreign operation will be profitable in two years.

Source: Information from "Radio Shack's Rough Trip," *Business Week,* May 30, 1977, p. 56.

1. How might planning be different in Europe than in the United States?
2. What recommendations would you have for Tandy after reading this chapter? Is he being optimistic or realistic in his planning?
3. What steps would you take to increase sales and profits? What would you want to know about the different European countries?
4. What implications does this case have for other international operations?

FOR YOUR CAREER

1. Trying to predict the future is difficult. Make certain you have contingency plans.
2. Believing in the accuracy of forecasting is like driving from Miami to Montreal and predicting on that basis how easy it would be to continue driving to the North Pole.
3. Planning is dynamic rather than static. One should not assume that a task is taken care of as soon as a plan is implemented. A plan should be used as a guide rather than viewed as an absolute.
4. The person who continued to make 1980 Summer Olympics souvenirs after President Carter declared a boycott of the games may have had a plan, but he also had his head in the sand.
5. A plan formulated without input from those who must implement it may be an exercise in futility.
6. Remember Murphy's basic law: Whatever can go wrong, will.

FOOTNOTES

1. "Sears, Roebuck & Co.," *Advertising Age,* September 6, 1979, p. 149; P. Drucker, *The Practice of Management* (New York: Harper & Bros., 1954); C. Looms, "The Leaning Tower of Sears," *Fortune* July 2, 1979, pp. 78–86; *Moody's Industrial Manual* (New York: Moody's Investor Service, 1979), p. 2974; and W. Christensen, "Long-Range Planning as Applied to the Allstate Group," in *Managerial Long-Range Planning,* ed. G. Steiner (New York: McGraw-Hill, 1963), pp. 98–114.

2. G. Steiner, *Top Management Planning* (New York: Macmillan, 1969), p. 7.

3. Ibid., p. 34.

4. Ibid.

5. Ibid., p. 35.

6. H. Ansoff, J. Avner, R. Brandenburg, F. Portner, and R. Radosevich, *Acquisition Behavior of U.S. Manufacturing Firms* (Nashville, Tenn.: Vanderbilt University Press, 1971); J. Eastlack, Jr., and P. McDonald, "CEO's Role in Corporate Growth," *Harvard Business Review* 48 (May–June 1970): 150–163; C. Reimnitz, "Testing a Planning and Control Model in Non-Profit Organizations," *Academy of Management Journal* 17 (March 1972): 77–87; S. Schoeffler, "Impact of Strategic Planning on Profit Performance," *Harvard Business Review* 52 (March–April 1974): 137–145; R. Stagner, "Corporate Decision Making," *Journal of Applied Psychology* 53 (February 1969): 1–13; and G. French, "The Payoff from Planning," *Managerial Planning* 27 (September–October, 1979): 6–12.

7. S. Thune and R. House, "Where Long-Range Planning Pays Off," *Business Horizons* 13 (August 1970): 81–87.

8. D. Herold, "Long-Range Planning and Organizational Performance: A Cross-Validation Study," *Academy of Management Journal* 15 (March 1972): 91–105.

9. Steiner, *Top Management Planning,* pp. 6–21.

10. J. Martin, "Business Planning: The Gap between Theory and Practice," *Long Range Planning* 16 (December 1979): 2–10.

11. B. Nanus, "The Future-Oriented Corporation," *Business Horizons* 18 (February 1975): 5–12;

F. Foreland, "Dialectic Methods of Forecasting," *Futurist* 5 (August 1971): 169–170; B. Cazes, "The Future of Work: An Outline of a Method for Scenario Construction," *Futures* 8 (October 1976): 405–410; and R. Linneman and H. Klein, "The Use of Multiple Scenarios by U.S. Industrial Companies," *Long Range Planning* 12 (February 1979): 83–90.

12. J. Balogna, "Why Managers Resist Planning," *Managerial Planning* 28 (January–February 1980): 23–25; H. Henry, "Formal Planning in Major U.S. Corporations," *Long Range Planning* 10 (October 1977): 40–45; R. Knoepfel, "The Politics of Planning: Man in the Decision Process," *Long Range Planning* 6 (March 1973): 17–21; P. Lorange, "The Planner's Dual Role—A Survey of U.S. Companies," *Long Range Planning* 6 (March 1973): 13–17; C. Saunders and F. Tuggle, *Long Range Planning* 10 (June 1977): 19–24; R. Taylor, "Psychological Aspects of Planning," *Long Range Planning* 9 (April 1976): 68–74; and P. Stonich, "Formal Planning Pitfalls and How to Avoid Them—Part 2," *Management Review* 64 (July 1975): 29–45.

13. J. Martin, "Business Planning: The Gap between Theory and Practice," *Long Range Planning* 12 (December 1979): 3.

14. J. Naor, "The Underlying Factor Approach—Some Long-Standing Ills of Long-Range Corporate Planning Revisited," *Managerial Planning* 27 (March–April 1979): 15–18.

15. P. Stonich, "Formal Planning Pitfalls and How to Avoid Them, Part 1," *Management Review* 64 (June 1975): 5.

Strategic Planning   CHAPTER 7

CONTENTS

The original draft of this chapter was written by Professor Sexton Adams of North Texas
State University.

Incorporated in 1900, the American Machinery and Foundry Company changed its name to AMF in 1970. In 1978 it had sales of $1.3 billion, for a net income of approximately $45 million. As a multinational company, it derived about 20 percent of its income from its overseas operations. About two-thirds of its total income came from consumer businesses, including these wholly owned subsidiaries: the Ben Hogan Company, maker of golf equipment; Head Sportswear, Inc., maker of skis, rackets, and sportswear; Voit, Inc., maker of a variety of balls, including basketballs and footballs; and Harley-Davidson, the only motorcycle manufacturer in the United States. The other third of AMF's income came from manufacturing electrical components, timers, filters, and automated machinery for the apparel, tire, baking, and tobacco businesses.

To make managing such a diversified organization easier, in 1978 AMF was divided into seven basic groups—five for the consumer business and two for the industrial. Within these seven groups there were either forty-one or fifty-four divisions, depending on how *division* is defined, and seventy-four manufacturing plants. Each month about 1,5000 financial statements and about 400 profit-and-loss statements were generated.

In the 1960s, in particular, the pressure was on for increasing sales and growth. Acquisitions and mergers with other companies brought growth, but income and profits suffered in the process, especially when sales reached the $1 billion mark in the early 1970s. Under a new chairman of the board and chief executive officer, AMF began to give attention to strategic planning for improving income and profits.

Among the strategic objectives AMF developed were: to grow at an annual earnings increase of at least 10 percent, to obtain an "A" rating on its debit securities (then rated "Baa"), and to balance the company about equally between leisure and industrial sales. Continuing with its two-thirds lei-

sure/one-third industrial split in sales was proclaimed unwise, since industrial sales were more profitable and less volatile than leisure sales. For example, AMF began to make mopeds, a recreational, or leisure product, in 1978, having forecasted sales of about 67,000 units. An unexpected flood of imports hit the market, however, and AMF sold only 52,000 units, which resulted in a shutdown of the production line. Industrial products rarely encountered such major, unforeseen changes in the marketplace.

To reach its new objectives, AMF needed detailed strategic plans for each business unit. Time horizons differed for each unit; they ranged from three years for a unit like Head sportswear to ten years for the unit making Harley-Davidson motorcycles, which require long, development lead times. Moreover, planning for each unit required a continuing dialogue between that unit's manager and top management. This was provided by management identifying key issues for each unit early in the year. The identification included potential opportunities and problem areas; each unit was to create a plan that addressed those key issues. Unit managers and top management then engaged in a number of discussions to modify the plans until they gained everyone's approval. The final step, near the end of the year, was to develop a budget for the next year. This budget translated the plan into specifics—the details of sales, revenues, and profits and the number of employees, and amount of capital and other expenditures required.

In 1978 the units of AMF were asked to submit contingency plans, or scenarios, instead of just one plan. Each year these scenarios have been refined and improved, and new ideas have emerged. Among them is the system created by one unit to activate certain trigger points when specific defensive steps need to be taken against a problem.[1]

This opening case raises several key questions which you should be able to answer after reading this chapter. The questions include:

1. What were the specific organizational strategies of AMF? How did the strategies influence what AMF actually did?
2. What is the relationship between organizational strategy, planning, and decision making?
3. How do contingency plans aid an organization? Explain.
4. What are your personal career strategies?

7

Chapter 6 examined planning in general. This chapter will explore in detail the way strategic planning is used to accomplish organizational objectives. It will look first at the concept of *strategy*, then at the process of strategic planning and the various forms it takes. After reviewing the strengths and weaknesses of strategic planning, the chapter will present some approaches to measuring the effectiveness of such planning.

THE NATURE OF CORPORATE STRATEGY

Strategy determines:

- Services or products
- Methods of production
- Sequence of major steps
- Targets to be achieved

Traditionally, the word **strategy** referred to management's actions in counteracting a competitor's success. Today's meaning is much broader: "Strategy refers to the formulation of basic organizational missions, purposes and objectives; policies and program strategies to achieve them; and the methods needed to assure that strategies are implemented to achieve organizational ends."[2] Essentially, two issues are involved: what the organization is to be and how it is to become what it is to be. In effect, strategy encompasses all the goals and major policies of the organization.[3] It covers the following four areas:

1. Services to be provided: What products or services will the organization sell or provide, and to which customers or clients?
2. Basic ways the services will be produced: What will the organization make, and by what processes will it make them? What will it buy? From which sources?
3. Sequencing and timing of major steps: Which actions should be taken early? Which should be deferred?
4. Targets to be met: What are the criteria for success? What levels of achievement are desired?[4]

Management's responses to these questions determine company strategy. Although there are a number of ways of formulating strategy, the chapter will concentrate on two: the outside-inside and the inside-outside approaches.

Strategy can be shaped by:

- Outside forces
- Inside forces

Outside-Inside Approach to Strategy In the **outside-inside approach** to strategic planning managers look first at the environment and then at the organization. They note shifting demands and trends relevant to the organization and plan internal changes to meet anticipated opportunities and problems. General Electric has been a pioneer in this approach.[5] Since 1970 the starting point for any planning cycle at GE has been long-term environmental forecasts that examine the entire economic-technological-social-political environment for a period of at least ten years. This four-sided framework is shown in Figure 7.1. In the social and political parts of the forecast, changing values and life-styles and possible new legislation are analyzed in terms of their relevance to the organization. This information is integrated with that obtained from the more traditional economic and technological forecasts to form the overall environmental forecasts.

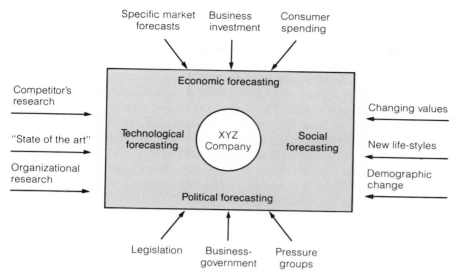

FIGURE 7.1 Four-sided framework for planning

Source: Adapted from Ian H. Wilson, "Socio-Political Forecasting: A New Dimension to Strategic Planning," *Michigan Business Review,* July 1974, pp. 19–20. Reprinted by permission from the July 1974 issue of the *University of Michigan Business Review,* published by the Graduate School of Business Administration, The University of Michigan.

The outside-inside approach was also used with success by a few sporting goods manufacturers in the early 1950s, when they predicted increased leisure time for consumers and began to establish their public image and product lines accordingly. When the demand for leisure-time products and services increased dramatically a few years later, these manufacturers were prepared to take advantage of it, while competitors faltered. This approach to strategic planning calls for insight on the part of corporate management and courage to act on that insight.

Inside-Outside Approach to Strategy In the **inside-outside approach,** managers look first at the organization, noting the particular skills that give it advantages over its competitors, and then at the external environment to determine how these skills can best be put to use. What does the organization have to offer that is unique? The answer to this question is the key to the direction all organizational planning should take. For instance, General Dynamics identifies its particular strength as aerospace engineering and manufacturing. Consequently, its planning is directed to fulfill the air defense needs of the United States and its allies, a purpose for which it is well equipped by its special technological skills. Often a combination of the outside-inside and inside-outside approaches is most successsful for strategic planning.

Developing Feasible Strategies Both the outside-inside and inside-outside approaches to strategic planning require a fit among a number of different factors, including: (1) potential needs or wants of the market, (2) environmental opportunities and constraints, and (3) organizational skills and resources. For feasible strategies, these and other factors must be analyzed.

Sometimes a strategy develops gradually over a period of time as a

Feasible strategies require a fit of different factors.

result of decisions made by management. This form of strategy emerges almost automatically as management meets the day-to-day requirements of doing business. Only when operations are viewed over a period of time can the formation of such a strategy be detected. Although this is the way many organizations have formed their strategy, today's managers feel that it is a poor approach in view of environmental and other complexities in the world. They prefer planned strategy.

Over a period of time an organization can slowly drift from its basic purpose and then suddenly realize that its organizational strategy is no longer working. Unless management periodically reexamines its relationships to the environment, its strategy may become obsolete and inapproproate. When this happens, the organization will decline.

Contingent Strategic Planning: Developing Scenarios In the past, strategic planning was usually based on one hypothetical, most probable, future environment. Now, because of a growing awareness that organizational planning should allow for unforeseen events of various kinds, many organizations develop contingency plans for a number of different future environments or alternative futures, called **scenarios.**[6] A plan is formulated for each scenario, as shown in Figure 7.2. Thus the organization is prepared to act as follows:

1. If the actual future environment is like Scenario A, follow Plan 1.
2. If the actual future environment is like Scenario B, follow Plan 2.
3. If the actual future environment is like Scenario C, follow Plan 3.

A recent survey showed that approximately 150 of the *Fortune* "1000" industrials are now using multiple scenario analysis (MSA) in their formal planning processes.[7] The survey also showed that many other organizations were seriously considering MSA and that the major reason more did not use it was that they did not know enough about it.

The organizations that used MSA usually included economic, technological, political, demographic, and ecological factors in their scenarios. The scenarios themselves were expressed mostly in qualitative and verbal terms rather than numerical ones, perhaps to prevent the blind spots that often occur when only numerical information is used.

Building a scenario entails: (1) identifying key variables that affect the organization, (2) developing different sets of assumptions about the future, (3) estimating how the key variables will change in the future, and (4) developing written descriptions of each of the predicted future environments. Although a large number of scenarios can be constructed, probably no more than three or four are useful. More than four will probably not be different enough from each other to be meaningful. Fewer than three, however, will probably fail to cover many future possibilities.

Each scenario should be plausible, neutral in tone, and written from the viewpoint of someone living in its environment. A scenario for a small, independent oil company might tell of better fuel consumption, resulting in slower company growth and lessened market demand and

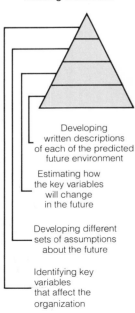

Building a scenario

Developing written descriptions of each of the predicted future environment

Estimating how the key variables will change in the future

Developing different sets of assumptions about the future

Identifying key variables that affect the organization

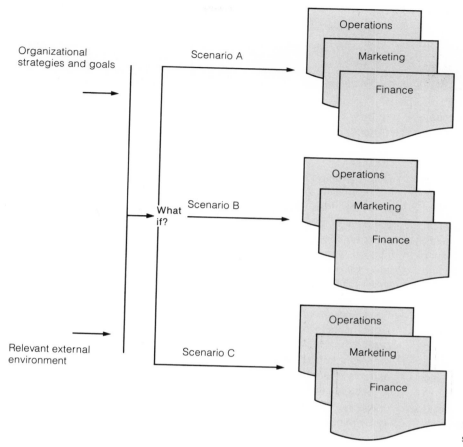

FIGURE 7.2 Alternative scenarios

indicating a need for fewer outlets and for lower prices through the use of self-service pumps. Another might describe the impact of electrically powered automobiles. Yet another might postulate the elimination of private automobiles from major cities because of an energy shortage.

THE STRATEGIC PLANNING PROCESS

As Chapter 6 stressed, there is no single formula for comparing formal, corporate planning systems. Many factors influence the development and implementation of a planning system. They include the values of the dominant coalition, the type of organization, whether the organization is centralized or decentralized, the types and variety of products and services, and past history and practice. Therefore, the planning system is tailored to the organization. Seldom are two systems exactly alike.[8]

On the Job

STRATEGIC PLANNING

Strategic planning means reconciling an organization's resources (capital and personnel, for example) with the threats and opportunities that exist in the organization's environment. Most organizations face similar challenges from their environments. These challenges can be classified into four categories: technological, economic, societal, and political.

Technology is critical for a variety of reasons. For the corporate strategist it is probably the fastest developing and most far-reaching challenge. In technology a threat to one organization is an opportunity for another. Someone will inevitably introduce a monumental improvement in some process or product. Breakthroughs in data and information processing, machine obsolescence, efficient uses of energy, and improvements in logistics

are only a few of a myriad of environmental threats and opportunities that confront corporate strategists.

Economics is another forum for the making or losing of corporate fortunes. Internalization of competition, unemployment, changes in discretionary income, inflation, and availability of capital funding are examples of areas critical to commercial operations. The development of Third World countries and trade agreements with new markets, such as mainland China, also represent important economic aspects of strategic planning.

Society itself is another major challenge. The quests for equality by minority groups and women, changing work and leisure patterns, and changes in the composition of consumers (male versus female, young ver-

sus old, married versus single) are a few examples. Accelerating crime rates and changing moral attitudes are other areas of concern to corporate strategists. The existence of X-rated films, massage parlors, casino gambling, narcotics, and sexually explicit magazines is evidence that changes in the public's attitudes are an opportunity for someone, somewhere.

The political climate includes import duties and quotas and tax legislation, safety legislation, and equal rights legislation. All these areas have had enormous impact on the operations of organizations in recent years.

The threats and opportunities mentioned here apply to all organizations. How the organizations meet them determine to a large degree the success or failure of individual organizations.

Organizing and implementing a formal strategic planning system is vital, but it is also one of the most difficult endeavors facing top management, particularly if the organization is large and diversified.

A starting point for understanding the elements of strategic, long-range planning is provided in the model of a company-wide planning process shown in Figure 7.3. This model demonstrates the relationships between the changing environments of the organization, its central purpose and objectives, the design and implementation of plans, and how coordination and control of the planning process are achieved. With Figure 7.3 as a base, the major elements of the strategic planning process will now be discussed.[9]

The plan
The plan for the plan
What will it achieve?
How will it be implemented?
How will it be organized?
Who will guide it?
What is the timetable?

The Plan for the Plan   One of the more difficult steps in developing a planning system is the first step—getting started. In essence, a plan for

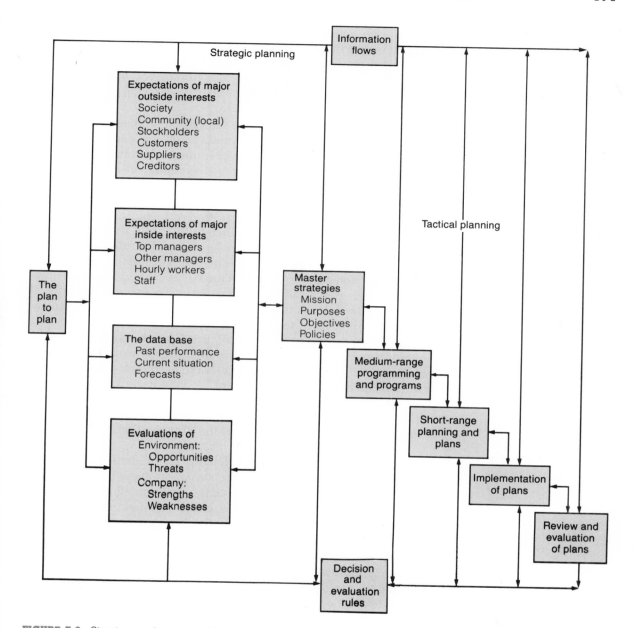

FIGURE 7.3 Structure and process of business company-wide planning
Source: Reprinted with permission of Macmillan Publishing Co., Inc. from *Strategic Planning: What Every Manager Must Know* by George A. Steiner. Copyright © 1979, The Free Press, a Division of Macmillan Publishing Co., Inc.

the plan is required. Management must define specifically what the plan is expected to achieve and how it will be put to use. A planning approach must be selected. The approach should include the method of organization and the person or persons who will guide the planning effort, along with a timetable for developing the plans. Decisions are required on whether there will be a planning staff or a separate planning department. If there is a corporate planner, what will be that person's responsibilities?[10] Or will the planning function be organized within an existing function, such as control, finance, or marketing?[11]

Corporate planning:

- Premises
- Master strategy
- Medium- and short-range plans
- Coordination
- Control
- Review

Developing Planning Premises   The four stacked boxes of Figure 7.3 illustrate some areas where premises, or assumptions, should be developed. These premises are basic to the planning effort and should embrace the economic, social, political, and technological considerations as well as assessments of the industry, the market, and competitors.

Specific plans ensue from these premises. Consequently, formal written statements presenting three or four different scenarios based on the premises about the future are useful, since in this form they are open to scrutiny by management and will likely be changed if relevant environmental factors change. Otherwise plans may be formulated on the basis of faulty or outmoded assumptions that are never examined. Many organizations find their plans failing without knowing specifically why. If the assumptions underlying the plans are formally written, the organization can detect the roots of the failure.

A significant aspect of the model in Figure 7.3 is the emphasis on the outside environment: "The strategic planning process would be invaluable to an organization if it did nothing more than force top management to be aware of its changing environment."[12] This part of the process is designed not only to help management anticipate both threats and opportunities facing the organization but also to allow management to examine the strengths and weaknesses of the organization.

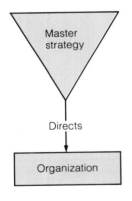

Determining the Master Strategy   The next major element of the strategic planning process can be called the master strategy. It concerns the basic mission or purpose of the organization and related specific objectives. An understanding of the basic mission enables management to deal with such questions as "What are the key success factors in our industry?" "What is the nature of the competitive environment?" "Are we capable of meeting our basic mission, given our objectives, capabilities, and opportunities?"

Identifying the major purpose of the organization causes top management to consider how the organization should carry out its activities in regard to customers, employees, suppliers, product quality, and pricing to best fulfill that purpose. Normally, that purpose is stated in such a way as to give broad general direction to the organization. For example, "We intend to be the recognized industry leader in new product development."

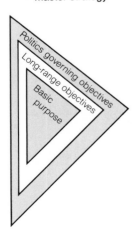

Specific, long-range objectives are established to harmonize with the basic purpose. They should, if possible, be stated in measurable terms so that management and employees know exactly what is expected of them. They usually are set in key areas such as return on investment (ROI), sales, and profits. (Objectives were discussed in Chapter 5.)

Overall policies are another component of the master strategy. They determine what resources will be deployed to achieve the long-range objectives.

Medium- and Short-range Plans After the master strategy has been developed, the logical next step is to develop and implement medium- and short-range plans. Tactical, or operational, planning is usually done at lower levels in the organization. Implementation planning is an integral part of comprehensive corporate planning and provides infomation for refining overall strategic plans and for developing overall operating plans and budgets for the company.

Coordinating and Controlling Planning After implementation plans are completed, they should be reviewed and coordinated along the various levels of management. Controls for measuring performance before and after implementation of plans must also be developed. (Controls will be discussed in more detail in Part IV of this book.)

In this stage, methods are developed by which the individual plans of each level of management in an organization are reviewed by the next higher level until all individual plans are ultimately coordinated and integrated within the overall comprehensive organizational plan. Effective function depends on this process of integrating individual operating and staff plans, reviewing and revising them in light of their effect on other plans and on company profits, and summarizing highlights of these plans and their budgets in a single overall organizational plan.

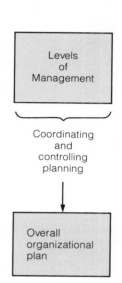

Review of Plans When formal planning as we know it was first introduced to organizations, the organizations tended to develop such plans and keep them intact for years. Today, most organizations review and revise their plans at least annually. This reviewing process gives an organization the flexibility to adjust to changing conditions, particularly if alternative scenarios are used in revising plans and creating new ones for the next year. Moreover, each reviewing process should lead to improved planning.

Significance of the Model The major significance of the strategic planning model is that it clarifies top management's responsibility for developing organizational strategy. It shows that a part of management's primary job is to continuously monitor the outside environment and evaluate how well the organization is meeting its core responsibilities. The strategic planning process provides a unified framework that allows managers to deal with major issues. It helps them recognize threats and opportunities from the external environment while it keeps their attention focused on the basic purpose of the organization. Strategic planning is an essential part of everything the manager does.

Approaches to planning:

- Top-down
- Bottom-up
- Team

FUNDAMENTAL APPROACHES TO FORMAL STRATEGIC PLANNING

There are several approaches to conducting formal planning. Four of them will be discussed here: the top-down approach, the bottom-up approach, the combination of top-down and bottom-up, and team planning.

Top-down approach

Top management
Lower-level managers develop plans within constraints of objectives set by top management.

The Top-Down Approach   In the **top-down approach,** top management gives specific guidance to lower-level managers regarding lower-level planning. A centralized organization using this approach would have top management developing the strategic objectives of the organization and the departments or divisions then developing their plans within these specific constraints.

An advantage of this approach is that in order to provide direction and control for departments and divisions to do their own specific planning, top management is forced to develop strategy for the way it will implement those plans to achieve its objectives. A major disadvantage is that lower-level managers sometimes feel constrained because of top-down direction. Flexibility can be lost for the sake of consistency.

Bottom-up approach

Top management
Lower-level managers develop plans without constraints or guidance and submit them to top management for approval.

The Bottom-Up Approach   The **bottom-up approach** to planning takes an entirely different tack—it is a form of decentralized planning. Lower-level managers develop their own objectives and plans, which are reviewed by top management and are either accepted or sent back to the division for modifications. (Top management, however, may reserve the responsibility of developing plans for acquisitions, investment, or refinancing.) In the extreme form of the bottom-up approach, top management provides no guidelines to the lower divisions for formulating their plans. In a modified version, which is more common, top management provides broad guidelines but asks the various divisions to develop their own specific plans.

Usually, certain information is requested from the divisions in the bottom-up approach, such as: major opportunities and threats, major objectives and strategies, sales profit, market share data, and capital requirements. This material is reviewed, perhaps modified, and developed into an overall corporate plan.

This approach is particularly helpful to an organization just getting started in planning, where top management may not be ready to give specific directions to the organization concerning objectives and strategies. They can rely on the divisions to develop tentative objectives and directions, which top management can then develop more fully as the planning system matures. This approach is also useful in that it provides a learning experience for division managers; and since they feel less constrained with less top-down direction, they may prepare better plans. A disadvantage is that the division managers may be uncomfortable without directions from top management. Another disadvantage is that without coordination at the top, the divisions may go in different, uncoordinated directions.

Combination of Top-Down and Bottom-Up Approaches A third approach to the development of a strategic planning system is the combination of the two approaches just described. This combination is used most often in large, decentralized organizations that have had experience in planning. The process can work in many ways, but generally top management will set objectives that allow the divisions considerable flexibility in developing plans, and then top management and division managers will work together to finalize these plans. This approach is appropriate for developing an objective such as return on investment when the performance of the division is measured by this standard. The advantage in using this approach is the improved coordination and increased participation that result from the intensive communication between top- and lower-level managers. Better, more creative plans usually occur in this atmosphere.

Team Planning Team planning, another approach to strategic planning, is particularly appropriate for relatively centralized organizations. In this approach the president meets regularly with a group of executives to discuss problems facing the organization and to devise strategic plans to deal with them. A formal planning committee chaired by the chief executive is sometimes used to develop the plans. The committee may set aside portions of meetings specifically for the planning or its members may periodically cloister themselves for a few days to plan. Another variation is for one executive to prepare a preliminary plan that is used by the other committee members as a basis for planning.

The team approach can be effective if there is a good relationship between the chief executive and the committee and among the committee members. On the other hand, an overbearing, authoritarian chief executive can spoil the effectiveness of this approach.

This section has described four basic approaches to strategic planning. Many modifications and variations of these approaches are possible, and there is no single method that is best for all organizations.

THE BASIC CYCLES OF CORPORATE STRATEGIC PLANNING

In most cases managers do not develop strategies and plans in isolation from each other. Rather, there is constant interaction among managers at all levels in the hierarchy, and a combination of top-down and bottom-up planning occurs. These interactions can be divided into three basic cycles, as shown in Figure 7.4.[13]

In the first cycle, top management and division managers meet together to set tentative agreements on overall strategies and objectives. Each division charter is defined broadly, and some general objectives and strategy are established. The functional managers at a lower level play a relatively minor part in this cycle. They may, however, be deeply

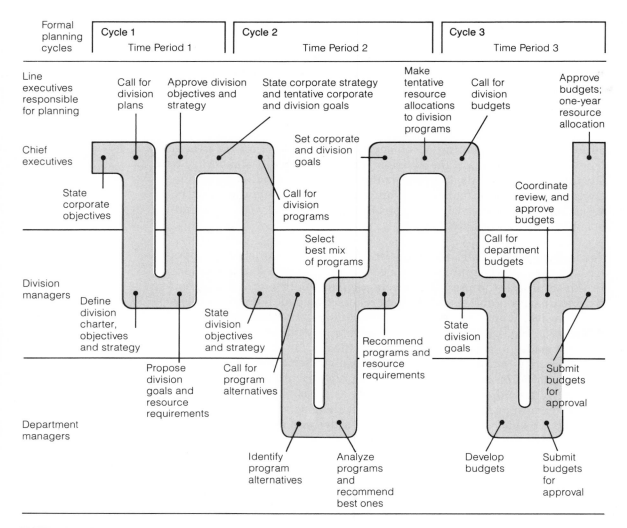

FIGURE 7.4 The cycles of planning

Reprinted by permission of the *Harvard Business Review*. Exhibit from "Strategic Planning in Diversified Companies" by Richard F. Vancil and Peter Lorange (January–February 1975). Copyright © 1975 by the President and Fellows of Harvard College; all rights reserved.

involved on an informal basis in that they may be expected to keep the division manager informed as to whether a certain objective is practical and attainable.

In the second cycle, functional department managers play a more important role than they do in the first cycle. Here each division manager sets tentative agreements with the department managers concerning each department's role in meeting divisional objectives. After this step, each department manager establishes tentative, alternative plans for carrying out that role. For example, the production manager might suggest that production can be increased by hiring more workers, providing additional training, increasing overtime, or purchasing additional equipment. The division manager would then choose the plan that would best contribute to divisional and top-level objectives and would submit a composite of the divisional and departmental plans to the top-level managers.

In the third cycle, the resources of the organization are tentatively allocated to division programs. Each division and functional department manager then develops specific budgets showing how the department or division intends to carry out its planned programs. After these budgets are discussed and the final budget is approved, funds are made available. The budget approval process and the amount of money actually received depend not only on the needs of the division or department but also on its manager's persuasiveness, political savvy, and influence within the organization.

Most budgets are for a one-year period. A shorter time span might cause erratic behavior, and a longer one might not allow for a timely review of progress. This chapter has discussed budgets as plans, but budgets also serve as a control process, as will be discussed in Part 4 of this book.

Source: © Rothco.

Strategic planning depends on the size of the organization.

STRATEGIC PLANNING IN DIFFERENT TYPES OF ORGANIZATIONS

There is no single planning system that suits every organization. The planning process always needs to be tailored to the particular organization. However, some features make certain systems more suitable for large, diversified organizations, medium-size organizations, or small organizations.

Strategic Planning in Large, Diversified Organizations Planning in large, diversified organizations tends to follow the cyclic model shown in Figure 7.4. Strategy in such an organization frequently evolves from interaction among the three levels: top-level managers and planning staff, division managers, and functional or department managers.

Top-level managers, together with the planning staff, decide on the organization's overall objectives, how resources will be acquired to attain these objectives, and how resources will be allocated among the various divisions. Middle-level managers formulate objectives and strategies within the framework of the overall strategic plans and determine the resource requirements needed to meet the objectives. Lower-level functional managers or department heads create the action programs by which their departments can contribute to the divisional objectives.

The planning process is competitive; in it plans and objectives are proposed, discussed, and approved. During each of the three planning cycles shown in Figure 7.4 the plans and objectives from the preceding cycle are discussed, modified, and elaborated on.

The process of strategic planning can offer many benefits to the organization beyond the plans it produces. Objectives developed at each level of the organization benefit the next higher level. The discussions among managers at different levels and the integration and coordination required for planning a budget tie the various levels of the organization into a unified whole. Thus the act of engaging in a planning process brings cohesiveness to a large organization.

Strategic Planning in Medium-Size Organizations For medium-size organizations, several different methods of formal planning may be suitable. These organizations may copy the more structured approach used by large, diversified firms, with some modifications, or they may use the approach designed for small organizations (which will be discussed later).

Many medium-size organizations use a variation of the bottom-up approach that can be called a middle-up approach, since the strength and expertise of the organization rest primarily in the functional areas of production, marketing, and finance. Top managment may call on the managers of these areas to develop objectives, assess environmental opportunitites and threats, and create budgets. The plans are then sent to top management to be consolidated into an overall company plan, sometimes with only minor modifications. With this approach, the knowledge of the middle manager is used extensively in developing the plan that will guide the medium-size organization on its future course.

Strategic Planning in Smaller Organizations For planning purposes, a small organization can be defined as one with fewer than five hundred employees or less than $500,000 in profits after taxes. A classic weakness in most small businesses is an almost total lack of long-range planning. The top executive in a small company may be aware that more time should be spent planning the future of the organization but under day-to-day pressure may let immediate problems push planning aside.

Although the general approach to planning is the same for organizations of all sizes, a small organization has some special problems such as:

1. Management resources that can be devoted to planning are limited.
2. Immediate survival is often the most pressing problem.
3. Capital is always limited.
4. Small businesses are most sensitive to minor changes in the market and they cannot sustain minor reverses.[14]

If planning is to be done at all, it must be scaled down to the limitations of time, energy, and data available, and it must be kept simple. Some basic questions should be asked by the small business planner at the start of the first major phase of the planning process—the development of overall planning premises, objectives, strategies, and policies. These questions are:

1. What business am I in now? What business should I be in five years from now? Who are my customers? Where is my market? What is my share of the market? What should it be?
2. What are my specific goals? What are my greatest strengths? Weaknesses? What action should be taken for product or service development now? In the future?
3. Are my personnel policies acceptable to employees?
4. How can growth or expansion be financed? What provisions have been made for setbacks? For taking advantage of opportunities?[15]

In order to answer these questions, the chief executive and others in a small organization are forced to think strategically. The next stage is to develop the detailed action plans needed to implement strategy.

STRATEGIC PLANNING—STRENGTHS AND WEAKNESSES

One way to understand strategic planning is to discover what managers and planners see as its strengths and weaknesses. A recent survey asked about three hundred managers and professional planners from a large number of manufacturing firms included in the *Fortune* "500" list to describe what they perceived as the strengths and weaknesses of long-range planning in their organizations.[16] As shown in Table 7.1 and 7.2,

TABLE 7.1   Areas of Long-Range Planning Strengths

	PERCENT OF INDIVIDUALS WHO MENTIONED THE PLANNING ASPECT	
	Planners	Managers
Planning prerequisites		
Strong top management support	21%	24%
High levels of participation by operating management	31	18
	52%	42%
Planning process		
Comprehensiveness and flexibility	15%	20%
Goal Identification	16	15
Regularity and formality	9	10
Consistency with company objectives	1	4
	41%	49%
Application of plans		
Integration with operating budgets	6%	2%
Utilization in performance evaluation	1	7
	7%	9%
Total	100%	100%

Source: Reprinted from K. Said and R. Seiler, "An Empirical Study of Long-range Planning Systems: Strengths—Weaknesses—Outlook," *Managerial Planning,* Vol. 28, No. 1 (July–August 1979): 24, by permission Planning Executives Institute.

the responses referred to either planning prerequisites, the planning process itself, or the application of plans.

Table 7.1 shows what were perceived as the major strengths of the long-range planning systems in the 68 organizations involved in this study. In terms of planning prerequisites, planners and managers agreed that top management support is a significant strength in their companies' planning efforts, although planners placed greater emphasis on this than did managers.

Both groups ranked the planning process as important, but more managers than planners believed that comprehensiveness and flexibility were important. Both groups rated the planning prerequisites and planning process as more important than the actual application of plans. Managers were more aware than planners that the application of plans— that is, how effectively plans are implemented—should be used to evaluate the performance of managers.

Table 7.2 shows the weaknesses in planning systems identified by both managers and professional planners. As can be seen by comparing the tables, the process of planning is viewed by a majority, especially

TABLE 7.2 Areas of Long-Range Planning Weaknesses

	PERCENT OF INDIVIDUALS WHO MENTIONED THE PLANNING ASPECT	
	Planners	**Managers**
Planning prerequisites		
Unreadiness for planning activities	16%	7%
Lack of top management support	11	4
Lack of operating managers' participation	4	3
	31%	14%
Planning process		
Unreliable data	8%	25%
Fragmented and inflexible	24	29
Noncreative, restraining growth	14	9
Incomplete and vague	4	6
Irregular and informal	2	5
	52%	74%
Application of plan		
Inapplicable for performance evaluation	10%	6%
Not integrated with the operating budgets	7	6
	17%	12%
Total	100%	100%

Source: Reprinted from K. Said and R. Seiler, "An Empirical Study of Long-range Planning Systems: Strengths—Weaknesses—Outlook," *Managerial Planning,* Vol. 28, No. 1 (July–August 1979): 25, by permission Planning Executives Institute.

managers, as the area of the greatest weaknesses, primarily because of the possibility of unreliable data and inflexible or fragmented plans. Managers appeared to be far more concerned about these problems than planners, probably because it is the managers who have to work with the plans.

Analysis of the questionnaires suggests that three unrelated factors are to blame for unreliable data and inflexible plans: (1) the lack of an overall corporate strategy, which makes the planning process more short-term than long-range; (2) a tendency to emphasize too much detailed data and analysis of numbers; and (3) the lack of thorough analysis and evaluation of alternatives (or different scenarios), causing a plan to rely too heavily on a single, detailed forecast.

In summary, the study indicated that a supportive managment attitude is the greatest strength a planning system can have. Weaknesses were seen as most likely to occur in the content of plans and in the process of planning. Both managers and planners, but especially manag-

Problems with long-range planning:

- Concentration on present
- Confusing planning studies with plans
- Lack of clear, attainable, and specific objectives
- Too heavy concentration on economic and technological factors
- Planning perceived as being concerned only with the future

ers, cited incompleteness, fragmentation, and inflexibility as the most common weaknesses of long-range plans.

MEASURING PLANNING EFFECTIVENESS

Chapter 6 showed the effectiveness of planning by comparing organizations on such gross measures as sales, earnings per share, and earnings on total capital employed. Nevertheless, ways to measure the effectiveness of a given strategic planning system are limited. Here are some guidelines to aid such evaluation.

1. Does the plan help the manager manage more effectively?
2. Does the plan elicit commitment from both the supervisor and the subordinates? Without this commitment, planning will not be effective.
3. Is the plan based on enough information to make it credible? Have planning premises been accurately developed? Were forecasting procedures appropriate? Have strategies been effectively developed, tested, and implemented?
4. Does the plan have a strategic focus? Are the organization's competitive advantages identified? Are potential opportunities and threats from the environment adequately documented?
5. Does the process of planning foster awareness of alternative possibilities for the future, and are the consequences of following various plans detailed for each scenario?
6. Does the plan focus the attention of management on critical issues, choices, and priorities?
7. Does the plan coordinate with the organization's system for allocating and committing capital funds? Is the paperwork manageable?
8. Can both the process of planning and the implementation of the plan accommodate a variety of managerial styles?
9. Does the planning process lend itself to becoming a natural part of both the formal and informal processes of the organization?[17]

Managers must constantly survey the planning process and evaluate, revise, and update it in order to maintain effectiveness.

SUMMARY

This chapter has expanded on the nature and process of strategic planning as described in the preceding chapter. The nature of corporate strategy involves decisions on what an organization is to be and how it will become what it is to be. One part of such strategy is to carefully examine the environment; another is to examine the organization itself in terms of strengths, weaknesses, and "fit" with the environment.[18]

As environmental conditions change, organizations are finding that they cannot depend on a single plan to serve satisfactorily over the years. Rather, contingency plans or scenarios are necessary to allow for different future conditions.

One model of strategic planning stresses the relationships between the changing environment of an organization, its basic purpose and objectives, the design and implementation of its plans, and the coordination and control of its planning process. Among the approaches to formal planning are the centralized top-down approach and the decentralized bottom-up approach. Many organizations use a combination of these or other approaches.

Strategic planning in large, diversified organizations is complex. The development of plans involves much interaction among top-, middle-, and lower-level managers before the

planning cycle is complete. Although the planning process is in many respects the same for large, medium, and small organizations, some planning problems are peculiar to the small organization.

Some major strengths and weaknesses of strategic planning have been seen by both managers and planners. In one study, both believed an appropriate planning process is highly important, perhaps more so than the actual application of the plans. Managers in particular saw the major weaknesses of strategic planning as being the possibility of unreliable data and inflexible, fragmented plans.

There are many ways to measure the effectiveness of plans within an organization.

STUDY QUESTIONS

1. Why has the emphasis on strategic planning increased over the last few years?
2. Describe the differences between the outside-inside and inside-outside strategies.
3. How might the passage of time affect plans?
4. In what way are the three planning cycles more applicable to a large rather than a small organization?
5. Explain why scenarios are being more widely used.
6. According to Chapters 6 and 7, how can planning be made more effective?
7. Evaluate this statement by the dean of a small college: "We are growing too fast to have the time to plan."
8. How might the strengths of long-range planning be preserved while the weaknesses are reduced?

Case for Discussion

$40 MILLION FOR A REAL SMOKE?

In 1977 R. J. Reynolds announced a $40 million promotion campaign to introduce a new cigarette, "Real."[19] In 1980 the *Wall Street Journal* ran an article titled "'Real' Cigarettes Prove True Disappointment Despite Their Merit." Reynolds had laid out millions of dollars to launch a label that smokers liked but would not buy. What happened?

For almost four years the project was a secret one, code-named RI. Fewer than fifty people within the company were aware of it. One of the

company's ceaseless consumer surveys had prompted the decision to bring out a "natural" cigarette. As the project continued, it was also decided to make Real into a low-tar cigarette. This was done because low-tar cigarettes had acquired an increased share of the market, from 5.7 percent in 1970 to 20 percent in 1977.

More than $1 million had been spent to develop the product before it was announced at a press conference in May 1977. Dozens of consumer polls were taken, and more than ten thousand smokers were asked to try different mixtures of tobacco. Based on the evidence, Reynolds had reason to hope that the cigarette would sell better than Merit, Winston, and Marlboro cigarettes.

A blitz advertising campaign for the second half of 1977 cost $40 million, the largest amount spent by any company for a single product for a period of only six months. In contrast, in 1975 the largest advertiser was Kellogg, which spent a total of $47.9 million for all its products. Kraft spent $46.7 million for all its products that year, and Wrigley spent $35.5 million.

The $40 million was used to buy 130 boxcars of display materials to be used by retailers; more than 25 million free sample packages; the biggest billboard overlooking Times Square; advertising in newspapers, radio, and television; and the summer-long services of more than 2,000 salespersons to call on the nation's more than 360,000 retail stores selling tobacco. As one executive said, "With 170 different brands out there, you have to shoot your way into the saloon."

The unprecedented barrage was calculated to help Reynolds, which already makes one out of every three cigarettes sold in the United States, gain an extra 1 to 2 percent of the highly profitable $18 billion cigarette market. Each percentage point is worth about $100 million a year in additional revenues, more than enough to justify the heavy front-end expenditures.

The initial advertising in June 1977 stressed that Real was a "natural" cigarette. A tobacco leaf rather than the customary picture of people appeared in the advertisements and on the package. In October, when sales were not up to expectations, the advertising approach was changed from stress on an all-natural composition to a focus on taste. In November a promotional campaign was established to give away 40 million coupons offering $1 off the carton price. In May 1978 yet another approach was tried. Still focusing on taste, the ads were headlined "Real's got strong taste. More like a high tar." A dune buggy soaring across the sand took the place of the tobacco leaf of the first advertisements.

A year after its introduction Real had about 0.5 percent of the market, and in 1980 it had about 0.4 percent of the market. Reynolds was ready to give up. One advertising executive suggested, "Real is to cigarettes what the Titanic was to sailing."

What had happened? The planning was based on four years of development work and a number of consumer polls, and it appeared solid. Marketers and securities analysts offer several explanations for the failure. One is that Real advertising failed to exploit the market in low-tar brands, although Real is low in tar content. Another is that Real entered the market toward the end of a flood of low-tar cigarettes (twenty-six low-tar brands in 1977) and may have gotten lost in the shuffle. Yet another is that Reynolds may have made a mistake by calling Real "all natural." One executive working for a competing firm suggested that "natural might appeal to health nuts and people who eat yogurt, but they aren't the kind of people who buy cigarettes." Whatever the reason, R. J. Reynolds was unable to buy its way into the market, and its planning was not successful despite the expenditure of many millions of dollars over three years.

Sources: A. Crittendenm, "$40 Million for a Real Smoke," *New York Times,* May 15, 1977, sec. 3, p. 1; P. Dougherty, "Real, a Low-Tar, High-Budget Smoke," *New York Times,* May 10, 1977, p. 10; "R. J. Reynolds Industries Inc.," *Advertising Age,* August 29, 1977, p. 170; J. Koten, "'Real' Cigarettes Prove True Disappointment Despite Their Merit," *Wall Street Journal,* February 26, 1980, p. 12; and "R. J. Reynolds Industries," *Advertising Age,* September 6, 1979, p. 144.

1. What does this case tell you about the planning process?

2. Cigarette packages in the United States carry the following:

> "Warning: The Surgeon General Has Determined That Cigarette Smoking Is Dangerous To Your Health."

Because of this warning, what social and environmental dilemmas might face cigarette companies?

3. What are the ethics of the advertising campaign Reynolds used for Real?

4. Based on what you now know about strategic and tactical planning, what would you have done in the situation, if you had been the president of R. J. Reynolds?

FOR YOUR CAREER

1. If you want to know more about planning, read such journals as *Business Horizons, Futures, Long Range Planning,* and *Managerial Planning.*

2. Planning is an expanding career area, particularly in large organizations. New products and the money to make them are an integral part of business planning. If you are interested in such a career, you may want to take additional courses in marketing, finance, and the behavioral sciences.

3. In your own strategic planning for your career, keep asking these questions: (a) Where am I now? (b) Where do I want to be? (c) What alternatives do I have? (d) How can I get to where I want to be?

4. When you are looking for a job, remember that starting salary is important. However, you should also evaluate the organization on how well it plans. Salary loses importance if one is laid off because the organization has not planned well.

5. Successful organizations often revise their long-range strategic plans because of environmental changes and changes in top management. To stay abreast of typical changes in strategic plans, see the corporate strategies section of each issue of *Business Week.*

FOOTNOTES

1. C. Loomis, "AMF Vrooms into Who Knows What," *Fortune,* April 9, 1979, pp. 76–88; and "AMF Incorporated," *Moody's Industrial Manual* (New York: Moody's Investors Service, 1979), p. 1401. In 1981 Harley-Davidson became independent of AMF.

2. G. A. Steiner and J. B. Miner, *Management Policy and Strategy* (New York: Macmillan, 1977), p. 7.

3. S. Tilles, "How to Evaluate Corporate Strategy," *Harvard Business Review* 41 (July–August 1963): 111–121.

4. W. H. Newman, "Selecting Company Strategy," *Journal of Business Policy* 2 (Summer 1972): 60–71.

5. "The Opposites: G. E. Grows while Westinghouse Shrinks," *Business Week,* January 31, 1977, p. 60.

6. B. Nanus, "The Future-Oriented Corporation," *Business Horizons* 18 (February 1975): 5–12; F. Foreland, "Dialectic Methods of Forecasting," *Futurist* 5 (August 1971): 169–170; and B. Cazes, "The Future of Work: An Outline of a Method for Scenario Construction," *Futures* 8 (October 1976): 405–410.

7. R. Linneman and H. Klein, "The Use of Multiple Scenarios by U.S. Industrial Companies," *Long Range Planning* 12 (February 1979): 83–90.

8. Steiner and Miner, *Management Policy and Strategy,* pp. 31–32.

9. G. A. Steiner, *Strategic Planning: What Every Manager Must Know* (New York: Free Press, 1979), p. 17.

10. R. W. Ackerman, "The Role of the Corporate Planning Executive," in *Strategic Planning Systems,* ed. P. Lorange and R. F. Vancil (Englewood Cliffs, N.J.: Prentice-Hall, 1977), pp. 157–158.

11. R. J. Mockler, *Business Planning and Policy Formulation* (New York: Appleton-Century-Crofts, 1972), pp. 18–19.

12. Ibid, pp. 6–7.

13. R. F. Vancil, and P. Lorange, "Strategic Planning in Diversified Companies," *Harvard Business Review* 53 (January–February 1975): 81–91.

14. Mockler, *Business Planning and Policy Formulation,* pp. 300–312.

15. G. A. Steiner, "Approaches to Long-Range Planning for Small Business," *California Management Review* 5 (Fall 1967): 3–16.

16. K. Said and R. Seiler, "An Empirical Study of Long-range Planning Systems: Strengths—Weaknesses—Outlook," *Managerial Planning* 28 (July–August 1979): 24–28.

17. W. A. Schassir, *Strategic Business Planning: Some Questions for the Chief Executive* (New York: President's Association, Chief Executive Officer's Division, American Management Association, 1976), as cited in Steiner, *Strategic Planning,* pp. 305–306.

18. A. H. Van de Ven, "Problem Solving, Planning and Innovation," *Human Relations* 33 (1980): 771–740; R. J. Kudla, "The Effects of Strategic Planning on Common Stock Returns," *Academy of Management Journal* 23 (1980): 5–20; F. H. Wu, "Incrementalism in Financial Strategic Planning," *Academy of Management Review* 6 (1981): 133–144; J. C. Camillus and J. H. Grant, "Operational Planning: The Integra-

tion of Programming and Budgeting," *Academy of Management Review* 5 (1980): 369–380; F. H. Mitchell and C. C. Mitchell, "Development, Application, and Evaluation of an Action-Reaction Planning Method," *Academy of Management Review* 5 (1980): 83–88; G. G. Alpander, "Human Resource Planning in U.S. Corporations," *California Management Review* 22 (1980): 24–32; and D. Horvath and C. McMillan, "Industrial Planning in Japan," *California Management Review* 13 (1980): 11–21.

Organizing

PART III

Staffing and Managing Human Resources

CHAPTER 8

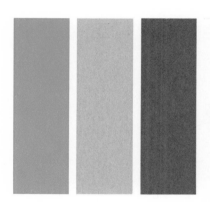

BUT WILL HE PUT IT IN WRITING?

Allan Jackson, chairman of the finance department for a large California university, received a telephone call from a professor at a moderate-sized university in the Midwest whom he knew slightly from meetings of professional associations. After the usual preliminaries, the caller said, "I'm calling because I'm a member of a search committee at our school. We are looking for a new dean for the school of management. As you may know, our ex-dean resigned to become president of XYZ University. James Jones is one of the applicants for the position. He gave your name as a reference, since he worked for you for about five years."

"I'll be happy to discuss him," said Jackson.

For the next fifteen minutes Jackson described his experiences with and impressions of Jones during the five years that Jones had been a member of the department. Jackson included his observations of Jones's classroom teaching, the results of student evaluations, Jones's behavior in and contributions to a number of committees to which Jackson and Jones had jointly belonged, and Jones's publication and research record.

At the end of conversation Jackson recommended that Jones not be hired as dean. The caller thanked him for his frankness and cooperation and asked if he would summarize their conversation in a letter. Jackson refused to do so, pointing out that under the Privacy Act of 1974 people have a legal right to examine letters of reference about themselves unless they have waived that right, which Jones had not. Jackson said that if the committee needed a formal letter, he would verify in writing the last salary, job title, and dates of employment for Jones, but no more.[1] He gave the caller the names of three other people to contact about Jones, since he was aware that he could possibly be biased.

This opening case raises several key questions which you should be able to answer after reading this chapter. The questions include:

1. What reasons might exist for an organization to provide only favorable references regarding previous employees?
2. What is the relationship between an employee's past performance and his/her future performance?
3. How can affirmative action programs affect an organization's staffing requirements?
4. What channels and methods do organizations use to recruit managers?

This chapter is about the process of getting the right people into the right jobs by means of proper selection, training, development, performance appraisal, and compensation. One approach to selection is, of course, reference checking. The preceding case illustrates the influence of recent laws and regulations on the process of checking references with employers. One might question whether Jackson was fair to Jones by refusing to put his comments in writing. Obviously Jackson was protecting himself from any unfavorable legal consequences of recommending that Jones not be employed as dean. One might also question whether it would be fair for the caller from the search committee to relate Jackson's orally expressed views to the rest of the committee. This chapter will briefly review some of the more important aspects of staffing, which can also be called the management of human resources.

THE IMPORTANCE OF STAFFING

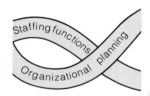

Staffing cannot be separated from *planning* for achieving organizational objectives.

Staffing: getting the right people at the right time for the right job legally.

Organizations cannot achieve their objectives without strategic planning and short-range planning, and staffing is an integral part of both types of planning (as shown in Figure 8.1).

In its broadest sense, **staffing** is "identifying, assessing, placing, evaluating and developing individuals at work" through such actions as "recruiting, selecting, appraising, and promoting individuals."[2] The basic purpose of staffing is to obtain the best available people for the organization and to foster development of their skills and abilities, which in turn helps the organization accomplish its objectives. Basically, good staffing puts the right people in the right jobs at the right time.

A Major Managerial Function Staffing is a major managerial function—one of the important things managers must do. Although they can get help from others, such as the personnel department, they retain the fundamental responsibility for staffing. Unfortunately, some managers neglect this responsibility or discharge it inadequately. Often they spend a great deal of time and effort deciding which machine to buy but relatively little time and effort selecting and training the person who will operate it.

Three Important Issues in Staffing The first issue in staffing is the very existence of the organization; without people, it does not exist. The second issue is that all the functions of staffing—selection, training, appraisal, promotion, and salary adjustment—must be performed properly for the organization to function effectively. Failure in any of these areas can result in many employees feeling trapped in jobs they do not like. They suffer, and so do those around them. The third issue is that the productivity of an organization depends on staffing decisions that place people in jobs they can competently handle.

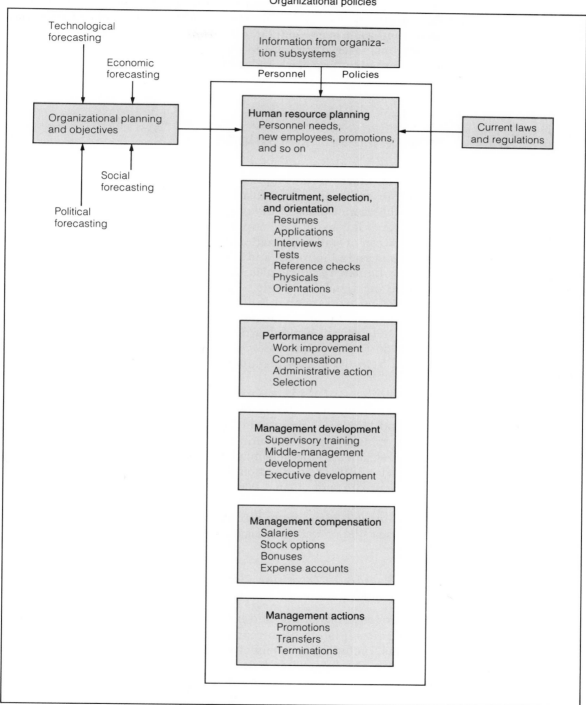

FIGURE 8.1 The staffing process

Steps in staffing

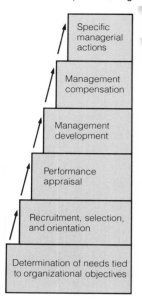

Specific managerial actions

Management compensation

Management development

Performance appraisal

Recruitment, selection, and orientation

Determination of needs tied to organizational objectives

Basic Steps in Staffing The basic steps in staffing are: (1) to determine staffing needs for accomplishing organizational objectives; (2) to recruit, select, and train personnel; (3) to regularly evaluate performance; (4) to develop managerial staff; (5) to periodically adjust compensation; and (6) to promote, transfer, and terminate employment of employees (whether for poor performance or retirement).

HUMAN RESOURCE PLANNING

Organizational planning begins with determining organizational objectives, then moves to developing strategies to achieve those objectives. **Human resource planning** must be a comprehensive, ongoing process tied to the overall plans of the organization. It must be continuous and systematic if it is to help accomplish organizational goals.[3] The relationship between overall organizational planning and human resource planning is shown in Figure 8.1 and is covered in more detail in Chapter 25.

When human resource planning is haphazard or neglected, many problems emerge. In one large corporation a department laid off a number of skilled workers on a Friday, and the following Monday another department of the same company asked the personnel department to immediately recruit a number of people with the same skills as those laid off on Friday. Unnecessary confusion and loss of productive time resulted from the lack of planning.

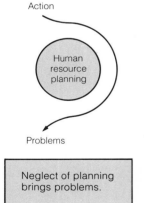

Action

Human resource planning

Problems

Neglect of planning brings problems.

Fundamentals of Human Resource Planning Effective human resource planning must start at the top, be tied to organizational objectives, and be closely monitored by top management, with each lower level of management contributing to the overall plan. Frequently, planning is relegated to the personnel department, with operating management giving little or no attention to its nature and scope. A study of 249 firms each with more than 1,000 employees showed that 96 percent of the firms assigned human resource planning to the personnel department.[4] For such planning to be done well, the head of the organization must insist that operating managers and personnel people work closely together.

Action

Human resource planning

Success

Major Factors to Consider Some factors to consider in human resource planning are:

1. Future cost, marketing, and income projections for the organization.
2. Realistic appraisals of current and projected human resource requirements, including numbers of people and skill levels.
3. Present and future trends in terms of equipment purchase, capital expenditures, sales, and production requirements.
4. Technological and other changes.
5. Present and future trends and demands for different skills and educational backgrounds.

6. Present and future trends in general economic conditions.
7. Present and potential legislation and attitude changes in the community and the nation.

An example of the effect of such factors is the federal legislation raising the mandatory retirement age from sixty-five to seventy that forced most organizations to change many of their hiring, promotion, and firing procedures. Another example is the rapid obsolescence of certain products and equipment that caused rapid shifts in human resource requirements.

Management Replacement Charts Identifying and grooming candidates for existing management positions is imperative for effective human resource planning. One way to handle this is to have each department or unit develop a management replacement chart similar to the one shown in Figure 8.2. This is simply a chart with all the managerial positions keyed to the promotability of each manager.

Figure 8.2 shows the present status of the staffing function of a particular unit. (For the purpose of this illustration, the possibility of someone being transferred from another division or employed from outside is ignored.) Unless further development work is undertaken for other managers in the unit, the most likely present successor is the engineering finance manager—who in turn has a successor ready for promotion and a backup for that position. But the finance manager of military production engines represents a major problem, not all of which is indicated by the chart. He is not doing his job and should be fired. Since he took over the position eight years ago, military production has become far more important; but he is simply not capable of handling the job. He was promoted to the position during a time of rapid expansion, when managers were scarce, but he has passed his level of competence. Since he has been with the company for many years, it will try to find him another position for which he is more suited. This will leave room for the person immediately below him to move up.

Problem of Charts There are dangers in using a management replacement chart. If its confidentiality is not maintained, some people will probably view themselves as "crown princes" and others will be utterly crushed. Furthermore, the simplification into four categories means that people may be stereotyped. Thus, while charts of this sort can be helpful, they must be backed up with complete data and specific plans of action for each individual.

Managers can certainly find other methods of human resource planning as well as these charts. Whatever the method, it is important that such planning be done, so that when a key person leaves, the organization is not at a loss for how to replace that person. Some organizations, both large and small, never recover from losing certain key people, because their human resource planning was haphazard. This planning must be viewed as a continuous task of management.

Factors in human resource planning:

- Financial projections for organization
- Current and projected staffing needs
- Changing technology
- Organizational trends
- Trends in exterior environment

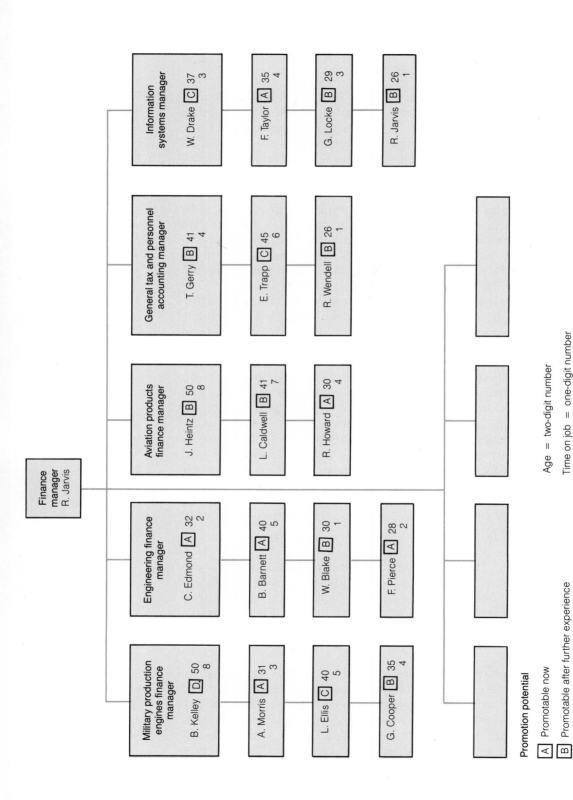

FIGURE 8.2 A partial management replacement chart

CURRENT LAWS AND REGULATIONS

As Figure 8.1 demonstrates, current laws and regulations must be considered in the staffing process. For example, civil rights laws and regulations not only forbid discrimination against minorities but also require affirmative action to reduce discrimination.

Affirmative action   **Affirmative action** refers to a positive plan to reduce or eliminate internal minority imbalances or inequalities.[5] Failure to do so can result in fines, loss of government support or contracts, or other actions. For example, AT&T agreed to pay more than $51 million in back wages to women and minority employees whose pay was arbitrarily low because of the company's discriminatory practices.[6]

> Organizations must be concerned with valid staffing procedures.

Types of Discrimination   There are two broad categories of discrimination in the United States—that against nonwhites, including blacks, Mexican-Americans, Asians, and American Indians, and that against women. Traditionally, nonwhite women have been the most discriminated against. Under affirmative action legislation, organizations must show specific evidence of attempts to hire minority employees in numbers proportionate to their level in the local population. For example, during the two years following their payment of back wages, AT&T increased the number of blacks and women in second-level management by 82 and 46 percent respectively, the number of men in clerical and operator jobs by 147 percent, and the number of women in craft jobs by 119 percent. Directory assistance from a male operator is no longer unusual.

Reverse Discrimination   The pressure for affirmative action has brought a growing number of charges of **reverse discrimination,** which can be defined as the preferential treatment of one group in reverse order to the original discrimination, rather than actions to create equal opportunity in place of the original discrimination. The best known case of alleged reverse discrimination is the Bakke case, in which an application by Alan Bakke to the University of California Medical School at Davis was turned down while at the same time, under a special quota program to help disadvantaged minority students, the school accepted sixteen Hispanic, black, and Asian-American students who were less qualified than Bakke. Thus the school's acceptance of them was a violation of his civil rights.

Bakke sued the University of California. The case went to the United States Supreme Court, where the primary issue was whether the Constitution permitted universities to give preference to minorities over whites in order to remedy the evils of past discrimination.

In mid-1978 the Court ruled that rigid quotas based solely on race were forbidden but that race was a legitimate element in judging students for admission, and it upheld the constitutionality of affirmative action programs. At present, the issue of whether reverse discrimination or equal opportunity is established by affirmative action programs has not been resolved, and future legal decisions will have a significant impact on selection procedures in all sorts of organizations.[7]

Recent Laws and Regulations   Many other laws and regulations also affect the staffing process. Some of them are:

1. The *Equal Pay Act* (*Fair Labor Standards Act*—1963), which forbids unequal pay for men and women doing equal work on jobs requiring equal skill, responsibility, and effort that are performed under similar working conditions. This act was amended in 1972 to include administrative, executive, and professional employees.
2. The *Civil Rights Act* (1964), which forbids discrimination in education and employment on the basis of race, sex, color, religion, and national origin.
3. The *Age Discrimination Act* (1967), which forbids all forms of discrimination in employment for persons between forty and sixty-five years of age.
4. The *Occupational Safety and Health Act* (*OSHA*—1970), which establishes mandatory safety and health standards in organizations, including work rules, job design, and the overall work environment.
5. The *Revised Order No. 4* (1971), under which the Department of Labor established detailed guidelines for affirmative action programs, including procedures and demonstration of good faith efforts.
6. The *Rehabilitation Act* (1973), which, among other rules, requires organizations to take affirmative action for employment of people with physical or mental handicaps. Specific regulations were developed and issued by the Department of Labor in 1976.
7. The *Employment Retirement Income Security Act* (*ERISA*—1974), which allows full vesting after ten years and establishes an insurance program to protect pension funds. (Vesting allows the employee to receive the employer's contributions to the pension fund if the employee terminates employment before retirement.)
8. The *Uniform Guidelines for Employee Selection Procedures* (1978), which established specific rules and guidelines on employment practices for the federal government and its contractors. The Equal Employment Opportunity Commission (EEOC) provided revised and tougher guidelines for the private sector and state and local governments.
9. *Changes in mandatory retirement rules*, under which people in most jobs cannot be forced to retire before age seventy (formerly sixty-five).

Federal and State Agencies Affecting Staffing   A number of federal and state agencies have been developed to police civil rights and other legislation. Among the most important federal agencies are the Equal Employment Opportunity Commission (EEOC), the Office of Federal Contract Compliance Programs (OFCCP) in the Department of Labor, and the Occupational Safety and Health Administration (OSHA) in the Department of Health and Human Services.

Equal employment laws and regulations are changing at a rapid rate. Managers need to be aware of the changes.

EEOC was created by the Civil Rights Act of 1964 to hear and investigate charges of minority discrimination. In 1972 it was given the additional power to go directly to the federal courts to enforce its decisions.

OFCCP was created in 1965 by Presidential Executive Order No. 11246 to enforce the requirement that organizations doing work for the federal government take affirmative action to reduce discrimination against women and minorities.

OSHA was created by the Occupational Safety and Health Act of 1970 to improve work rules, job design, and the work environment. It is responsible for drawing up regulations and guidelines for occupational safety and health.

Because of the complexity and importance of staffing, managers at all levels have immediate responsibility for staffing within the law. Top management must establish policy and make certain it is carried out. Middle- and lower-level managers must implement the policy and recommend necessary changes. As mentioned earlier, the personnel department can assist with the staffing process, but the ultimate responsibility rests with the managers.

RECRUITMENT AND SELECTION

As with other aspects of staffing, recruitment and selection should be tied to the overall objectives of the organization. This means that each job should be carefully analyzed and that appropriate requirements should be set before candidates are recruited.

Recruitment is the process of attracting candidates from either inside or outside the organization who are qualified for and interested in the position. **Selection** is the process of choosing the most qualified candidate. Many organizations like to promote from within whenever possible because this practice creates executive continuity, career development paths, a high level of morale, and job satisfaction. But promotion from within has drawbacks as well. Each position can be filled by only one person, so the candidates who are passed over for promotion may become unhappy. Moreover, internal candidates may be less qualified than candidates from outside the organization.

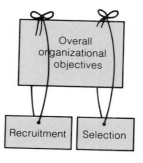

Recruitment Outside the Organization An important reason to recruit outside the organization is that many organizations have systematically, even if inadvertently, discriminated against potential managers because of sex, color, age, religion, and so on. Now their available pool of potential middle- and upper-level managers is primarily white men. To ensure that women, minorities, the handicapped, and other groups have an equal chance at becoming managers, they must aggressively recruit such people from the outside.

Approaches to Recruitment Figure 8.3 is a diagram of the recruitment and selection process. The management replacement chart or its equiva-

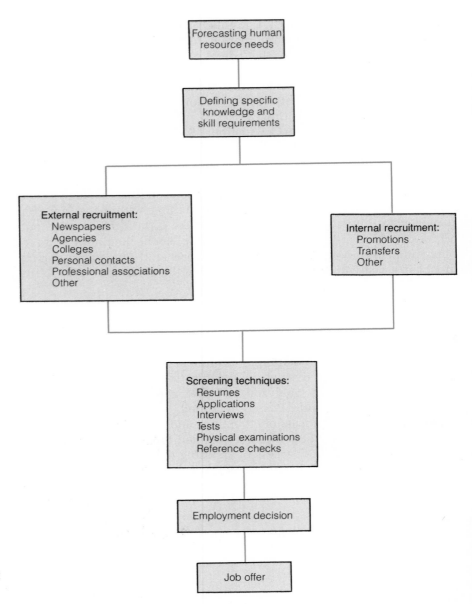

FIGURE 8.3 Frequently used steps in recruitment and selection

lent is one tool for recruiting and selecting from within. Another tool is job posting—the posting in prominent places of all open positions. Recruiting from outside the organization is done with the help of colleges, private employment agencies, state employment agencies, professional associations, other employees, and newspaper advertisements. For all forms of recruitment the legal requirements are becoming stricter and stricter. A 1974 law stipulates that certain organizations doing work for the federal government must list job openings with the local office of the state employment agency. Other regulations require certain organizations to advertise in minority or special group journals.

Recruitment: The More Realistic, the Better The recruiting process is also becoming more realistic. In the past, organizations tried to sell themselves to prospective candidates. Now they aim to provide a realistic preview of the job, so that both they and the candidates can make a better choice. Studies suggest that when clear and realistic information about the job is given, the number of applicants remains the same but the turnover rates for those hired are reduced.

In the early 1970s the U.S. Army Intelligence Corps changed its description of the desired candidate for a particular job from "an individual of high character and good intelligence with better than average ability to communicate" to "a college graduate in liberal arts who has previously demonstrated outstanding fluency and command of both spoken and written English, and can type at least 40 words a minute." This type of change leads to a better match of candidates and jobs.

In another situation, a bank personnel manager found that having applicants read job descriptions before being interviewed helped the recruitment and selection process. After reading the job description, some applicants would screen themselves out, saying, "I don't think this is the type of job I am looking for."

Selection as a Series of Hurdles The traditional managerial selection process is a series of hurdles: résumés, applications, personal interviews, reference checks, physical examinations, and even psychological testing. (A sample résumé is given in Figure 8.4.) Most research on selection indicates that none of these steps is very accurate.[8] For example, studies suggest that impressions gathered from résumés are not accurate for predicting job performance. The well written and well designed résumé attracts favorable attention regardless of the candidate's qualifications for the particular job; yet it is these qualifications that usually determine job success.

The *application*, a printed form that asks for biographical and other information about a candidate, is one of the most widely used tools for selection from outside the organization. The forms vary considerably according to organization and job level. Few organizations have attempted to demonstrate that their applications ask for information relevant for predicting success on the job. Some types of questions are, of course, common to all application forms and are essential for screening candidates. Others, however, such as questions about race, color, religion, age, physical or mental handicaps, marital status, and previous convictions for crimes are now required by law to be proved as job related or removed from the form.

The use of *psychological testing*, another selection tool, is declining. Recent Supreme Court rulings state that such tests can be used for employment decisions only if they are proved to predict job performance, do not discriminate, and are job related.

Janet M. Gulick
Mill Pond Road
Chagrin Falls, Ohio 21212

Home telephone: 216/444-9393
Office telephone: 216/777-8484

Objective: To assume a position of responsibility in the financial department of
                    a manufacturing, processing, or service organization. Ultimate goal:
                    upper-level managerial position.

Education: Case Western Reserve University, B.A. in Finance, May 1979 (cum
                    laude). Course work included corporate finance, investments,
                    internal finance, management accounting, organizational studies,
                    and computer science. Was member of University Debate Team,
                    Academic Affairs Council, Student Governance Board.

Experience:
January 1979 to   Western Federal Savings and Loan, Cleveland, Ohio. *Lending
present   Officer,* responsible for managing operation of the home
                    improvement loan department; duties include qualifying loan
                    applications, supervising disbursement of $300,000 per month, and
                    soliciting new accounts.

1976–1979   Ajax Construction Company, Omar, Ohio. Four consecutive summers
                    of increasing responsibilities. Advanced from general laborer to
                    carpenter to detail planner and layout designer. Increasing ability to
                    plan, organize, and control was required.

1975   Avis Car Rental, Omar, Ohio. Summer employment, included vehicle
                    cleaning and inspection.

1974   Omar Market, Omar, Ohio. Summer employment as cashier and
                    bagger.

Interests: Captain of the swimming team at Omar High School and a member
                    of the varsity baseball team. Also editor of the yearbook. Other
                    interests include classical music, woodcraft, tennis, and softball.

References: Supplied on request.

FIGURE 8.4 A sample résumé

Interviews are perhaps the most widely used selection technique. They can be relatively unstructured and nondirective or highly structured and patterned. A structured interview probes predetermined areas according to a detailed checklist. Most research suggests that the interview is not very accurate in predicting job success unless the interviewer is well trained and uses a structured format. To offset possible biases on the part of the interviewer, more than one interviewer should be used and as many different selection methods as possible should be employed. "The more carefully clues about an applicant are checked against other information, the higher the validity (accuracy) of the selection procedure is likely to be."[9]

Assessment Centers—A Popular Approach to Selection One way to check clues about an applicant against other information is through assessment centers. Most centers are company operated, although some are independent. Companies usually either set aside particular offices or reserve educational or other facilities for the purpose. Many organizations (such as AT&T, IBM, Sears, General Motors, Standard Oil, General Electric, Ford, the IRS, and the U.S. Department of Agriculture) are now using this approach for selecting, identifying, and developing managers.[10] The use of such centers is spreading because research suggests that they are appropriate for essentially everyone. The centers help managers make decisions about placement, job rotation, training, and development. For example, GM is now using assessment centers to select hourly workers for some of its new plants.

There is no best procedure for assessment centers to follow. But in general the chosen procedure should incorporate some or all of these six steps:

1. Ten to twelve people are assessed at the same time. They may be outside applicants or current employees being considered for promotion or development.
2. The people participate in a number of activities for $1\frac{1}{2}$ to $3\frac{1}{2}$ days.
3. The activities include interviews, leaderless group discussions, working through collections of memorandums and papers typical of a manager's incoming mail, business games and other simulation exercises, and a variety of aptitude or other tests.
4. The people are interviewed and observed by trained staff people, often including managers, personnel people, and psychologists.
5. Observers and interviewers pool their combined judgments to develop a joint report, frequently with recommendations for development, on each individual being assessed.
6. Based on the managerial level of each participant, the staff members conduct follow-up developmental discussions with the person and frequently offer specific plans for the individual's development.

A series of studies suggest that assessment centers are generally more accurate than other selection processes in predicting managerial potential. They can also have a positive impact on the individual. For example, after a comprehensive developmental discussion, one young manager who was being assessed by General Electric remarked: "I had been thinking of leaving the company. In fact, I have an excellent job offer right now. But I think I will stay with GE because the company shows so much interest in me as an individual."

APPRAISAL—EVALUATING THE MANAGER'S PERFORMANCE

Performance appraisal is a formal, written process for the periodic evaluation of managers' performance that is necessary if organizational goals are to be reached.[11]

Objectives of Performance Appraisal   The purposes of performance appraisal are:

Objectives of performance appraisal:

- Work improvement
- Salary administration
- Information storage for administration
- Isolation of training needs
- Selection of new employees

1. *Work improvement.* To improve, a subordinate needs feedback about personal performance.
2. *Salary administration.* To determine appropriate salaries, the manager needs to review the performance of subordinates.
3. *Information storage for administrative action.* Most organizations need data about employees to be used in future administrative actions such as promotion, demotion, or transfer.
4. *Isolation of training needs.* Clear, current information about the strengths and weaknesses of the organization's members is needed if the organization is to create appropriate and timely development and training programs.
5. *Selection of new employees.* Prediction of future performance is based largely on understanding of past performance. Thus employers use appraisals of current employees to validate tests that will be applied to new employees.

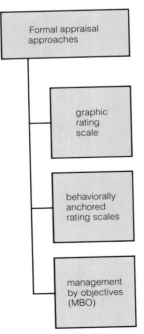

These objectives of performance appraisal have been affected by federal legislation. Equal Employment Opportunity Commission actions and court decisions have shown organizations that they must have fair and accurate records of employee performance if they are to defend themselves against possible charges of discrimination in promotions, salary increases, and discharges. Legally, performance appraisals must be shown to be job related. Thus the appraisal rating method must be developed from comprehensive and thorough job analysis, and the ratings themselves must be free of racial, sexual, or other bias and must be collected and scored under standardized conditions.[12]

Most organizations have a formalized appraisal program for lower- and middle-level management, usually in the form of rating scales or essay evaluations or a combination of the two.[13] Achievement of performance goals is a major point in any appraisal. Most appraisals are conducted yearly or semi-yearly.

Of the many kinds of formal appraisal approaches in use, only three will be described here: the graphic rating scale, behaviorally anchored rating scales, and management by objectives (MBO). The most frequently used approach is the *graphic rating scale*. With this method, the person doing the rating places checkmarks on the appraisal form 40 indicate performance in a number of different areas such as quality of work, quantity of work, job knowledge, cooperation, and dependability. The degrees of merit being checked may run from "consistently low" to "outstanding" or from "far below standard" to "well above standard." Figures 8.5 and 8.6 show two types of rating forms. Figure 8.5 is from a large organization, and it rates managerial and administrative personnel. Figure 8.6 is a form used by a savings and loan to rate nonmanagerial employees.

A serious problem with graphic rating scales is that terms like *below standard* and *above standard* can mean different things to different people. The accuracy of such scales can be improved by carefully training managers and others who are doing the rating.

Improving Appraisal Attempts to improve the traditional graphic rating scale have included the development of *behaviorally anchored rating scales*, which are designed to be more job related, to reduce the amount of judgment required by the rater, and to be less open to the charge of discrimination.[14] A behaviorally anchored rating scale for a supermarket checker is shown in Figure 8.7.

Five basic steps are used in the development of such scales:

1. Managers or others who know the job describe specific incidents or examples of ineffective and effective behavior on the job.
2. Those who are developing the scales group the examples into five to ten performance categories.
3. A second group of managers or others who know the job sort the examples into the performance categories. If the people disagree about any example, it is dropped.
4. The second group then rate, on a seven to nine point scale, how effective the examples are in terms of performance. They keep only those items on which there is general agreement.
5. Finally, the rating instrument is developed. Specific incidents are placed on the scale as a result of their rating in Step 4. In the supermarket study, seven dimensions were identified: conscientiousness, knowledge and judgment, skill in human relations, skill in operation of the cash register, skill in bagging, organizational ability in the checkstand work, and skill in monetary transactions.

Following these five steps will help validate the performance appraisal method.

Behaviorally anchored rating scales have not been used extensively for appraising managers. However, as more organizations find it necessary to prove the accuracy and validity of performance appraisal in terms of civil rights, the use of this approach is likely to increase.

A third type of formal appraisal is *management by objectives (MBO)*, which was described in detail in Chapter 5. An effective MBO program consists of periodic manager-subordinate meetings designed to accom-

BOSTON COLLEGE
EMPLOYEE APPRAISAL AND DEVELOPMENT PLANNING

EMPLOYEE'S NAME _____ DEPARTMENT _____
                        last   first   m.i.

POSITION _____ DATE ENTERED POSITION _____

1. MAJOR STRENGTHS — What have been the employee's assets and chief abilities in present job? (Cite specific job accomplishments)

_____
_____
_____
_____
_____
_____
_____
_____
_____
_____
_____

2. AREAS NEEDING IMPROVEMENT — Where did employee exhibit need for improvement? In what specific areas is improvement needed? (Cite specific assignments which could have been more effectively performed, for example.)

_____
_____
_____
_____
_____
_____
_____
_____
_____
_____
_____

3. PERFORMANCE CHANGES — What specific performance changes have you observed over the past year? Include both positive and non-positive changes.

_____
_____
_____
_____
_____

4. DEVELOPMENT PLANNING — What specific steps are being taken or planned to effect employee's improvement on present job and preparation for further responsibilities? What would be needed to enhance promotability?

_____
_____
_____
_____
_____

FIGURE 8.5 Performance appraisal form from Boston College, Boston, Massachusetts

plish organizational goals by mutual planning of the work, a review process, and mutual solving of problems that arise in the course of getting the job done.

The Appraisal Interview   The *appraisal interview* should be an open discussion between the manager and the subordinate regarding strengths, weaknesses, and areas needing improvement. Although a majority of companies using performance appraisals report that managers conduct such interviews, the discussions are not always fruitful. Indeed, some studies have found that formalized performance appraisals

5. GENERAL APPRAISAL FACTOR RATINGS — Check appropriate box for applicable factors. Empty boxes may be used to include other factors unique to position or situation (e.g. ability to meet deadlines, counseling skills, communication skills, etc.)

	UNSATIS-FACTORY	NEEDS IMPROVE-MENT	GOOD	COMMEND-ABLE	DISTIN-GUISHED
QUANTITY — Capacity for meeting workload demands of responsibilities.					
QUALITY — Accurate, complete work free of frequent or costly error, professionalism, level of work standards.					
INITIATIVE — Ability to be a self-starter, supervise self, take action on own.					
JUDGMENT — Analytical ability, common sense, ability to make sound decisions/recommendations, determine priorities and foresee ramifications.					
CREATIVENESS — Ability to come up with original thinking, new ideas, innovative suggestions.					
ATTITUDE — Degree of conscientiousness, willingness, dependability and general approach to position.					
INTERPERSONAL SKILLS — Ability to interrelate harmonously with peers, subordinates, superiors, students, or public.					
PLANNING & ORGANIZATION — Ability to observe, analyze, plan work, organize & delegate to subordinates, utilization of time.					
LEADERSHIP — Ability to win confidence and cooperation of, and train and develop subordinates.					
CRITICAL EFFECTIVENESS — Ability/willingness to confront, control, resolve any disciplinary/remedial situations.					
OVERALL RATING —					

APPRAISED BY _____ DISCUSSED WITH EMPLOYEE _____

      Supervisor   Date   Date

6. EMPLOYEE'S COMMENTS — What are your views of your performance? To what degree do you concur or not concur with this appraisal? How do you feel your supervisor or others can assist you in developing your present and/or future performance?

_____

_____

_____

_____

_____

_____

_____

_____

_____

_____

_____

_____

_____

EMPLOYEE'S SIGNATURE _____ DATE _____

4/78 Office of Personnel Relations

do more harm than good.[15] For example, subordinates' defensiveness to criticism of their performance increased in direct proportion to the number of criticisms made.[16] Part of the problem is that performance appraisal programs developed for one purpose have been used for others. One organization instituted a pay for performance program with salary levels determined strictly by ratings. A young engineering graduate did an outstanding job during his first six months with the company, and at his six-month review his manager gave him a substantial salary increase—15 percent. During the discussion, however, the young engineer found that he had received a "D" (below average) rating. Although he

PERFORMANCE APPRAISAL REPORT	TO BE FILLED IN BY IMMEDIATE SUPERVISOR	RETURNED
NAME OF STAFF MEMBER		DATE EMPLOYED
DIVISION/DEPARTMENT/BRANCH		DATE OF LAST APPRAISAL

1 POSITION TITLE (IF THE POSITION TITLE IS NOT SELF-EXPLANATORY, BRIEFLY DESCRIBE JOB FUNCTION OR RESPONSIBILITIES)

− AREAS FOR DISCUSSION −

2 INDICATE, BY CHECKING THE APPROPRIATE BOX, THE LEVEL WHICH MOST ACCURATELY DESCRIBES THE EMPLOYEE'S PERFORMANCE IN THE AREA BEING RATED. BASE YOUR JUDGEMENTS UPON OBSERVED PERFORMANCE IN THE PRESENT POSITION.

GENERAL	Not Applic-able	Out-Standing	Satis-factory	Improve-ment Needed	Unsatis-factory	4 IDENTIFY THE EMPLOYEE'S PRINCIPAL STRENGTHS:
PRODUCTION LEVEL						
QUALITY LEVEL						
ACCURACY AND ATTENTION TO DETAILS						
PERFORMANCE UNDER PRESSURE						
WORK ORGANIZATION						
WORKING WITHOUT SUPERVISION						
WORKING WITH OTHERS						
WRITING EFFECTIVELY						
ORAL COMMUNICATION						
ADAPTING TO NEW ASSIGNMENTS						5 IDENTIFY THE EMPLOYEE'S PRINCIPAL IM-PROVEMENT NEEDS:
TECHNICAL KNOWLEDGE/SKILLS						
KNOWLEDGE & APPLICATION OF POLICIES						
CREATIVE PROBLEM SOLVING						
PREPARING REPORTS & DOCUMENTS						
METHODS AND COST SENSE						
COOPERATING WITH OTHER UNITS						
RELIABILITY						
TRAINING STAFF *						
MOTIVATING STAFF *						6 IDENTIFY THE SPECIFIC STEPS TO BE TAKEN TO IMPROVE THE EMPLOYEE'S JOB PERFORMANCE:
DELEGATING DUTIES & AUTHORITY *						
* For Supervisors Only						
CUSTOMER CONTACT						
COURTESY TO CUSTOMERS						
MAINTAINING RAPPORT WITH CUSTOMERS						
ADDRESSING CUSTOMER NEEDS						
SEEKING NEW BUSINESS PROSPECTS						
SKILL IN CLOSING NEW BUSINESS						
CROSS-SELLING INSTITUTIONAL SERVICES						
USE THE BLANK LINES BELOW TO ADD OTHER IMPORTANT JOB AREAS						

3 OVERALL PERFORMANCE EVALUATION: IN SUMMARIZING THIS EMPLOYEE'S PERFORMANCE, HEAVILY WEIGHT THOSE FACTORS MOST IMPORTANT TO PERFORMANCE IN THE POSITION AND THEN MARK THE APPROPRIATE BOX.

FAILS TO MEET THE MINIMUM REQUIREMENTS OF THE JOB	
MEETS THE REQUIREMENTS OF THE JOB	
CONSISTENTLY PERFORMS ABOVE THE REQUIRED LEVEL	

☐ Probationary   ☐ Regular   ☐ Merit   OVER ▶

FIGURE 8.6 Performance appraisal form from First Federal Savings and Loan Association of Alexandria, Virginia

was doing excellent work, he could not be given an "A" rating, his manager explained, because this would force the manager to increase his pay by 50 percent—and no one in the company had ever gotten that large a raise. Although the engineer was pleased with the 15 percent increase, he soon quit, because he did not want to have a below average performance rating on his record.

To make good use of performance appraisals, a manager should first determine what is to be accomplished in the case of each subordinate and then choose the most suitable method of appraisal. Different objectives require different methods. MBO, for example, may be appropriate

EMPLOYEE'S COMMENTS: Are you in general agreement with the present appraisal? ☐YES ☐NO If "NO", please explain:
7

STAFF MEMBER'S SIGNATURE	DATE

8

RECOMMENDATION
(Comments required below)

☐ Promotion

☐ Salary increase from_____to_____

☐ Continue in present position

☐ Transfer

☐ Terminate

SUPERVISOR'S COMMENTS:
9

PRINT NAME	SIGNATURE	TITLE	DATE

COMMENTS OF NEXT MANAGEMENT LEVEL:
10

PRINT NAME AND TITLE	SIGNATURE	REVIEWED-PRESONNEL	DATE

for improving work performance, while graphic rating scales or other approaches may be more effective for determining promotions, salary increases, and other personnel actions. Also, the appraisal interview for salary action should be separate from the one for improving work performance. If the same data are used for both, their effectiveness is diluted the second time around.

Accurate performance appraisals are a major tool for helping subordinates improve job performance. They also are a key to accurate and adequate management compensation, which will be discussed later in the chapter.

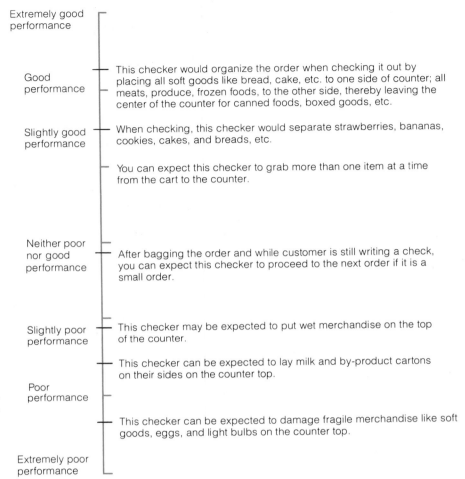

FIGURE 8.7 A behaviorally anchored rating scale for a supermarket checker

Source: Lawrence Fogli, Charles Hulin, and Milton R. Blood, "Development of First-Level Behavioral Job Criteria," *Journal of Applied Psychology* 55 (February 1971): 7. Copyright 1971 by the American Psychological Association. Reprinted by permission.

MANAGEMENT DEVELOPMENT

Management development:

- Improves skills
- Improves current performance
- Improves future performance

One of the reasons for using replacement charts, assessment centers, and appraisal programs is that they help identify where job performance can be improved. In a quickly changing world, managers need continual updates on information, techniques, and skills.[17] Development should thus take place continually and throughout the organization.

In a sense, all development is self-development; yet the organization has a powerful effect on certain kinds of development. For example, the first year in a management job can affect a person's future promotions, job success, and salary levels.[18] The greater the organization's expectations of the individual on the first job, the more likely the person is to be successful later. That the first job is important is demonstrated by an organization that had consistently high turnover among recent college graduates in their first year with the company. The organization restructured its entry-level jobs to make them more challenging, and turnover dropped to almost zero.

Management development is training or other processes to improve manager's knowledge, skills, and job performance and to prepare the managers for promotion. *Development* refers to both individual managers and groups of managers in this context.

Self-development, the primary approach to management development is explained in detail in Chapter 19. Other approaches come from the organization. They include development on the job through counseling and coaching programs and development off the job through courses, conferences, and executive seminars. As Table 8.1 indicates, management development should be tailored to the levels of the positions as well as to the needs and career stages of the individual managers. For example, many organizations have entry-level development programs, middle-management development programs, and executive development programs.

First-Line Supervisory Training College graduates should be encouraged early in their careers to develop specialties in which they can apply the concepts and knowledge they obtained in school. A specialty provides an entrance into first-line supervisory positions. However, overspecialization can trap a person by making him or her indispensable in a particular area, so it is best to acquire a new specialty after a few years.

When a college graduate is assigned to a first-line supervisory position, that person's practice of management begins. The individual at this career stage needs to develop action skills—skills in developing and accomplishing approved plans and programs within an established budget and in obtaining and using help from others, including staff and service groups. In addition, the individual needs information about the organization in general, the department, and the particular unit; knowl-

Individual in organization with inadequate management development

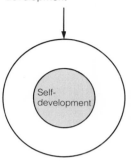

Individual in organization with effective management development

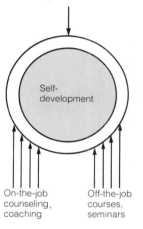

On-the-job counseling, coaching

Off-the-job courses, seminars

TABLE 8.1 Developmental Needs in Early, Middle, and Late Career

STAGE	TASK NEEDS
Early career	**1.** Develop action skills.
	2. Develop a specialty.
	3. Develop creativity, innovation.
	4. Rotate into new area after two to five years.
Middle career	**1.** Develop skills in training and coaching younger employees.
	2. Train for updating and intergrating skills.
	3. Develop broader view of work and organization.
	4. Rotate into new job requiring new skills.
Late career	**1.** Shift from power role to consulting role; offer guidance and wisdom.
	2. Begin to establish self in activities outside the organization, starting on part-time basis.

Source: Adapted and modified by permission from Douglas Hall, *Careers in Organizations* (Pacific Palisades, Calif.: Goodyear Publishing, 1976), p. 90.

edge of how to recruit, train, and motivate subordinates; understanding of the labor contract if there is a union; and the ability to cooperate with other departments and units.

Much of the training at this level comes directly from the immediate supervisor through example and explanation, although large organizations often have training programs for new supervisors in such areas as company policies, communications, motivation, and labor law applying to the organization. Supervisors should encourage creativity and innovation and should provide an atmosphere of support and freedom. Two freedoms that should be given are the freedom to learn from mistakes and the freedom to develop self-confidence. Supervisors should also help inexperienced managers learn how to communicate with, instruct, and motivate subordinates and how to cooperate with peers. Thus, although each individual is responsible for personal development, upper-level managers can greatly influence recent college graduates.

Middle Management Development   Most people entering middle management ranks are supervisors who have achieved specific goals in such major areas as budgeting, production, and expense control. Middle managers need to know a great deal about the practical side of management; yet they tend to lose contact with the day-to-day functions of workers. Managers at this level must (1) develop skills in training and coaching others, particularly young employees; (2) update and integrate their own skills; (3) develop a broad view of work and of the organization; and (4) know general management theory and understand the overall functions of managers.

The knowledge required at this level involves a broad background in such areas as finance, behavioral sciences, and planning for and coordinating different units. This kind of knowledge is hard to learn on the job; it can often be taught best through in-house seminars and courses, where managers can learn from give-and-take with other managers in structured situations. Another method is for managers to attend courses arranged by universities, associations, or consultants. Outside "live-in" programs have the most prestige and are the most attractive. Still another method is planned job rotation, which gives managers experience in different areas of the organization and helps them avoid overspecialization.

Executive Development   The executive level usually encompasses plant, functional, and division managers who are in line for positions such as general manager, executive vice-president, or president. These people need to have the knowledge, skills, and ability to move from managing a relatively specialized area into managing a larger and broader area of the organization. Thus they require training and development in the management of functions with which they are not familiar. These functions include the strategic direction of the organization and the handling of certain areas outside the organization, such as work with trade associations, relationships with the financial community and with other countries, and lobbying.

As with middle managers, special courses, seminars, and on-the-job training can be helpful to executives. Managing special task forces, sitting in on contract negotiations, and handling special assignments are among the tasks that can be used to train people at this level.

At all levels in the organization, the immediate supervisor must make certain that potential managers are being developed among subordinates. In the press of other business, this development may not occur without the reminder that performance appraisal and reward systems provide.

The Importance of Mentors Evidence is growing that college graduates who rise more rapidly than their peers through the managerial ranks have one or more mentors.[19] A **mentor** is an older executive who takes a personal interest in the younger person's career and provides guidance

"I'm sorry. All the openings for clock watchers, woolgathers, time wasters, and goof-offs have been filled. We do have, however, several openings for workaholics."

Source: Reprinted by permission of the Chicago Tribune–New York News Syndicate, Inc.

and sponsorship. The first fifteen or so years of a management career is a time of learning and growing—and it is then that a mentor is needed. By the age of about forty, those who are destined for the highest executive ranks are already in positions of some power and no longer need a mentor. Research indicates that those who benefit most from one or more mentors feel the strongest obligation to extend mentoring to others. Chapter 19 describes the influence and importance of mentoring in more detail.

MANAGEMENT COMPENSATION

Managers receive many forms of **compensation**—direct or indirect, immediate or deferred, rewards, some of which are monetary. One type of compensation, psychological income, includes achievement, power, prestige, challenge, and respect. Monetary types of compensation are often enough used to satisfy not only basic physiological and security needs but also needs for recognition, achievement, and growth. A salary increase does more than pay the bills; it lets the manager know that good job performance is recognized and appreciated.

Three basic and related decisions must be made about any form of wage payment:

1. What is the job worth in comparison to other jobs in the organization?
2. What is the job worth in comparison to other jobs in the community (or other areas)?
3. What is the individual worth on the particular job (how much should the individual be paid and in what form)?[20]

What Is the Job Worth?—Internal Comparison   All organizations have some form of job evaluation. When a manager decides that an engineer's job is worth more than a buyer's job, that is job evaluation. Of course, usually a systematic process is followed. First, job descriptions are prepared and approved for each job in the organization. Then these descriptions are compared to other jobs in terms of their importance. Finally, jobs of approximately equal importance and difficulty are placed in particular grades or levels. For example, in the federal government all jobs under civil service have been described, evaluated, and graded from GS–1, the lowest, to GS–15, the highest. (Higher graded jobs—previously GS–16 to GS–18—are in the senior executive service.) Frequently, organizations have different job evaluation plans for managerial, clerical, and blue-collar workers.

What Is the Job Worth?—External Comparison   Each job grade usually has a minimum starting salary and a maximum salary. The minimums and maximums are frequently determined by salary surveys and reviews of what other organizations are doing. For hourly and clerical workers, they are often done on a community or local basis; for managers and executives, they are often done on a national or international basis.

Pay scales at the World Bank, for example, are set after a survey of comparable jobs in a number of developed countries.

In the federal government, comparisons are done at the national level, since the government competes with employers across the country. General Schedule Grade GS–13 is the beginning of the professional, middle-to-high-level management ladder. At this grade are positions such as agricultural economist, hospital administrator, and supervisory auditor. In 1949 the beginning annual salary for that level was $7,600. In 1969, after the first comparison salary survey, the beginning salary for the level was $16,760. In 1977 the beginning salary was increased to $26,022, and in 1981 it was $32,048. The U.S. Bureau of Labor Statistics conducts the national surveys each March, and the GS levels are adjusted on the basis of the surveys.

What Is the Individual Worth?   A civil service professional or manager whose job is rated GS–13 can be paid anywhere from $32,048 to $41,660. Where an individual is placed in that range depends on the person's experience and ability. Thus performance appraisal is one method of setting salaries, and most organizations try to link pay to performance. Many organizations also have a number of other ways of paying managers in addition to straight salary, including stock options, bonuses, consulting, and other fringe benefits.

Management compensation:

- Salary
- Stock options
- Bonuses
- Consulting
- Additional fringe benefits

Stock Options   Managers are often given the option to buy shares of stock in the company at a price lower than the market value. If the shares are going up in value, the manager can buy them at the lower price, hold them for a period of time, sell them at a profit, and pay a relatively low income tax on the profit because it is taxed as capital gains.

Bonuses   Bonuses are usually granted for outstanding performance. They can be in the form of cash or company shares. They can be given in the current year, distributed over a period of years, or deferred until after retirement, when the executive is earning less money and will pay less tax on the income received.

Expense Accounts   In theory, expense accounts are not compensation, since managers are to use them for entertaining customers or others.

Consulting   Some organizations retain executives as consultants. This is a form of deferred wage payment that enables the executive to receive pay at a time when total income (and therefore the tax rate) is lower.

Additional Fringe Benefits   Pensions, life insurance, health insurance, executive dining rooms, free automobiles—all are examples of fringe benefits that add to the total compensation package. A number of organizations even have barbershops where managers can get haircuts free or at a low price. In many executive dining rooms, meals cost less than in comparable restaurants.

TABLE 8.2   The Millionaires' Club—1980's Highest Paid U.S. Executives

		SALARY	BONUS	SALARY AND BONUS	LONG-TERM INCOME	TOTAL COMPEN-SATION
				(THOUSANDS OF DOLLARS)		
1. Robert A. Charple, pres.	Cabot	$ —	$ —	$ 799	$2,531(1)	$3,330
2. Edward M. Gibbs, exec. v-p (3)	NL Industries	155	128(1)	283	2,942	3,225
2. C. C. Garvin Jr., chmn.	Exxon	640	275	915	2,145(1)	3,060
4. John C. Kenefick, pres.	Union Pacific	249	325	574	2,480	3,054
5. Fred L. Hartley, chmn. & pres.	Union Oil of Calif.	440	825	1,265	1,761	3,026
6. David S. Lewis, chmn. & CEO	General Dynamics	400	55	455	2,557	3,012
7. James H. Evans, chmn. & CEO	Union Pacific	385	550	935	1,863	2,798
8. J. E. Swearingen, chmn.	Standard Oil (Ind.)	380	—	380	2,207	2,587
9. Ned Tanen, pres.	MCA (Universal Pictures)	330	—	330	2,137(5)	2,467
10. Ray C. Adam, chmn. & CEO	NL Industries	345	317(1)	662	1,707	2,369
11. W. J. McDonald, sr. v-p	Union Pacific	181	225	406	1,655	2,061
12. Robert Anderson, chmn. & CEO	Rockwell International	415	450	865	1,164	2,029
13. Donald P. Kelly, pres. & CEO	Esmark	—	—	1,647(2)	314(1)	1,961
14. F. C. Osment, exec. v-p	Standard Oil (Ind.)	258	—	258	1,631	1,889
15. J. R. Lesch, pres. & CEO	Hughes Tool	—	—	418	1,452	1,870
16. Pierre Gousseland, chmn.	AMAX	405	360	765	936	1,701
17. John F. Bookout, pres. & CEO	Shell Oil	—	—	740	960	1,700
18. Andrew Heiskell, chmn. & CEO (4)	Time	—	—	437	1,245	1,682
19. R. O. Anderson, chmn. & CEO	Atlantic Richfield	—	—	754	896	1,650
20. Louis W. Cabot, chmn.	Cabot	—	—	508	1,105(1)	1,613
21. William D. Manly, sr. v-p	Cabot	—	—	365	1,186(1)	1,551
22. Ray A. Burke, sr. v-p	Union Oil of Calif.	224	286	510	1,031	1,541
23. John Towers, pres.	AMAX	305	270	575	939	1,514
24. G. G. Zipf, vice-chmn., pres. & COO	J. Ray McDermott (Babcock & Wilcox)	—	—	300	1,186	1,486
25. Rawleigh Warner Jr., chmn.	Mobil	498	530	1,028	427	1,455

(1) Includes value of performance award units expensed in 1980, but not total value received in 1980. (2) Includes performance award payments. (3) Resigned Sept. 4, 1980. (4) Retired Oct. 1, 1980. (5) Reflects accelerated vesting of shares under incentive stock plan.

Data: Sibson & Co.

Thus there are a number of ways managers can be paid in addition to straight salary. In many instances, the additional compensation is not only a performance measure but also a way of reducing the income tax paid by managers. Top executives are very well paid, which explains why their companies try to help them minimize their taxes. (Table 8.2 shows the twenty-five highest paid U.S. executives in 1980.)

PROMOTION, TRANSFER, AND TERMINATION

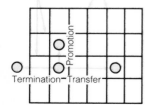

Managers do not necessarily stay in the same jobs forever; they may be transferred, promoted, or terminated. A **transfer** is a move to another job, usually without an increase in either status or pay. As Table 8.1 suggests, job transfer or rotation is a good way of avoiding overspecialization. Transfers also can occur when the individual and the job are not properly matched; at times an individual may perform poorly in one job but well in another.

A **promotion** is a move to another job, usually higher in the organization and with an increase in status and pay. It is a reward for accomplishment. Besides higher pay, it brings other tangible forms of recognition such as greater challenge, prestige, and opportunities for further recognition and responsibility.

However, one problem with promotions is the ever-decreasing number of higher positions open to people. While there are usually many first-line supervisors, there is only one president. It is thus impossible for everybody to make it to the top. The Horatio Alger tradition of striving for the top has caused a great deal of psychological damage in this country, particularly among people who want to move up but are incapable of handling high-level jobs. Fortunately, not everyone wants to be at the top. For example, a university school of management with almost a hundred faculty members had only two apply for the position of dean. Furthermore, one of the outside candidates for the position was the vice-president of a large industrial organization who decided that he wanted to get out of the rat race of being a top executive.

Termination is action by the organization to remove an individual from the organization. One form of termination is, of course, retirement. Most large organizations and many small ones have compulsory retirement programs. (Many also have pension programs to supplement retirees' social security income.) The retirement age of sixty-five was established many years ago in Germany, at a time when that was the average life expectancy of a man. Now that the average life expectancy is much longer, compulsory retirement programs are being thoroughly reviewed at both federal and state levels. In fact, as mentioned earlier, federal legislation has raised the mandatory retirement age to seventy for most organizations.

Some terminations come about because the work force has become more mobile.[21] Particularly in high technology organizations, such as those in electronics and aerospace industries, managers can move easily from one firm to another. In the 1960s it was not unusual for such firms to get a contract, hire professional managers and other workers, and then lay off workers when the contract was completed. This process is still occurring but to a lesser degree. At times, however, an organization may simply have more managers and other employees than either work or sales can justify.

Dismissal   The unhappiest form of termination is dismissal, or firing. Many reasons exist for this action: corporate mergers, relocation of facilities, across-the-board cutbacks, poor job performance, mismatching of the job and the individual are a few. Sometimes firing can be avoided by a transfer to another job or by special development programs to help the employee improve performance.

Although most managers dislike firing as much as they would dislike being fired, this process is sometimes necessary. Occasionally, being

Equal employment laws apply to:

- Promotions
- Transfers
- Terminations

fired from a job will jolt an individual into reappraising personal strengths, weaknesses, and potential. Many organizations help those who are terminated find new jobs through the use of career placement counselors. One follow-up study of 250 managers who had been fired found that 88 percent had been placed in higher paying jobs than those they were fired from. Clearly, being fired can have good results for people who have valuable talents and skills to begin with and who are willing to evaluate themselves constructively after termination and then work hard at finding a good job.[22]

SUMMARY

Staffing is an important managerial function, since organizations cannot exist without people. There are a number of laws, rules, and regulations affecting the selection, promotion, transfer, training, and retention of employees at all levels. Managers must be aware of them if they are to perform the staffing function well.

The effective manager makes certain that planning for human resources is closely tied to the overall long- and short-range plans of the organization or unit. In what direction is the organization going? What changes are anticipated for the future? Only when these and other questions are answered can the manager effectively plan for human resource needs. The planning can be formal or informal, but it must be systematic and ongoing.

Recruitment and selection are often done through processes that are insufficient and sometimes even inaccurate. Research indicates that the results of most selection processes do not highly correlate with later job success. Thus the effective manager does not rely on one process but considers job requirements, multiple interviews, and well-conducted reference checks as well. In addition, the manager should be aware of new or changed laws and regulations that affect both the recruitment and selection processes. Given all the areas that must be considered, the manager may want to hire an expert to oversee these procedures.

Many organizations conduct performance appraisal unsystematically. They also provide little or no feedback to employees about their performance. The effective manager sees careful performance appraisal as an essential part of the job and uses MBO or similar approaches to coach and counsel subordinates about improving job performance. The manager also uses carefully developed rating scales for areas such as salary decisions.

In one sense, all development is self-development. Yet, the organization influences the individual's self-development, and the manager has a responsibility to help subordinates improve their job knowledge and skills and prepare for promotion. This help can be given in the following ways: (1) by coaching and counseling, (2) by providing an example for subordinates, (3) by encouraging subordinates to attend internal or external courses, (4) by providing opportunities for job rotation, and (5) by being alert to any other way that will give subordinates an opportunity to grow.

Compensation is an important aspect of staffing. The effective manager makes certain that the organization's plan for evaluating jobs is accurate and that salaries are in line with salaries for similar jobs both inside and outside the organization. Furthermore, the manager must reward good performers and explain to others how they can improve. Studies and interviews have shown that one of the most difficult aspects of managerial jobs is explaining to subordinates the areas in which they are not performing well. Ineffective managers tend to ignore this important task.

Judgment regarding promotions is important; not everyone is promotable. The manager must carefully review subordinates for promotability and candidly discuss opportunities with them. When terminations are necessary, the manager should act humanely. Research has shown that subordinates who are fired often can be helped to find another job that better fits their qualifications.

Finally, the manager needs to review and update the entire staffing process on an ongoing basis to make certain that the human resources of the organization are used wisely.

STUDY QUESTIONS

1. At the beginning of the chapter, you were asked if you had ever applied for a job. If you have, how would you assess that recruitment and selection process on the bases of what you have learned from this chapter?

2. How are recruitment, selection, and performance appraisals of college students similar to what the chapter has described for employees? How are they different?

3. Visit an organization's personnel office to see what steps are followed in staffing. Report on the procedure used.

4. Assume that you are asked to improve the recruitment and selection process of a firm. What will you want to know about the current process in order to determine how it can be improved?

5. What are some of the effects of laws and regulations on staffing? What implications (beyond those described in the chapter) do they have for the manager?

6. Why might a manager neglect some aspects of the staffing process? Which steps are most likely to be neglected? Explain.

7. Based on your reading so far, describe some ways to change the development process for first-level, middle-level, and upper-level management.

8. How important is a person's first job? What effect does the supervisor have on a person's future success?

Case for Discussion

THE PROMOTION

Maureen Thomas was a supervisor for the National Municipal Bank, one of the largest banks in the country. She began working there as an executive secretary after receiving her bachelor's degree from the University of California. The job gave her a good insight into the bank's activities. After three years she asked that she be considered for the next opening in management. A few months later, she became a supervisor in operations, where she worked with five male supervisors. The six supervisors formed a cohesive group, enjoyed their work, and liked the department head, James Bedford.

After three more years Bedford became an officer of the bank. A great deal of speculation arose as to who would succeed him as the department head. Five of the six supervisors, including Thomas, were capable of handling the job, and all five wanted it. Rumor had it that either Jim Johnson or Jack Burton would get the job; both men were highly regarded by both supervisors and employees.

However, on a Monday morning Thomas was called into the office of the bank's executive vice-president. Much to her surprise, the vice-president told her that she would be promoted to department head as Bedford's replacement. He also said that she had been found to be as capable as any of the other supervisors and that her work had been praised by top management. Then he added that the bank had very few women in management and wanted to start promoting women as a matter of policy.

Thomas was told that as soon as her promotion was announced, she should call a meeting of the other supervisors and communicate clearly that (1) she was the boss, (2) her sex was not a factor in the promotion, and (3) she would be as objec-

tive as anyone else in the new job. The vice-president closed the meeting by explaining that success in the department head job could be the beginning of a major career with the bank and that top management and others would be closely watching her over the next few months.

1. Was Maureen Thomas promoted because she was the most qualified supervisor? Explain.

2. What might be the reactions of the other supervisors?

3. What should Thomas say and do at her first meeting with the supervisors?

FOR YOUR CAREER

1. Affirmative action means actively looking for and recruiting women and members of minority groups. Check with the Equal Employment Opportunity Commission (EEOC) for guidelines on where to begin such recruitment.

2. Many questions that used to be common on applications and in interviews are now illegal. Ask the EEOC for a list of these questions, and *memorize* them so that you will be sure not to ask them.

3. Mot interviews are poor predictors of later success. If you are interviewing people for an important job, enlist the aid of other interviewers. Ask them to write down their impression, and then discuss the candidates with them.

4. As the case at the beginning of the chapter indicates, written letters of reference tend to contain little information. Try to generate your own sources of information, and telephone rather than write.

5. Since we all tend to be biased, if more than one reference is to be checked on a particular person, try to have different people make the calls.

6. Look for time gaps in résumés or on applications. Check on them during the interview. Reference checking in these areas is particularly helpful.

7. Keep comprehensive records when recruiting and selecting, particularly for important jobs. You may have to defend yourself against charges of either discrimination or reverse discrimination.

8. One of the best ways to improve the selection process is to accurately describe the job to applicants. Most interviewers do not really interview; instead they tend to "sell" the job.

9. When you are starting your career, find a good mentor for yourself. Later in your career, be prepared to serve as a mentor to someone else.

FOOTNOTES

1. L. Wangler, "References Dry Up," *Wall Street Journal,* January 6, 1976, p. 1.

2. B. Schneider, *Staffing Organizations* (Pacific Palisades, Calif.: Goodyear Publishing, 1976), p. 3.

3. D. Reid, "Human Resource Planning: A Tool for People Development," *Personnel* 54 (March–April 1977): 41–50; R. Fried, "Organizational Charts from Computerized Personnel Data Systems," *Personnel Journal* 56 (June 1977): 284–288; L. Tracey, "The Control Process in Personnel Management," *Personnel Journal* 55 (September 1976): 446–450; A. T. Hollingsworth and P. Preston, "Corporate Planning: A Challenge for Personnel Executives," *Personnel Journal* 55 (August 1976): 386; and J. Gilbreath, "Sex Discrimination and Title VII of the Civil Rights Act," *Personnel Journal* 56 (January 1977): 23–26.

4. A. Janger, *Personnel Administration: Changing Scope and Organization* (New York: National Industrial Conference Board, 1966), p. 25.

5. G. Gery, "Hiring Minorities and Women: The Selection Process," *Personnel Journal* 53 (December 1974): 906–909; J. Straka, "Guidelines on Affirmative Action Recruiting," *Personnel Administrator* 20 (April 1975): 36–39; and W. Hubbartt, "The State Employment Service: An Aid on Affirmative Action Recruiting," *Personnel Administrator* 22 (April 1977): 289–291.

6. "Goals That Look Like Quotas," *Time,* January 29, 1973, p. 77.

7. C. Faulk and U. Lehner, "The Bakke Ruling," *Wall Street Journal,* June 29, 1978, p. 1; and M. Miner and J. Miner, *Employee Selection and the Law* (Washington, D.C.: Bureau of National Affairs, 1978), p. 42.

8. N. Schmitt, "Social and Situational Determinants of Interview Decisions: Implications for the Employment Interview," *Personnel Psychology* 29 (Spring 1976): 79–101; O. Wright, Jr., "Summary of Research on the Selection Interview since 1964," *Personnel Psychology* 22 (Winter 1969): 391–413; F. Gaudet and T. Casey, "How Much Can You Tell from a Resume?" *Personnel* 36 (July–August 1959): 62–65; and E. Burack and R. Smith, *Personnel Management: A Human Resource Systems Approach* (St. Paul: West Publishing, 1977).

9. W. French, *The Personnel Management Process* (Boston: Houghton Mifflin, 1978), p. 234.

10. J. Huck and D. Bray, "Management Assessment Center Evaluations and Subsequent Job Performance of White and Black Females," *Personnel Psychology* 29 (Spring 1976): 13–30; J. Hinrichs and S. Haanpera, "Reliability of Measurement in Situational Exercises: An Assessment of the Assessment Center Method," *Personnel Psychology* 29 (Spring 1976): 31–40; and D. Bray, R. Campbell, and D. Grant, *Formative Years in Business: A Long Term AT&T Study of Managerial Lives* (New York: Wiley, 1974).

11. A. Locher and K. Teel, "Performance Appraisal—A Survey of Current Practices," *Personnel Journal* 56 (May 1977): 245; D. McGregor, "An Uneasy Look at Performance Appraisal," *Harvard Business Review* 35 (May–June 1957): 89–94; E. Huse, "Performance Appraisal—A New Look," *Personnel Administration* 30 (March–April 1967): 13–18; W. Bigoness, "Effect of Applicant's Sex, Race, and Performance on Employer's Performance Ratings—Some Additional Findings," *Journal of Applied Psychology* 61 (January 1967): 80–84; and L. Crooks, ed., *An Investigation of Sources of Bias in the Prediction of Job Performance: A Six Year Study* (Princeton, N.J.: Educational Testing Service, 1972).

12. W. Holley, H. Field, and N. Barnett, "Analyzing Performance Appraisal Systems: An Empirical Study," *Personnel Journal* 55 (September 1976): 457; and W. Holley and H. Field, "Performance Appraisal and the Law," *Labor Law Journal* 26 (July 1975): 423–430.

13. "Management Performance Appraisal Programs," *Personnel Policies Forum,* Survey No. 104 (Washington, D.C.: Bureau of National Affairs, January 1974), pp. 1–3.

14. L. Fogli, C. Hulin, and M. Blood, "Development of First-Level Behavioral Job Criteria," *Journal of Applied Psychology* 55 (February 1971): 3–8; P. Smith and L. Kendall, "Retranslation of Expectations: An Approach to the Construction of Unambiguous Anchors for Rating Scales," *Journal of Applied Psychology* 47 (April 1963): 149–155.

15. "Management Performance Appraisal Programs"; and Huse, "Performance Appraisal—A New Look."

16. E. Huse and E. Kay, "Improving Employee Productivity through Work Planning," in *The Personnel Job in a Changing World,* ed. J. Blood (New York: American Management Association, 1964), pp. 301–312; and Locher and Teel, "Performance Appraisal—A Survey of Current Practices."

17. H. Hague, *Executive Self Development* (New York: Halstead Press, 1974); D. Moment and D. Fisher, *Autonomy in Organizational Life* (Cambridge, Mass.: Schenkman Press, 1975); H. Levinson, "A Psychologist Looks at Executive Development," *Harvard Business Review* 40 (September–October 1962): 69–75; V. Walter, "Self-Motivated Personal Career Planning: A Breakthrough in Human Resource Management," *Personnel Journal* 55 (March 1976): 112; R. Howe, "Building Teams for Increased Productivity," *Personnel Journal* 56 (January 1977): 16; and C. Reeser, "Managerial Obsolescence—An Organizational Dilemma," *Personnel Journal* 56 (January 1977): 27.

18. D. Berlew and D. Hall, "The Socialization of Managers: Effects of Expectations on Performance," *Administrative Science Quarterly* 11 (June 1966): 207–223.

19. G. Roche, "Much Ado about Mentors," *Harvard Business Review* 57 (January–February, 1979): 14–31; D. Levinson, *The Seasons of a Man's Life* (New York: Knopf, 1978); and R. Kanter, *Men and Women of the Corporation* (New York: Basic Books, 1977).

20. "Job Evaluation Policies and Procedures," *Personnel Policies Forum,* Survey No. 113 (Washington, D.C.: Bureau of National Affairs, June 1976); D. Belcher, *Compensation Administration* (Englewood Cliffs, N.J.: Prentice-Hall, 1974); W. French, *The Personnel Management Process* (Boston: Houghton Mifflin, 1978); and E. Lawler, Jr., *Pay and Organizational Effective-*

ness (New York: McGraw-Hill, 1971).

21. E. Jennings, *The Mobile Manager* (New York: McGraw-Hill, 1967).

22. M. Rogers, "Outplacement Specialists, Professional Help for Disabled Careers," *Master in Business Administration* 11 (July–August 1977): 13–15.

Organizational Design— Basic Principles

CHAPTER 9

CONTENTS

THE OSAGE PLANT

Amco, Inc., has about seventy manufacturing plants in the continental United States and ten other countries. One plant is located in the small town of Osage, about a hundred miles from Seattle, Washington. The plant manufactures a variety of industrial and consumer products and has about three hundred employees, including engineers, accountants, salespeople, and factory workers. Figure 9.1—the organization chart of the Osage plant—shows that six managers report to the plant manager, who in turn reports to a division manager.

The plant occupies a modern leased building only two years old. The plant manager, who has been on the job about six months, was promoted from the position of manufacturing manager after the previous plant manager died. As is common for new plants, the Osage plant was losing money. The new plant manager, however, was determined to make the plant profitable as soon as possible.

With the approval of those employees directly reporting to him, he brought in a consultant. The consultant interviewed a number of people, including the manager's immediate subordinates, and reported, orally, that while the plant personnel were hardworking and dedicated, management did not seem to agree on plant objectives and mutual responsibilities.

As a result of the report, the management group (consisting of the plant manager and six subordinate managers) decided to spend three days away from the plant to develop ways of working more effectively together. First they attempted to identify plant objectives. Although overall objectives had been established previously, they discovered they either did not understand them or did not agree with them. Together, the group formulated objectives they could agree on and then began to discuss mutual responsibilities.

FIGURE 9.1 Organization chart of the Osage plant

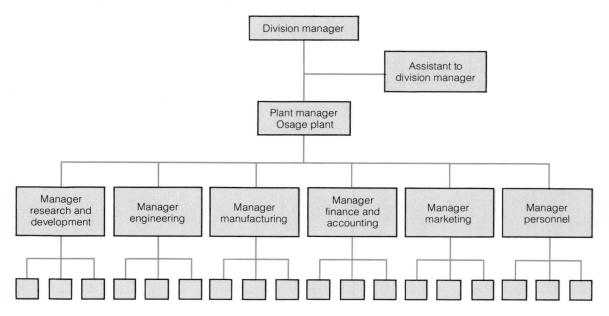

This discussion revealed more disagreements. The manager of finance and accounting began describing his job as he saw it, based primarily on Amco's carefully prepared job description; before he got very far, several people interrupted to express contradictory ideas. It took almost three hours for the job to be defined to the satisfaction of all seven managers, and each of the other job descriptions took about the same amount of time. The resulting job descriptions sounded very different from those given by the organization, which had spelled out relationships mostly to subordinates rather than to peers.

Next, the group redefined organizational goals on the basis of the new job descriptions. And finally, it identified the major problems facing the organization and developed approaches to solving them.

After this meeting, the managers reported that they were working much better with each other. Clarification of each one's responsibilities had been difficult but worthwhile for the Osage plant.

This opening case raises several key questions which you should be able to answer after reading this chapter. The questions are:

1. How can organizations such as Amco, Inc., determine if they have the best organizational design?
2. What determines what type of design an organization should have?
3. Are there any similarities between a local restaurant and General Motors in terms of organizational design? Explain.
4. In what ways can work or groups in an organization be specialized?

Organizations have parts that must be coordinated.

Structure is the essence of defining and coordinating the parts of the organization.

In the preceding case the plant manager and the six subordinate managers together form a complete system; each individual manager is a subsystem. The system was faced with two fundamental tasks—proper division of labor (specialization) and coordination of the work (integration) to accomplish the organization's objectives. Even a system this small had difficulty with specialization and coordination. The larger the system, the more difficult these tasks become. Consider, for example, the organizational problems of managing the federal government with its countless departments, bureaus, agencies, and services.

To function effectively, organizations must be properly designed. This chapter will examine the basic principles of specialization and coordination. Its ideas are only guides, however, since organizations constantly change. As symptoms of organizational problems appear, managers study them, make adjustments, and check to see if the problems have been solved. The process can entail major reorganization and constant tinkering (small readjustments). The plant manager of the Osage plant made a small adjustment by bringing in a consultant and by holding the out-of-plant meeting—which led to a major reorganization.

The subject of organizational structure is sufficiently important to require two chapters—this one for basic information that applies to most organizations and the following one for addressing specific situations. This chapter takes a closed system approach to organizational problems in that it offers the basic principles of the internal structure of organizations. Chapter 10 takes an open system approach, discussing environmental factors that affect organizational structure and design. Thus, the *unity of command,* a principle of internal structure that suggests that an individual should have only one boss, will be discussed in this chapter, since it is valid for most circumstances. The *matrix* design, on the other hand, involves an individual having two or more supervisors. Because it violates the principle of unity of command, it is preferable for certain, special situations and will be discussed in Chapter 10.

THE IMPORTANCE OF STRUCTURE

Essence of structure

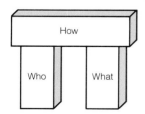

Organizational structure is the framework of the formal relationships among various tasks, activities, and people in the organization. Organizations and their subunits are designed by managers to accomplish certain goals. Thus the organizational design states the nature and degree of division of labor that will be used and choreographs the coordination of efforts to reach desired results. Essentially, basic managerial decisions are *who* will do *what* and *how* they will do it.

Proper structure determines how effectively and efficiently an organization will perform. It was the basic structure of the British army that brought it defeat at the beginning of the American Revolution in the spring of 1775. The army had been trained to fight in a rigid formation, firing in volleys under command, so bright red uniforms had been chosen to make it easier to keep in close formation. But this structure, effective for the open battlefields of Europe, was disastrous for the battles at Lexington and Concord. The Americans hid behind trees and rock walls rather than "standing up to fight." As a result, a relatively small number of men, many of them militarily untrained farmers, soundly defeated a much larger number of trained, professional British soldiers.

Particularly in the past fifty years, many people have tried to identify the key principles for managing and designing organizations, with little agreement. In 1961, in an article called "The Management Theory Jungle," Harold Koontz, a noted college professor, described a number of different schools of management theory.[1] Twenty years later he followed this with another article pointing out that the number of schools had increased and the controversy had heightened rather than being resolved.[2] The trend for organizations to become more complex and heterogeneous contributes to the general disagreement on theories. Some ideas touted as effective worked only because they were applied under a certain combination of conditions that are not likely to be repeated in other organizations. Researchers of organizational design are finding it necessary to examine more and more variables. As knowledge expands, simple answers to fit all situations are becoming rare.

To add to the general complexity, proper organizational design demands examination not only of the organization itself but also of major environmental forces, both local and international. Among these forces are technological, industrial, moral, scientific, racial, and political factors. Continual change, both inside and outside the organization, is causing managers to redefine the ways in which they manage.

Of major importance is that the manager have a good grounding in basic principles in order to develop strategies for designing an organizational structure that is appropriate for rapidly shifting environments. "Effective organization design results not from the blind use of management principles, but from managers matching appropriate principles with particular conditions facing the organization."[3]

SPECIALIZATION AND COORDINATION

In order to accomplish its objectives, every organization (except for the very smallest) faces two basic problem areas—specialization, or **division of labor,** and coordination. The greater the need for specialization, the greater the need for coordination. Chapter 2 briefly described the gains in productivity attained by the Arsenal of Venice in using a relatively simple form of both specialization and coordination to build and equip naval galleys for the defense of the Venetian merchant fleet.

Specialization is necessary because organizations take on tasks that require a wider variety of skills than can be found in one person. Moreover, as workers specialize, they often increase their expertise and productivity and are able to develop work methods that are well suited to the tasks they perform. Special procedures and machinery often make it easier to train new workers in a specialty than in a generalized job. Nev-

Specialization helps define the parts.

Two basic problems
of organizations

Specialization
Coordination

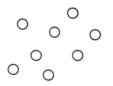

Specialization

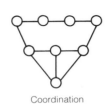

Coordination

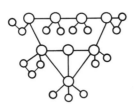

Increased specialization . . .

increases need
for coordination

Types of departmentation:

- Function
- Product
- Geography
- Client
- Persons
- Time

ertheless, as will be shown later, over-specialization can be detrimental to both the individual worker and the overall productivity of the organization.

In this chapter specialization will be viewed in the context of larger units, or groups rather than at the level of the single worker.

HORIZONTAL SPECIALIZATION

Clustering, assigning, and grouping of work activities have been discussed for many years.[4] When performed throughout an organization, this type of specialization is called departmentation. **Departmentation** is the establishment of a distinct area, unit, or subsystem of an organization over which a manager has authority for the performance of specified activities and results.

As Figure 9.2 shows, there are many **types of departmentation,** particularly function, product, geography, client, persons, and time. Most organizations use a combination of approaches to departmentation, shifting from one to another as necessary. Each approach has its advantages and disadvantages.

Basic Types of Departmentation *Functional departmentation,* one of the most common types of departmentation, is grouping activities according to similar work, skills, knowledge, and technology. This approach is particularly appropriate in manufacturing organizations, where it has two important advantages. It makes certain that the interests of vital departments such as manufacturing, marketing, and finance are represented to top management, and it minimizes costly duplications of expensive equipment. For example, having a centralized X-ray department in a hospital is more effective than having X-ray machines scattered throughout.

Disadvantages of the functional approach are overspecialization and the development of narrow viewpoints. The same problem will be perceived by marketing people as a marketing problem and by manufacturing people as a manufacturing problem.

Product departmentation is the grouping of activities around a particular product or product line. Each department is relatively self-contained, with its own manufacturing, purchasing, accounting, personnel, and sales units. The advantages of this approach are that it allows more attention to be given to each product line, it improves coordination of functional activities, and it places greater responsibility for profits and overall operations at the divisional level. Disadvantages are the strong possibility of duplication of effort and the obstacles posed to centralized management control. The trend in U.S. and European industry has been toward product departmentation, particularly for conglomerates, which have a number of very different product lines.

Geographical departmentation, the grouping of activities by territory or geographical location, is common among such diverse organizations

Type of department	Basic definition	Examples of organization chart
1. Function	Similar work activities	
2. Product	Product or service provided	
3. Geography	Location of production, sales, elementary schools	
4. Client	Client or customer needs	
5. Number of persons	Reduced span of management	
6. Time	Time that work is scheduled	

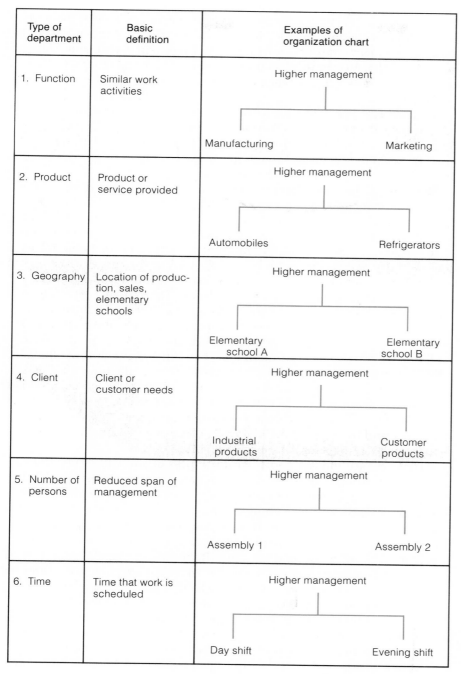

FIGURE 9.2 Basic forms of departmentation (specialization)

as schools and sales forces of every type. Elementary schools are usually established by neighborhood. McDonald's found that three-quarters of its customers came into the restaurants in conjunction with some other activity, so it began to build restaurants in areas of high customer activity—sometimes within blocks of each other in order to capitalize on different traffic patterns.

Geographical specialization is often reasonable for some parts of an organizational unit but not for that unit as a whole. For example, the overall finance function of an organization would probably suffer if split apart geographically, even though geographical separation of some accounting functions might be useful.

Departmentation by *client* means specialization according to the needs of customers or the paths by which customers are reached. This type of specialization is helpful if an organization has clients with markedly different needs. For example, a sales force may be divided into those calling on private individuals, those calling on commercial accounts, those calling on industrial accounts, and those calling on government agencies. This approach to departmentation is necessary for some types of organizations—for example, the federal government, which needs a Department of Labor, a Department of Agriculture, and so on in order to minister to the needs of diverse groups of people. Disadvantages are increased difficulty in coordination and the possibility of underutilization of specialized groups when times or conditions change.

Large organizations use all types of departmentation.

Departmentation by numbers of persons involves placing a number of persons doing essentially the same job under different supervisors. This form of specialization usually occurs within departments or units. For example, the U.S. Army is organized into squads, platoons, companies, and so on; and in large offices, clerks are often grouped into a number of sections with a supervisor for each section.

As the next section will show, most complex organizations use all or a number of these approaches to departmentation. The manager's task is to decide which approach is best, given a particular set of circumstances. For example, a company's manufacturing unit may be designed according to function, while its sales department is specialized by geographic area. Managers must understand the uniqueness of a particular organization's or unit's situation and structure its resources accordingly.

Organizations often change types of departmentation.

Structural change occurs frequently in many organizations. Large firms typically make major structural changes about every other year; and the larger the organization, the more it usually changes. During the last decade, nine out of ten of the largest U.S. organizations have made such changes, as did sixteen out of the next twenty-five largest. Management's reason for making such changes is to accommodate changing conditions inside and outside the organization and thus increase the organization's effectiveness.[5]

Examples of Departmentation Figure 9.3 shows examples of different types of departmentation in a large, hypothetical organization. The organization is involved in both industrial products (such as the manu-

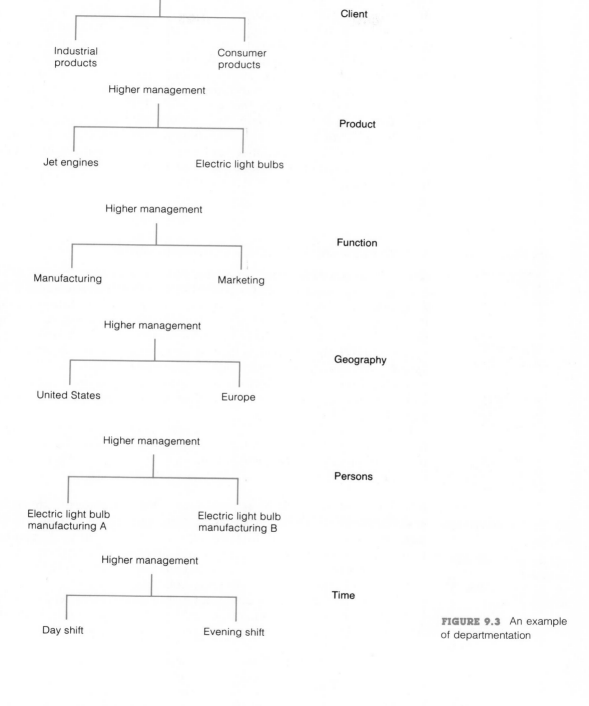

FIGURE 9.3 An example of departmentation

facture of jet engines) and consumer products (such as light bulbs). As a result, departmentation is by client and by product. In the electric bulb division there is further departmentation, this time by function—that is, manufacturing and marketing. And the marketing department is divided geographically, with different units for the United States and Europe.

Because electric light bulb manufacturing involves a number of similar machines and a relatively large number of people, departmentation at this level is by person, with a different supervisor for each of two groups of people doing essentially the same work. Differentiation is also by time, with both a day shift and a night shift, each requiring a manager.

Although Figure 9.3 is a simplification, it shows the types of specialization, or departmentation, that can be instituted at the discretion of the manager. The hypothetical organization shown could just as easily have been organized differently; the manager decides how to departmentalize.

Vertical coordination

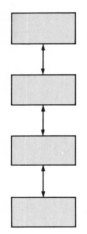

PRINCIPLES OF VERTICAL COORDINATION

Vertical coordination is the linking together for common action of superiors and subordinates and of units and subunits at different levels of the organization. After the organization has been specialized into subunits, it must be reunited or coordinated. Vertical coordination assumes that there is a hierarchy of objectives and a hierarchy of authority and responsibility. Higher-level objectives are broad; lower-level objectives are specific. Each subsystem should have objectives that are consistent with, and subordinate to, the objectives of the next higher administrative unit; and the higher the level, the more authority and responsibility the manager of the unit should have.

Given these hierarchies, vertical coordination is accomplished through the application of a number of basic principles. These principles include span of management, delegation, unity of command, and the scalar principle.[6]

Principles of vertical coordination:

- Span of management
- Delegation
- Unity of command
- Scalar principle

Authority, Power, and Responsibility   **Organizational authority** is the right to make decisions, to take action, and to use and expand resources. As will be shown, lines of authority link the different organizational units together. Unclear lines and delegation of authority are a major source of confusion and lack of coordination in an organization.

Power and authority are frequently confused. (Chapter 20 will thoroughly distinguish between different types of power.) One type of power is the ability to force others to do something; it does not imply authority. An airplane hijacker may have power but certainly does not have organizational authority.

Authority on the part of one person or unit in an organization cannot exist without acceptance on the part of others.[7] A supervisor's authority does not come into being until subordinates acknowledge that authority by taking the actions desired. The difference between power and authority is important, since "the power concept directs our attention to the dominating part in a relationship, whereas the concept of authority emphasizes the importance of the subordinate's acceptance."[8]

Responsibility is the obligation of subordinates to exercise authority delegated to them by their supervisors in a way that will attain the results expected. It is the accountability for attaining objectives, using resources, and following policies and procedures.

Span of Management One method of coordinating is to make a single manager responsible for coordinating the work of subordinates. If the work is simple and independently performed, the manager can successfully orchestrate the work of many subordinates. If the work is interdependent and complicated, a single manager can supervise only a few subordinates. However many subordinates are supervised by each manager, the result is the creation of organization levels.

The **span of management** is the number of subordinates supervised. (In much of the literature, it is called the span of control, but the span is one of management, not merely control, which is only one aspect of management.) As the number of subordinates increases *arithmetically,* the number of relationships between the manager and the subordinates increases *geometrically.* For example, if a manager has four subordinates, the theoretical number of relationships between the manager and subordinates is 44; eight subordinates means 1,080 potential relationships.

Theorists still debate about how many subordinates should report to a single manager. (A recent review of the literature revealed more than 255 articles or books on the subject.)[9] The evidence suggests that the proper span of management depends on many factors, among them:

1. *The manager's ability.* Some managers are more capable than others of supervising a large number of people.
2. *The nature of the work.* The more simple, routine, and repetitive the work, the greater the possible span of management.
3. *The degree of interdependence among units.* The more interdependent the units, the greater the need for coordination and the smaller the optimal span of management.
4. *The organization's efficiency.* The more efficient the organization and the greater the competence of its members, the larger the possible span.[10]

In sum, the span of management is best determined by the situation. If a manager appears harried, perhaps the span should be reduced. If the subordinates appear harried, perhaps the span is too small and the manager is too closely riding herd on them.

Delegation Because no manager, including the chief executive officer (CEO), can make all the decisions necessary for the functioning of an organization, especially the numerous day-to-day ones, it is necessary to delegate some decision-making authority to subordinates. The process

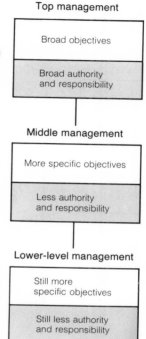

Factors determining span of management:

- Manager's ability
- Nature of work
- Degree of interdependence among units
- Organization's efficiency

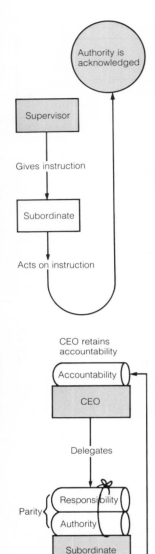

Authority is acknowledged

Supervisor

Gives instruction

Subordinate

Acts on instruction

CEO retains accountability

Accountability

CEO

Delegates

Parity {

Responsibility

Authority

Subordinate

Makes and implements decision

Consequences of decision

Principles of delegation:

• Parity
• Accountability

of **delegation** involves the assignment of tasks, the determination of expected results, and the granting of authority to accomplish the tasks. Two important principles of delegation are parity and accountability.

Parity means that a subordinate should receive sufficient authority to implement a decision along with the responsibility for the decision. Two classic propositions of management are that it is meaningless to delegate responsibility without authority, and it is dangerous to delegate authority without responsibility.

Accountability means that even though decision-making authority and responsibility can be delegated, the CEO remains ultimately accountable. In one respect, this means that while the responsibility for making decisions can be delegated, the responsibility for the consequences of the decisions cannot. As two respected management authors put it, "Likewise, *the responsibility of the subordinate to his superior for performance is absolute*, once he has accepted an assignment *and no superior can escape responsibility for the organization activities of his subordinate.*"[11]

From a closed-system point of view, these statements about delegation are correct. However, from an open-system point of view, such absolute distinctions are unsuitable. The concept that authority must be equal to responsibility is one of the most cherished ideas of the classical management theorists. However, the responsibility of a manager operating in a subsystem within the larger system is to get a particular job done. This effort requires ongoing negotiations with subsystems over which the manager has no formal authority. Therefore, the manager's effectiveness depends in part on skill in negotiation, compromise, and persuasion of others. Thus, while the accepted principles of delegation are generally valid, they cannot be uniformly applied to all situations at all times.[12]

But even knowing the principles and the situations in which they should be applied does not guarantee delegation will be successful. A few common reasons for potential failure are:

1. Too much work was dumped on the person at one time.
2. The individual was required to do too much too fast.
3. The individual did not fully understand what was required.
4. Performance expectations were unrealistic.
5. Contingencies were not provided for.
6. Overall performance expected from the subordinate was not explained.
7. Progress toward accomplishment of objectives was not monitored.
8. Unanticipated problems were not provided for.
9. In the past there were no adverse consequences for nonperformance.

Unity of Command The **unity of command** principle suggests that no organization member should report to more than one supervisor for any single function, as Figure 9.4 shows. The more complete and clear an individual's reporting relationship to a single boss is, the less chance of

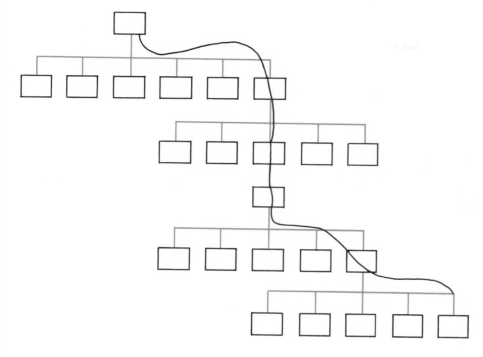

FIGURE 9.4 Unity of command and scalar principle

conflict in instructions and the greater the feeling of personal responsibility for results. However, as Chapter 1 pointed out, managers meet and are influenced by many other people, since most organizations consist of a number of subsystems interacting with each other. This classic principle of unity of command helps clarify the relationship between supervisors and subordinates—but only when it takes account of the many formal and informal relationships managers have with others. The seven managers at the Osage plant, for example, influenced each other; and this influence was considered in the action taken by their supervisor to clarify relationships all around.

The Scalar Principle The **scalar principle** states that authority and responsibility should flow in an unbroken line from the top to the bottom of the organization. The more clearly this line is manifested, the more coordination, responsible decision making, and organizational communication there will be. This principle is really an extension of the unity of command principle, as Figure 9.4 shows. It argues for a clearly defined hierarchy of authority in an organization. Again, the principle is helpful only as a general guideline. It does not take into consideration the idea that the organization's subsystems are interdependent and interrelated. Even those who originally proposed the principle recognized that for everything to go up and down the chain of command would be cumbersome. Nor does the principle allow for the formal and informal pressures from peers and other groups. Moreover, lines of authority and responsibility are seldom clear-cut and easily identifiable except in the smallest of operations.

PRINCIPLES OF HORIZONTAL COORDINATION

Horizontal coordination

Principles of horizontal coordination:

- Functional authority
- Line and staff relationships
- Centralization and decentralization
- Use of committees and task forces

Although the principles of vertical coordination (coordination from the top down) may be sufficient to govern small organizations, coordination across the organization is necessary as well for any organization that is too big for the top manager to have a basic understanding of all its functions. **Horizontal coordination** is the linking together of managers, units, and subunits across the organization for the purpose of common action. Organizational authority is involved in any type of formal coordination, but it is less evident in horizontal than in vertical coordination.

There are many different methods of horizontal coordination. Rules, procedures, budgets, and similar impersonal approaches will be discussed in the section on controlling, which is one form of horizontal coordination. Coordination through informal processes will be described in Chapter 16 on managing groups.

This section will first briefly describe functional authority, then outline several managerial approaches to horizontal coordination, including line and staff, decentralization, and task forces and committees. Chapter 10 will amplify some of these approaches and will elaborate on specialization and coordination in relation to the political, technological, and economic environment.

Functional Authority **Functional authority** is the authority to prescribe practices, procedures, policies, or other matters to units or groups not in the direct chain of command (as shown in Figure 9.4). The unity of command and scalar principles are manifested here, since such authority is delegated by higher-level management. For example, functional authority may be delegated to the personnel department to develop and prescribe the use of an application blank for all clerical applicants to any department in the organization. Also, although a line manager may have the organizational authority to employ an engineer, the personnel department may specify the beginning salary to be paid, so that wage and salary practices are coordinated across the organization. As another example, in order to maintain standardized accounting practices the controller may receive functional authority to prescribe how accounting records will be kept throughout a number of the organization's divisions.

Line and Staff Relationships In the formal organization, the term **line** describes the relationship in which a supervisor has the organizational authority—**line authority**—to direct a subordinate. Line authority is therefore a direct extension of the unity of command and scalar principles. The term **staff,** on the other hand, describes the relationship in which the staff is to serve and advise a line manager.

The distinction between line and staff frequently blurs.[13] Line functions typically are viewed as those directly responsible for attaining the organization's objectives; staff functions are seen as assisting the line functions. Thus departments such as manufacturing and sales are said to perform line functions, whereas departments such as purchasing, accounting, advertising, personnel, and quality control are said to perform staff functions. However, splitting up line and staff by departments is not accurate. When the purchasing department, for example, is classified as performing staff functions (since purchasing is considered secondary to production), it is cast in the advisory role, with the implication that it is less essential than line functions. But the purchase of materials, parts, and other items is just as necessary to an organization as manufacturing or other production operations. (Indeed, in some organizations, the advertising department's budget is larger than that of the production department.)

Line and staff functions are better distinguished from a systems viewpoint, in which they are defined as residing not in departments but in the relationships among departments. For example, according to the unity of command and scalar principles, the personnel manager is a line manager in functions regarding subordinates over whom the manager has organizational authority—that is, subordinate managers who answer to the personnel manager and who in turn have their own subordinates. But when the personnel manager advises the production manager, the personnel manager is performing staff functions. If, in turn, the production manager advises the personnel manager or the chief executive, this advice is also a staff function. These relationships are shown in Figure 9.5.

As previously indicated, units classified as performing staff functions are sometimes delegated functional authority. In addition, where functional authority has not been officially delegated, it is sometimes assumed. For example, an assistant to a chief executive may open a request with, "The president wants . . ." In one instance the president may have really authorized the request, but in another the authority may have been assumed by the assistant. The receiver of the request has no way of knowing which is the case. Consequently, the more clearly spelled out the functional authority is, the better.

Centralization and Decentralization   Organizational **centralization** and **decentralization** refer to the degree to which authority is retained at the top of the organization (centralization) or delegated to lower levels (decentralization). Figure 9.6 shows the distribution of authority and delegation in a relatively centralized organization versus a relatively decentralized organization. As the figure shows, the more the scope of authority is spread throughout the organization, the more decentralized the organization is.

A move toward decentralization is often wise for a large company. U.S. Steel improved its profits by decentralizing one area of its business in 1974. Two operating divisions and five sales divisions were converted

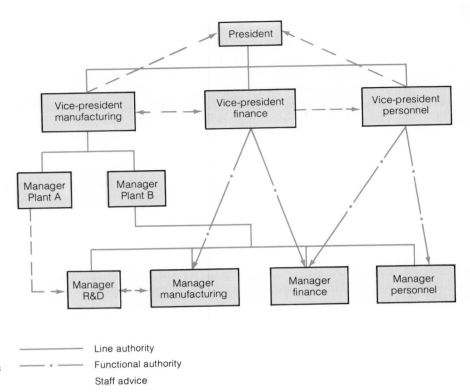

FIGURE 9.5 Line versus functional authority

— Line authority
—·— Functional authority
Staff advice

into five almost autonomous profit centers. The changed structure, bringing authority and power into divisions that formerly had no profit responsibility, was successful.[14]

Determining the appropriate level of decentralization can be difficult, however. The more decentralized an organization is, the more prone it is to duplication of effort; consequently, excellent coordination is needed among the decision makers. Some organizations decentralize too far and have to reorganize in order to achieve adequate coordination. The F. W. Woolworth Company, for example, found that consolidating and centralizing its extremely decentralized purchasing, distribution, and merchandising operations resulted in greater efficiency and reduced cost.[15]

FIGURE 9.6 High centralization versus high decentralization

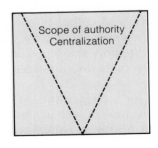

Board of directors
Top management
Middle management
First-level employees
Employees

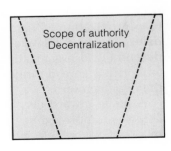

On the Job

CENTRALIZATION AND DECENTRALIZATION AT ITS BEST

What bothered me was that there was no means to make the changes in our business philosophy and the response to our publics which I felt were paramount to the long-term health and growth of the corporation. In theory, the GM system of business management featured two functions: centralized policymaking and control, and decentralized operations. The latter meant that the operating decisions for the day-to-day running of the business were made at the divisional level. It was here that you smelled the clay in the styling studios; ran the plants where engines were built, body panels stamped out and cars and trucks assembled; created the advertising campaigns; worked with the dealers and managed all of the physical aspects which took a product from design to production to retail sale.

To coordinate all the company's many and varied divisions and operations, and to direct them toward the overall good of the corporation, general policy guidelines and controls were formulated and administered within which the divisions ran their own businesses. This policy and control function was the responsibility of corporate management, and exercised through a series of committees composed generally of men who had made their marks in the divisions. Once "upstairs" on The Fourteenth Floor, the men who sat on these committees were supposed to draw upon their operating experience to plan the growth of the business and control the company. The success of General Motors in the past had come from a finely tuned balance between this centralized control and the decentralized operations.

Source: J. Patrick Wright, *On a Clear Day You Can See General Motors* (New York: Avon Books, 1980), p. 7.

Chapter 10 will discuss the factors that determine the right degree of decentralization for an organization.

Use of Committees and Task Forces The use of committees, task forces, and similar groups will be discussed more thoroughly in Chapters 10 and 16. This chapter will demonstrate that such approaches are widely and successfully used for coordinating the units or subunits of an organization.[16]

Task forces can be critical to organizations such as General Motors.

One reason such groups are effective is that most problems require more judgment, knowledge, and experience than is possessed by one person. Another is that a committee provides viewpoints from several different organizational units. The usefulness of committees for coordinating organizational activities is generally acclaimed. In one study about 90 percent of the respondents felt that committees promote coordination among departments.[17] In another study the use of a special task force composed of representatives from several different organizational units was able to increase the quality of manufactured products by more than 60 percent, which resulted in a considerable saving to the organization.[18]

On the Job

TASK FORCES AT WORK

. . . GM has found . . . ways to bring in fresh ideas and visions. Over the years it has hired several new vice presidents from outside—Fuller was one—to take charge of areas where new thinking was clearly needed. And in the early Seventies, it set up a series of new links with the outside world, including the public-policy and science-advisory committees, and the environmental-activities and industry-government relations staffs. It also created a strategic-planning department to develop models of the future.

Consultations with Outsiders

Run by the best people GM could attract, the staffs and committees opened the company's eyes as never before to the outside world, and GM's managers took their recommendations seriously. Former Chairman Richard C. Gerstenberg cites a striking example of the committees' effectiveness. At one of its earliest meetings in 1970, the public-policy committee, which consists of GM's outside directors, met with a group of researchers at the technical center to discuss issues of auto safety and air pollution. Afterward, the research

staff concluded that it needed to consult with some outside scientists to broaden its knowledge. The people it subsequently got, including Charles H. Townes, a Nobel Prize-winning physicist at the University of California, and Lee A. DuBridge, past president of Caltech, eventually became members of the science-advisory committee. On their recommendation, Gerstenberg notes, GM drastically increased its research spending. Today the research staff is 2½ times bigger than in 1971, and engages in an immense variety of basic as well as applied research projects . . .

Source: Excerpted from Charles R. Burck, "How GM Stays Ahead," *Fortune,* March 9, 1981, p. 54. Reprinted by permission *Fortune* Magazine.

THE DYNAMICS OF SPECIALIZATION AND COORDINATION

To understand more clearly the dynamics of specialization and coordination, we will examine the job of a first-level (operations) supervisor in a modern mass production organization. The supervisor is in charge of manufacturing parts for the fuel control system of a jet engine and of managing workers and activities at the operations level.[19]

The first-line supervisor interacts with:

- The boss
- The union
- Specialists
- Workers
- Peers

The supervisor's job is a specialized one, but it also requires interaction and coordination with a wide variety of people, including (1) the boss to whom the supervisor formally reports, (2) a wide variety of specialists, (3) other first-line supervisors to which the individual's department relates, (4) the workers themselves (about sixty of them), and (5) the shop steward and other union members in a union-organized plant. All these people and groups have certain expectations about the supervisor, and the supervisor has certain expectations about them. Studies show that supervisors in similar jobs have an average of 457 interpersonal contacts during each eight-hour day, although most of these contacts last for only one or two minutes.[20] Figure 9.7 gives an idea of the network of relationships, although the diagram is simplified.

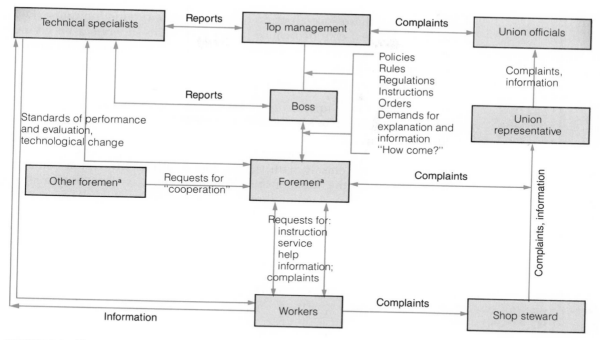

FIGURE 9.7 The many forces affecting the foreman

[a]The word *foremen* is used here because it is the word used in the original source. It corresponds to the term *first-level supervisors* used elsewhere in the text.

Source: Reprinted by permission of the publishers from *Man-in-Organization: Essays of F. J. Roethlisberger* (Cambridge, Mass.: Belknap Press of Harvard University Press, 1968), p. 327. First published in Fritz J. Roethlisberger, "The Foreman: Master and Victim of Double-talk," *Harvard Business Review* 13 (Spring 1945): 286. Copyright © 1945, 1968 by the President and Fellows of Harvard College.

The Boss   The relationship with the boss is part of the line of organizational authority that runs directly to top management. It involves both specialization and coordination. The first-level supervisor receives specific orders, approval, recognition, pay increases, and possible promotions through the immediate supervisor.

Technical Specialists   The first-level supervisor is in contact with a wide variety of specialists—inspectors, design engineers, production control schedulers, efficiency and standards specialists, personnel representatives, methods and repair people, and methods engineers, for example.

Many of these specialists exercise functional authority over the first-level supervisor by originating the standards of performance for the unit. These standards, to which all workers in the unit must conform, are often set by the specialists without consultation with the supervisor. For example, the supervisor must adhere to a budget established by the accountants, a production schedule established by production control, and quality standards established by the quality control unit.

Although these specialists do help coordinate production units, they (or their bosses) can also cause problems for the supervisor by giving information directly to higher levels of management without also informing the supervisor.

Other First-Level Supervisors   The term *foreman* in Figure 9.7 corresponds to the term *first-level supervisor* or *supervisor* used elsewhere in this text. As suggested by the figure, because an organization is a complex, interrelated set of subsystems, the supervisor of one department must work very closely with supervisors of other units. Such contacts help coordinate the work of the different units. They can be formal or informal, one-on-one or conducted in committee meetings. They are essential to the supervisor's job. An assembly line supervisor cannot wait until the time of assembly to find out if the proper parts have been manufactured elsewhere in the plant or if parts have been purchased as scheduled. Many lateral relations, seldom formally defined, provide this kind of information at the time that it is needed. Their effective functioning depends on good relationships among supervisors.

Workers   The first-level supervisor must translate into action the expectations of various groups in the organization. Policies, rules, standards, and regulations originated by these groups must be upheld by the workers subordinate to the supervisor. Since most people do not like to conform to rules they have not contributed to forming, the supervisor's task of obtaining the workers' whole-hearted cooperation is difficult.

The Union   The role of the supervisor is further complicated in a unionized plant. The union contract is usually signed by a top-management negotiating team and contains a comprehensive set of rules, procedures, and policies mandating how the supervisor deals with the unionized workers. As Figure 9.7 shows, union officials, including the shop steward, are entitled to make many demands on the supervisor.

The process of dealing with these varied expectations from different sources requires that the supervisor constantly organize and reorganize in order to fine-tune the unit's responsiveness. Reorganizing includes shifting employee assignments to accommodate new methods or comply with union seniority rules. It may even entail retraining workers for new assignments and expanding or narrowing the span of management of group leaders. Other adjustments may involve borrowing materials from other units during a time of shortage or taking corrective action when the manufactured parts are not up to standards set by quality control experts (which may occur when a design is changed by design engineers). Thus the first-level supervisor constantly reorganizes the unit on the basis of ever-changing information from a variety of sources.

The first-line supervisor must be:

- A good boss
- A good worker

ORGANIZATION CHARTS AND MANUALS

A model is a representation of reality. An **organization chart** is a graphic model of a formal organization and has two basic purposes: it shows who is accountable to whom (the scalar principle); and it shows, in abbreviated form, who does what in the organization. For example, the organization chart for the Osage plant (Figure 9.1) reveals that six managers report to the plant manager, and it shows what each is responsible for—one for manufacturing, another for marketing, and so on. It also shows that the plant manager is accountable for the operation of the entire plant and is responsible to a division manager.

Several conventions are used in preparing organization charts:

1. The individual positions on the chart are usually represented by a rectangle, although a circle or triangle is sometimes used. Committees or several executives in the same position occupy one rectangle.
2. The vertical arrangement of the rectangles usually shows relative positions in the organization's hierarchy. The most powerful position is normally at the top of the organization chart. (Some organization charts are circular or read from left to right, with the power emanating from the left.)
3. Direct organizational relationships are shown by solid lines between positions; they indicate who reports to whom.
4. Functional or advisory authority is usually shown by dotted or broken lines.
5. Lines of authority usually enter at the top center of the rectangle and leave at the bottom center; they do not run through the box. An exception is the staff assistant or "assistant to" position, which may enter the side of the rectangle (see Figure 9.1).

The organization chart shows formal work relationships among managers and others, can help orient new members, and can identify what changes have occurred in the organization and where. In this sense an organization chart serves as a method of communication.

The *organization manual* goes even further as a model of the organization. Through its job descriptions, it shows the duties performed (thereby defining the scope and limits of the various jobs), the extent of authority held by individual managers, and the relationships among positions.

There are a number of disadvantages to both organization charts and manuals, chief of which is their expense to develop and maintain. More importantly from a systems point of view, neither organization charts nor manuals can represent the dynamic, ongoing process of interaction among the organization's different subsystems with a dependable degree of accuracy. In the Osage plant case a great deal of misunderstanding existed about duties and responsibilities despite detailed position descriptions, organization charts, manuals, and formal objectives.

One reason organization charts and manuals can be misleading is that they show only the formal organization, not the informal organization

Organization charts are maps of the organization.

Charts, like maps, are not always correct or always used.

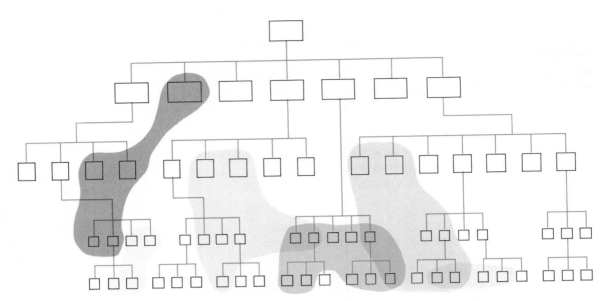

FIGURE 9.8 The formal and informal organization

that evolves spontaneously from the ways in which employees at all levels interact and work with each other.[21] These informal connections help satisfy people's needs for relatedness, security, friendship, and growth. They do not have official rules or formal work managers. Indeed, sometimes they work against the organization. There are many well-documented cases of output restriction and other negative actions taken by informal organizations.

Figure 9.8 is a hypothetical organization chart. The solid lines represent lines of authority, and the rectangles show who reports to whom. The shaded areas indicate patterns of interaction not prescribed by the formal organization that cut across formal organizational lines. Everyone knows of examples. The student whose friend works in the registrar's office may get information about grades long before the official grade notification is sent out. The person who knows the mechanic at the local service station or garage receives faster and better service than the one who does not. (Informal organizations will be discussed more thoroughly in Chapter 16.)

SUMMARY

In order to accomplish their objectives, organizations have to achieve the proper degree of specialization and coordination. Both can present problems. Specialization, or division of work, is usually accomplished through departmentation. For example, organizations can be specialized according to function, product, client, geographical area, number of persons, and time. With specialization comes the need for coordination. All other things being equal, the greater the degree of specialization, the greater the need for coordination or integration.

Different methods of coordination are required for different types of departmentation. Vertical coordination is based on the hierarchy of authority and concerns span of management, delegation, and unity of command. Horizontal coordination is based on the pattern of functional authority and concerns line and staff relationships, centralization and decentralization, and the use of committees and task forces.

The dynamics of organizing are ongoing and constantly changing. In a specialized job at the bottom of the management hierarchy, a supervisor must coordinate the requests and expectations of a variety of individuals and groups.

The principles discussed in this chapter have emerged from observations of similarities among organizations throughout a number of years. Because every organization has its unique aspects, none illustrates these principles perfectly. Nevertheless, in a general sense they explain the workings of most organizations. The principle of unity of command, for example, does express the usual relationship between supervisor and subordinate, even though it does not take into consideration group dynamics, the power of the informal organization, and the many relationships the manager has with others (as shown in Figure 9.7).

STUDY QUESTIONS

1. What are two basic tasks of organizations that are potential problem areas?
2. List and give examples of six methods of horizontal specialization.
3. How does authority differ from power?
4. What does *span of management* mean? What factors should be considered in establishing the span of management?
5. Give an example of each of the basic principles of coordination (not using any of the examples in the text).
6. What distinguishes line and staff functions? What is the purpose of each of these types of functions?
7. What difficulties might arise if unity of command and the scalar principle were used as absolutes?
8. Can an organization exist without structure? Explain.
9. In what ways is an organization chart helpful? In what ways is it misleading?

Case for Discussion

THE CASE OF DALTON'S DILEMMA

Dalton Manufacturing Company produces widgets. These widgets require four processes before they are ready to ship to wholesale outlets for distribution. They must be formed, painted, tested, and boxed. In the past, employees have performed all four processes themselves, each employee being responsible for the forming, painting, testing, and boxing of a certain number of widgets a day.

Employees receive incentive pay for each widget they ship in excess of the standard.

The general manager of the company, Ann Wyatt, has suggested that many more widgets could be produced if the work were specialized. Some employees could form the widgets, others paint them, others test them, and others box them for shipment. Wyatt has pointed out that when each employee performs all the processes, there is a good deal of time lost in going from one process to the other.

The president of the company thinks Wyatt's suggestion has merit but wonders whether the employees will object strongly to such a major change. Naturally, a new incentive program would be devised so that no employee would receive less money than before. Still, the president hesitates to implement the change.

1. What would be your recommendation to the president?
2. If the specialization plan were adopted, what employee reactions would you anticipate and how would you handle them?
3. If you were convinced that employee reactions would be very negative, would you adopt the changes anyway?
4. How much influence should employees' preferences have on decisions involving technological progress?
5. What are the societal implications of this case?

FOR YOUR CAREER

1. In general, the greater the division of labor, the greater will be the need for coordination.
2. In general, the greater the interdependence of the subunits, the greater will be the need for coordination.
3. Organizational structure has a strong impact on human behavior. Many so-called personality conflicts really are problems of organizational structure.
4. Organizing is not a one-time process but is constant, sometimes requiring major restructuring and other times requiring fine-tuning.
5. Principles of organizational structure are only guides for understanding the dynamics of the organization, not absolute rules to be followed. The effective manager constantly attempts to improve the organizational process.
6. The informal organization may have more influence on behavior than the formal one. The good manager keeps informed of its workings.
7. Frequently, more gets done through the informal organization than through the formal one. The good manager builds a network of contacts throughout the organization so as to work within the informal organization when necessary.

FOOTNOTES

1. H. Koontz, "The Management Theory Jungle," *Journal of the Academy of Management* 4 (December 1961): 174–188.
2. H. Koontz, "Commentary on the Management Theory Jungle—Nearly Two Decades Later," *Management: A Book of Readings,* 5th ed., ed. H. Koontz, C. O'Donnell, and H. Weinrich (New York: McGraw-Hill, 1980), pp. 18–26.
3. J. Slocum, Jr., and D. Hellriegel, "Using Organizational Design to Cope with Change," *Business Horizons* 22 (December 1979): 66.
4. H. Fayol, *General and Industrial Management* (New York: Pitman Publishing, 1949); L. Gulick and L. Urwick, eds., *Papers on the Science of Administration* (New York: Institute of Public Administration, 1937); Max Weber and Talcott Parsons, eds., *The Theory of Social and Economic Organization,* trans. A. Henderson and T. Parsons (New York: Oxford University Press, 1947); and E. Holdaway, "Dimensions of Organizations in Complex Societies: The Educational Sector," *Administrative Science Quarterly* 20 (March 1975): 37–58.

5. D. Ronald, "Reorganizing for Results," *Harvard Business Review* 44 (November–December 1966): 96–104.

6. L. Urwick, ed., *The Golden Book of Management: A Historical Record of the Life and Work of Seventy Pioneers* (London: N. Neame, 1946); J. Mooney and A. Reiley, *Onward Industry* (New York: Harper & Bros., 1931); L. Urwick, *The Theory of Organization* (New York: American Management Association, 1952); V. Graicunus, "Relationship in Organizations," in *Papers on the Science of Administration,* ed. L. Urwick and L. Gulick (New York: Institute of Public Administration, 1937); L. Urwick, "The Manager's Span of Control," *Harvard Business Review* 34 (May–June 1956): 39–47; and W. Suojanen, "The Span of Control—Fact or Fable," *Advanced Management* 20 (November 1955): 5–13.

7. C. Bernard, *The Functions of the Executive* (Cambridge, Mass.: Harvard University Press, 1950).

8. B. Abrahamsson, *Bureaucracy or Participation* (Beverly Hills, Calif.: Sage Publications, 1977), p. 163.

9. D. Van Fleet and A. Bedeian, "A History of the Span of Management," *Academy of Management Review* 3 (July 1977): 356–372.

10. R. Carzo, Jr., and J. Yancuzas, "Effects of Flat and Tall Organization Structure," *Administrative Science Quarterly* 14 (June 1969): 178–191; G. Fisch, "Stretching the Span of Management," *Harvard Business Review* 41 (September–October 1963): 74–84; and G. Bell, "Determinants of Span of Control," *American Journal of Sociology* 73 (July 1967): 100–109.

11. H. Koontz and C. O'Donnell, *Essentials of Management* (New York: McGraw-Hill, 1974), p. 202.

12. E. Huse and J. Bowditch, *Behavior in Organizations: A Systems Approach to Managing,* rev. ed. (Reading, Mass.: Addison-Wesley, 1977).

13. G. Fisch, "Line/Staff Is Obsolete," *Harvard Business Review* 39 (September–October 1961): 79–81.

14. "A Steelman Steps Up the Pace at U.S. Steel," *Business Week,* March 9, 1974, pp. 154–155.

15. "The Problems That Are Upsetting Woolworth's," *Business Week,* June 29, 1974, p. 73.

16. J. Presley and S. Keen, "Better Meetings Lead to Higher Productivity: A Case Study," *Management Review* 64 (April 1975): 16–22; R. Tillman, Jr., "Committees on Trial," *Harvard Business Review* 38 (May–June 1960): 6–16.

17. Tillman, "Committees on Trial."

18. E. Huse, "The Behavioral Scientist in the Shop," *Personnel* 42 (May–June 1965): 50–57.

19. Although the job is an actual one, many of the concepts are based on a classic article by F. J. Roethlisberger, "The Foreman: Master and Victim of Double-Talk." The article was first published in the *Harvard Business Review* in the Spring issue of 1945 (Vol. 13, pp. 283–298) and then republished twenty years later as a classic in the September–October 1965 issue (Vol. 43, pp. 22–52). The article itself is well worth reading for its illustration of the complexity of organizations and of managerial jobs, even at the first level of supervision.

20. O. Ponder, "Supervisory Practices of Effective and Ineffective Foremen" (Ph.D. diss., Columbia University, 1968).

21. E. Bakke, *Bonds of the Organization* (New York: Harper & Bros., 1957); D. Katz, "The Motivational Basis of Organizational Behavior," *Behavioral Sciences* 9 (April 1964): 130–145; F. Jasinski, "Adapting Organizations to New Technology," *Harvard Business Review* 37 (January–February 1959): 79–86; K. Davis, *Human Relations at Work* (New York: McGraw-Hill, 1962), p. 236; and R. Van Zelst, "Sociometrically Selected Work Teams Increase Production," *Personnel Psychology* 5 (Autumn 1952): 175–185.

Organizing Effectively CHAPTER 10

CONTENTS

THE REORGANIZATION OF ELECTRONIC PRODUCTS

The electronic products division of Alpha Corporation, a large multinational company, was organized along functional lines. It included research, product development, manufacturing, marketing, sales (organized on a geographic basis), finance, and personnel departments. The division manufactured a variety of electronic instruments and components.

Because the division had experienced turbulent business conditions and poor performance for three years, its general manager called in a consultant from the home office to discuss what he saw as a problem in intergroup relations. The manager believed that there were many conflicts among the various functional groups in the division and that these conflicts were severely hampering the division's product development efforts, which required cooperation and coordination among all the functional groups.

The consultant suggested an analysis and examination to see if the poor relationships were a problem or a symptom. The consultant observed divisional meetings, looking at both content and process. He interviewed about forty managers, supervisors, and key individuals, and he gave each of them a questionnaire to complete. The problem soon became clear. The consultant found that the division was highly specialized and that the managers and others were highly motivated but that the overall design of the division needed to be improved. The primary coordination (integration) was through the division manager, who held frequent meetings with his top staff and others to discuss and coordinate all product development activities in the division. This was not sufficient, however, Poor intergroup relations were symptoms: poor organizational design was a cause.

At the suggestion of the consultant, the areas of the division that were concerned with new product development were reorganized into product teams (one for each new product) to bring about better coordination. Members of the teams were selected on the basis of the clarity and certainty of the function involved. For example, the less-known and less-certain functions of research and development were generally represented by a scientist or a development engineer. Well-established and well-known functions such as finance and manufacturing were represented by individuals at higher levels in the organization, such as the plant controller or production superintendent. Coordination of each team was the responsibility of a market development representative. The consultant trained the coordinators and served as a process observer at meetings of the project teams.

Thus the coordination was now being performed not only through the management hierarchy but also through project teams led by representatives of market development. Each of the project teams was phased out when the particular new product was developed. The initial diagnosis period lasted approximately six months. The program to change the organizational structure took approximately a year.

Follow-up studies were done eighteen months and two years after the project began. In the year after the program was implemented, nine complex products were introduced; this compared to a total of five new products in the previous five years. Intergroup friction dramatically declined, morale increased, and profits rose. The revised design resulted in better performance, greater commitment to the decisions made, and more professional and interpersonal competence. As a result of the success of the project, nineteen project teams were established in five major divisions of the corporation.[1]

This opening case raises several key questions which you should be able to answer after reading this chapter. The questions include:

1. How can departments in an organization such as Alpha Corporation be coordinated?
2. Should a secondary school system in Great Falls, Montana, be organized the same way as one in Chicago or New York City? Explain.
3. When are project teams, like those in Alpha, most effective? How can an organization decide if it should use project teams?
4. Is it ever advisable for one person to work for two bosses? Explain.

10

The essence of designing organizations is determining the appropriate structure and strategy.

Often, the more appropriate the structure, the more effective the organization.

The electronic products division of Alpha Corporation is discussed here for two main reasons. First, its story shows that organizational design is a powerful influence on the behavior of individuals and groups. As the organizational design changed for the better, so also did the employees' behavior.

Second, this case is a reminder that organizational structure is the result of human thought. Organizations are designed by managers and are therefore changeable (although frequently they are not regarded that way).

Organizational design is a matter of managerial choice. Intelligent choices, however, require knowledge of alternative structures.[2] Given this knowledge, the manager can select the system or subsystem design that best fits organizational strategy and managerial values. Therefore, this chapter will examine a number of alternative structures.

While Chapter 9 discussed organizational design from a relatively closed-system approach and provided some basic principles of organizing, this chapter views organizational structure and design from a more open-system approach. Many factors influence design; some of the more important are size, operations technology, and environment. This chapter offers a brief historical background and then examines the factors influencing structure. It concludes with suggestions for organizational design at the top, middle, and lower management levels.

EVOLUTION OF ORGANIZATIONAL STRUCTURE

Compared with today, large organizations before World War II were less complex, producing a relatively few number of products. Appropriately, most of them were functionally organized. With the postwar economic boom came increasing organizational complexity, caused in part by a proliferation of product lines. The functional approach was inadequate for maintaining managerial direction and control in the midst of this complexity, and many organizations changed from functional to product-based structures during the late 1950s and early 1960s. Restructuring according to product lines usually followed the pattern set by General Motors and DuPont, in which product divisions were established with division managers accountable for the operations of each. For most organizations, the reorganization was successful.

In the mid 1960s conditions changed again. Capital investment projects became longer-range, more elaborate and expensive, and needing longer-range planning. Division managers could not make such major decisions involving the organization's limited resources independently. A partial recentralization of corporate decision making was required. The result was that neither staff (planning) nor line (division management) could be held clearly responsible for medium- and long-range performance.

In the 1970s, new problems that further threatened the autonomy of product divisions arose. Many organizations were now international in scope, and requirements imposed by foreign governments made it more difficult for U.S. organizations to maintain the integrity of divisional structure on a worldwide basis. Moreover, on the domestic scene, greater centralization was called for to meet a variety of government regulations, including equal opportunity and affirmative action, safety, and environmental requirements. For example, the mileage and emissions standards imposed on the automobile companies severely reduced divisional autonomy. In addition, more rapid changes in products and accelerated product line obsolescence meant that the home office had to involve itself more in engineering and manufacturing issues.

Through the 1970s and early 1980s the pace of change continued to be rapid, partly because of political (local and international), technological, scientific, racial, and moral factors in the environment. Social responsibility involvement increased; for example, organizations were expected to improve the quality of work life for employees. Such increased demands deepened the complexity of organizational structure, leading, in part, to the management theory jungle described in Chapter 9.[3]

Meanwhile, as the next section will show, research on organizational structure was increasing geometrically. As a result, although the basic principles described in Chapter 9 were still applicable, managers were also establishing various new types of organizational structure, including matrix organizations (described later in this chapter). The problems were becoming more complex and the answers less clear.

RECENT FINDINGS ON EFFECTIVE ORGANIZING

As organizations have become more complex, so also have studies on organizational design. This section briefly reviews some recent findings on organizational efficiency and effectiveness that are relevant to the basic principles described in the last chapter. These findings support what practicing managers have intuitively known—that no single organizational structure is best for all organizations in all situations. Rather, the most appropriate structure for a given organization or unit depends both on the objectives of the organization and on factors such as size, technology, rate of change in the environment, and types of interdependence within the organization.[4]

Factors influencing organizational structure:

- Organizational objectives
- Size
- Operations technology
- Environment
- Types of interdependence within organization

Size and Structure The **size** of an organization usually is measured by the number of people working for the organization in a single location. Although the classification is arbitrary, small organizations usually have from 1 to 250 employees, medium-sized organizations have 250 to 1,000, and large organizations have more than 1,000. There are other ways to measure size—revenue, sales, assets, and so on—but the relationships among these measures are usually highly correlated with each other.

Categorizing size (small, medium, or large) is difficult, since it is relative. An accounting firm with 4,000 to 5,000 employees worldwide is indeed large. Another type of organization with that number of employees might not be considered large. McDonald's is a large corporation even though it has only a few people at any single location. In contrast, the General Electric plant in Cincinnati, Ohio, has thousands of employees in a single location.

Size profoundly affects structure. Usually, as size increases, the organization tends to become more formal and complex—to have more rules and more formal positions, ranks, subunits, and sections within subunits. And as departmentation (structural differentiation) increases, the administrative staff and the administrative hierarchy also increase.

In general, the larger the number of people, the less easy it is to relate informally. Therefore, the greater the size of the unit, the greater the need for formal procedures to deal with employee interrelationships and the flow of communications. As the number of employees increases, more formal approaches to control are necessary, including written rules, job descriptions, and increasing levels of hierarchy.[5]

C. Northcote Parkinson has developed what is known as Parkinson's Law. In his book of that name, he suggests that every unit tends to build up its importance by expanding the number of its employees. Parkinson's Law states that the number of people in a given department has no relationship to the amount of work that must be done. In order to improve their own status, managers are motivated to endlessly expand their own staffs. However, this grand strategy is seldom revealed because the additional employees make work for one another through the division of labor. According to Parkinson, "An official wants to multiply subordinates, not rivals."[6]

Size has probably been studied more intensively than any other factor that influences the structure of an organization. Its effect on organizational effectiveness and efficiency, is not as easily studied, perhaps because it cannot be separated from the effects of other powerful factors, including technology and environment.

Operations Technology and Structure Most studies on technology have focused on **operations technology,** which includes the tools, mechanical equipment, actions, knowledge, or material used in the production or distribution of a good or service. All organizations have some kind of operations technology.

The term includes managerial and nonmanagerial knowledge or experience, a range of equipment from simple to complex, widely varying production techniques, and a variety of materials. An individual weaving a rug on a hand loom is using relatively simple technology, while an operator in the control room of an automated refinery is using complex, sophisticated technology. Both are involved in operations technology.

Early studies of the effect of technology on organizational structure were done by several management researchers, including sociologist Joan Woodward and her associates.[7] Woodward developed a scale for measuring technological complexity and found that differences in complexity accounted for differences in organizational structure.

Definition of operations technology:

Tools, mechanical equipment, actions, knowledge, or material used in the production of a good or service

She placed organizations into three major production categories: unit and small batch, large batch and mass production, and continuous process. The major distinction among these three operations was the extent to which the processes for manufacturing the product were standardized and automatic. She found that unit and small batch organizations were the least standardized and that continuous process organizations were the most automatic and thus the most technologically complex—as Figure 10.1 shows.

Woodward's scale is still relevant. Unit and small batch organizations are primarily involved in made-to-order items, such as custom clothing, custom furniture, and specialized electronic equipment. Their technology requires workers who are expert in a given craft or skilled in using various simple tools. Large batch and mass production organizations include automobile companies, mass-produced clothing manufacturers, large bakeries, and industrial equipment manufacturers. Such organizations usually have highly mechanized production processes. In an automobile plant, for instance, one or more cars a minute may go past the assembly line worker. The work requires machine operators who are trained to perform very few operations. Automated, or continuous process, production calls for the worker to monitor an automatic ongoing process, such as a production process in an oil refinery or a pharmaceutical or chemical plant. At an oil refinery the product flows continuously, regulated by a set of automatic operations. Process production does not require craft workers or assembly line workers. Instead it requires technicians—workers trained to monitor operations and make adjustments as necessary.

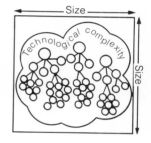

Ratio of managers and supervisors to total personnel increases as technological complexity increases. Size may not.

Although organizational design in each of these categories varied a great deal, the design of organizations with above average commercial success tended to conform to elements typical for a particular category. Thus Woodward concluded not only that technology does affect structure but that within each production category, it is a key to the best organizational design. Therefore, organizational success is related to appropriate structure, which in turn is related to the technology used. For example, Woodward found that the ratio of managers and supervisors to total employees and the number of levels in an organization increased as the technological complexity increased but that there was no significant relationship between size and technological complexity. This pioneering study firmly established the importance of technology's influence on organizational design.[8]

Recent years have brought more knowledge about the relationships between technology and organizational structure, and the effective man-

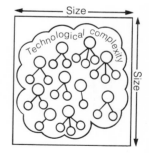

Unit (craft)	Mass (mechanized)	Process (automated)
Craft workers	Machine operators, assembly line workers	Technicians, monitors

FIGURE 10.1 Increasing technological complexity

ager can experiment with different designs based on this knowledge. Among the relationships are:

1. The more routine and well-known the technology, the greater the formalization and bureaucratization of the organization. Conversely, the more uncertain and complex the technology, the less rigid the rules and regulations.
2. Technology has a greater effect on relatively small, production oriented units than on upper levels of organizations and on units normally considered staff function units.
3. Most firms have several different technologies, and these affect the structure of the different subunits.
4. In considering the effect of technology, it is useful to distinguish among at least three levels of organization—the individual, the subunit, and the organization as a whole.

These recommendations may not seem particularly helpful at this point, but they will be amplified later in the chapter—after more of the structural aspects of organizations are explained.

Environment and Structure   Organizations depend on exchange with the outside environment. Their units must deal with both external and internal environments. This section will examine the effect of environmental certainty or uncertainty on organizational structure, as shown in Figure 10.2.

Environmental variability, which has gained attention as a factor contributing to uncertainty for organizational decision makers, refers to the degree of change faced by an organization or its units.[9] It includes at least three factors: (1) the frequency of changes in the relevant environment, (2) the degree of difference involved in each change, and (3) the degree of predictability in the overall pattern of change.

Organizations making matches, bottles, cans, manhole covers, and toothpicks experience relatively little change. Their customers and competitors are fairly well known, and there is little technological innova-

FIGURE 10.2 A continuum from certain to highly uncertain environment

Stable, certain environment	Highly unstable, uncertain environment
Few changes in products and services	Frequent changes in products and services
Known and stable competitors and customers	Changing or new competitors
Little technological innovation	High degree of technological innovation
Formalized and centralized structure	Dynamic and flexible structure

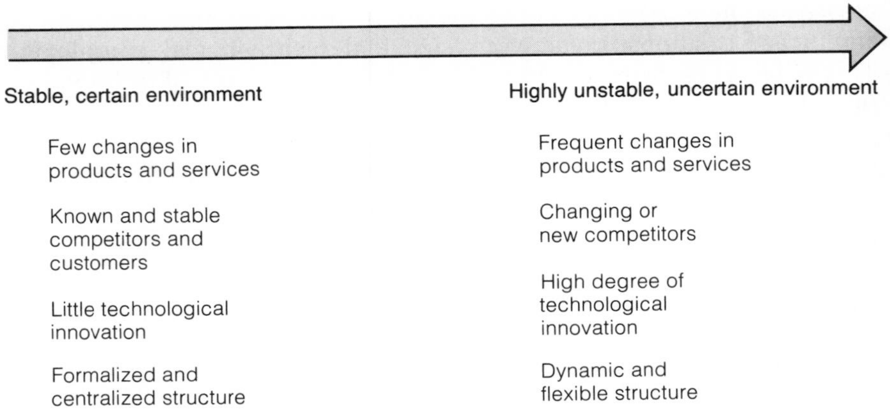

tion. Burlap bags and cotton twine can be made on machines that are sixty or seventy years old. But organizations involved with plastics, electronics, solar power, and nucleonics experience great uncertainty and rapid changes. Technological breakthroughs occur frequently. For example, the organizations manufacturing minicomputers are constantly changing their products.

Few organizations exist in a completely stable environment. Changes in laws and regulations, such as those on air pollution and retirement age, affect many organizations. Further, an individual organization may exist in several environments. The General Electric division that makes electric toasters may exist in a more stable environment than the division engaged in research on solar energy. The Corning Glass division that makes hospital instruments and electronics equipment may be in a less certain environment than the division making television screens.

Research has suggested that organizations (or their units) should be designed differently, depending on how unstable and unpredictable their environments are. Figure 10.3 shows the two extremes of design— the mechanistic and the organic.[10]

The **mechanistic** type of organization is highly bureaucratic, characterized by precise job descriptions, fixed authority and responsibility, specialized tasks, and a clear hierarchy of control. Information filters up through the hierarchy, and instructions flow down. The responsibility for overall knowledge and coordination rests exclusively at the top. This type of organization is suitable when markets and technology are well established and show little change over time.

The **organic** type has less formal job descriptions, less fixed authority, more participation of more employees in decision making, and greater emphasis on adaptability. Individuals can communicate with others in the organization besides their immediate supervisors, subordinates, and colleagues. Power derived from expertise is greater than that derived from position in this type of organization. The organic style is most appropriate when unstable environmental conditions constantly pose novel problems.

Almost all organizations need a combination of these two extreme styles, particularly for their organizational units, each of which exists in an environment of its own. In the case of Alpha Corporation's electronic products division a mechanistic and bureaucratic structure was modi-

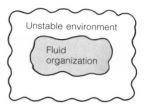

Relationship between organization structure and environment

Stable environment

Structured organization

Unstable environment

Fluid organization

Mechanistic
(certain) environment

Moderate
environment

Organic
(uncertain) environment

Knowledge at top
Formal authority
Rules for decisions
Specified communications patterns
Specialized and defined tasks

Knowledge spread through organization
Situational authority
Autonomy of decision making
Freedom of communication
Uncertain tasks

FIGURE 10.3 The continuum from mechanistic to organic organizations

fied to a more organic structure that was better suited to the rapid environmental and technical changes facing that division.

Degrees of Environmental Certainty   Lately, the importance of the environment has been studied in more detail. In one study three industries were selected to form a continuum from the certain to the uncertain environment, as shown in Figure 10.4.[11] An environment with a high degree of certainty is typified by that of the container industry. Sales are relatively predictable, the industry has had only a few innovations over time, the technology is stable, and only a few new firms have been established.

On the highly uncertain side of the continuum is the plastics industry. In its unpredictable environment there are frequent and rapid innovations, and an organization's position in the market can suddenly drop if it does not quickly respond to innovation by competitors and changing needs of customers.

The food industry is represented as being midway between the two extremes. The environment is moderately certain. Although there is innovation and sales do change over time, the future is relatively predictable.

The study analyzed successful and unsuccessful firms in each of these three categories and found that there were major differences in two important factors: differentiation and integration.

Differentiation—A Type of Specialization   **Differentiation,** one type of specialization, is "the difference in cognitive and emotional orientation among managers in different functional departments."[12] The more uncertain the environment, the more differentiated or specialized was the successful firm. Uncertainty necessitates more differentiation.

The container organizations have little need for differentiation. Their environment is stable, their technology established. In such organizations, the bureaucratic hierarchy, with rigid job specifications and procedures, is more successful. For the plastics organizations, on the other hand, innovation is continually needed to meet changing customer demands. Such innovation requires a great degree of differentiation and specialization in such units as marketing, science, and production.

Integration (Coordination)   The greater amount of differentiation or specialization, the greater the need for integration, or coordination.

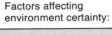

Factors affecting environment certainty:

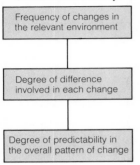

Frequency of changes in the relevant environment

Degree of difference involved in each change

Degree of predictability in the overall pattern of change

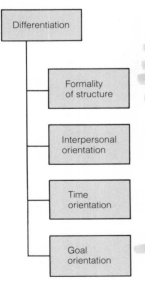

Differentiation

Formality of structure

Interpersonal orientation

Time orientation

Goal orientation

FIGURE 10.4 Industries at different places on the environmental continuum

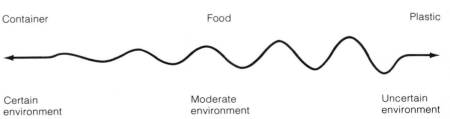

Integration is "the quality of the state of collaboration that exists among departments that are required to achieve unity of effort by the demands of the environment."[13] In other words, once the organization has been differentiated (specialized), it must be integrated (coordinated).

Table 10.1 shows the different integrative approaches used by the high-performing organizations in the three major industries of this study. In the container firms, which had low differentiation (5.7), integration was achieved through a mechanistic approach. Direct managerial contact, a bureaucratic hierarchy, and a paper system of specifying jobs, rules, and procedures—these are sufficient to coordinate the work in such organizations. There are few innovations, so top management is concerned primarily with the quality of goods produced and the scheduling of deliveries. If communication and coordination begin to break down, managers can coordinate tasks through bureaucratic rules.

In the moderately certain environment of the food industry, such procedures are helpful but not sufficient in themselves to provide integration. Temporary cross-functional teams were used by the successful organizations in this study. *Integrators*—individuals specifically responsible for coordinating the interdependent activities of various departments—were also necessary. Integrators' functions can be classified as neither line nor staff. Rather, they constitute a separate class, one with enough knowledge and delegated authority to issue the instructions that will cause the various line managers to work together to achieve the organization's objectives.

In the highly uncertain environment of the plastics industry, the successful organizations in this study were more highly differentiated (10.7)

Differentiation:

The difference in cognitive and emotional orientation among managers in different functional departments

Relatively stable environment

Relatively unstable environment

TABLE 10.1 Comparison of Integrative Devices in Three High-Performing Organizations

	CONTAINER	FOOD	PLASTICS
Degree of differentiation [a]	5.7	8.0	10.7
Major integrative devices	(1) Direct managerial contact	(1) Individual integrators	(1) Integrative department
	(2) Managerial hierarchy	(2) Temporary cross-functional teams	(2) Permanent cross-functional teams at three levels of management
	(3) Paper system	(3) Direct managerial contact	(3) Direct managerial contact
		(4) Managerial hierarchy	(4) Managerial hierarchy
		(5) Paper system	(5) Paper system

[a] High score means greater actual differentiation.

Source: Reprinted by permission of Harvard University Press from *Organization and Environment* (p. 138) by Paul R. Lawrence and Jay W. Lorsch, Boston, Mass.: The Division of Research, Graduate School of Business Administration, Harvard University. Copyright © 1967 by the President and Fellows of Harvard College.

Integration:

The quality of the state of collaboration that exists among departments that are required to achieve unity of effort by the demands of the environment and required more integration. To make certain that interdependent departments would coordinate their activities and respond quickly to changing environmental demands, these organizations used all the integrative approaches used by organizations in the other two industries and, in addition, established permanent cross-functional teams and formal departments of integration.

The concepts of differentiation and integration are analogous to those of division of labor and coordination. In terms of organizational design, however, they have more meaning, since they can be more specifically defined and measured.

The case of the electronic product division of Alpha Corporation shows how an understanding of these concepts of organizational design was applied to indirectly change the intergroup relations of people. The general manager made a conscious choice to change the organizational design rather than trying to directly change the interactions of the people. The results were improved intergroup relations, increased motivation and morale, and a productive handling of conflict—all of which enabled the company to introduce nine complex new products in one year as compared to a total of five in the previous five years.

In summary, a mechanistic structure with little differentiation is more effective for an organization or unit in a stable, known environment. More dynamic, uncertain environments require more differentiation and correspondingly more integration.[14]

Types of Interdependence within the Organization   As we have seen so far, many factors are involved in specialization and coordination, one of the most obvious being the number of units or subsystems involved. Usually, the greater the number of units, the more difficult is coordination. Another major factor is the pattern of interdependence among the units.[15] Three basic patterns can be identified: pooled, sequential, and reciprocal.

Pooled interdependence exists when two or more units interact with the central organization but not with each other. Managers and workers at one McDonald's restaurant, for example, interact little or not at all with their counterparts at another restaurant. However, the restaurants are interdependent in that one must succeed if the other is to succeed. On the performance of both (and of all other McDonald's restaurants) rests the success of the total organization. In this type of interdependence, each part of the organization contributes to the whole, and each is supported by the whole. Since the subsidiary units do not interact with each other but only with the home office, their functions can be coordinated through standardized instructions issued from the home office.

Sequential interdependence exists when one unit must act before another unit can accomplish its tasks; each unit is interdependent with the one that precedes it and succeeds it in the flow of work. The outputs from Unit A become inputs for Unit B. Both contribute to and are sustained by the entire organization; thus the interdependence is both pooled and sequential. The order of the interdependence can be clearly

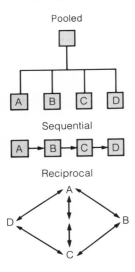

Patterns of
interdependence:

Pooled

Sequential

Reciprocal

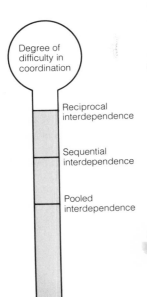

Degree of
difficulty in
coordination

Reciprocal
interdependence

Sequential
interdependence

Pooled
interdependence

specified. For example, a hospital dietary department must prepare meals before the people on the nursing floors can serve them. The production department must make the widget parts before they can be assembled by another unit.

Coordinating sequentially interdependent units requires more effort, more planning, and more managerial contact than coordinating units in pooled interdependence. There are more important lateral (as opposed to vertical) relationships, and conflict is more likely to occur.

Reciprocal interdependence exists when the outputs of each unit provide inputs for all others. As Figure 10.5 shows, all units exist in mutual interdependence. An example is the relationship between marketing, research and design, and manufacturing in product innovation. Each of these functions affects both of the others and is in turn affected by each of them. Another example is the maintenance and operations groups of an airline. The maintenance group's output is an input for operations—a usable aircraft. After the plane has been flown, the maintenance group receives an input—an airplane needing maintenance.

Reciprocal interdependence incorporates pooled and sequential interdependence. Coordination requires mutual adjustment by all units. This type of interdependence demands the most effort at communication and decision making, and it entails the greatest likelihood of conflict because of the greater number and complexity of relationships involved. The frequency of interaction and the importance of that interaction further complicate the task of coordination. Moreover, the information transmitted among reciprocally interdependent units tends to be more complex and uncertain and requires more time and effort for sorting out, understanding, and resolving conflicting points of view.[16] The increased importance of lateral (as opposed to vertical) relationships noted in the

Coordination in reciprocal interdependence is made difficult by:

- Frequency of interaction
- Importance of interaction
- Complexity of information exchanged in interaction

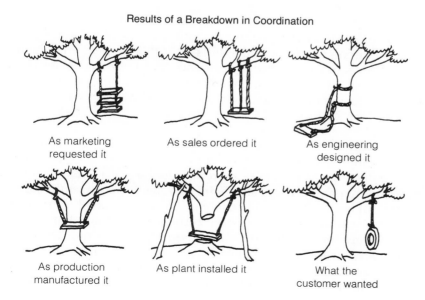

Results of a Breakdown in Coordination

As marketing requested it

As sales ordered it

As engineering designed it

As production manufactured it

As plant installed it

What the customer wanted

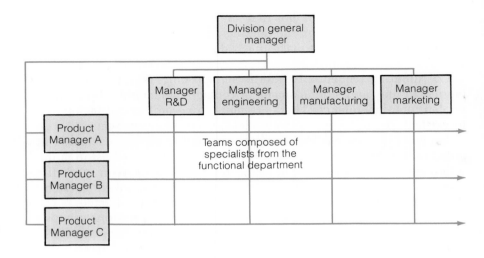

FIGURE 10.5 A matrix
organization

discussion of sequential interdependence is even stronger in the case of reciprocal interdependence.

A CONTINGENCY APPROACH TO ORGANIZATIONAL DESIGN

Contingency approach to organizational design:

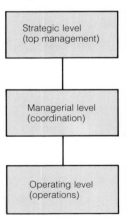

The findings presented thus far on organizational structure and design constitute only a brief review of the abundant research that has been done. However, even this brief review conclusively demonstrates that there is no single best design for all organizations. Thus a contingency approach is appropriate for determining what structure an organization or unit should have—that is, the structure should be contingent (dependent) on a number of factors, including size, technology, environment, and interdependence of the units. A further consideration in organizational design is provided by evidence that these and other factors may not affect all levels of the organization in the same way.[17] Put another way, top-, middle-, and first-level managers may have different sets of factors to consider.

Top Management—The Strategic Level   At the top management level, size and environment may be more important than technology, since top-level managers must keep informed about the external environment. From an open-systems point of view, management must continually gather information on economic and energy conditions, changing attitudes toward work, social responsibility, and the growing number of environmental and civil rights groups and issues. The organization's structure should help ensure this gathering of information.

At this level, size can be controlled by departmentation or other structural devices. For example, the automotive division of General Motors is decentralized into a number of operating divisions such as Chevrolet, Buick, and Cadillac. Although the automobile names and designs are somewhat different, the Chevrolet division of General Motors is essentially the same as the Cadillac division. The organization charts of the two divisions are very similar. In each division employees with the same functional specialties are grouped together—assembly workers in one subdivision, engineers in another, and so on. Yet overall policy issues from a centralized top management, which coordinates the different automotive divisions. Top management is aware of the differing environments and technologies in these divisions. Some operate in fairly stable environments and with stable technologies, whereas others have quickly changing environments and technologies.

At one time General Electric had almost two hundred operating divisions—far too many to coordinate effectively. In 1970 the company began reducing the number of these units. Eventually there were about forty-three, each a strategic business unit with market challenges and problems in common with the others. Several years later the interdependence between the units was accommodated by grouping them into six major sectors, according to industrial products and components, consumer products and services, power systems, and the like. Each of the six major sectors could operate relatively independently of the others.[18] The reorganization, completed in 1977, resulted in increased sales and profits.

Source: Reprinted by permission of the Chicago Tribune–New York News Syndicate, Inc.

HOW A WINNING FORMULA CAN FAIL

Transplanting a winning corporate culture to a sleepy company is not easy, as William Hartman, chairman of Interpace Corp., may have discovered. Hartman, the former president of International Telephone & Telegraph Corp.'s Grinnell Corp., has spent the last seven years attempting to transform Interpace, a mini-conglomerate that manufactured products as diverse as teacups and concrete pipes, into a dynamic company centered in the residential and commercial construction business. He used a formula that worked well for ITT that consisted of viewing assets primarily as financial pawns to be shifted around at the chief executive's will, of compelling managers to abide by financial dicta, and of focusing on financial results.

The goal seemed reasonable. But its implementation has been fraught with problems. Hartman lopped off what he regarded as "mediocre, unsuccessful businesses" and acquired new ones in a field he knew—residential construction products. He also chose to replace 35 members of a 51-man management team, enduring the personnel turmoil that accompanies such a move. His emphasis on financial management has not brought about the gains he sought. Nor is the company positioned yet in businesses of great future promise.

All of this is evidence that what worked for one company in the 1960s may not work for another company two decades later.

Bad timing To be sure, Hartman's attempts at realigning the company could not have come at a worse time. As interest rates soared, crushing the market for housing products, they also prevented Interpace from expanding its industrial products business, which accounts for 9% of sales, through acquisition. This latter goal was conjured up as a secondary strategy when Hartman's primary strategy went awry. Thus, for all his emphasis on financial concerns, the company has done poorly since 1975. With sales from continuing operations up 81% to $352 million, net income has nudged up only 10% to $15 million, and return on sales in 1980 was a mediocre 4.3%.

The financial picture is only one part of the problem. Executives were lured to the Parsippany (N.J.) company, says one former executive, in the hope that the ITT style of management would produce a company in the billion-dollar sales category. But with Interpace locked in its current dilemma, some have left, including Arthur W. DeMelle, chief financial officer, and Valentine Tackowiak, vice-president for human resources, who had

worked with Hartman at Grinnell. Indeed, since divestiture of the retail and commercial china operations and the salt and other nonmetallic mineral divisions, Hartman sees his staff as underutilized.

Hartman's abortive attempt to interject Interpace in Kennecott Corp.'s bidding war for Curtiss-Wright Corp. last year is almost certainly a tacit acknowledgment of that work-load vacuum. The unsolicited offer to trade Interpace's stock for CW's was quickly withdrawn when Hartman got no response.

Hartman adopted more than financial criteria from his ITT days. He apparently has modeled his management style after that of Harold S. Geneen, who built ITT almost from scratch using autocratic methods. Says Charles A. Gallagher, a former vice-president and 24-year Interpace veteran who left within a year of Hartman's arrival: "He demanded a lot more of people and was not willing to spend time to develop them." Even Executive Vice-President John F. Maypole, 41, who joined Interpace in 1966, notes that Hartman is a "demanding, difficult man, who expects a lot and does not tolerate lack of performance."

"Getting to goal" Demanding high performance can be a key to successful operations, but only if corporate goals are clearly communicated. Hartman demanded detailed plans to fit the financial goals he imposed on his managers, but some executives claim he kept his strategic goals to himself. Typical of that style was his decision to sell Interpace's oldest business, Lock Joint Products Div., earlier this year, without informing the division chief until the very last minute. Yet Hartman concedes that his greatest managerial problem has come from getting "frustrated when people don't see the important factors in getting to goal," when he himself has "such a clear intuitive view of where we are going."

Yet even this intuitive view has not always paid off. To counteract the dips in utility construction orders, Hartman chose to enter the equally cyclical residential and commercial construction markets with which he was familiar. But Mason D. Reed Jr., 51, vice-president of corporate planning and development, admits that Interpace's present results are "unsatisfactory," and its product lines—Mansfield Sanitary (toilets) and Hart & Cooley and Tuttle & Bailey (heating and air-conditioning equipment)—are not in growth areas.

Hartmen feels the pinch but is still intent on growing by acquisition, rather than by developing

Interpace's existing businesses, except for electric utility insulators. This time he wants to expand deeply into industrial products, an extension of the plan he announced in 1979, which has been implemented only minimally.

By moving into industrial products, Hartman is drawing both on his Grinnell past and Interpace's experience with two small product lines—chemical processing pumps and ceramic sealers, and a recently acquired foundry. Reed says Interpace would like to imitate fastgrowing $835 million Dover Corp., manufacturer of hydraulic elevators, pumps, and petroleum processing equipment, which has achieved success from less cyclical areas.

"Management horsepower"

Observers of Interpace are puzzled, however, by Hartman's lunge last December for Curtiss-Wright, a $362 million company. For Hartman the attraction was obvious: Curtiss-Wright's Dorr-Oliver Inc. subsidiary, which accounted for half its revenues through the sale of industrial processing equipment. Far from viewing it as a drawback, Curtiss-Wright's size was seen as an opportunity by Hartman. The one Interpace weakness Hartman admits to is the high caliber of its "management horsepower,"

capable of operating a company twice its size and of absorbing a large acquisition. In 1980 he boasted to stockholders that Interpace's experience in divesting itself of $70 million in assets at book value made him confident that it could acquire large companies and "spin off things we didn't care about."

But those statements cloak a floundering acquisition program. Aside from the $2 million purchase of a pump line last December, he has made no acquisitions in two years. Corporate planner Reed notes that the high multiples of good companies, selling at 13 to 15 times earnings, make acquisitions difficult.

Paying such high prices could limit Interpace's other financial goals. Hartman's objectives are a 6% return on sales, up from 4.3%; an increase in return on investment to 14% from 6.6%; and an almost doubling of return on equity to 18%. All of those goals presuppose that inflation will decline to 8% or 9% and that housing starts will increase from the current 1.2 million to 2 million by 1983.

Shrinking back to size   While waiting for that to happen, Hartman has not been idle. By the middle of this year, he will have divested 75% of Interpace's original assets, including its core

On the Job

HOW A WINNING FORMULA CAN FAIL (Continued)

division, Lock Joint Products, which last year contributed 27%, or almost $100 million, to revenues and 30% to earnings. That will provide some cash for acquisitions, but will not make it any easier for him to acquire companies, given their current high prices.

With Lock Joint gone, Interpace will shrink to $250 million, the same size it was when Hartman took it over. Right now, the shifting of assets does not appear to have improved the company noticeably. But Hartman is still betting on a changed economy to prove his strategies right. Whether he can sustain his management team long enough for that to occur remains to be seen.

Source: "How a Winning Formula Can Fail," reprinted from the May 25, 1981, issue of *Business Week* by special permission, © 1981 by McGraw-Hill, Inc., New York, NY 10020. All rights reserved.

From the point of view of top management, units operating in stable environments and with known technologies should be formalized and centralized with task-centered leadership. Those operating in uncertain environments and with changing technologies should be structured in a more organic and less bureaucratic fashion.

In the case of the electronic products division of Alpha Corporation, the first, and unsuccessful, attempt to solve the problems in intergroup relations was through the management hierarchy, vertical information systems, and meetings at the division manager level. The reorganization that solved the problems created a more flexible and decentralized structure, one that allowed for self-contained tasks and reliance on lateral relationships.

Middle Management—The Coordinating Level At the middle-management level of all departments, managers face different types of uncertainties depending on their particular task environments. Therefore, it is important that an organization be ready to adopt different managerial practices and systems as each middle manager tries to cope with each set of uncertainties. Managers operating in stable task environments (such as General Electric's steam turbine department) will probably find a mechanistic structure most effective, whereas those dealing with less stable environments (such as General Electric's defense and power systems) should choose a more organic structure.

Matrix When the environment is uncertain and the technology complex, lateral coordinating approaches may be more important than vertical ones. In fact, a number of new approaches are being developed to handle problems that neither the functional organization (organizational units formed of different specialists) nor the product organization (different specialists in the same unit) seems capable of handling. One new approach is the **matrix organization,** a device for integrating the activities of different specialists while maintaining specialized organizational units. Figure 10.5 offers an example of this type of organization.

The matrix organization came into prominence in the 1960s, when the U.S. Department of Defense and the aerospace industry began using it.[19] Combining the functional and the project types of structure, it is often used in project, program, and product management. For example, it is suited for coordinating efforts on large, complex projects involving a number of product lines. It is also useful for projects that have a limited time span and that need different people for each phase of the work.

Under a matrix organization, people can be shifted around as necessary while still belonging to their functional department. To illustrate: An organization may have certain people prepare bids on projects. When the contract is accepted, engineers, scientists, and other workers may then be assigned to one or more of the tasks. The manager responsible for a specific project may also purchase certain needed services from elsewhere in the organization. The functional managers, in turn, depend on this income to maintain their departments' operations (as shown in Figure 10.5).

Modified forms of matrix organizations are often used. In the area of manufacturing, matrix approaches are followed by such industries as aerospace, chemicals, electronics, and pharmaceuticals. In the area of service, they are followed by banking, retailing, construction, health, and brokerage organizations. Even the accounting and advertising fields are using matrix organization. Hospital nurses and social workers report to a single administrator but work in departments such as obstetrics, medicine, surgery, and psychiatry. Matrix and similar forms of organization are a practical way to focus attention simultaneously on a specific desired goal, on complex technical issues, and on the unique requirements of customers, particularly in areas requiring a high degree of information-processing capability. Of course, they have disadvantages too. They often force professionals and other employees to work for more than one boss and within teams whose existence is limited by the project itself. Collaboration and constructive conflict resolution are imperative under such conditions but also difficult to achieve.

Still, when properly used, a matrix organization can ensure that the information flow is channeled to and from the appropriate people. In one situation, an organizational redesign to take advantage of a matrix approach increased effectiveness in designing and producing hospital and medical electronic instruments. The rate of new product introduction to manufacturing more than doubled. Manufacturing efficiency, measured in terms of actual costs versus predicted costs for the first month of manufacture, rose from an average of 20 percent before the matrix organization was installed to an average of 80 percent afterwards.[20]

Shift from Function to Matrix There is disagreement on precisely what constitutes a matrix structure. Many instances of resource sharing are called matrix. This structure is difficult to define because it represents a continuum of possible structural arrangements. For example, the coordination devices of organizations can be placed on a scale of increasing complexity:

Rules and programs

Hierarchy

Plans

Direct contact

Liaison

Task force

Teams

Integrators

Integrating departments

Matrix organization[21]

An organization or unit might appear anywhere on the scale, depending on the information-processing demands of its environment. Thus a natural progression exists from the functional to the matrix organization, as Table 10.2 shows.

Function The functional organization is most effective when it has a relatively narrow range of products that require little change, with a

TABLE 10.2 Determinants of the Stages of Matrix Organization

FORM	DETERMINANTS
Function	1. Efficiency as a success criterion 2. Competitive advantage along a single parameter (technology, price, performance, delivery) 3. Markets relatively predictable 4. Narrow range of products with long time horizons
Project	1. Several simultaneous success criteria: performance, cost, price, schedule, technology, efficiency 2. Moderate market change 3. Differentiated clients and markets 4. Moderate number of products (projects) 5. Specified time horizons for each client or project 6. Interconnectedness between outside and focal organization
Product/Matrix	1. Innovation as a success criterion 2. Differentiated products, markets, customers 3. High variability and uncertainty in product-market mix 4. Time horizons for product varying from medium to long
Matrix	Same as product/matrix

Source: Adapted by permission from Harvey F. Kolodny, "Evolution to a Matrix Organization," *Academy of Management Review* 4 (October 1979): 551.

predictable market and a competitive advantage based on factors like technology or price. The container industry—with its relatively mechanistic organizational structure and reliance on rules. hierarchy, and direct managerial contact—would fit in this category.

Project At the next level of complexity there are more product lines; a number of success criteria need to be applied simultaneously; and interdependence is reciprocal, so that problems cut across department lines. Here a vertically structured hierarchy cannot respond quickly enough to the rapidly changing requirements of coordination. The answer may be to develop a *project organization,* which decentralizes the processes of decision making and assigning of specific projects or tasks to a coordinator, often called a project manager or integrator. In this way decision making related to such issues as performance, delivery, and cost is coordinated at the level where the knowledge necessary for the decisions can be closely monitored. Such project arrangements are usually temporary and are dissolved when the project is completed.

Product/Matrix Further down the continuum is a stage where innovation becomes important. Markets, products, and customers are highly differentiated and diverse; the time structure is relatively long, and there is a great deal of uncertainty and variability in the mix of products and markets. The product/matrix organization is appropriate at this stage. It is a relatively permanent structure designed for developing a product, idea, or a particular type of technology. In this organization a product manager becomes a mini–general manager, a person responsible for the complete business—for its profit and loss, for its success and failure, and for its future potential as well as its current operations.[22]

Additional support systems are necessary in product/matrix organizations, since many people are now reporting to more than one boss (product and functional managers). Dual evaluation and reward systems and dual accounting and control systems need to be developed, and job descriptions need to be less specific and more general, focusing on results more than tasks.

Matrix There is little difference between product/matrix and matrix organizations except that the matrix structure generally receives more formal recognition from top management. Also, product managers may be able to subcontract for services, either from the functional managers or from outside the organization.

Since much of the decision making has been decentralized, top management in both product/matrix and matrix organizations has more time to interact with the external environment. Conflict is frequently resolved through a complex and changing variety of task forces, team meetings, multiple team membership, and a variety of other approaches. "The design becomes more a 'logic of change' and less a 'logic of control.'"[23]

In summary, different environmental and strategic conditions deter-

Scale of complexity of coordination devices for organizations from bottom to top:

Matrix organization
Integrating departments
Integrators
Teams
Task force
Liaison
Direct contact
Plans
Hierarchy
Rules and programs

mine at what stage of organizational design—ranging from product or functional to matrix—an organization or its subunits are.

First-Level Management—The Operating Level   First-level management is concerned with the actual production of goods and services. At this level size is especially important because it affects the way people work together (group dynamics). Environment is also important. It affects the kind of work being done and, at this level, frequently consists of other units of the organization as well as the external environment. The type of technology, another factor, helps determine structure, which in turn affects the behavior of employees. The smaller the subunit, the more it is influenced by the technology.

Additional contingency approaches are used at the operating level. Among them is the **sociotechnical approach,** which is concerned with organizing and matching the technology (work flow and information flow) and the people. In most instances it involves creating relatively autonomous groups of employees who are collectively responsible for their output.

Two early studies involved coal in England and weaving in India. In both situations, new and modern equipment had been introduced, and the change in technology had been accompanied by a change in job structure. The jobs, which were set up according to U.S. and British standards regarding the division and specialization of work, were fractionalized and did not allow a group structure to emerge. Productivity decreased sharply, and absenteeism and turnover increased.

In both instances it was recommended that the jobs be restructured to build on work teams. Members of the newly formed teams had the necessary ability and resources to do the job and to coordinate efforts. In the coal mining industry output rose from 78 percent to 95 percent; in the weaving industry it rose from 80 percent to 95 percent. Turnover and absenteeism dropped correspondingly. In the weaving industry a follow-up study sixteen years later found that the levels of performance had remained relatively constant through the years.[24]

The results of these and similar studies made the idea of autonomous production groups popular throughout Europe, particularly in the Netherlands, Scandinavia, and Great Britain. Such groups are relatively self-governing in that they make many of their own decisions. A publication from Norway reports on the success of projects conducted from 1964 to 1972 for manufacturers, banks, hotels, shipyards, and other organizations. A similar publication from Sweden reports on the relative success of about five hundred different projects.[25]

Production groups should consist of people whose work is interdependent. They should be separated from other production centers so they can operate with relative independence. Their goals should be spelled out in clear, simple terms. Such groups enable supervisors to delegate authority and thus to devote more time to overall development and planning. Often, development groups coordinate the work of several production groups, as shown in Figure 10.6.

Sociotechnical approach considers:

- People
- Technology

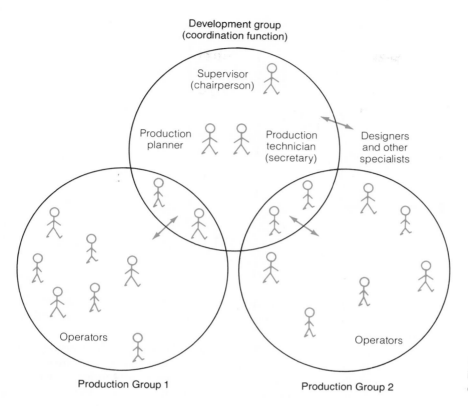

FIGURE 10.6 Interlocking production and development groups

Two of the better-known programs involve the redesign of work at Saab and Volvo plants. The widely publicized Volvo plant at Kalmar, Sweden, is designed so that different work teams are responsible for specific installations on the car (for example, the electrical system, controls, and instrumentation). One first-level supervisor and one industrial engineer or technician supervise two to four teams. Supervision focuses primarily on overall quality and on making certain that each team has the necessary equipment.

A Saab engine assembly factory experimented with another type of work design. After considerable discussion the decision was to have teams of three or four workers completely assemble each engine. A number of engineering problems had to be solved before this approach became possible, but eventually the design shown in Figure 10.7 was developed. A large conveyor loop close to the work area brings in the engine block and takes out the completed engines. Each work group has a U-shaped guide track in the floor. Trucks can easily come in to furnish the necessary parts without disturbing the assembly group.

This plant has been criticized, however. For example, a group of U.S. workers visited the plant and reported that the work pace was too fast and the lunch breaks too short. Immediately after the visit a Saab executive commented that the U.S. workers had not stayed long enough to

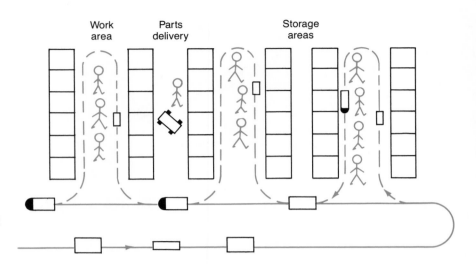

FIGURE 10.7 Redesigned area for engine assembly at Saab

become completely proficient and that that was one reason they felt the pace was too fast. Others have criticized the team approach in general for its potential loss of accountability.[26]

Sociotechnical systems are used much more often in Europe and Great Britain than in the United States. In the past few years, however, a quiet revolution has been taking place in a number of American organizations, which have tended to establish sociotechnical systems. "They have designed, built, and managed one or more new plants in a manner that is both revolutionary and at the same time very much in tune with the state of the art in management theory."[27] Among these organizations are General Motors, General Foods, Procter & Gamble, Sherwin-Williams, PPG Industries, The Mead Corporation, TRW, Rockwell, and Shell Canada, Ltd., as well as a host of smaller organizations. Some have created more than one new-design plant based on the sociotechnical approach. It is estimated that at least 30 of such large organizations as those named have at least 1 of these plants operating and that altogether there are about 150 of them. General Motors alone has built about 20.

This trend has been called a quiet revolution because it has generated so little fanfare. One reason for the lack of publicity is that organizations have discovered that the new approach gives them a competitive edge. For example, one U.S. organization found that the introduction of autonomous work groups resulted in a 17 percent increase in productivity. Absenteeism dropped 50 percent, quality increased 50 percent (that is, there were 50 percent fewer rejects), and employee satisfaction and morale increased.[28]

Sociotechnical and related approaches are being used in older plants too. General Motors, for example, did some major restructuring along these lines in its North Tarrytown, New York, plant. The change involved 4,000 people: 3,500 hourly and 500 salaried workers. In the early 1970s the plant was in serious trouble, with deep hostility between union and management, a staggering absentee rate, high operating costs, and as many as 2,000 labor grievances on the docket at any time. General Motors considered closing the plant.

Instead a joint union-management quality of work life project was started. By late 1979 both the union and management pronounced the project a success.[29] Absenteeism had dropped from more than 7 percent to about 2 percent. At the end of December 1979 only 32 grievances remained on the docket (compared to 2,000 seven years earlier). Quality of performance improved. The plant had been one of the poorest; recently it won an award from General Motors for its quality performance. There was no strike or work stoppage for seven years. General Motors is now deeply involved in work restructuring and quality of life projects in a number of its other plants.

Sociotechnical systems and related approaches are powerful tools of organizational design, particularly at the worker level. But changes in one subsystem can have negative effects on other subsystems. For example, traditionally trained managers often resist the apparent loss of their authority and responsibility, under a sociotechnical type of system in which new support systems are needed and new styles of supervision are required. One major corporation that has built fifteen such new-design plants has found this problem serious enough to limit its supervisory personnel for the new plants to those already experienced in the sociotechnical approach.

SUMMARY

This chapter has discussed the gradual evolution of new approaches to organizational design that have stemmed from the growing size and complexity of many organizations and the wealth of information gained from research on the relationship between organizational design and effectiveness. Particularly since World War II, management has had to resort to new types of structures to cope with new problems arising from increased complexity.

Although countless factors bear on organizational structure, four are critical: size, technology, stability of the environment, and internal interdependence of the organizational units. Not only does each affect organizational design but, to make matters more complex, the interaction among all four factors also has an effect.[30]

Practicing managers know intuitively that

no single organizational structure is best for all organizations. Rather, the best structure is contingent on the circumstances. For example, a mechanistic design is best for an organization or unit existing in a stable, known environment, whereas a more organic structure is appropriate for unstable, turbulent environments.

Situational factors apply differently to different levels of management. For example, top-level, strategic management can control size by the way the organization is subdivided, as the General Electric example showed. Particularly at the middle-management level, organizational structure can vary from functional or product to matrix, depending on a number of factors. For first-level management, the type of technology and type of interdependence among units determines which structure works best, from the traditional one person—one job to autonomous work groups based on sociotechnical principles. Many large organizations are now constructing new plants designed on the new sociotechnical type of approaches.

Perhaps the most important point of this chapter is that a manager should not accept current organizational designs without question but should constantly be testing and questioning, tinkering and modifying, in order to come up with the best design possible, given current knowledge, the particular situation, and the organization's values.

STUDY QUESTIONS

1. List two fundamental reasons for the increasing attention to organizational design.
2. Do managers really have a choice in the design of organizations and their units?
3. What are the four major factors described in this chapter as affecting organizational structure?
4. Explain the contingency approach.
5. A paper mill that has been in operation for ten years has two identical machines making newsprint. Would you recommend a mechanistic or an organic management style for the organization? Explain.
6. What other approaches might have been considered in the case of the electronic products division of the Alpha Corporation?
7. Under what conditions would you recommend the use of a matrix organization? Under what conditions might it be harmful?
8. Why does a vice-president of industrial relations at one organization prefer that traditional managers not be recruited for the new plants the organization is building?
9. What personal values do you hold that might make you prefer either a mechanistic or organic structure as an employee? As a manager?
10. Pick an organization with which you are familiar. Would you recommend any changes in its structure? Explain.
11. In a matrix organization employees often work for more than one boss. Does this violate the principle of unity of command? Elaborate.
12. Compare and contrast *differentiation* and *integration* with *division of labor* and *coordination*.

Case for Discussion

MANAGERIAL CHOICE

You are the manager of the materials control department for a small plant of about three hundred people, and you report directly to the plant manager. The plant makes a variety of electronic testing instruments, some of which are used to test blood and urine samples and others to test water samples for chemical impurities. Although the plant manufactures a number of different instruments, there are only four basic types. Most of the parts used in one type are not used in the others, although there is some overlap.

Your department has four essential functions—purchasing, plant scheduling, inventory control, and expediting, as shown by the organization chart in Figure 10.8. (Expediting involves finishing and shipping a product faster than normally scheduled or speeding parts delivery.) The purchasing unit is responsible for all the plant's purchases. The purchases include a variety of electronic parts (such as printed circuits, transistors, and resistors) as well as raw materials, clerical supplies, and everything else needed to operate

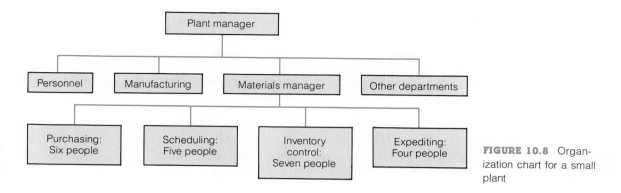

FIGURE 10.8 Organization chart for a small plant

the plant. There are six people in the purchasing unit, which is headed by a team leader. The people are experienced enough that each can buy almost everything needed by the plant.

The plant scheduling unit has five people, headed by a team leader. The basic responsibility of this unit is to prepare the manufacturing schedules for the plant. As orders come in, they must be scheduled to be processed through the plant. Each manufacturing area needs to know when to start production on a particular order and when to complete it.

The inventory control unit has four people and is headed by a team leader. There are frequent modifications of the instruments made by the plant. As a result, the inventory can be overloaded with some items and understocked with others. One of the responsibilities of the inventory unit is to suggest to the manufacturing, research, and development departments that a change in an instrument might make a particular part obsolete. Then the department involved can delay the change until arrangements are made to either use up the parts before they become obsolete, see if they can be returned to the manufacturer, or use them in another instrument.

The expediting unit has four people and a team leader. Because of frequent changes and because new instruments may not have detailed parts lists until just before going into manufacturing, the job of this unit is to expedite such parts. In addition, sometimes there are rush orders. Therefore, the expediters often work directly with the manufacturing people to finish an order quickly and send it out.

As the manager of the materials control department, you are aware that the way you are organized is common in your industry and in the rest of the corporation. However, a number of parts shortages have caused delays in production, and many schedule changes have been made because of the parts shortages or rush orders. In addition, you believe that the expediters do not like their jobs, because the work is not very challenging. Finally, you know that the different groups seem to have problems communicating across functional lines. Indeed, sometimes you wonder if any of them know what the others are doing.

You have just come from a meeting with the plant manager, who has suggested that you think of other ways of structuring the department.

1. What problems does the present structure solve? What problems does it create?
2. What are some other ways of organizing?
3. What are the advantages and disadvantages of the other approaches?

FOR YOUR CAREER

1. The structure of an organization should not be derived from either abstract principles or intuition but from the organization's strategy, markets, technology, and task environment.

2. Frequently what are diagnosed as personality clashes are really problems in organizational design.

3. The cause of a problem should be diagnosed before any tinkering is done with the organizational design to deal with symptoms.

4. Some managers never think of changing the structure; others change it almost without thought. Be wary of both extremes.

5. Rather than trying to create an organizational design, meant to last indefinitely, managers should be prepared to constantly and deliberately experiment with new organizational approaches.

6. Proper timing is one of the keys to success in organizational redesign. Usually the time to suggest a change is when there is a problem, not when the organization is functioning well.

7. A good design may take years to fully implement.

FOOTNOTES

1. Papers presented at the Symposium on Improving Integration between Functional Groups—A Case in Organization Change and Implications for Theory and Practice, Division of Industrial and Organizational Psychology, American Psychological Association, Washington, D.C., September 3, 1971: M. Beer, "Organizational Diagnosis: An Anatomy of Poor Integration"; G. Pieters, "Changing Organizational Structures, Roles and Processes to Enhance Integration: The Implementation of a Change Program"; A. Hundert, "Problems and Prospects for Project Teams in a Large Bureaucracy"; S. Marcus, "Findings: The Effects of Structural, Cultural, and Role Changes on Integration"; and P. Lawrence, "Comments."

2. J. Child, "Organizational Structure, Environment and Performance: The Role of Strategic Choice," *Sociology* 6 (January 1972): 2–22; P. Khandwalla, *The Design of Organizations* (New York: Harcourt Brace Jovanovich, 1977); D. Hickson, D. Pugh, and D. Pheysey, "Operations, Technology, and Organizational Structure: An Empirical Reappraisal," *Administrative Science Quarterly* 14 (September 1969): 370–397.

3. H. Koontz, "Commentary on the Management Theory Jungle—Nearly Two Decades Later," in *Management: A Book of Readings,* 5th ed. ed. H. Koontz, C. O'Donnell, and H. Weinrich (New York: McGraw-Hill, 1980), pp. 18–26.

4. V. Sathe, "Contingency Theories of Organizational Structure," in *Managerial Accounting: The Behavioral Foundations,* ed. J. Livingstone (Columbus, Ohio:

Grid, 1975), pp. 51–63; Child, "Organizational Structure, Environment and Performance"; and J. Ford and J. Slocum, Jr., "Size, Technology, Environment and the Structure of Organizations," *Academy of Management Review* 2 (October 1977): 561–575.

5. P. Blau and R. Schoenherr, *The Structure of Organizations* (New York: Basic Books, 1971); J. Child, "Managerial and Organizational Factors Associated with Company Performance: Part I," *Journal of Management Studies* 11 (October 1974): 175–189; J. Child, "Managerial and Organizational Factors Associated with Company Performance: Part II," *Journal of Management Studies* 12 (February 1975): 12–28; and M. Meyer, *Bureaucratic Structure and Authority* (New York: Harper & Row, 1972).

6. C. N. Parkinson, *Parkinson's Law* (Boston: Houghton Mifflin, 1957), p. 5.

7. J. Woodward, *Management and Technology* (London: Her Majesty's Stationery Office, 1958); J. Woodward, *Industrial Organization* (London: Oxford University Press, 1965).

8. Hickson, Pugh, and Pheysey, "Operations, Technology, and Organizational Structure"; E. Chapple and L. Sayles, *The Measures of Management* (New York: Macmillan, 1961); C. Perrow, *Organizational Analysis: A Sociological View* (Belmont, Calif.: Wadsworth, 1970); J. Thompson, *Organizations in Action* (New York: McGraw-Hill, 1967); P. Blau et al., "Technology and Organizations in Manufacturing," *Administrative Science Quarterly* 21 (March 1976): 21–40; D. Comstock and W. Scott, "Technology and the Structure of Subunits: Distinguishing Individual and

Workgroup Effects," *Administrative Science Quarterly* 22 (June 1977): 177–202.

9. Child, "Organizational Structure, Environment and Performance."

10. T. Burns and G. Stalker, *The Management Innovation* (New York: Barnes & Noble, Social Science Paperbacks, 1961).

11. P. Lawrence and J. Lorsch, *Organization and Environment: Managing Differentiation and Integration* (Boston: Harvard University, Graduate School of Business Administration, Division of Research, 1967).

12. Ibid., p. 11.

13. Ibid.

14. Comstock and Scott, "Technology and the Structure of Subunits"; C. Derr, "An Organizational Analysis of the Boston School Department" (Ph.D. diss., Harvard University, Graduate School of Business Administration, Boston, 1972); W. Brown and J. Blandin, "Coping with Uncertainty: Some Cross-Cultural Comparisons," *Journal of Business Research* 4 (May 1976): 163–174; A. Reudi, "Cultural Factors in Contingency Theory: A Comparative Study of Six U.S. and One German Plastics Producers" (Ph.D. diss., Harvard University, Graduate School of Business Administration, Boston, 1972); and E. Nielson, "Contingency Theory Applied to Small Business Organizations," *Human Relations* 27 (April 1974): 357–359.

15. J. Thompson, *Organizing in Action* (New York: McGraw-Hill, 1967).

16. J. Galbraith, *Organization Design* (Reading, Mass.: Addison-Wesley, 1977).

17. R. Duncan, "Multiple Decision-Making Structures and Adapting to Environmental Uncertainty: The Impact on Organizational Effectiveness," *Human Relations* 26 (March 1974): 273–291; J. Galbraith, *Designing Complex Organizations* (Reading, Mass.: Addison-Wesley, 1973); and Galbraith, *Organization Design.*

18. "Mastering Diversity at GE," *Dun's Review,* December 1978, pp. 30–32; and P. Wiggins, "U.S. Oil Companies Dominate Sales List," *New York Times,* March 19, 1980, p. D1.

19. S. Davis and P. Lawrence, *Matrix* (Reading, Mass.: Addison-Wesley, 1977); Galbraith, *Organization Design;* T. Moore and B. Lorimer, "The Matrix Organization in Business and Health Care Institutions: A Comparison," *Hospital and Health Services Administration* 21 (Fall 1976): 26–33; and W. Goggin, "How the Multidimensional Structure Works at Dow Corning," *Harvard Business Review* 52 (January–February 1974): 54–65.

20. E. Huse and J. Bowditch, *Behavior in Organizations: A Systems Approach to Managing* (Reading, Mass.: Addison-Wesley, 1977), pp. 479–481.

21. J. Galbraith, "Matrix Organization Designs," *Business Horizons* 14 (February 1971): 29–40; and Galbraith, *Organization Design.*

22. H. Kolodny, "Evolution to a Matrix Organization," *Academy of Management Review* 4 (October 1979): 547.

23. Ibid., p. 549.

24. E. Trist and K. Bamforth, "Some Social and Psychological Consequences of the Long Wall of Goal Setting," *Human Relations* 4 (January 1951): 1–8; A. Rice, *Productivity and Social Organizations: The Ahmedabad Experiment* (London: Tavistock Publications, 1958); and E. Miller, "Socio-Technical Systems in Weaving, 1953–1970: A Follow-up Study," *Human Relations* 28 (August 1975): 348–386.

25. "Work Research Institutes—Projects: 1964–1972," mimeographed (Oslo: Work Research Institutes, n.d.); and D. Jenkins, ed., *Job Reform in Sweden: Conclusions from 500 Shop Floor Projects* (Stockholm: Swedish Employer's Confederation, 1975).

26. "Doubting Sweden's Way," *Time,* March 10, 1975, p. 40; and E. Jacques, "The Importance of Accountability," *International Management* 32 (July 1977): 43–45.

27. E. Lawler III, "The New Plant Revolution," *Organizational Dynamics* 6 (Winter 1978): 3.

28. E. Huse and M. Beer, "Eclectic Approach to Organization Development," *Harvard Business Review* 49 (September–October 1971): 103–112.

29. R. Guest, "The Quality of Work Life—Learning from Tarrytown," *Harvard Business Review* 57 (July–August 1979): 76–87.

30. For an extensive review of the current literature on organizational design, see K. S. Cameron, "Domains of Organizational Effectiveness in Colleges and Universities," *Academy of Management Journal* 24 (March 1981): 25–47; L. E. Davis, "Optimizing Organization—Plant Design: A Complementary Structure for Technical and Social Systems," *Organizational Dynamics* 8 (Autumn 1979): 2–15; D. A. Nadler and M. L. Tushman, "A Model for Diagnosing Organizational Behavior," *Organizational Dynamics* 9 (Autumn 1980): 35–51; P. Gringer, S. Al-Bazzoz, and M. Y. Ardekani, "Strategy, Structure, the Environment, and Financial Performance in 48 United Kingdom Companies," *Academy of Management Journal* 23 (June 1980): 193–220; K. G. Provan,

"Board Power and Organizational Effectiveness among Human Service Agencies," *Academy of Management Journal* 23 (June 1980): 221–236; H. R. Bobbitt, Jr., and J. D. Ford, "Decision-Maker Choice as a Determinant of Organizational Structure," *Academy of Management Review* 5 (January 1980): 13–24; L. J. Bourgeois III, "Strategy and Environment: A Conceptual Integration," *Academy of Management Review* 5 (January 1980): 25–40; and R. A. Pitts, "Toward a Contingency Theory of Multibusiness Organization Design," *Academy of Management Review* 5 (April 1980): 203–210.

Controlling

PART IV

Fundamentals of Control

CHAPTER 11

CONTENTS

LAVELLE'S PRIVATE WAR

In August 1971 General John Lavelle took command of all the U.S. Air Force units in the Vietnam conflict. At the time, bombing raids in North Vietnam could be conducted only with White House approval or as "protective reaction strikes." Such strikes could take place only if a target, usually a missile battery, had fired or was preparing to fire on a U.S. plane.

General Lavelle saw the North Vietnamese building up their forces along the border and requested approval to bomb. Refused approval, he decided to take matters into his own hands. From November 1971 to March 1972, when he was recalled, he secretly sent his planes north to bomb selected but unauthorized targets. The official report of each unauthorized mission was falsified, and the strike was referred to as a protective reaction strike.

The White House and the Pentagon might never have heard of Lavelle's private war except for the fact that an Air Force sergeant in Vietnam heard his immediate commander say that even the president did not know what was going on. The sergeant wrote Iowa Senator Harold Hughes to find out "if this falsification of classified documents is legal and proper." Within hours the Air Force inspector general was on a plane to Saigon.

The inspector general pinpointed 147 unauthorized raids in which Lavelle had chosen his own targets, and there may have been many more. During the four months in question, Lavelle's planes reported 1,300 protective reaction strikes. How had Lavelle managed to conduct so many strikes in violation of White House rules before he was caught? The general and his subordinates had developed a double accounting system. The Air Force required reports on all missions, which were checked to make certain that the rules had not been violated. However, Lavelle and his subordinates completed two sets of reports for each strike—one true and the other false. The true reports detailed damage done to North Vietnamese airfields, supply dumps, and the like. The false reports detailed protective reaction strikes and were forwarded to the Pentagon. Both sets were kept in South Vietnam—some in Lavelle's office.

In November 1971 Henry Kissinger began secret peace talks in Paris. In that same month the general began his extracurricular activities with strikes at three North Vietnamese airfields. Thus the White House and Pentagon lost control of air activities at the same time that negotiations began. Indeed, it is possible that Lavelle's raids contributed to the mysterious breakdown of the secret peace negotiations. When delicate coordination was most needed between the civilian and military areas of government, it was lost because of vital series of controls was not functioning effectively.

Lavelle was removed from command and given the choice of retiring from the Air Force or taking a lesser position at the pay and rank of a major general (two stars). He chose to retire. The Department of Defense kept silent on the real reason for this retirement. It announced on April 7, 1972, that the general was "retiring for personal and health reasons."[1]

This opening case raises several key questions which you should be able to answer after reading this chapter. The questions include:

1. Have you ever ignored or objected, as Lavelle did, to a control? If so, what were your reasons?
2. What are some of the controls that already affect your life?
3. What negative reactions can control produce in employees?
4. How do organizations control the behavior of their employees?

The opening case shows both the need for information and control systems and the difficulty of coordinating and controlling the different activities within an organization. The overall policy was clear: There must be civilian control over the military. The established procedure was clear: All but protective reaction strikes had to be approved in advance by Washington. The rule was specific: Detailed reports were to be sent to Washington for review. But the elaborate control system was ineffective for four months. In fact, if someone had not blown the whistle, the deception might never have been discovered. The important issues to be covered in this chapter are the need for information and control systems in organizations, the purposes they serve, the design of effective controls, the types of controls, and some of the reasons for the ineffectiveness of controls.

WHAT IS CONTROLLING?

Establishment of organizational objectives and plans is of little value if the plans are not adequately carried out to achieve objectives.[2] Any plan is only as effective as management's ability to carry it out; planning itself is not an end. To be effective, management must be able to measure performance, determine if and where deviations from the plan are occurring, and take corrective action. Knowing how effectively the planned activities are being carried out is essential to achieving the plan's objectives. Therefore, decision making, establishing objectives, planning, and controlling are highly interrelated—as Figure 11.1 shows.

The development of computers has made possible faster and more effective control processes. For example, one objective of airlines is to fill all seats for every flight but not to overbook. Hotels and motels want to fill all their rooms but not have more guests than available rooms. The computerized reservation systems of airlines and major hotel and motel chains allow ticket clerks, reservation clerks, and managers to determine immediately whether a seat or room is available and to confirm a reservation in seconds. This ability is taken for granted today, but a few years ago such an approach to control was not possible.

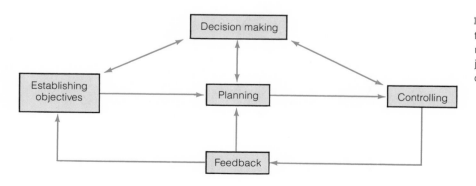

FIGURE 11.1 The relationships among decision making, establishing objectives, planning, and controlling.

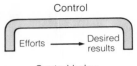

Control

Efforts ⟶ Desired results

Control helps ensure that results are attained.

The examples given here help show the difference between managerial control and control by nonmanagers. According to two management researchers: "In the literature relating to organizational behavior, there is ambiguity in the use of the word control. The confusion arises largely because to control can also mean to direct. Precisely defined, **control** refers solely to the task of ensuring that activities are producing the desired results."[3] (Boldface added.) Although managers set objectives, many other people control activities or processes. For example, the airline reservation clerk who tells a potential passenger that all the seats are booked is controlling behavior. The technician who sits at the console of an automated refinery is controlling processes.

Managerial control differs from nonmanagerial control by virtue of its extra duty of **directing,** which includes leading, developing, training, and motivating subordinates. Figure 11.2 shows how directing is related to control. Performed by managers only, directing overlaps controlling, since establishment of any monitoring approach usually means directing the activities of another person. Directing stresses personal approaches while control stresses impersonal ones. One *controls* the output of a refinery, but one *directs* the people in the refinery.

THE DIFFERENCE BETWEEN STRATEGIC PLANNING AND MANAGEMENT CONTROL

Although planning and controlling are clearly related, as shown in Figure 11.1, they differ in many respects.[4] Table 11.1 summarizes some of these differences.

Although strategic planning is continuous, it tends to proceed in spurts, since problems, opportunities, and innovative ideas do not occur according to a set schedule. The taking of the U.S. hostages in Iran in

FIGURE 11.2 The relationship between directing and controlling

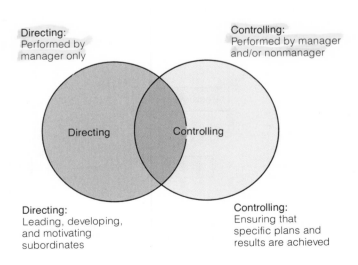

Directing:
Performed by manager only

Controlling:
Performed by manager and/or nonmanager

Directing

Controlling

Directing:
Leading, developing, and motivating subordinates

Controlling:
Ensuring that specific plans and results are achieved

TABLE 11.1 Some Distinctions Between Strategic Planning and Management Control

CHARACTERISTIC	STRATEGIC PLANNING	MANAGEMENT CONTROL
Focus of plans	On one aspect at a time	On whole organization
Complexities	Many variables	Less complex
Degree of structure	Unstructured and irregular; each problem different	Rhythmic; prescribed procedures
Nature of information	Tailor-made for the problem; more external and predictive; less accurate	Integrated; more internal and historical; more accurate
Communication of information	Relatively simple	Relatively difficult
Purpose of estimates	Show expected results	Lead to desired results
Persons primarily involved	Staff and top management	Line and top management
Number of persons involved	Small	Large
Mental activity	Creative; analytical	Administrative; persuasive
Source discipline	Economics	Social psychology
Planning and control	Planning dominant, but some control	Emphasis on both planning and control
Time horizon	Tends to be long	Tends to be short
End result	Policies and precedents	Action within policies and precedents
Appraisal of the job done	Extremely difficult	Much less difficult

Source: Reproduced by permission from Robert Anthony and John Dearden, *Management Control Systems: Text and Cases* (Homewood, Ill.: Richard D. Irwin, 1976), p. 13.

late 1979 and the Russian invasion of Afghanistan in early 1980 caused many organizations to reexamine their strategic plans. Because of the complexity of such planning, no effective overall approach, such as a mathematical model, can be developed. Indeed, attempts to apply such a formal approach might stifle the creativity necessary for developing planning scenarios.

The forecasts, estimates, and scenarios used in strategic planning are intended to show the *expected* results of a plan. In contrast, the management control process and the data it generates are intended to influence managers to take actions that will cause *desired* results. Thus in the management control process the question discussed is: How tight should the operating budget be? Should the goals be set so high that they can be achieved by only an exceptional manager, or should they be set where they can be achieved by an average manager? In the strategic planning process a different question is asked: What is the operating budget likely to be?

External information is vital to strategic planning. Market analyses, news on social changes, reports on new laws and regulations, and information about technological developments and about competitors are all

Forecasts, estimates, scenarios

Attempt to see

Expected results

Management control process

Attempts to cause

Desired results

Conflict between
strategic planning
and management
control process

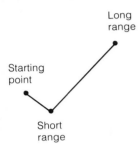

Action to increase
long-range profit
may reduce short-
range profit.

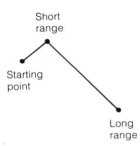

Action to increase
short-range profit
may reduce long-
range profit.

relevant, although much of the data will be imprecise and uncertain. These types of information are used to form estimates, usually long-range, of probable events. In the management control process, the relevant information is mostly internal, consisting of cost accounting, bank balances, and so on, and is expected to be accurate. Predicting how much one will earn ten years from now is a totally different matter from guessing at what one has in the bank today. In the first case some uncertainty is acceptable and, indeed, unavoidable; in the second, it is inexcusable.

Although all managers should be involved in planning, top management and staff planners are more deeply involved in strategic planning than other managers. Indeed, many middle- and lower-level managers may not be aware that a specific plan is being considered. Also, planning by lower-level managers is usually of shorter range and more detailed than that of top management, and it would be unwise for such planning to claim too much of top management's attention.

At times strategic planning and management control activities can conflict. For example, a manager may spend time thinking about the future that should be spent controlling current practices and operations. The reverse is also true. Furthermore, some actions taken to benefit strategic, long-range plans may cause immediate profits to drop. Certainly time and money spent on research and development of new products or services and on advertising are immediate costs for long-range gains. One of the central problems of the entire management process is that of striking the right balance between strategic (long-range) and operating (short-range) considerations.

THE BASIC CONTROL PROCESSES

The basic purpose of control is positive in that it focuses on achieving organizational objectives.[5] The best control process is forward looking; it prevents deviations from plans or objectives by anticipating their occurrence. The next best process detects variations as they occur and corrects them before they are fully established. The poorest process points up problems after they have developed. The latter process is one of the reasons that control is sometimes seen as a negative function. Controls that catch deviations only after they have occurred can lead to casting blame.

To illustrate: Most organizations have as one of their objectives the safety of employees. In one firm a tank had to be cleaned periodically. Even when empty it contained potentially dangerous fumes. Rules specified that the employee cleaning the tank had to wear a gas mask. He also had to wear a rope around his body under his arms; an employee at the top of the tank held the rope. The worker could thus be quickly pulled out if he were overcome by fumes. One day the foreman noticed that someone was cleaning the tank. The person was wearing the rope, but there was nobody standing at the top of the tank to pull it up in an

Three types of control
processes:

• Steering controls
• Yes-no controls
• Post-action controls

emergency. The foreman immediately rushed off to find the culprit. He did not realize that his leaving the scene violated the rule that someone had to be near the tank at all times while it was being cleaned. The foreman had lost sight of the positive side of controlling—in this case the goal of safety.

There are at least three basic types of controls: (1) steering controls, (2) yes-no controls, and (3) post-action controls.[6] Although the three are related, they will be described separately.

In **steering controls** corrective action is taken as necessary to ensure desired results while the operation is in progress. For example, in the Mars landings and Venus probes in-flight corrections were made while the spacecrafts were on the way to their destinations. As another example, the market research of an organization wishing to bring out a new product indicates that, to be competitive, the product must not cost more than a certain amount. Using standard cost control information, labor and other costs are estimated as the project begins. If the predicted cost is too high, steps are taken to reduce it before actual production. Steering controls offer the best opportunity for achieving desired results, because they provide for corrective action at the time it is most effective.

Yes-no controls report whether the completed work is acceptable or unacceptable before final action is taken with it. Quality inspection and legal approval of contracts are examples of such controls, which are essentially safety devices. A parachute is either properly packed or not. Yes-no controls would be unnecessary if steering controls were always effective. But since steering controls are often too expensive or not fully reliable, yes-no controls are frequently needed.

Post-action controls compare results after final action to a standard of desired results. School report cards, budgetary controls, and final inspections are examples of these controls. Although post-action controls cannot change results or initiate new results, they are useful in rewarding individuals for good performance and in providing planning data for steering controls.

All three control processes are necessary for an effective control system; each has a purpose. (Figure 11.3 shows the interrelationships among them.) Because steering controls are usually the most forward

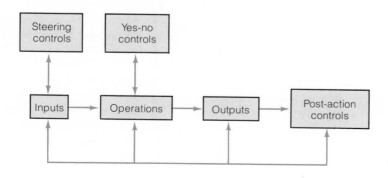

FIGURE 11.3 The interrelationships among the different types of controls

On the Job

TRUST: THE NEW INGREDIENT IN MANAGEMENT

Microscopically examining Japanese management practices to discover the secrets of that nation's high productivity has become almost an obsession in U.S. business circles. Treatises on the atmosphere of trust implicit in Japanese management-labor relations are crowding other business books off the shelves. But with all the savants' pronouncements on participatory management, one important element has been almost totally ignored: Japanese managers trust not only their workers but also their peers and superiors.

The existence of that all-encompassing trust leads to a simplified organizational structure that has helped many Japanese companies become low-cost producers. Because Japanese companies assume that personnel at all levels are competent—and, above all, trustworthy enough to have the company's best interests in mind—they do not employ highly paid executives whose only jobs are to review and pass on the work of other highly paid executives. They do not write job descriptions giving managers authority for specific fiefdoms and putting them into conflict with managers of rival fiefdoms. Instead, their operations are lean at the staff level and rich at the line level—where profits are made.

"The Japanese firms may well

have more people, but they are in profit related jobs," notes William H. Newsman, a professor at Columbia University's business school. "The Japanese will train their smartest engineers to identify problems, then put them on the shop floor. In the U.S. they'd be sitting at a desk reviewing things."

"Big Brother syndrome"
Slowly, U.S. business experts are recognizing the bottom-line impact that a preponderance of "reviewers" can have. The addition of layers of highly paid executives to Sears, Roebuck & Co.'s corporate headquarters—rather than to its stores—has helped turn the mammoth retailer into one of the highest-cost merchandisers in the country. And U.S. auto makers are beginning to see connections between Japanese structural organization and low costs. Japanese foremen, for example, report directly to plant managers, while American foremen must wade through three extra layers of management. Not surprisingly, the Japanese can make a car and ship it here for $1,500 less than it costs a U.S. auto maker to produce and sell a comparable vehicle.

At Ford Motor Co., there are 11 layers of management between the factory worker and the chairman, while Toyota Motor Co. makes do with six. Now Ford's

management has come to the uncomfortable conclusion that this excess layering has had two negative results: high overhead and a morass of red tape.

The company recently increased by several million dollars its plant managers' spending authority in order to push decision-making further down the hierarchy. And Ford is starting to disband some of the corporate subcommittees that traditionally had reviewed divisional decisions. "We've had Big Brother syndrome, looking over each others' shoulders, checking and rechecking," admits William J. Harahan, Ford's director of technical planning. "I suggest that we can no longer afford these layers of manufacturing management."

Theory Y management   Clearly, Ford is moving toward what Douglas McGregor would describe as a Theory Y approach to management. McGregor has postulated that a Theory X manager—until recently, a typical American manager—works on the premise that employees cannot be trusted to do their best and thus must be given specific orders and close supervision. A Theory Y manager, by contrast, believes that people want to work hard and respond best to a participatory managerial style. This theory, almost always cited in terms of individual managerial approaches, can easily apply to a corporate culture. Japanese companies, thus, would be Theory Y companies throughout their hierarchies and would require fewer purely supervisory layers.

Instinctively, the Japanese recognize that a Theory Y approach must be a two-way street. Japanese companies are as conscious of their employees' interests as they expect employees to be of theirs. Work force layoffs are rare, and, similarly, Japanese managers are almost never pushed out. Promotions and raises are based as much on seniority and teamwork as on individual performance. "The Japanese managers do not feel they must constantly cover themselves or be caught up in an individually competitive position to get ahead," maintains Harry Levinson, head of the Levinson Institute, a psychological consulting firm. Adds Junichi Nakamura, general manager for Mitsubishi International Corp. in New York: "There is pride and even sibling rivalry, but there is a family consciousness. Everyone believes that his colleagues and superiors care about his welfare."

It would be unrealistic to expect this atmosphere to exist in an American corporation. Nonetheless, Japanese companies that hire Americans in their U.S.

operations manage quite effectively without cadres of supervisors in their executive suites. The presidents of both Quasar Co. and Matsushita Industrial Co. find it comfortable to work with only one vice-president and to have 10 or more managers reporting to them.

Matrix management These companies and others like them operate in a manner highly reminiscent of the American concept of matrix management. That concept requires design engineers, production managers, and marketing specialists, for example, to iron out their differences on priorities and scheduling long before their recommendations are passed upward. Implementing a matrix structure has proved to be inordinately difficult in the hierarchy-conscious U.S. business culture, but it is the natural order of things in Japan. Japanese employees learn the intricacies of other departments before they are permitted to specialize. Thus they are sympathetic rather than suspicious of their counterparts by the time they have become managers.

Both Quasar and Matsushita are seeking ways to emulate that approach by educating their American managers in the profit-and-loss ramifications of operations outside their sphere. "I now have managers all the

way down to product-line level who realize the P&L implications of our whole operation and thus [fully understand interrelationships] outside their immediate areas," says Alex Stone, Quasar's president.

No one suggests that the quick fix of a training program can achieve the results garnered from an environment that fosters lifetime security and trust. But it is important for U.S. managers to realize that, at least to a certain extent, it can happen here. There are enough American companies that have tried some small part of the Japanese method to prove that point. Dana Corp., for one, has been existing with only five levels of management between the chief executive and the shop floor, and Chairman Gerald B. Mitchell says his immediate goal "is to reduce this to four." Hewlett-Packard Corp. has been able to dispense with accounting experts who arbitrate transfer prices between divisions supplying goods to each other by establishing a simple formula based on fully loaded factory cost less a percentage negotiated between the departments. Sums up a consultant who has studied the company: "It works because the department heads trust each other."

Still, it will take a while before American business culture moves firmly into the camp of

looking and effective, more emphasis will be placed on them than on the other two in the rest of this chapter.

THE BASIC ELEMENTS OF CONTROL

Elements of control processes:

- Standards
- Results versus standards
- Corrective action

Controlling is a universal management function.[7] Its basic elements remain the same no matter what is being controlled. They are: (1) establishing standards, (2) measuring the results of activities against these standards, and (3) taking necessary corrective actions when deviations from standards occur. Figure 11.4 shows these basic elements.

Element 1: Establishing Standards **Standards** are units of measurement against which results are compared. The general objectives for the organization or unit that are established by the planning process need one or more standards. Without such standards, control is impossible. The basic purpose of control is to make certain that goals are achieved, and standards are necessary to judge how well results fulfill those goals.

Some standards are concrete measurements such as quantities of

FIGURE 11.4 The basic steps in the controlling process

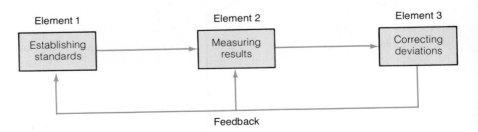

products, units of output service, number of clients seen, turnover rate, absentee rate, hours worked, and money spent and received. Other standards are relatively intangible and can be measured only indirectly. One example is job satisfaction, which can be measured by using absentee and turnover rates. Another tool of indirect measurement is the questionnaire.

Whenever possible, standards should point to key result areas. For example, the J. C. Penney stores measure productivity in two key areas—sales per square foot and sales per labor hour. Using computerized cash registers, Penney's can provide managers with almost instant information on total footage and hours of labor. Managers can use the information to decide if slow-selling goods should be replaced with faster-moving items and to pinpoint areas of high and low productivity.[8]

Element 2: Measuring the Results of Activities against Standards

Ideally, the measurement of results against standards involves steering controls. This allows **deviations**—variations from a plan—to be detected in time to make corrections. Frequently, alert managers can predict deviations from information they have gathered through the grapevine. News that a competitor is bringing out a new product or that a vendor's employees are planning to strike signals a deviation. News that President Carter was ordering a boycott of the 1980 Summer Olympics in Moscow because of the Soviet Union's invasion of Afghanistan caused a number of U.S. companies to stop making Olympic souvenirs.

Measuring results is facilitated by arranging data into a scale of performance that can be developed by collecting data on results and then comparing them with the data of the control standards. When planning has been performed well and objectives are clearly expressed in measurable terms, developing such a scale is easy. Data collection should be thorough to afford an accurate comparison.

In some areas performance cannot be accurately measured. For example, one goal may be to accelerate management development. Although the number of people attending management development courses can be counted, the count does not indicate the quality of the training. In other areas accurate measurements are too costly. A large department store chain developed an elaborate procedure for determining whether to accept or reject returned merchandise only to discover that the cost of maintaining the system was far greater than the cost of simply accepting all returned merchandise.

Control is more difficult when outputs are not tangible.

Measurement of tangible results, such as the production rate for a mass-produced item, requires relatively little effort. But what standard can a hospital manager use to measure, for example, the overall competence of the social work director? And can the social work director measure the results of a psychiatric social worker assigned to the family of a mental patient?

In these situations managers must discuss relatively intangible standards with their subordinates. Management by objectives may help develop mutual agreement about the job and about how well it is being done, but in many instances "managerial controls over interpersonal relationships must continue to be based upon intangible standards, considered judgment . . . and even, on occasion, sheer hunch."[9]

Corrective action involves:

• Analysis of cause
• Initiation of action
• Expected results forecasted

Element 3: Correction of Deviations The final element of the control process is to correct significant deviations from desired results. This process includes both a decision-making and an action-taking phase. First, a decision is made on what the deviation is—what problem it represents—and what must be done to correct it. Care must be taken at this stage to separate symptoms from causes. A jump in absenteeism may be the result of a flu epidemic rather than a sign of dropping morale.

Second, corrective action is initiated. This may involve redrawing plans, modifying the objective, adjusting standards, or changing some key factor in the general situation. In the case of General Lavelle, the corrective action, which came months after the deviation began, was to recall the general.

Since controls do not always succeed in their purposes, after corrective action is taken, new forecasts of expected results should be made. If necessary, a new cycle of planning and controlling should be started.

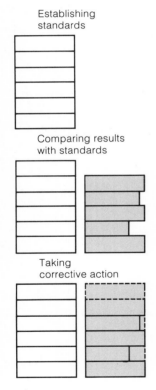

Establishing standards

Comparing results with standards

Taking corrective action

Control processes need not be highly complex. Indeed, effective controls can be very simple and still include the basic elements of establishing standards, measuring results, and taking corrective action. To illustrate: A restaurant owner suspected that the night watchman was stealing liquor and drinking it on the job. Controlling the drinking was probably not possible, but reducing the theft (establishing standards) was. The restaurant manager introduced a control process. Every night, just before leaving the restaurant, he would turn every two whiskey bottles behind the bar at a forty-five-degree angle to each other. The next morning he could immediately tell which had been moved (comparing results against standards). For several days he made such remarks to the night watchman as: "Hobby, how was the Four Roses last night?" or "I see you had Canadian Club this time." (This was corrective action.) The control process stopped Hobby from stealing whiskey, but it did not stop him from continuing to drink. Eventually, he was fired for drinking on the job (whiskey that he had bought elsewhere). Thus the final corrective action was discharge.[10]

CONTROL AS A FEEDBACK PROCESS

For the purpose of clarity the three basic control elements have been described in sequence, as though they were independent of each other. In reality, however, the elements are highly interrelated through the principle of feedback, illustrated in Figure 11.5.[11] A furnace demonstrates this principle when feedback informs the thermostat to turn the furnace on or off. Many physical, biological, and social systems also operate this way. Managerial control follows a similar process.

Management by exception is used when things go wrong, not right.

Lack of effective feedback and information flow was one of the major

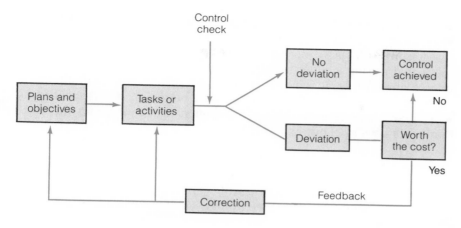

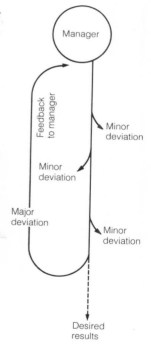

FIGURE 11.5 Control as a feedback process

causes of the failure of the W. T. Grant Company, a national chain of dime stores, when it went bankrupt in 1975.[12] According to testimony offered in court, Grant's buyers often had to ask their suppliers for figures on Grant's inventory, since they had no accessible data of their own. Store managers did not have the information or authority to control the stock in their own stores, and control on credit purchases was so poor that about 20 percent of all credit purchasers never paid their bills and the delinquencies were never detected.

But as Figure 11.5 suggests, the manager cannot and should not receive feedback about every minor deviation from plans. Thus the guideline for establishing feedback loops is whether knowledge of the deviation is worth the cost.

This system for relaying information on only the significant deviations to the manager is called **management by exception**, or the exception principle. It is so designed that the manager will receive no feedback information as long as the operation is proceeding close to plan. Consequently, the manager can concentrate attention on serious exceptions. If the cost of labor in an organization deviated from standard by 5 percent that would probably constitute a serious exception and the manager would be alerted. However, if the cost of postage deviated from the budget by 15 percent for a particular month, no feedback would be warranted.

INDIRECT AND DIRECT CONTROL

The two basic types of control—ways of making certain that future action is corrected or improved so as to achieve desired results—are indirect and direct control.[13] In **indirect control** the cause of an unsatisfactory result is traced to the responsible person, who is advised to correct or improve specific activities or practices. In **direct control** undesirable results are reduced by helping managers attain more knowl-

Indirect control improves managerial procedures.

Direct control improves managerial skills.

edge of management concepts and increase their skill in management techniques. In other words, better managers bring about better results, so direct control fosters internal changes in the individual manager that make that person a better manager. Indirect control, on the other hand, effects changes in specific processes and procedures external to the manager in order to help the manager do a better job. Indirect control is used more frequently and is usually what is meant when the word control is used without explanation.

Indirect Control   Most organizations have thousands of different standards for evaluating performance, including measurements of time, cost, quality, and quantity. Indirect control is appropriate for correcting deviations from these standards. Two human causes of deviations are uncertainty and lack of experience, knowledge, or judgment.

Uncertainty   As explained in Chapter 4, plans and decisions are created under conditions of certainty, risk, or uncertainty. Under conditions of certainty, the facts are known; under conditions of uncertainty and of risk, probabilities rather than facts must be used as a basis for planning. Decisions made under conditions of uncertainty or risk (risk being an extreme form of uncertainty) are usually directed by a combination of hunch, intuition, and judgment. Indirect control is ineffective in these situations, because it cannot make corrective adjustments for problem-causing events that cannot be predicted. Tracing the cause of the problem to the responsible person is irrelevant if unforeseen circumstances are the culprit.

Lack of Experience, Knowledge, or Judgment   A manager's lack of experience or knowledge of the work of a particular unit may cause some deviations from plans, especially when decisions must be made under conditions of uncertainty. However, years of experience in that unit's work is not sufficient to qualify an individual as a general manager. Good judgment is even more important than experience. A lack of experience or knowledge, can be remedied more easily than a lack of the maturity and wisdom necessary for good judgment. A person lacking experience can be transferred into a position that will provide it; a person lacking knowledge can receive further training; but continuing errors of judgment, particularly at the lower levels, may warrant demotion or dismissal.

A problem with indirect controls is that they are based on some false assumptions. One is that performance can always be measured. Sometimes, particularly under conditions of uncertainty, it cannot. Another is that personal responsibility for deviations can always be pinpointed. Government action, sudden moves by competitors, or unforeseeable disasters (such as the burning of a plant) can disrupt the best plans and controls, with no one in the organization being at fault. Still other false assumptions are that the time and expense of the controls are always warranted and that mistakes can always be detected in time to correct them. If the assumptions about indirect controls were all true, direct controls would be less important. Since they are not all true, however, indirect controls (which are always necessary) should be used in conjunction with direct controls, and direct controls should receive the greater emphasis.

Direct Control Direct control is based on the principle that no substitute exists for the intelligent use of fundamental management principles at all managerial levels: "The higher the quality of managers and their subordinates, the less will be the need for indirect controls."[14] Improving direct control means improving the quality of managers and their subordinates. This approach is forward looking in that it attempts to prevent the amount and degree of undesirable results.

At each managerial level there are various ways to improve the quality of performance. They include planned manager development programs, multidisciplinary trouble-shooting task forces, special project assignments, cross-functional task force study teams, ongoing appraisal, management by objectives, and planned job rotation.

An example of direct control follows: A certain company believed that a young salesperson had the potential to become a general manager. To give her the needed experience, the company planned a series of job rotations to various functional areas. First it made her the accountant for a small plant. Although she had had no actual accounting experience, she was trained for two weeks by the plant accountant (who was in turn being rotated to a different job). After working as plant accountant for about a year, the young woman was moved to the position of first-level manufacturing supervisor in a larger plant. Other carefully planned transfers followed, all designed to give her broad experience before her length of employment warranted a salary too large for these positions.

Another example of direct control involves an entire work force rather than one potential manager. In this case sociotechnical approaches (described in Chapter 9) were used to structure work so that deviations were corrected by direct control within the work group rather than by external, indirect control. A large petrochemical plant is the scene of this event, and 150 employees are involved. Instrumentation and equipment costs for the plant required a capital investment of over $2 million per employee.[15] Everything possible in this continuous process plant is routinized and computerized. The plant is run primarily by remote control from a central control room. Experience has shown that higher levels of technology, usually accompanied by large capital expenditures (exactly the case in this plant), actually increase the dependence of the organization on its workers, even though the opposite is intended. (The near-catastrophe at the Three Mile Island nuclear power plant is one illustration.) As a result, a decision was made at this plant to train the work force to work in teams to handle the unexpected events that could not be handled by computers. This is a direct control procedure. (This plant will be discussed further in Chapter 13.)

Direct and indirect control are the two major types of control—one

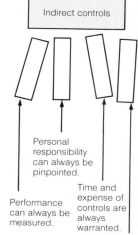

Indirect controls are based on some shaky assumptions.

Indirect controls

Personal responsibility can always be pinpointed.

Performance can always be measured.

Time and expense of controls are always warranted.

Mistakes can always be detected in time to correct them.

focused internally and the other externally. Other, specific types of controls are focused on different organizational areas or subjects, as described in the next section.

TYPES OF CONTROLS

The pervasiveness of control systems is such that we are all affected by some of them. Every time we stop for a traffic light, we are affected by a process for controlling traffic. The checkout counter at the local supermarket is a control process for ensuring that the store is paid for the goods it provides. Registration for courses at a university is a control process to ensure accurate records for charging tuition and maintaining transcripts.

Controls vary from very simple to highly complex. Their basic purpose is to prevent deviation from goal attainment. Among the many specific types of controls are (1) organizational structure and design, which determines reporting relationships and job design; (2) organizational norms and values; (3) production control, which is concerned with the scheduling (times and routes) for any product—from peanut butter to movies; (4) inventory control, which is concerned with the number of things produced; (5) quality control, which applies to both services and goods; and (6) budgetary control, which involves income, expenses, and similar matters.[16]

Types of control:

- Organizational structure
- Norms/values
- Production
- Inventory
- Quality
- Budgetary

Organizational Structure and Design **Organizational structure,** the overall design of the organization, determines reporting relationships and job design. It influences the work flow, the information flow, and the behavior of people on the job. It is a powerful control mechanism. In the past, there was little solid research to indicate the best way of using organizational structure to improve the function of organizations, subunits, and individual jobs. Today, however, certain principles of structure have been identified that motivate employees, lessen tension and frustration among them, and make the organization more effective.[17] (This topic is covered in more detail in the Chapters 12 and 15.)

Organizational Norms An **organizational norm** is a rule that tells the individual how to behave in a particular group or organization. Much of the organization's control is exercised through the use of norms. The norms may be formalized in written manuals, codes, and orders, or they may be less tangible. The strength of their influence does not depend on the degree of their formalization. Bankers in Boston tend to wear three-piece, pinstripe suits even in hot weather while bankers in California tend to dress more comfortably, but the norms that govern this matter are not written or even discussed. They are tacitly understood and obeyed.

Figure 11.6 shows the way the norms of an organization control the behavior of an individual member. The circle represents the vast range of human behavior. Out of this range the organization will reward a certain subset, will be indifferent to a second subset, and will oppose a

On the Job

FUNDAMENTALS OF CONTROL

In modern society, almost every aspect of social life is subject to control. We awake to the control of alarm clocks. The clothes we put on and even the breakfast we eat are controlled. Some control is imposed by government (for example, registering cars and licensing the people who drive them) and some by tradition, morality, good taste, or convention (for example, wearing clothes even in the hottest weather).

Although we do not like to think of ourselves as being "under control," most of us realize that control contributes greatly to society and, of course, to the organizations within it. Chaos would result if people could operate cars at any speeds they liked and could disregard stop signs and traffic lights.

In a work situation, nothing could be accomplished without control. Products could not be manufactured; services could not be rendered. Occasionally someone says that organizations and employees should be subject only to self-control because people are responsible and would conduct themselves in a reasonable manner. No one seriously suggests, however, that a society could prosper under self-control conditions. Imagine even a town in which all conduct were subject only to self-control.

Limits to the amount of control that a society or an organization can impose on its members should exist. But although control limits discretionary behavior to some degree, it also *allows* for responsible behavior. Therefore, it is something an organization or a society must have.

---

third subset. The norms of the organization, combined with the norms of the larger society, specify which behaviors belong to these subsets.[18]

In the diagram some of the symbols $(+, -,$ and $0)$ are out of place. They represent the mistakes that occur because of the imperfection of human systems (such as sending an innocent person to prison or failing to audit the returns of someone who cheats on income taxes).

Production Control **Production control,** an essential part of any organization, is concerned with the functions necessary to produce goods or services. It is production control that makes sure classes are scheduled correctly so that students and faculty come together at the right time and place. For manufacturers, production control is a complex process involving many aspects of the work flow. It is responsible for ensuring that operations are performed in the right sequence, that the right parts are ready at the right time, and that machines are properly loaded.

Inventory Control **Inventory control,** which is used by all organizations, is concerned with making certain that the right amount of raw materials, work in progress, and finished goods are available. A supermarket manager who orders too little milk runs the risk of losing sales; one who orders too much milk runs the risk of spoilage and waste. Universities know that not all the students they admit will actually enroll.

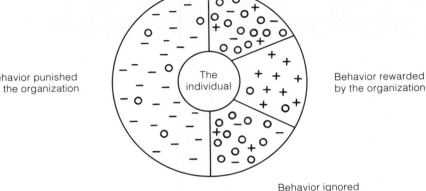

FIGURE 11.6 The normative model of control

Source: Adapted with permission from Gerhard E. Lenski, *Human Societies* (New York: McGraw-Hill, 1970), p. 75.

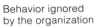

+   Behavior that is rewarded
O   Behavior that is ignored
−   Behavior that is punished

As a result, the admissions office admits more than the university can actually handle, using pre-controls based on past experience to try to get the right number actually admitted. Airlines, hotels, and motels have a complex inventory control process to ensure maximum use of facilities.

In large, complex organizations, inventory control is more difficult than it is in small ones. However, sophisticated methods have been developed for determining the proper level of inventory for literally hundreds of thousands of different parts.

Quality Control **Quality control** is concerned with the quality of goods and services provided. It ranges from the relatively simple to the highly complex. A relatively simple quality control model is a student's grade point average. A university sets a minimum standard and reviews the student's average to ensure that he or she is performing in an academically satisfactory manner. A slightly more complex example of quality control is the McDonald's hamburger. McDonald's uses a computer to maintain tight quality control of the size and content of the hamburgers, each of which must be 1.6 ounces in weight, 0.221 inches thick, and 3.875 inches wide when raw.

Budget Control Every organization has a **budget control** among its other financial controls. The budget is a statement of the future revenues and expenses of the organization. It provides perhaps the clearest quantification of the organization's plans, and it controls financial and other resources. (Budgets will be discussed in more detail in the following chapter.)

TEN CHARACTERISTICS OF EFFECTIVE CONTROLS

Managers need good control systems to help them make certain that results conform to plans. Much of the time and effort spent on accounting, statistics, and other planning approaches in an organization contributes to this control system. Each organization is different, and each has control systems specific to it; however, ten basic characteristics of effective controls have been identified[19]:

1. *Controls must be tied to the needs and nature of the activity.* The type of control system must be determined by the particular job that needs to be done. A marketing department, for example, may use controls for product introduction and for specific advertisements. A vice-president in charge of manufacturing generally uses more sophisticated and broad-ranging controls than a shop floor supervisor. Large businesses need different control systems than small ones. The more the control reflects the nature of the specific plan, the more effective it is.

2. *Controls must indicate deviations promptly.* The ideal control system detects potential deviations before they become actual ones. Although it is important to know when things have gone awry, it is better to know beforehand that they are likely to go wrong.

3. *Controls must be forward looking.* Closely related to the preceding characteristic is the concept of using forecasting as a method of control. Usually there is a time lag between a deviation and a corrective action. For example, although accounting reports are usually accurate, they occur after the fact. The manager may, however, want to forecast the future (with all its potential for error) rather than wait for an accurate report about which little can be done.

4. *Controls must point out critical exceptions at important points.* The manager cannot watch everything. As mentioned earlier, the *exception principle* must therefore be applied to factors that are critical in comparing results against predicted plans. The more the manager concentrates on important exceptions, the more effective are the control results.

5. *Controls must be reliable.* Accuracy in reporting results is essential. As computers are used more widely in organizations, information transferral improves, but reliability of data decreases. One way of increasing the reliability of data is to make certain that those providing the data do not perceive its ultimate use as being punitive to them. We all hate to testify against ourselves.

6. *Controls must be valid.* The validity of a control refers to how well it measures what it is supposed to measure. Counting the number of different clubs used by a golfer gives no idea of the person's score and is an invalid control. One of the best examples of deliberate mismeasurement occurred a few years ago. Two cars were entered in an international road trial. One was from Russia, and the other was from the United States. The U.S. car won, but the Russian press reported that "while the Russian car had finished second, the Amer-

Controls are critical determinants of peoples' behaviors.

ican car came in next to last."[20] Although the figures were accurate and the reporting reliable, the conclusion was not valid.

7. *Controls must be flexible.* As Chapter 7 showed, we live in an uncertain world. Because of this, it is unwise to make controls too objective and inflexible. Unforeseen circumstances usually alter any situation to some degree. One way of maintaining flexibility is to have alternative plans (and controls) for various possible situations. A sure sign of an organization that has inflexible controls is the failure to remove obsolete ones. For example, a large insurance company handles pension plans for a number of organizations. On one such plan is the notation, "Before taking any action on this plan, see John Doe." At one time, there had been a problem with the pension program, and the control of seeing John Doe was instituted. John Doe eventually left the company, but five years later the useless control was still in writing.

8. *Controls must be economical.* Controls are a means to an end, not an end in themselves. Obviously, a control process should not cost more than the results it controls. The effective manager carefully reviews control systems to ensure that they are cost effective, and one way of doing this is to eliminate controls in unimportant areas. One executive vice-president spent many hours a week reviewing expense accounts of salespeople and other employees. During a period of two years he changed not a single expense account; yet he continued the reviews. From the viewpoint of the total organization, his time could have been more profitably spent in other activities.

9. *Controls must be understandable.* In this age of complex mathematical formulas, charts, and computer printouts, a tendency has arisen to develop controls that are not understandable by those who use them or by those affected by them. In one organization a question-and-answer session revealed that the supervisors did not understand the budget and cost systems, although they had not previously indicated this. "Furthermore, since the answers that they received to their questions were invariably phrased in technical engineering and accounting terms, it is doubtful that their comprehension had increased very much by the end of the meeting."[21] If the control system cannot be understood and easily used by those involved, it is a liability rather than an asset.

10. *Controls must indicate corrective action.* A good control indicates not only when deviations occur but also how they should be corrected. A control is of value only if it allows decisions to be made before a crisis develops.

SUMMARY

Establishing goals and objectives, creating plans to meet those objectives, and designing controls to ensure that desired results are at-tained are all essential functions of the effective manager. Objectives, plans, and controls are linked together by a number of complex and interrelated decisions made on the basis of information received from an uncertain and turbulent environment. The manager must be able to adjust to different contingencies and be ready to change plans, objectives, and controls as necessary.

The three basic control processes are steering controls, yes-no controls, and post-action controls. Steering controls offer the greatest opportunity for bringing actual results close to desired results, because they provide a way to take corrective action while the activity is still going on.

The control process has three basic elements: establishing standards, measuring the results of activities against these standards, and taking necessary corrective actions when deviations from standards occur. These three elements are interrelated through the principle of feedback.

There are two basic types of control—indirect control and direct control. Indirect control traces the cause of an unsatisfactory result to the responsible person and advises that person to change procedures as appropriate, while direct control is a process of developing better managers.

Within these two major categories of control, there are a number of specific types. They include production control, inventory control, quality control, and budget control. Chapter 12 will describe other control techniques in greater detail.

There are ten characteristics of effective controls. Every organization and unit is unique and requires its own control systems, but managers should keep these ten basic characteristics in mind when designing such control systems.

STUDY QUESTIONS

1. What are the relationships among decision making, establishing objectives, planning, and controlling?

2. How does directing differ from controlling?

3. Why are forward looking controls important?

4. What are the basic differences among the three different control processes?

5. What are the basic elements in control?

6. How does direct control differ from indirect control?

7. Describe the characteristics of effective controls.

8. Interview managers and employees of both large and small organizations. Ask them about what techniques the organizations use to control their work and what they think about them. Do managers have the same opinions as employees? Explain.

9. Design a control system for a course you are taking. Relate the control system to objectives and planning.

Case for Discussion

THE FLYBALL GOVERNOR

James Watt faced a problem in 1788. Although he had successfully harnessed the energy of boiling water in his steam engines, a human operator was still needed to adjust the engine's throttle for increased or decreased power as the situation demanded it. This was particularly true when the steam engine was used to power other machines. The human operators often could not react quickly enough to adjust the power levels at the right time. Watt searched for a solution that would not only provide better regulation of the throttle but would also free the human operator for other tasks. The invention he created to solve the problem was the flyball governor, a device (illustrated in Figure 11.7) that is still used today. The flyball governor is geared to the main drive shaft of the steam engine. It rotates as the steam engine operates. If the engine speeds up, the governor rotates more rapidly. If the engine slows down, the governor rotates more slowly. The governor's rotation controls the power level of the engine.

As can be seen in the figure, two metal balls are attached to the governor by movable rods. When the governor's rotation speeds up, inertia causes the metal balls to move away from the governor's central shaft. When rotation slows, the balls move closer to the central shaft.

The governor also moves up and down as it rotates, tending to move upward as its speed increases and downward as its speed declines. Since it is connected to the engine's throttle by a metal rod that pivots on a fulcrum, the amount of fuel or steam furnished the engine will increase or decrease depending on the position of the governor. The position of the governor is determined by its speed of rotation, which in turn is determined

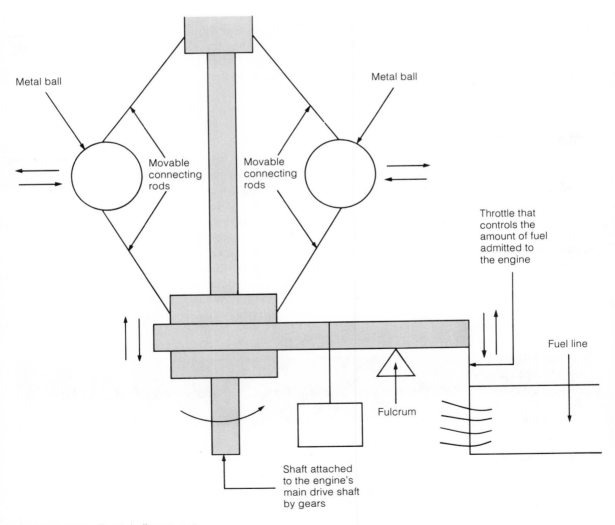

FIGURE 11.7   The flyball governor

by the speed of the engine's operation. Thus the flyball governor keeps the engine operating at a constant speed by adjusting the amount of fuel it receives.

This mechanism met Watt's objectives, includ-

ing that of freeing the human operator for other tasks. The flyball governor is one of the first control devices designed to be almost totally self-regulating.

Sources: F. Ross, Jr., *Automation: Servant to Man* (New York: Lothrop, Lee, and Shepard, 1958), pp. 7–9; and D. Woodbury, *Let Erma Do It: The Full Story of Automation* (New York: Harcourt, Brace & World, 1956), pp. 31–33.

1. Can you think of any ways in which human behavior is controlled in the same way the flyball governor controls a steam engine?

2. Would a manager want to exert control as continuously over employees as the flyball governor does over the steam engine? What would the gains and losses be from doing so?

3. What differences are there between human systems like organizations and mechanical devices, like the steam engine? Do these differences have any implications for control?

FOR YOUR CAREER

1. Controls are necessary because, as Murphy's Law suggests, whatever can go wrong, will.

2. Direct control is ideal, but we do not live in a perfect world. Trusted employees have been known to embezzle money.

3. Too often we do not examine whether controls are worth the cost. They should be economical.

4. Controls need to be positive and flexible. Controls that are too negative and inflexible tend to be ignored or, worse, subverted.

5. A feedback process should provide information directly to the person most affected by it. We can all learn from our mistakes if we get the right information.

FOOTNOTES

1. "Lavelle's Private War," *Time,* June 26, 1972, p. 14; "The Private War of General Lavelle," *Newsweek,* June 26, 1972, pp. 17–18; and George C. Wilson, "Washington: The Lavelle Case," *Atlantic Monthly,* December 1972, pp. 6–27.

2. P. Dauten, Jr., H. Gammil, and S. Robinson, "Our Concepts of Controlling Need Re-thinking," *Journal of the Academy of Management* 1 (December 1958): 41–55; W. Jerome, Jr., *Executive Control—The Catalyst* (New York: Wiley, 1961); E. Lawler, III, and J. Rhode, *Information and Control in Organizations* (Pacific Palisades, Calif.: Goodyear Publishing, 1976); and R. Dewelt, "Control: Key to Making Financial Strategy Work," *Management Review* 66 (March 1977): 18–25.

3. G. Giblioni and A. Bedian, "A Conspectus of Management Control Theory: 1900–1972," *Academy of Management Journal* 17 (June 1974): 293.

4. R. Anthony and J. Dearden, *Management Control Systems: Text and Cases* (Homewood, Ill.: Richard D. Irwin, 1976); and R. Anthony, *Planning and Control Systems: A Framework for Analysis* (Boston: Harvard University Graduate School of Business Administration, Division of Research, 1965).

5. E. Strong and R. Smith, *Management Control Models* (New York: Holt, Rinehart and Winston, 1968); and H. Koontz and C. O'Donnell, *Essentials of Management* (New York: McGraw-Hill, 1974).

6. W. Newman, *Constructive Control: Design and Use of Control Systems* (Englewood Cliffs, N.J.: Prentice-Hall, 1975); and H. Koontz and R. Bradspies, "Managing through Feedforward Control," *Business Horizons* 4 (June 1972): 25–36.

7. R. Mockler, *The Management Control Process* (New York: Wiley, 1961); and W. Newman, *Constructive Control: Design and Use of Control Systems* (Englewood Cliffs, N.J.: Prentice-Hall, 1975).

8. "J. C. Penny: Getting More from the Same Space," *Business Week,* August 18, 1975, pp. 80–88.

9. Koontz and O'Donnell, *Essentials of Management,* p. 368.

10. R. Albanese, *Management: Toward Accountability and Performance* (Homewood, Ill.: Richard D. Irwin, 1975), p. 189.

11. S. Beer, *Decision and Control* (New York: Wiley, 1966).

12. S. Slom, "Grant Testimony Shows It Lacked Curbs on Budget, Credit and Internal Woes," *Wall Street Journal,* February 4, 1977, p. 1.

13. Koontz and O'Donnell, *Essentials of Management,* pp. 403–413; and E. Huse, "Putting in a Management Development Program That Works," *California Management Review* 9 (Winter 1966): 73–80.

14. Koontz and O'Donnell, *Essentials of Management,* p. 406.

15. L. Davis and C. Sullivan, "A Labor-Management Contract and Quality of Working Life," *Journal of Occupational Behavior* 1 (January 1979): 15–28.

16. X. Gilbert, "Does Your Control System Fit Your Business?" *European Business* 37 (Spring 1973): 69–76; A. Tannenbaum, *Control in Organizations* (New York: McGraw-Hill, 1969); and B. Reimann and A. Negandhi, "Strategies of Administrative Control and Organization Effectiveness," *Human Relations* (May 1975): 475–486.

17. P. Lawrence and J. Lorsch, *Organization and Environment: Managing Differentiation and Integration* (Boston: Harvard University Graduate School of Business Administration, Division of Research, 1967).

18. G. Lenski, *Human Societies* (New York: McGraw-Hill, 1970), pp. 73–77.

19. Koontz and O'Donnell, *Essentials of Management,* pp. 362–365; and R. Fulmer, *The New Management* (New York: Macmillan, 1974), pp. 260–261.

20. Fulmer, *The New Management,* p. 259.

21. E. Caplan, *Management Accounting and Behavioral Science* (Reading, Mass.: Addison-Wesley, 1971), pp. 68–69.

Selected Control Techniques

CHAPTER 12

CONTENTS

CONTROLLING AT GENERAL ELECTRIC

Now beginning its second century of operation, General Electric is reaping the fruits of a major organizational restructuring begun in 1970 and completed in 1977. This restructuring resulted from a strategic planning system for making the company more effective in dealing with a changing environment. By 1976, six years after restructuring had begun, the company was achieving record results. In 1978, the year after the reorganization was completed, record results had been achieved for the third straight year. Sales were close to the $20 billion mark, and earnings moved up from $4.79 a share in 1977 to $5.39 in 1978 (compared to $1.98 a share in 1968, shortly before the reorganization began). The year of 1979 was the fourth straight year of increases. Sales were almost $22.5 billion (up 14 percent from the previous year), and earnings increased by 15 percent, making GE the tenth largest U.S. nonfinancial corporation.

GE recognized its need for a new organizational structure to afford better managerial control in the late 1960s. It had grown into the most diversified company in the world, producing everything from industrial diamonds, aircraft engines, microwave ovens, and refrigerators to electric carving knives, buses, steam turbines, locomotives, and heat pumps. Moreover, its heavy emphasis on research and development continually led it into new ventures. Its diversity was not well controlled, and some of its ventures were costly. For example, in the 1960s GE plunged into computer manufacturing and lost its shirt, eventually being forced to withdraw from that business.

Between 1965 and 1970 earnings were relatively flat, while return on investment and profit margins dropped. Meanwhile, top management was finding it impossible to keep informed on all the activities of the different operating units. As a result, funds were often improperly allocated, particularly those for capital expansion.

The restructuring begun in 1970 reduced the number of operating units from about two hundred to forty-three, each of which became a strategic business unit (SBU). Although a unit might comprise several departments, all its departments faced common market challenges and problems, allowing common planning strategies.

The workload at the top was still overwhelming. Top management wrestled with mountains of detail coming in from operating units around the world. To help them, GE set up a new layer of management just below the top. The business was divided into six major sectors—consumer products and services, power systems, industrial products and components, technical systems and materials, international, and Utah International, Inc. (a recently acquired mining company). Except for the Utah sector, each was headed by an executive who assumed much of the decision-making responsibility and also helped coordinate strategic planning. Not only was the load at the top reduced, but new synergies in operations were achieved in such areas as advertising, marketing, and joint ventures between different units.

Now GE's planning for each year starts in the January of the year before, when the SBUs begin drawing up their plans, taking into account political, economic, social, and technological factors. The plans usually include some new or revised programs. Each plan goes to the sector executive to whom the unit reports. Then, working closely with the managers of different units, the sector executive draws up a master plan and budget.

Top management receives the six sector plans and budgets together with summaries of the unit plans and budgets on which they are based. In November or December, the top policy group makes the final allocations of funds to the SBUs for the coming year. The allocations are based on each SBU's potential contribution to the overall sales and profits of the company. They provide a major control on what each SBU will do during the year.[1]

This case raises several critical questions which you should be able to answer after reading this chapter. The questions include:

1. How do budgets such as those used at General Electric help control the behavior of its employees?
2. What is the relationship between plans, goals, objectives, and organizational control? Explain.
3. What are some of the things you do to control the behavior of others? How effective are you in controlling others?
4. How can supervisors best control their employees?

12

Chapter 11 discussed the general principles of control. Using the GE case as a guide, this chapter will discuss some specific control techniques being used to manage organizations.

As the GE case demonstrates, structure is important to control. GE had to reorganize before top management was able to establish control of the sprawling organization. Essential to control is a structure that allows managers to plan what needs to be done and then use various types of controls (steering, post-action, and yes-no) as appropriate to ensure that events are proceeding according to that plan or that the manager is notified if events warrant a change in the plan.

Since structure is so consequential to control, this chapter will first examine some key elements of structure. Then it will look at budgets, a widely used form of financial control. (The structure of an organization must be established before its budgets can be prepared.) Since budgets are closely tied to planning, they can serve as steering or post-action controls. The chapter will also examine some widely used types of non-budgetary financial controls and will briefly review several goal-directed controls.

RESPONSIBILITY CENTERS

Any organization of more than a few people requires proper specialization or departmentalization—that is, structure—for work to proceed efficiently and for controls to be established. The pattern of departmentalization should be kept as simple as possible, or control can become unwieldy, as it did for GE when departmentalization had created two hundred diverse units.

The term **responsibility center** denotes any organization or unit that is headed by a manager responsible for that unit.[2] The responsibility centers making up an organization are known as departments or units. The SBUs described in the GE case are responsibility centers.

Responsibility centers can form a hierarchy. At the lowest level in the organization they might consist of one work shift or other small organizational unit headed by a lower-level manager. For example, the head nurse in a hospital is in charge of a responsibility center. At higher levels several of these smaller units might constitute a responsibility center. To top management and the board of directors, the entire organization is a responsibility center. Usually, however, the term is used for smaller, lower-level units.

All responsibility centers have objectives that are intended to help the organization as a whole achieve its broad objectives. Another characteristic of a responsibility center is that it has inputs of goods, services, or other resources and that it exists to produce outputs of goods or services. With this general description of a responsibility center as a guide, four

Responsibility centers include:

- Expense centers
- Profit centers
- Revenue centers
- Investment centers

The original draft of this chapter was written by Professor Allen C. Bluedorn of the University of Missouri–Columbia.

types of centers important to management control systems will be described: expense centers, revenue centers, profit centers, and investment centers.

Expense Centers   In an **expense center** the control system measures inputs or expenses (that is, costs) in monetary terms but does not measure outputs of goods, services, or other resources in the same way. Every responsibility center has outputs; that is, it does something. In expense centers, however, it is neither necessary nor feasible to measure these outputs in monetary terms. For example, it would be extremely difficult to measure the contribution of the main library to a university or the value of the accounting department to a company, though both are unarguably necessary to their respective organizations. In this type of responsibility center costs need to be watched and controlled, but measuring output would be impractical if not impossible.

Many, but not all, expense centers are also cost centers. A cost center is a device that is used in a full-cost accounting system to identify costs that are later to be charged to specific cost objectives.

Engineered expense centers should be distinguished from *discretionary cost centers.* Engineered costs, such as the costs of raw material or of direct labor, can be closely estimated by the manager and are expressed as standard costs. The competence of the manager of an engineered expense center can be evaluated by the degree to which actual costs are kept at or below standard. Discretionary costs cannot be reliably estimated in advance or even measured in monetary terms. Staff units responsible for industrial relations, research and development, and legal matters are examples of discretionary cost centers. Their costs depend in large part on the manager's judgment or discretion.

Revenue Centers   The **revenue center** is a responsibility center in which income or revenues are recorded. Thus outputs are measured, although no formal attempt is made to directly relate them to inputs (costs). (When costs are matched against income, the unit is a profit center, which will be described next.) Marketing and sales units are revenue centers. A branch sales office prepares budgets and sales quotas, both for the revenue center as a whole and for the individual sales people in the branch office. Records of actual sales or orders are compared with these budgets. To match costs against income, however, would be misleading, because the branch office has little or no influence over such factors as product design, product cost, or marketing strategy. Control of revenue centers is the same as for expense centers.

Profit Centers   Profit is the difference between revenues (income) and expenses (costs). A **profit center** measures performance in monetary terms of this difference between its outputs (revenues) and inputs (expenses). These measurements are one indication of how successful the profit center is and of how well its manager performs.

Whenever an organizational unit is given responsibility for earning a

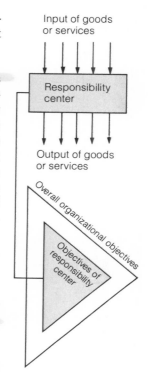

Input of goods
or services

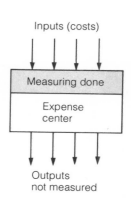

Inputs (costs)

Outputs
not measured

Cost centers and expense centers may be identical.

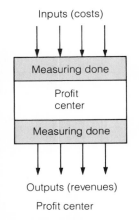

Inputs (costs)

Profit center

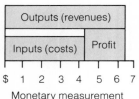

Outputs (revenues)

Profit center

Profit centers can motivate managers.

profit, a profit center is established. For example, each McDonald's restaurant is a profit center. In a different type of organization, such as a divisionalized corporation, each division may be a profit center. Each of the SBUs in GE is a profit center.

Profit centers are established when an organization or a division of it is charged for expenses and credited for revenues. A service department of an organization, such as the maintenance department, is sometimes a profit center in that it charges for or sells its services to other responsibility centers. In many universities, the bookstore is a profit center. Sometimes the manufacturing department of an organization becomes a profit center by charging the sales department for its output and recording its income from such transactions. In essence, the manufacturing department is selling its output to the sales department, and the more it sells, the higher its profits (although these profits are, of course, distinct from the profits of the organization as a whole and serve mainly to motivate employees within that center).

Such sales are also possible between different departments and are known as *transfer prices*. Usually they are the subject of much haggling, since each manager—both the buyer and the seller—is highly motivated to make that particular unit look good. As one GE executive said, "We have more trouble haggling over transfer prices than we do if we just go out and buy on the open market."

Investment Centers An **investment center** is a responsibility center in which the manager is responsible for the use of assets as well as revenues and expenses. It not only measures the money value of inputs and outputs, it also reviews how those outputs compare with the assets needed to produce them. An investment center is expected to produce a satisfactory return on the assets employed in it.

General Electric's SBUs are investment centers. So are McDonald's franchises. The profit generated by a McDonald's restaurant hides the true cost of going into business. The cost of the franchise itself must be taken into account as an investment.

Except in a few service organizations in which the amount of capital acquired is minor, an important objective of any profit-oriented organization is to earn a satisfactory return on the investment. The true profit made from a McDonald's franchise is made the same way a profit is made in purchasing high quality stocks or bonds or in buying a hardware or laundry business.

In larger organizations the measurement of the assets employed is called the *investment base*. Experts disagree on what is the best way to calculate the investment base. Once calculated, however, the base is related to profit in one of two major ways: through the percentage return or investment or through residual income. The **return on investment (ROI)** is a ratio, or fraction. The numerator is the income of the investment center, and the denominator is the assets employed. A McDonald's manager can take the profits for a year, or other suitable period of time, and divide them by the total investment. The results can then be compared to those of other restaurants in the chain or to other forms of investment as one index of success. One McDonald's manager found that after all his hard work, his ROI was less than it would have been if he had invested in a good mutual fund. He sold out and took up another line of work.

Residual income is a dollar amount rather than a ratio. It is computed by subtracting an interest charge from the net income. The residual income can then be used to make the same kinds of comparisons as are made with the ROI.

ROI is more widely used than residual income because it allows organizations to quickly find out when an investment center, such as a division or department, is unprofitable. When organizational units have widely differing amounts of capital investments or different profit objectives, however, the residual income method is preferable, because it provides a common standard for comparing such units. (Return on investment will be discussed in further detail later in the chapter.)

Clear identification of the various types of responsibility centers is essential for proper management control. For example, during the seven years of its reorganization, GE was able to identify forty-three strategic business units that it then combined into six major sectors. This identification was necessary before management could coordinate the planning and control that were so successful.

BUDGETS

A **budget** is a plan for a given future period that is stated in numerical (usually financial) terms. A household budget itemizes the sources of income for a family and describes how the income will be spent: so much for housing, food, utilities, transportation, clothing, entertainment, education, and so on.

Budgets can serve as:

- Plans
- Controls

The use of budgeting procedures for control purposes was first developed by the governments of several European countries during the eighteenth and nineteenth centuries. Budgeting procedures in the United States were haphazard and unsystematic until 1921, when Congress passed the Budgeting and Accounting Act. This act required the president to submit a budget with estimates of revenues and expenditures to Congress each year.[3]

The basic purpose of the budget is to improve operations. It represents an ongoing effort to specify actions needed to get the job done in the best possible way. An organization's budget is a detailed plan showing how funds will be spent on capital goods, labor, raw materials, and the like and how the funds for the expenditures will be obtained. Budgets should be thought of not as a way of limiting expenditures but as a management tool for obtaining the most productive and effective use of the organization's resources.

Budgets should be seen as opportunities rather than as constraints.

PLANNING AND BUDGETS

The budgeting process is closely tied to the planning process, as shown in Figure 12.1. Thus budgets are used as both planning and control devices.[4] As the figure shows, the first step in creating a budget is to establish overall objectives. The statement of objectives gives rise to the long-range plan (as discussed in the chapters on planning). For the organization in Figure 12.1 part of the long-range plan is a long-range sales forecast. The forecast requires a product mix strategy that predicts the number and types of products that will be produced in both the near and far future.

Within the framework of the long-range plan, short-term forecasts and budgets are developed. For the organization in the figure, a short-term sales forecast is developed. This forecast provides a basis for (and is

FIGURE 12.1 The relationships among organizational goals, plans, and budgets

Source: From *Managerial Finance,* Sixth Edition, by J. Fred Weston and Eugene F. Brigham. Copyright © 1978 by the Dryden Press, a division of Holt, Rinehart and Winston. Copyright © 1962, 1966, 1969, 1975 by Holt, Rinehart and Winston. Reprinted by permission of Holt, Rinehart and Winston.

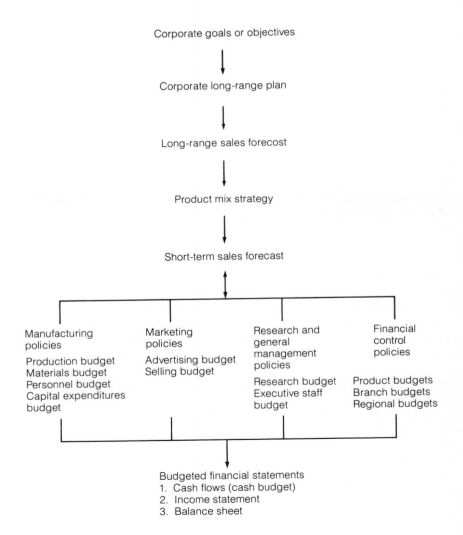

dependent on) the broad range of policies shown in the lower portion of the figure.

Manufacturing policies cover the different types of equipment needed, the layout of the plant, requirements for materials and personnel, and manufacturing arrangements. Quality and durability of items needed should be noted in these policies, as *should* quantities needed. *Marketing policies* state whether the organization will sell directly or through wholesalers, and they cover the pricing of products and set forth budgets for advertising and selling. Because an organization needs to continually upgrade its present products and develop new ones, *research policies* are also needed. *General management policies* specify the amount and degree of centralization or decentralization, the size of the corporate versus the divisional staff, pay levels and other reward procedures, and procedures for recruitment, selection, training, and development of employees. Finally, *financial policies* tie into the organization's goals and long-range plans. They cover many different kinds of budgets and financial ratios.

All these policies—manufacturing, marketing, general management, research, and financial—produce a variety of budgets. The production budget reflects the predicted use of labor, materials, parts, and facilities, each of which is the subject of a separate budget. Thus within the production budget there is a personnel or labor budget, a materials budget, a parts budget, and a facilities, or long-run capital expense, budget. Also, in marketing a number of different budgets are required; they cover advertising on TV, on radio, and in other media. Executive and general office requirements are reflected in the general administrative budget system, which may include, for example, one budget for recruitment costs and another for training and development.

To be most effective, each budget should be produced by means of planning and control approaches that anticipate and adapt for change. In today's economic environment, organizations are subject to complex pressures from competition, legislation, and other sources. The budget and control process can help managers plan ahead for changes necessitated by these pressures.

Internally, as Figure 12.1 shows, the budgeting process improves coordination. It provides an integrated picture of all the organization's operations research, engineering, personnel, production, marketing, and administrative areas.

> Plans and controls should never become fixed and rigid.

TYPES OF BUDGETS

The varieties of budgets are numerous.[5] Rather than trying to describe all the myriad types, this section will focus on three important ones that correspond to three types of responsibility centers. They are: expense budgets, revenue budgets, and profit budgets. It will then examine deviations from budgets and recent innovations in budgets.

Expense Budgets   An **expense budget** is a plan for a future period detailing the projected costs or expenditures for a specific responsibility center. Many college students operate on a simplified expense budget, since their expenses are higher than their income. Loans and parental subsidies are not technically income.

An organization's expense budgets are a key factor in its success. Since there are usually many more expense centers than revenue or profit centers, expense budgets affect a far higher percentage of employees and a higher percentage of managerial and supervisory personnel than almost any other type of budget. Many times manufacturing, personnel, legal, quality control, inspection, finance, and accounting departments have no identifiable revenue although they all have expenses. Therefore, these departments will not have revenue budgets but will have expense budgets.

Particularly for production operations, the proper way to express an expense budget is in terms of physical quantities and unit prices. For example, a manufacturing manager may control the amount of material and labor, expressed in physical terms, such as number of units or number of hours worked. The actual pay rate may be controlled by the union contract and may not be under the individual supervisor's control.

Revenue Budgets   A **revenue budget** is a plan for a future period detailing the projected income for a specific responsibility center. In a manufacturing company, such a budget usually consists of the expected quantity of sales multiplied by the expected unit selling price of the organization's products. An accounting, consulting, or legal organization might project revenues based on the number of consulting hours multiplied by consulting rates. A hospital might project income based on many factors involving admissions, prescriptions, X-rays, and so on.

Types of budgets:

- Expense budgets
- Revenue budgets
- Profit budgets

Manufacturing companies frequently establish revenue budgets for each sales office and even for individual salespeople; they are, in effect, sales quotas. Although the revenue budget is highly important, perhaps even the most critical part of a profit budget, it is also highly uncertain since it requires an attempt to predict the future. Revenue budgets for organizations in a stable, known environment are more cetain than those for organizations in an unstable, turbulent market.

Most organizations can control to some extent the factors that affect sales (revenue), such as advertising, service, and personnel training. However, sales and marketing managers usually have less control over sales than operating managers do over costs and so are not expected to be as closely on target as operating managers. As a result, revenue budgets are less useful than cost budgets for managerial evaluation.

Of course, organizational units such as district sales offices have expenses as well as revenues for salaries, travel, and advertising. Revenue centers have budgets for these expenses also. Thus revenue centers are also cost centers. However, the expenses cannot be subtracted from revenues to reveal profit, because the expenses do not include the cost of goods sold. If they did, the centers would be profit centers rather than revenue centers.

Profit Budgets A **profit budget** includes expense and revenue budgets in a single statement. Individual departments with profit budgets—indicating that they control both their income and their costs—are usually found only in large organizations. The clearest illustration is that of an operating division where the manufacturing, marketing, engineering, and staff departments all report to a single manager as in the SBUs at General Electric. Under these circumstances, the manager can be held responsible for both output (sales) and costs. Furthermore, profit can be calculated by subtracting the costs from the revenues.

Because there are ways of temporarily increasing profits, such as reducing maintenance, the success of a department or unit that operates as a profit center cannot be evaluated solely on the basis of its annual profit. The control process must consider not only whether or not the budgeted profit level was achieved, but also whether it was achieved according to plan, without resorting to steps of temporarily increasing the profit.

Deviations from Budgets Budgets are predictions of the future and thus are subject to change. Consequently, in most organizations managers are not automatically denounced for not meeting the budget in every minor revenue and expense category. This is particularly true for managers at the higher levels. Managers are not expected to pass up unforeseen opportunities, for example, because of a blind adherence to the budget. Moreover, the budget limitations should not prevent the manager from dealing with unforeseen problems in the best way possible. Most organizations are careful not to prohibit explainable deviations from budgets, though they may require that managers obtain permission in advance for major deviations. Deviations are not necessarily good or bad; they are simply signs that investigation is needed.

One should avoid the attitude of a certain division sales manager who was proud that for the last ten years he had never deviated one penny from his expense budget. In his case, the budget had become the end, rather than the means, a goal in itself rather than a tool to achieve the goal of increased sales. This manager was eventually replaced on the grounds of lack of initiative and lack of creativity.

Many organizations have seasonal peaks and valleys in revenues and costs. A resort restaurant has most of its business (and expenses) in July and August. For these organizations flexible budgets (sometimes called variable budgets) are more useful than fixed budgets. A *flexible budget* relates costs to overall units of volume rather than to any particular fixed volume or time. It allows for variation in some types of costs at different levels of output. For example, a department store's budget may allow for employing extra workers just before Christmas to handle the increased volume of sales.

INNOVATIONS IN BUDGETS

Although organizations have been using budgets for many years, innovations still occur. The government sector has been particularly innovative in recent years. Two techniques popularized by the government are the planning-programming-budgeting system (PPBS) and zero-base budgeting (ZBB).

Planning-Prgramming-Budgeting System (PPBS) PPBS received national attention when Secretary of Defense Robert McNamara introduced it to the Department of Defense (DOD) in 1961. This system was instituted because previous budgeting systems had resulted in unnecessary duplication among the different military services. They had also failed to provide for the long-range consequences of short-range budgetary decisions. Finally, the previous budgeting systems had given too little priority to the effectiveness of weaponry and personnel acquired by the DOD. PPBS was seen as strong in all the areas where other systems had been weak.

In the late 1960s PPBS reached its peak of popularity when President Johnson ordered all departments in the federal government to adopt it. For reasons that will be discussed later, it subsequently lost some popularity, at least the federal government, and was abandoned by most departments and agencies in 1971.[6] It is still being used in some government institutions, however, and in many types of educational institutions because of its many advantages over traditional budgeting systems.

The PPBS approach to budgetary control consists of five major steps:

1. Program objectives are specified. The organization or unit analyzes what it is trying to accomplish in order to make sure that nothing is overlooked.
2. Proposed or ongoing activities are examined to ensure that they are promoting the ultimate objectives of the organization.
3. Program costs are projected for several years into the future, since many projects that organizations undertake have deceptively low short-run costs but are prohibitively expensive in the long run. Developing a feasibility study for a dam (a short-term cost) is much less expensive than actually building the dam (the long-term cost).
4. Alternatives are analyzed. Various projects are compared with each other to determine which will contribute the most to the overall objectives of the organization and at what cost.
5. PPBS is made an integral part of all budgetary processes in the organization, standardizing budgeting procedures and providing the entire organization with its benefits.[7]

Along with its many advantages, PPBS has a number of shortcomings.

1. It emphasizes what is to be accomplished (strategic goals) at the expense of delineating how the goals are to be accomplished.

2. It forces managers to make policy decisions very early, often too early for a well-reasoned decision.
3. It is not always beneficial to the lower-level managers who must implement hastily made policy decisions of higher-level managers.
4. It fails to provide the means to evaluate the impact of budgets on various programs.
5. It concerns itself with new or expanding programs to such a degree that evaluation of older, established programs is neglected.[8]

Despite its faults, PPBS has produced such positive results as an overall increase in efficiency, more critical evaluations of programs, and the impetus to establish concrete and specific goals.[9]

Zero-Base Budgeting (ZBB)   As the popularity of PPBS waned, a new system called zero-base budgeting (ZBB) was developed and implemented with apparent success in many organizations. It was first employed on a large scale at Texas Instruments. Its potential gained national attention during the presidential campaign of 1976, when Jimmy Carter said that, if elected, he would implement it for the federal government just as he had for the state of Georgia while he was governor.[10]

ZBB is a system whereby each department of an organization must start its budget anew each year. Each year it must analyze every program and justify every proposed expense. ZBB contrasts dramatically with traditional methods of budgeting, in which a new year's budget is based primarily on the preceding budget. The traditional approach is called incrementalism, because it causes budgets to change each year only by modest increments, although occasionally there are slight decreases. ZBB produces more changes in budgets. It proceeds by three basic steps: developing decision packages, ranking decision packages, and allocating resources.

Developing Decision Packages   A decision package is a written description of a single specific activity within an organizational unit. Its purpose is to provide management with all relevant information about the activity or program so that its costs and benefits, can be compared with others within the unit regarding the potential consequences if it is not continued, and how it could be replaced by other activities.

Ranking Decision Packages   A decision package is created for each activity (down to a certain level) performed by the organization. Each decision package is ranked in order of its decreasing benefit to the organization. Rankings made by lower-level managers are reviewed by higher-level managers. Ultimately, all rankings are reviewed by top management.

Allocating Resources   After the organization's activities have been ranked, resources are assigned to them. Higher ranked activities, of course, tend to receive more of the organization's resources. Activities

ZBB
emphasizes
how

PPBS
emphasizes
what

Way to achieve goals

Goals

with lower ranks may not be funded as quickly, and activities with extremely low ranks may not be funded at all.

Advantages of ZBB are that it concentrates on the means to achieve the organization's goals, not stopping at merely defining them (as PPBS does), it serves as a working tool for lower-level managers, and, perhaps most importantly, it provides a way to review programs and activities in their entirety.

ZBB's disadvantages are primarily ones of cost. It requires more time and people than the traditional methods. When the city of Wilmington, Delaware, adopted the ZBB system, it devoted 50 percent more time to the process than it had to previous systems. When the U.S. Navy tried ZBB on its $10 billion budget for operations and maintenance, it sent 2,000 pages of documentation to Congress compared to the 150 pages under its old system.[11] These examples illustrate the increased costs associated with ZBB. A manager who is considering the adoption of ZBB should weigh the benefits of the system against the increased costs.

NONBUDGETARY RESOURCE CONTROLS

Nonbudgetary controls:

- Break-even analysis
- Performance ratios
- Audits

Previous sections of this chapter have focused on the budgetary aspects of controls that stem primarily from responsibility centers. A wide variety of resource controls are nonbudgetary in nature. Only a few of the more important ones will be discussed: break-even analysis, performance ratios, and auditing.

Break-even Analysis Although break-even analysis is a technique often used to help plan budgets, it is discussed here with nonbudgetary control techniques because it is not a budgeting technique in itself. **Break-even analysis** is an analytical technique for examining the relationships among fixed costs, variable costs, and profits. The analysis is based on the assumption that managers of an organization wish to have the organization make a profit or at least minimize its losses. This technique allows managers to determine the amount of profit or loss an organization will experience on the basis of its level of production.

Although the analysis can be performed entirely by mathematics, without the use of a graphic display, the break-even chart introduced in 1914 is a very useful device.[12] An example of the chart is given in Figure 12.2.[13]

The vertical axis in the chart represents the dollar value of income and costs. The horizontal axis represents the number of units produced and sold. The chart can be adapted for service organizations by changing units produced to an appropriate volume of business dimension. Since the amount of profit or loss at any level of production is figured simply by subtracting the organization's total costs from its total income, the value of break-even analysis is that it allows managers to calculate total costs and the organization's income at a given level of production.

An organization's total costs are the sum of its fixed and variable

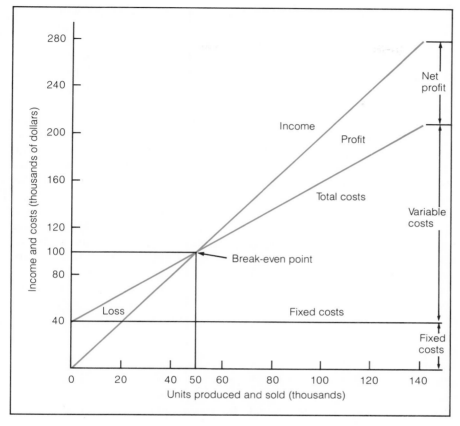

FIGURE 12.2 Break-even chart

Source: From *Managerial Finance,* Sixth Edition, by J. Fred Weston and Eugene F. Brigham. Copyright ©️ 1978 by the Dryden Press, a division of Holt, Rinehart and Winston. Copyright ©️ 1962, 1966, 1975 by Holt, Rinehart and Winston. Reprinted by permission of Holt, Rinehart and Winston.

costs. **Fixed costs** are expenses that remain unchanged regardless of the level of production. Typical examples are depreciation on plant and equipment, loan payments, rental expenses, salaries of upper-level management (within limits), and general office expenses. In Figure 12.2, the fixed costs amount to $40,000, as shown by the horizontal line.

Variable costs are expenses that increase as the volume of production increases. Examples are raw materials, wages, and sales commissions. In the figure variable costs are computed at $1.20 per unit produced, so total costs per unit increase by that amount. Production is predicted at sales of $2 per unit, so the total income is shown as a straight line that varies directly according to production. Since the organization is receiving $2 of income for every $1.20 paid out, the slope (or the rate of ascent) of the total income line is steeper than that of the total costs.

The total cost line and the income line in the figure intersect at 50,000 units of production. This point is called the *break-even point,* the point at which costs exactly equal income. The area between the intersecting lines and below the break-even point represents a net loss to the organization since costs exceed income. In the same way, the area between the two intersecting lines above the break-even point represents a net profit for the organization since income exceeds costs in varying degrees.

Break-even analysis is helpful in setting production quotas and rates. The break-even point is the minimum production level needed to avoid losing money. Also, to increase production to a satisfactory profit level may require additional capitalization through loans, and break-even analysis can help management determine the amount of money it needs to borrow.

Some warnings are appropriate for a discussion of break-even analysis. For most organizations, the information required to develop the analysis is complex. The linear (straight line) functions for costs and income shown in Figure 12.2 are reasonably accurate within limits but lose accuracy as the lengths of the cost and income scales increase. More complex, nonlinear curves may then be required.[14] Also, regardless of the sophistication of the functions used in the model, it is still based on assumptions and estimates. (For example, wage rates, the number of units that can be sold at a certain price, and the price of raw materials are all estimates, not facts.) This means that the principle well-known to computer programmers—GIGO (garbage in, garbage out)—could seriously distort the results of the analysis. Put another way, the analysis will be only as good as the assumptions and estimates on which it is based.

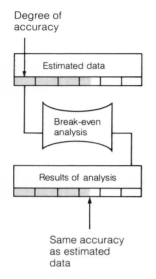

Degree of accuracy

Estimated data

Break-even analysis

Results of analysis

Same accuracy as estimated data

Performance ratios:

- Liquidity
- Quick
- Leverage
- Activity
- Profitability
- ROI

Performance Ratios   Ratios are an important and widely used form of both steering and post-action controls. They entail comparisons of selected financial values to evaluate the overall performance of an organization. They allow comparison of the organization's earlier performance with its later performance and also with the performance of other, similar organizations.[15] Ratios make figures more meaningful. For example, $5 million annual sales for a hardware store might be high in relationship to other hardware stores but low for an oil company. (Exxon had more than $84 billion in sales in 1979, while Mobil had almost $48 billion.) **Ratio analysis** selects two significant figures from a financial statement and shows their relationship in terms of a ratio or percentage, thus allowing the manager to more accurately assess performance of the organization.

Although there are many different kinds of ratios, they can be classified into four general categories: liquidity, leverage, activity, and profitability. Each of these types of ratios gives managers information about a different aspect of the organization's performance, and together the four types provide an overall picture of the organization's financial condition.

A *liquidity ratio* measures an organization's ability to pay its short-term debts. Two commonly used liquidity ratios are the current ratio and the quick ratio (also called the acid test ratio). The *current ratio* is calculated by dividing the organization's current assets (cash, inventories, accounts receivable, and so on) by its current liabilities (such as accounts payable and short-term notes payable):

$$\text{Current ratio} = \frac{\text{Current assets}}{\text{Current liabilities}}.$$

The ABC Hardware Store has current assets of $320,000 and current liabilities of $80,000. Thus, according to the formula, its current ratio is $320,000 ÷ $80,000 = 4.0. Since the average for other hardware stores is 3.79, we know that ABC has an above average current ratio.

The *quick ratio* is calculated in the same way as the current ratio, with one change. Inventory is no longer considered a current asset and must be subtracted from current assets. The reason for this difference is that a company's inventory is often the least liquid of its assets.

$$\text{Quick, or acid test, ratio} = \frac{\text{Current assets} - \text{inventory}}{\text{Current liabilities}}.$$

The ABC Hardware Store's quick ratio is $320,000 − $100,000 ÷ $80,000 = 2.75. These ratios inform us that the store could pay off short-term debts without relying on the sale of inventory and thus is solvent.

A *leverage ratio* compares the amount of an organization's financing from its owners (stockholders, partners) with the amount provided by creditors. The leverage ratio indicates the organization's ability to pay total or long-term debts. While there are a number of specific ratios used to measure leverage, the simplest and most straightforward is the *debt ratio*. This ratio is calculated by dividing an organization's total debt (current liabilities, bonds, and so on) by its total assets:

$$\text{Debt ratio} = \frac{\text{Total debt}}{\text{Total assets}}.$$

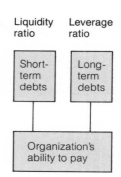

Liquidity ratio   Leverage ratio

Short-term debts | Long-term debts

Organization's ability to pay

The lower the ratio, the safer the firm's position. The ABC Hardware Store's ratio is 40 percent ($130,000 ÷ $325,000 = 0.4). Since the average for hardware stores is 10 percent, the firm's long-term debt may be too great.

Activity ratios indicate an organization's efficiency in utilizing its resources. There are a number of activity ratios, but most of them compare the organization's sales with some component of its assets. A frequently used activity ratio is the *inventory turnover ratio*, which is calculated by dividing the organization's sales by its inventory:

$$\text{Inventory turnover ratio} = \frac{\text{Sales}}{\text{Inventory}}.$$

This ratio shows whether an organization's inventories are too large or too small. In the case of ABC, the ratio is $700,000 ÷ $100,000 = 7, which compares favorably with the hardware store average of 3.9. A low ratio, such as 1.9, might indicate that some of the inventory is becoming obsolete or consists of items that will not sell.

Profitability ratios measure how profitable a company's overall performance is. In general, they compare returns generated on sales and investments. One such ratio is the *gross operating margin*, which is calculated by dividing sales into the gross operating profit and shows the extent to which unit selling prices can decline without causing a loss from operations profits. Another profitability ratio is the *sales margin*, which shows the profitability of overall sales and is calculated by dividing net income by sales.

Return on Investment (ROI) Return on investment is a profitability ratio that has become so popular that it merits separate discussion.[16] **Return on investment (ROI)** is the rate of return that an organization or a division has realized from the capital allotted to it. For this ratio, data should come from a relatively large segment of an organization, because the smaller the unit, the less accurate the ratio will be. Since the ROI ratio shows how effectively capital is being employed in various areas, it is helpful for establishing balance in the use of an organization's facilities.

The general ROI ratio is calculated by dividing the organization's net profit after taxes by its total assets:

$$\text{ROI} = \frac{\text{Net profit after taxes}}{\text{Total assets}}.$$

The DuPont Corporation has elaborated on this method in order to provide a more complete utilization of the information that is usually available to organizations. The DuPont system for calculating overall ROI is presented in Figure 12.3. As indicated in the figure, the final computation required in the DuPont method is:

$$\text{ROI} = \frac{\text{Profit}}{\text{Sales}} \times \frac{\text{Sales}}{\text{Investment}},$$

or profit margin divided by turnover. Since the sales terms in both ratios can be canceled, the formula reduces to:

$$\frac{\text{Profit margin}}{\text{Capital turnover}} = \text{ROI},$$

which is essentially the same as the original ROI formula. The DuPont system is significant because it specifies how to calculate the various components of the formula.

Using Financial Ratios In using any of the financial ratios, it is often useful to compare an organization's score with the scores of other similar organizations. Industry averages for many of the most common ratios are available from several sources. For example, *Dun's Review*, published by Dun & Bradstreet, annually reports thirteen ratios for twenty-two categories of manufacturing. Dun and Bradstreet publishes other ratios as well, and quarterly reports are made by such sources as the Federal Trade Commission. Public and university libraries can provide more information.

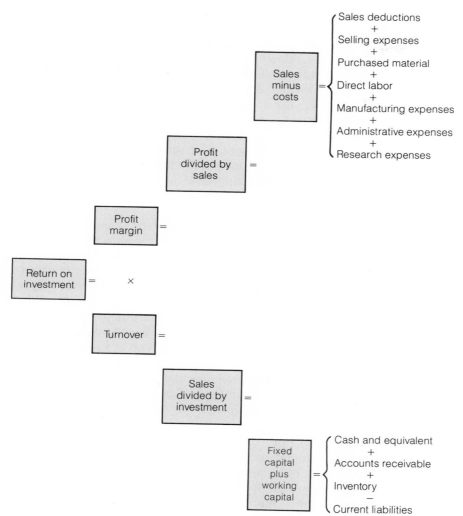

FIGURE 12.3 The return on investment equation

Source: Reprinted by permission of the publisher from Reginald L. Jones and H. George Trentin, *Budgeting: Key to Planning and Control,* © 1971 by American Management Association, Inc., p. 166. All rights reserved.

Financial ratios are often used in the control process as performance goals or as criteria for decision making. For example, an organization might regulate its volume of production so as to keep its inventory turnover ratio above or below a certain level. Financial ratios can be extremely valuable for this purpose, but when they are used too inflexibly, they can impede an organization's long-term success.

An example of the inflexible use of financial ratios is the way DuPont, the major innovator in the use of the ROI ratio, established a criterion of developing only those new products that seemed likely to produce an ROI ratio of at least 20 percent. Because of this criterion, DuPont passed up opportunities to develop xerography and the instant developing camera. Since the outcomes of these two decisions were poor in retrospect,

DuPont now uses ROI level as a general guideline rather than as a hard-and-fast rule.[17]

The ROI of the H. J. Heinz Company was markedly reduced (by a total of $8.4 million after taxes) during the period of 1971–1978, when some managers who had already made their sales or profit goals for a particular year surreptitiously switched records of their earnings in excess of those goals into following fiscal years to help ensure full compensation for those years under the company's extensive managerial bonus system. In addition, managers made prepayments to vendors with the agreement that the money or its equivalent in goods or services would be returned at a later date. The time of repayment was chosen by the manager to boost income when the division appeared to be falling short of its targets.[18]

Auditing   A third general approach to nonbudgetary financial control is *auditing*, which has traditionally been defined as the objective examination of the honesty and fairness of the presentation of the financial statements initially prepared by management.[19] *External auditing* is essentially a verification of the financial statements and is performed by a public accountant or accounting firm. *Internal auditing* is performed by accountants employed within the company. In addition to checking the accuracy of the financial data, internal auditing is used to check compliance with plans, policies, and procedures. Each type of auditing is useful for organizations. In both, the operating principle is that of accountability—the principle that people are more likely to behave in a desired fashion if they know that their behavior will be checked (audited) and that they will be held responsible for it.

Management audits
should have:

- Objective qualities
- Past, present, and future performance
- Useful results

The Management Audit   Both internal and external audits have traditionally dealt with financial records and statements. Since the Great Depression of the 1930s, however, a different type of audit, the management audit, has gained popularity. A **management audit** is a systematic procedure for examining, analyzing, and appraising management's overall performance.[20] Like the more traditional financial audit, management audits may be conducted by either internal personnel or external specialists. Regardless of who performs it, a good management audit possesses three fundamental characteristics:

1. It addresses objective and measurable issues.
2. It is concerned only with past and present performance, leaving future concerns to the manager.
3. It yields results and conclusions that are understandable and usable by relevant audiences.

GOAL-DIRECTED CONTROLS

So far this chapter has discussed control techniques that emphasize the management of organizational resources. A second family of techniques emphasizes control through the setting and analysis of both individual and organizational goals. Since the two most prominent of these techniques—management by objectives (MBO) and the program evaluation and review technique (PERT)—are described in detail elsewhere in the book (Chapters 5 and 14, respectively), only a brief summary of each technique will be provided here.

Goals provide for direction and control.

Management by objectives, or MBO, as it is more commonly known, is a technique for defining specific goals for employees and motivating the employees to achieve them. MBO is used primarily at managerial and professional levels. It usually involves three distinct endeavors. First, the individual manager's area of responsibility is defined. This task usually requires the participation of both the manager and the immediate superior. Second, mutually agreed upon standards and priorities for performance are set. Finally, a work plan is developed for achieving the mutually agreed upon goals in the defined area of responsibility.

MBO helps improve performance by ensuring that managers know what they are expected to do and how well they are expected to do it. In addition, the process provides managers with feedback on their performance and helps superiors provide instruction and advice in a supportive, nonthreatening manner.

The program evaluation and review technique (PERT) was originally developed to help the U.S. Navy manage very large and complex construction jobs. The basic function of PERT is to provide a detailed analysis of all the tasks required to complete a job. Thus the manager must describe each task and draw up a network diagram of the relationships among all the tasks (usually expressed by showing the sequencing of the tasks and the time required for each). With this diagram, the critical path (usually the sequence of activities that will take the longest time to complete) can be determined. Decisions about the overall project are then made within the constraints provided by the critical path.

SUMMARY

In the case of General Electric, at the beginning of the chapter, sales and earnings remained relatively flat until the company began reorganizing to better synchronize planning and control. The clear implication of this case for the manager is that planning, control, and organizational structure are highly interdependent.

Budgets are tied to the long-range plans of responsibility centers. Responsibility centers are the essential building blocks of an organization. They represent areas or units of an organization for which assigned managers are held accountable. A budget is a plan for a given future period and serves as both a steering control and a post-action control. Among the many different types of budgets are expense, revenue, and profit.

Since a budget is a plan for the future as well as a control process, deviations from the budget should be expected, because the future is never totally predictable. Managers should take advantage of opportunities when they arise even if it means deviation from the budget. Of course, significant deviations should be explained.

The modern manager should be familiar with innovations in budgeting—particularly the planning-programming-budgeting system (PPBS) and zero-base budgeting (ZBB)—and be ready to use whatever systems are most helpful to the particular organization or department.

Nonbudgetary resource controls are tools for both planning and control. Break-even analysis can help both the planning and controlling processes by clarifying the relationship between production and fixed and variable costs. Performance ratios serve as yardsticks for comparing the performance of an organization over time and against the performance of other, similar organizations. Return on investment (ROI) can provide managers with information on how well capital is being employed. Finally, the management

audit is a valuable tool for examining the management process itself.

Thus managers have access to a wide range of tools for determining whether goals are being met and for showing where corrective action is necessary. The manager who appreciates the importance of control and understands general control principles will develop and utilize specific techniques to implement such control.[21]

When budgeting controls are required, specific methods such as ZBB and PPBS are useful. For a more general approach to the control of resources, three of the more popular methods are break-even analysis, performance ratios, and auditing. If controlling by organizational and individual goals rather than by resources is desirable, MBO and PERT are helpful systems.

STUDY QUESTIONS

1. Describe a responsibility center.
2. Explain why the concept of a responsibility center is important.
3. Define *budget*. What are some major types of budgets?
4. In what way are planning and budgets related?
5. How is a break-even analysis performed?
6. What types of decisions does break-even

analysis help a manager make?
7. Describe the different types of performance ratios and explain their uses. Give an example of each type.
8. Where can information about the performance ratios of many companies be found?
9. Describe the different types of auditing.
10. Explain how a revenue center differs from a profit center.

Case for Discussion

PHANTOMS FILL BOY SCOUT LISTS

For most of this century, the Boy Scouts have been a tradition in the United States. The very term *scouting* conjures up images of camping, hikes, canoe trips, and troop meetings. After a four-month investigation, however, the *Chicago Tribune* reported another side of scouting— massive cheating on the part of paid professional staff members to make new enrollment quotas.

In 1968 the Boy Scouts of America (BSA) announced a campaign called *Boypower, 76*. The $56 million national program was to expand the BSA by more than 2 million members by 1976—to enroll one-third of all eligible boys eight to twenty years old. The program was designed to attract all nationalities and colors. Part of the campaign (programs for the poor) was federally funded.

By 1974 the program was far behind schedule, and professionals within the BSA were cheating extensively even in the federally funded programs to meet to Boypower quotas imposed on them. Many past and present BSA professionals claimed that, under pressure from the top, membership quotas were met with nonexistent boys in existing units or boys belonging to nonexistent units.

The investigation indicated that the cheating had little or no effect on existing Scout programs operated by adult volunteers. Once begun, the troops, packs, and posts operate almost independently of the professional organization. For example, the 15 Cub Scouts meeting weekly in a Detroit church were unaware that official Scout reports showed their unit as having 65 members.

The investigation suggested that the cheating was nationwide and that the worst of it occurred in the federally funded programs. These programs pay Scout dues and fees for inner-city blacks and Latinos, many of whom live in housing projects.

In Chicago, for example, a suppressed audit of the BSA showed that while the official membership figure was 75,000, the actual number was less than 40,000. The Scout official who ordered the audit was quietly transferred elsewhere. An independent report in the New York area in 1971 by the Institute of Public Affairs suggested that many Scout officials believed the pressure to meet membership quotas resulted in a "numbers game and a possible cause of paper troops." The report was never released to the public.

The inflation of membership was greater in the inner city than in the suburbs. The investigation reported that a Detroit supervisor told staff members to meet quotas even if they had to register bodies in cemeteries. Another professional reported that of the 3,000 Scouts on the books in Fort Dearborn in 1972, only 300 existed.

A professional staff member received a letter indicating that enrollment at camp was below acceptable limits and that failure to show dramatic progress could result in his being fired. The staff member replied that he could not send boys to camp when they existed only on paper. He had been transferred into the district a few months earlier and had discovered that 33 of its 47 registered units did not exist.

Sources: D. Young, "Phantoms Fill Boy Scout Rolls," *Chicago Tribune,* June 9 and 10, 1974; E. E. Lawler III and J. G. Rhode, *Information and Control in Organizations* (Santa Monica, Calif.: Goodyear Publishing, 1976); and C. Cammann and D. Nadler, "Fit Control Systems to Your Managerial Style," *Harvard Business Review* 54 (January–February 1976): 65–72.

1. Assuming that the investigation was correct, what could have caused the cheating?
2. What does this case show about control processes?
3. If you were the chief executive of the Boy Scouts, what would you do differently at the start of the campaign? After the investigation?

FOR YOUR CAREER

1. There is a saying, "Figures don't lie, but liars figure." Don't hesitate to check things out further if you suspect something is wrong.
2. One marketing executive was proud of the fact that he had never gone over budget. In the process of being a slave to the budget, however, he had missed a number of excellent marketing opportunities.
3. Frequently the best type of control is a proper organizational structure. One organization lost five engineering managers in six years; it finally redesigned the engineering department.
4. When numbers are overemphasized, the less easily quantifiable goals, such as management development, may be neglected.
5. Frequently the purpose of controls is forgotten in the process of implementing them. They are guides to attaining objectives, not ends in themselves. Technique should never supplant purpose.

FOOTNOTES

1. "Mastering Diversity at GE," *Dun's Review,* December 1978, pp. 30–32; "The Fortune Directory of the 500 Largest U.S. Industrial Corporations," *Fortune,* May 7, 1979, p. 272; and P. Wiggins, "U.S. Oil Companies Dominate Sales List," *New York Times,* March 19, 1980, p. D1.

2. C. Walker, "An Overview of Responsibility Accounting," in *Controller's Handbook,* ed. S. Goodman and J. Reece (Homewood, Ill.: Dow Jones–Irwin, 1978), pp. 567–617; R. Anthony and J. Dearden, *Management Control Systems: Text and Cases* (Homewood, Ill.: Richard D. Irwin, 1976); and R. Anthony and J. Reece, *Management Accounting: Text and Cases* (Homewood, Ill.: Richard D. Irwin, 1975).

3. W. Rautenstrauch and R. Villers, *Budgetary Control* (New York: Funk and Wagnalls, 1968); and G. Steiner, "Program Budgeting," *Business Horizons* 8 (Spring 1965): 43–52.

4. J. F. Weston and E. F. Brigham, *Managerial Finance,* 6th ed. (Hinsdale, Ill.: Dryden Press, 1978).

5. R. Jones and H. Trentin, *Budgeting: Key to Planning and Control* (New York: American Management Association, 1971); Goodman and Reece, *Controllers Handbook;* and G. Welsch, *Budgeting: Profit Planning and Control,* 4th ed. (Englewood Cliffs, N.J.: Prentice-Hall, 1977).

6. A. Schick, "A Death in the Bureaucracy: The Demise of Federal PPB," *Public Administration Review* 26 (March–April 1973): 146–156.

7. R. Anthony and R. Herzlinger, *Management Control in Nonprofit Organizations* (Homewood, Ill.: Richard D. Irwin, 1975).

8. P. Pyhrr, *Zero-Based Budgeting* (New York: Wiley, 1973), pp. 140–142.

9. Ibid., pp. 148–149.

10. "What It Means to Build a Budget from Zero," *Business Week,* April 18, 1977, pp. 160–164; "What Zero-Base Budgeting Is and How Carter Wants to Use It," *U.S. News & World Report,* April 25, 1977, pp. 91–93; P. Phyrr, "Zero-Base Budgeting," *Harvard Business Review* 48 (November–December 1970): 111–121; L. Cheek, *Zero-Base Budgeting Comes of Age* (New York: American Management Association, 1977).

11. "What It Means to Build a Budget from Zero."

12. Rautenstrauch and Villers, *Budgetary Control,* p. xxv.

13. Weston and Brigham, *Managerial Finance,* 6th ed. p. 72.

14. Ibid., pp. 72–82.

15. R. Mockler, *The Management Control Process* (New York: Appleton-Century-Crofts, 1972); and S. Goodman, *Financial Manager's Manual and Guide* (Englewood Cliffs, N.J.: Prentice-Hall, 1973).

16. R. Mockler, *The Management Control Process;* Weston and Brigham, *Managerial Finance,* 6th ed.; and Jones and Trentin, *Budgeting: Key to Planning and Control.*

17. "Lighting a Fire under the Sleeping Giant," *Business Week,* September 12, 1970, pp. 40–41.

18. T. Pretzinger, Jr., "Results in Probe of Heinz Income Juggling Expected to Be Announced by Early April," *Wall Street Journal,* March 18, 1980, p. 7.

19. A. Holmes and W. Overmeyer, *Basic Auditing,* 5th ed. (Homewood, Ill: Richard D. Irwin, 1976)

20. R. Doades, "The Mentality of Management Audits," *Public Utilities Fortnightly,* February 16, 1978, pp. 25–28; *Management Audit Questionnaires (Eleventh of a Series)* (New York: American Institute of Management, 1961); and R. Zilly and V. Meyers, *Management Audit for Small Construction Firms* (Washington, D.C.: Government Printing Office, 1979).

21. E. Flamholtz, "Organizational Control Systems as a Managerial Tool," *California Management Review* 12 (1979): 50–59; R. E. Cole, "Learning from the Japanese: Prospects and Pitfalls," *Management Review* (September 1980): 22–28, 38–42; H. C. Jain, "Workers' Participation versus Managerial Control," *Journal of Contemporary Business* 8 (1980): 137–152; S. Kerr, and J. Slocum, "Controlling the Performance of People in Organizations," in *Handbook of Organizations,* ed. W. Starbuck and P. Nystrom (University Press, 1981); and R. K. Sarin, "Performance-Based Incentive Plans," *Management Science* 26 (1980).

Designing Effective Control Systems

CHAPTER 13

CONTENTS

THE DENVER BRONCOS

On August 14, 1959, Lamar Hunt, the millionaire son of Texas billionaire H. L. Hunt, announced the formation of the American Football League. Having been denied expansion franchises in the established National Football League, he and his associates had formed their own league. Their original plan called for franchises in Dallas, Denver, Los Angeles, New York, Boston, Buffalo, Houston, and Minneapolis, but the Minneapolis group later withdrew when it was invited to join the National Football League in 1961, and Oakland took its place. On September 9, 1960, the first official game of the American Football League was played. The Denver Broncos defeated the Boston Patriots in Boston, 13–0.

The Denver franchise was owned by Lee Howsam and his two sons. The Howsam family had gained experience in professional sports by managing a minor league baseball team, the Denver Bears. The Howsams owned the stadium in which the Broncos would play. It was conveniently located close to downtown Denver, but it was small, barely accommodating 30,000 spectators.

To manage the football team, the Howsams hired Dean Griffing, a former football player at the University of Kansas and a coach and general manager for more than twenty-five years in the Canadian Football League. Griffing's most recent position had been that of manager of the city of Saskatchewan's football team. He hired his former coach there, Frank Filchock, to coach the Broncos. The team's first quarterback was ex-Saskatchewan quarterback Frank Tripuka. Partly because the Howsam family had considerably strained its resources, Griffing and Filchock adopted a managerial strategy focused primarily on controlling the team's costs.

The decision to tightly control costs produced a number of decisions unique for a football team. Mush was the main meal served at the training table. Only one set of jerseys was purchased for each player; the same jerseys were used for both home and away games. The coaching staff consisted of only three people—Griffing and two assistants. Griffing's attitude toward the team's operation was best revealed by his reaction to the injury of the team's only middle linebacker. When quarterback Tripuka asked Griffing to check the waiver list (a list of players available from other teams at a minimal cost) for potential linebackers, Griffing replied, "We don't need any; we have plenty of players here."

The Howsams lost $250,000 during the first year; the team won only four games and averaged only 13,000 spectators per game. Discouraged, and with their resources strained, the Howsams sold the team to another group of Denver people. The sale was not completed until May 1961—too late to make any significant changes in the team's basic strategy for the upcoming year—and a second poor season ensued, with only three games won and an average of 14,000 spectators per game.

After the second season, the new owners replaced Griffing and Filchock. They also changed the organization's strategy to provide much more money for improving the team by hiring better players, and more coaches and buying better equipment. Results were immediate. The Broncos won seven games during their first season under the new strategy and averaged 25,000 spectators per game, an increase of about 11,000.[1]

This opening case raises several key questions which you should be able to answer after reading this chapter. The questions include:

1. One strategy of the Denver Broncos was based on controlling costs. On what other bases can strategies be established?

2. What ways, in addition to strategy, can organizations control the behavior of their employees and departments?

3. Do you agree on disagree with the statement "I can't influence you if I don't allow you to influence me"?

4. What behavior of employees shouldn't organizations be allowed to control?

13

The first owners of the Broncos succeeded in implementing their strategy of controlling costs. However, the team's performance needed controlling as well, and in this they failed. Their actions are an example of what Peter Drucker calls doing things right but not doing the right things.[2] What they chose to perform was performed well (minimizing the team's cost), but they did not perform what was most important (leading the team to success). They could have used steering controls to good effect and learned that desired results were not going to be achieved in any area other than cost control. Post-action controls would have been ineffective. The Howsam family was forced to sell the team after losing $250,000.

The previous two chapters have focused on the fundamentals of control and have reviewed the application of some control techniques. This chapter will discuss the steps in designing and using effective control systems. First, each step will be examined in detail. Then the influence of the psychological contract on the behavior of people within the organization will be explored. Evidence suggests that people behave as they are expected to behave. Workable and just psychological contracts are based on this evidence.

Control can be seen as one-sided (one person in a relationship wields the control, and the other is affected by it) or as a process of mutual influence. The third major section of this chapter examines some of the consequences of these two different viewpoints of control. The next section examines some newer approaches to control evolving from belief in the validity of the psychological contract and the idea of control as a process of mutual influence. The final section considers which behaviores are appropriate for organizations to control.

DESIGNING EFFECTIVE CONTROL SYSTEMS

As Chapter 11 pointed out, there are many different kinds of control systems, including financial (such as budgets) and nonfinancial (such as production, inventory, and quality control). That chapter also briefly described the basic elements in controlling. This chapter will use those elements to develop an overall approach to designing control systems of all types.[3]

Some managers believe that responsibility for control belongs essentially to the controllers and accountants of an organization, probably because financial controls are the most emphasized type. Certainly financial controls are important; often they set the resource limits within which managers must work. Nevertheless, many control methods exist—more nonfinancial ones than financial—that all managers at all levels should exercise to successfully carry out their activities.

Such important factors as employee turnover, absenteeism, produc-

The original draft of this chapter was written by Professor Allen C. Bluedorn of the University of Missouri–Columbia.

tivity, sales force performance, plant safety, public relations, new product development, product quality, and market share all frequently need to be controlled by nonfinancial means. Indeed, in the case of the Broncos, nonfinancial controls were more needed than financial ones.

As shown in Figure 13.1 certain basic steps characterize good control systems. They include defining results to be obtained, looking for predictors, developing feedback methods, developing standards, specifying information flows, and taking corrective action when necessary.

Define Desired Results The control process is established to ensure that activities are proceeding in such a way that they will produce desired results. There are three crucial aspects to this process: completeness, objectivity, and controllability.

Completeness refers to how broadly and inclusively the control system measures the behaviors involved. For example, a control device that emphasizes the importance of current sales at the expense of considering

FIGURE 13.1 Basic steps in the control process

factors in long-term goodwill with customers may be viewed by a sales representative as incomplete and therefore may be resisted.

Objectivity refers to collecting information in such a way that personal biases have minimum influence on what is collected. A count of the number of customers handled at a teller's window in a bank is relatively objective; rating the goodwill of those customers is relatively subjective.

Controllability refers to the amount of influence those being controlled have on the control system. It is difficult for a lower-level manager to influence the year-end profits of General Electric, but the same manager would find it much easier to influence the travel budgets for subordinates.

The more complete, controllable, and objective control systems are, the more cooperation they will receive from managers and others, and the more effective they will be. Completeness is sometimes more important than total objectivity. Cost control for the Broncos was objective but not complete. The contributions of such organizational units as law, research and development, and advertising are difficult to measure objectively. So are those of management development and community relations. When subjective judgments are unavoidable, they should be widely communicated and open to discussion.

Link Objectives to Individuals   Managerial control is intended to influence the behavior of people. Thus clearly defined responsibility centers are important, because they allow organizational objectives to be translated into specific measures to be enacted by each manager. For example, measures related to income and expense can be tailored to the specific responsibility center. Control becomes operational only when specific goals are assigned to specific individuals.

Consider Interrelationships   From a systems point of view, all units in an organization are interdependent. The interrelationships must be considered in establishing the three aspects of an effective control system. In one organization that ignored such interdependencies, managers were heard to say, "To hell with you. I have my own score card to worry about." There was little cooperation until the control system was changed.

Look for Predictors of Results   An effective managerial control system continually monitors how actual results are approaching desired results. This requires good predictors of results and often involves the use of steering controls, which allow for early corrective action.

Recognizing good predictors requires experience. An experienced manager knows that one customer complaint is probably insignificant whereas several may indicate a problem with product quality that will require corrective action. As another example, an experienced manager knows that increased absenteeism may be due to a flu epidemic and therefore temporary; increased absenteeism coupled with increased tar-

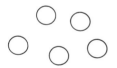

Organizational objectives

Managers

Control becomes operational when objectives are linked to individuals

Specific objectives

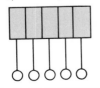

Assigned to managers

diness may indicate a more serious problem with long-term effects on productivity.

Examples of good predictors abound. Most college texts, including this one, are reviewed before publication by knowledgeable people who serve as predictors in that they signal the need for corrective action before results are final. Also, the drop in sales of U.S. cars in 1980 is a valid predictor of future declining sales unless corrective action is taken. Clearly, the sooner such signals operate, the easier it is to take the corrective action.

In certain repetitive operations post-action controls are more appropriate than steering controls and serve as predictors for future operations. For example, in making newsprint, a bad batch of paper can be compared against desired results (post-action control), and corrective action can be taken for the next operation. These post-action controls sometimes even afford improvement on desired results when comparisons between operations suggest ways to improve the next operation.

Who Should Look for Predictors? The individual whose performance is being measured is best qualified to identify the appropriate predictors, perhaps in conjunction with another knowledgeable person or persons involved in a mutual influence process.[4] When it is possible to custom-fit standards for each person, there is more cooperation from each person in meeting the standards and thus in employing predictors for that purpose. For example, specific sales quotas negotiated with individual sales representatives are more likely to be accepted than a standard sales quota applied to all salespeople. Also, individuals object less to control

Goods predictors enhance likelihood of desired results.

Standards can be jointly set by supervisor and subordinate.

"This sugar substitute is perfect except for one thing. It's salty."

Source: Current Contents, March 30, 1981, p. 15. © 1981 Sidney Harris/*Current Contents.*

procedures developed by their immediate supervisors than to control procedures established and administered by an outside staff group.

Develop Composite Predictors A composite predictor is timely, reliable, and comprehensive, and it does not entail unreasonable expense.

Timeliness Is Critical "Above all, a management control system must be current."[5] However, promptness is relative. Deviations in a nuclear generating plant may need to be identified in seconds or less, while other types of deviations may be allowed to go undetected for months or years. The reorganization of General Electric into strategic business units and major sectors (discussed in Chapter 12) took years to accomplish, but it resulted in increased sales and higher earnings. Attempts to predict the results of such actions in days or months would have been misleading. Information can be too old or too current, depending on the activity being measured.

To be *reliable*, a measure should be consistent. Some predictors can be used as early warnings but are not consistently valid. For example, a few customer complaints may serve as a warning to investigate product quality but do not constitute a reliable predictor of problems requiring corrective action.

A *comprehensive* measure is one that uses a variety of significant indicators. In the Sears case described in Chapter 6 too much attention was paid to sales volume and too little to the relation of sales to profitability; predictors were not comprehensive. A comprehensive measure does not emphasize short-term profitability more than long-term results. When predicted results cover only one or a few factors, a manager is tempted to deal with only those few factors. Balanced effort requires a relatively broad index. A quarterly report that is devoted to profit considerations and does not mention employee morale or customer goodwill is unbalanced. In the case of the Denver Broncos predictors used by the manager were reliable but not comprehensive.

The *expense* of a measure should not exceed the value of the information it provides. As noted in Chapter 6, one large department store chain developed an elaborate plan for controlling customer returns. Before the control plan was implemented, its cost was calculated and found to be greater than adopting a policy of accepting all returns without question.

For repetitive operations, sampling may be an appropriate form of reasonably priced control. Sophisticated techniques have been developed for the sampling process. The Internal Revenue Service cannot afford to audit all income tax returns, so it has indicators to highlight suspicious returns.

Develop Standards for Each Predictor and Desired Result Standards are the units of measurement against which results can be compared. Two major and related factors involved in establishing standards

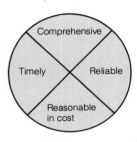

Characteristics of a composite predictor

Comprehensive

Timely

Reliable

Reasonable in cost

Feedback should be:

- Timely
- Reliable
- Comprehensive
- Inexpensive

are how high the standards should be set and who should participate in determining them.

Standards that are perceived as too difficult to attain discourage employees. People are reluctant to attempt to reach a goal that they believe is impossible. On the other hand, goals that are too easy invite mediocre performance. The best performance is elicited by standards that are seen as difficult but achievable. Research suggests that people often perform best when they feel that they have about a 50/50 chance of achieving the goals.[6]

Only those who know the job can set goals at the proper level of difficulty. Therefore, ideally, the immediate supervisor should set the standards, with the participation of those whose performance is being measured. Typically, standards are set from above, and the cooperation of those who must meet them is assumed. However, participation by those involved is highly desirable, not only for the information they can contribute but also because they are more likely to perceive the standards as reasonable and try to meet them when they know what information was used to formulate them. For example, studies show a strong relationship between the amount of participation in establishing budgets and the degree of motivation in keeping to them.[7]

Nevertheless, although such participation is desirable, it is not always necessary. If standards are complete, comprehensive, and controllable, they may be perceived as reasonable and be accepted even without participation. The greatest resistance to standards appears to occur when they are established by a mistrusted outside group rather than a trusted, well-informed supervisor. In these cases, employees often make a game of "beating the standards." An example of too-high standards, set by an outside group and not accepted by employees, follows.

In an organization that worked with precious metals, a stringent control system was imposed by an engineering group on the production workers. Under these standards, any wastage of precious metals was severely reprimanded. Much of the building was on piles over a reservoir that had to be drained one summer. In the mud under the building about $50 million of gold and other precious metals was found in the form of improperly made parts. Over the years, the workers, with the tacit approval of their foremen, had simply thrown their mistakes into the water rather than face reprimands.

Specify Information Flow Prompt and accurate feedback of results is probably the best single way of improving performance. Lack of it causes distress. For example, college students are unhappy if they do not receive their test grades before taking another test. A number of studies have shown that people will work harder and longer when they are informed of the results of their actions.[8] Unfortunately, in many organizations the information flow is not well designed for proper feedback.

Chapter 11 suggested that control information can be given to any of the following: (1) staff units, (2) high-level line managers, (3) the manager of the organizational unit being measured, and (4) the individuals

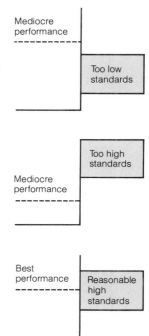

Standards should be reasonably difficult.

Participation increases joint ownership of standards and goals.

Control information can go to the:

- Staff
- Managers of the unit
- Top-level managers
- Employees

in the groups being measured. Control processes must be tailored to specific organizations, so no single description exists of who should get the information. Generally, it is the individual or group who can make the most meaningful use of the data.[9] In many organizations just the opposite occurs, and those who are directly involved in a job are the last to know whether it has been done well or poorly.

Whenever possible, information should be fed back to the person making operating decisions, since this is the person who is able to take immediate action when it is needed. There are two basic sources of feedback information: the work itself or an agent of the work, such as the immediate supervisor, a staff group, or a formal information system. The work itself is the best source. Supervisors tend to be poor at giving feedback information to their subordinates.[10] Usually they are uncomfortable dispensing both positive and negative feedback and have a relatively poor sense of timing.

Feedback can often lead to improved performance.

Control data should be received by the immediate supervisor as well as by the person directly responsible for the particular task, but not necessarily in the same form. The supervisor needs this information to ensure that corrective action will be or has already been taken by the subordinate.

In many instances control information is obtained by staff groups before managers or employees have received it. Sometimes this advantage is used to make the individual staff unit look good at the expense of the manager or the organizational unit. Data developed and used in this way are frequently distorted, particularly with regard to internal audits. Such manipulation of data is widespread among managers and employees, which drastically weakens the control process. This situation often results from using control information to catch people in their mistakes rather than to improve overall function of the unit involved.

Evaluate and Take Corrective Action   The final step in the control process is to correct significant deviations of actual results from desired results. If the steps described thus far for developing an overall control system have been properly executed, frequently the manager only has to ascertain that corrective action has been taken, making this last step unnecessary.

Particularly for steering controls, the first action taken should be to investigate early warnings. In the case of the Denver Broncos, for example, the Howsams should have heeded early warnings about the team's performance. As indicated earlier, many predictors are not reliable, so corrective action should not be taken until enough evidence points to its necessity. A major pitfall for the supervisor is to move too quickly, interfering with the subordinate manager's job and causing frustration and annoyance. Most professional people, including managers, interpret interference as a lack of confidence and trust. A wise supervisor gives subordinates a chance to implement corrective action themselves.

In corrective action haste can make waste.

Yes-no controls do not allow work to proceed to the next step until the work has been verified as satisfactory. Work that does not pass yes-no controls frequently requires immediate corrective action. Again, the wise supervisor will allow subordinates to perform the corrective action.

Post-action controls are used when results are completed and compared to the established standards. Although in the narrow sense of the term, corrective action is not possible at this time, post-action controls do serve two major purposes. First, they provide a guide for distributing rewards or punishments. For example, after the World Series in baseball is over, the winning team gets a larger portion of the series money than the losing team. In organizations, wage incentives, managerial bonuses, and other rewards are often based on knowledge furnished by post-action controls—for example, whether the sales quota was met.

Post-action controls are also tied to planning. Failure to make the sales quota or to produce the budgeted profit may spark alternative plans, prompting a new forecast of expected results. Thus a new cycle of planning and controlling is necessary.

DIFFERENCES IN DESIGN FOR THE THREE CONTROL PROCESSES

Chapter 11 described three control processes: steering controls, yes-no controls, and post-action controls. To review briefly, steering controls are controls in which results are predicted and corrective action is taken while the operation or task is being performed. Yes-no controls indicate that the work is either acceptable or unacceptable. Post-action controls compare results to a standard when the action or task is completed.

Much of the focus in the preceding section has been on steering controls, which are more sophisticated and have more elements than post-action and yes-no controls. Yet all three processes are important.

All managerial controls require that desired results (whether predicted or actual) be defined, standards established, and the information flow specified. Post-action controls include evaluation but not necessarily corrective action, since the activity has already been completed. (Corrective action might be taken in repetitive actions, however.) Yes-no controls may or may not result in evaluation and corrective action, since a no in some instances simply stops the action or kills the project. Evaluation may show that re-work can overcome the reasons for the no.

Combining several measures into composite predictors or feedbacks is not a necessary step in yes-no or post-action controls, but it is the step that usually provides the greatest potential for improving a control system.

CONTROL AND THE PSYCHOLOGICAL CONTRACT

As briefly mentioned in Chapter 11, much of an organization's control is exercised through the use of norms. A *norm* is a rule that tells the individual how to behave in a particular group or organization. How do

Employees will perform within their psychological contracts, but it is hard to get behavior outside the contract.

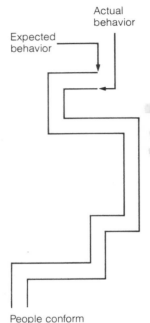

Actual behavior

Expected behavior

People conform to expectations.

Three types of power:

• Coercive
• Utilitarian
• Normative

Three types of involvement:

• Alienative
• Calculative
• Moral

norms get established? A major way is through the **psychological contract,** which is the sum total of the expectancies of the individual and the organization about one another. The psychological contract is an excellent tool for explaining how people behave in organizations. To a relatively high degree, people behave in different organizations and situations in the way they are expected to behave. For example, how often does a student walk around in a college classroom while a class is in session?

A classification system has been developed to illustrate how the psychological contract affects behavior. As shown in Table 13.1, the system identifies three types of power used by organizations and the response of employees to that power.[11] The first is *coercive power*—power through the possible application of force or other negative rewards. The second is *utilitarian power*—power that comes from rational-legal authority and the use of economic rewards such as salaries and bonuses. The third is *normative power*—power based on status, intrinsic value rewards, and charismatic leadership style. Many organizations rely heavily on one of these three types of power to achieve control, and many others use more than one type.

The second part of this classification system is an involvement factor that indicates how an organization member reacts to the control technique used. If the organization exercises primarily coercive power and authority, as do jails, penal institutions, concentration camps, and slave labor camps, the employee is likely to become *alienated*—an intensely negative reaction—and psychologically withdraw from that organization.

If an organization exerts primarily rational-legal authority and uses economic rewards in exchange for performance (*utilitarian* power), the reaction of the employee is primarily calculative—a fair day's work for a day's pay.

College and universities, religious institutions, professional associations, and ideologically based political organizations are examples of organizations that use normative power; membership in the organization or the opportunity to perform a task or function for it has intrinsic value. The response is a moral one. Frequently the person is willing to accept lower economic rewards or even none (as is the case with a vol-

TABLE 13.1 Predominant Types of Responses to Different Psychological Contracts

TYPES OF POWER/CONTROL USED	TYPES OF INVOLVEMENT		
	ALIENATIVE	CALCULATIVE	MORAL
Coercive	x		
Utilitarian		x	
Normative			x

Source: Adapted from Amitai Etzioni, *A Comparative Analysis of Complex Organizations,* rev. ed. (New York: Free Press, 1975), p. 12.

unteer in a political campaign). Members belong because they value the goals of the organization, enjoy fulfilling those goals, and consider it morally right to do so.

Table 13.1 suggests that there are nine potential types of relationships between an individual and an organization. The three just described (and marked by "x" in the table) represent workable and just psychological contracts. The kind of involvement expected by the organization fits with the kinds of rewards it gives and the kind of authority it exercises. If a manufacturing company uses primarily scientific management, rational-legal authority, and economic rewards, for example, it should expect a calculative type of involvement from its members. If the same organization asks its members to be loyal, to be morally involved, and to enjoy their work, it may be asking more than it is willing to give.

The influence of the psychological contract on the behavior of members of the organization cannot be overestimated. A number of studies support the proposition that organizations with workable psychological contracts, such as those marked by "x" on the diagonal in Table 13.1, perform better than others.[12] In one review of reasons for turnover among life insurance salespeople, industrial employees, supermarket employees, and nurses, there was clear evidence that new employees often quit their jobs because they expected a different psychological contract than the organization provided.[13]

Another report demonstrates the change in behavior of newly hired supervisors in a juvenile correctional institution, which was basically an alienative organization.[14] Before employment, questionnaires and other information suggested that the new supervisors were likely to be open to change and innovation and to be humanistic. After employment, the opinions of the new supervisors changed radically to conform with the attitudes of the other employees in the correctional institution; they had become much less humanistic and were now taking a basically punitive approach. In other words, the new supervisors had adjusted to the psychological contract in the institution and had changed their attitudes and behavior to conform to the behavior that was expected of them.

Thus the psychological contract helps explain why employees behave as they do. One of the ways to change behavior is to change the contract. More participation, for example, brings more involvement.

CONTROL AS MUTUAL INFLUENCE

In addition to the psychological contract, another major concept that sheds light on the impact of control on the performance of organizations is that of mutual influence.[15] Much discussion on control in the literature is based on the **fixed-pie assumption** of power and influence—the assumption that the amount of control held by people is a fixed quantity and that increasing the power of one group or individual (for example, a worker) automatically decreases that of another (for example, a manager). Technically speaking, this approach is known as a zero-sum gain.

Fixed-pie assumption

Manager A loses exact amount of power that Manager B gains.

Expanding-pie assumption

Total amount of control in organization can be increased indefinitely.

Control can be distributed throughout the organization.

If one person wins, another loses, and subtracting what one gains from what the other loses equals zero. We are familiar with zero-sum games in sports. If one team wins, another loses.

In contrast to this zero-sum or win-lose situation, in which one person must lose some control in order for another's control to be increased, the **expanding-pie assumption** postulates that the total amount of control in an organization can be increased indefinitely. If this assumption is correct, and there is evidence for it, one member of an organization can gain a greater amount of control without reducing the amount of control exercised by anyone else in the organization. The implications of this veiw are that everyone in an organization could expand individual control.

The following two cases illustrate the difference between the type of one-way control that accompanies the fixed-pie assumption and the mutual influence type of control that operates along with the expanding-pie assumption. The control room of the ill-fated Three Mile Island nuclear plant was designed by engineers with little input from the operators who were to use the controls. As a result, some important and closely related controls were located as many as eighty feet apart. Furthermore, the nearly universal color convention of using red to mean stop or danger and green to mean go ahead or clear was reversed in some areas. In contrast, in a different nuclear plant, two adjacent, identical-looking handles had dramatically different functions—to raise or lower the control rods that would start or stop the nuclear reaction. To avoid confusion, operators suggested putting a rounded Michelob beer tap knob on one control and a flat Heineken handle on the other. At first, the plant management rejected the idea, since it violated the original design, but later the management agreed that the shape coding made sense.[16] In the Three Mile Island plant, control was perceived as a one-way street; in the other plant, mutual influence allowed better control.

The **control graph** is a method of measuring the total control in an organization and exploring its relationship to performance. An example is shown in Figure 13.2. The control graph works the following way. Members of an organization are asked to respond to a questionnaire regarding how much say or influence various levels of authority have in the organization. The levels are usually as follows: top management, plant managers, department heads, supervisors, and workers. Averages are calculated of the amount of control each group is believed to have, and a graph is drawn.

In the example in Figure 13.2, top management is perceived to have a great deal of control, although not as much as the plant managers. Department heads, supervisors, and workers have lesser amounts. More important than the slope of the curve is the height of it, or the amount of area under the curve. This shows how much total power is seen to exist in the organization. Some organizations are seen as having significantly more total power than others. The greater the perceived amount of power (which is available to various employees), the greater the effectiveness of the organization and the greater the member satisfaction. When asked how much influence or power each of the different hier-

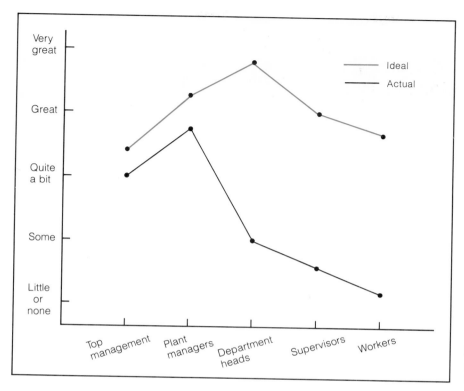

FIGURE 13.2 Hypothetical control graph of an industrial firm

archical levels should have, organization members almost always want more influence not only for their own level but for all other levels as well. They obviously do not view control as a win-lose situation.

The control graph in Figure 13.3 shows that high performing insurance agencies were seen as exercising more total control than medium to low performing agencies. (Note the greater area beneath the curve of the high performing agencies.) This factor, the amount of total control, appears to be the most important in determining organizational performance. The relative amounts of control perceived for various levels of management are similar for the high and the medium to low performers. Regional managers were seen to exert the most control, followed by the home office, the agents, and the district managers. Thus, who is perceived as exercising the most control is not nearly as important for an organization's success as how much control everyone together is exercising.

In the insurance organization shown in Figure 13.3 influence scores obtained one year were compared to performance factors obtained a year later.[17] The results confirmed that the more widely the total control was distributed, the higher the performance.

So far the chapter has considered the impact of control on the performance of the organization as a whole. Control also has specific impacts on individual performances, which in turn further affect the over-

On the Job

DESIGNING CONTROL SYSTEMS

A critical factor in any well designed control system is the element of potential. Many people think of control as someone looking over their shoulder and inspecting everything they do. But control systems have only a single purpose: to minimize deviations from some desired behavior or outcome. Direct supervision of every activity is unnecessary, excessive, and shortsighted.

Imagine a situation in which every time you drove your car you were followed by a police officer. Or picture every tax return being audited by the Internal Revenue Service.

The effectiveness of such efforts would be great. There would be little deviation from speed limits, and income would be honestly reported. But the cost of the efforts would be prohibitive and would outweigh any possible benefits.

Most organizations do not rely on personal observation; instead they rely on potential. For the government it is enough that people realize they *could* be penalized for deviating from the guidelines. They *could* be caught speeding; they *could* be audited. For most people that potential is sufficient to encourage adherence to standards.

True, people occasionally exceed the posted speed limits, and they exaggerate a bit on their tax returns. They do not, however, drive ninety-five miles an hour on a road posted for forty-five; nor do they claim pets as deductions on their tax returns. Potential is sufficient to remind most people of the limits imposed on them.

A key part of potential is that we never know when the inspection will come. They are not sure if they are in a speed trap; they are not sure if their tax return will be audited. This is an important principle. Suppose I could assure you that you would never be cited for speeding or that your tax return would never be audited. What would you do?

---

all performance of the organization. These individual impacts will now be discussed.

The impact of control on individuals can be either positive or negative, depending, in part, on the organization's general approach to control. The expanding-pie approach seems to be related to positive impacts more often than is the traditional zero-sum view. One model of human growth explains why this is so. According to this model, people at birth are dependent and submissive, have few abilities, have superficial abilities, and have a very short time perspective. As they grow older, these characteristics change. Infant dependency becomes a desire for independence and control over one's affairs. Abilities increase in number and sophistication, and time perspectives lengthen significantly.[18]

The zero-sum assumption forces managers to keep control at ever higher levels, forcing greater dependency on those at lower levels. The expanding-pie approach allows all employees to increase their influence and control, which usually involves the use of more sophisticated abilities over a longer time span. Obviously, the expanding-pie approach fits the stage of the human growth model that represents most people of an age to work. Clearly, the owners and the manager of the Denver Broncos

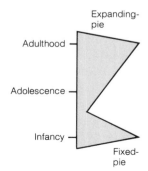

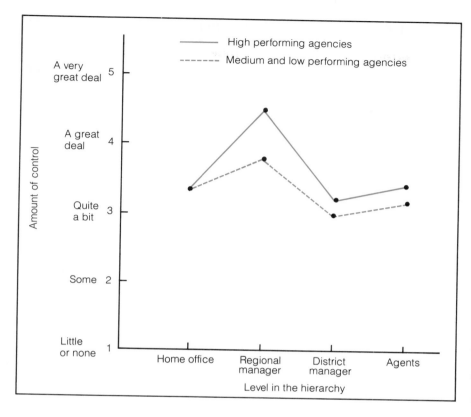

FIGURE 13.3 Control graphs of high and medium/low performing insurance agencies

Source: Adapted from Arnold Tannenbaum, *Control in Organizations* (New York: McGraw-Hill, 1968), pp. 52 and 117.

did not believe in the expanding-pie approach, since they did not allow the players or the quarterback any influence in important decisions.

Job enrichment, a successful managerial technique discussed in detail in Chapter 22, can be explained as an application of the expanding-pie approach to increasing organizational control. When a job is enriched, the amount of control associated with it is increased, as are the number and the sophistication of abilities required. With the expansion of the job in this way, the length of time over which activities must be planned also increases. Thus the human growth model fits very well with the expanding-pie approach to organizational control and helps explain why job enrichment is such a valuable management technique.

A number of research studies have shown the advantages of the expanding-pie approach either directly or indirectly. In one, a review of more than a thousand employees in about a hundred jobs in more than a dozen organizations showed that high satisfaction, high performance, and low absenteeism were associated with jobs perceived as meaningful, with a high degree of responsibility and knowledge of results. Responses were more positive in people indicating strong growth needs than in those indicating weaker growth needs.[19] Another study that compared a number of different work groups in four organizations confirmed the hypothesis that individuals given more opportunities for growth and responsibility on the job would demonstrate greater maturity and less dependence in job behaviors.[20]

Many of the negative connotations of the word *control* come from reactions to the zero-sum assumptions about control. Two of the more serious results often associated with the zero-sum approach are alienation and deviance. The alienation encountered in the model of control and involvement shown in Table 13.1 was described as an intense negative reaction on the part of individuals. *Deviance* is the violation of organizational rules. When employees feel strongly enough about rules, or when rules interfere with getting the job done, the rules get bent or broken. The Heineken and Michelob handles in the nuclear power plant are an example. Significant evidence also exists that employees who exercise insufficient amounts of control in their jobs often engage in *ritualism*; they follow rules even when the rules impede the achievement of the organization's goals.[21]

Control, particularly that achieved in a zero-sum manner, may provoke the seriously negative reactions of alienation, deviance, and ritualism. Nevertheless, a certain amount of control is necessary to avoid other negative consequences. This point is illustrated well by the analyses performed by the French sociologist, Emile Durkheim, almost a century ago. Durkheim found a consistent pattern of higher suicide rates where people did not have sufficient rules to control their behavior (a condition Durkheim called *anomie*). Suicide rates were lower where more guides to behavior existed.[22] Particularly in a zero-sum situation, too little control can be as harmful as too much.

Employees want some degree of control on the job as well as off the job.

Deviance and ritualism are ways to gain some control on the job.

SOME NEWER APPROACHES TO CONTROL

The two preceding sections present abundant evidence that the best way for an organization to change human behavior is for it to change the psychological contract. This is particularly true because of today's increasing emphasis on the quality of work life. The concept of the psychological contract and the concept of the expanding-pie approach to control are closely related. As the nature of the psychological contract moves from coercive to normative, there is less of a zero-sum approach to control and more emphasis on the expanding-pie approach. Indeed, in the United States, the nature of the psychological contract is slowly moving from coercive/utilitarian to utilitarian/normative. As organizations increasingly expect their members to be committed to organizational goals and to value their work, management must change its part of the psychological contract to give employees at all levels more opportunity for self-control through personal involvement, autonomy, decision making, and growth.

Indeed, a recent review reports that a quiet revolution has occurred in a number of U.S. organizations in the past decade.[23] During this time, many of them have designed, built, and managed one or more new plants. The organizations are extensive and varied; they include General Foods, General Motors, Procter & Gamble, PPG Industries, Sherwin-Williams, Cummins Engine, H. J. Heinz, the Mead Corporation, Dana Corporation, TRW, Rockwell, and a host of smaller organizations. A number of them have started more than one new-design plant. At this stage, no one knows how many organizations have initiated new-design plants or how many actually exist; a guess is that at least twenty-five organizations have at least one plant and that more than a hundred plants are currently in operation. General Motors alone has built about twenty of them.

The new plants are built around teams that are relatively self-managing and self-controlling. The teams are responsible for a whole product or unit, and they can decide who performs which tasks on a given day. In many cases they set their own production goals. Frequently they are responsible for purchasing, quality control, and the control of absenteeism. The new plants require a new style of managing, since the teams are relatively self-controlling. Thus most are staffed with relatively recent college graduates.

The Three Mile Island nuclear plant, as discussed earlier, had been designed without input from the operators. This, along with the complexity of the control room, may have led to operator mistakes. A typical control room includes a panel about eight feet high and sometimes a hundred feet long, covered with long rows of meters and control handles, many of which look the same except for small labels that are hardly readable. At Three Mile Island, it was reported, "The operators quickly become familar with the frequently used controls and displays by position, but they sometimes cannot find the less familiar displays or controls for minutes at a time, because designers have located these devices on the basis of available panel space rather than for the operator's convenience."[24]

Contrast this approach to the design of a new chemical plant by Shell Canada, Ltd. Instrumentation and equipment costs for the plant required a capital investment of approximately $2 million per employee for approximately 150 employees.[25] Active work on the design of the plant began in 1975. Previous work had convinced Shell management that the higher levels of technology that were usually accompanied by large capital expenditures actually increase rather than decrease the dependence of organizations on their workers. (The 1979 grounding in the United States of the McDonnell Douglas DC–10 for safety inspections is one illustration.) As a result, Shell decided to involve the union and the operators as full partners in developing the basic design of the organization, jobs, training, and the physical layout, including controls. One of the reasons for the increased dependence of the organization in this plant is that every programmable task has been built directly into the system; it has been either taken over by machines or regulated by the computer. What is left are the unprogrammable tasks, such as monitoring the flow, diagnosing problems, adjusting equipment, fine-tuning, and maintaining the system. These are skilled tasks requiring quick judgment. If output is to be maintained, these tasks must be done well. The involvement of the union and the operators has significantly reduced the cost of operating the plant.

Three Mile Island is an illustration of zero-sum control. The Shell plant is an illustration of expanding-pie, direct, reciprocal control.

BEHAVIORS CONTROLLED BY ORGANIZATIONS

Much of the discussion thus far has centered on who is in control of organizations and what the results of control are for both the individual and the organization. This section will specify which employee behaviors organizations attempt to control. Obviously, the issue of which behaviors are properly subject to organizational control and which are not is also involved. Two principles of bureaucracy noted in Chapter 2 are that individuals will have personal freedom and will become members of organizations on the basis of freely negotiated contracts. The implication is that individuals have an inviolate private life beyond the legitimate influence of the organization. Likewise, they have a public organizational existence properly subject to control. Problems occur because the boundary between these two areas is not distinct and because it changes as the culture changes.

In the 1950s William H. Whyte made an impressive attempt to address this issue in his classic book, *The Organization Man*. An editor of *Fortune* magazine, Whyte was distressed by a general trend he observed in twentieth century America. This trend was the increasing dominance of a social ethic different from the individual or Protestant ethic of the nineteenth century. Whyte saw the social ethic, in the extreme, as advocating a general submission to the desires and values of groups at the expense of the individual. Although he viewed this trend as covering all social life, he believed it was most powerful in organizations. Whyte believed that too many parts of life, including housing, education, religion, and family, focused on and accommodated to the demands of work organizations. Although it is almost thirty years old now, his book is valuable reading because its statement of the issues is clear and surprisingly relevant to contemporary affairs.

In 1977 the *Harvard Business Review* conducted a survey of its subscribers about the type of control issues addressed by Whyte.[26] The survey presented respondents with short descriptions of realistic but problematic business situations. The respondents then answered questions about what action they would take and what action they thought would be taken in the larger business community. In general, the respondents showed a consistently strong concern for the rights and dignity of employees. The issues they considered included disobedience to unethical instructions, employee participation in decision making, the privacy of personnel records, standards of dress, political activity, and product safety. Unfortunately, the respondents also indicated that their respective organizations had substantially less concern for employee rights than they as individuals did. They believed that there should be more freedom from control than currently existed in those organizations. Thus it is obvious that there are many types of behaviors over which organizations have a dubious right, if any at all, to exercise control.

SUMMARY

As the previous two chapters demonstrated, good controls are essential for a well-run organization. Everyone wants controls as a guide to appropriate behavior and action. The college student who is assigned a term paper without guidelines (steering controls) is unhappy with the instructor. A well-designed budget that is clearly understood is an invaluable help to the good manager.

Yet the word *control* frequently has a negative connotation. One reason for this is the over-emphasis on financial controls that often exists in organizations. Controls are needed in all areas of the organization, and many are not financial in nature. A related reason for a negative perception of control is that many controls, financial and otherwise, are not well designed. The over-emphasis on cost in the controls employed by the first owners of the Denver Broncos is an example.

The good control systems, whether financial or nonfinancial, requires a clear definition of results. The control system must be complete, objective, and controllable. (The system for the Broncos was objective and controllable, but not complete.) Good predictors that are comprehensive, timely, reliable, and cost effective need to be developed. Standards that are difficult enough to be challenging but not unachievable and that are accepted by those who must meet them also need to be developed. Clear information flows need to be established, so that the appropriate people can take corrective action when necessary.

Under such controls, a great deal of behavior is still left to the discretion of the individual. Therefore, the psychological contract is of great importance. In a sense, organizations get the behavior that they ask for, either explicitly or implicitly. An organization using coercion will get alienation from its members. An organization that uses utilitarian, economic rewards and punishments will get, in return, calculative behavior—"What's in it for me?" Organizations that want committed, self-motivated behavior need to have psychological contracts that allow opportunities for participation and responsible autonomy.

The control graph is another way of viewing the same phenomenon. One assumption about control is that it is a fixed-pie, win-lose process. Organizations operating under this assumption tend to have psychological contracts that result in alienative or calculative behavior. Many of the negative concepts of control come from this win-lose assumption, in which controls are often seen as personally degrading or punitive.

The second assumption about control is that it is a process of mutual influence—the expanding-pie concept. A number of research studies have linked high satisfaction and performance to this concept. Organizations operating under this assumption of control tend to move toward a psychological contract that is more calculative/moral than alienative/calculative.

A quiet revolution is occurring in a number of U.S. organizations. They are increasingly recognizing the mutual dependence of management and workers, and they are moving from the fixed-pie to the expanding-pie assumption of control. As a result, a number of new plants are using teams that are relatively self-managing and self-controlling. The dependence is even greater in high technology organizations, where programmable tasks have already been computerized.

The modern manager does not take the design and implementation of control systems lightly. Controls are vitally necessary, and it is imperative that they be properly designed to fit the situation.

STUDY QUESTIONS

1. What are the basic elements of an effective control system? Explain the importance of each.
2. Why should interrelationships of individuals, groups, or responsibility centers be considered in designing control systems?
3. Define *psychological contract*. Give examples of the contract from your own experience.
4. Your behavior and the behavior of others usually change in different types of situations. Explain why this is true.
5. Differentiate between the fixed-pie and the expanding-pie assumptions of control. Think of examples from your own experience and describe your reactions to each.
6. Describe how a certain type of psychological contract is related to the expanding-pie assumption of control.
7. Should an organization attempt to control any behavior that is seen as being in its best interest to control?
8. Describe the psychological contract that the players on the Denver Broncos believed they had under the team's first owners. Do you see the contract as being appropriate? Explain.

Case for Discussion

OUTSIDE ACTIVITIES

This chapter described a *Harvard Business Review* survey of attitudes toward employee rights. One of the issues addressed in the survey was the possibility of organizations attempting to exert control over the private lives of their members. One of the scenarios used in the survey is reproduced here, along with the respondents' answers to questions about the scenario.

> Several top executives of a company in a large city are disturbed by community activist organizations that are protesting the treatment of minority groups. The executives feel that the activists, while abstaining from violence, are doing more harm than good to the schools, urban renewal programs, public transportation, and retail business. The chief executive himself has articulated his fears about the activists at local business meetings. However, a young official in the personnel department thinks that the activists are on the right track. He goes to work for the leading activists organization, spending many evening and weekend hours doing unpaid volunteer tasks. Occasionally

he is quoted in the newspaper and identified with the employer company.

> The personnel director of the company comes under pressure from several senior executives. They urge him to warn the young official either to stop working for the activists or resign. How should he answer them?

If you were the personnel director, which of the following possible responses would come closest to the answer you would make?

RESPONSE	PERCENT WHO CHOSE THE RESPONSE
1. "This is a question for the chief executive to decide, not you or me."	5%
2. "People in this company and especially in this department should be free to express their opinions on public problems.	

I'll go to bat for the young man as a matter of principle."   19%

3. "As long as this person keeps doing a good job for the company, I shall not interfere."   6%

4. "I agree it's bad business for the chief executive to be saying one thing and a lesser official to be saying just the opposite. I'll tell the young man he's got to stop."   8%

5. "As long as this person keeps doing a good job, and until there is some concrete factual evidence that the company's public image is being hurt by his association with the activists, I shall not interefere."   62%

Source: D. Ewing, "What Business Thinks about Employee Rights," *Harvard Business Review* 55 (September–October 1977): 87.

1. Which response would you have chosen?
2. Are there other possible responses to the young official's action.
3. Do you think management has any legitimate reason for reaction in *any* way to the young official's activities? Explain.
4. Would possible action by a prospective employer inhibit you from becoming involved in this type of activity?
5. What would you do if you were the young official and the company said, "Stop doing this type of thing or you're fired"?

FOR YOUR CAREER

1. Too much emphasis on short-range success can hamper longer-range success.
2. Remember the earlier statement of one foreman: "Just tell me what you want my boss to look good on, and I'll see that it happens."
3. Most of us feel more comfortable with controls as guides to our behavior. If you don't agree, think of a freshman course where the instructor, at the beginning of the semester, asks the students, "What shall we study this semester?"
4. If you encounter personnel problems as a manager, you may want to take another look at the psychological contract as perceived by the workers.
5. The control process can be motivating, particularly if the standards are known, fair, and challenging and if the feedback is immediate. The popularity of electronically controlled TV games confirms this point.

FOOTNOTES

1. B. Curran, *The $400,000 Quarterback or The League That Came in from the Cold* (New York: Signet Books, 1969); and G. Sullivan *Touchdown: The Picture History of the American Football League* (New York: G. P. Putnam and Sons, 1967).
2. P. Drucker, *Management* (New York: Harper & Row, 1973), p. 45.
3. This section is based primarily on W. Newman, *Constructive Control: Design and Use of Control Systems* (Englewood Cliffs, N.J.: Prentice-Hall, 1975); and E. Lawler III and J. Rhode, *Information and Control in Organizations* (Pacific Palisades, Calif.: Goodyear Publishing, 1976).
4. C. Argyris, "Human Problems with Budgets," *Harvard Business Review,* 31 (January–February 1953): 97–110.
5. E. Schleh, *Management by Results* (New York: McGraw-Hill, 1961), p. 179.

6. E. Locke, "Toward a Theory of Task Motivation and Incentives," *Organizational Behavior and Human Performance* 3 (May 1968): 68–106; D. McClelland, "Some Social Consequences of Achievement Motivation," in *Nebraska Symposium on Motivation,* ed. M. Jones (Lincoln: University of Nebraska Press, 1955).

7. D. Searfoss and R. Monczka, "Perceived Participation in the Budget Process and Motivation to Achieve the Budget," *Academy of Management Journal* 16 (December 1973): 541–554; and K. Milani, "Budget-Setting, Performance, and Attitudes," *Accounting Review* 50 (April 1975): 274–284.

8. E. Locke and J. Bryan, "The Directing Function of Goals in Task Performance," *Organizational Behavior and Human Performance* 4 (1969): 35–42; A. F. Smode, "Learning and Performance in a Tracking Task under Two Levels of Achievement Information Feedback," *Journal of Experimental Psychology* 56 (October 1958): 297–304; and E. A. Bilodeau, I. McD. Bilodeau, and D. A. Schumsky, "Some Effects of Introducing and Withdrawing Knowledge of Results Early and Late in Practice," *Journal of Experimental Psychology* 58 (August 1959): 142–144.

9. H. Koontz and C. O'Donnell, *Essentials of Management* (New York: McGraw-Hill, 1974); and E. Huse, "Putting in a Management Development Program That Works," *California Management Review* 9 (Winter 1966): 73–80.

10. M. Greller and D. Herold, "Source of Feedback: A Preliminary Investigation," *Organizational Behavior and Human Performance* 13 (April 1975): 244–256; and L. Porter, E. Lawler III, and J. Hackman, *Behavior in Organizations* (New York: McGraw-Hill, 1975).

11. A. Etzioni, *A Comparative Analysis of Complex Organizations,* rev. ed. (New York: Free Press, 1975); and E. Schein, *Organizational Psychology,* 3d ed. (Englewood Cliffs, N.J.: Prentice-Hall, 1980).

12. Ibid.

13. R. Scott, "Job Expectancy—An Important Factor in Labor Turnover," *Personnel Journal* 55 (May 1972): 360–363.

14. C. Perrow, "Reality Adjustment: A Young Institution Settles for Humane Care," *Social Problems* 14 (Summer 1966): 69–79.

15. A. Tannenbaum, ed., *Control in Organizations* (New York: McGraw-Hill, 1968); A. Tannenbaum, *Hierarchy in Organizations* (San Francisco: Jossey-Bass, 1975); and A. Tannenbaum, "Control in Organizations: Individual Adjustment and Organizational Performance," *Administrative Science Quarterly* 7 (June 1962): 236–257.

16. D. Sobel, "Accidents Blamed on Faulty Designs," *New York Times,* April 1, 1980, p. C1.

17. E. Yuchtman, "Control in an Insurance Company: Cause or Effect," in Tannenbaum, *Control in Organizations,* pp. 125–128.

18. C. Argyris, "Personality and Organization Theory Revisited," *Administrative Science Quarterly* 18 (June 1973): 141–167.

19. J. Hackman, G. Oldham, R. Janson, and K. Purdy, "A New Strategy for Job Enrichment," *California Management Review* 17 (Summer 1975): 57–71.

20. E. Huse and P. Price, "The Relationship between Maturity and Motivation in Varied Work Groups," *Proceedings of the 70th Annual Convention of the American Psychological Association,* Chicago, September 1970, pp. 587–788.

21. R. Merton, *Social Theory and Social Structure* (New York: Free Press, 1968), pp. 185–214; and R. Kanter, *Men and Women of the Corporation* (New York: Basic Books, 1977), pp. 192–193.

22. E. Durkheim, *Suicide,* trans. J. Spaulding and G. Simpson (New York: Free Press, 1966).

23. E. Huse, *Organizational Development and Change* (St. Paul, Minn. West Publishing, 1980).

24. T. Sheridan, "Human Error in Nuclear Power Plants," *M.I.T. Technology Review* 82 (February 1980): 22–34.

25. L. Davis and C. Sullivan, "A Labor-Management Contract and Quality of Working Life," *Journal of Occupational Behavior* 1 (January 1979): 25–38.

26. D. Ewing, "What Business Thinks about Employee Rights," *Harvard Business Review* 55 (September–October 1977): 81–94.

Analytical Aids to Decision Making, Planning, and Controlling

CHAPTER 14

CONTENTS

NATIONAL AIRLINES

The world fuel crisis in late 1973 had a dramatic impact on the airline industry. In the five months between December 1973 and May 1974, fuel prices for airlines in the United States soared from an average of 14 cents a gallon to 22 cents a gallon. Furthermore, the federal government limited each airline's monthly supply of jet fuel to a percentage of the amount used in 1972.

The result was chaos. Fuel vendors were often unable to supply fuel at certain cities. Schedules were changed, and fuel allocation did not match the revised schedules. There were excess allocations to some cities and shortages at others. The airlines planned their monthly fuel purchases poorly. Many times the supply was gone by the middle of the month. This resulted in canceled flights, exorbitant prices paid for immediate purchases, and tremendous increases in operating costs. Fuel became the largest percentage cost of operations, rising to 18 percent for domestic air lines.

Using a mathematical technique called linear programming, National Airlines was able to improve fuel availability and to reduce its cost. The first month National used the approach, June 1974, its fuel costs dropped to an average of 14.4 cents a gallon, compared to an average of 22.5 cents a gallon for ten other airlines (including American, United, and Trans World). The model is still being used.

Building the model was not easy. One factor that had to be considered was aircraft rotation—a chain of flights, or legs, that each aircraft follows. For example, a DC-10 may leave Los Angeles as Flight 36, arrive at Fort Lauderdale, and then leave Fort Lauderdale as Flight 144. After a few days, the same aircraft may return to Los Angeles to become Flight 36 again. In the meantime, other DC-10s are following the same rotation, since Flight 36 is a daily flight.

Other factors were the price, availability, and vendor allocations of fuel at each station; the minimum and maximum quantity of fuel the aircraft could carry; the maximum landing weight allowed at a station; and the fuel consumption of various planes and flights. An aircraft's fuel consumption is a function of its weight, flight altitude, and speed and of the weather. If the price of fuel is lower at the first of several stations in an aircraft rotation, it may seem logical to purchase the maximum amount of fuel there and then tanker the additional fuel for later flights (tanking can be costly). However, the extra fuel adds weight to the plane, which causes extra fuel to be burned on the first leg. The extra fuel also results in additional consumption for all the following flight legs on which the fuel is tankered. Clearly, then, the entire flight pattern must be considered in figuring fuel costs.

Solving the problem (and building the model) involved approximately 800 constraints and 2,400 variables for a flight schedule of 350 legs, 50 station/vendor combinations, and multiple types of aircraft. But this effort was apparently worthwhile. National's fuel management and allocation model has resulted in substantial savings. For example, during price negotiations with a vendor, the model allows National to determine the effect of proposed price and supply changes on the total system. It also allows the company to quickly analyze alternative flight schedules in order to determine their effect on current fuel contracts and allocation levels at each station.[1]

This opening case raises several key questions which you should be able to answer after reading this chapter. The questions include:

1. Why do individuals and organizations resist using operations research techniques? Explain.
2. What prompted National Airlines to use linear programming? In what other ways could National have used linear programming?
3. What are some organization-wide problems that operations research techniques can help solve?
4. Why haven't mathematical and other analytical approaches always lived up to their promise?

14

The National Airlines case illustrates the complex interrelationships among decision making, planning, and controlling. The company's fuel management and allocation model helps its managers decide how and where to schedule aircraft and how to save money on fuel—the single highest expense in operating an airline today. The model is also a tool for planning and controlling. Indeed, it is difficult to separate the three functions.

This chapter will describe various analytical aids of value to the manager: operations research, time-event-network analysis, and decision trees. Although most managers will never become experts in all the approaches, they should at least be aware of their existence.

MODELS

Models are representations of real situations or objects.[2] They can take various forms. *Scale models* are physical replicas of real objects; a child's toy truck is a scale model of a real truck, for example. *Analog models* are physical, but they represent something that does not have a physical appearance. A thermometer is an analog model for temperature, and an automobile speedometer is an analog model for speed. The position of the mercury in the thermometer represents temperature, and the position of the needle on the dial represents the automobile's speed.

Mental models are the assumptions we make about people, things, and situations with which we come into contact. A person standing on the corner of a busy street uses a mental model of the expected situation to decide when it is safe to cross to the other side. Likewise, a manager uses a mental model of how the organization and its units operate to make decisions.

People have models of events and theories of why events are what they are.

Descriptions of these models usually use a shorthand system of symbols and mathematical relationships or expressions known as *mathematical models*. The mathematics may be simple, as in a graph or chart, or complex enough to require knowledge of calculus.

The difference between a manager's mental (qualitative) model and a mathematical (quantitative) model is shown in Figure 14.1. When a problem is identified, the manager attempts to solve it on the basis of experience and judgment. If the problem is sufficiently complex, quantitative analysis can be of great help.

Mathematical models also make it possible to infer new information about the real system. For example, the National Airlines model is able to account for the important factors in determining the lowest fuel cost as well as fuel availability. This could not be done without the model, because the number of factors involved is too great to be calculated without a computer.

Simulation models are numerical models that represent some dynamic process. With the values of starting conditions, variables, and influencing factors, these models can simulate a process over time. Some

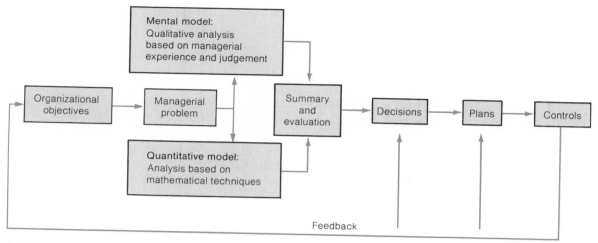

FIGURE 14.1 A comparison of qualitative and quantitative models

simulations can be manually performed, but those for more complex processes need a computer.

Simulation models that are both physical and mathematical have been used for many years to train astronauts for moon landings. The astronauts enter a replica of the space vehicle, where they are given, by computer, a variety of situations to deal with. The computer is pro- grammed to react to the astronauts' actions as though these actions were actually controlling the space vehicle. A serious mistake by an astronaut automatically aborts the mission. Some other simulation models are: (1) a model to simulate traffic flow in a city, (2) a model of corporate financial operations, (3) a model of a baseball game in its complete form, and (4) a model of the number of people at supermarket checkout sta- tions and the service provided at those stations.

In general, experimenting with models requires less time and is less expensive than experimenting with the real object or situation. Of course, the accuracy of the conclusions and decisions based on a model depends on how well the model represents the real situation.

Models and theories are critical in helping manag- ers improve performance.

OPERATIONS RESEARCH (OR)

Operations research (OR) is: "(1) an application of the scientific method to (2) problems arising in the operations of a system which may be represented by means of a mathematical model and (3) the solving of these problems by resolving the equations representing the system."[3] Also known as management science, it is an approach that builds mathe- matical models and uses mathematical techniques to help organizations solve complex problems. The discipline developed about the time of World War II.

National Airlines used OR when it developed a mathematical model to decide how to save money. Two other applications of OR follow:

1. A model was developed to simulate the solid waste disposal system in Cleveland, Ohio. By applying the model to the real system Cleveland's solid waste managers were able to reduce the annual budget of $14.8 million in 1970 to a low of $8.8 million in 1972. The total savings in a four-year period, based on the 1970 budget, were $14.6 million. The solid waste work force was reduced from 1,640 to 850, and the collection routing system was completely redesigned. The management structure of the Cleveland Division of Solid Waste Collection and Disposal was reorganized to take advantage of and to supplement the major operational changes.[4]

2. Logs arriving at a mill making plywood were of different woods, sizes, and lengths. Intuition and experience had been used to determine the best way to make plywoods that would be suitable for a variety of orders. In 1967, however, the mill developed a linear programming model that determined the optimum balance among the different types of plywood and an annual operating plan. Under the plan, the mill's production is scheduled on a biweekly basis. A monthly financial report analyzes the effects of price, wood, product demand, and other variables. As a result of the program, the contribution margin of the mill—sales income minus wood costs—increased by an average of $1 million per year between 1970 and 1975 as compared to the base year 1969.[5]

OR has been applied to a variety of problems, such as establishing inventory levels, allocating advertising budgets among different products, setting time standards as a basis for costs and labor efficiency controls, and determining proper distribution of warehouses. Its application requires analysis of the functioning of the system, construction of a mathematical model, and a solution that results in greater ability to plan and control the operations of the system. The solution is obtained by solving the mathematical equations representing the system.

OR techniques can help solve at least six organization-wide problems: inventory, allocation, waiting lines, scheduling, replacement, and competition.[6] Although these problems will be described independently for the sake of convenience, from a systems point of view they are usually interrelated. For example, inventory problems may be closely related to scheduling problems.

Problems solved by OR techniques:

- Inventory
- Allocation
- Waiting lines
- Scheduling
- Replacement
- Competition

Inventory By defining *inventory* as idle resources, resources can then be defined as anything usable for obtaining something of value—such as people, money, machines, and material. Inventory involves the balancing of conflicting objectives. Because of their complexity and size, many organizations must maintain enormous inventories. The shortage of a critical part may halt production, and shortages of goods may turn customers to new sources of supply. However, certain costs are attached to maintaining a large inventory. Storage, handling, insurance, taxes, obsolescence, and interest on capital are some of them.

Allocation Allocation entails organizing resources in order to maximize the overall efficiency of the organization. The problems are encountered when resources are scarce and have to be allocated among several groups in order to accomplish an objective.

Waiting Lines An almost universal problem is waiting lines. They exist at the bank teller's window, at the supermarket checkout counter, at telephone and telegraph switching stations, and at loading platforms. Airplanes wait for runways, commuters wait for buses, and machines wait for repair. Any time there is a wait, a potential waiting line problem exists.

Scheduling The order in which operations or tasks occur can be important. Many products require operations on more than one machine. When this situation exists, the material flow needs to be sequenced to provide maximum utilization of the different machines. One class of scheduling problems involves sequencing jobs through a succession of stations, such as grinding, polishing, and shipping.

Replacement Parts or equipment break down or wear out over time; people leave; equipment becomes obsolete. An organized plan for repairs or replacements is essential and should stipulate the proper time for replenishing capital equipment or other earning assets. Such timing is not always easy to determine. Consider, for example, a television commercial as a deteriorating asset. When should it be replaced?

Competition In many situations, a conflict of interest exists among parties competing for a common resource. Examples are athletic competition, collective bargaining, military deployment strategy, political campaigning, pricing strategy, and market share. In these situations, two or more units are trying to achieve conflicting objectives. When the decisions made by a competitor can materially influence a decision, the behavior of the competitor must be included as part of the decision environment. Thus the problem is to develop decisions and strategies that will minimize losses and maximize gains. In competitive bidding for a contract, for instance, each bidder must consider the strategies of the other bidders.

SELECTED TOOLS AND TECHNIQUES
USED IN OPERATIONS RESEARCH

Many tools and techniques have been developed in OR, and more are constantly being created.[7] Most are mathematically based. The logical structure, precision, and convenience of the language of mathematics are great assets to a model.[8] This section will briefly describe such OR techniques as probability theory, queuing, and game theory. It will give short examples of approaches such as linear programming, PERT, and decision trees. No attempt will be made, however, to cover all existing approaches.

Probability Theory   **Probability theory,** which serves as the basis for many OR applications, is a way of computing the outcomes of decision alternatives by using statistical and other procedures for estimating the degree of risk. It provides ways to measure the likelihood of occurrence of events or environmental states. Specifically, a *probability* is the proportion of times under identical circumstances that the event can be expected to occur. The long-run frequency of occurrence is referred to as **objective probability.** Flipping a coin to see who buys the coffee is one of the simplest forms of objective probability, since the probability is one-half for getting heads. This can be verified by tossing a coin many times and observing that heads appear about half the time.

Insurance companies use a more complex form of probability. Although they cannot predict the death of any particular individual, they have developed life expectancy averages for various age groups on the basis of careful statistical analysis, and rates are set according to the probable age of death for individuals in each age category. Statistical quality control is another application of probability theory. In many organizations, inspecting each item produced would be prohibitively costly or even physically impossible. But a detailed inspection of a small sample makes it possible for a manager to predict the approximate number of defective products that will be produced.

Probability values can also be subjective, formed primarily or solely on the basis of personal judgment and experience. **Subjective probabilities** are used for events that have no meaningful long-run frequency of occurrence. Many business decisions involve one-time situations that are impossible to repeat exactly and require subjective probabilities. A wildcat oil driller, for example, may have only enough money to drill one well and must judge carefully where to sink the well. The owner of a small clothing store who wishes to expand must use subjective probability to determine where to locate a second store.

Most organizational decisions involve an element of chance. Both objective and subjective probability theory can be used to change a blind gamble to a calculated risk. Probabilities are fundamental to decision making. The process of developing them is a huge topic in itself and outside the scope of this book.

Queuing   A queue is a waiting line, and **queuing theory** is the study of waiting lines. The problem to be solved by a queuing theory is that of determining the optimum number of facilities to maintain when the need for them varies randomly. In the case of supermarket checkout counters, for example, there may be long waiting lines of customers at some times and few or no customers at other times.

This is a matter of economics, and it involves tradeoffs. Each checkout line costs money to maintain, but waiting lines also cost money. People who have to wait too long at supermarkets, drugstores, or banks may take their business elsewhere. A manager must determine the most economical queuing system—the system of service facilities that will take care of those people who often wait for service. With enough facilities, almost all waiting could be eliminated, along with the irritation, unpleasantness, and monetary losses they engender. But extensive service facilities involve large installation, operation, and maintenance costs.

Queuing theory is concerned with balancing the expected waiting costs and the expected service costs. The manager's objective is to determine the queuing system that minimizes the total expected cost. A number of mathematical approaches provide the answers; the best approach depends on the complexity of the problem.[9]

Game Theory   **Game theory** is used to develop a mathematical approach for maximizing gains or minimizing losses regardless of counter moves by competitors. Most organizations compete with other organizations. Their product, service, promotion, distribution, and pricing strategies usually are created in a competitive environment. Game theory attempts to predict the rational moves of people in competitive situations. Its purpose is to develop long- or short-term strategies that combine low costs with high gains. Game theory is used most widely in war games. But it is also used in organizations that must adjust their actions to respond to their competitors' actions and reactions. Thus it attempts to predict the reactions of competitors to a price increase, a new advertising campaign, or the introduction of a new product and to provide guidelines for effective strategies against those reactions. Unfortunately, competitive situations often involve a large number of variables, and the mathematics of game theory has not been developed far enough to deal with more than relatively simple problems in decision making and strategy. Still, under conditions of uncertainty, experienced managers can use game theory to effectively supplement their own knowledge, hunches, and intuition.

Linear Programming   **Linear programming** is a mathematical technique applicable when the relationships among variables can be expressed as directly proportional (linear) functions. *Linearity* means that a change in one variable must produce a directly proportionate change in another, the result being a straight line. A number of linear functions generally operate at the same time.

Every linear programming problem consists of a mathematical statement called an *objective function;* this function is to be either maximized or minimized, depending on the nature of the problem (for example, profit would be maximized but cost would be minimized. Also involved is a *set of constraint equations* specifying the quantities of the different resources available and the proportion of each resource necessary to make a unit of the item of interest. (Units might be manufactured parts, time, personnel policies, advertising time or space, inventories, or the blending of raw materials.)

Linear programming models are most helpful in situations where the required information can be expressed in mathematical terms, the variables are interrelated, and the resources are in limited supply. An example of a problem that linear programming could solve is the optimum scheduling of parts in a manufacturing plant with many machines operating at varying rates of speed and with thousands of parts to be processed. One machine may process Part A at the rate of 2,000 pieces per hour and Part B at the rate of only 250 pieces per hour. Where the human mind could not by itself work out the best combination of parts and machines and timing for each operation, linear programming, using complex mathematics, can provide the information that enables such scheduling to be made. National Airlines used linear programming to devise its plan for significantly reducing fuel costs.

The technique can be used for such diverse tasks as determining the most profitable product mix, scheduling inventory, planning manpower management, locating warehouses, and calculating whether it would be more efficient for a product to be manufactured or bought. It has been used for pollution control, rezoning of school districts, legislative redistricting, personnel allocation, capital budget allocation, and financial portfolio selection.

The Graphic Method of Linear Programming   The graphic method is seldom used because it applies only to problems involving no more than two decision variables (or three variables for three-dimensional graphing). It is described here in detail, however, because it provides an insight into the nature of linear programming and illustrates what takes place in the more widely used simplex method explained later in this chapter.[10]

The Skillco Corporation manufactures a wide variety of products. One small plant concentrates on two basic products, alpha (A) and beta (B). The unit contributions (unit selling prices minus unit variable costs) are $10 for alpha and $12 for beta. Each product has to be worked on by the plant's three production departments. The time requirements for each product and the total time available in each department are shown in Table 14.1. Skillco wants to maximize its profit by getting the best mix of alpha and beta within the constraints of the plant.

Z (total contribution) = $10A + $12B,

with the following constraints or limitations:

2A + 3B ≤ 1,500
3A + 2B ≤ 1,500
 A + B ≤ 600
where:

A = the number of units of alpha
B = the number of units of beta

TABLE 14.1 Hours Required for Products, by Department

DEPARTMENT	HOURS REQUIRED		HOURS AVAILABLE PER MONTH
	ALPHA	BETA	
1	20	30	1,500
2	30	20	1,500
3	10	10	600

The first equation, which deals with total contribution (Z), is an equality. The next three are inequalities. The inequality sign, ≤, meaning "is equal to or less than," is used so that Skillco can produce any combination of products that will be either equal to or less than the available stated hours in each department. In this sense, an inequality is less restrictive than a corresponding equality. For this reason, most constraints in a linear programming problem are expressed as inequalities that set upper and lower limits rather than exact equalities. A step-by-step procedure follows for stating and solving a problem by the graphic method of linear programming.

1. *State the problem in mathematical terms.* The objective function shows the relationship of output to contribution (Z = $10A + $12B). The three inequalities refer to the time used in making one unit of each of the products on the left-hand side of the inequality and the total time available in the department on the right-hand side. The total hours for making both products must be equal to or less than the time available in each department. All three inequalities represent capacity restrictions regarding output, not contribution.

   The values calculated for both products must be positive because a unit of product is either produced or not produced. Therefore, all elements in the solution of a linear programming problem need to be equal to or greater than zero. Stated mathematically the problem is:

Maximize:

$$Z = \$10A + \$12B.$$

Constraints:

$$2A + 3B \leq 1,500$$
$$3A + 2B \leq 1,500$$
$$A + B \leq 600$$
$$A \geq 0$$
$$B \geq 0$$

2. *Plot constraint equations.* The constraint equations are next graphed. Alpha is shown on the X axis of the graph, and Beta appears on the Y axis. All three inequalities can be drawn on the graph by locating their two terminal points and joining them by a straight line. For example, the first equation was 2A + 3B ≤ 1,500. If all the time in

department 1 is used to make alpha units and if no betas are made, then 750 units of alpha can be made. This is calculated as follows:

$$2A + 3(0) \leqslant 1,500$$
$$2A \leqslant 1,500$$
$$A \leqslant 750$$

Using the second equation, the second point can be computed in the same manner, this time with all the hours available used to make the maximum number of units (500) of beta and no units of alpha. The results are graphed in Figure 14.2.

The same procedure is used for the other two inequalities, which are shown in Figure 14.3. In order to complete the manufacturing of both products, all three departments must be used. Therefore, the feasible solution area is the shaded area in Figure 14.3. It contains all possible combinations of the two products that satisfy the original inequalities.

If a combination of output for both products results in a solution outside the striped area, one or more of the constraints has been violated. If management decides to make 100 units of alpha and 550 units of beta (point K in Figure 14.3), the time required is available in department 2 but not in departments 1 or 3. This solution is not feasible on the basis of the existing constraints.

3. *Plot the objective function.* The objective function can be plotted by assuming some arbitrary total profit figure and then solving for the axis coordinates. As described earlier, the objective function is given as $Z = \$10A + \$12B$.

The total contribution is made equal to some minimum dollar amount, such as $1,200, that is easily attainable within the given constraints. To plot this equation, one can write it as $\$1,200 = \$10A + 12B$. Then one can locate two terminal points and

FIGURE 14.2 Graph of equation $2A + 3B = 1,500$

Source: Robert J. Thierauf, *An Introductory Approach to Operations Research* (New York: Wiley, 1978), p. 191. Reproduced by permission.

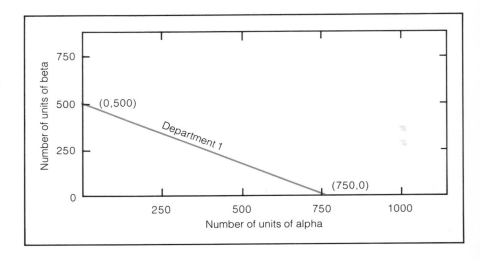

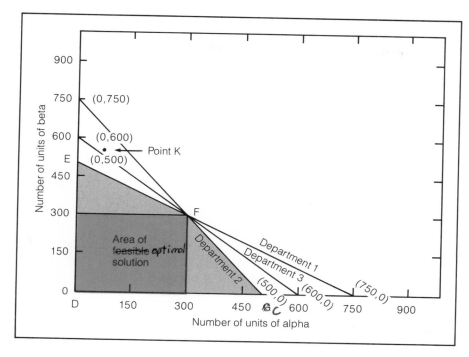

FIGURE 14.3 Graph of problem constraints (step 2)

Source: Robert J. Thierauf, *An Introductory Approach to Operations Research* (New York: Wiley, 1978), p. 191. Reproduced by permission.

join them with a straight line. The calculations are performed as follows. When A = 0:

$1,200 = $10(0) + $12B
        B = 100 units of beta.

When B = 0

$1,200 = $10A + $12(0)
        A = 120 units of alpha.

The area of feasible solutions (D, E, F, and C) has been taken from Figure 14.3 and is shown with the contribution equation in Figure 14.4. A parallel line can then be drawn from the original objective function line to the farthest point in the feasible solution area. Another approach is to use higher amounts for the contribution and compute new values for the two products, alpha and beta. A series of objective function lines can be drawn to locate the farthest point from the origin (point D), as shown in Figure 14.4. The combination line farthest from the origin contains all possible combinations of alpha and beta that will provide the greatest possible contribution. In the given problem, point F is the farthest point in the area of feasible solutions. Thus it represents the most profitable combination of products. The colored lines in Figures 14.3 and 14.4 show this best combination—300 units of alpha and 300 units of beta.

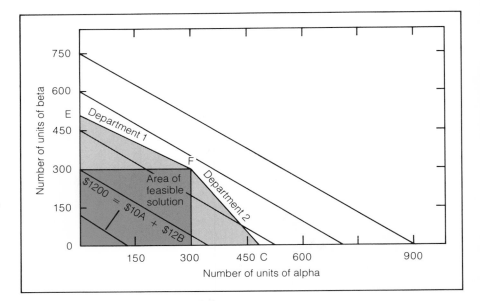

FIGURE 14.4 Objective function plotted (step 3)

Source: Robert J. Thierauf, *An Introductory Approach to Operations Research* (New York: Wiley, 1978), p. 192. Reproduced by permission.

4. *Solve the simultaneous equations.* In this problem the values for both products can be read off the graph. In most cases the graphical approach is not sufficiently accurate; therefore, the final step is to solve simultaneously the equations that intersect at point F. The equations for departments 1 and 2 are solved simultaneously in the following way:

$$2A + 3B = 1,500 \text{ (department 1):} \qquad 2A + 3B = 1,500$$
$$3A + 2B = 1,500 \text{ (department 2):} \qquad \underline{-2A - 4/3B = -1,000}$$
$$B = 300$$

When 300 is substituted for B into the equation for department 2, $3A + 600 = 1,500$, and the value for A is thus 300. By using the total contribution equation, $Z = \$10A + \$12B$, the total contribution is ($\$10 \times 300$) + ($\$12 \times 300$), which comes to $6,600.

Simplex Method   Most linear programming problems are too complex to be solved graphically, so the simplex method is used instead. This method is an algebraic procedure that progressively approaches an optimum solution through a series of repetitive operations. In the same fashion as the graphic method, it explores solutions at each intersection of the constraint equations. With the use of calculations based on matrix algebra, an optimum combination can be found. The simplex method can solve a problem involving any number of variables and constraints, but in most cases the computations are sufficiently complex that a computer is used.

Time-Event-Network Analysis   A number of techniques have been developed for planning and controlling the time periods within which work activities are to be accomplished. The simplest scheduling

method is jotting down an appointment on a calendar. More complicated methods involve complex mathematical or computer techniques
for analyzing, designing, and controlling large-scale activities.

Gantt Charts The Gantt chart, developed by Henry L. Gantt, is one of the
simplest and most useful aids in scheduling activities over time. The
first step in preparing the chart is to list the project's individual tasks.
The second step is to plot these tasks against time. The last step is to
compare actual progress with the schedule. Figure 14.5 is a simple Gantt
chart showing the construction of a small grain elevator with three silos.
Actual Gantt charts are often more complicated than the one shown.
Project are usually broken down into many more tasks—among them,
the different steps required to construct the foundation and install the
plumbing, electrical wiring, heating system, water system, and even the
office furniture.

PERT An even more advanced technique is the Program Evaluation and
Review Technique (PERT).[11] Developed by the navy in 1957–1958, it is a

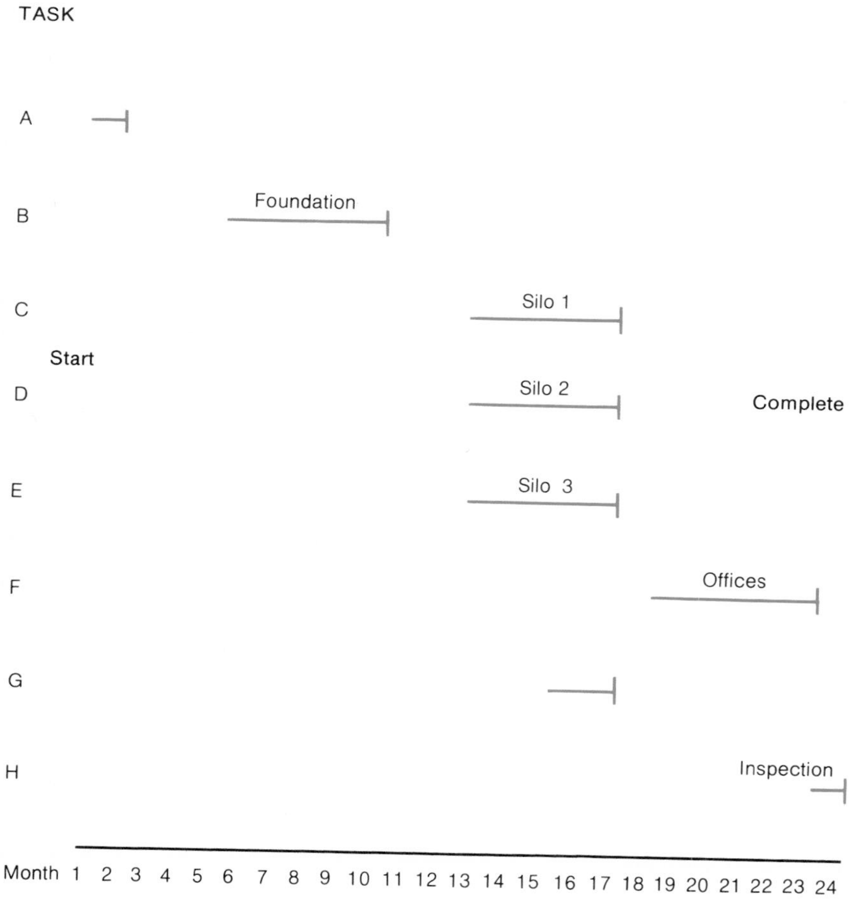

TASK

FIGURE 14.5 A simpli-
fied Gantt chart

A

B — Foundation

C — Silo 1

Start

D — Silo 2 — **Complete**

E — Silo 3

F — Offices

G

H — Inspection

Month 1 2 3 4 5 6 7 8 9 10 11 12 13 14 15 16 17 18 19 20 21 22 23 24

relatively new tool for planning, decision making, and control. PERT builds on the ideas of the Gantt chart but shows more clearly the interrelationship of events and activities. Specifically, **PERT** provides management with an operational network that relates the activities of a project in a time frame, thereby allowing the identification of the project's critical and subcritical stages. The navy began using PERT to plan, schedule, and control the development of the Polaris submarine. Building the submarines involved approximately 250 prime contractors, more than 9,000 subcontractors, and hundreds of thousands of individuals. The navy credits PERT with the successful completion of the Polaris two years earlier than originally scheduled. PERT and similar programs have since been adopted by many other organizations, including those in the fields of manufacturing, construction, and health care.

PERT is a way to plan programs that have specific objectives and specific, measurable results. It facilitates decision making, planning, and control primarily by controlling time and in some cases by controlling cost. PERT is usually used for complicated projects that require a great deal of coordination to be completed on time. It has been used in the construction of new buildings, aircraft, missiles, and highways; the design of buildings; the timing of important activities in mergers; and the development and distribution of new products. It tends to be a single-use plan, since it generally plans and controls nonrepetitive projects. PERT plans can have a number of steps. Some highly simplified ones follow.

1. *Identifying all activities.* PERT builds from basic groupings of work —jobs or tasks that are components of a project. Such groupings, called **activities,** take time and usually consume money, material, or labor. Table 14.2 shows that the first activity is to prepare the site for the grain elevator, and the second is to complete the foundation.
2. *Estimating time between activities.* The second step is to estimate how long it will take to complete each activity before the next one can be started. Those familiar with the particular program may wish to make three time estimates for each definable activity: (a) the minimum (most optimistic), which assumes that no problems will occur;

TABLE 14.2   Building a Small Grain Elevator (Times Given in Months)

ACTIVITY	EXPECTED TIME	MINIMUM TIME	MAXIMUM TIME	PRECEDING ACTIVITIES
A. Prepare site	2	2	3	
B. Complete foundation	6	5	7	A
C. Complete silo 1	7	6	9	B
D. Complete silo 2	8	6	9	B
E. Complete silo 3	7	7	8	B
F. Construct offices	7	7	8	C
G. Construct railroad siding	4	2	5	B
H. Inspect	1	0.5	2	All

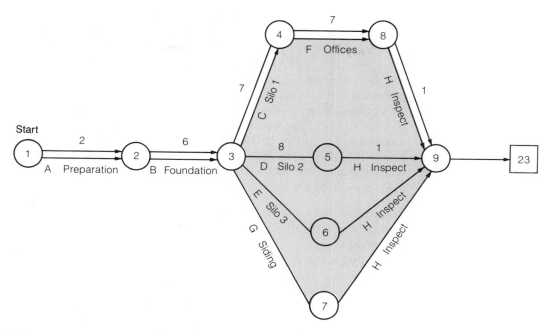

FIGURE 14.6 A PERT diagram for the building of a grain elevator (time given in months, for a total of twenty-three months)

(b) the maximum (most pessimistic), which assumes that all potential problems will indeed occur but that no major disaster will take place; and (c) the likeliest. The three times can be combined using probability estimates. The most probable time for site preparation in Table 14.2 is two months. The box at the end of Figure 14.6 shows that the project is expected to take twenty-three months to complete.

3. *Developing the PERT network.* An example of developing the network is shown in Figure 14.6. The circled numbers, called **events,** signal the completion or starting points of one or more activities. They are only points in time and consume neither time nor resources. They serve mainly as project milestones and provide a logical glue for connecting the different activities. Normally they are numbered serially from start to finish of a project.

In Figure 14.6 activities are represented by arrows. The tail of each arrow represents the beginning of the activity, and the head represents its completion. The shape, length, and position of the arrows are unimportant.

Activities in a PERT network should be related to each other in order of their occurrence. As many activities as possible should be performed at the same time. For example, after the site is prepared and the foundation laid, the three silos and the railroad siding can be started at the same time. The construction of the offices, on the other hand, must wait for the completion of silo 1.

4. *Identifying the critical path.* The **critical path** is the longest set of adjoining activities, or path, in a project management (PERT/CPM) network. The estimated project duration is the time it takes to traverse this path. Delays along the path cause delays in the entire project; delays along other paths are generally not as important, since the paths are not as long as the critical path. (The critical path in Figure 14.6 is shown by the double arrows.) For example, the railroad siding for the freight cars in the example of Figure 14.6 takes only four months to complete. If construction of the siding were to begin immediately after completion of the foundation, a delay would have little effect on the entire project. A delay in completing silo 1, however, would be critical.

The simple PERT discussion here is intended only to provide a general familiarity with PERT/CPM. Most PERT analyses have hundreds or thousands of events and require a computer for calculations. In real life, each activity shown in Table 14.2 would be broken down into a number of subactivities.

PERT has been modified in a number of ways, one of which is called PERT/COST. Here costs as well as time are included in the network. In the example that appears here, the construction of the railroad siding might be postponed for a time so it can use the same equipment that was used in building the silos, thereby cutting costs.

A major advantage of using PERT or its modifications is that it forces advance planning and examination of critical areas, including the use of forward looking decisions, plans, and controls, particularly for single-use plans. PERT can also be used to study a recurring sequence of events to see that there is no time lost in the procedures. It is not a cure-all, however; it simply establishes better conditions for employing sound decision-making and control techniques.

Decision Trees   A **decision tree** aids in planning by providing a method for identifying and choosing among available alternatives. The use of probability in decision making under conditions of uncertainty or risk was discussed earlier. A decision tree is a relatively simple and understandable way of using probability. It mathematically factors the degree of risk into a business decision. It is designed to help the manager "consider various courses of action, assign financial results to them, modify these results by their probability, and then make comparisons."[12]

One way to explain a decision tree is by example. When Acme Hardware Stores decided to build another store, preliminary market research and other information indicated that the two best towns in which to build were Centerville and Easthaven. Zoning ordinances, construction costs, the price of land, and accessibility to the main warehouse were approximately the same in both towns. Those reporting on these locations, however, disagreed on which was the best. A decision tree was developed as shown in Figure 14.7 to compare the two locations.

The usual steps in constructing a decision tree are:

1. *Identifying the possible actions and the possible outcomes (events) associated with each action.* In the Acme situation only two alternatives existed—building the new store in Centerville or building it in Easthaven.

2. *Estimating the probability of each outcome and assigning it a value, called the expected value, calculated by multiplying its estimated payoff by its probability of occurring.* (Expected value is used because under conditions of risk or uncertainty no outcome is certain.) The president of Acme and his staff combined their best judgment based on their accumulated experience to develop the subjective probabilities of first-year profits at both Easthaven and Centerville shown in Figure 14.7. (Subjective probabilities were discussed earlier in this chapter.)

3. *Identifying the action with the highest expected value.* This action usually the best choice. Reading from right to left on the decision tree ("rolling back") in Figure 14.7, the highest expected value belongs to Centerville.

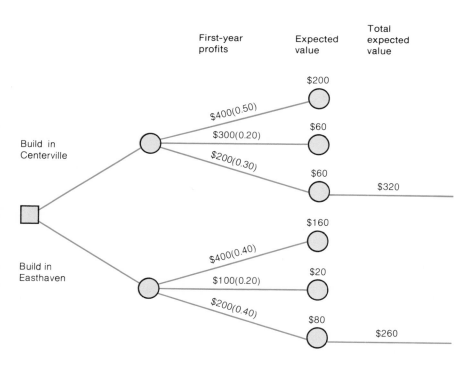

FIGURE 14.7 Where to build a hardware store (dollar amounts indicated in thousands)

☐ Indicates a choice mode.

◯ Indicates a chance mode.

Before Acme's president made a decision based on the decision tree, he learned of new projections for population growth in Easthaven attending new industry and development plans. He asked that the decision tree be extended for two years using this new information. As shown in Figure 14.8, expected values at the end of two years showed the Easthaven location to have the greatest payoff (the best outcome). Projected two-year profits for Easthaven were $520,000, compared to only $450,000 for Centerville.

From the data in Figure 14.8, the Easthaven location appears the better choice. However, the president and his advisers still had to use judgment (subjective probabilities) before making the final decision, since (1) a two-year projection is more uncertain than a one-year one, (2) the company might want the potential extra cash that the Centerville store would provide during the first year, and (3) the Easthaven location also had the possibility of an expected value as low as $160,000—lower than any expected value for the Centerville location. These and other variables were included in a more complex decision tree (not shown here), and the ultimate choice was Easthaven.

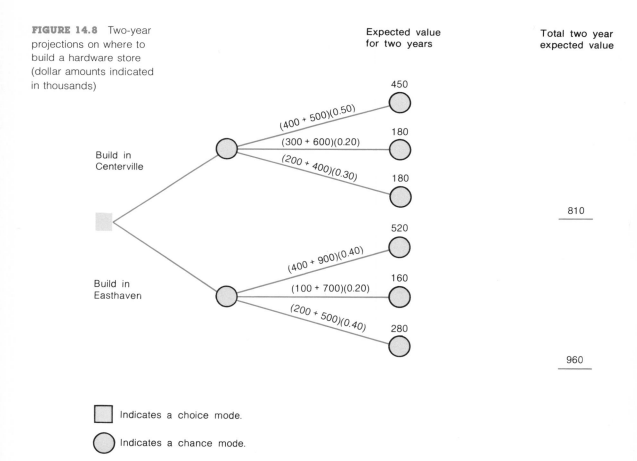

FIGURE 14.8 Two-year projections on where to build a hardware store (dollar amounts indicated in thousands)

Expected value for two years

Total two year expected value

Build in Centerville

(400 + 500)(0.50) 450

(300 + 600)(0.20) 180

(200 + 400)(0.30) 180

810

Build in Easthaven

(400 + 900)(0.40) 520

(100 + 700)(0.20) 160

(200 + 500)(0.40) 280

960

☐ Indicates a choice mode.

◯ Indicates a chance mode.

The decision tree can be used for many complex marketing, advertising, investment, equipment purchase, pricing, new venture, and other decisions. It clarifies for the manager the major alternatives and reminds the manager that decisions should allow for future events. Having the probabilities of different events expressed in concrete form helps the manager estimate just how likely a particular decision is to bring the desired outcome. Without this help, the best estimate is much less accurate. Thus decision trees force managers to plan and to analyze alternatives carefully and facilitate accurate judgment.

Decision trees are helpful in other ways too. Some managers tend to be conservative. Knowing that a single failure can generate losses that may ruin their careers, they choose actions with low personal risk, even if other actions have more potential benefit for the organization. Conversely, other managers act impulsively. They fail to think through the consequences of their behavior and therefore choose actions with great risk. Decision trees discourage either approach by forcing managers to delay their decisions until they have carefully examined alternatives.

LIMITATIONS OF OPERATIONS RESEARCH

As the examples have shown, operations research can be helpful in decision making, planning, and controlling. In large organizations, however, its application is limited. One reason is that large organizations are complex, and the number of relationships among all the factors of a problem is huge. In the case of National Airlines thousands of variables had to be considered in minimizing the cost of jet fuel, and this was a concern of only a small part of the total organization. Another limitation is that many important managerial decisions involve factors that cannot be quantified. While OR can help establish the economic level of raw material inventory, individual judgment is required to estimate the consequences of an impending steel strike. Indeed, one study found that decision makers sometimes do as well, if not better, than the quantitative models developed to aid or replace them.[13]

C. Jackson Grayson, a noted practitioner of operations research, did not use the technique when he headed the U.S. Price Commission's endeavor to set up and monitor price controls from 1971 to 1973. He deemed the OR approach unsuitable for this situation, which required fast action on large-scale problems with political implications. In a thoughtful review, Grayson gave five reasons that many managers avoid using operations research:

1. *Time shortage.* Gathering the data and building a model for OR can be time-consuming, and managers frequently need to make quick decisions.
2. *Difficulty of gathering data.* A great deal of time and effort are required to gather the data necessary for building an effective OR model.

3. *Resistance to change.* Managers have their own approaches to problems and often resist new ones. The situation is not helped by the tendency of mathematicians (OR practitioners) to use abstract language in describing the different approaches and advantages of OR.

4. *Long response time.* Operations research is methodical, involving a number of clear-cut steps; and managers view OR as too slow to give them solutions to problems when they need them.

5. *Oversimplification.* Operations research deals with mathematics and mathematical models, and many organizational problems (such as politics and power struggles) are hard or impossible to quantify. In most cases, these kinds of considerations are entirely excluded from the model. When this happens, the optimum solution according to the model is not really optimum. Furthermore, managers prefer not to look for optimum solutions but instead seek those that satisfice (explained in Chapter 4) and that account for the myriad of conflicting objectives.

Grayson suggested that OR practitioners become more sensitive to managers' needs and preferences—to their personal styles, their immediate and quickly changing problems, and their complicated, ill-defined environments. The way to do this is to work more closely with managers and gain a first-hand understanding of managerial approaches and concerns.[14]

SUMMARY

A few of the analytical aids available to managers are probability theory, linear programming, queuing, game theory, time-event-network analysis, and decision trees. (The National Airlines case demonstrated how linear programming was used to control fuel costs and avoid disrupted flights.) Clearly, however, there are times when knowledge of specific events must override the use of sophisticated techniques.

Probability theory is used to measure the chances of events occurring. It is critical to many organizations, especially insurance companies. Queuing theory is concerned with determining the optimum number of facilities to maintain, for example, the number of tellers needed to service a bank's customers. Game theory is a mathematical approach for specifying the gains and losses an organization will incur in implementing a strategy when competitors make rational decisions. Linear pro-

gramming is an analytical aid used by organizations in deciding on how to maximize or minimize such things as profits or costs. The organizations use a particular set of linearly related variables such as type of product, size of advertising budget, and location of distribution centers. The two other decision-making aids, decision trees and time-event-network analysis, are essentially pictorial descriptions of decision points and the events and times attached to each of them.

A problem in the use of the analytical tools available today is the gap between managers and trained mathematicians or computer experts. Managers frequently have little understanding of or appreciation for the complexities of mathematics. They tend to be action oriented, wanting their problems to be solved quickly. Operations researchers, on the other hand, tend to have little understanding of and appreciation for the nature and urgency of managerial problems. More reflective than managers, they seek the optimum solution and, in the pursuit, sometimes become more concerned with the elegance of the solution than with its practicality. When data are limited for a decision, the manager must supplement them with judgment based on knowledge and experience. Computerized models, however, are not very flexible; and if important data are either unknown or cannot be measured precisely, they cannot be put on a computer, and their existence is ignored in the computer's calculations.

Managers should be knowledgeable about the effectiveness and limitations of mathematical models. They should know when to ask for this type of help and when to rely instead on experience, intuition, and personal judgment.

STUDY QUESTIONS

1. Assume that no other airline besides National is using a mathematical model for reducing fuel costs. List all possible reasons that such an approach might have been rejected. How valid do you think each reason is? Explain.
2. Describe the various types of models discussed in the chapter. Which of them can be helpful to managers? Explain.
3. What are the six organization-wide problems that OR techniques can help solve?
4. In what way can OR be helpful in planning? In decision making? In controlling?
5. Mathematical models are abstractions of reality. Explain how this is true with regard to linear programming and network analysis.
6. Describe various uses of PERT.
7. Explain how decision trees can help managers.
8. Identify the major reasons that managers often do not accept and effectively use quantitative methods.

Case for Discussion

DECISIONS AT B-MART

The manager of a local B-Mart is planning to have a sale on pocket calculators. The store has budgeted $1,250 for advertising, not including preparation of the ads, and has asked the Acme Advertising Agency to handle the job. Acme has ten days before the sale is to take place.

Acme estimates that the average newspaper will produce $4,000 in sales and that the average radio spot will produce $5,000 in sales. The current standard rates are $40 for each newspaper ad and $125 for each radio spot. A newspaper ad will take about a day to prepare and a radio spot only half a day. Acme can work on only one ad at a time.

Acme recommends that all the B-Mart advertising monies be spent on radio spots since they produce higher dollar sales. Ten radio spots, which will use up the entire $1,250 budgeted for advertising, will according to Acme, produce total sales of $50,000. The manager of B-Mart mentions the proposal to one of the department managers, who returns an hour later with the following analysis:

It is clear that you want to maximize the money you will realize as a result of these newspaper and radio ads. In mathematical terms, your goal is:

Maximize $5,000R + $4,000N,

where R and N are the number of radio spots and the number of newspaper ads, respectively. Now, you can't choose just any number for R and N. You have limitations. The first limitation is your

budget. You have only $1,250 to spend. This limi-
tation can be expressed mathematically as

$40N + $125R ≤ $1,250,

since you would pay $40 for each newspaper ad
and $125 for each radio spot. For example, if you
choose to have five newspaper ads and three
radio spots, the formula will be

$40(5) + $125(3) = $575,

which is less than $1,250.

This is not your only constraint, however. The
advertising company needs time to prepare ads. It
takes a full day for a newspaper ad to be prepared and a half day for a radio spot, and there
are only ten days available. Mathematically, this
can be expressed as

N + 0.5R ≤ 10.

What you must do is find the best N and the best
R to make the following true:

$40N + $125R ≤ $1,250
N + 0.5R ≤ 10.

(Of course, N and R cannot be negative numbers.) You can get your answer in a variety of
ways. The easiest is to find values that fulfill both
the limiting inequalities. This is done by solving
the two simultaneous equations—the result of
which is that N = 6 and R = 8. This gives you a
sales values of

$4,000(6) + $5,000(8) = $64,000.

In other words, by using six newspaper ads and
eight radio spots you can top Acme's estimate of
$50,000 in sales and at the same time come in
slightly under budget:

$40(6) + $125(8) = $1,240.

The manager doesn't know whom to believe. Help
her by answering the following questions.

1. Do the department manager's suggested values fulfill the constraints? Are there other values that will?
2. What would be the effect of hiring an advertising company that could do more ads in the ten-day
   period than Acme can?
3. Which decision-making approach is being used by Acme?
4. Which decision-making approach is being used by the department manager?
5. What if the sales are only $42,000 as a result of the ads? Is the linear programming model wrong?
   Explain.

FOR YOUR CAREER

1. Don't discount the value of experience and judgment. One company president told a market analyst, "I
   don't like your figures. Go back and get me some better ones." He suspected the lack of validity of
   the first set of figures on the basis of his experience and judgment. His judgment was subsequently
   confirmed.
2. Mathematics can be helpful, but be sure to check the assumptions on which they are based.
3. Good managers do not have to be experts in operations research and other mathematical techniques,
   but they know when to call on the help of those who are experts in such approaches.
4. The computer is here to stay. It is a powerful tool to analyze data. If you don't know its strengths and
   limitations, you should.
5. People say that analytical aids to decision making, planning, and control are time-consuming. On the
   other hand, their office walls often sport signs that say: "Why is there never time to do it right the first
   time but always time to do it over?"
6. OR techniques are designed to discover the optimum answer to a problem, but for some problems an
   optimum answer is not desirable or possible.

FOOTNOTES

1. D. Darnell and C. Loflin, "National Airlines Fuel Management and Allocation Model," *Interfaces* 7 (February 1977): 1–16. This paper is a condensed version of an original paper delivered at the 16th Agifars Symposium in Miami, Florida, September 1976.

2. D. Smith, *Quantitative Business Analysis* (New York: Wiley, 1977); D. Anderson, D. Sweeney, and T. Williams, *An Introduction to Management Science: Quantitative Approaches to Decision Making* (St. Paul: West Publishing, 1976); and R. Gue and M. Thomas, *Mathematical Models in Operations Research* (New York: Macmillan, 1968).

3. C. W. Churchman, R. Ackoff, and E. L. Arnoff, *Introduction to Operations Research* (New York: Wiley, 1957), p. 18.

4. R. Clark and J. Gillean, "Analysis of Solid Waste Management Operations, Cleveland, Ohio: A Case Study," *Interfaces* 6 (November 1975): 32–42.

5. D. Kotak, "Application of Linear Programming to Plywood Manufacture," *Interfaces* 7 (November 1975): 56–68.

6. R. Ackoff and P. Rivett, *A Manager's Guide to Operations Research* (New York: Wiley, 1963).

7. Smith, *Quantitative Business Analysis;* J. Boot and E. Cox, *Statistical Analysis for Managerial Decisions* (New York: McGraw-Hill, 1970); and H. Raiffa, *Decision Analysis: Introductory Lectures on Choices under Uncertainty* (Reading, Mass.: Addison-Wesley, 1968).

8. R. Hartley, *Operations Research: A Managerial Emphasis* (Pacific Palisades, Calif.: Goodyear Publishing, 1976); and H. Lyon, J. Ivancevich, and J. Donnelly, Jr., *Management Science in Organizations* (Pacific Palisades, Calif.: Goodyear Publishing, 1976).

9. F. Hillier and G. Lieberman, *Introduction to Operations Research* (San Francisco: Holden-Day, 1967), pp. 379–471.

10. This section is based primarily on R. Thierauf, *An Introductory Approach to Operations Research* (New York: Wiley, 1978), pp. 185–219; and L. Lapin, *Quantitative Methods for Business Decisions* (New York: Harcourt Brace Jovanovich, 1976), pp. 207–232.

11. F. Levy, G. Thompson, and J. Wiest, "The ABC's of the Critical Path Method," *Harvard Business Review* 41 (September–October 1963): 99–110; D. Malcolm, J. Roseboom, C. Clark, and W. Fazar, "Applications of a Technique for Research and Development Program Evaluation," *Operations Research* 7 (September–October 1959): 646–699; and W. Merten, "PERT and Planning for Health Programs," *Public Health Reports* 81 (May 1966): 524–532.

12. E. McCreary, "How to Grow a Decision Tree," *Think Magazine,* March–April 1967, p. 13.

13. R. Woolsey, "A Candle to St. Jude, or Four Real World Applications of Integer Programming," *Interfaces* 2 (February 1972): 20–27.

14. C. J. Grayson, Jr., "Management Science and Business Practice," *Harvard Business Review* 51 (July–August 1973): 41–48.

Directing

PART V

Individual Motivation and Performance CHAPTER 15

THE YOUNG FOREMAN

Tom, a recent college graduate, was made foreman of an assembly line that put together automatic transmissions for an automobile company. The assembly line was located in a relatively isolated part of a large factory. The jobs of the twenty men of the assembly line had been carefully designed by industrial engineers so that fifty automatic transmissions could be produced each hour. This number was the standard for men working at a normal pace, allowing for an hour break for lunch and ten-minute rest breaks in the morning and afternoon. According to factory rules, the assembly line could be shut down only during those breaks.

Tom soon realized that the standard was not being met. Instead of fifty units per hour, only thirty-seven were being produced. New to the job, he was concerned that he would be criticized for failing to meet the standard. He checked the production records and found that the standard had never been met; in fact, the average of thirty-seven transmissions per hour had been maintained since the last design change of the transmission (more than a year ago), when the standard of fifty had been prescribed.

While in college, Tom had studied the effects of participation and feedback on employee motivation. So he decided to call a meeting and ask for suggestions from the workers. The first meeting was not very productive, but Tom did get a few suggestions. One was that the men be provided stools. Tom got the stools and allowed each worker to stand or sit as he desired.

The second meeting was more productive. Tom brought up the difference between the thirty-seven units being assembled and the standard of fifty and asked for suggestions. The men said that the job was boring and that an occasional break beyond the scheduled ones would be helpful. Forgetting the factory rule that the assembly line could be shut down only during prescribed times, Tom made a deal with the workers. When they completed fifty units in a given hour, they would get the rest of that hour off. Within two weeks the men were taking only thirty-five minutes to produce the standard; the other twenty-five minutes were spent on breaks.

Tom and the workers realized that this situation could not continue. Although the assembly line was relatively isolated, Tom was getting complaints from other foremen that his men were sitting around too much. They renegotiated their deal. This time productivity went to sixty-five units per hour with a ten-minute break every hour. All went well until the plant superintendent, who had heard of the increased production, decided to pay an unannounced visit. Unfortunately, he came just when the line was being shut down at an unauthorized time. After watching the men on their break, he shouted that assembly lines should not stop and that the men were being paid to *work* eight hours a day.

As a result, the men went back to working their full eight hours, and production went back to thirty-seven units per hour. Tom was eventually able to convince the superintendent that if the men produced fifty units an hour, they should be given some time off; but the superintendent insisted that they at least had to give the appearance of being busy. Production again rose to fifty units, and Tom and his workers developed ways of looking busy during their breaks.

This case raises several key questions which you should be able to answer after reading this chapter. The questions include:

1. Do all employees respond favorably to participation as they did when Tom asked his workers for their ideas and suggestions? Explain.
2. Should employees be allowed to determine at what pace they want to work?
3. Is money really the most effective way by which to get employees to perform?
4. Are satisfied employees more productive than dissatisfied employees? Explain.

This case illustrates several points that will be covered in detail in the chapter. First, managers are responsible for motivating people. They must provide the right conditions for people to work together, and they must coordinate the workers' efforts. Second, different people have different ideas about motivation. Third, as the situation changes, people's behavior also changes. Finally, although people are not always motivated in the desired direction, they are always motivated in some direction; that is, they behave in ways that are intended to satisfy needs and to reduce the tension of those needs, as Figure 15.1 shows.

Motivation is the "conditions responsible for variation in the intensity, quality, and direction of ongoing behavior."[1] **Performance** is the behavior that a person selects on the job to meet or achieve personal goals. Motives, which are internal, can be distinguished from external conditions and forces that determine how a person acts in a given situation. In the case of the new foreman, the motivation shifted as the external conditions changed, and the behavior changed as the motivation changed. Individuals perform in ways that help satisfy needs, and they avoid activities that do not satisfy needs or that result in punishment. Performance is based on the individual's perception of the situation, as shown in Figure 15.2.

The individual's perception of the situation includes what is seen as the degree of probability of reaching the objectives set by the manager or the organization and also the potential for extrinsic and intrinsic rewards. **Extrinsic rewards** are rewards given by the organization, such as pay, promotion, praise, tenure, and status symbols. When a person acts to receive an extrinsic reward (say money or a better job) or to avoid punishment (say loss of money or criticism), that person is *extrinsically motivated.*

Intrinsic rewards cannot be given by the organization; they must originate within the person.[2] Among them are feelings of accomplishment, enjoyment of the work, and self-esteem. A person who acts for no externally given reward is *intrinsically motivated.* The activity is a reward in itself, because it produces intrinsic rewards. Jigsaw puzzles provide this type of satisfaction.

Extrinsic and intrinsic rewards motivate performance only if the performance appears necessary to obtain them. Organizations can directly control extrinsic rewards such as pay, but their influence on intrinsic rewards is indirect.

Managers cannot change people; they can only change behavior. To

Motivation depends on:

* Motives/needs
* Intrinsic rewards
* Extrinsic rewards

Performance depends on:

* Motivation
* Ability

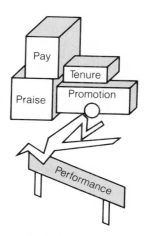

Extrinsic motivation

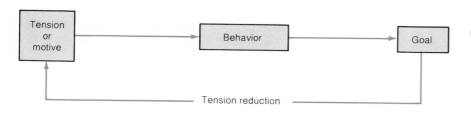

FIGURE 15.1 Motivation to achieve a goal

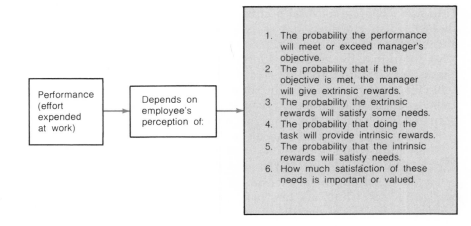

FIGURE 15.2 The motivation to work

Intrinsic motivation

do this they usually must change the *work situation*—the place and the circumstances of work—so it will allow people to satisfy work-related needs through performance. The balance of the chapter will look at some of the needs people have and will examine how work situations can be changed to satisfy these needs. Several different models of motivation will be described. As used in this chapter, the word *model* means a mental representation or idea of why people behave as they do. (Clearly, Tom and the plant superintendent were using different models.) The chapter will differentiate between content and process models, although basically they differ only in their relative focus, and they overlap considerably. **Content models** focus on the wants and needs that individuals are trying to satisfy (achieve) within the situation. **Process models** focus on how managers can change the situation to better tie need satisfaction to performance. The manager must consider both areas of focus if performance is to be improved.

THE CONTENT MODELS OF MOTIVATION

Two content models of motivation are discussed in this section. The first, the **need hierarchy model,** describes a hierarchy of needs existing within people. The second, the **motivation-hygiene model,** describes factors in the workplace that dissatisfy people and factors that motivate them.

The Need Hierarchy Model The need hierarchy model, developed by psychologist Abraham Maslow and adapted for use in management by psychologist Douglas McGregor, suggests that:

1. Adult motives are complex. No single motive determines behavior; rather, a number of motives operate at the same time.

2. Needs form a hierarchy. In general, lower-level needs must be at least partly satisfied before higher-level needs emerge.
3. A satisfied need is not a motivator. If a lower-level need is satisfied, a higher-level need emerges. In a sense, humans are always wanting something.
4. Higher-level needs can be satisfied in many more ways than can the lower-level needs.

The five need levels are physiological, safety (security), social (affiliation), ego (esteem), and self-actualization (or developmental).[3] Their sequence and relative importance are shown in Figure 15.3.

The *physiological* level includes the universal needs for food, clothing, and shelter. These needs must be met, at least partly, before higher-level needs emerge. The need for *safety* has been interpreted by recent writers to include more than freedom from physical harm—freedom from job layoffs and loss of income as well. In most Western countries both physiological and safety needs are satisfied for most people. The importance of these needs can be seen in the widespread emphasis on job tenure, savings accounts, and various types of insurance.

The *social* level includes the need to belong—to be accepted by others and to give and receive friendship and love. In the case at the beginning of the chapter, Tom may have been tapping into social needs in his discussions with the workers on how fast they should work and how they could appear busy.

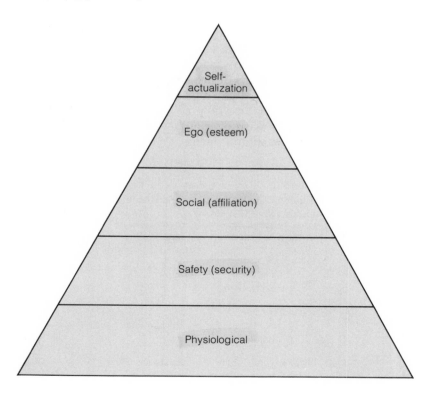

FIGURE 15.3 The need hierarchy

The *ego* level involves the need to have a firm, stable, and reasonably high evaluation of oneself. This level has both internal and external aspects. The internal aspect is a personal feeling of self-worth, an assurance of one's achievement, knowledge, and competence. The external aspect involves receiving appreciation, recognition, and respect from others.

At the social level of need a person wants only to be accepted; at the ego level a person wants to be admired or at least perceived as competent. Tom probably increased the ego satisfaction of the assembly line workers, while the plant superintendent probably threatened it.

At the fifth and highest level, **self-actualization,** individuals are concerned with achieving their full potential through self-development, creativity, and psychological health. The need cannot be completely satisfied by any job. Many people never attempt to satisfy the need, because they remain preoccupied with satisfying the lower-level needs. Maslow estimated some years ago that in the United States 85 percent of physiological needs, 70 percent of safety needs, 50 percent of social needs, 40 percent of ego and esteem needs, and only 10 percent of self-actualization needs were being satisfied.[4] Although the percentages may have changed, they probably are very similar.

Three need levels:

- Existence
- Relatedness
- Growth

The need hierarchy has been modified by later research indicating that the five levels can be reduced to three levels of core needs: existence, relatedness, and growth (**ERG**).[5] The first level, *existence,* includes the physiological (survival) and safety categories, among them fringe benefits, pay, and working conditions. The second level, *relatedness,* includes the social and esteem levels. The basic ingredient of this need is mutuality, or sharing, with such significant persons as family members, coworkers, subordinates, supervisors, and friends. The third level, *growth,* involves the individual's desire to be self-confident, productive, and creative. It includes the desire to engage in tasks that require the full utilization of abilities and that develop additional capabilities or skills. As Table 15.1 shows, there is an overlap between the growth need and Maslow's ego and self-actualizing needs.

TABLE 15.1 A Comparison of the Need Hierarchy and the Existence, Relatedness, and Growth (ERG) Model

MASLOW/McGREGOR	ERG
Self-actualization	
Ego ← Self-esteem / Social esteem	Growth
Social affiliation	
Safety ← Interpersonal / Material	Relatedness
Physiological	Existence

The need hierarchy is a general proposition supported by only a few studies; indeed, some studies do not support the proposition.[6] Managers using the theory should try to determine the motivational state of their employees before attempting to develop better performance. They should ask whether basic needs are being satisfied. Do the employees seem to seek opportunities to take on greater responsibilities, thereby increasing growth or self-esteem?

Care should be taken not to overgeneralize from the model. A number of different needs may be in operation at any one time, and not all of them can be satisfied simultaneously. Some aspects of the job may be more satisfying than others; and although some motives are involved only with job behavior or performance, others may be reserved for behavior off the job. For example, as mentioned earlier, it is impossible for a job to completely satisfy the self-actualization or growth needs.

A few years ago people were enjoying themselves at a popular Boston nightclub called the *Coconut Grove* when suddenly a fire broke out. We can assume that they attended the nightclub to satisfy social, status, and esteem needs. The fire threatened their physiological and safety needs. People rushed to the exists in a panic, only to find that the doors opened inward rather than outward. Their rush was so great and their panic so strong that they would not move back to allow the doors to be opened. They literally clawed, fought with, and trampled each other in their effort to escape the flames. Relatedness gave way to the struggle for existence, and the result was that hundreds of people died. This incident is an example of what can happen when one set of needs is suddenly threatened. (The *Coconut Grove* disaster is the primary reason that doors on most modern buildings now open outwards.)

The Motivation-Hygiene Model About twenty years ago Frederick Herzberg and his associates asked engineers and accountants what they liked and disliked about their work. After analyzing the data, Herzberg concluded that there were two vital kinds of factors in any job: hygiene and motivation. The motivation-hygiene model is based on the idea that one set of job characteristics determines the degree of worker dissatisfaction (hygiene), and another set determines the degree of positive satisfaction (motivation). In other words, the hygiene factors can be changed to reduce worker dissatisfaction, but these changes are not sufficient to create motivation. The *hygiene factors* involve the context in which the work is performed. They include company policy and administration; job security; interpersonal relations with supervisors, peers, and subordinates; salary; and working conditions. Herzberg's findings suggested that if these conditions were poor, they could lead to physical or psychological withdrawal from the job. The improvement of conditions is a little like vaccination; it can keep someone from getting sick, but it doesn't make the sick person well—hence the term *hygiene*.

The conditions surrounding the job (the hygiene factors) must be adequate before a person is motivated to work, but other factors are necessary to produce that motivation.

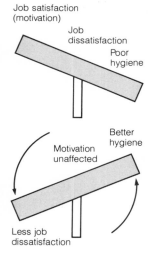

Motivation factors
Sense of achievement, recognition, advancement, enjoyment of work personal growth, sense of responsibility

Hygiene factors
Company policy, salary, job security, co-worker relations, working conditions

Hygiene factors must be adequate before motivation factors can operate.

Job satisfaction (motivation)

Job dissatisfaction

Poor hygiene

Better hygiene

Motivation unaffected

Less job dissatisfaction

Improving hygiene factors can reduce dissatisfaction but cannot produce motivation.

These *motivation factors* include a sense of achievement, recognition, advancement, enjoyment of the work itself, the possibility of personal growth, and a sense of responsibility. By increasing job satisfaction and motivation and improving mental health, these factors tend to increase productivity.

To briefly summarize Herzberg's findings, what motivates employees toward effective work is a job that is challenging and that encourages feelings of achievement, growth, responsibility, advancement, earned recognition, and enjoyment of the work itself. What disinclines them are primarily factors that are not directly part of the job itself, such as poor working conditions, bad lighting, insufficient coffee breaks, lack of opportunity to socialize, unpleasant work rules, unneeded titles, a rigid seniority system, low wages, and a lack of fringe benefits.[7]

A 1971 *Atlantic Monthly* quotes a supervisor addressing assembly line workers, "You don't think. . . . You're just an automated puppet." A worker responds, "That's all I'm working for—my paycheck and retirement." The article goes on to describe an employee who began shooting at everybody in white shirts with an M–1 carbine. In a few minutes three men were dead. At his trial the worker was found innocent because of temporary insanity. After viewing the factory where the man worked, one juror was heard to remark, "Working there would drive anyone crazy." The worker was reinstated, (although not in the same job).[8]

The findings use to postulate a motivation-hygiene model have been extensively criticized.[9] One of the most serious criticisms is that the way in which the information was gathered (interviews) may have distorted the findings. Since people usually attribute good results to their own efforts and blame others for bad results, it is possible that these interviews provided inaccurate information. The more the research approach used to create a motivation-research model varies from Herzberg's, the more likely it is that the conclusions will also vary.

Nevertheless, the model demonstrates that not all factors in the workplace have the same potential for motivating behavior. It also presents the useful generalization that any job has both satisfying and dissatisfying features for the employee. Furthermore, it suggests that increasing pay or improving working conditions will not automatically increase motivation; they may decrease dissatisfaction but may not affect work performance at all. Despite its many weaknesses, the model has been used successfully as a practical guide for redesigning some jobs.[10] (The subject of job design is discussed in greater detail in Chapter 22.)

The Relationships among the Content Models Although the models discussed so far have different sources, they showed marked similarities, as Table 15.2 indicates. The left-hand column is the need hierarchy, with the higher-order needs (starting with self-actualization) at the top and the lower-order needs at the bottom; the middle column is the ERG model; and the right-hand column is the motivation-hygiene model.

There are some obvious likenesses. The hygiene factors are roughly equivalent to the lower-level hierarchy needs, and the motivational fac-

TABLE 15.2 A Comparison of the Maslow/McGregor, ERG, and Herzberg Models

MASLOW/McGREGOR	ERG	HERZBERG
Physiological needs	Existence needs	Pay; job security; work conditions
Safety needs	Existence needs	Relationships with boss, coworkers Company policy; job hazards
Social needs	Relatedness needs	Recognition from others
Ego needs	Growth needs	Achievement Advancement
Self-actualization needs	Growth needs	Growth potential; work itself

tors are roughly equivalent to the upper-level hierarchy needs. All the models are slanted toward humanistic concerns; that is, they assume that most people want more self-esteem, which is achieved through greater opportunity for achievement, advancement, and responsibility. This assumption is clearly not true for all people. For example, some who were severely abused as children or who come from deprived homes may have learned to avoid advancement and responsibility.

The manager using the content approaches should analyze the working conditions and other circumstances surrounding the job to determine if they are satisfactory. If they are, the manager should try to provide opportunities for interesting work, earned recognition, and additional responsibility for those willing to accept it. In the case at the beginning of the chapter, Tom could not change the design of the assembly line, but he was able to improve some of the working conditions and provide additional responsibility and recognition. For example, he gave the men a say in how many units they would produce, and he recognized and rewarded them when they achieved the production goal.

THE PROCESS MODELS OF MOTIVATION

The content models of motivation provide some idea of the needs people try to satisfy. However, they are not explicit in showing how people attempt to satisfy needs at work or how managers can change the work situation to enable employees to satisfy needs through improved job performance.

The process models of motivation are more explicit in these areas. This section examines two of them: the positive reinforcement model and the expectancy model.

PR

Focus

Desired behavior → Desired outcome

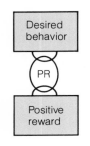

Desired behavior

PR

Positive reward

PR attempts to link behaviors to rewards.

The Positive Reinforcement Model The **positive reinforcement model** involves the use of positive rewards to increase the occurrence of the desired performance. It is based on two fundamental principles: (1) people perform in ways that they find most rewarding to them; and (2) by providing the proper rewards, it is possible to improve performance. A positive reinforcement (PR) program focuses on the job behavior that leads to desired results rather than on the results directly. It uses rewards rather than punishment or the threat of punishment to influence that behavior and attempts to link specific behaviors to specific rewards. This model operates according to the *law of effect*, which states that behavior that leads to a positve result tends to be repeated, while behavior that leads to a neutral or negative result tends not be be repeated. Thus an effort is made to link behavior to its consequences.

A PR program is installed by four basic steps, as shown in Figure 15.4: (1) conducting a performance audit, (2) establishing performance standards or goals, (3) giving feedback to employees about their performance, and (4) offering employees praise or other rewards tied directly to performance.[11]

Conducting a Performance Audit Performance audits examine how well jobs are being performed. Without them, many managers believe that their operations are going better than they actually are. Emery Air Freight Corporation conducted a performance audit on the way it was shipping packages. The cost of freight is considerably reduced if all the small packages going to a particular city are put in large containers. The managers involved in this part of the operation estimated that large containers were used in shipping about 90 percent of the time. The audit showed, however, that the actual figure was only 45 percent.[12] If possible, workers should be involved in performance audits, since they know more about the job than anyone else.

Establishing Performance Standards or Goals Standards are the minimum levels of performance accepted. They should be set after a performance audit and be tied directly to the job. The goals should be measurable and attainable, and the standards should be challenging but not impossible to reach; perfection is never possible. Standards are best formed on the basis of observation and common sense, and they should be as precise as possible. "Better identification with the organization" and "increased job satisfaction" are too general to be standards.

Where possible, the workers should help establish their standards. In

FIGURE 15.4 Steps in a positive reinforcement program

This is a linear diagram. From a systems point of view, each step may have unintended consequences.

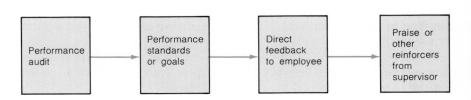

the case at the beginning of the chapter, the standard of fifty automatic transmissions per hour was not accepted by the workers until they participated in the decision making. Production eventually climbed to sixty-five units as a result of the workers' involvement. It would have been impossible for Tom to set a higher standard, such as eighty units. When the workers' involvement was again reduced, productivity dropped. At Emery Air Freight, the employees in the Chicago customer service department set and reached a standard higher than the one management would have set for giving customer answers within a specified time period.[13] However, time does not always allow for giving employees all the information they need to establish a reasonable standard.

Giving Feedback to Employees about Their Performance The third step in a positive reinforcement program is to give workers the basic data they need in order to keep track of their own work. The standards of performance for many jobs are not clearly stated; even when clearly stated, they are seldom available to the worker. A woman in an insurance company described her routine as follows: "I glance through the form to see if it is completely filled out. Then I separate the blue copies from the yellow copies and put them in different piles." When asked the purpose of the form, how it was used, and where the different copies went, she reported that she did not know. She had no idea if the information on the form was accurate, and she did not know the consequences if the form was incompletely or incorrectly filled out. All she knew was that each line of the form had to have something on it or be returned to another department.

Performance should be measured against standard, and employee should be given direct feedback.

Performance standards are ineffective without constant measurement and feedback. The feedback should be neutral rather than evaluative or judgmental and, if possible, should come directly to the worker rather than to the supervisor. Prompt, direct feedback refers, of course, to knowledge of results, one of the most important learning principles. Feedback allows the worker to know whether performance is improving, remaining the same, or getting worse.

In the relay assembly test room described in connection with the Hawthorne studies in Chapter 2, operators assembled small relays for telephone equipment. Continuously operated recorders counted each relay assembled by each worker. Readings were taken every half hour, and "at the end of each day, a report specified the total number of relays each worker had completed, type of relay, total time for sets of 50, and time breaks."[14] The workers freely discussed their performance. For example, on April 19, 1929, at about 4:30 P.M., Operator 3 said, "I'm about 15 relays behind yesterday." Operator 5 reported, "I made 421 yesterday and I'm going to make better today."[15] It has since been suggested that this prompt feedback was one of the reasons for the increased productivity revealed in the Hawthorne studies.

Performance keys:

• Rewards
• Punishments
• Clear performance specifications
• Feedback
• Goals

Offering Employees Praise or Other Rewards Tied Directly to Performance As explained earlier, positive reinforcement involves the use of positive rewards to increase the occurrence of the desired performance. The fourth step in a positive reinforcement program—offering employees praise or other rewards tied to performance—is the most important one. If the reward is praise, it should be expressed in specific quantitative terms. "Keep up the good work, Chris" is too general. A better form of praise is: "Mary, I liked the imagination you used in getting the product packed. You are running fairly consistently at 97 percent of standard. After watching you, I can understand why."

One of the most common rewards is money. Although money is very effective as a motivator, many organizations cannot afford to use it that way often. Other rewards can be just as effective, though. They include praise and recognition tied to the specific job behavior, the opportunity

"I FIND THIS WORK TRULY FULFILLING IN MANY WAYS — THERE'S THE EXERCISE, THE SENSE OF ACCOMPLISHMENT, AND, MOST IMPORTANT, THE OPPORTUNITY TO MAKE LOTS OF NOISE."

to choose activities, the opportunity to personally measure work improvement, and the opportunity to influence both coworkers and management.

Rewards for specific performance should be given as soon as possible after the behavior has taken place. Reinforcement should be more frequent at the beginning but can become less frequent and more unpredictable after the desired performance level is reached.

There are several different types of reward schedules, among them continuous reinforcement and partial reinforcement. Under **continuous reinforcement** the employee is reinforced every time the correct performance occurs. When this schedule is used, performance improves rapidly but can regress just as rapidly when the reinforcement is removed. In addition, managers find it difficult or impossible to continuously reward performance. Therefore, managers should use **partial reinforcement,** rewarding correct behavior only part of the time. There are a number of partial reinforcement schedules, perhaps the most effective being the variable ratio schedule. Under this schedule, reinforcement is given after an average number of desired responses but not precisely at that average point; rather the time of dispensation varies somewhere around the average point so that it cannot be predicted exactly.[16] In most organizations pay occurs on a fixed interval schedule, such as once a week or once a month; pay increases and promotions occur on a variable interval schedule; and praise, recognition, and similar rewards occur on a partial reinforcement schedule.

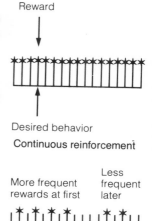

Continuous reinforcement

Partial reinforcement

The six basic rules for using reinforcement are:

1. *Do not reward everyone the same way.* Using a defined objective or standard, give more rewards to the better performers.
2. *Recognize that failure to respond also has reinforcing consequences.* Managers influence subordinates by what they don't do as well as by what they do; lack of reward thus can also influence behavior. Managers frequently find the job of differentiating among workers unpleasant but necessary. One way to differentiate is to reward some and withhold rewards from others.
3. *Tell people what they must do to be rewarded.* If employees have standards against which to measure the job, they can arrange their own feedback system to let them make self-judgments about their work. They can then adjust their work patterns accordingly.
4. *Tell people what they are doing wrong.* Few people like to fail; most want to get positive rewards. A manager who withholds rewards from subordinates should give them a clear idea of why the rewards are not forthcoming. The employees can then adjust their behavior accordingly rather than waste time trying to discover what behavior will be rewarded.
5. *Do not punish anyone in front of others.* Constructive criticism is useful in eliminating undesired behavior; so also is punishment, when necessary. However, criticizing or punishing anyone in front of others lowers the individual's self-respect and self-esteem. Further-

more, other members of the work group may sympathize with the punished employee and resent the supervisor.

6. *Be fair.* Make the consequences equal to the behavior. Do not cheat an employee out of just rewards; if someone is a good worker, say so. Some managers find it difficult to praise; others find it difficult to counsel or tell an employee about what is being done wrong. A person who is overrewarded may feel guilty, and one who is underrewarded may become angry.[17]

In the case at the beginning of the chapter rewards were closely related to the desired performance. As soon as the agreed-upon quantity of units was assembled, the men took their break. When the managers and employees at Emery Air Freight understood that only 45 percent of the packages were being shipped in containers, and feedback and positive reinforcement were given, the workers soon hit the standard of 95 percent. The change resulted in savings of about $65,000 per year.[18]

The manager using the positive reinforcement model should first examine the job (audit the performance) to determine standards, preferably with the assistance of the employees. Then the manager should establish methods of getting direct feedback to employees about individual or group performance. Finally, the manager should provide positive reinforcement as employees come closer to the standard, shifting perhaps from a continuous to a partial reinforcement schedule as they get very close to the standard. At the beginning, the manager might have to look carefully for even small changes in behavior in order to give positive reinforcement; otherwise behavior might not improve.

Expectancy keys:

- Perceptions
- Effort-performance relationships
- Performance-reward relationships
- Performance
- Outcomes/preference
- Equity
- Satisfaction
- Choice

The Expectancy Model The expectancy model of motivation, designed by Victor Vroom, has been the subject of a great deal of research and attention since its development. The **expectancy model** suggests that people are motivated at work to choose among different behaviors or intensities of effort if they believe their efforts will be rewarded and if the rewards they expect to get are important to them. The three primary factors in this model are choice, expectancy, and preference.[19] **Choice** is the freedom to select from among different possibilities or alternatives. People can usually choose from among a wide range of behaviors. They choose to come to work or to call in sick and to work hard on the job or to take it easy, for example. The men in the case at the beginning of the chapter initially chose to hold productivity down to thirty-seven transmission assemblies per hour and later chose to increase productivity to sixty-five units per hour. Working harder led to rest breaks (positive outcome) but may also have led to more fatigue while working (negative outcome). A student may decide to study hard to get a good grade in a particular course (positive outcome) but may have to pass up going to a party (negative outcome). Sometimes the choice is relatively simple, as in these examples. Other times it is more difficult, as in choosing a career.

Expectancy is the belief, expressed as a subjective estimate or odds, that a particular act will or will not be successful. Individuals who want to attain a particular goal must usually expend some effort to do it. However, people have certain expectations or beliefs about whether their behavior will be successful. If they see the odds as zero, they will not even try.

The expectancy model was explained the following way to a group of managers meeting in a conference room. A thousand dollars was offered to anyone who could, without special help, kick the ceiling with either foot. When no one even tried, it was pointed out that everyone had subjectively estimated that the odds of kicking the ceiling were zero and on the basis of this expectancy had made a choice not to attempt it.

As with positive reinforcement, the standards of an expectancy model should be seen by the employees as challenging but attainable. The probability of accomplishing a task must be relatively low for a feeling of achievement to be imparted.

Preferences involve valuing some rewards more highly than others and avoiding punishment. In the case at the beginning of the chapter the opportunity to take a break was a valued reward for which the men were willing to work harder.

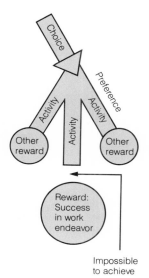

Impossible to achieve

The expectancy model of behavior suggests that people will work (behave) to accomplish goals that satisfy certain needs. The goals may be either ends in themselves or means to an end. For example, an engineer attempting to solve a technical problem worked on Saturdays and Sundays until the problem was solved. Coming to work on the weekend was his *choice*, based on his *preference* for solving the problem rather than enjoying some other activity. His *expectation* that he would solve the problem was necessary for this choice and preference to operate.

The process of choice, expectancy, and preference can be expressed in five propositions:

1. Behavior is directed toward satisfying needs by means of achieving certain goals. The goals may be valued for themselves or because they lead to still other goals, such as passing a course to get a diploma to get a better job.

2. The behavior must be seen as a way of making the goal possible, or it will not be chosen. Working harder resulted in a rest break for the factory workers in the chapter opening case. Working on weekends helped the engineer solve a difficult problem. Studying harder usually results in higher grades. In all these cases the behavior chosen is considered likely to achieve the desired outcome.

3. In most circumstances, individuals can choose among a range of different behaviors to reach certain outcomes. For example, assume that a student wants high grades. One way to achieve the grades is to study hard, another way is to take easy courses, a third way is to cheat, and a fourth way is to join a study group. Moreover, alternatives can be mixed. The student can take easy courses, study hard, and cheat.

4. The more an individual perceives a desired outcome as a direct result

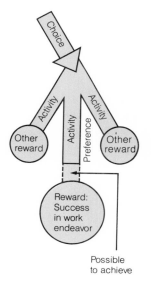

Possible to achieve

of personal behavior, the greater the motivation. For example, if everybody has job security for minimum effort, there is little motivation to work hard for that outcome. However, motivation may exist to work hard for other outcomes, such as a pay increase, promotion, or increased recognition and praise from the boss.

Positive outcomes include:

- Job security
- Praise
- Salary
- Promotion
- Fairness
- Freedom
- Respect
- Job variety
- Challenge
- Participation

5. Most behaviors have both positive and negative outcomes. Working harder, as in the case of the engineer working on weekends, may lead to solving the problem quicker (positive outcome) but may also lead to fatigue (negative outcome) or loss of social life (negative outcome). However, the engineer clearly felt that the positive outcome was greater than the negative outcome in working hard to solve the problem. There was little payoff for the men assembling the automatic transmission to work harder until they got rest breaks as the positive outcome of their work.

The expectancy model can be summarized by stating that performance at work is a function of the expectation that a desired outcome will be achieved and of a preference for that particular outcome over other desired outcomes. The outcome that the performance is directed toward is also a function of an expectation that it can indeed be achieved.

People are constantly making choices based on the subjective probability that what they do will have a payoff. The situation illustrated in Figure 15.5 is that of a married woman, with two young children, who recently graduated from law school. She has an unsatisfied need for

FIGURE 15.5 An expectancy model of motivation

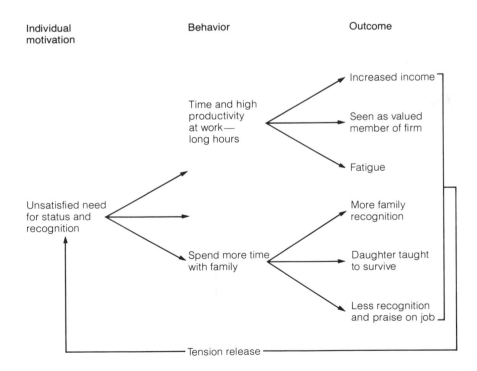

status. This need can be satisfied by obtaining the high regard of those with whom she works in the prestigious law firm (job) or by being seen as an attentive, caring wife and mother (family life). She can choose to work harder at the law firm, which may result in the desired outcome of increased status but also may bring negative outcomes of fatigue and emotionally impoverished family life. Or she can choose to spend fewer hours at work and devote more time to her family, which may gain her increased appreciation from family and friends but cause her to lose prestige at work.

Consciously or subconsciously, she will probably work out the subjective answers to a series of questions before making a choice. What is the probability (expectancy) that harder work will lead to greater status on the job? What is the probability (expectancy) of receiving more recognition from the family by spending more time with them? By teaching her daughter to swim? Although an individual may not be aware of mentally calculating the relative values of these choices, the calculations are nevertheless proceedings.

In other words, in making choices, people constantly ask themselves, "What is the payoff for me?" The diagram in Figure 15.5 is, of course, oversimplified. The complexity of human beings is such that a number of needs are usually in operation at the same time. The model effectively shows, however, that needs are considered in light of the best known subjective probabilities and that particular behaviors are chosen to bring about outcomes that satisfy those needs. Behavior choices depend on what the individual perceives as the greatest reward. Obviously, this varies from individual to individual. Some students occasionally skip an eight or nine o'clock class in order to sleep longer; others never do.

The expectancy model forces the manager to focus on a fundamental managerial problem. If workers are to be motivated to perform satisfactorily on the job, they must see a clear-cut payoff. If they do not, it is the manager's responsibility to either change the work situation to provide such a payoff if none exists or clarify for the workers the path to that payoff if it does exist. (Some suggestions for solving this problem are made at the end of the chapter; other suggestions—the path-goal approach—are described in Chapter 17.)

Neither the positive reinforcement model nor the expectancy theory model has been subjected to rigorous research in business and similar organizations. However, such research has begun and thus far suggests that both show promise of being valuable techniques.

TOWARD AN OVERALL APPROACH TO MOTIVATION

There are some similarities and some differences among the four basic models of motivation discussed so far.[15] Figure 15.6 shows the basic similarities, which are of more value to the reader's understanding of motivation than are the differences.

Some areas of motivation are controlled by individuals, each of whom

Areas within or controlled
by the employee

Areas that can be clarified
by the manager or situation

Areas that can be affected
by the manager or the situation

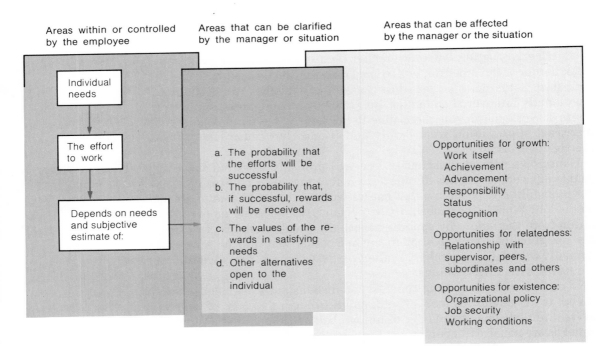

Individual
needs

The effort
to work

Depends on needs
and subjective
estimate of:

a. The probability that
   the efforts will be
   successful
b. The probability that,
   if successful, rewards
   will be received
c. The values of the re-
   wards in satisfying
   needs
d. Other alternatives
   open to the
   individual

Opportunities for growth:
   Work itself
   Achievement
   Advancement
   Responsibility
   Status
   Recognition

Opportunities for relatedness:
   Relationship with
   supervisor, peers,
   subordinates and others

Opportunities for existence:
   Organizational policy
   Job security
   Working conditions

FIGURE 15.6   The motivation to work

comes into any situation with different needs and abilities. Individuals decide whether to put forth the effort to work, basing their decision not only on their needs and abilities but also on their subjective estimates. They decide what rewards they value and whether the effort is worth the reward. These are subjective perceptions.

Managers, on the other hand, have greater control over the situation. When the managers at Emery Air Freight learned that the percentage of packages shipped in larger containers was only 45 instead of the 90 percent they had predicted, they were able to take precise corrective action and bring the percentage up to their standard.

Managers should recognize individual differences and capitalize on everyone's strengths.

Managers often are inaccurate in their estimate of the relative importance to employees of various rewards and working conditions. Frequently, they spend large sums of money trying to motivate employees without first learning what employees view as valuable and determining how performance can be tied to attainment of those rewards. The Christmas turkey given to all employees has little effect on performance throughout the year.

An example of misjudgment occurred in the dietary department of a hospital. The majority of the department's employees were women of about fifty years old. Each Christmas the head dietician gave out large mesh stockings filled with hard candies, chocolates, and oranges. The employees lined up, accepted their Christmas stockings, and thanked the dietician. What she never knew was that this gift actually embarrassed the employees; they felt they were being treated like children, but they were too polite to say so.

The employees' estimates of the value of a reward and the amount of effort necessary to achieve it are of necessity subjective. Nevertheless, the manager can be influential in helping to clarify the relationship between effort and reward. The manager can, for example, establish situations where the goals are clearer and the feedback on performance is faster and more direct. Thus the areas listed in the right-hand column of Figure 15.6 are more directly affected by the manager or the organization than by the employee. The manager can (1) make certain that standards are clear and that the employee receives feedback regarding performance, (2) create opportunities to make the work more interesting, (3) design jobs so that they contain more opportunities for responsibility or achievement, and (4) provide recognition or provide the opportunity for the employee to obtain gratification from the work itself or from the reward system.

A sales manager can make certain that sales quotas are clear and attainable, perhaps by soliciting the help of the salespeople in setting the quotas. When a quota is reached, the manager can give praise and recognition that goes beyond the gratification the salesperson may receive from reaching or exceeding the quota.

A survey of a manufacturing situation showed that skilled machinists were not receiving recognition for good work. Their supervisor said, "Why should I praise them? They are getting paid for it." This is an example of an ineffective manager with no understanding of human motivation.

Individuals have available a wide range of behaviors that they will not use in the work environment if they are not rewarded in that environment. Therefore, the impact of organizational conditions on the individual cannot be overstressed. For example, the opportunity to develop meaningful relationships with others is important to some people. The manager can establish working conditions that provide this opportunity on the job satisfaction of such social needs to job performance. One of the reasons for increased productivity in the case at the beginning of the chapter may have been the increased opportunity of the workers to satisfy social needs after reaching the agreed-upon standard. Finally, the manager and the organization affect job security and working conditions by formulating and administering organizational policy.

THE RELATIONSHIP BETWEEN JOB SATISFACTION AND PRODUCTIVITY

The relationship between job satisfaction and productivity is not completely clear. For a long time, people felt that high levels of satisfaction caused high productivity. Then other studies suggested that there was no consistent relationship between job satisfaction and productivity. Still later work suggests that while high performance is related to intrin-

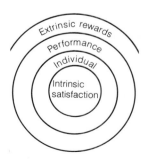

Extrinsic rewards increase performance, and better performance provides intrinsic satisfaction.

sic satisfaction, extrinsic rewards such as pay, praise, and recognition are what lead to higher performance levels.[21] In other words, paying someone well or giving praise and recognition tends to increase the performance level, and the higher performance level increases the intrinsic satisfaction.

Thus, rather than trying to make employees happy (intrinsically satisfied), the manager should concentrate on creating conditions that inspire high performance. Out of increased productivity will usually come increased job satisfaction.

SUMMARY

Motivation is the conditions responsible for the intensity, quality, and direction of ongoing behavior. These conditions are both intrinsic and extrinsic to the individual. Performance at work is a result of the individual's needs, beliefs, and attitudes and of the situation in which the person works. Since most people who work are mature adults, there is relatively little managers can do to directly change their behavior. However, managers can change the conditions under which the people work, and changing these conditions frequently changes people's behavior.

The different models of motivation overlap considerably. The content models tend to focus directly on people's needs, while the process models tend to focus more on behavior and the work situation. Clearly, attention must be paid to both the person and the situation. There is no single, comprehensive, well-supported model to which all subscribe; yet the different approaches agree in enough areas to give some overall guidelines.

People have numerous and complex needs. No single motive determines behavior; usually a number of motives operate at the same time. Satisfied needs are not motivators, but lower-level needs must be satisfied for higher-level needs to emerge. In this sense, people can be described as always wanting something. Each person has a unique set of needs that are satisfied or unsatisfied at any particular time. Therefore, managers should work at understanding their own motives.

The better they understand themselves, the better they can understand others.

The individual has a wide choice of behaviors in most work situations; among them are the choices of whether to come to work or not and whether to work hard or take it easy. The decision to engage in one behavior results from a consciously or unconsciously made choice among different probabilities that needs will be satisfied. These choices are affected by many factors, including the work situation, other people, and the individual's own experiences. Some behaviors are motivated by avoidance of loss; for example, the individual may come to work to avoid being fired. Other behaviors, especially those involving better-than-average performance, result from attempts to satisfy such complex needs as relatedness, status, and growth.

The manager should examine the range of choices within the work situation. What alternatives do people have? Which alternatives may lead to increased performance. How can employees be encouraged to choose them?

Behavior changes as situations change. Although there are always technological and other constraints, the manager does have some control over work situations. Within the limits of those constraints, the manager should examine what can be done in any job situation to allow for more direct need gratification that will lead to better performance. The manager can help motivate employees by clarifying which specific behaviors will lead to specific rewards. To the greatest extent possible, the manager should ensure that rewards are closely tied to performance.[22]

In summary, for workers' performance to improve, the manager must define superior performance for the workers and reward superior performers more than others. The link between superior performance and reward must be as clear as possible. Also, rewards should be those that satisfy needs that employees consider important.

STUDY QUESTIONS

1. What is a model of motivation?
2. List and give examples of the levels in the need hierarchy.
3. What are some difficulties in applying the need hierarchy model?
4. How do the hygiene and motivational factors differ?
5. Describe the basic relationships among the content models of motivation.
6. How do the content and process models of motivation differ?
7. Describe the basic characteristics of the positive reinforcement model of motivation.
8. What are the basic steps in constructing a positive reinforcement model?
9. Describe and give examples of the three basic features of the expectancy model of motivation.
10. What can a manager do to motivate people?
11. Interview a number of managers (managers of pharmacies, grocery stores, service stations, fast food restaurants, and the like). Ask them what outcomes their subordinates value most.
12. Ask the same managers to describe a time when they felt especially good about their jobs and a time when they felt especially bad about their jobs. How do their answers relate to what you have learned in this chapter?
13. Ask the same managers to describe their own motivation. Is there a difference between how they perceive their subordinates' motivation and their own motivation? If there is a difference, how would you explain it?
14. Take a work situation with which you are familiar, and assume you are the manager. How would you change the situation to provide more opportunity for need gratification on the job?

Case for Discussion

WHAT IS GOOD PERFORMANCE?

"Jay, I hate to drop in unexpectedly like this, but if you have a minute, there's a problem I'd like to discuss with you", said Karen Whitman, regional sales manager, to Jason Bovar, vice-president of sales for Dalton Manufacturing.

"I do have a meeting in a few minutes, Karen, but what's on your mind?"

"Well, I'm having some problems with one of our newer salespeople. She is not fitting into our system. Actually, there's both good and bad news. Her sales are quite good. As a matter of fact, she is number two in total sales for the last quarter, and frankly, she'll soon be number one."

"You're talking about Jane Elliott," interrupted Bovar. "I could hardly help noticing her early performance. What's the bad news?"

"She is causing me a lot of trouble with my other salespeople. Not surprisingly, they are somewhat jealous of her, but the problem runs much deeper than that. They think she gets special treatment—mostly because she disregards nearly all our rules."

"For instance?"

"She never attends sales meetings. She travels in her personal car almost exclusively, which is expressly against our policy. She refuses to carry our entire line of products. She tells me confidentially that some of the stuff is second rate and that she would have trouble servicing accounts if she sold it. So she won't even carry it in her case. While I must admit that I've not personally heard it, the rumor is that her sales pitch is decidedly different from the one we encourage in our training sessions. She has on occasion given credit for items that were recently out of warranty. I could go on and on. The point is that she is definitely 'doing her own thing.' My other people are complaining because thus far I have been hesitant to take any action against her. I have talked with her on several occasions about these problems. She inevitably smiles understandingly and promises to stay in line. However, she doesn't change. Jay, the thing is getting out of hand. What do you think I should do?"

1. If you were the vice-president, how would you counsel your sales manager?
2. Has the organization failed to control Jane Elliott properly?
3. Do you interpret Elliott's behavior as being arrogant and lacking in commitment to the organization? Is she insensitive to the problems of the organization and, more particularly, to the sales manager?
4. How should organizations deal with higher performers who are not good team players?
5. What psychological contract did Elliott perceive she had established?

FOR YOUR CAREER

1. Don't fall into the trap of thinking that everyone is motivated by the same things that you are. Try to figure out what needs and motives are most important to those people with whom you work—boss, peers, and subordinates.
2. When needs are satisfied, others emerge. Watch for this in people, remembering, again, that their needs are not necessarily the same as yours.
3. The saying "Different strokes for different folks" makes sense. Within the confines of any situation, be willing to give different rewards to different workers. You will have to exert some effort to discover the "different strokes" that you can use to influence the behavior of your boss, peers, and subordinates.
4. You get what you reward, not necessarily what you expect. If you see behavior that you don't expect, ask yourself what rewards are available to that person and adjust them accordingly to encourage more desirable behavior.
5. Avoid the error of single-cause labeling, as in assuming that someone is of lazy character because he or she is not motivated at work. The person may be highly motivated to leave work early and exert impressive energy in some more rewarding activity.
6. If you want to improve employees' performance, ask yourself whether the job or conditions surrounding it can be redesigned to provide more challenge, recognition, and responsibility. You can change the situation more easily than the people—and a changed situation often changes the behavior of the people.
7. Remember, people will satisfy their needs. Such needs can be satisfied in ways that help the organization or in ways that hinder or even sabotage it.

FOOTNOTES

1. W. Vinake, "Motivation as a Complex Problem," in *Nebraska Symposium on Motivation,* ed. M. Jones (Lincoln: University of Nebraska Press, 1962), p. 3.

2. E. Lawler III, and J. Rhode, *Information and Control in Organizations* (Pacific Palisades, Calif.: Goodyear Publishing, 1976).

3. A. Maslow, *Motivation and Personality* (New York: Harper & Bros., 1954); and D. McGregor, *The Human Side of Enterprise* (New York: McGraw-Hill, 1960).

4. Maslow, *Motivation and Personality.*

5. C. Alderfer, *Existence, Relatedness and Growth: Human Needs in Organizational Settings* (New York: Free Press, 1972); L. Waters and D. Roach, "A Factor Analysis of Need Fulfillment Items Designed to Measure Maslow Need Categories," *Personnel Psychology* 26 (Summer 1973): 185–190; and D. Hall and K. Nougaim, "An Examination of Maslow's Need Hierarchy in an Organizational Setting," *Organizational Behavior and Human Performance* 4 (February 1968): 12–35.

6. Ibid.

7. F. Herzberg, B. Mausner, and B. Snyderman, *The Motivation to Work* (New York: Wiley, 1959); and F. Herzberg, "One More Time: How Do You Motivate Employees?" *Harvard Business Review* 46 (January–February 1968): 53–62.

8. W. Serrin, "The Assembly Line," *Atlantic Monthly,* October 1971, pp. 62–68.

9. B. Hinton, "An Empirical Investigation of the Herzberg Methodology and Two-Factor Theory," *Organizational Behavior and Human Performance* 3 (August 1968): 286–309; E. Locke, "Satisfiers and Dissatisfiers among White-Collar and Blue-Collar Employees," *Journal of Applied Psychology* 58 (February 1973): 67–76; and D. Ondrak, "Defense Mechanisms and the Herzberg Theory: An Alternate Test," *Academy of Management Journal* 17 (March 1974): 121–147.

10. R. Ford, *Motivation through the Work Itself* (New York: American Management Association, 1969); M. Myers, *Every Employee a Manager* (New York: McGraw-Hill, 1970); and W. Paul, K. Robertson, and F. Herzberg, "Job Enrichment Pays Off," *Harvard Business Review* 41 (March–April 1969): 61–78.

11. A. Bandura, *Principles of Behavior Modification* (New York: Holt, Rinehart and Winston, 1969); W. Nord, "Beyond the Teaching Machine: The Neglected Area of Operant Conditioning in the Theory and Practice of Management," *Organizational Behavior and Human Performance* 4 (November 1969): 375–401;

W. Hamner, "Worker Motivation Programs: Importance of Climate, Structure and Performance Consequences," in *Contemporary Problems in Personnel: Readings for the Seventies,* ed. W. C. Hamner and F. Schmidt (Chicago: St. Clair Press, 1974), pp. 280–401; R. Beatty and C. Schneier, "A Case for Positive Reinforcement," *Business Horizons* 2 (April 1975): 57–66; and H. Wiard, "Why Manage Behavior? A Case for Positive Reinforcement," *Human Resources Management* 11 (Summer 1972): 15–21.

12. E. Feeney, "At Emery Air Freight: Positive Reinforcement Boosts Performance," *Organizational Dynamics* 1 (Winter 1973): 41–50.

13. Ibid., pp. 47–48.

14. H. Parsons, "What Happened at Hawthorne?" *Science* 183 (March 8, 1974): 924.

15. F. Roethlisberg and W. Dickson, *Management and the Worker* (Cambridge, Mass.: Harvard University Press, 1961), p. 74.

16. W. C. Hamner, "Reinforcement Theory and Contingency Management in Organizational Settings," in *Organizational Behavior and Management: A Contingency Approach,* ed. H. Tosi and W. C. Hamner (Chicago: St. Clair Press, 1974), pp. 86–111.

17. Ibid.

18. Feeney, "At Emery Air Freight," p. 42.

19. V. Vroom, *Work and Motivation* (New York: Wiley, 1964); and L. Porter and E. Lawler III, *Managerial Attitudes and Performance* (Homewood, Ill.: Dorsey press, 1968).

20. Nord, "Beyond the Teaching Machine."

21. A. Brayfield and W. Crockett, "Employee Attitudes and Employee Performance," *Psychological Bulletin* 52 (November 1955): 396–424; J. Wanous, "A Causal-Correlational Analysis of the Job Satisfaction and Performance Relationship," *Journal of Applied Psychology* 59 (April 1974): 139–144; and J. Dermer, "The Interrelationship of Intrinsic and Extrinsic Motivation," *Academy of Management Journal* 18 (March 1975): 125–129.

22. For a review of the most recent techniques and approaches to understanding human motivation and behavior see L. E. Davis, "Individuals and the Organization," *California Management Review* 12 (Spring 1980): T. R. V. David and F. Luthans, "A Social Learning Approach to Organizational Behavior," *Academy of Management Review* 5 (April 1980):; L. Greenhalgh, "A Process Model of Organizational Turnover: The Relationship with Job Security as a

Case in Point," *Academy of Management Review* 5 (April 1980):; S. A. Stumph and P. K. Dowley, "Predicting Voluntary and Involuntary Turnover Using Absenteeism and Performance Indices," *Academy of Management Journal* 24 (March 1981): 148–163; T. A. Daniel and J. K. Esser, "Intrinsic Motivation as Influenced by Rewards, Task Interest, and Task Structure," *Journal of Applied Psychology,* 65 (October 1980): 566–573; J. S. Paimonte, "An Employee Motivational System That Leads to Excellent Performance," *Personnel* 56 (1980): 55–66; R. S. Cheloha and J. L. Farr, "Absenteeism, Job Involvement, and Job Satisfaction in an Organizational Setting," *Journal of Applied Psychology* 65 (August 1980): 467–473; C. C. Manz and H. P. Sims, Jr., "Vicarious Learning: The Influence of Modeling in Organizational Behavior," *Academy of Management Review* 6 (January 1981): 105–114; D. B. Fedor and G. R. Ferris, "Integrating OB Mod with Cognitive Approaches to Motivation," *Academy of Management Review* 6 (January 1981): 115–126; and G. P. Latham and E. A. Locke, "Goal-Setting—Motivational Technique That Works," *Organizational Dynamics* (Autumn 1979): 68–80.

Managing Groups

CHAPTER 16

CONTENTS

THE HOVEY AND BEARD COMPANY

The Hovey and Beard Company manufactured a variety of wooden toys, including animals and pull toys. After the toys were cut, sanded, and partially assembled in one area, they were sent to the paint room. There they were individually dipped in shellac and painted by eight workers. The toys were usually two-colored; and since only one color could be applied at a time, the painting process had to be repeated for each additional color.

For many years the toys were made almost entirely by hand. Then, to meet the demand of increased sales, the painting operation was changed. The eight painters were now lined up alongside an endless chain of continuously moving hooks that carried the toys into a long oven. Each worker sat at an individual painting booth, which was designed to be a backstop for excess paint and to carry away fumes. The worker would take a toy from a tray, place it in a jig (a holding device) inside the paint booth, spray on the proper color, and then hang the toy on the hook passing by. The engineers had carefully calculated the rate at which the hooks moved so that when each person was fully trained, the chain going into the oven would have a toy on each hook.

The paint room workers were on a group bonus plan; they received additional pay when the standard, or quota, was exceeded. However, the engineers calculated that the workers would not reach full productivity for about six months. Consequently, they were given a learning bonus that was scheduled to be reduced regularly until it stopped completely at the end of the six months. In this way the workers would not initially lose any income; but as their productivity went up, they also would not need the supplement.

At the end of the second month trouble was obvious. Production was low, and there were bitter complaints that the speed of the line was too fast. The workers were angry at both the engineers and the supervisor, and several of them quit. One worker, Helen, was especially vocal and was seen by management as a ringleader who was holding back the group's productivity.

The supervisor asked the personnel department for advice, and personnel suggested a meeting with the painters. In the course of several such meetings, Helen made the painter's point clear. They believed they could keep up the pace some of the time but not all day long. As a result of the meetings, the workers were given the authority to regulate the speed of the line, and a control was installed in Helen's booth. The workers also had a number of meetings of their own to discuss how the speed of the line should be varied during the day.

Productivity soared. Two months before the scheduled ending of the learning bonus, the group was painting toys at a level about 40 percent above what had been expected under the original arrangement. Bob, one of the painters, remarked, "I always knew we were the best group in the plant!"

Now, the painters were earning more than many skilled workers in the rest of the plant. Management was besieged by complaints from other departments. Finally, the plant superintendent, without consulting anyone, revoked the learning bonus and removed the control from Helen's booth. The hooks moved again at the constant speed. Helen and Bob objected, but the decision stuck. Within a month, six of the eight painters left, including Helen and Bob; the supervisor quit in about two months. Production dropped well below the previous levels, and some members of the group were no longer speaking to each other.[1]

This case raises several critical questions which you should be able to answer after reading this chapter. The questions include:

1. How can groups help and hinder a manager?
2. What can a manager do to ensure that groups help rather than hinder efforts of the organization?
3. Does your behavior change when you are in different groups? Explain how and why.
4. What characteristics do groups need in order to be effective?

16

What happened in the Hovey and Beard case? Why did the eight painters first complain, then increase productivity, and finally reduce productivity? Understanding group behavior and the properties of groups—the subject matter of this chapter—is essential to being both a good manager and an effective member of groups. However, before embarking on that subject, let us see how the principles explained in earlier chapters apply to this discussion.

Chapter 1 showed that about half a manager's time is spent in meetings. Almost all these meetings involve groups of people getting together to solve problems or make plans. Thus the manager is frequently a member of a group with other managers, or peers. The eight painters in the Hovey and Beard case also attended meetings—some of them formal, such as those with the supervisor, and some of them informal, such as those where they decided how fast the hooks should move—and they also were members of a group.

Chapter 2 examined early studies of the Hawthorne plant of Western Electric; these studies demonstrated that groups have a powerful effect on human behavior. Chapter 15 suggested that people are motivated to act a certain way within a given situation. For their behavior to change, the situation must be changed. However, any change has both intended and unintended consequences. For example, in the Hovey and Beard case, the supervisor focused primarily on the painters' complaints. The actions he took increased their productivity, but they also resulted in the unintended consequence of higher than normal pay for the workers.

The superintendent unilaterally changed the situation again for a number of reasons: (1) the wage structure of the plant was upset, (2) the prestige of the engineers had suffered, and (3) some of management's prerogatives were apparently being taken over by employees. His decision essentially ignored the groups' needs and focused on the needs of the larger organization. While it solved some of the organizational problems, it also had unintended consequences—the supervisor and most of the painters quit, and productivity dropped.

Small groups are important in affecting behavior. A 1972 bibliography listed more than five thousand articles and books on the subject, and more work has been done since.[2] It is clear that knowledge about group dynamics and behavior is tremendously important to the effective manager, who must know when to make unilateral decisions and when to rely on groups, including meetings and committees. The effective manager is also an effective group member. As mentioned earlier, approximately half a manager's time is spent interacting with others—peers, other managers, specialists, and others in the work flow process—at a lateral level.

In one organization, sales districts were divided into fourths in terms of total sales. The least effective sales teams (the bottom fourth) cost the organization about $1 million in profits each year when compared to the higher-performing teams. The two distinguishing features of the higher-performing sales teams were team cohesion and leadership.[3]

The rest of this chapter will examine some principles of group dynamics with the objectives of learning how to manage a group and becoming a more effective group member. Accomplishing these objectives requires an awareness of the group as a part of the larger organization with which it interacts.

WHAT IS A GROUP?

A **group** is "any number of people who: (1) have a common purpose or objective, (2) interact with each other to accomplish their objective, (3) are aware of one another, and (4) perceive themselves to be a part of the group."[4] Throughout our lives we belong to many different groups. Families are groups; so are scouts and similar organizations. Friendship clubs, chess clubs, and drama and music organizations are all groups.

This text concentrates primarily on groups at work. In most organizations, getting the work done requires group efforts. Managing an individual requires an understanding of individual dynamics, and managing a group requires an understanding of group dynamics.

In the definition of a group, "any number of people" cannot be taken too literally, since at some point the number of people may become too large to fit the rest of the definition. Clearly, all the people in the United States cannot interact with each other although they do form a group as a nation. Every group has a common objective, but the individuals belonging to it may have other, personal objectives as well. An insurance salesperson may join the high school PTA to help promote the school's welfare. But belonging to the PTA may also provide contacts for insurance sales.

Perhaps it is the awareness of each other that most clearly differentiates a group from an aggregation of people. Unless people are aware of each other and of the fact that they are a group, they will not interact in the way that accomplishes the common objective.

The interaction can be over a long or a short period of time. A line of people were waiting to purchase tickets for a rock concert. Although the people had a common purpose, buying tickets, they were not a group. Suddenly two people tried to crash the line. About eight of the people in line immediately banded together to stop the gate crashers. At that moment a group was formed. After the group succeeded in repelling the invaders, its members continued talking to each other. But the common purpose, keeping out the gate crashers, was gone, and the group reverted to an aggregation. In this example the aggregate of people became a group when they suddenly perceived themselves as a group.

There are many different kinds of groups and many different ways of classifying them. This text will concentrate on the formal and informal groups that exist in organizations. **Formal groups** are established by the organization to accomplish specific tasks. They include **command groups,** which consist of managers and their direct subordinates, and **committees** and **task forces,** which are created to carry out specific organizational assignments or activities. Command groups and committees

Groups are composed of people who:

- Share goals
- Interact
- Identify with each other
- Are aware of each other

Types of formal groups:

- Command
- Committee
- Task force

usually continue in existence, while task forces usually are established to solve a particular problem and then are disbanded.[5] Committees and task forces frequently cut across organizational lines, as Figure 16.1 shows.

The boards of directors of large organizations usually have committees to review worker compensation and public policy issues. Audit committees to review financial considerations are now almost universal; in fact, organizations whose shares are sold on the New York Stock Exchange are required to have them. Approximately 80 percent of top management people are members of one or more committees, as are some 75 percent of middle-level managers and 50 percent of lower-level managers. Over 30 percent of nonmanagement personnel also belong to committees.[6]

Task forces, or project teams, are usually formed to solve a problem or perform an activity that involves a number of organizational units. In one organization, for example, task forces composed of managers and technical experts from the research, development, marketing, production, and purchasing departments are formed to make certain that each

FIGURE 16.1 A command group and a task force or committee

The individuals within the dotted lines belong to both a command group and a task force.

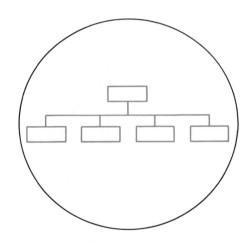

Command group

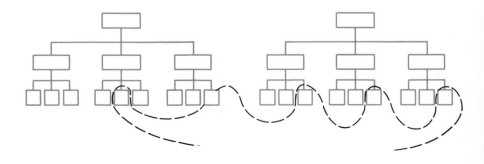

new product is moved smoothly from the idea stage through the production stages and into the marketplace.

Informal groups appear within the organizational structure but are formed by the individuals of the group rather than by management. Indeed, such groups may or may not be approved by management. Many informal groups are formed to satisfy social needs on the job. Sometimes they are formed to hold production at a certain level; at other times they attempt to accomlish a certain task better. In one rigid bureaucratic organization, a group of middle- and lower-level managers meet approximately once a week to cut through the company's red tape and coordinate their efforts more effectively.

ACTIVITIES, INTERACTIONS, AND SENTIMENTS

The eight painters in the Hovey and Beard case constituted a formal task group established by management. The terms described in this section—activities, interactions, and sentiments—will help explain the behavior of that group. **Required activities** are formally assigned tasks. **Required interactions** take place between employees when one person's required activity follows or is influenced by the required activity of another. This interaction can be either verbal or nonverbal. **Sentiments** are the attitudes of like or dislike, approval or disapproval, that people have toward each other. Activities and interactions can be seen, while sentiments must be inferred from behavior.[7]

At the beginning of the Hovey and Beard case, the activity is clear—hand painting of toys—but little is revealed about interactions or sentiments. After the activity is changed to a more automated operation of spray painting, required interactions occur. **Emergent interactions** follow. They are informal interactions that occur in addition to the required ones, and they result from changes in either formal or informal activities or sentiments. For example, when the painters began to talk to each other about working conditions, their interactions were informal, emergent interactions. They went beyond those interactions formally required by the organization. Moreover, they led the workers to changed feelings or sentiments about each other and the organization. Helen emerged as the informal task leader and Bob as a social leader. The group members began to have more positive feelings about each other and more negative ones about their supervisor. **Emergent activities**—informal actions that occur in addition to required activities—followed the emergent interactions and changed sentiments.

Figure 16.2 shows the interactions among required and emergent activities, required and emergent interactions, and sentiments. In the painters' situation, when the change in required activities allowed the group to control the speed of the line, their activities, interactions, and sentiments changed again. Their discussions focused less on complaints and more on how to increase productivity; their interactions—both required and emergent—focused on what the speed of the line should be.

Group components:

- Activities
- Interactions
- Sentiments

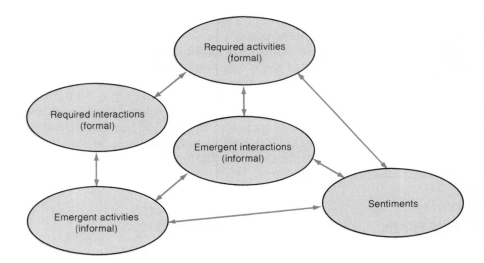

FIGURE 16.2 Interactions among required and emergent activities, required and emergent interactions, and sentiments

Their sentiments also changed; the painters felt better about themselves and about their supervisor. When the superintendent stepped in to make a unilateral change in their required activities, the painters' interactions and sentiments changed again.

To summarize, required activities lead to required interactions, which in turn lead to sentiments. Sentiments then produce emergent (informal) activities and emergent (informal) interactions, which in turn lead to changed sentiments. For example, after the last change, the supervisor and six painters quit (changed activities and sentiments); and some members of the group were no longer speaking to each other (changed sentiments). As the figure indicates, it is difficult to determine cause and effect. Rather, from a systems point of view, the activities, interactions, and sentiments are both causes and effects of each other.

WHAT GROUPS OFFER INDIVIDUALS

As Chapter 15 suggested, people have many needs, only a few of which can be satisfied in isolation from others in our complex modern society. If we are hungry, we can satisfy our need for food merely by eating. However, the apparently simple process of satisfying need is intricately involved with other people. We need money to buy food, and in order to have money, we must work for it or have someone give it to us. Very few people can live in isolation. Most needs can be satisfied only with or by other people. A discussion follows of the types of needs that groups help individuals to satisfy.

Safety and Security Belonging to a group is important for safety and security. Children soon learn to protect each other in group fashion. A grade school teacher who asks a class, "Who did that?" will probably receive no answer. Teenagers struggling for individual independence use the group as a source of social support to protect them from the uncertainties of the rest of the world.

Group support is also necessary to adults in organizations. Both formal and informal groups serve to protect individuals and help them deal with the formal organization or the environment. Union membership, seniority, and other such measures help satisfy safety and security needs. The need for physiological as well as psychological support from groups exists in dangerous jobs such as coal mining or fire fighting. Here the groups are extremely important to the workers. A fire fighter who does not cooperate with the group is ostracized. Among coal miners in England, group structures were disrupted when an attempt was made shortly after World War II to combine small work teams into larger crews with more technical equipment. The result was a reduced output of coal until the small group concept was reintroduced in a modified form.

One of the chief causes of casualties among untrained troops in battle is called "bunching up." People who are in danger need to be physically close to one another, even if they know that this increases their collective danger. Studies of soldiers in World War II showed that men who belonged to cohesive groups were more confident of being able to perform well in battle, less fearful, more responsible for carrying out their duties, and less likely to surrender under stress than were men who did not belong to such groups. The studies also showed that, as a determinant of behavior, the group was more important than loyalty to country or orders received from military supervisors.[8] In recognition of this fact, the U.S. Army instituted the "buddy system," whereby at least two people work together.

Relatedness People are social beings. Belonging to groups satisfies a number of social needs. Many studies have shown that high turnover, absenteeism, and alienation are closely related to the inability to belong to groups. Emotional support from a group is especially helpful when people are under stress. The importance of relatedness needs was highlighted in both the Korean and Vietnam conflicts. U.S. prisoners of war who were in solitary confinement were more likely to go beyond official policy (soldiers were to give only name, rank, and serial number) in talking to their captors.[9] Many of them seemed to have an overwhelming compulsion to talk when taken to an interrogater, even knowing that the questioner was the enemy. A person isolated from human communication and companionship simply loses touch with reality.

Higher-Level Needs Groups can also satisfy higher-level needs such as status, esteem, and growth. For example, recognition can be given only by others; it cannot be generated within oneself. In the case of the eight painters, a great deal of recognition and pride in accomplishment were generated within the group when the workers were allowed to determine their own pace. Productivity soared, only to drop dramatically when the superintendent took that responsibility away from them.

Accomplishing Organizational Objectives   Most organizational tasks require the coordinated effort of a number of people to maintain productivity and reach organizational goals. The formal or informal group can be extremely helpful in solving specific work problems or in keeping the individual from making mistakes on the job.

Groups perform a number of functions in accomplishing organizational objectives. One major function is training new members in how to get the job done. In theory, the organization is responsible for training employees to do new tasks or jobs, but it is the effective work groups within the organization that help the employee learn how to interact with the rest of the organization and how to get the job done. Sociologist William F. Whyte describes work groups in the restaurant industry:

> In restaurants we studied, management trained the waitresses to work together and help each other. They were taught to consider two, three, or more stations as a unit and to divide the work among themselves in the most efficient manner. . . . The waitresses help only those girls who will return the favor. . . . The girl who helps nobody can get nobody to help her, and she drops behind and has trouble with her service. The girl who gives help gets help in return.[10]

The group, together with the manager, can also help clarify the job to be done. *Goal clarity* exists when the task of the group is clearly identified, and *goal-path clarity* exists when the manner of completing the task is clearly defined. The individual's motivation to work is situation dependent and affected by both informal and formal groups. The individual subjectively estimates whether an effort will be successful and bring forth rewards. The manager must clarify the goal and the manner of attaining it, but the groups to which the individual belongs also have tremendous impact on the individual's subjective estimates, and the group can contribute greatly to the clarity of the work goal. Studies have shown that groups with clearly specified goals are more highly motivated and work more effectively than groups where the goals are not clear.[11] Groups operate both to reach goals and to establish or clarify them.

CHARACTERISTICS OF EFFECTIVE WORK GROUPS

An effective work group develops clearly defined goals, maintains adequate resources to accomplish them, and functions as a team whose members participate fully in group discussions. Some of the factors that influence group effectiveness are norms, cohesion, cohesion process and leadership.

Group Norms   Over time, groups tend to develop norms, or standards of behavior. A *norm* is a rule that tells the individual how to behave in a particular group. To understand the idea of norms, consider an individual who belongs to a church group, a family group, a bowling group, and a task group. That person probably behaves somewhat differently in each group because of the norms of each group.

Some norms are formal rules, dictated by the organization, that have been accepted by the group. If a formal rule is not accepted by the group, it is not a norm. In one organization, for example, there was a formal rule that workers had to wear safety glasses at all times. The rule was constantly violated until the manager held a group meeting. The group decided that safety glasses should be worn in particular areas and when working on particular machines. The rule then became a norm and was followed by all the workers. Other norms are informal rules that emerge from the interactions and sentiments of the group members. For example, in the Hovey and Beard case, the group of painters developed a rule (norm) of high productivity when they were allowed to regulate the speed of the line of hooks.

Norms have certain characteristics. First, they are developed only for behavior that the group deems significant. Although interactions and activities are prescribed by the organization, the emergent activities, interactions, and sentiments of the group are what determine whether a rule becomes a norm. For example, one group may have a norm of high productivity, while another in the same organization, subject to the same formal rules, may not.

Another characteristic of norms is that they can apply to all members of a group or to certain members only. A norm that states how one person will interact with others is called a role; to phrase it another way, a role is the behavior expected of an individual in a given position by the other members of the person's group. For example, the manager is expected to behave differently from the other members of a work group. A new member of a work group may be expected to follow the norms more closely than a more senior and liked member.

Some norms are of central importance—accepted by almost everyone in the group—while other norms are of less importance.[12] A **pivotal group norm** is a norm to which every member of the group must conform. For example, it may be essential to perform at the highest level one is capable of all the time. A **relevant group norm** is not as central as a pivotal norm; following it is seen as not absolutely essential but as worthwhile and desirable. For example, a relevant group norm may include being on time to meetings. While not performing well may be seen as a sign of disloyalty to the group, not attending a meeting may be seen as simply having something more important to do.

Each group member has several choices about behavior. One choice is complete conformity, where the individual accepts all the norms of the group. Another is creative individualism, where the individual accepts all pivotal norms but reserves the right to reject specific relevant norms. The third choice is rebellion, where all the group's values and norms are rejected. Creative individualism appears to be the best choice for both the individual and the group. Rebellion causes the individual to leave or to be expelled from the group, and complete conformity reduces the individual's ability to influence the group.

Group members

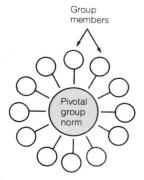

Seen as essential. Every group member conforms.

Group members

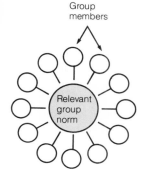

Seen as desirable but not essential. Not every member conforms.

On the Job

GROUP NORMS AT WORK

One summer during my college days I worked as a bulk hand press printer with a major paper products company. My job was to operate, along with two other workers, the press that printed information on bulk ice cream containers—usually the company's name, address, and commercial message.

The three-person crew, consisting of two press operators and one packer, was paid a specific rate per hour plus a bonus for exceeding the standard quota. The bonus was directly related to the over-quota production; 20 percent over the quota resulted in 20 percent more pay.

One person would remove the flat twenty-gallon ice cream containers from a large box that held about five hundred of them and would place them in a holding device that could handle about twenty-five containers at a time. The holding device would feed the containers, one at a time, into the press, which would imprint up to three colors on each container. The containers would emerge on a twenty-five foot long conveyer belt that would take them through a dryer and on to another person, who would repack them into a large box.

When the box was full, one of the two press operators would remove it from the packing platform and place it on a flat pallet.

When the pallet was loaded with six full boxes of printed containers, a fork-lift driver would take it to the loading platform for shipment and would drop off an empty pallet.

During my first month on the job I worked with the regular full-time press operator and packer. The job was not very demanding. In fact, by alternating jobs, two people could do the job of three and each person could therefore take a twenty minute break each hour. Even with breaks, the three of us averaged about a 30 percent bonus each week. At the beginning of the fifth week the regular press operator went on vacation and was replaced by a college student. It didn't take us long to determine that with a little extra effort we could get an even larger bonus. We increased our pace, and by the end of the first week we had earned a 50 percent bonus. At the beginning of the sixth week we had one 80 percent bonus day. We were looking forward to returning to college with our tuition money and some to spare.

However, as we were leaving that evening, one of the regular operators on the next shift looked over our production report and explained that we had been working too hard. We told him that we were trying to earn as much as we could during the

summer for our college tuition and that we figured that if we wanted to put in the extra effort to earn a good bonus, we would do so. The regular operator replied. "It don't look good to have such a big bonus."

When we reported for work the next day, we found that the ink holders and rollers had not been cleaned by the preceding shift. We had to clean them before we could start our run. We also found that we were to run one large order with no ink color changes. (We were allowed twenty minutes for color changes—time to clean the rollers and put in new colors of ink. We could do the procedure in about five minutes, and the extra fifteen minutes had been adding to our over-quota production.) Even without the color-change time, though, we managed to have a 50 percent bonus day. The night crew checked our production and claimed we were still working too hard.

The following day, the rollers were again dirty when we arrived. To add to our problems one fork-lift operator was so busy that sometimes we had to wait for containers to print. The other fork-lift operator was so busy he often didn't pick up the full pallets. That made it necessary for the press operator to move the boxes of printed containers from the packing platform to the floor and then to load them on the pallet when it arrived. Finally, the regular member of our crew, the packer, decided that he couldn't keep up with the packing of the containers. They would fall to the floor, and we would have to help pick them up and pack them.

From that day, the other crews began to check our production, which by this time was only about 15 to 20 percent above quota, and ask how we were doing. After about five or six days of working harder and earning less bonus, we agreed that perhaps we had been working too hard. The next day the rollers were clean when we arrived and the fork-lift operators were not as busy. We didn't have to wait for containers very often, and pick-ups were fairly regular. After a few days of experimenting, we found that if we averaged about 30 percent bonus we didn't have any problems.

A norm among most blue-collar workers is that they wear colored work shirts rather than white shirts to work. The story is told of one worker who began wearing a white shirt and a tie to work (a norm of most management people). Puzzled and uncertain of how to treat this deviant behavior (creative individualism), management eventually promoted the individual to assistant foreman (thereby legitimating the white shirt and tie).

Conformity to norms is not usually blind, slavish, and unthinking; nor is it only a function of the norm's centrality. Conformity also depends on the group itself, the individual, and situational factors. For example, intelligent people are less likely to conform to norms than those who are less intelligent. Conformity can also be affected by the size of the group. For example, groups of more than four or five people tend to have less uniform conformity than smaller groups. The larger the group, the more likely that subgroups or cliques will form around a mutual rejection of certain relevant group norms.

Most norms allow for a certain range of deviation beyond which some form of punishment is supplied. In an organization that had periodic union strikes one member of a work group consistently crossed the picket line and worked. When all had resumed work, the other members punished the deviant by never speaking to him and by causing occasional so-called accidents in his vicinity. Sometimes a piece of heavy metal would be dropped close enough to the deviant worker that he only narrowly escaped injury. Periodically, the organization would buy him a new toolbox because the old one would be crushed by a heavy object dropped by someone who had tripped in just the right place.

A manager coming into an organization is a formal leader of one group and a member of many groups. Among the manager's most important tasks are learning the norms of the different groups, finding out

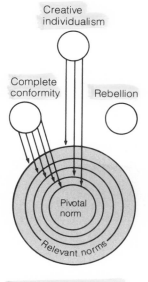

Individual's reactions to norms:

- Conformity
- Creative individualism
- Rebellion

which are central and which are not, and determining the degree of conformity required and the degree of nonconformity allowed. Norms can be detected through observation. Do people at a meeting wait for the boss to speak first? Are they on a first-name basis? Do they arrive on time for meetings? Is disagreement or controversy encouraged, or are people overly courteous? What style of clothing is preferred? The manager can also ask discreet questions, such as, "How do we usually handle this?"

The effective manager works to change norms that hinder the accomplishment of organizational goals. For example, if a work group has a norm of low productivity, the manager should explore the reasons for this norm and look for ways of changing the situation in order to change the norm. A new manager should above all attempt to earn the trust of subordinates. A high level of trust increases the manager's ability to change norms.

Group Cohesiveness   **Group cohesiveness** is the degree to which group members are motivated to remain within the group and, in consequence, to behave in similar ways. In Figure 16.3, the pluses indicate cohesiveness causes more harmonious behavior in group members. A cohesive group is able to act as one body to attain its goals. In addition, the more cohesive the group, the more likely it is to satisfy the individual needs of its members. Group cohesiveness develops out of the activities, interactions, and sentiments shown in Figure 16.2. A number of factors determine the degree to which a group is cohesive.

First, the *size* of a group affects its cohesion. Depending on the purpose for which it is formed, it should be neither too small or too large. A group of only two or three people may not have enough available skill to accomplish a complex task; consequently, the group may break down in failure. On the other hand, if the group becomes too large, communications within it may become less effective, and individual members may

Cohesiveness is positive interpersonal attraction.

Factors in cohesiveness:

- Size
- Proximity within group
- Geography within group
- Geography in relation to other groups
- Outside pressure
- Success in accomplishing group goals

FIGURE 16.3   Norms and cohesiveness affect behavior

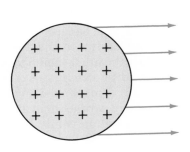

Behavior of cohesive group

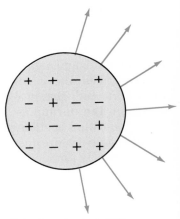

Behavior of group with low cohesiveness

not have enough opportunity to satisfy their personal needs. Also, people in large groups tend to form subgroups, which lowers the cohesiveness of the group as a whole.

The *proximity* and *geography* of the members of a group also influence cohesiveness. People who work closely together in the same geographical location tend to form more cohesive and effective groups than do people who are geographically separated. The increased opportunity for face-to-face contact provided by proximity is highly important. Particularly under such conditions of proximity among group members, isolation of the group from other groups enhances cohesiveness. A small, isolated work group can become highly cohesive in working toward its common goals and demand a great deal of conformity from its members.

Outside pressure also contributes to group cohesiveness. Banding together against a common enemy is one of the best ways known to make a group forget its common differences and become cohesive. For many work groups outside pressure can come from union-management conflict, competition with other groups, reaction against a supervisor, or mistrust between two groups. In the Hovey and Beard case, group cohesiveness first began to build as the painters banded together against the supervisor and the engineers who redesigned the job.

The more cohesive a group, the more its members subscribe to group norms, behave in similar ways, and are motivated to accomplish group goals. When these goals are accomplished, group cohesiveness increases; failure to accomplish them reduces cohesiveness. In the Hovey and Beard case cohesiveness led to high productivity, which in turn increased cohesion. When the situation was changed and the group could no longer control the speed of the moving hooks (failed in its endeavor), the group lost cohesiveness, and many of the workers quit.

From the manager's point of view, group cohesiveness can sometimes be helpful and sometimes harmful. A cohesive group is necessary to accomplish organizational goals; however, it may decide to work *against* management (by establishing group norms of low productivity, for example).

When a group is too cohesive, or clubby, new ideas may be rejected too quickly. As group members become excessively close, they may generate a feeling of "we know best." In this stage, called *groupthink*, there may be a tremendous desire for unanimity. The feelings of solidarity and loyalty to the group may override the motivation to evaluate different courses of action logically and realistically. The principles of groupthink have been used to explain a number of unfortunate and highly significant decisions made by top-level government administrators.

The effective manager works at building a cohesive group whose energies are directed toward accomplishing organizational goals. Passing along information, getting the resources for the group to accomplish the task, and holding frequent open meetings are some of the ways the manager can build cohesiveness. Groupthink can be avoided by encouraging open discussion of conflicting points of view.[13]

GROUP CONTENT AND PROCESS

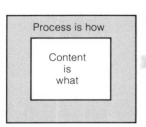

Content is the subject matter of a meeting or the object of a task. **Process** is the way the content is discussed by the committee or handled in accomplishing the task. In other words, content refers to what is being done, while process refers to how it is done.

To understand what makes a group or management committee more or less productive requires an understanding of both content and process. A management committee may have one or more of the following general purposes (types of content):

1. Solving a problem and making a decision that affects all members.
2. Identifying and recommending a particular course of action.
3. Developing a list of alternative actions to be considered by group members.
4. Exchanging information and ideas, with the primary objective being mutual understanding.

A number of approaches have been developed to describe group process. One of the more effective ones distinguishes among task accomplishment activities, group building activities, and self-serving activities.[14]

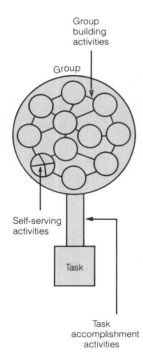

Task accomplishment activities are activities directed at helping the group accomplish its goals. They include initiating, orienting the group to its goals, coordinating, and giving and seeking information. In the Hovey and Beard case, Helen was the most involved with task accomplishment activities. Initially, she complained about the working conditions, and later she controlled the speed of the line from her booth.

Group building activities, or maintenance activities, are any activities that allow the group to maintain itself by helping to satisfy members' needs and by fostering cooperation among members. A group can become more effective by using humor to reduce tensions, by harmonizing ("I don't think you two are really as far apart as you think"), and by encouraging people to participate ("What about your ideas, Beth?"). All these activities are attempts to build better group relationships so that the group can maintain itself. In the Hovey and Beard case, Bob tended to be the social, or group building, leader.

Group members also satisfy their needs through **self-serving activities,** activities that satisfy individual needs at the expense of the group. These activities include dominating, attention getting, aggression, and withdrawal. They can be disruptive and can reduce the ability of the group to attain its formal or primary objectives.

Managers need to understand the difference between content and process in order to help the group become more effective. If a group is engaged in too much task activity and not enough building activity, its effectiveness can be reduced. If group members are interrupting each other, not listening, or shooting down one anothers' ideas, the group may suffer from too much concentration on the task and not enough group maintenance. Conversely, too much maintenance activity can detract from the task. Self-serving activities are usually symptoms of unsatisfied, probably valid personal needs, and the manager should try to understand and deal with them. A summary of these three sets of activities is presented in Table 16.1.

Because people are emotional as well as rational beings, they sometimes cannot separate content from process. A sure sign that a group is in trouble is for someone to suggest, "Let's leave emotions out of this and stick with the facts." Such a comment is clear evidence that group maintenance or building activities are being neglected. Emotions are indeed facts. The neglect of group building activities reduces the effectiveness of many group and committee meetings. The effective manager is one who can diagnose whether content and process are in balance.

TABLE 16.1 Group Member Activities

TASK ACTIVITIES	MAINTENANCE ACTIVITIES	INDIVIDUAL ACTIVITIES
1. *Initiating:* Proposing tasks, goals, or actions; defining group problems; suggesting a procedure.	2. *Harmonizing:* Attempting to reconcile disagreements; reducing tension; leading people to explore their differences.	1. *Aggression:* Deflating others' status; attacking the group or its values; joking in a barbed way, or with semi-concealed hostility.
2. *Informing:* Offering facts; giving expression of feeling; giving an opinion.	2. *Gate keeping:* Helping to keep communication channels open; facilitating the participation of others; suggesting procedures that permit sharing remarks.	2. *Blocking:* Disagreeing and opposing beyond reason; resisting stubbornly the group's wish for personally oriented reasons; using hidden agenda to thwart the movement of a group.
3. *Clarifying:* Interpreting ideas or suggestions; defining terms; clarifying issues before group.	3. *Consensus testing:* Asking to see if a group is nearing a decision; sending up a trial balloon to test a possible conclusion.	3. *Dominating:* Asserting authority or superiority to manipulate the group or certain of its members; interrupting contributions of others; controlling by means of flattery or other forms of patronizing behavior.
4. *Summarizing:* Pulling together related ideas; restating suggestions; offering a decision or conclusion for group to consider.	4. *Encouraging:* Being friendly, warm and responsive to others; indicating by facial expression or remark the acceptance of others' contributions.	4. *Out-of-field behavior:* Making a display of one's lack of involvement; abandoning the group psychologically while remaining physically with it; seeking recognition in ways not relevant to group tasks.
5. *Reality testing:* Making a critical analysis of an idea; testing an idea against some data; establishing the feasibility of an idea.	5. *Compromising:* When one's own idea or status is involved in a conflict, offering a compromise that yields status; admitting error; modifying in interest of group cohesion or growth.	5. Using the group to advance one's personal interests that are unrelated to the group's task—for example, advertising a brother's insurance agency or a wife's stockbrokerage house.

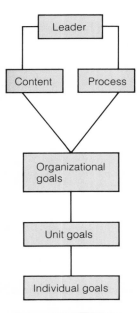

The task of the leader is to help the group reach organizational, unit, and individual goals through attention to both content and process.

GROUP LEADERSHIP

An effective work group accomplishes a task, provides its members with social satisfaction, and enjoys, as a whole, a sense of contribution and growth. For a group to attain organizational or unit goals as well as the personal goals of individual group members, attention must be paid to both content and process. This requires **leadership**—the dynamic in which group behavior is influenced in a certain direction. (Leadership is so important that Chapter 17 is devoted to it.)

Leadership is frequently assumed to rest in one particular person, who occupies a formal position as leader. However, in practice, leadership functions are not always performed by the same person. Rather, leadership can be seen as a quality of the group or as "a set of functions which must be carried out by the group."[15]

In addition to the formal leader, informal leaders frequently emerge from the activities, interactions, and sentiments of the ongoing group. These leaders may focus on helping the group accomplish either its work tasks or its social goals. Usually one person emerges as the informal task leader, and a different person becomes the informal social-emotional (group maintenance) leader. In the Hovey and Beard case the supervisor was the formal leader, Helen was an informal task leader, and Bob was the informal social leader.

In many cases the formal instructions that come from the supervisor are supplemented by informal help from an informal leader, as Figure 16.4 shows. The informal leader may well be lower in official status than the formal leader. For example, during World War II a lieutenant commander in the U.S. Navy who had no experience in managing dry docks was put in charge of a large dry dock. He found that his chief petty officer, an enlisted man, knew all the details of the work to be done, and soon he had delegated most of the actual supervision to the enlisted man.

MANAGING EFFECTIVE MEETINGS

The purpose of a work group is to perform a task—to accomplish a specific objective. The group can be a task force established temporarily to

FIGURE 16.4 The formal and informal leader

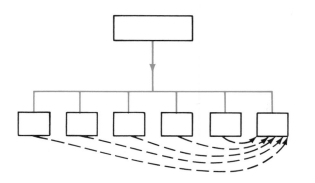

Formal leader

(official instruction, help, guidance, and supervision)

Informal leader

(informal, unofficial help, guidance, and support)

solve a particular problem and then disbanded, or it can be an ongoing group consisting of a manager and subordinates who have regular staff meetings or of a standing committee established to deal with an ongoing series of tasks. The individuals in any type of group have unique personal needs and varying commitments to the task. Therefore, the group has a multiplicity of objectives, some organizational and some personal.

Managers spend up to half their time in meetings of various kinds. Although meetings can be an important source of communications, an aid to decision making, and a motivator, too often they are instead unproductive. Managers view many of them as a waste of time. Although there is no simple approach to an effective meeting, there are some general guidelines that a chairperson can use.[16]

Considerations for effective meetings:

- Leadership
- Agenda
- Consensus
- Size
- Physical surroundings
- Summary and clarification
- Content and process

Leadership The formal chairperson of a meeting needs to recognize that leadership will naturally shift throughout the meeting and should not be artificially controlled by one person. The chairperson should be able to identify and work with informal leaders especially task and group maintenance leaders. The meeting will benefit from a chairperson who is a careful, judicious listener open to suggestions from other group members.

Agenda The agenda and purpose of the meeting should be clear to all participants. Moreover, all should know their expected roles in the meeting. The importance of a clearly defined agenda and well informed participants cannot be overstressed. If one topic should be given priority for discussion, this too should be made clear to the participants. Any group tends to wander from topic to topic, so the chairperson's job is to keep the discussion on track to accomplish the main purposes of the agenda.

When possible, the agenda for the meeting, together with any supporting information, should be distributed before the meeting. This gives committee members an opportunity to study and think about the material beforehand, making the contributions at the meeting more valuable.

Consensus Chapter 4 described a number of decision styles. Essentially, participation can be limited to the manager or chairperson making the decision alone, or it can extend to the entire group sharing the problem and the manager or chairperson accepting a decision that has its support. In this event the chairperson should strive for a decision by consensus.

Consensus means full participation by all group members until they have become committed to a decision. Consensus means not that everyone agrees with the decision but that all group members accept it and will carry out their roles in implementing it. Consensus can be reached only when group members freely express their opinions and actively work together to reach a mutually pleasing decision. Such techniques as voting and compromising, which tend to bury conflict, are not appropriate here. Rather, a full airing of facts and thorough discussion are invited. The consensus approach tends to extract the full resources of every member both in making the decision and in acting on it later. Members are requested to state their reasoning when they express agreement or disagreement in the meeting.[17]

Size   The size of the committee should be based in part on its authority and responsibility. If its task is difficult or complex, the committee should have enough experts to be able to approach the problems from several different angles. Generally, fewer than five members reduce the group's effectiveness, while more than fifteen tend to break into subgroups. Most committees operate best with five to ten members.

Physical Surroundings   The physical layout of a meeting, such as seating arrangements, affects behavior. In many instances the seating arrangement is approximately triangular, with subordinate managers sitting along the base of the triangle and the chairperson or boss sitting at its apex. If the chairperson is sitting behind a desk, this creates both physical and psychological barriers. Such an arrangement, which is usually seen as formal, may be satisfactory for formal pronouncements from top management, but it is not conducive to a problem-oriented discussion. A circular pattern makes it easier for the participants to see or talk to each other and creates a more informal atmosphere.

Summarizing and Clarifying   During the meeting the chairperson should periodically summarize the discussion and restate what appears to be the current position of the committee so as to make certain that the task remains clear and that the discussion does not wander.

Focusing on Both Content and Process   People frequently assume that only the overt content of a matter need be addressed and that emotions can be safely ignored. Yet nothing inhibits discussion more than ignoring the emotions of the discussants.

   Focusing only on content means that group members can become overly concerned with the task issues and fail to examine the way these tasks will be managed. This is a common failing of committees.

   To avoid this error, the chairperson should refrain from dominating the meeting and should actively encourage even quiet members to present their ideas. In addition, the chairperson should resist the temptation to accept the first feasible solution presented and should aim to generate as many feasible alternatives as possible. Otherwise, premature majority votes may reduce creativity and constructive conflict. The nominal group technique is effective in soliciting ideas from everyone, including the more timid members of the group.

SUMMARY

A manager is, by definition, a formal leader of a work group as well as a subordinate reporting to an upper-level manager (and thus a member of another formal work group). In addition, a manager is a member of many different formal or informal groups at the lateral or peer level. Indeed, managers may be involved with as many as forty or fifty different groups, both inside and outside the organization. As a leader of one group and a member of others, an effective manager needs to have a clear understanding of group dynamics and the characteristics of effective and ineffective groups.

The effective manager is aware that prescribed activities and interactions lead to emergent activities, emergent interactions, and sentiments. As a result, the manager must try to prescribe activities and interactions that will yield the type of emergent activities, interactions, and sentiments that will promote the cohesiveness of the group. This requires establishing goals for the group or using the group to help establish goals, depending on the situation.

Group norms have a powerful effect on behavior. The effective manager observes and watches for group norms and earns the trust of subordinates in order to be able to influence their norms. Cohesive groups can do a better job than uncohesive groups of attaining organizational goals. Thus the manager should work at establishing conditions that promote group cohesiveness while avoiding groupthink. The manager should also be ready to change the geography of the group if that is needed and practical, since geography is an important factor in cohesiveness. Another way the manager can foster cohesiveness is to have frequent meetings and promote open discussion and honest differences of opinion.

The effective manager (1) understands the difference between content and process and uses the knowledge to diagnose why a group is not performing as effectively as it could, (2) pays attention to the norms of different groups in order to behave more effectively within them, (3) helps new members understand the norms and standards so they can be effectively integrated into the group, and (4) is aware of the interface between groups. The supervisor in the Hovey and Beard case worked only with one particular group and lost sight of the consequences of that group's behavior on the other groups in the organization.

All organizations have informal groups. The effective manager recognizes this and works with such groups and with their informal leaders. The manager cannot personally satisfy the needs of all members. Indeed, the norms of many groups require that the manager maintain a certain psychological distance from members. Thus the manager should help the informal leaders satisfy the needs of individuals in the group. Furthermore, the manager should try to keep formal activities from unnecessarily disrupting the informal organization and should make use of the influence of the informal group by integrating its objectives with those of the formal group.

STUDY QUESTIONS

1. What are the key elements of a group?
2. How do command groups differ from committees?
3. How does a formal group differ from an informal one?

4. Explain the interdependence of activities, interactions, and sentiments.
5. Explain why it is important to understand the concepts of group norms and cohesiveness.
6. Distinguish between formal and informal lead-

ership. Are both necessary? Explain.

7. In what ways does group process affect the tasks of the group?

8. List some group building activities.

9. List some self-serving activities.

10. Under what circumstances might a work group have low productivity as its norm? Under what circumstances might it have high productivity?

11. What are the major characteristics of effective groups? Describe some effective and ineffective groups you have known. Can you identify some reasons for their effectiveness or ineffectiveness?

12. Think of a group with which you have been familiar over a period of time. Explain the relationships among its activities, interactions, and sentiments.

13. When you were in high school, did your parents affect your behavior more or less than your peer group did? Explain.

14. Observe a work group of some kind. Can you identify specific group task, group building, and self-serving activities?

Case for Discussion

AJAX CONSTRUCTION COMPANY

Since Ajax's construction work usually increased during the summer, the company normally employed extra help for that time. This year one of the extra workers was Bill Marston, an architectural design student who was interested in gaining practical construction experience. Ajax needed some college graduates on its permanent staff and planned to consider him for employment after his graduation if his performance that summer warranted it. Marston had an athletic scholarship at his university and was in good enough physical condition to do the heavy construction work demanded of summer employees.

After he was hired, Marston was interviewed by Scott Drake, a construction foreman. Drake was impressed by Marston's apparent ability and agreed to assign him to one of his own crews. After several days of orientation, all new employees were assigned to work teams, each of which had an experienced group leader. The foreman usually saw little of the new employees after that, because he gave the assignments to the group leaders.

After about three weeks Marston approached Drake. He was upset and told Drake that he would either have to quit or else take a chance of being fired or hurt. He explained that the harder he worked on the job, the less popular he was with the others in the work crew. No one would eat lunch with him or talk to him. He had gone to the group leader to ask if his work was unsatisfactory or if there was some other problem. The group leader explained that his work was satisfactory but that the pace he was setting was too high and was going to put someone else out of a job. He then advised Marston to either slow down to the rate of the others or take the chance of an "accident" happening to him.

1. How does a group exert pressure on a newcomer to conform to group norms?

2. Should Marston take the group leader's advice seriously?

3. How does an organization get into a situation where employees dictate productivity rates?

4. What would you do if you were Scott Drake and had a number of different work teams under your management?

FOR YOUR CAREER

1. If you want to influence a group, make certain its informal leaders are on your side.

2. If a group is not productive or is actively working against the organization, ask yourself what needs its unproductive activities are serving.

3. Join as many different informal groups as you can. Frequently, membership in such groups is the most effective way of cutting through the red tape of large organizations.

4. In any meeting that you attend, practice paying attention to both the content and the process. The better you become at observing process, the more effective you can be as a group chairperson or member.

5. If you want to learn more about yourself in action, use a cassette tape recorder to tape your meetings and later listen to yourself. Be sure to tell people what you are doing and why you are doing it.

FOOTNOTES

1. Adaptation from pp. 90–96 in *Money and Motivation: An Analysis of Incentives in Industry* by William Foote Whyte. Copyright 1955 by Harper & Row, Publishers, Inc. Reprinted by permission of the publisher.

2. N. Knowles and H. Knowles, *Introduction to Group Dynamics,* rev. ed. (New York: Association Press, 1972).

3. J. Zenger and D. Miller, "Building Effective Teams," *Personnel* 52 (March–April 1974): 20–29.

4. E. Huse and J. Bowditch, *Behavior in Organizations: A Systems Approach to Managing,* rev. ed. (Reading, Mass.: Addison-Wesley, 1977), p. 160.

5. D. Cartwright and D. Lippitt, "Group Dynamics and the Individual," in *Organizational Psychology: A Book of Readings,* rev. ed., ed. D. Kolb, I. Rubin, and J. McIntyre (Englewood Cliffs, N.J.: Prentice-Hall, 1974); R. Napier and M. Gershenfeld, *Groups: Theory and Experience* (Boston: Houghton Mifflin, 1974); R. Likert, *New Patterns of Management* (New York: McGraw-Hill, 1961); R. Likert, *The Human Organization: Its Management and Value* (New York: McGraw-Hill, 1967); and G. Farris, "Organizing Your Informal Organization," *Innovation* 25 (October 1971): 2–11.

6. R. Tillman, "Committees on Trial," *Harvard Business Review* 40 (May–June 1960): 8.

7. J. Seiler, *Systems Analysis in Organizational Behavior* (Homewood, Ill.: Dorsey Press 1967); G. Homons, *The Human Group* (New York: Harcourt, Brace and Co., 1950); and M. Shaw, *Group Dynamics: The Psychology of Small Group Behavior* (New York: McGraw-Hill, 1976).

8. S. Stouffer et al., *The American Soldier: Combat and Its Aftermath* (Princeton, N.J.: Princeton University Press, 1949); and E. Shils, "Primary Groups in the American Army," in *Continuities in Social Research: Studies in the Scope and Method of the American Soldier,* ed. R. Menton and P. Lazarsfeld (New York: Free Press, 1954), pp. 16–39.

9. W. Dean, *General Dean's Story* (New York: Viking Press, 1954); E. Schein, "The Chinese Indoctrination Program for Prisoners of War," *Psychiatry* 19 (May 1956): 149–172; and E. Kinkead, *In Every War but One* (New York: Norton, 1959).

10. W. Whyte, *Human Relations in the Restaurant Industry* (New York: McGraw-Hill, 1948), p. 124.

11. A. Cohen, "Situational Structure, Self-esteem and Threat-Oriented Reactions to Power," in *Studies in Social Power,* ed. D. Cartwright (Ann Arbor, Mich.: Institute for Social Research, 1959); and B. Raven and J. Rietsema, "The Effects of Varied Clarity of Group Goal and Group Path upon the Individual and His Relation to the Group," *Human Relations* 10 (February 1957): 29–44.

12. E. Schein, "Organizational Socialization and the Profession of Management," in *Organizational Psychology,* rev. ed., pp. 1–15.

13. C. O. O'Donnell, "Ground Rules for Using Committees," *Management Review* 50 (October 1961): 63–67; and A. Filley, "Committee Management: Guidelines from Social Science Research," *California Management Review* 13 (Fall 1970): 13–21.

14. Zenger and Miller, "Building Effective Teams"; and O'Donnell, "Ground Rules for Using Committees."

15. C. Gibb, "Leadership," in *Handbook of Social Psychology,* 2d ed., ed. G. Lindzey and E. Aronson (Reading, Mass.: Addison-Wesley, 1954), p. 884.

16. R. Golde, "Are Your Meetings Like This One?"
Harvard Business Review 50 (January–February
1972): 68–77: S. Larson, "The Behavioral Side of
Productive Meetings," *Personnel Journal* 59 (April
1980): 292–295; G. Manners, Jr., "Another Look at
Group Size, Group Problem Solving, and Member
Consensus," *Academy of Management Journal* (December
1979): 715–724; and G. Prince, "How to Be
a Better Meeting Chairman," *Harvard Business Review*
47 (January–February 1969): 98–108.

17. D. Fisher, *Communication in Organizations* (St. Paul
Minn.: West Publishing, 1981), pp. 224–225.

Leadership

CHAPTER 17

CONTENTS

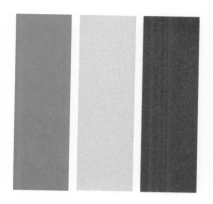

THE NEW CAPTAIN

In July 1918, a young captain took over his first command. The captain was Harry S Truman, and he later became president of the United States. The command was Battery D of the 129th Field Artillery, an outfit known as "Dizzy D" because of its bad reputation. Many of the men in the outfit were well educated; several had attended Rockhurst College, a Jesuit college in Kansas City. Nevertheless, they were "wild." Battery D had had four previous commanding officers, none of whom could control the men.

Truman reported later that he had never been so scared in his life as when he was told of the assignment. He explained to the colonel who had made the assignment that he might just as well go home, then and there. One of the men in the outfit reported that a great deal of resentment had been generated by the knowledge that Captain Truman had been assigned to them. There was talk of causing trouble, even of mutiny.

Although the men stood at attention when Captain Truman took command, their resentment and hostility were clear. They figured he could do nothing to reestablish control, and if he thought he could, he was mistaken.

From their past experience, the men in Battery D expected to get chewed out. They knew they deserved it from the new commander because of their past conduct. Captain Truman, however, did not say a single word. He walked up and down the lines about three times, looking directly at each man. Only then did he speak. His only word was, "Dismissed."

As the men went back to their barracks, they felt that they had been given a kind of benediction (most of them were devout Irish Catholics) and a fresh start.

Many years later, Judge Albert Ridge of the federal district court in Kansas City and a veteran of Company D said, "From that time on, I knew that Harry Truman had captured the hearts of those Irishmen in Battery D, and he never lost it. He has never lost it to this day."

As a matter of fact, Truman kept in touch with the "boys from Battery D" all the rest of his life. Of course, if he had not been a good leader, that first meeting would not have had a lasting effect. After all, Battery D had already gotten rid of four commanding officers before Truman took over.[1]

This case raises several critical questions, which you should be able to answer after reading the chapter. The questions are:

1. Do some people have charisma? Was Captain Truman a charismatic leader?
2. What makes a good leader? Do good managers have to be good leaders?
3. Does a good leader have to change personal behavior under different conditions?
4. Are good leaders born, or can they be made?

17

Leadership is important, as the preceding case shows. **Leadership** is the ability to persuade others to do something. Although it is one of the most studied aspects of management, it may be the least understood. For example, a recent book that summarizes leadership reaseach has 150 pages of bibliography listing over 3,000 studies. The last chapter of the book suggests that only a beginning has been made in understanding leadership.[2]

A person who has a leader's title may not have leadership ability. (Battery D resisted the control of four leaders before Truman.) Popularity is not the same as leadership ability. Sometimes a person is popular only because he or she agrees with everyone to avoid conflict.

MANAGERIAL AUTHORITY AND SOURCES OF POWER

As the Truman case indicates, there is a difference between authority and power. **Authority** is the right to command and exact obedience from others. It comes from the organization, and it allows the manager to use power. **Power** is the exercising of influence or control over others. Authority allows managers to make decisions that guide the actions of others. Power enables them to carry out those decisions. The four officers before Truman all had authority but no power to back it up. In contrast, terrorists who have hijacked a plane may have a great deal of power but no authority. There are at least five types of social power: legitimate power, expert power, charismatic power, reward power, and coercive power.[3]

Legitimate power is the power that comes when the organization's authority is accepted. The manager has the authority that goes with the position in the organization and the power of the organization. Truman, for example, had both legitimate authority and legitimate power. Legitimate power, then, is power that stems from either implicit or explicit rules. Police, parents, teachers, managers—all have legitimate power, but only when their authority is accepted.

Expert power is the power of knowledge. It comes from specialized knowledge and skills that are important in getting a job done. Credibility accrues to the person with professional expertise, leading other individuals to trust that person's judgments and decisions. Physicians, lawyers, computer programmers, chemists, financial analysts, and purchasing agents are all people with expert power.

Managers do not always have expertise in every phase of their work. The dean of a university division cannot be an expert in all the subjects being taught. However, the manager can and should draw on the expert power of specialists in particular fields.

Charismatic power is the power of attraction or devotion—the desire of one person to admire another. In an organization it is the positive attraction a subordinate feels toward a manager. On the manager's part it is identification power, relationship power, or the power to be attractive. In effect, the subordinate is saying, "I want to be like the manager; con-

Authority is the right to give orders.

Power is the ability to enforce them.

Types of power:

- Legitimate
- Expert
- Charismatic
- Reward
- Coercive

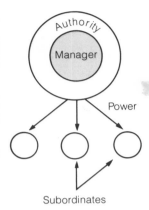

Legitimate power

Authority without power

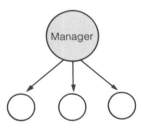

Power without authority

sequently, I want to act as the manager does.'' The more subordinates identify with the boss, the more they internalize the boss's expectations. They then act as their own boss, behaving in ways they think the supervisor will want.

Reward power is the present or potential ability to award something for worthy behavior. The manager has the power to give or retain tangible rewards such as promotions, raises, time off, desirable work assignments, office space, and secretarial help. Of course, the manager's awards can also be psychological: approval, praise, appreciation, and recognition, for example. For reward power to be effective, the subordinate must be confident that the manager controls access to rewards through either authority or upward influence. Reward power can increase legitimate and charismatic power.

Coercive power is the ability to threaten or punish. Tangible punishments include dismissal, demotion, a low rating, less satisfying work assignments, and poor references if the subordinate leaves. Psychological punishments include criticism, snubs, and avoidance. To some degree, reward and coercive powers overlap, since one form of punishment is the withholding of rewards. However, evidence has shown that reward power is more effective in getting a subordinate to do something, while coercive power is more effective in getting the subordinate to refrain from doing something. Generally, coercive power is of less value than reward power. The latter increases the self-esteem of the individual, while the former reduces it. Overuse of coercive power can result in hostility, withdrawal, rule breaking, and a reduction of legitimate and charismatic power.

A case earlier in this text described an organization dealing with precious metals that enforced extremely detailed rules and severe punishments for wastage of these metals. Indeed, every fraction of an ounce of the metal had to be accounted for. Part of the manufacturing plant was built on pilings over a pond. Eventually it became necessary to drain the pond, at which time literally millions of dollars of precious metals were revealed partially buried in the mud. For years, rather than be caught and reprimanded for making a mistake, workers had been dropping their mistakes into the water and falsifying records to conceal the losses.

Some types of power can be exercised by peers and groups who have no legitimate power or authority. A maintenance manager can reward another manager by giving high priority to that person's request. Because of expert knowledge a market research analyst can influence the direction of an organization. An informal group leader who has more charismatic power than the manager can cause a work slowdown.

While the different formal leadership styles have been thoroughly studied, little research exists on how informal leaders gain and use power. Yet understanding how managers can do a better job of leading in various situations requires more attention to the way power is distributed among group members.[4]

The effective manager must be able to differentiate among subordinates who can work independently, those who need the participation of others, and those who need direct and forceful supervision. Further-more, any manager who cannot be both a formal and an informal leader must learn to work with informal group leaders in order to accomplish organizational goals.

FORMAL AND INFORMAL LEADERSHIP

There is a major difference between formal and informal leadership. As explained earlier, leadership is the ability to persuade others to do something. A manager is a **formal leader** by virtue of the authority coming from the organization; that is, a formal leader is usually selected by the organization.

An **informal leader** is chosen by an individual or group. Thus all managers are leaders if their authority is accepted, but not all leaders are managers. In the book *Tom Sawyer*, Aunt Becky was acting as a manager when she told Tom to whitewash the fence. When Tom was able to get others to whitewash the fence for him—indeed, to consider the job a privilege—he was acting as an informal leader.

Being a leader means being accepted.

As a formal leader, the manager influences others to help accomplish the goals of the organization or unit. The person who leads a wildcat

"It's my game. I'll determine corporate policy!"

strike is a leader who is working against the formal goals of an organization. By defining *leadership* as influence over others, we can see that most people are leaders at one time or another. Formal leadership which comes from legitimate authority and power, may last over a long period of time. Informal leadership, which confers no established position on the person who wields it, may shift quickly from that person to another. The ideal manager is one who is simultaneously the formal leader and the informal leader of the group.

APPROACHES TO LEADERSHIP BEHAVIOR

Most of the better-known approaches to managerial leadership focus on one or more of three basic factors: people tasks, personality attributes, and situational factors.

Personality Attribute Approaches Much of the early work on leadership consisted of trying to identify the personality traits inherent in good managers. The primary result of this work was a long list of traits with little evidence that they were related to effective leadership. Such research continues and is becoming more sophisticated, but results are still inconclusive. The most frequently mentioned attributes of an effective leader are fairness, intelligence, general knowledgeability, understanding, perception, and delegativeness. The most frequently mentioned attributes of a poor leader are poorness at communicating, indecisiveness, lack of leadership, and self-centeredness.[5]

One difficulty in assessing leadership ability according to personality attributes is that the mere possession of a trait does not guarantee its successful use for the purpose of leadership. Many highly intelligent people, for example, do not make good managers. Sometimes people with the right traits for being effective managers do not want to be managers or do not really want to be effective. One comprehensive review suggests that leadership characteristics and the demands of the situation combine to determine the effectiveness of a given leader in a given group.[6]

People/Task Approaches A number of studies have examined people and task relationships under the terms of consideration and initiating structure.[7]

Consideration reflects the extent to which individuals are likely to have job relationships characterized by mutual trust, respect for subordinates' ideas, and consideration of subordinates' feelings. **Initiating structure** reflects the extent to which individuals are likely to define and structure their roles and those of their subordinates toward goal attainment.[8] Both terms will be used frequently throughout this chapter. Other factors important to leadership are job level, subordinates' expectations of how leaders should behave, subordinates' need for information, per-

Approaches to leadership consider:

- People
- Tasks
- Personal attributes
- Situational factors

ceived independence of subordinates, upward influence of leaders, and task characteristics such as job clarity and job pressure.

Theory X and Theory Y One of the more influential writers on leadership is psychologist Douglas McGregor, whose primary focus is consideration. McGregor categorizes managers as holding one of two basic beliefs or assumptions about subordinates—called Theory X and Theory Y—that directs their managerial style or strategy. He believes that Theory X assumptions, which are basically authoritarian, are held by a majority of the industrial managers in our society. Theory Y assumptions, held by fewer managers, are more egalitarian.[9]

Typical **Theory X** managers believe that people dislike work and will avoid it whenever possible. Such managers view themselves as part of an elite group that wants to lead and take responsibility, while the larger mass of other people want to be directed and to avoid responsibility. Theory X managers therefore see a need for strong controls and direction achieved through coercion and punishment if people do not work properly and monetary rewards if they do.

In contrast, **Theory Y** managers believe that people will usually work hard and assume responsibility provided they can satisfy personal needs in the process. Therefore, the two categories of leaders (the elite) and followers (the masses) that Theory X managers posit do not exist for Theory Y managers. Theory Y managers believe that performance is based more on internal than on external controls. (See Figure 17.1 for a comparison of the two theories.)

McGregor reports that Theory X assumptions are widely used but are outdated, especially given society's push toward increased education and emphasis on the need for more individual responsibility. In addition, he finds that following Theory X assumptions can demotivate people and become a negative self-fulfilling prophecy. McGregor points out that the Theory X and Theory Y approaches are not managerial strategies as such but tend to influence managerial styles.

An important implication of McGregor's postulation of Theory X and Theory Y managers is that all managers need to examine carefully their own assumptions about the motivation of others. However, the appropriate leadership style may depend partly on the situation. For example, McGregor was a college professor when he first described Theory X and Theory Y. After six years as president of Antioch College, he wrote:

I believed, for example, that a leader could operate successfully as a kind of adviser to his organization. I thought I could avoid being a "boss." Uncon-

Theory X:
- People avoid responsibility
- People are motivated by money

Theory Y:
- People seek responsibility
- People want to work

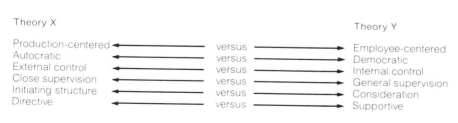

Theory X

Production-centered	versus	Employee-centered
Autocratic	versus	Democratic
External control	versus	Internal control
Close supervision	versus	General supervision
Initiating structure	versus	Consideration
Directive	versus	Supportive

Theory Y

FIGURE 17.1 The continuum from Theory X to Theory Y

sciously, I suspect, I hoped to duck the unpleasant necessity of making difficult decisions, of taking the responsibility for one course of action among many uncertain alternatives. I thought that maybe I could operate so that everyone would like me—that good "human relations" would eliminate all discord and disagreement.

I couldn't have been more wrong. It took a couple of years, but I finally began to realize that a leader cannot avoid the exercise of authority any more than he can avoid responsibility for what happens to his organization.[10]

The Managerial Grid The **Managerial Grid** suggests that managers must be concerned about both production (structure) and people (consideration).[11] Concern for production covers a wide range, including efficiency and workload, units of output, number of creative ideas developed, quality of policy decisions, and thoroughness of staff services. Indeed, concern for production covers any human accomplishment within the organization, whatever the assigned tasks or activities. Concern for people implies an acknowledgment of the personal worth of the individual and thus a concern for good working conditions, job security, a fair salary structure and adequate fringe benefits, and conditions that will foster the individual's personal commitment to doing a good job and encourage harmonious social relationships.

9,9 managers:

- Show concern for people
- Show concern for productivity

Figure 17.2 shows how concern for production relates to concern for people. The vertical axis indicates concern for people, ranging from very little (1) to a great deal (9). The horizontal axis indicates concern for production, also ranging from very little (1) to a great deal (9). A manager with little concern for production or for people (a 1,1 manager) does little except pass along orders and carry messages between subordinates and upper-level managers. A manager with a great deal of concern for people and little concern for production (a 1,9 manager) tries to provide subordinates with comfortable, secure, and easy working conditions. Many 1,9 managers feel that the demands of the organization are harsh and unnecessary. Thus they try to avoid any production pressure that is high enough to reduce their personal acceptance by subordinates. In effect, they assume that by providing acceptance and understanding, they will receive loyalty; and out of loyalty, subordinates will do their jobs. They believe there is little need to emphasize responsibility and accountability, that happy workers will produce well without pressure.

The manager with little concern for people but a great deal of concern for production (the 9,1 manager) assumes that individual needs always conflict with the organization's production needs. Thus the 9,1 manager does not even consider the needs of individuals but concentrates on getting the work done. This manager does the planning and expects the subordinates to follow the rules, directives, and schedules laid out for them.

The manager with a great deal of concern for both people and production (the 9,9 manager) does not assume that the needs of the organization

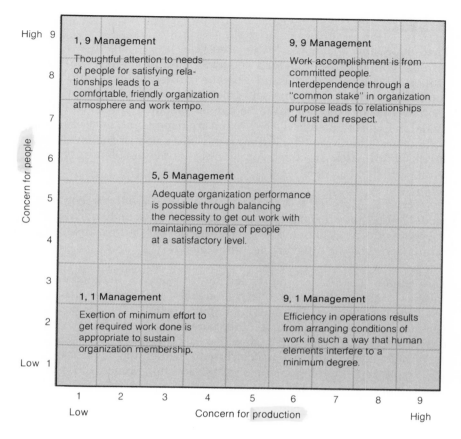

FIGURE 17.2 The Managerial Grid®

Source: Robert R. Blake and Jane S. Mouton, *The Managerial Grid* (Houston: Gulf Publishing, 1964), p. 10. Reproduced with permission. See also *The New Managerial Grid* (Houston: Gulf Publishing, 1978), p. 11.

and the needs of people are inevitably distinct from one another. Believing that the two sets of needs can be integrated, the basic aim of the 9,9 manager is to develop cohesive work teams with both high productivity and high morale through efforts to gain commitment, involvement, mutual trust, goal setting, creativity, and two-way communication.

The Managerial Grid is perhaps the most popular of all the approaches to leadership. According to the Grid, the 9,9 style is the optimum leadership approach. Many organizations have even used training programs to develop 9,9 managers.

According to Blake and Mouton, "this is the one best style of exercising most effective leadership; what changes with the situation is the tactics of its application."[12] Thus two managers can be 9,9 but behave in entirely different ways. The Managerial Grid is, after all, an attitudinal and conceptual description of leaders, not a behavioral one. Specific behaviors, however, can be predicted on the basis of knowledge of a manager's attitudes toward and concepts of people and productivity. Thus there can be a single "best" style of managing, although the specific behaviors may vary with the situation.

CONTINGENCY MODELS

Theories X and Y and the Managerial Grid are, in effect, models that assume there is a best style for a manager or administrator. Two recently proposed leadership models are based on a different idea—that there are conditions under which one set of behaviors is more appropriate than another and that those conditions can be specified. These **contingency models** suggest that effective behaviors are dependent, or contingent, on a number of conditions, including the leader's power, the level and status of subordinates, and the favorableness or unfavorableness of the situation.

Fiedler's Contingency Leadership Model **Fiedler's contingency model** holds that a manager's effectiveness depends on two main factors: the motivational system of the leader and the extent to which the situation is favorable or unfavorable to the leader.

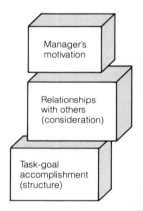

The Leader Leaders are motivated by satisfaction obtained from two sources—relationships with others (consideration) and task-goal accomplishment (structure). The relationship-motivated manager obtains satisfaction from maintaining good interpersonal relationships with subordinates. The task-motivated manager obtains satisfaction from the accomplishment of the goal. According to Fiedler, managers receive satisfaction from both relationship and task accomplishments, but the relative importance of each source varies for each manager and may also vary according to the situation.

Managers are motivated by two sources of satisfaction; the relative importance of each depends on the manager's personality and on the situation.

The Situation The contingency theory suggests that relationship-motivated leaders are more effective than task-motivated leaders in moderately favorable situations and that task-motivated leaders are more effective in either highly favorable or highly unfavorable situations. The favorableness of the situation depends on three factors:

1. *The quality of leader-member relations*—the warmer and friendlier the relationships, the more favorable the situation.
2. *The nature of the tasks*—the more structured and routine the tasks, the more favorable the situation.
3. *The position power of the leader*—the more position power, the more favorable the situation. The leader's power includes legitimate, expert, charismatic, reward, and coercive power.

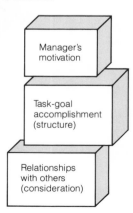

Fiedler has developed questionnaires and ratings to measure the manager's basic motivation and the favorableness of the situation. The results of the questionnaires and ratings are combined to show the degree to which a situation is favorable or unfavorable. Figure 17.3 illustrates the appropriate leadership style for situations varying from highly unfavorable to highly favorable.

The figure indicates what was mentioned before, that task-goal managers perform best in situations that are either very favorable or very

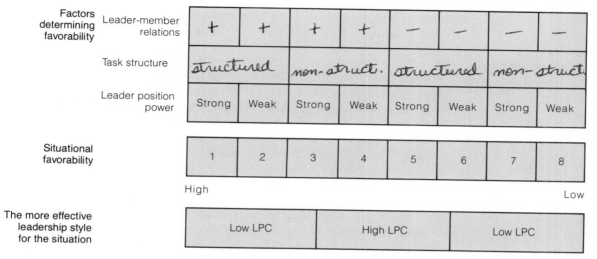

Factors determining favorability	Leader-member relations	+	+	+	+	−	−	−	−
	Task structure	structured		non-struct.		structured		non-struct.	
	Leader position power	Strong	Weak	Strong	Weak	Strong	Weak	Strong	Weak

Situational favorability	1	2	3	4	5	6	7	8

High   Low

The more effective leadership style for the situation	Low LPC	High LPC	Low LPC

FIGURE 17.3 Group performance and leadership style

unfavorable to the manager. In situations of intermediate difficulty, the relationship- or people-centered manager is more effective. Fiedler found this to hold true, in general, in his studies of such varied groups as B–29 bomber crews, open-hearth steel workers, general managers, sales display teams, service station managers, high school basketball teams, boards of directors, and church leaders.

• Match the leader with the situation.

Relationship-motivated managers take a somewhat nondirective role, asking others in the group to share in the decision-making process and interacting with subordinates in a relatively considerate, permissive, human relations—oriented fashion.[13] This managerial approach is effective in a situation where, for example, a manager with good interpersonal relationships is developing a new policy that will have a great impact on the work group. At this stage the situation is relatively unstructured but moderately favorable, and it is appropriate for the manager to consult with subordinates and consider their thoughts and ideas. Once the new policy is settled and approved, the situation becomes favorable for the manager to become more task-goal oriented so as to enforce the policy.

When Truman took over Battery D, the situation was highly unfavorable. Leader-member relations were poor, and Truman had poor position power. To have asked for cooperation (consideration) from the men in Company D would have been disastrous. Truman's task-goal approach, however, using his position power and authority, was effective in changing the unfavorable situation into a favorable one.

Recent research challenges some aspects of Fiedler's model.[14] Nevertheless, the model illustrates how managers can and should vary their style to fit particular situations.

The Path-Goal Model Robert House has developed a path-goal model of leadership by defining the relationship between leader behavior and subordinate work attitudes and performance as situational. The essential ingredient of the **path-goal model** is that the leader smooths the path to work goals and provides rewards for achieving them. In developing the model, House returned to the expectancy model of motivation (see Chapter 15), under which people are assumed to have needs and to want to work (behave) in a way that accomplishes goals that satisfy those needs. Thus the path-goal model, like the contingency model, is based on the situation rather than on a single kind of leadership. This model also makes use of positive reinforcement (see Chapter 15).

The first concept of the path-goal model is that the leader motivates subordinates by clarifying the path to personal rewards that results from attaining work goals, as shown in Figure 17.4. The path is clarified by eliminating confusing or conflicting ideas that the subordinate may hold. In other words, it is the manager's task to provide the subordinate with a better fix on the job and on the relationship of performance to both positive and negative reinforcement.

The second concept is that when the path-to-goal relationship is clarified—when the job requirements are highly structured—additional structure by the manager is unnecessary. Indeed, if too much structure is provided by the manager, worker satisfaction although not necessarily performance, will decline.

The final concept is that managers who attempt to satisfy subordinates' needs will increase performance if the reward is related to the desirability of the effort and of the goal. That is, the manager must offer a reward only if the subordinate actually accomplishes the task. The reward can be relatively simple, such as praise, or require more effort to arrange, such as a pay increase or promotion.

The degree to which the subordinate sees certain job behaviors as leading to various rewards and the desirability of those rewards to the individual (preference) largely determine job satisfaction and performance. The leadership style that motivates subordinates is the one that clarifies the kind of behavior most likely to reap those rewards.

Managers should vary their style for each subordinate. For example, subordinates with high needs for affiliation will be satisfied with a considerate leader. But subordinates with a high need for achievement will probably prefer a task-oriented leader. The path-goal model forces the leader to consider the individual subordinate as well as the situation.[15]

In one organization, to combat a high turnover rate, an unusual training program was used to help reduce anxiety in new employees. The employees were told clearly what their supervisor expected of them. They were told also that they would not be expected to become immedi-

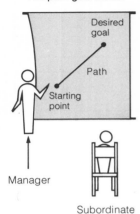

The path-goal model

Desired goal

Path

Starting point

Manager

Subordinate

Leaders should:

- Clear paths
- Clarify goals
- Provide rewards
- Provide support
- Analyze the situation, task, and employees' needs

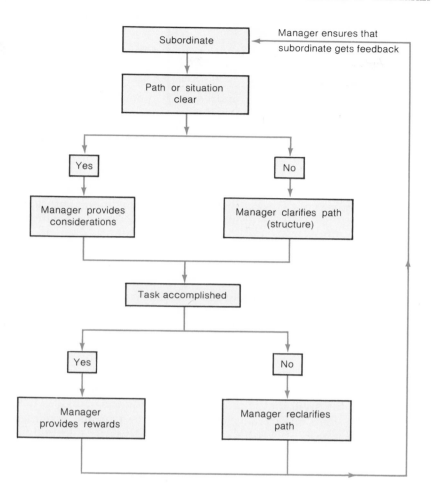

FIGURE 17.4 The path-goal relationship

ately proficient at the job, but at the same time they were given specific steps for gaining proficiency. The results were dramatic. Workers given this orientation reached job competence more quickly and made fewer errors than those who had received conventional on-the-job training. The special orientation had told the new workers what to expect and what their rewards for good performance would be. In addition, the orientation constituted a supportive introduction to the organization.[16]

The path-goal theory of leadership is a new one, backed by relatively little research. Early findings have been encouraging, though. In general, workers on highly structured tasks have reported high satisfaction when their leader uses a supportive rather than a directive style, but they are not necessarily more productive. Workers on highly unstructured tasks are more productive when the leader uses a directive style, but they do not necessarily report more satisfaction.

SOME SUGGESTIONS FOR MORE EFFECTIVE LEADERSHIP

Fundamentally, the role of the leader is to coordinate human and material resources for the accomplishment of a task—to get things done through others. No one yet has formulated a clear prescription for how a manager can lead effectively. Hundreds of leadership studies have produced results that are often contradictory and confusing. At least one valid concept has emerged, however—that a given style of supervision can be effective in one situation but lead to low performance in a different situation. This finding has led to the situational, or contingency, approach to leadership, which argues that appropriate leadership behavior is a function of many factors. Among them are the characteristics of the leader, the type of decision that needs to be made, the nature of the work situation, the leader's upward influence in the organization, the subordinates' abilities and values, the climate of the organization, and the expectations and influence of peers, as shown in Figure 17.5.

Leader Characteristic The more types of power a formal leader wields, the more successful his or her leadership. Some types of power usually accompany each other. Legitimate, reward, and coercive power tend to be vested in a formal leadership position; charismatic power and expert power generally have to be earned. Managers should remember that many subordinates have expert power and should be willing to respect such power and avail themselves of that expertise.

Although to some degree people can appropriate their choice of leadership styles, the style that is most natural to the individual is usually more effective than one chosen for manipulative reasons. A manager's best approach is to begin with the style that feels most comfortable and then vary it when the individual or the situation seems to call for a particular other style.

FIGURE 17.5 Factors determining the appropriate leadership behaviors

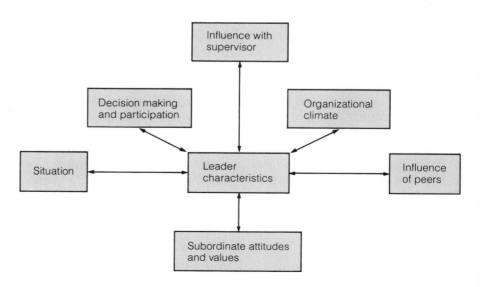

Decision Making and Participation   In situations where the manager has the necessary information and expertise and does not need to acquire subordinates' acceptance of decisions in order to implement them, the most appropriate action may be for the manager to make the decision without consultation and announce it to subordinates only if necessary. The more complicated a problem and the more widespread its consequences, the less likely the manager is to possess all the necessary expertise. Also, the more subordinate acceptance is needed to carry out a decision, the more participation should be solicited from those participants. Thus managerial decision making can extend on a continuum from no outside participation, to merely informing subordinates of an already made decision, to discussing the decision with subordinates and perhaps modifying it, to involving subordinates in making the decision. This contingency approach is discussed in more detail in Chapter 4.

Nature of the Work Situation   When the work is simple, highly structured, and routine, considerate or supportive leadership may be more salutary than directive leadership. Since workers frequently find highly routine jobs boring and unrewarding, frequent contact from the supervisor is likely to be seen as oversupervision or even harassment. In this type of work situation workers prefer a supervisor who does not seem to be constantly looking over their shoulders. For example, warehouse workers and secretaries often appreciate a considerate as opposed to a directive boss in order to compensate for the routineness of their work and the necessarily frequent interactions with their boss.

When the work is less structured, subordinates may appreciate more specific direction from their immediate boss. Here the supervisor who gives subordinates guidance and direction is seen as helpful rather than oppresive. In this type of work situation the directive leader actually contributes a satisfying work experience for the workers. When people do not know what needs to be done, the manager can be more effective by structuring the task than by being warm and friendly. Consideration and praise, though, can come both during the task and after the task has been completed.

Upward Influence of Supervisor   The degree to which a supervisor is seen by subordinates as being able to obtain valued work-related goals and rewards from higher-level management may also influence the effectiveness of that supervisor's leadership. The considerate supervisor who is upwardly influential can act as a negotiator between higher-level management and subordinates. Supervisors who can give their subordinates desirable rewards have more power than those who cannot. Indeed, sometimes the time spent negotiating with top management may be more valuable for one's leadership than the time spent directing workers' activities. The supervisor who is seen by subordinates as having little upward influence may also be seen as having little power, particularly legitimate, reward, and coercive power. The effective manager pays attention to developing upward influence.

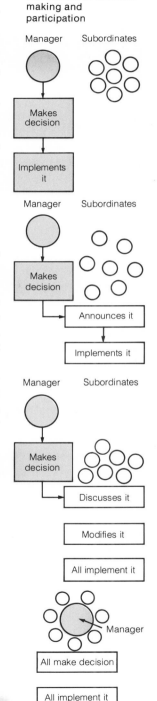

Continuum of decision making and participation

On the Job

DEERE & CO. FARM-MACHINERY LEADERSHIP HELPS FIRM WEATHER THE INDUSTRY'S SLUMP

MOLINE, III.—William A. Hewitt still has the notes he made to himself more than 25 years ago when he became president of Deere & Co., the farm-equipment maker.

His top goal then, "to lead the industry," has long since been accomplished, as Deere, with 30% or more of the nation's farm-equipment production, has replaced International Harvester, with 20% of this market (although Harvester's main business now is trucks).

With its overall sales of $6 billion a year, Deere is nearly 20 times bigger than when Mr. Hewitt became president in 1955, succeeding his father-in-law, the late Charles Deere Wiman.

Deere's strength as the industry leader stood it in good stead during last year's recession. Farm-equipment sales were depressed by the embargo on grain shipments to the Soviet Union, a slump in commodity prices and soaring interest rates. Deere's earnings fell 26% to $228.3 million, or $3.72 a share, in the fiscal year ended last Oct. 31.

But this slump from the year-

earlier record profit was mild compared with the showings of competitors International Harvester, Massey-Ferguson Ltd. and White Motor Co., all of which slipped into considerable financial trouble. Through the slump, securities analysts say, Deere may have increased its market share, because it could continue financing of machinery sales, while some competitors were hampered in raising capital.

"There is only one top-quality company in farm machinery, and that's Deere," says Michael Braig, an analyst for McDonald & Co. of Cleveland. Others say that Deere has made a few mistakes. Its foreign operations have been less than spectacular so far, for example, and it occasionally brings out a line of tractors before the markets are ready.

Family Affair But its overall success isn't questioned, and most agree that a main factor in that success is Mr. Hewitt, now 66 years old and chairman of the company that was started 144 years ago by John Deere, inventor of the first steel plow suitable for tilling the rich soil of the prai-

ries. Mr. Hewitt is the fifth—and probably the last—in a line of family members to run the company.

Under Mr. Hewitt, Deere has excelled in mass-producing such things as its big green tractors and combines and large implements such as planters and cultivators. The bigger the equipment, the more profitable as a rule, Mr. Hewitt observes.

Bigger machinery goes hand in hand with the trend to fewer and larger farms in the U.S. It requires large acreage to justify the $70,000 to $100,000 cost of a large new tractor or combine.

Deere's competitors may have fallen on hard times, but they aren't to be counted out. International Harvester predicts it will eventually overtake Deere in farm machinery again. Ben W. Warren, president of Harvester's agricultural-equipment group, says the company has stepped up its development of new farm equipment and has bolstered manufacturing and marketing.

Rotary Combine Harvester, for one thing, is trying to dominate the market for the rotary combine, which it claims yields 5% more grain because the grain is threshed several times. The rotary combine also is said to perform better than conventional combines on hilly ground. But it usues more energy and has more trouble when the grain is wet.

Deere isn't saying whether it will market a rotary combine. "My guess," one securities analyst says, "is that Deere will come out with its rotary combine within two years, if customers want them, and try to benefit from competitors' early mistakes."

Mr. Hewitt led Deere's diversification into production of construction and forestry equipment, which now represents about $1 billion of the company's annual sales. Caterpillar Tractor Co. remains a strong No. 1 in construction equipment, with Deere and the J.I. Case unit of Tenneco Inc. neck and neck for No. 2.

While Deere is trying to make further inroads in construction equipment, Caterpillar appears to be coveting the farm-equipment business by testing prototypes of large farm tractors. Analysts doubt that Caterpillar plans any major move into the farm-equipment business, but one suggests Caterpillar may be trying to warn Deere against further invasions of its turf.

Meantime, Deere is proceeding with a $2 billion capital-spending program to automate plants and increase capacity, at a time when some competitors are retrenching. Deere's spending on research and development, representing about 4% of sales, also exceeds that of most competitors.

"Deere uses money as a competitive weapon very effectively," says Eli S. Lustgarten, an analyst for Paine Webber, Mitchell Hutchins Inc. "As a result, I'll be surprised if the company doesn't substantially increase its market share by 1985."

Deere's success under Mr. Hewitt is attributed largely to a strong dealer network. After he took over, the company trimmed its dealerships to fewer than 2,500 from 10,000, concentrating on the financially stronger ones and backing them with faster parts supplies and other services.

The strong dealer network also is credited with bolstering the resale market for Deere machines. Anthony Mohr, a dealer at Eldridge, Iowa, asserts that a large Deere tractor will usually fetch several thousand dollars more at resale than competitors' models.

Mr. Hewitt, who reluctantly left his native San Francisco for Moline when he joined Deere, devoted considerable attention to the building of a new complex of headquarters buildings, designed by the late architect Eero Saarinen and by his partner, Kevin Roche.

As he escorts a visitor around the headquarters, Mr. Hewitt points out features that helped win awards for the building. He notes, for instance, that the building is designed so that at any place a worker can see the surrounding countryside. Having a first-class work place, he says, gives employees pride in their work and raises their sights.

"Being the best can be important," Mr. Hewitt says, "like in a race where no one remembers who took second place."

Supportive — More skilled, more ambitious

Leadership style — Subordinate's abilities and values

Directive — Less skilled, less ambitious

Subordinates' Abilities and Values Consideration on the part of the manager and participation from the subordinates are most profitable for the work unit when subordinates are competent, desire responsibility and independence, and are looking for promotion and advancement. This type of subordinate wants to satisfy social and ego needs through job accomplishment and will perform better under a supportive leadership style than under a directive leadership style. A supportive leader provides the considerate behavior that this type of employee needs to help satisfy social needs; and the opportunity to regulate one's own activities that comes with increased employee participation helps this type of employee satisfy ego needs.

Not only does the best leadership style vary from group to group because of the overall abilities and values of the subordinates involved, but it also may vary within a group according to the individual subordinate involved. Generally, the more skilled and capable employees require less directive supervision, whereas new, untrained employees require a more directive approach that emphasizes goal clarification.

In many instances the style of supervision acts as a self-fulfilling prophecy. The manager who expects more motivation and autonomy from subordinates generally obtains it.

The overall abilities and values of subordinates in a group also help determine what kind of informal leadership prevails. (Chapter 16 described informal leadership.) The effective manager will identify and enlist the cooperation of these informal task and social leaders. Whatever the manager's leadership style, their support can be of tremendous assistance.

Organizational Climate Every organization has its own climate or personality, which influences the expectations and behavior of its members. Formal leaders cannot act in ways that are too inharmonious with the climate, although they can use their personal style to modify it.

In a very restrictive, autocratic climate, for example, employees are likely to have negative attitudes toward the organization and low job satisfaction, innovation, and productivity. The manager cannot completely change this climate but can temper it, since there will usually be some opportunities to allow extra freedoms and self-regulation to subordinates. However, the manager needs to be careful not to overstep the bounds and be seen as violating the norms of the organization.

Expectations and Influence of Peers In addition to leading a group, managers also belong to a group. This group has norms set partially by its supervisor and partially by its members, who are managers on a peer level with each other. These managers are an important source of motivation and rewards for each other. The opinions of colleagues heavily influence behavior. A manager who is practicing consideration when other managers are focusing on more directive, task-oriented behavior may shift style if other managers comment, "You're being too easy on your people" or "Why are you holding so many meetings? Around here,

On the Job

TELLING OFF BOSS PAYS FOR OVERWORKED EMPLOYEE

The window panes shuddered as Janet Cooper (not her real name) slammed the front door shut. For the fourth night this week, her family had to eat dinner without her while she worked late in her office.

Her promotion to the business analysis group of a Connecticut-based Fortune 100 company was testimony to outstanding reviews during the four years since she graduated from Columbia University with her MBA degree.

As one of four senior financial analysts in her department, her new assignments gave her the opportunity to become involved in new areas. She didn't mind the responsibilities or increased challenges, but she felt her boss was insensitive to the demands placed upon her.

At first the workload seemed evenly distributed. But for the past four weeks she bitterly watched as her peers departed hours before her while she buried her thoughts in net present values, pay back periods and internal rates of return. Although externally self-controlled, the pressures within were manifesting themselves as non-voiced antagonisms toward her superior. In the morning she resented going to work and was on the verge of resigning.

Janet reasoned that if her manager didn't like her she would go elsewhere. One afternoon, Janet met a former classmate for lunch. The classmate held a similar position in a neighboring firm. Janet sought her friend's help in exploring a new opportunity with the latter's employer.

When the classmate asked Janet what her boss said when she confronted him with the inequities in the workload, Janet fell silent. She confided that she never thought to discuss it with him. She just assumed that he didn't care and for some reason "had it in" for her.

The following week began no differently than the previous ones. New assignments continued to appear on Janet's desk, and she still missed dinners with her family. But she increasingly thought about what her friend had said.

On Thursday of that week, she commandeered an hour of her boss's time and proceeded to bare her soul. Weeks of pent-up pressures and antagonisms rolled out. To her surprise, her manager genuinely professed that he was not aware of her feelings. He explained to her that because of her excellent academic background, because of the praise from former superiors, and because of his own high regard of her, he counted on Janet more than his other subordinates. Since she never protested to him, or even voiced the slightest complaint, he assumed she was quite satisfied with the assignment given her. He acknowledged that he spent more time with her peers, but that was because they required more guidance.

That meeting was a turning point in Janet's relationship with her manager. She still continued to be assigned the most important projects in the department, but the workload was more evenly distributed.

Janet still—and rightfully so—believed that her manager erred in not being more responsive to all the people under him.

But she also now understood that she too was in error. Every manager-subordinate relationship requires continual feedback.

She certainly had no regrets that she did do just that. Several months later, Janet was promoted to the new position of supervisor, with two assistants reporting to her.

Source: Stanley Herz, "Telling Off Boss Pays for Overworked Employee," Reporter Dispatch, White Plains, N.Y., January 18, 1981. Stanley Herz is a principal of Herz, Stewart & Company, an executive search firm headquartered in Stamford, Connecticut.

we tell people what to do." The effective manager does not stray too far from the norms set by peers but also refrains from blind imitation of the management styles of others.

SUMMARY

The crucial tasks of a manager are to assist, motivate, and control subordinates in order to attain organizational objectives. This can often be facilitated by helping subordinates gain personal satisfaction in the process of accomplishing the organization's objectives.

No single factor can explain the performance of a group; nor is there a single comprehensive theory of leadership. Nevertheless, different studies reveal enough consistencies to yield some guidelines for effective leadership. Two general propositions that emerge from the literature on leadership are:

1. The more subordinates depend on the manager for needed or valued services, the higher the potential for a positive relationship between the manager's behavior and the subordinates' performance and satisfaction.
2. The more the manager is able to give subordinates needed, valued, or expected rewards, the higher the potential for a positive relationship between the manager's behavior and the subordinates' performance and satisfaction.[17]

Some principles that managers should understand in order to put these two propositions into effect follow.[18]

Power The more power managers have, the greater their potential to influence others. (Some suggestions for increasing power are spelled out in Chapter 20.) Managers can increase their expert power by becoming more knowledgeable about their own operation and by cultivating experts outside their unit. They can increase legitimate, reward, and coercive power by showing subordinates that they have influence with higher-level managers,

especially by getting payoffs such as raises, for subordinates. They can increase charismatic power by the appropriate use of rewards and by getting to know subordinates as individuals.

Diagnosis The good manager needs to be an effective diagnostician, ready to vary the style of supervision with the situation. When the job is simple, routine, and structured, considerate leadership will probably promote better job performance and satisfaction than directive leadership. For less structured tasks, more direction is usually appreciated, with consideration and feedback employed after successful completion of the task.

Feedback Accurate and nonthreatening feedback to the individual about performance is important. Most managers cannot give complete feedback to all subordinates; therefore, effective managers must try to design tasks so that feedback is provided through the task itself or through appraisal or other approaches.

Rewards Part of feedback should be rewards that are closely tied to task accomplishment. Effective managers reward successful accomplishment as soon as possible. By knowing their subordinates well, managers can provide different types of rewards to different types of people to great effect. Praise (which is not used enough in most organizations) is one reward that is effective with most people. Opportunities for increased responsibility, achievement, and interesting work are other potential rewards.

Influence of Subordinates With the exception of Fiedler's leader-member relations, little attention has been given to the upward influence of subordinates. Effective leaders recognize the validity of this influence when, for example, the task is complex and the manager does not have all the required expertise or when consensus of the work group is necessary for satisfactory completion of a task.

Personal Qualities Effective managers act naturally and do not try to manipulate their subordinates. They recognize that subordinates are subject to a variety of pressures and they try to identify and allow for these pressures in the way they direct the group.

Avoiding Value Judgments Effective managers try to diagnose the causes of undesirable behavior rather than make value judgments about the employees demonstrating it. For example, automatically classifying a subordinate as lazy without attempting to analyze reasons for the unsatisfactory performance reduces the possibility of changing that behavior.

STUDY QUESTIONS

1. What different types of power can one person exercise over another? Are they interrelated? Explain.
2. How does formal leadership differ from informal leadership?
3. How does Theory Y differ from Theory X? Are their concepts oversimplified? Explain.
4. What are the two basic principles underlying the Managerial Grid? How do they compare to the basic principles of McGregor's approach?
5. How do McGregor's and Blake's approach to leadership differ from the contingency approaches?
6. What distinction can be made between leading and managing?
7. What aspect of Fiedler's theory suggests that a research director should use a leadership

style different from that of an accounting clerk's supervisor?
8. Interview several people, asking them to describe situations where someone's attempt to influence them was successful or unsucessful. Analyze the reasons for the success or failure of the influence attempt.
9. Some managers reject participative approaches such as Theory Y as being unrealistic. Advocates of participation argue that those who oppose it are authoritarians who are afraid to change their style. Comment on these views.
10. Describe how a college professor would conduct classes following each of the major Managerial Grid leadership styles.
11. Describe how a college professor would conduct classes using the path-goal approach.

Case for Discussion

THE FOUNDERING FIRM

In January 1974 duPont Walston went out of business. The Wall Street stockbrokerage firm had 138 branch offices. After a merger, it had been taken over by H. Ross Perot, a naval academy graduate and data-processing multimillionaire. On the first day after the merger, all the male employees were told to get short haircuts and to wear dark suits and bow ties. Mustaches and beards were prohibited. Two black men with Afro hair styles quit immediately.

No form of dissent was tolerated. For example, eight of the directors were fired for having opposed Perot's takeover of the firm (all were employees as well as directors). Nearly all the employees in research and in certain sales and operations areas were fired. Those who expressed dissent or even made suggestions were fired. Perot made it clear that he distrusted the employees, and he tried to force the staff into a paramilitary mold with strict rules and regulations that applied to everyone.

Employees were told to forget about small investors and to go after company presidents and other big investors. However, many of the big investors were already tied up with other brokers. Further, as a former executive pointed out:

There is a big difference between the computer business and stockbrokerage. In the computer business, you can make a one-time big sale to a customer and then perform service under a long-term contract. In the brokerage business, you can make a sale once, but after every sale you have to do it all over again because there are a number of other brokerage firms after the same account. Perot could not see the difference until it was too late. You can't adapt computer-selling methods to Wall Street.

A training program was instituted that included teaching employees how to sleep. Management forced trainees to sign an agreement to repay the organization for part of their training if they did not stay for three years. For example, a trainee who quit right after graduation would owe the organization $25,000. Trainees who did not sign were fired.

Employees were called up during off hours and asked to report to someone at work immediately for trivial matters. When the wives started complaining, that particular form of harassment stopped. Increasingly, employees objected to being treated "like plebes at the naval academy." Finally, a general exodus began. The replacements at the home office were more amenable to the paramilitary regime. However, they did not bring in the revenues. The exodus increased. In May 1973 the manager of the Decatur, Illinois, branch office along with ten salesmen and three operating workers quit to join a competitor. Only the receptionist stayed on. In Hartford fourteen employees quit to join a competitor when a new manager was put in charge.

The firm was losing money at a faster and faster rate. After a lengthy discussion over the weekend of January 19–20, the directors voted to go out of business.

Source: Adapted from R. Rustin, "Critics Say Heavy Hand at Helm Led to Collapse of duPont Walston," *Wall Street Journal*, February 26, 1974. Reprinted by permission of *The Wall Street Journal*, © Dow Jones & Company, Inc. 1974. All rights reserved.

1. Which approach to leadership did Perot use?
2. What motivational needs in employees were satisfied? What needs were not satisfied?
3. What types of power did Perot use?
4. What alternative leadership approaches could Perot have used?
5. Was there a difference between authority and influence in this situation?

FOR YOUR CAREER

1. A leadership style is effective if it fits the leader's personality, the characteristics of subordinates, and the work situation. Don't be afraid to experiment with leadership styles until you find one that fits all three of these factors.
2. No single leadership style is ideal for all occasions, just as no leader is perfect for all groups. Discover under which circumstances your own leadership style—that is, the one most natural to you—is most effective.
3. The most effective leadership style is the one you feel most comfortable with. Artificial behavior and manipulativeness are quickly noticed and resented.

4. Perhaps the most effective motivator at your disposal is honest praise.

5. Enlist the assistance of the informal leaders in the group. They can ensure your success or failure as a formal leader.

FOOTNOTES

1. Adaptation by permission of Berkley Publishing Corporation from *Plain Speaking: An Oral Biography of Harry S Truman* (p. 96) by Merle Miller. Copyright © 1973, 1974 by Merle Miller.

2. R. Stogdill, *Handbook of Leadership: A Survey of Theory and Research* (New York: Free Press, 1974).

3. J. French and B. Raven, "The Basis of Social Power," in *Group Dynamics: Research and Theory,* 3d ed., ed. D. Cartwright and A. Zander (New York: Harper & Row, 1967).

4. G. Farris, *Leadership and Supervision in the Informal Organization,* Working Paper No. 655-73 (Cambridge, Mass.: Massachusetts Institute of Technology, 1973).

5. Adapted from L. Sank, "Effective and Ineffective Managerial Traits Obtained as Naturalistic Descriptions from Executive Members from a Super-Corporation," *Personnel Psychology* 27 (Autumn 1974): 423–434.

6. Adapted from Stogdill, *Handbook of Leadership*.

7. R. Stogdill and A. Coons, *Leader Behavior: A Description and Measurement,* Research Monogram 88 (Columbus, Ohio: Bureau of Business Research, Ohio State University, 1957); R. Stogdill, *Individual Behavior and Group Achievement* (London: Oxford University Press, 1959); A. Korman, "Consideration, Initiating Structure and Organizational Criteria—A Review," *Personnel Psychology* 19 (Winter 1966): 349–361; R. House, A. Filley, and S. Kerr, "Relation of Leader Consideration and Initiating Structure to R and D Subordinates' Satisfaction," *Administrative Science Quarterly* 16 (March 1971): 19–30; S. Kerr and C. Schriesheim, "Consideration, Initiating Structure, and Organizational Criteria—An Update of Korman's 1966 Review," *Personnel Psychology* 27 (Winter 1974): 555–568; and C. Schriesheim, R. House, and S. Kerr, "The Effects of Different Operationalizations of Leader Initiating Structure: A Reconciliation of Discrepant Results," *Academy of Management Proceedings,* New Orleans, Louisiana, August 10–17, 1975, pp. 167–170.

8. E. Fleishman and S. Peters, "Interpersonal Values, Leadership Attitudes and Managerial Success," *Personnel Psychology* 15 (Summer 1962): 43–44.

9. D. McGregor, *The Human Side of Enterprise* (New York: McGraw-Hill, 1960); and D. McGregor, *The Professional Manager,* ed. D. McGregor and W. Bennis (New York: McGraw-Hill, 1967).

10. D. McGregor, "On Leadership," *Antioch Notes,* May 1954, pp. 2–3. Used by permission of Antioch University.

11. R. Blake and J. Mouton, *The Managerial Grid* (Houston: Gulf Publishing, 1964); L. Barnes and L. Greiner, "Breakthrough in Organization Development," *Harvard Business Review* 42 (November–December 1964): 133–155; R. Blake and J. Mouton, *Corporate Excellence through Grid Organization Development: A Systems Approach* (Houston: Gulf Publishing, 1968).

12. R. R. Blake and J. S. Mouton, "Toward Resolution of the Situationalism vs. 'One Best Style . . .' Controversy in Leadership Theory, Practice and Research," paper from Scientific Methods, Inc., 1981.

13. F. Fiedler, *A Theory of Leadership Effectiveness* (New York: McGraw-Hill, 1967); G. Graen, K. Alveris, J. Orris, and J. Martella, "Contingency Model of Leadership Effectiveness: Antecedent and Evidential Results," *Psychological Bulletin* 74 (October 1970): 285–296; S. Shiftlett and S. Nealey, "The Effects of Changing Leadership Power: A Test of Situational Engineering," *Organizational Behavior and Human Performance* 7 (June 1972): 371–382; F. Fiedler, "Predicting the Effects of Leadership Training and Experience from the Contingency Model: A Clarification," *Journal of Applied Psychology* 57 (April 1973): 110–113; F. Fiedler and M. Chemers, *Leadership and Effective Management* (Glenview, Ill.: Scott, Foresman, 1974); J. Stinson and L. Tracey, "Some Disturbing Characteristics of the LPC Score," *Personnel Psychology* 27 (Autumn 1974): 477–485; D. Hovey, "The Low-Powered Leader Confronts a Messy Problem: A Test of Fiedler's Theory," *Academy of Management Journal* 17 (June 1974): 358–362; F. Fiedler, "Engineer the Job to Fit the Manager," *Harvard Business Review* 43 (September–October 1965): 118; and F. Fiedler, "The Leadership Game: Matching the Man to the Situation," *Organizational Dynamics* 4 (Winter 1976): 6–15.

14. C. Schriesheim and S. Kerr, "Theories and Measures of Leadership: A Critical Appraisal of Current and Future Directions," in *Leadership: The Cutting Edge,* ed. J. Hunt and L. Larson (Carbondale: Southern Illinois University Press, 1977).

15. R. House, "A Path-Goal Theory of Leader Effectiveness," *Administrative Science Quarterly* 16 (September 1971): 321–338; R. House and T. Mitchell, "Path-Goal Theory of Leadership," *Journal of Contemporary Business* 3 (January 1974): 81–98; Stogdill, *Handbook of Leadership;* J. Stonson and T. Johnson, "The Path-Goal Theory of Leadership: A Partial Test and Suggested Refinement," *Academy of Management Journal* 18 (June 1975): 242–252; H. Sims, Jr., and A. Szilagyi, "Leader Structure and Subordinate Satisfaction for Two Hospital Administrative Levels: A Path Analysis Approach," *Journal of Applied Psychology* 60 (April 1975): 194–197; and A. Downey, J. Sheridan, and J. Slocum, "Analysis of Relationships among Leader Behavior, Subordinate Job Performance and Satisfaction: A Path-Goal Approach," *Academy of Management Journal* 18 (June 1975): 252–262.

16. E. Gomersall and M. Myers, "Breakthrough in on-the-Job Training," *Harvard Business Review* 44 (July–August 1966): 62–72.

17. S. Kerr, C. Schriesheim, C. Murphy, and R. Stogdill, "Toward a Contingency Theory of Leadership Based upon the Consideration and Initiating Structure Literature," *Organizational Behavior and Human Performance* 12 (August 1974): 62–82.

18. C. C. Manz and H. P. Sims, Jr., "Self-Management as a Substitute for Leadership: A Social Learning Theory Perspective," *Academy of Management Review* 5 (July 1980): 361–368; J. A. Waters, "Managerial Skill Development," *Academy of Management Review* 5 (July 1980): 449–454; R. C. Liden and G. Grosen, "Generalizability of the Vertical Dyad Linkage Model of Leadership," *Academy of Management Journal* 23 (September 1980); 451–465; G. Hofstede, "Motivation, Leadership, and Organization: Do American Theories Apply Abroad?" *Organizational Dynamics* 9 (Summer 1980): 42–63; M. M. Petty and N. S. Bruning, "A Comparison of the Relationships between Subordinates' Perceptions of Supervisory Behavior and Measures of Subordinates' Job Satisfaction for Male and Female Leaders," *Academy of Management Journal* 23 (December 1980): 717–725; A. D. Szilagyi, "Causal Inferences between Leader Reward Behavior and Subordinate Performance, Absenteeism and Work Satisfaction," *Journal of Occupational Psychology* 53 (March 1980): 195–204; and R. J. Klimoski and N. J. Hayes, "Leader Behavior and Subordinate Motivation," *Personnel Psychology* 33 (Autumn 1980): 543–556.

Communications

CHAPTER 18

CONTENTS

THE PLUMBER

A plumber from New York developed what he thought was an excellent method for cleaning drains. He wrote the Bureau of Standards to tell them that he was using hydrochloric acid and to ask them if it was harmless. The bureau replied, "The efficacy of hydrochloric acid is indisputable, but the chlorine residue is incompatible with metallic permanence."

The plumber wrote back, thanking the bureau for agreeing with him. Alarmed by his response, the bureau wrote another letter, saying, "We can-not assume responsibility for the production of toxic and noxious residues with hydrochloric acid, and we suggest that you use an alternative procedure." The plumber wrote again, explaining how happy he was to learn that Washington still agreed with him.

At this stage, the bureau resorted to simple terms: "Don't use hydrochloric acid. It eats the hell out of the pipes." Finally, the plumber understood the bureau's message.[1]

This case raises several critical questions which you should be able to answer after reading this chapter. The questions include:

1. Was the plumber a poor listener or was the Bureau of Standards a poor communicator?
2. What does it take to be a good communicator? Can employees be trained to be good communicators?
3. Is two-way communication always better than one-way communication? Explain.
4. How can negative feedback best be given? Do employees desire negative feedback? Explain.

18

Both the plumber and the Bureau of Standards thought they were communicating with each other when, in fact, they were not. Communications were not effective until the bureau used words that the plumber could understand. This chapter will explore the importance of information and communications in organizations, describing (1) different types of communications, (2) barriers to effective communications, (3) ways of analyzing and better understanding the communications process, and (4) ways of improving the process.

THE IMPORTANCE OF INFORMATION

Having the right information at the right time is vital to an organization. **Information** is the knowledge or other data pertinent to the individual or organizational unit. Decision making, establishing organizational objectives, planning, and controlling cannot take place without accurate and timely information.

Information serves not only to motivate behavior but also to aim it in the proper direction.[2] For example, a truck driver receives visual information that the truck is moving off the highway onto the shoulder of the road. The information not only motivates the driver to take action but also serves to guide the action (turning the wheel in the direction that will bring the truck back onto the road). A manager receives information that the volume of bank loans is falling off and is motivated to take action to increase the number of loans and guided to accomplish this by discussing the situation with subordinates.

As explained in Chapter 1 and elsewhere, managers are the nerve centers of the organizational unit. In order to get the job done well, they must obtain and give information horizontally, downward, and upward. In the liaison role, managers communicate horizontally with others; they are nerve centers in touch with a variety of other nerve centers. As monitors, they must continually get information from and give information to horizontal and lower levels to ensure that the unit is operating properly. As disseminators, they must make certain that subordinates and others are informed of pertinent information. Frequently this requires feeding the unit information that has been obtained from people at the same and higher levels. As spokespersons, managers must speak for and represent the unit to others at both the same and higher levels. All these roles require that managers be excellent communicators.

Managers are:

- Communicators
- Disseminators
- Spokespersons
- Monitors
- Nerve centers

WHAT IS COMMUNICATIONS?

Communications is the process by which information is exchanged and understood by two or more people, usually with the intent to motivate or influence behavior. As people interact with others to work and to solve problems, they communicate ideas, attitudes, and feelings. If the communications are effective, the work is performed more efficiently and problems are solved more quickly. Thus a positive relationship exists between good communications and productivity.[3]

Communications can be either formal or informal. *Formal communications* follow lines of authority prescribed by the organization. For example, Mike gets Reports A and B but is not on the list for Report C. Christine has access to payroll information, but Leslie is not allowed such information. *Informal communications* need not follow organizationally prescribed lines of authority. Usually, they take place on a person-to-person basis. Because prescribed information channels are frequently slow and incomplete, the manager needs to develop a network of informal communications at all levels.

Most people think of communications as a simple process, but it is actually quite complex, and the probability for sending or receiving the wrong message is great.[4] How often have you heard someone say, "But that's not what I meant"? How often have you given people what you thought were clear directions yet they lost their way?

The main elements of the communications process, shown in Figure 18.1, are the sender, the transmitter, the message itself, noise, and the receiver. Secondary elements include the source of information, the characteristics of the sender and receiver, and the climate and environment of the communications. A simplified explanation of the communications process follows.

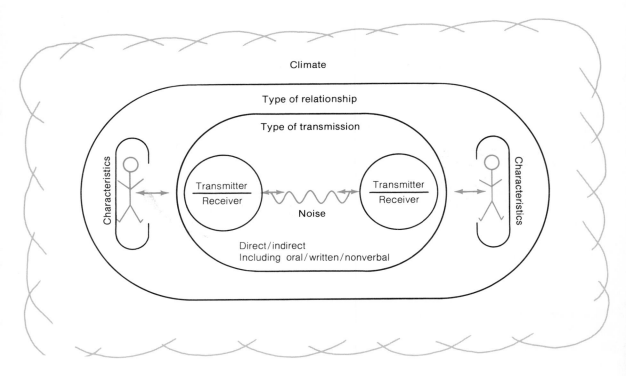

FIGURE 18.1   The communications process

An individual has an idea. The idea exists in the person's brain and must be coded into some form of oral, written, or other language, which is then transmitted. If the coding, transmitting, or decoding process is faulty, there is noise in the system. When this occurs, the message may not be received, a wrong word may be used, or the right word may be misinterpreted. If and when the message is received by the other person, it must be decoded in that person's brain, where it then forms a message. If the communication has been effective, the message received is the same as the one transmitted.

A number of factors can cause the message to be lost at some point in the communications process. Since the process is a two-way one (as presented by the double-headed arrow in Figure 18.1), the possibilities for misunderstanding are doubled.

Sometimes covert messages are sent along with overt messages.

Characteristics of the Sender The message originates with the sender (although, as Figure 18.1 shows, the sender can also become the receiver). Since the vast majority of communications are two-way, the terms *sender* and *receiver* can often be used interchangeably.

The prior contacts between two or more people influence all subsequent communications. Thus time and effort are well spent developing mutual trust and identifying areas of present and potential agreement. People are often unaware of some of their actions. To become an effective sender, one should cultivate senstivity to the impact of actions on others and responses of others and thus increase self-awareness. This will in turn increase the ability to send clear and inoffensive messages.

Sending the Message Messages can be of two types. In the *overt* message, the stated idea is the only one sent to the other person. If a person says to a service station attendant, "Fill the gas tank with regular," the message is clear, simple, and unaccompanied by any other message.

Frequently, however, a *covert*, or hidden, message accompanies the overt message. Sometimes the covert message is in the emotional overtones of the overt message and may or may not be received. It is important to be tuned into both types of messages. In many cases it is the covert message that carries the primary weight of the entire message's meaning.

For example, a junior accountant may complain, "My desk is too small." The overt message is, "My work requires more space." However, since desk size may also indicate status, the covert message may be, "I'm not getting the recognition I should be getting." Both messages must be received for effective communication.

As Table 18.1 shows, there are a number of methods for sending messages. The three basic ones are oral, written, and nonverbal. Nonverbal messages may be sent alone or may supplement oral messages; often they are sent unconsciously or covertly. In addition, there are a number of communications channels. A **communications channel** is the way in which information reaches the receiver. The choice of channel affects

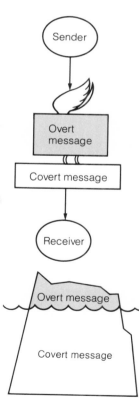

Often the covert message is the largest part of the entire message sent.

TABLE 18.1 Some Types of Communication

Oral
    Personal — face-to-face
    Personal — telephone
    Group
    Public address system
    Closed circuit television
Written
    Personal — letters, notes
    Organizational — general announcements, newsletters
    Outside the organization
Nonverbal
    Body language — body and eye movements, facial expressions, hand signals, voice
        (pitch, volume), touch, smell, taste
    Mechanical — sirens, traffic lights, horns
    Symbolic — status (office size, desk size, carpet, badge), religious (bible, rosary, medal)
    Pictorial (no smoking, smoking, no trucks)
Mixed
    Most oral and written communications include nonverbal cues or components
    Written messages may be accompanied or followed by oral explanations

the accuracy of communications and the degree to which the receiver responds to them. The advantages and disadvantages of the various communication methods are explained below.

Oral Communications Oral communications have the advantage of speed. They allow more interaction between the communicants, since response and counter-response can be immediate. In addition, they create an informal atmosphere, particularly if conducted face-to-face. Their chief disadvantage is that they have no permanent record and may be forgotten.

> I know that you believe you understand what you think I said but I am not sure you realize that what you heard is not what I meant.

The environment of oral messages affects their efficacy. If the boss stops at the subordinate's office or desk, the two are likely to interact on a more nearly equal basis than if the subordinate has to see the boss by appointment. Placing a telephone call personally is much more informal than having a secretary place it. In some organizations the manager who picks up the phone first (after the secretary has placed or received the call) is considered the loser in a covert power struggle.

In most organizations the flow of communications downward or laterally is considerably better than the flow of communications upward. Used properly, one of the chief advantages of oral communications is its superiority at moving messages upward.

The president and executive vice-president of a large eastern university make it a practice to walk (separately) through the campus at least once a day. As the vice-president puts it, "I pick different hours of the day so that I don't run into the same people." Both also drop into the faculty dining room or one of the student dining halls on random occasions to have lunch with random groups of faculty and students. They report being able to obtain or pass on information in this way that would be impossible to transmit or receive by more formal methods.

Written Communications One advantage of written communications is that they leave both sender and receiver a record of the message. Another advantage is that the process of writing a message encourages clear thinking. Written communications are best for transmitting policies and procedures, which remain in effect for a considerable period of time, and technical material such as engineering, legal, or financial data, which would be nearly impossible to transmit orally.

One of the disadvantages of written communications is its danger of being misunderstood, especially when there is no opportunity to ask questions. Another is that the information contained in written messages can become accessible to the wrong people or at the wrong time. Unfortunately, many organizations tend to rely too much on this form of communication. Some people want everything in writing so they can prove they have been following directions. Frequently such over-reliance is a result of the lack of trust and openness in the organization.

In many cases written and oral approaches should be combined. For example, if a person in one department has to send a memo on a sensitive matter to a person in another department, a draft of the memo should be prepared and discussed with the other person before it is written in final form. This way the possible misinterpretations of the memo can be eliminated.

Which is better—oral or written communications? As already suggested, written communications may be better if a formal record must be kept, but oral communications are generally faster and more interactive. Probably a combination of the two is best for most circumstances. For example, a formal policy or procedure may be written and then orally explained to those affected; this method allows questions and answers to be exchanged. Most research studies on communication indicate that greater satisfaction, understanding, and retention occur with oral communications than with written ones.

Nonverbal Communications **Nonverbal communications** are messages transmitted without words. As Table 18.1 shows, there are several types of such communications. A fire alarm, a police siren, a traffic light—each has its own message. A drawing of a lighted cigarette with a large X drawn through it clearly conveys the message "no smoking."

One important type of nonverbal communication is **body language,** in which thoughts, feelings, and intended actions are "read" by other people. Most situations require the use of words; however, words are often insufficient to convey the entire message. Particularly in face-to-face communications, only about 35 percent of the message is transmitted through words. The rest either gets lost or is communicated in nonverbal ways.[5]

Included in body language are voice tones, facial expressions, eye

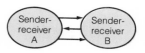

Oral communications

Speed and interaction

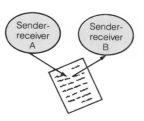

Written communications

Permanence

In body language one gesture may have several meanings, and several gestures may have the same meaning.

movements, and hand and body movements. Meanings in body language, however, are not always consistent. For example, nodding the head up and down is the usual nonverbal sign of agreement. However, if a supervisor is communicating an unwanted message, subordinates may nod their heads to avoid verbal agreement. In this instance, the nod means "Yes, boss, I hear you," but not "I agree with you."

Not only can a gesture change meanings according to the situation, but different gestures can be used for the same meaning. Frustration, for example, can be indicated by clenching hands tightly, throwing pencils, running a hand through the hair, rubbing the back of the neck, or breathing quickly and shallowly. Meditation can be indicated by stroking the face or chin, closing the eyes, or frowning. Suspicion or doubt can be shown by pulling on or rubbing the ear with the index finger or thumb, glancing sidewise, peering over the top of glasses, frowning, or averting the eyes.

Openly displayed arms and hands, particularly if hands are open, with palms up, usually indicate sincerity and openness. Crossed arms or legs indicate possible defensiveness, stubbornness, or withdrawal. In one meeting, for example, the boss had been talking for forty-five minutes. Although the fourteen subordinates were apparently listening intently, most were leaning back in their chairs, and all had their arms crossed. Several had tightly closed fists or were tightly grasping their arms. Ten seconds after the boss said, "I want to get your opinions," all fourteen were leaning forward with their arms and hands on the table.

Nonverbal communications are often just as meaningful as words. For years Ted Williams held the record for paying the largest fine ever levied against a professional baseball player. The fine was for arguing with an umpire. During the argument Williams had not spoken a word; the entire content of his message to the umpire was through a single gesture.

Just as people learn to recognize and use words, so do they learn body language. Consciously or unconsciously, they note whether the verbal and nonverbal messages agree. When they receive conflicting messages, they tend to rely more on the body language than on the verbal information. Indeed, body language is generally more accurate than other signals because it is performed unconsciously. Close attention to body language helps improve communications skills.

> Do what I say, not what I do.

Noise—Communication Barriers

Barriers to communication, or **noise,** are any factors that limit or distort messages. Some always exist. They include filtering, selective perception, semantics, jargon, information overload, rumors, and value judgments. Sometimes, the barriers are physical—for example, bad telephone connections or the loss of the audio on a television. However, physical barriers are less serious than others.

Filtering occurs when the sender intentionally sifts or modifies the message so it will be seen more favorably by the receiver. For example, subordinates communicating with managers tend to make the information conform to what they feel the managers want to hear. Many employ-

> Barriers:
> - Filtering
> - Selective perception
> - Semantics
> - Jargon
> - Information overload
> - Rumors
> - Value judgments

ees feel that if they communicate openly, they cause themselves trouble. In addition, lower-level managers who want to get promoted tend to filter information transmitted upward.[6]

The same filtering process distorts downward communications. Supervisors frequently avoid giving subordinates information that may be threatening to subordinates' self-esteem, and they tend to screen any other information moving downward. For some supervisors, knowledge equals power.

To reduce filtering by subordinates, a manager should create an environment in which subordinates will not expect punishment for disclosing information. In addition, a manager should avoid practicing filtering and should give subordinates the information they need to do their jobs and make certain that the communications process is two-way.

Selective perception is the tendency to perceive only part of a message even though the entire message was delivered.[7] People often hear what they want to hear and see what they want to see, ignoring information that conflicts with their beliefs and expectations. For example, subordinates tend to hear information that they think is of the most interest to the boss and forget information that they deem less important.

One of the most common reasons for selective perception is a poor self-concept on the part of either the sender or the receiver. Individuals with a poor self-concept tend to see communications as vaguely threatening and so block out part of the information. During a recent electrical power failure, a mother, anxious about her child, called him. The child responded plaintively, "Mommy, I didn't do it!" The mother's concern was perceived by the child as a threat.

Figure 18.2 illustrates the tendency toward selective perception. What message is in the triangles? Most people would say "all in the family" and "once in a lifetime." But look again, saying aloud each word, one at a time. What is really written there?

One way to reduce selective perception is to develop **empathy**—an understanding of other people's viewpoints. Managers, for example, can

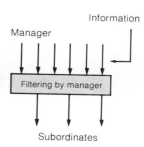

Information
Manager

Filtering by manager

Subordinates

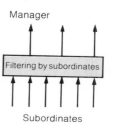

Manager

Filtering by subordinates

Subordinates

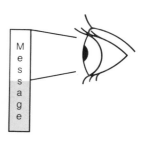

Selective perception

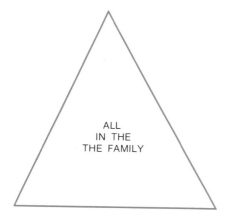

ALL
IN THE
THE FAMILY

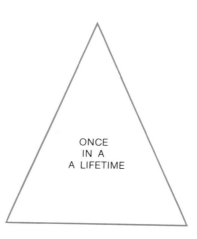

ONCE
IN A
A LIFETIME

FIGURE 18.2 What is the message?

On the Job

"BIG JIM" IS WATCHING AT RMI CO., AND ITS WORKERS LIKE IT JUST FINE

NILES, Ohio—When James Daniell arrived here nearly four years ago to take over as president of RMI Co., the gloom was knee-deep and rising.

RMI, an integrated titanium producer and a unit of U.S. Steel Corp. and National Distillers & Chemical Corp., had suffered big losses. The company was about to be convicted of price fixing. Management was lackluster, and employe morale was in the dumps.

Since then, RMI has done a flip-flop. Unit sales last year were up 500% from 1976, and productivity has soared. In late 1978, the company reported its first quarterly profit in four years. It's tempting to search for a sophisticated answer for the turnaround: an expensive consulting study, perhaps, or a couple of super-smart MBAs.

Big Jim Speaks   Well, the titanium market has improved, but forget the rest. Mr. Daniell cred-

its most of the improvement to an employe relations program that is pure corn—a mixture of schmaltzy sloganeering, communication, and a smile at every turn.

"If You See a Man Without a Smile, Give Him One of Yours," says a big sign hanging on a factory wall. "People Rarely Succeed at Anything Unless They Enjoy Doing It," says another. The slogans are signed: "Big Jim."

Mr. Daniell was captain of the Cleveland Browns professional football team in 1945, which probably accounts for the rah-rah style and such homilies as: "I'm the quarterback, I make the calls, the union is the line, and my management team, the backfield, will get through the holes they open."

"Believe it or not, for a big, dumb football player I have a philosophy," Mr. Daniell adds. "Do unto others as you would have them do unto you."

Union in the Know   This new low in cliches has helped produce a new high in morale. "He calls us into meetings and lets us know what's going on, which is unheard of in other industries," says Charles Corman, president of the Clerical and Technical Union local.

Robert Paul, a Lockheed Corp. vice president and an RMI customer, calls the Daniell method, "A management approach this whole country needs to get production up."

The company's logo, a yellow smile face, grins from stationery, from the front of the factory and from workers' hard hats. Mr. Daniell has renamed the Niles headquarters, Smiles, Ohio.

Riding through the factory in a golf cart, Mr. Daniell, 62 years old, waves and jokes with workers. He says he knows all 700 Niles employes by name. "If I don't wave to these people, they pout," he says.

help subordinates see the broader picture of what must be accomplished by the work group, thereby reducing the subordinates' selective perception. Beyond that, each person as an individual can attempt to consider the position of the other person and adjust personal behavior accordingly.

During the energy crisis in 1973 a high-level conference on energy was held at the White House on a cold day in November. Each government official arrived in a chauffeur-driven limousine. During the meeting the engines were kept running and the heaters were kept on to keep the cars warm. After the meeting the officials returned to their warm cars as passersby stared and news cameras clicked. These public servants were apparently unaware of the inconsistency in suggesting that other people do all they could to conserve energy while they themselves wasted it in keeping their cars warm. They lacked empathy.

Semantics is the study of meaning in language. Most messages are sent in words, and words often are not precise. Many words carry different meanings for different people. For example, one dictionary lists 14,000 meanings for the 500 most used words, an average of 28 meanings per word![8]

In addition to impreciseness, another semantic barrier is **jargon**—overly specialized or technical language. The incident at the beginning of the chapter illustrates the obstructive use of jargon. The meaning of "the chlorine residue is incompatible with metallic permanence" exists but is not readily understandable. The words chosen to convey the information act as a barrier to communication. Professional and highly technical groups tend to develop specialized language that cannot easily be understood by others. A visitor to an industrial firm picked up a copy of the weekly plant newspaper and was unable to understand most of it because of the heavy use of initials, abbreviations, and technical words. When asked about the meaning of some of the terms, the editor responded, "I don't understand them either. I just print the stories as they are sent in."

Communications can be improved by avoiding jargon. Many states, for example, now require that insurance policies and warranties be written in clear, simple language, so their purchasers can understand them.

Information overload, another communications barrier, is an excess amount of incoming information—too much to be handled. Some managers are literally swamped with information. One study reports a manager receiving approximately six hundred pages of computer printout each day. The information detailed the location of materials, the output of each production line, and other operational information. Rather than trying to wade through the information, the manager arranged to have it removed with the trash once a month.[9]

The first step in reducing information overload is to determine which reports and messages are unnecessary. The person in charge of compiling a periodic, lengthy report found a unique way to convince her boss that the report was unnecessary (or at least unread). Without telling anyone, she inserted a line on page eleven of each of five reports: "I will pay fifty dollars to anyone who reads this sentence." Nobody responded. After the fifth report had been issued with this insert, she told her boss about it and he agreed to discontinue the lengthy report.

Yet another source of noise in the system is **rumors**—unconfirmed messages passed from person to person. Formal communications channels are often short-circuited by the *grapevine*, which is a valuable way of informally getting information to those who need it. However, many

Grapevines are effective ways to communicate; managers should prune and care for them.

On the Job

THE AIR-CONDITIONED CAFETERIA

In December 1974 the executive management committee of the Berkshire Stove and Range Company recommended to the president that the employee cafeteria be air-conditioned. The committee's recommendation was based on the fact that the temperature in the foundry and other production areas often reached more than 100 degrees Fahrenheit; and because company profits for the fiscal year had been good, the committee felt that the employees were entitled to benefit from the profits. The air-conditioned cafeteria would represent management's appreciation of the employees' good work. The recommendation was approved and implemented.

At the end of the following year the committee reviewed the company's operation for the past year. Again, profits were high, labor productivity had been good, and labor turnover had been low. The committee unanimously agreed that the employees deserved additional recognition for their work, and the group considered how to show management's appreciation. Since the company cafeteria had been air-conditioned during the past year on the recommendation of the committee, the chairman and other members wondered if this sort of action was appreciated by the employees. In the course of discussion the chairman asked the personnel director to send a questionnaire to a sample of fifty employees in order to obtain their reaction to the air-conditioned cafeteria. The committee agreed to meet again in two weeks to hear the report from the personnel director.

The personnel director mailed a simple form to fifty employees; it asked for the following information: "Please state your reaction to the air-conditioned cafeteria." Of the fifty forms mailed, forty-six were returned. The answers could be classified generally as follows.

REACTION	TOTAL NUMBER
a) "I didn't know it was air-conditioned."	16
b) "I never eat there."	8
c) "I wish the entire plant were air-conditioned."	8
d) "If management can spend money like that, they should pay us more."	6
e) "That is a cafeteria for management people."	4
f) "It's O.K."	2
g) Miscellaneous comments.	2

rumors passed through the grapevine are inaccurate. They are prevalent when people are confused about what is happening in the organization or when they feel powerless to affect their own future. Passing on a rumor is a means of reducing anxiety about the subject of the rumor.

Since the grapevine will always exist and rumors will inevitably crop up, the effective manager uses the grapevine to get accurate information to people. A casual comment to one or more persons may take care of a problem without the need for more formal action. Also, the effective manager is alert to inaccurate rumors and counters their spread by transmitting correct information on the subject.

Value judgments, also a communications barrier, are statements or beliefs based on or reflecting the individual's personal or class values. The statements "workers aren't motivated any more" and "Jim is lazy" are judgments. They reflect someone's opinion but are not necessarily factual (even if others agree). Such judgments are frequently treated as fact, however, and people do not search further for more accurate information.

Communications can sometimes literally break down; the phone may go dead or the TV may lose the audio. Most of the time, however, the term *communications breakdown* or the statement "we need better communications" is used in the value judgment sense. When two departments or workers are feuding, the communications are operative but ineffective in helping the organization reach its goals. The term *communications breakdown* usually refers to the symptoms of value judgments being used as a barrier to effective communications.

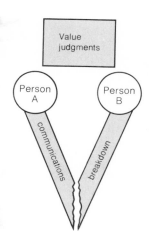

Value judgments can render communications ineffective.

THE IMPORTANCE OF CLIMATE IN COMMUNICATIONS FEEDBACK AND LISTENING

A number of studies have shown that the climate of an organization is important to all parts of the communications process, including feedback.[10] Especially in interpersonal communications, trust is a vital part of a good climate. There are a number of ways that the communications process can be used to build either a supportive climate (which increases trust and receptiveness to feedback) or a defensive climate (which decreases trust and increases defensiveness and resistance).

Threatening or defensive climates are created by judgmental rather than supportive communications. For instance, the comment "Your typing is terrible" is more judgmental than "There are two typing errors per page in this report." The second statement contains verifiable data, which increases the accuracy of the communication and reduces its threat.

In other areas, communications can be changed from judgmental to supportive if they are shifted to an emphasis on problems, detachment shifted to spontaneity and empathy, superiority in attitude shifted to equality, and certainty shifted to provisionalism. "You're wrong" (certainty) arouses a different reaction from "I wonder if we have thoroughly identified the problem" (provisionalism).

Feedback properly given and received can increase trust and reduce dependence. Typically, feedback involves an offer by one person to another, "Here's what I think you should do . . ." The typical response is, "Thanks, but the reasons that won't work are . . ." There is a difference between simple assistance and developmental help in giving feedback. *Simple assistance* means doing the task for the other person (which tends to increase that person's dependence on the helper). Some examples are a father tying a child's shoelace, a person giving a panhandler money for a cup of coffee, or a supervisor handling a difficult problem with a subordinate's customer. *Developmental help* means working with others to help them increase their capability for handling similar problems in the future. Two examples are a mother helping a child deal with lack of acceptance by other children and a secretary helping a saleswoman see that she is hurting her chances of making a sale by calling too frequently on the secretary's boss.

Effective Feedback[11]   Whether negative or positive, feedback is not always easy to provide. Fortunately, several characteristics of effective feedback have been determined. First, effective feedback is specific rather than general. Telling someone that he or she is dominating the conversation is probably not as useful as saying, "Just now you were not listening to what the other said, but I felt I either had to agree with your arguments or face attack from you."

Second, effective feedback focuses on behavior rather than on the person. It reports what a person does rather than judging what a person is. Thus a supervisor might say that a person talked more than anyone else at a meeting rather than that he or she is a loudmouth. The former statement allows for the possibility of change; the latter implies a fixed personality trait.

Effective feedback also takes into account the needs of the receiver of the feedback. Feedback can be destructive when it serves only the evaluator's needs. Too often it is used to gratify the evaluator's desire to "cut a person down to size." Its purpose should be to help, not to hurt, the receiver. Furthermore, it should concern behavior that the receiver can change. Frustration is the only result of reminding people of shortcomings they cannot control.

Feedback is most effective when it is solicited rather than imposed. To get the most benefit, receivers should formulate questions for the evaluator to answer and should actively seek feedback.

Sharing information is more useful feedback than giving advice, since it allows receivers to decide for themselves the changes to make in accordance with their own needs. Feedback should be well-timed, too. Usually immediate feedback is most useful—depending, of course, on the person's readiness to hear it, the support available from others, and so on.

Effective feedback provides the amount of information the receiver can use rather than the amount the evaluator would like to give. Overloading people with feedback reduces the possibility that they will use it effectively. Evaluators who give more than can be used are often satisfying needs of their own rather than trying to help the other person.

Feedback is most effective when it answers questions of *what* and *how*, not *why*. Telling people what their motivations or intentions are tends to alienate them and creates a climate of resentment, suspicion, and distrust; it does not contribute to learning or development. It is dangerous to assume knowledge of why a person says or does something. If evaluators are uncertain of receivers' motives or intent, the uncertainty itself is feedback and should be revealed.

Effective feedback improves employee performance and satisfaction.

Finally, feedback should be checked to ensure clear communication. One way of doing this is to have the receiver try to rephrase the feedback, to see if it corresponds to what the evaluator had in mind. No matter what the intent, feedback is often threatening and thus subject to considerable distortion or misinterpretation.

Effective Listening A supportive climate is also enhanced by effective listening. The average person, however, has only about 30 percent listening efficiency. Studies indicate that people spend about 40 percent of the workday listening. Considered together, these two facts suggest that the average person is only 30 percent efficient for 40 percent of the workday. From a business and personal standpoint this could have disastrous results.

Among the essential responsibilities of the manager are to develop employee potential, delegate responsibility, and achieve cooperation. The ability to listen intelligently and carefully is necessary to discharge these responsibilities. Intelligent listening is **active listening.** Basically it requires that the listener try to grasp what the speaker is communicating by looking at the issues involved from the speaker's point of view. More than that, the active listener conveys to the speaker that this attempt is being made.

Most messages have two components: the content and the feeling or attitude underlying the content. Both are important; both give the message meaning. For example, a computer engineer may say to her manager, "I've finished that installation." The content of this message is obvious and perhaps calls for a response—another work assignment from the manager.

Suppose, on the other hand, that the computer engineer says, "Well, I'm finally finished with that damned installation." The content is the same, but the total meaning of the message is significantly different. Here, insensitive listening can hurt the relationship between the manager and the computer engineer. If the manager responds by simply giving the engineer another work assignment, will the employee feel that her total message was received? Will she feel free to talk to the manager? Will she feel better about the job? Will she be anxious to do good work on the next assignment? Active listening on the part of the manager could have changed the answers to all these questions.

Sometimes the content of a message is far less important than the feeling that underlies it. If, for instance, the computer engineer had said, "I'd like to give that customer to our competition," responding to content would be obviously absurd. But a manager who responds to the disgust or anger at the difficulty of dealing with that customer recognizes the meaning of the message.

Different messages have different proportions of these two components of content and meaning. The active listener tries to receive the total meaning of each message, asking: What is this person trying to tell me? What does this mean to him or her? How does this situation look from this person's viewpoint?

Active listening:

• Try to grasp speaker's point of view
• Be sensitive to feeling component as well as content
• Respond to feeling component where appropriate
• Note all nonverbal communication

Not all communication is verbal. Hence, active listening requires that people become aware of several kinds of nonverbal communication. Hesitation in speech can reveal much. So can tone of voice. The speaker may express certain points loudly and clearly and mumble others. Facial expressions, body posture, hand movements, eye movements, and breathing all help to convey the total message.

SUMMARY

Managers spend a large percentage of their time communicating with others inside and outside the organizational unit. Thus communications take place upward, downward, and horizontally. As the nerve center of the unit, the effective manager develops good communications skills and a broad network of contacts on both a formal and an informal basis.[12]

This chapter contains many suggestions for improving communications and communications skills. The terms *sender* and *receiver* are used almost interchangeably, since most communications are a two-way process. Furthermore, most suggestions for improving two-way communications can also be used for improving one-way communications. Ten ways to improve communications are:

1. *Develop self-awareness.* The effective manager develops awareness of actions and their impact on others. At times, nonverbal messages contradict oral or written messages. Awareness of one's own needs and values affords control over the messages sent.

2. *Develop awareness of the other person's point of view.* Before sending a message, look at it from the receiver's point of view. Attempt to understand the other person's position, and convey something of help or value to that person in the message. Messages are usually well received and acted upon when they contain something of either immediate or long-range value to the person receiving them.

3. *Avoid value judgments.* Value judgments such as "people are not motivated" only add noise to the system. Since they deal

with symptoms rather than causes, they should not be used.

4. *Be clear and thorough.* Make certain what is to be communicated, and then make it clear to the receiver. Use simple language and concrete terms.

5. *Be concise and correct.* Get to the point, make certain the information is correct, and don't exaggerate.

6. *Choose channels carefully.* Oral communications are faster than written ones, but written communications provide a permanent record. For important messages, use more than one channel. Face-to-face oral communications, for example, can be backed up with written records.

7. *Support communications with action.* Many managers say one thing but do another. People tend to discount a message when they believe the attitudes or actions behind it contradict it. Obtain feedback on important communications to see if the entire message was received and to make certain that appropriate action was taken.

8. *Develop a supportive climate.* Without knowing it, managers often send messages in ways that increase others' defensiveness. Description, problem orientation, spontaneity, equality, and provisionalism create a supportive climate. Evaluation, control, strategy, superiority, and dogmatism establish a defensive climate for receiving communications.

9. *Improve listening and feedback skills.* Managers find it difficult to listen well. Indeed, in many interpersonal communi-

cations neither person really listens to the other. Become an active listener. Look for both overt and covert messages, for both content and feeling components. Listen with empathy; assume the other person's role, viewpoint, and emotions. Make sure that the speaker knows you have received the full message.

10. *Check the effectiveness of the messages.* Some managers can learn more effective communications techniques by tape recording themselves as they communicate with others. Generally, people do not ob-

ject to being recorded if they know why the tape is being made. (Managers who tape record their communications often are amazed at some of the things they have done or said without knowing it.) Ask questions; seek feedback. One of the most important elements in human interaction is communication. Effective communication leads to good relationships and good results. Effective managers use the tools of effective communication; they are both good senders and good receivers.

STUDY QUESTIONS

1. As a sender, you can use either written or oral communications. Which do you prefer? Why?
2. As a receiver, do you prefer written or oral communications? Why?
3. List what you think are the most important barriers to communications. What suggestions do you have for reducing these barriers?
4. Describe some mixed messages you have received and some you have sent.
5. Find a group of people. Sit close enough to observe their behavior but far enough away

that you cannot hear their conversation. What can you tell from the nonverbal behavior you observe? For example, are the people comfortable, tense, happy, sad?

6. What nonverbal ways do you have of communicating? Observe yourself, and ask a friend to observe you in order to get the information.
7. Do you make many value judgments? Listen for statements by others that reflect value judgments. What effect do such statements have on you?

Case for Discussion

THE FURNITURE STORE

One summer when I was in college four other students and I worked at a furniture store having a "going out of business" sale. Although the store had sold only wholesale, when the owners decided to close the business, they opened their doors to the public.

The owners had never dealt with retail customers, so they hired professionals to run the sale for them; and the professionals hired us. Sam was our boss, Bill was Sam's boss, and Jim was Bill's boss.

At first the work went smoothly. We did as Sam

directed. Then Jim and Bill began to have us rearrange whatever we had just done, contradicting what Sam had told us and commenting that Sam didn't know what he was doing. This, of course, bothered us, especially when it began to happen frequently.

Some days we were sent to the warehouse to uncrate merchandise and then back to the store to arrange the furniture on the sales floors. If Jim saw us resting, he would immediately ask what we were doing. Sometimes he would even peer around corners to watch us. He never let us do things on our own; he always wanted Sam to be with us, and we would have to check with him if Sam was not around. We finally reached the point where, when our work was done, we would stay out of Jim's sight. Otherwise, he would have us do some little senseless job just to keep us busy. He told us that we had been hired to work and that he would make sure we did.

After a few weeks I noticed that three cliques had formed; the other college students and I formed one clique, the people hired to run the sale formed another, and the owners and original salesman formed the third. The owners wanted things done one way and the professionals another. Soon they were talking behind one another's backs. This was bad for us, for we were given contradictory orders by two or three people, and we were inevitably yelled at by those whose orders were not carried out. Once, for example, an argument arose between one of the owners and Jim because the owner had sent us to another one of his stores and Jim was angry that we didn't get some work done at our regular store. That

time he told us not to listen to what the owners said.

Another time one of the students got into an argument with Sam. The student had done something his own way, and Sam was angry because he had not been consulted. Eventually, the student was fired. We were told that it was because he was a bad worker, but we found out later it was because the professionals thought he was too outspoken. After that, we never offered any ideas or suggestions.

After about a month and a half we got a small raise, thanks to Bill. But this only added to our headaches. Every time we would make a mistake, Bill would say that he had thought we were worth the raise but now he was not sure.

By summer's end the situation had deteriorated to the point where we did not talk to the bosses. We just listened to our orders, carried them out (whether they made sense or not), and left at the end of each day. The only reason I stayed on was that I needed the money and it was too late in the summer to look for another job.

1. What was the climate of this organization?
2. What sorts of messages were being sent?
3. How does communication affect behavior?

FOR YOUR CAREER

1. You are not communicating effectively until the other person understands you.
2. Remember that most people retain only 30 percent of what they are told.
3. You communicate as much nonverbally as verbally; remember, actions speak louder than words.
4. Managers spend a majority of each day communicating with others. More effective communicating skills can significantly increase their productivity.
5. To be an effective manager and communicator you need to emphathize with your listener.
6. The status and authority differences between manager and employees are critical barriers to effective communications. As manager, you must assume responsibility for overcoming these barriers.
7. One of the most critical types of communication a manager can give an employee is feedback, positive as well as negative.

FOOTNOTES

1. Adapted from *Power of Words,* p. 259, copyright 1953, 1954, by Stuart Chase. Reprinted by permission of Harcourt Brace Jovanovich, Inc.

2. D. Nadler, *Feedback and Organization Development* (Reading, Mass.: Addison-Wesley, 1977); E. Lawler and J. Rhode, *Information and Control in Organiza-*

tions (Santa Monica, Calif.: Goodyear Publishing, 1976); and W. Newman, *Constructive Control: Design and Use of Control Systems* (Englewood Cliffs, N.J.: Prentice-Hall, 1975).

3. C. Barnard, *The Functions of the Executive* (Cambridge, Mass: Harvard University Press, 1938); R. Carter, *Communication to Organizations: A Guide to Information Sources* (Detroit: Dale Research, 1972); J. Franklin, "Down the Organization: Influence Process across Levels of Hierarchy," *Administrative Science Quarterly* 20 (June 1975): 153–163; S. Hayakawa, *Language in Thought and Action,* rev. ed. (New York: Harcourt Brace Jovanovich, 1972); R. Huseman, J. Lahiff, and J. Hatfield, *Interpersonal Communication in Organizations: A Perceptual Approach* (Boston: Holbrook Press, 1976); and E. Rogers and R. Rogers, *Communication in Organizations* (New York: Free Press, 1976).

4. V. Balachandran and S. Deshmuch, "A Stochastic Model of Persuasive Communication," *Management Science* 22 (April 1976): 829–841; G. Chapel, "Speechwriting in the Nixon Administration," *Journal of Communication* 26 (Spring 1976): 65–79; F. Roethlisberger, "Social Behavior and the Use of Words in Formal Organizations," in *Interpersonal Behavior and Administration,* ed. A. Turner and G. Lombard (New York: Free Press, 1969); C. Shannon and W. Weaver, *The Mathematical Theory of Communication* (Urbana, Ill.: University of Illinois Press, 1949); and J. Wiemann and M. Knapp, "Turn-Taking in Conversations," *Journal of Communication* 25 (Spring 1975): 75–93.

5. H. Herzfeld, "The Unspoken Message," *Small Systems World,* February 1977, 12–14; R. Harrison, "Non Verbal Communication," in *Dimensions in Communication,* ed. J. Campbell and H. Harper (Belmont, Calif.: Wadsworth, 1970); F. Davis, *Inside Intuition: What We Know about Nonverbal Communications* (New York: McGraw-Hill, 1973); and J. Fast, *Body Language* (New York: M. Evans, 1970).

6. W. Read, "Upward Communication in Industrial Hierarchies," *Human Relations* 15 (January 1962): 3–15; and G. Gemmill, "Managing Upward Communications," *Management Review* 59 (May 190): 26–27.

7. J. Bruner, "Social Psychology and Perception," in *Readings in Social Psychology,* 3d ed., ed. E. Maccoby, T. Newcomb, and E. Hartley (New York: Holt, Rinehart and Winston, 1958), pp. 85–94; J. Bruner and C. Goodman, "Value and Need as Organizing Factors in Perception," *Journal of Abnormal and Social Psychology* 42 (January 1947):

33–45; M. Cook, *Interpersonal Perception* (Middlesex, *Superior-Subordinate Communication in Management* (New York: American Management Association, 1961), pp. 61–72; R. Rosenthal, *Experimenter Effects in Behavioral Research* (New York: Appleton-Century-Crofts, 1966); and S. Dornbusch et al., "The Perceiver and the Perceived: Their Relative Influence on the Categories of Interpersonal Cognition," *Journal of Personality and Social Psychology* 1 (January 1965): 433–440.

8. E. Huse and J. Bowditch, *Behavior in Organizations: A Systems Approach to Managing,* rev. ed. (Reading, Mass.: Addison-Wesley, 1977), p. 150.

9. J. Ivancevich, A. Szilagyi, and M. Wallace, *Organizational Behavior and Performance* (Santa Monica, Calif.: Goodyear Publishing, 1977), pp. 404–405.

10. J. Gibb, "Defensive Communication," *Journal of Communication* 11 (Summer 1961): 44–49; M. Greller and D. Herold, "Sources of Feedback: A Preliminary Investigation," *Organizational Behavior and Human Performance* 13 (March 1975): 244–256; D. Hellriegel and J. Slocum, Jr., "Organizational Climate: Measures, Research and Contingencies," *Academy of Management Journal* 17 (June 1974): 255–280; and C. Rogers, "Barriers and Gateways to Communication," *Harvard Business Review* 30 (July–August 1954): 44–49.

11. Adapted by permission from R. S. Schuler, *Personnel and Human Resource Management* (St. Paul, Minn.: West Publishing, 1981), p. 239.

12. C. A. O'Reilly, "Individuals and Information Overload in Organizations," *Academy of Management Journal* 23 (December 1980): 684–696; J. H. Gaines, "Upward Communication in Industry," *Human Relations* 33 (December 1980): 929–942; M. L. Tushman and R. Katz, "External Communication and Project Performance: An Investigation into the Role of Gatekeepers," *Management Science* 26 (November 1980): 1071–1085; F. B. Felson, "Communication Barriers and the Reflected Appraisal Process," *Social Psychology Quarterly* 43 (June 1980): 223–233; D. R. Ilgen and W. A. Knowlton, Jr., "Performance Attributional Effects on Feedback from Superiors," *Organizational Behavior and Human Performance* 25 (June 1980): 441–456; A. S. Baron, "Communication Skills for the Woman Manager—A Practice Seminar," *Personnel Journal* 59 (January 1980): 55–63; J. T. Samaras, "Two-Way Communication Practices for Managers," *Personnel Journal* 59 (August 1980): 645–648; and J. F. Kikoski, "Communication: Understanding It, Improving It," *Personnel Journal* 59 (February 1980): 126–131.

Career Planning and Development

CHAPTER 19

CONTENTS

THE INTERVIEW

Every spring, recruiters from a variety of organizations visit college campuses to interview students for possible jobs with their organizations. Table 19.1 lists typical questions asked by these recruiters. Many of the questions, or variations on them, are also asked by interviewers when an employee is thinking about changing jobs or moving from one organization to another.

To be properly answered, a number of the questions require that the students have some insight into their abilities and motivations. They also suggest the wisdom of having at least a tentative career plan. Indeed, the process of answering the questions can help in formulating a career plan or in sharpening or focusing an existing one.

TABLE 19.1 Typical Questions Asked by Interviewers

1. *What do you want to do, and why?*
(Employers want to know long- and short-range objectives and career plans.)

2. *How and why did you choose your major field?*
(They want to know what stimulated you in the particular direction.)

3. *Tell me about yourself.*
(They want only important points, such as key influences of your early home environment, why you chose the university you are attending and what is motivating you to choose a career.)

4. *Why are you interested in our organization?*
(They want you to know something about their organization, such as whether it is expanding or the key products or services it provides. They would like to see you tie this in with your own vocational objectives and in other ways show that you are interested in their particular organization.)

5. *Why isn't your grade record better? Or, for students with a B or higher average: Why didn't you participate in more extracurricular activities?*
(They don't want alibis or rationalizations. Instead, they prefer that you tell them where you rank in class and why you are involved or not involved in extracurricular activities.)

6. *What courses did you like best, and why? What courses did you like least, and why?*
(Again, they want you to tie your answer in with your objectives. The answer "I don't know why" shows no ability to discriminate, evaluate, or make decisions.)

7. *What are the three most important characteristics for success in your chosen field?*
(It is best to think out in advance the characteristics that fit in with your own strengths and to show how you possess these characteristics.)

8. *What do you see as your particular strengths and weaknesses?*
(Your answers should be tied to Questions 1 and 7. Be honest and specific without telling the interviewer everything about yourself.)

9. *What have you learned from previous job experiences?*
(If you have no job experience, discuss what you have learned from volunteer work, campus activities, and other sources. Don't be afraid to admit that there is still a lot for you to learn. As much as possible, relate this question to Questions 1 and 7.)

10. *How do you expect to achieve your job and career objectives?*
(Bring out what you hope to learn on the first job, how long you expect to stay at that level, and what you think is the next job level you should move to. Be as realistic as possible.)

11. *Why should we hire you?*

(Summarize your interests and assets and show how they fit the employer's job requirements. An effective closing will help you get an invitation to visit the employer or an offer for employment.)

Note: Each interviewer is different. Some interviewers may ask none of these questions, but most will ask questions that are closely related to them.

Source: Adapted and modified from J. Steele, Director, Career Planning and Placement, Boston College, personal communication.

This case raises several critical questions which you should be able to answer after reading this chapter. The questions include:

1. What are your career goals? What are your personal goals?
2. What questions are interviewers likely to ask when you look for a job?
3. In what ways can you learn about jobs and which ones may be the most appropriate for you?
4. How can career managment activities enhance your chances of having a successful career?

19

Career planning and development is important for a number of reasons. From the personal point of view, it can help people put their abilities, interest, and motivations to the best possible use. From an organizational point of view, it can help managers do a good job of managing and developing subordinates. This chapter provides an overview of the process of planning a career.

CAREER CONSCIOUSNESS

The choice of a career is more important to college students today than it was in the 1960s, when activism over social issues was more common. Then only about half the college students viewed their education as preparation for a successful career. But by 1973 the proportion had jumped to two-thirds, and it has continued to increase.

One of the most important reasons for this increased concern about careers is that the job market for college graduates has changed. During the 1960s, the rapidly growing economy stimulated a demand for college graduates to fill an increasing number of professional and managerial positions. In some fields, the shortages were so great that high-level positions often had to be filled with underqualified individuals. With the economic slowdown beginning in the early 1970s, the growth in demand for professionals and managers came to a halt just as the annual supply of college graduates was increasing at a rapid pace.[1]

The relative oversupply of graduates is likely to continue. In 1970 there were about 30 million workers in the 25 to 44 age range; they constituted about 35 percent of the work force. In 1990, about 60.5 million workers are expected to be in this age range, and they will constitute about 60 percent of the work force. The 25 to 44 age range is called *prime* because people of these ages are perceived as being ambitious, wanting advancement, and having skill. The tremendous increase of people in this age range will mean increasing competition for scarce jobs, particularly since these workers will, on the average, be better educated than many of their superiors.[2]

Careers are a life-long set of job experiences.

Career management means managing your job experiences.

Given the difficulties of finding jobs appropriate to their abilities, knowledge, and skills, it is understandable why college students have become job conscious. However, a career is much more important than finding a first job. For the purposes of this text, a **career** is "the sequence of behaviors and attitudes associated with past, present and anticipated future work-related experiences and role activities as perceived by either the individual or some other observer."[3] Thus a career is work-related and lifelong. As Table 19.1 shows, it has to do with both short- and long-range objectives, with particular choices, with the development and achievement of career choices, and with past and future experiences. It does not have to do with success or failure, the type of work in which a person is engaged, or activities engaged in outside of work.

Careers are important for most people because work itself is important. People want not only to make their own living but also to work at something that gives meaning to their lives. They want a sense of worth and uniqueness from their career. Generally, a career shoud meet a number of psychological needs and desires (as described in Chapter 15). They include:

1. The need for mastery or achievement related to ideas, situations, people, or other aspects of work.
2. The need for approval and recognition from supervisors, fellow workers, spouses, and others who are significant in one's life.
3. The need for social relationships. People at work are usually members of social units and feel they are part of a group.
4. The need for prestige or status. If properly chosen to fit the individual, a career can bring feelings of accomplishment, prestige, and status.
5. The desire for social equality and personal liberation. This desire seems particularly important for women and minorities. The first woman airline pilot in the United States was employed in 1973. Before then, pilots were always men. Under pressure from the Equal Employment Opportunity Commission, United Airlines agreed to actively recruit and hire qualified women and minorities.[4]

If these needs and desires are to be met, careful planning is necessary to ensure proper career development. **Career development** is "a developing, progressing process whereby an individual proceeds from a point of having no career direction to that of attaining a career consistent with his or her interests, abilities, and aspirations."[5] Many people think of career development as taking place very early in life, usually by the age of 20. As will be seen in the next section, however, career development is actually a long-term process.

CAREER STAGES

Just as there are stages people go through when growing up, so there are stages in careers. Generally, career stages follow a broad pattern.[6]

The Broad Pattern Although different researchers use different models, there appear to be three broad career stages—establishment, advancement, and maintenance. When young managers first enter an organization, becoming established and integrated is of primary concern to them. Their entry can be a stressful experience, and those who adjust best during this stage are those who can most easily deal with the insecurity and uncertainty that a new environment produces.

Once established and integrated into the organization, the young managers become concerned with achievement and promotion. At this stage advancement is very important for satisfying the need for achievement and a positive self-image.

Many managers reach a limit to advancement; the limit can be either organizational or personal. Some organizations have little turnover and

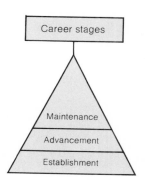

therefore little opportunity for promotion or advancement. On the personal side, some managers continue to grow while others reach a plateau, stagnate, or even decline. Many managers whose growth has ceased encounter a midcareer crisis when they realize that their goals either have been achieved or are unattainable. Some older managers feel that their knowledge and skills are obsolete, that their mobility is limited, and that they cannot compete in the job market. Consequently, they become more concerned about security than growth.

The Levinson Model Psychologist Donald Levinson has suggested that there are a number of basic stages and transitions in life: childhood and adolescence, novice, early adulthood, middle adulthood, and late adulthood. These are shown in Table 19.2.

Each stage begins as the one before is terminated. Thus there is a transition (and usually a crisis) period between stages. This section will briefly describe the stages, focusing primarily on the tasks to be performed in the transition between childhood and early adulthood—the novice stage.[7]

Age 0–22: Childhood and Adolescence During the stage from childhood to adolescence, the individual explores the world. The early adult transition, beginning at about age 17 and lasting to about age 22, is when the individual begins to form the adult personality and to make choices that will establish membership in the adult world. This stage involves pulling up roots and breaking away from family ties. Those who assert their independence at this time become gradually more self-sufficient and confident than those who prolong family ties.

Age 17–45: The Novice Phase and Early Adulthood The second and probably most dramatic stage of the life cycle is early adulthood. The body is at its peak functioning. In the early part of this period, the **novice phase,** major choices are made in areas such as occupation, marriage, and style of living—all of which form the preliminary adult identity. In terms of a career, the individual first becomes established at a junior level and then advances up formal or informal ladders until about age 40, when, if progress has been satisfactory, a new stage begins. If progress has not been satisfactory, the individual may become involved in radical job changes.

There are many tasks common to this novice phase; among them are

TABLE 19.2 Career Stages and Transitions

STAGES	TRANSITIONS
0–22 Childhood and adolescence	17–22 Early adult transition
17–45 Early adulthood	17–33 The novice phase
40–65 Middle adulthood	40–45 Midlife transition
65–? Late adulthood	60–65 Late adult transition

learning to relate to authority figures, forming peer relationships with adults of both sexes, and relating as an adult to people of different ages. Four developmental tasks are critical. They are:

1. Forming a dream—that is, developing an idea or vision of the kind of adult life the individual wants to lead. The dream usually starts out in a vague fashion and becomes sharper and clearer with age. Individuals who have a clearly delineated dream and who attain it are likely to feel successful. Those whose dreams remain vague or who fail to attain them are likely to feel unsuccessful regardless of their actual accomplishments.

2. Forming a **mentor relationship**—that is, finding a person, usually several years older, who can help the individual facilitate the realization of the dream. The relationship, which can be formal or informal, involves teaching, counseling, guidance, advising, and sponsoring. A major function of the mentor is to help the individual move away from dependency on parents and toward interaction as a peer with other adults.

3. Forming an occupation (as opposed to choosing an occupation, since the formation usually occurs over a number of years). Some individuals make early career choices and become physicians, lawyers, and the like. Most make their initial serious choice somewhere between the ages of 17 and 29 but try several different directions to sort out interests, discover various occupations, and eventually commit themselves to one of them. Occupational skills, credentials, and values must be developed.

4. Forming love relationships. Establishing relationships such as marriage is one of the tasks that appears to be important in moving into the adult world.

Age 40–65: Middle Adulthood The midlife transition, lasting from about age 40 to 45, involves the termination of early adulthood and the beginning of middle adulthood. It marks a potential midlife crisis, depending on how the novice phase is completed. Managers who are satisfied with their career to date will generally continue to be effective, developing pride in their achievements and experience. If the novice stage has not been satisfactory—if the dream is not in the process of being accomplished—a midlife crisis may emerge. Feelings of sadness, resentment, and frustration may develop. The crisis is often expressed by such behavior as a sudden job change, excessive drinking, a dramatic change in life-style, or other dramatic breaks with the past.

Age 56–?: Late Adulthood The late adulthood stage usually involves retiring from formal employment and (if earlier stages have proceeded well) satisfying certain needs and desires not satisfied earlier. Frequently this stage requires finding a new balance of involvement with society and the self. Many creative and intellectual works have been produced by people in their sixties, seventies, and eighties. (See Figure 19.1 for an indication of all the stages.)

The novice phase:

- Forming a dream
- Forming a mentor relationship
- Forming an occupation
- Forming love relationships

Stage	Age	
	75	
Late adulthood	70	Maintenance Decline Retirement
	65	
	60	Advancement Maintenance Stability Decline
	55	
Middle adulthood	50	Advancement Stability Decline
	45	
	40	Establishment and advancement
	35	
	30	Trial work period Possible establishment
Early adulthood	25	
	20	Initial work exploration Development of identity Pre-entry
	15	
Pre-adulthood	1	Childhood
	0	

FIGURE 19.1 Broad career stages

The Dalton, Thompson, and Price Model Three business professors—Gene Dalton, Paul Thompson, and Raymond Price—have developed a model that suggests there are four successive career stages: apprentice, colleague, mentor, and sponsor. Each stage involves different tasks, types of relationships, and psychological adjustments.[8]

Apprentice A young professional who enters an organization is an

apprentice—a beginner or learner under the direction of others. The individual must learn to perform some of the organization's tasks competently and must learn how to get things done through formal and informal channels. Many activities are routine, so the individual must be aggressive in searching out new and more challenging tasks.

The primary relationship of an apprentice is that of a subordinate to others. Thus ideally the new employee will work with a mentor who can counsel and sponsor. The presence or absence of a mentor can strongly influence the course of later career development.

Psychologically, the individual must adjust to the dependence involved in being a subordinate and be able to take supervision while at the same time exercising directed initiative and creativity. Many new employees expect to head their own projects or be able to work without taking orders and are psychologically unprepared for the apprentice role. A young, newly employed engineer was shocked to discover he would not even have a desk of his own.

The Dalton, Thompson, and Price model of career stages

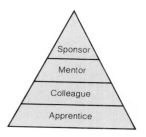

Colleague The individual who develops a reputation for being technically competent and able to work independently has entered Stage 2 (the colleague stage). To reach this stage, the individual needs a set of special skills or fund of knowledge. For example, someone working in a bank may concentrate on loans to utilities or systems analysis and computer programming or may develop skills in dealing with cutomers or clients. The individual should avoid becoming overly specialized but should develop a solid base of competence and expertise visible to those higher in the organization. At this stage the individual also needs ongoing peer relationships that can be used to get the job done better. The critical psychological events are the move from dependence to independence and the development of self-confidence.

Mentor Successful entry into Stage 3 (the mentor stage) means assuming responsibility for directing, guiding, influencing, and developing others, either directly as a manager or more informally as part of the work process. Interests and capabilities are broadened at this stage, and contact with others inside and outside the organization and its units may be increased. Activities may involve helping others get salary increases, obtaining contracts, and getting budgets approved.

Relationships with others change at this stage as a result of the changed activities. The individual assumes responsibility for the work of others. Interpersonal skills become highly important in supervising, coordinating, and delegating work and setting objectives. The psychological events are the willingness and ability to build the confidence of junior people and to take the responsibility for the output of others. Some very competent people are not psychologically suited for these demands and prefer to remain in Stage 2 in a situation that allows them to exercise broad influence without requiring much supervisory responsibility.

Sponsor   Not all people reach Stage 4 (the sponsor stage). The clearest characteristic of the sponsor stage is the influence the individual has on the direction of the organization or a major unit of it. This influence does not need to come directly through line management positions. Instead it may be manifested by developing new ideas for products, markets, or services and by interfacing and negotiating with key people in the environment.

At this stage the individual usually engages in at least one of three roles: manager, idea innovator, and internal entrepreneur. Many upper-level managers are in this stage, and so are idea innovators. Internal entrepreneurs are people who have new ideas or who get ideas from the innovator and then have sufficient influence to bring people, resources, and money together to execute the ideas and thus affect the direction of the organization.

Key work relationships at this stage may involve the selection and development of others. Outside relationships are critical both for gathering current information and for giving the organization visibility. Essential psychological achievements are learning to resist second-guessing subordinates and others on operating decisions and learning to use power to form strong political alliances.

A strength of the Dalton, Thompson, and Price model is that it avoids the fallacy that career development consists only of moving up the managerial hierarchy. The model suggests instead that individuals can be successful at the colleague, mentor, and sponsor levels, depending on their own needs and aspirations.

THE FIRST JOB

A career involves a sequence of jobs or stages, and the first job can influence the rest of that sequence. This section will examine several aspects of the initial job experience that can pose both problems and opportunities for the entire career.

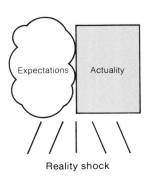

Reality shock

Reality Shock   Many college graduates enter the world of work with unrealistic information or expectations. The result is **reality shock,** a situation where the actuality does not agree with the expectations. One factor contributing to reality shock is the rosy view of the organization painted by recruiters. Another factor is the lack of work challenge that typifies an entry-level job. Many new graduates expect to have a great deal of challenge and responsibility on their first job and find that they are really apprentices working under close supervision, their abilities underutilized.[9]

There are a number of ways in which reality shock could be reduced. Recruiters and others in the organization could provide a more realistic view of the organization and more challenging work. The new employee, on the other hand, could more carefully explore the organization before entering it and, once there, could seek out innovative, challenging work. Students also need to understand that when they accept a particular job, they may tend to idealize it while downgrading other jobs. They need to prepare for the perceptual distortion (reality shock) that can occur.[10]

The First Supervisor As mentioned earlier, the first supervisor can greatly affect the career of the new recruit. The supervisor has a great deal of control not only over job assignments but also over organizational rewards and therefore is in a key position to launch and direct a subordinate's career development. Moreover, the first supervisor can serve as a mentor and role model and thus exert a tremendous positive influence on the subordinate. Such supervisors have been shown to figure largely in the management career progress of their subordinates.[11] In fact, the influence of this type of supervisor is just as important as the influence of job assignments on the later careers of managers. The best mentor and role model is the supervisor who demonstrates competence, who has influence with superiors, and who provides stimulation, support, and feedback to subordinates.

The first boss can also negatively affect the career of the new employee. Many managers have a stereotyped image of recent college graduates, viewing them as overly ambitious and unrealistic in their expectations, too theoretical and naive to be given a challenging initial assignment, too immature and inexperienced to be given much responsibility, and unskilled in communications. Treatment based on these assumptions can stifle the career development of the young subordinate.[12]

If such is the situation, the new recruit should find a mentor elsewhere in the organization, transfer to another department, or find another job. In one case a new employee found a mentor who was manager of another department. She was able to go to the other manager to discuss work assignments and to get advice and criticism. Eventually the other manager acted as a sponsor to get the new employee transferred to another unit in the organization. Thus the individual was able to overcome the initial handicap of an unhelpful supervisor by exercising her own initiative.

Critical to your career are:

- Your first job
- Your first supervisor
- Awareness of norms and values of the organization

ORGANIZATIONAL SOCIALIZATION

A person's life history and career can be seen as a series of passages from one role or level to another, with each passage stimulating an adjustment that can affect the person's identity, values, attitudes, and behavior. The discussion of the first job makes it clear that the passage from the role of college student to that of employee can be crucial to career development. It is primarily during the first job experience that the new employee undergoes **organizational socialization,** which means learning not only the role requirements of the job but also the values and behavior norms of the organization.[13]

Organizational socialization: Conforming to norms of organization at beginning of first job.

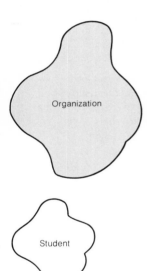

Anticipatory socialization: Conforming to norms of organization before beginning first job.

Organizations typically have a unique, well-defined subculture with norms for the behavior and interaction of the employees. For example, employees of one organization are fond of saying, "There is a right way, a wrong way, and the X Company way." Knowing the norms of a particular company is essential for succeeding at that company or, sometimes, even for obtaining a job with it. A man applying for a high-level administrative position in a large, conservative organization has little chance of being considered for the job if he appears in a checked suit and flowered shirt and tie.

The process of socialization can start even before the first job begins. Called **anticipatory socialization** (presocialization), it involves the adoption of attitudes, values, and identity perceived to be associated with a role before assuming that role. During the course of their education students learn some attitudes, values, and identities associated with particular occupational or organizational roles. They can learn more about particular organizations by talking to other students and by interviewing with recruiters from a number of organizations before taking the first job. Anticipatory socialization helps smooth the passage from the student role to the first work role.[14]

The idea of presocialization (anticipatory socialization) is to shortcut the socialization process by recruiting those who are already acquainted with many of the norms of a particular job or profession. In the process, however, a benefit may be lost—the importation to the organization of new ideas and new sensitivities.

Cultural anthropologists have noted that many cultures that have not developed by Western standards tend to restrict the migration of strangers into their midst. More developed cultures, on the other hand, allow strangers to enter and influence them.

Strangers often bring innovation, new curiosity unconstrained by "the way it has always been." A static culture must rely on those already immersed in the culture for development. Imagine the state of preindustrial Japan if it had maintained its policy of denying foreigners access to its shores. If this cultural anthropological phenomenon is applied to business, excessive presocializations might be viewed as more detrimental than helpful.

EQUAL EMPLOYMENT AND CAREERS

In many U.S. organizations, entry to and advancement in the management hierarchy has been limited to white Anglo-Saxon men. Many capable people have been excluded from pursuing careers in management because they do not conform to pivotal norms (pivotal norms were discussed in Chapter 16) regarding race, religion, or sex. To some extent, this situation is changing. Largely stimulated by federal and state equal employment legislation, organizations have begun to alter their hiring and promotion practices to comply with affirmative action programs. A major goal of such programs is to move more women and minorities into management-level positions. However, radical changes in employment practices have created new problems—not only for organizations but also for the careers of those directly affected by the changes.[15]

Tokenism Some minorities and women are hired simply as an effort at **tokenism**—a way of meeting the organization's obligations to affirmative action programs. The token person is usually put in a highly visible or specially created position but has little power or opportunity for advancement. Tokenism takes its toll in extreme psychological stress even when some career success is attained. Tokenism will likely diminish when minorities and women gain a substantial percentage of management positions. An increase in their numbers in such positions will also provide a support group for any remaining victims of tokenism.[16]

Lack of Mentors or Role Models A factor contributing to the stress of a token person is the lack of a mentor or role model that is usually associated with tokenism. As already seen, a mentor is vitally important to career success. Only recently, however, have management programs for women been developed to help socialize them into their new roles. Without a role model, the token person is a pioneer of sorts, required to break through barriers to gain respect. The task is especially difficult when the token person is a new college graduate with little previous experience. However, in time this difficulty too will ease, as minorities and women rise in the management hierarchy and thus act as mentors for those below them.[17]

Leadership Problems Prejudice still operates against women and minorities in management. It is manifested not only by superiors but also by peers and subordinates. Those who are the objects of such prejudice consequently lack influence in decision making in the work group and are limited in the exercise of leadership. Here again, it is the recent college graduates among minorities and women who are most likely to encounter this problem, although it also exists at higher levels.[18] In an unguarded moment, a hospital administrator recently told a woman manager that she could never become an assistant administrator, in spite of her obvious qualifications, because "people don't like to work for a woman."

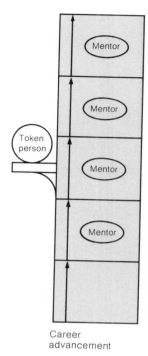

Career advancement

The token employee is hired for a highly visible position, cut off from further advancement, and lacking mentors.

Problems in equal employment:

- Tokenism
- Lack of mentors or role models
- Poor leadership

THE DUAL-CAREER FAMILY

With ever-increasing numbers of women responding to career opportunities, the number of dual-career families is increasing rapidly. The dual-career family is susceptible to stresses beyond the usual ones associated with work. There is no perfect strategy for coping with such problems. The most important ingredient for success is the spouses' willingness to discuss and agree on a strategy. For example, two college professors who are married to each other have decided that if they must leave a particular geographic area, they will take turns in picking the new location. If it is the wife's turn and she takes a teaching job in another geographic area, the husband will attempt to find work there. Concrete strategies for dealing with actual or potential problems created by the dual-career family include:

1. *Limiting either family or career demands.* This can mean having no children or having only one child, thereby placing greater emphasis on the career. Conversely, it can mean emphasizing the family and limiting the career growth for both husband and wife. Day-care centers for children and flexible or part-time work schedules can be employed in these options.

2. *Shifting the stages of work and family events.* The family, as well as the career, develops in stages, and the demands change for each stage. Thus husband and wife can postpone the child rearing stage until after they are both established in their careers, or they can postpone their periods of maximum work involvement until the children have grown up enough to be somewhat independent.

3. *Segmenting or compartmentalizing work and family activities so that both need not be dealt with at the same time.* There can be a total concentration on the career during working hours and a total involvement with the family the rest of the time. This is not new for women. What is new is the meshing of both partners' schedules in the dual-career family.

4. *Husband and wife participating in a joint venture.* Establishing a small family business is one way in which both husband and wife can work toward career success. However, in a joint venture it may be difficult to segment work and family concerns (and there is a possible problem of personal competitiveness).

5. *Pursuing completely independent careers.* Adaptations to this career strategy include the use of full-time child care and long-distance commuting. The strategy can be satisfactory for those who do not need to form close relationships but may not work well for others.

    Some commuting couples who are separated because of geographically distant jobs appear to have successful marriages despite (or because of) the separation, but for most people separation increases stress.[19]

Clearly, many strategies are available to cope with dual-career problems. The best strategy, of course, is one that can be modified as necessary. In one case a man received a lucrative job offer requiring a move to an area where his wife would have had little opportunity to move up in her own career. If the situation had occurred a few years earlier, they agreed that there would probably have been little discussion, and they would have automatically moved to the new location. In this instance, however, the husband turned down the job offer. Both spouses feel that the decision has strengthened their marriage.

DEVELOPING INITIAL PERSONAL CAREER PLANS

Careers, even managerial careers, often evolve more out of accident than design. Some people are remarkably lax in making major career decisions, passively letting changes in the external environment determine the organization they work for or the types of jobs they accept.[20] As one manager in a large organization put it: "Why should I worry? The company knows about me and will advance me when I am ready." Far too many people are like this manager. They fail to take the initiative in career planning, preferring to wait for someone else to act or for some event to spur them to action. One modern text on career planning suggests that "most people spend less time gathering and consciously analyzing data on possible occupations to enter than they do on the cars they buy."[21]

Another mistake many people make is to view an early career decision as immutable. Frequently actions during the ages of 17 to 35 are exploratory. One woman who had a master's degree in social work left a successful career in that field at the age of 34 to become a caterer. Her catering business is highly successful, and she is enjoying her new career.

Developing Self-Awareness Self-knowledge is central to developing a personal career plan. In fact, career choice is often determined primarily by one's self-concept.[22] One good beginning to planning a career is to obtain career counseling and guidance. This service, or information about it, is often provided on campus. Self-administered career planning exercises can also be useful. Two of the best known of these exercises are to write the kind of obituary that you would desire for yourself at some specific time in the future and to write the kind of feature article that you would like to see about yourself on the front page of your local newspaper in ten years. Many of the questions in Table 19.1 can be helpful too, as can talking to instructors and friends about your strengths and weaknesses. Finally, many universities now offer courses in career planning and development. Whatever approach you use, the key objective is to identify your capabilities and your interests.

Learning about Jobs and Organizations Another kind of necessary knowledge concerns jobs and organizations. As in obtaining self-awareness, this kind of knowledge entails a learning process. Specific information about many organizations and the types of graduates they hire can be obtained from the *College Placement Annual*, a publication that is usually available in the college placement office. Another source of information about the job market is the U.S. Department of Labor's *Monthly Labor Review*, which details the industries where jobs are most and least abundant. For example, the number of accountants, bank and finance managers, health administrators, and computer systems analysts is expected to increase by 1985, while the number of college teachers, postmasters, and funeral directors is expected to decrease.[23]

Steps to developing initial personal career plans

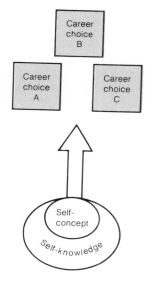

Self-concept often determines career choice; thus self-knowledge is important for a good career plan.

On the Job

WHEN YOU BECOME MANAGEMENT

"I'm probably the youngest general foreman in the plant. . . . I'm in the chassis line right now. There's 372 people working for us, hourly. And thirteen foremen. I'm the lead general foreman. . . .

"If you're a deadhead when you're an hourly man and you go on supervision, they don't have much use for you. But if they know the guy's aggressive and he tries to do a job, they tend to respect him. . . .

"When I came here I wanted to be a utility man. He goes around and spot relieves everybody. I thought that was the greatest thing in the world. When the production manager asked me would I consider training for a foreman's job, boy! My sights left utility. I worked on all the assembly lines. I spent eighteen months on the lines, made foreman, and eighteen months later I made general foreman. . . .

"A lot of the old-timers had more time in the plant than I had time in the world. Some of 'em had thirty, thirty-five years' service. I had to overcome their resentment and get their respect. I was taught one thing: to be firm but fair. Each man has got an assignment of work to do. If he has a problem [derived from the work], correct his problem. If he doesn't have a problem, correct him.

"If an hourly man continued to let the work go, you have to take disciplinary action. You go progressively, depending on the situation. If it was me being a young guy and he resented it, I would overlook it and try to get him to think my way. If I couldn't, I had to go to the disciplinary route—which would be a reprimand, a warning.

"If they respect you, they'll do anything for you. Be aggressive. . . . I have to know each and every one of my foremen. I know how they react, all thirteen.

"There's a few on the line you can associate with. I haven't as yet. . . . The more you get to know somebody, it's hard to distinguish between boss and friend. This isn't good for my profession. We work together, we live together. But they always gotta realize you're the boss.

"I want to get quality first, then everything else'll come. The line runs good, the production's good, you get your cost and you get your good workmanship.

When they hire in, you gotta show 'em you're firm. We've got company rules . . . that we try to enforce from the beginning.

"The case begins with a reprimand, a warning procedure. A lotta times they don't realize this is the first step to termination. . . . If you catch a guy stealing, the first step *is* a termination. In the case of workmanship, it is a progressive period. . . .

"There's an old saying: The boss ain't always right but he's still the boss. He has things applied to him from top management, where they see the whole picture. A lot of times I don't agree with it. . . .

"Prior to going on supervision, you think hourly. But when you become management, you have to look out for the company's best interests. You always have to present a management attitude.

"Out here, it's a big job. There's a lot of responsibility. It's not like working in a soup factory, where all you do is make soup cans. If you get a can punched wrong, you put it on the side and don't worry about it. You can't do that with a five-thousand-dollar car."

Source: Wheeler Stanley, quoted in *Working: People Talk about What They Do All Day and How They Feel about What They Do* © 1972, 1974 by Studs Terkel. Reprinted by permission of Pantheon Books, a division of Random House, Inc.

Personal work experience in part-time, summer, or volunteer jobs can be invaluable in choosing the type of job or organization most appropriate for a specific career. Before even going to college, one young woman took a volunteer job at a day-care center for abused children to help her decide whether her thoughts about becoming a child psychologist were realistic. The experience confirmed her dream and made her more certain about her career.

The job hunter should acquire as much information as possible about prospective employers and types of organizations. Interviews with recruiters can begin even before serious interest has developed about a particular job. People who actively learn about jobs and organizations before completing college are in a good position to begin career planning.

Determining Initial Career Plans For some, formulating career plans is relatively easy and quick. For others it is a complicated process that can last a number of years. The assumption that most people have made firm career choices in their early twenties is wrong. The first serious choice sometimes occurs between 17 and 29, but even when it is definitive and successfully enacted, it is sometimes followed by another career choice, also successfully enacted. An individual may take several years to determine interests, to discover the most suitable occupations, and to become committed to one of them.

As mentioned earlier, the first job is highly important, since it is there that the individual begins the process of actual, rather than anticipatory, socialization. It is also there that the individual begins, as an apprentice, to perform organizational tasks competently. Competence in critical tasks of the organization is essential for an individual to begin developing a reputation for knowledge and ability.

There is disagreement as to whether people should specialize early. A *Business Week* article suggests that experience should be sought in several fields, such as manufacturing, sales, and finance. It adds: "Get out of your specialty fast, unless you decide that's all you ever want to do. This means rapid rejection of the notion that you are a professional engineer, lawyer, scientist, or anything but a manager."[24] More formal research suggests that "it is often advisable to become a specialist, at least temporarily, and gain a reputation for competence within that specialty. . . . A person who has done outstanding work in one area is more likely than a jack-of-all-trades to gain visibility in a large organization."[25]

This contrasting advice points up the importance of a mentor who can guide, counsel, and support the new college graduate. Almost all the research agrees that the first supervisor is highly important in career development or planning. Should this person be unable or unwilling to undertake the mentor role, the individual just starting out should actively look for someone else to do so on either a formal or an informal basis.

Career planning and development clearly extend beyond the first job. Many individuals shift from one job and organization to another in the search for opportunities to fulfill their dreams and to advance. But many managers settle in one job and give little thought to ongoing career planning. In fact, "most managers, when asked how much time they spend on their own career planning, are surprised to realize how little they do. Usually they spend far more time managing their subordinates' careers than their own."[26]

Choosing a career and becoming successful in it involve a number of important steps, including self-knowledge and organizational knowledge, skills in interviewing and resume writing, socialization without the loss of independence, finding a mentor, and plotting a continuing career path.

SUMMARY

As suggested by the questions in Table 19.1, people should have a certain degree of self-awareness and at least a tentative career plan before looking for a job. A tentative career plan is also helpful in determining which courses to take in college and which types of jobs to look for after college. Firm evidence exists that proper career planning allows an individual to make the best use of abilities, values, interests, and motivations. Those who do not plan properly may wind up desperate.

The evidence is also clear that career development depends heavily on the first job and the first supervisor. It is here that organizational socialization takes place and that the new employee has the opportunity to look for, and work with, a mentor. People who do not

have good mentors are less likely to satisfy their dreams and to become successful in a chosen career.

The process also works the other way. The effective manager is one who can serve as a mentor to newer, younger subordinates. The manager who is on the wrong career track finds it difficult to serve as a role model, since he or she is likely to feel frustrated and unhappy rather than calm and confident.

Career planning and development is an extended process. Managers need to think about their own careers as well as those of their subordinates. One of the most important characteristics of the effective organization is the ability to select, develop, and place the right people in the right jobs.

STUDY QUESTIONS

1. How well have you planned your own career? What steps should you take to make certain you are headed in the right direction?

2. Interview friends and acquaintances. How well have they planned their careers?

3. How do you feel about a working spouse? How might your feelings and attitudes affect your dual-career family if you had one?

4. What are your expectations about your first job? How can you check to see if they are realistic?

5. Go to the alumni office and find the names of five recent graduates of your school. Call them and ask about their experiences after they accepted their first job.

6. Discuss your career plans with the placement director, a professor, or some other knowledgeable person. What have you learned about your career possibilities?

7. What problems do women and members of minority groups face in their careers with organizations? Discuss.

Case for Discussion

THE RAYMOND CHEMICAL COMPANY

After receiving B.S. and M.S. degrees in industrial engineering from a well-known eastern university, Larry Jones, joined the Buffalo plant of the Raymond Chemical Company. Jones, who had been at the top of his graduating class, was considered a very promising addition to the staff, and the plant manager felt that his knowledge of mathematical techniques would be valuable in solving a number of pressing problems.

He was assigned initially to an experimental group that had earned the reputation of being able to solve the toughest of technical problems. He fit in well with the group, and he soon was seen as a first-rate idea person in a very idea-conscious group. One of Jones's early contributions, a mathematical model of materials flows, caught the attention of factory manager Charlie Jenison. Jenison, who was second in command at the Buffalo plant, asked Jones to become his assistant, and Jones accepted.

As Jenison's assistant, Jones came up with a number of interesting ideas. Though his suggestions were not always immediately workable, they were invariably thought-provoking. Jenison felt that with more practical experience Jones would soon be ready for a top-level management job. He proposed to Jones that he transfer to the inventory control department, where he could serve as assistant to the manager, Allan Wilkinson. Though it was never mentioned by Jenison, Jones knew that Wilkinson had only four years to go until retire-

ment, and he believed that he was being groomed to be Wilkinson's successor.

In the inventory control group problems arose from the start. Wilkinson persistently harassed Jones and delighted in presenting him with problems almost impossible to solve. Wilkinson then taunted him with comments such as, "Your bright ideas aren't too good under real conditions." When Jones developed new approaches, Wilkinson blocked their use by saying that they were not practical. He did allow Jones to introduce one system, but it contained some costly bugs. Wilkinson ordered it removed with the comment, "I told you it wouldn't work." After a few months on the job, Jones was either ignored by Wilkinson or given only routine work.

One evening he decided he had had enough. He waited for Jenison after work and told him about his difficulties with Wilkinson. When he asked to be reassigned, Jenison assented and suggested a transfer to the job of assistant manager of production control. Jones agreed, and left Jenison's office feeling much less frustrated.

The following morning Jones learned that the production control department was headed by Phil Burgess, a man who had only five years left until retirement and who, for all practical purposes, was another Wilkinson. Jones was upset. He wondered why Jenison, whose judgment he respected, had transferred him to Burgess's department.

Source: The case and the questions following it are adapted from John G. Hutchinson, *Organizations: Theory and Classical Concepts* (New York: Holt, Rinehart and Winston, 1967), pp. 32–33. Reprinted by permission of Jean M. Hutchinson, executor, estate of Prof. John G. Hutchinson, deceased, Graduate School of Business, Columbia University.

1. Why do you think Jenison did what he did?

2. Assuming Jones wishes to stay with the Raymond Chemical Company, what do you suggest he do to make his new assignment less frustrating?

3. If you were Jones, would you stay with the company? Explain.

FOR YOUR CAREER

1. Getting a sponsor in an organization is important to the success of your career in that organization.
2. It pays to work hard and be aware of the key people in the organization.
3. Your first job is critical. Choose it carefully. Gather as much information as you can regarding what you will be expected to do, whom you will work with, and how your boss will deal with you.
4. You are responsible for your career. Only you can determine whether a particular organization suits you.
5. Advancement usually takes longer than anticipated. Organizations change but often more slowly than planned.
6. A career is a set of lifelong experiences in organizations. Since you will probably work in organizations, it pays to plan your experiences there so they they will be rewarding.
7. Being mobile—ready to leave a job or an organization when appropriate—along with being a good performer and being visible, help ensure you of having many career opportunities.

FOOTNOTES

1. D. Yankelovich, "Turbulence in the Working World—Angry Workers, Happy Grads," *Psychology Today,* December 1974, pp. 81–87.
2. J. Flint, "Oversupply of Young Workers Expected to Tighten Jobs Race," *New York Times,* June 25, 1978, p. 1.
3. R. Kopelman, Baruch College, City University of New York, personal communication.
4. M. Satchell, "Now Women Pilots Get Their Turn with the Airlines," *Parade,* June 25, 1978, pp. 4–5.
5. T. Bachhuber and R. Harwood, *Directions: A Guide to Career Planning* (Boston: Houghton Mifflin, 1978), p. 2.
6. E. Erickson, *Childhood and Soceity,* 2nd ed. (New York: Norton, 1963); D. Super, *The Psychology of Careers* (New York: Harper & Bros., 1957); and E. Schein, *Career Dynamics: Matching Individual and Organizational Needs* (Reading, Mass.: Addison-Wesley, 1978).
7. D. Levinson, *The Seasons of a Man's Life* (New York: Knopf, 1978); D. Levinson, "Growing Up with the Dream," *Psychology Today,* January 1978, p. 20; and G. Sheehy, *Passages* (New York: Dutton, 1976).
8. G. Dalton, P. Thompson, and R. Price, "The Four Stages of Professional Careers—A New Look at Performance by Professionals," *Organizational Dynamics* 6 (Summer 1977): 19–42: G. Dalton and P. Thompson, "Accelerating Obsolescence of Older Engineers," *Harvard Business Review* 49 (September–October 1971): 57–68; and P. Thompson and G. Dalton, "Are R&D Organizations Obsolete?" *Harv-*

ard Business Review 54 (November–December 1976): 105–117.
9. A. G. Athos and L. B. Ward, *Student Expectations of Corporate Life: Implications for Managerial Recruiting* (Boston: Harvard University, Graduate School of Business Administration, 1972); J. P. Wanous, "Realistic Job Previews for Organizational Recruitment," *Personnel* 52 (April 1975): 50–60. J. P. Wanous, "Organizational Entry: Newcomers Moving from Outside to Inside," *Psychological Bulletin* 84 (July 1977): 601–618; P. J. Manhardt, "Job Orientation of Male and Female College Graduates in Business," *Personnel Psychology* 25 (July 1972): 361–368; and D. A. Ondrack, "Emerging Occupational Values: A Review and Some Findings," *Academy of Management Journal* 16 (September 1973): 423–432.
10. D. E. Berlew and D. T. Hall, "The Socialization of Managers: Effects of Expectations on Performance," *Administrative Science Quarterly* 11 (June 1966): 207–229; and R. J. Campbell, "Career Development: The Young Business Manager," paper presented at Longitudinal Approaches to Career Development symposium, American Psychological Association annual meeting, San Francisco, 1968.
11. D. W. Bray, R. J. Campbell, and D. L. Grant, *Formative Years in Business: A Long-Term AT&T Study of Managerial Lives* (New York: Wiley-Interscience, 1974).
12. E. E. Jennings, *Routes to the Executive Suite* (New York: McGraw-Hill, 1971); E. H. Schein, "How to Break in the College Graduate," *Harvard Business*

Review 42 (November–December 1964): 68–76; and J. S. Livingstone, "Pygmalion in Management," *Harvard Business Review* 47 (July–August 1969): 81–89.

13. E. H. Schein, "Organizational Socialization and the Profession of Management," *Industrial Management Review* 9 (Winter 1968): 1–15; J. Van Maanen and E. H. Schein, "Career Development," in *Improving Life at Work: Behavioral Science Approaches to Organizational Change,* ed. J. R. Hackman and J. L. Suttle (Santa Monica, Calif.: Goodyear Publishing, 1977).

14. D. T. Hall, *Careers in Organizations* (Pacific Palisades, Calif.: Goodyear Publishing, 1976).

15. G. W. Bowman, "What Helps or Harms Promotability?" *Harvard Business Review* 42 (January–February 1964): 6–26; and R. M. Powell, *Race, Religion and the Promotion of the American Executive,* Monograph No. AA-3 (Columbus: Ohio State University, College of Administrative Science, 1969).

16. R. M. Kanter, "Tokenism: Opportunity or Trap?" *MBA* 12 (January 1978): 15–21; and B. Rosen and T. H. Jerdee, "Sex Stereotyping in the Executive Suite," *Harvard Business Review,* 52 (March–April 1974): 45–48.

17. "Why Women Need Their Own MBA Programs," *Business Week,* February 23, 1974, pp. 102, 107; and Kanter, "Tokenism: Opportunity or Trap?"

18. J. E. Haefner, "Sources of Discrimination among Employees: A Survey Investigation," *Journal of Applied Psychology* 62 (June 1977): 265–270; W. C. Hamner et al., "Race and Sex as Determinants of Ratings by Potential Employers in a Simulated Work Sampling Task," *Journal of Applied Psychology* 59 (December 1974): 705–711; S. A. Richards and

C. L. Jaffee, "Blacks Supervising Whites: A Study of Interracial Difficulties in Working Together in a Simulated Organization," *Journal of Applied Psychology* 56 (June 1972): 234–240; and Rosen and Jerdee, "Sex Stereotyping in the Executive Suite."

19. L. Bailyn, "Accommodation of Work to Family: An Analysis of Couples with Two Careers," in *Working Couples,* ed. R. Rappoport et al. (New York: Harper & Row, 1978); D. T. Hall, "A Model of Coping with Role Conflict: The Role Behavior of College Educated Women," *Administrative Science Quarterly* 17 (December 1972): 471–486; and L. Bailyn, "Career and Family Orientations of Husbands and Wives in Relation to Marital Happiness," *Human Relations* 23 (February 1970): 97–113.

20. A. Roe and R. Baruch, "Occupational Changes in the Adult Years," *Personnel Administration* 30 (July–August 1967): 26–32.

21. Hall, *Careers in Organizations,* p. 39.

22. A. Korman, "Self-esteem as a Moderator of the Relationship between Self-perceived Abilities and Vocational Choice," *Journal of Applied Psychology* 51 (February 1967): 65–67; and A. Korman, "Toward a Hypothesis of Work Behavior," *Journal of Applied Psychology* 54 (February 1970): 31–41.

23. "Where the Jobs Will Open Up over the Next Decade," *U.S. News & World Report,* December 27, 1976, pp. 82–83.

24. "Plotting a Route to the Top," *Business Week,* October 12, 1974, p. 128.

25. Dalton, Thompson, and Price, "The Four Stages of Professional Careers—A New Look at Performance by Professionals," p. 26.

26. Hall, *Careers in Organizations,* p. 40.

Management and the Environment

PART VI

Values, Power, and Ethics

CHAPTER 20

CONTENTS

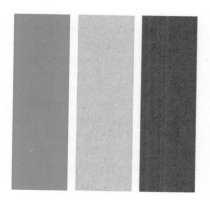

A CRISIS OF CONSCIENCE

Universal Neucleonics was the parent company for a number of wholly owned smaller companies, among them Quasar Stellar. The president and the controller of Quasar Stellar sent regular monthly reports to the parent company. Over a period of time they began to distort the reports to reflect their operation more favorably. They inaccurately reported the status of projects, and they grossly inflated actual and projected earnings. When the true figures were revealed, the year-end earnings of Universal Neucleonics were considerably lower than had been previously predicted. Shortly thereafter, Quasar's president and controller resigned.

Why had the deception been perpetrated? To find out, corporate headquarters interviewed five of the company's key managers: William Heller, vice-president of engineering; George Kessler, vice-president of manufacturing; Peter Loomis, vice-president of marketing; Paul Brown, vice-president of industrial relations; and Donald Morgan, chief accountant. The first four men had all reported directly to the president; the fifth had reported directly to the controller. All five had had access to information showing that the monthly reports were distorted, but none had reported the true state of affairs to corporate management.

Following is a brief summary of the interviews.

William Heller, vice-president of engineering: I was initially skeptical when the decision was made to shift from a subcontractor approach to bidding on primary contracts. Then I became very enthusiastic. The really big ones we tried for were the Apollo and LEM (lunar landing craft) contracts. If we had gotten one or both of these contracts, the engineering department would have been right out in front. Looking back, I was shortsighted and did not take into consideration the potential impact on both engineering and other parts of the company. I am an engineering manager, not a business manager. As a result, when things went wrong, I accepted the business decision to modify the re-

ports. Actually, I tried not to know what was in the reports. I wouldn't want a subordinate of mine second-guessing me and going around me. Perhaps the solution would be to have the corporation use an internal audit team.

George Kessler, vice-president of manufacturing: I was opposed from the beginning. Not long after we had a series of meetings, I was no longer involved in what went into the reports. I knew they were padded, but I wanted to work within the system. No self-respecting manager would go around his boss. Perhaps a solution would be to have the monthly report routinely include minority reports as the Supreme Court does. Another solution might be to have each manager report routinely to his counterpart at corporate headquarters.

Peter Loomis, vice-president of marketing: I had only been with the company nine months and perhaps I was overly optimistic about our odds of getting those two contracts. But there was a lot of pressure from corporate headquarters to try for both. Once the decision was made, we couldn't back down or we would lose face. Headquarters decided that this was the direction we would go. When things went wrong, they looked for scapegoats to sacrifice. I had to support my boss and be loyal to him. Besides, how much should personal morality enter into business decisions?

Paul Brown, vice-president of industrial relations: At first, people were really enthusiastic. It was like they were smoking pot. Then, when the trouble began to show up, a lot of people began to leave. I think that some of the people stayed only out of loyalty to their boss and the company.

Donald Morgan, chief accountant: We report only on data given to us. Our job is not to set policy or to question management decisions. Our job is to follow instructions.[1]

This case raises several critical questions, which you should be able to answer after reading this chapter. The questions include:

1. What are some examples of political behavior in organizations? Is political behavior good or bad?
2. Are business people more or less ethical than the population as a whole? Explain.
3. Should organizations have written standards of values and ethics? Why?
4. What are your own personal values and ethics?

20

The opening case, which shows real managers in a real situation, demonstrates how values can affect behavior and how managers can exercise power. What might have happened if the chief accountant had reported to the parent company that the figures were incorrect? How ethical was the managers' behavior?

This chapter will critically examine the influence of values, power, political tactics, and ethics on managerial behavior, focusing primarily on the individual. The large issue of the social responsibility of organizations will be discussed in Chapter 23.

THE IMPORTANCE OF VALUES

Many managers feel that their behavior is objective—that they gather the facts and then make rational decisions. This attitude is valid, however, only if the managers understand that their personal values and beliefs are among the facts. One of the most pervasive values learned in early childhood is that "squealing" is wrong. G. Gordon Liddy, one of the first people sentenced as a result of the Watergate burglary, marched off to jail proud of the fact that he had not squealed. There was evidence that, had he chosen to talk, he would have received a shorter jail sentence. The message in the case at the beginning of this chapter is that some managers will refuse to squeal even if their refusal may harm the company. This is clear evidence of behavior being affected by values rather than being completely objective.

Of course, some people do blow the whistle—for example, A. Earnest Fitzgerald, a deputy for management systems in the air force. In 1965 Fitzgerald was earning $31,000 a year. He blew the whistle on a $2 billion cost overrun on the C–5A (a transport plane), a fact that the Pentagon was apparently trying to conceal from Congress. He soon lost his job. In 1969 General Motors recalled 2.4 million Chevrolets to repair a faulty design that let carbon monoxide filter into the automobile. The recall cost was reported to be over $100 million. Edward Gregory is the safety inspector who repeatedly warned the company that the autos were unsafe. When he got no results from GM, he contacted Ralph Nader. After several reported deaths from carbon monoxide poisoning, the automobiles were recalled. At last report, Gregory was still working for General Motors (perhaps because he is a member of the autoworkers' union).

Relatively little is known about whistle blowers, but they seem to have a high degree of personal responsibility and ethics. Frequently they suffer retaliation by being transferred, demoted, isolated, cut off from responsibility, or fired. For example, shortly after Fitzgerald reported on the C–5A overrun, he was transferred to examining the cost problems of bowling alleys in Thailand and was no longer invited to management meetings.[2]

Values are relatively permanent ideals (or ideas) that influence and shape the nature of people's behavior and determine what they will consider desirable or undesirable, good or bad. People use values as guides when they are faced with a choice among various actions. Values are usually acquired early in life; they reflect family and educational background and are influenced by peers, teachers, and the culture.[3]

The Role of Values In stressing the role of values in influencing behavior, psychologist Robert McMurray has suggested that many problems involving people arise in the area of values. Examples of these problems are (1) the factory owner who is usually rational but who will go out of business rather than be forced to negotiate with a union, (2) the scientist who becomes a poor security risk because of misguided idealism, (3) the factory worker who welds pop bottles inside the body of the automobile just for kicks, (4) the labor leader who starts a costly strike just to show his muscle, and (5) the intellectuals and politicians who push for confiscatory taxes because they believe that profits are unethical.[4]

A study of more than a thousand managers concludes that:

1. Most managers are pragmatic; that is, they have values that contribute to success. A smaller number of managers have ethical-moral values. For them, the important ideas are those that they view as being morally right rather than successful.
2. Value systems vary widely among managers.
3. Personal values affect corporate strategy and goals as well as day-to-day decisions.
4. The personal values of individual managers have both a direct and an indirect effect on organizations.
5. Personal values are in turn influenced by organizations.
6. Differences and similarities of values help explain both conflict and cooperation among managers.[5]

Aids to success

According to a twelve-year study, values appear to be related to success. The more successful managers adhere to the values they learned in early life. They have certain values in common, such as a belief in the importance of integrity and of being fair to others; they have a sense of personal worth; and they believe in promoting the general welfare of the organization. Less successful managers are less interested in helping humanity or the organization than in helping themselves. They are more concerned about their financial security and avoiding problems or conflict in their immediate work situation.[6] The managers in the case at the beginning of the chapter appear much more concerned with keeping their jobs and staying out of trouble than with promoting the general welfare of the organization.

Values as Influence Values often influence behavior through behavior channeling and perceptual screening, as shown in Figure 20.1.[7] **Behavior channeling** is the idea that actual behavior is consistent with values. Behavior is channeled toward or away from particular actions as a result of the direct influence of values on behavior. If morality is im-

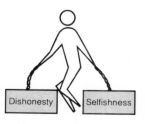

Hindrances to success

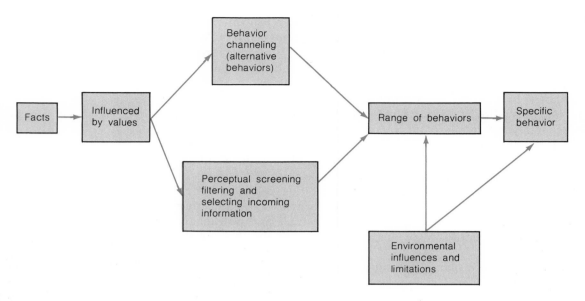

FIGURE 20.1   Values as influence

Behavior channeling: Values influence behavior.

Perceptual screening: Values influence perception.

portant to a manager, then the manager will be channeled away from immoral behavior, however he or she defines it.

Behavior channeling affects managerial behavior in the following areas: decisions on policy, solutions to problems, and acceptance of or resistance to organizational goals and pressures. Strong behavior channeling values prevented the managers in the case at the beginning of the chapter from reporting the distortions in the reports.

Values have a more indirect effect on behavior through **perceptual screening,** which means that values influence what the individual sees and hears. Perceptions can be highly inaccurate when personal values cause an individual to filter out or emphasize certain parts of incoming informtion. This can cause widely varying interpretations of the same information. A story is told about three managers who heard their work groups laughing. The first manager thought, "They are laughing because they are happy and productive." The second manager thought, "They are laughing because they are goofing off." The third managers thought, "They are laughing at *me*." The values of each of these managers prompted a totally different reaction to the same input.

Perceptual screening influences how managers assess interpersonal relationships, work situations and problems, and their own or their organization's success or failure. Evidence of perceptual screening can be seen in the case at the beginning of the chapter—particularly in the chief accountant's statement, "Our job is to follow instructions," and the engineering vice-president's statement, "Actually, I tried not to know what was in the reports."

THE IMPORTANCE OF POWER AND POLITICS

Power is "the ability of a person or group, for whatever reason, to affect another person's or group's ability to achieve its goals (personal or collective)."[8] In simpler terms, it is the ability to influence or control others.

As Chapter 17 pointed out, there is a difference between power and authority. *Authority* is the right to command and exact obedience from others, and it comes from the organization. Indeed, organizations have a hierarchy of authority. *Power,* however, is a broader concept than authority.[9] Power comes from many sources, including expert knowledge and friendship. Some managers, have much more power then others despite an equal amount of authority. Power is often seen as being immoral. The statement "power corrupts, and absolute power corrupts absolutely" summarizes the feelings of many. This feeling about the nature of power even influences many of those with power to deny that they have it. Whether or not they admit it, managers value power more than other people; and better managers tend to value it more highly than other managers.

Many nonmanangers have little or no authority but a greal deal of power. For example, a particularly insensitive person was hired by a medium-sized organization to be the manufacturing manager. Within a short period of time, he had alienated all the secretaries, including the president's. He never understood why it took so long to get an appointment with the president, why he did not receive important information, why memos to him were lost, and why telephone calls were not returned. Needless to say, he did not last very long in the organization. Because the secretaries lacked authority, he had failed to recognize their power which was substantial. Unfortunately for them, many managers are slow to recognize power where it exists without authority.

The Two Faces of Power One of the reasons emigrants came to the United States was to escape oppression. In a pluralist society people become uneasy when a political party becomes too strong or when an individual seems to be acquiring too much power. There was a public outcry, for example, when President Nixon attempted to change the uniforms of White House guards to those resembling the uniforms of the Swiss Guards at the Vatican. The plans for new uniforms were soon quietly withdrawn.

A way to avoid seeing power only in a negative light is to realize that there are **two faces of power.**[10] The *negative face* involves personal domination of others. If one person wins, another loses. The most direct and least socialized form of power is seen in direct physical aggression, where the loser is forced to submit to the winner. At the managerial level the negative face of power is more subtle. In an extreme case the powerful individual may be seen as superhuman, and those over whom the power is exercised may feel loyalty, devotion, and submissiveness. One

Definition of power:

- Ability to influence or control others
- Comes from many sources

Definition of authority:

- Right to command and exact obedience from others
- Comes from the organization

characteristic of both Hitler and Lenin was the ability to sway their audiences in mass meetings. Their power compelled loyal obedience.

The *positive face* of power is socially desirable, since this type of power is exercised not for personal benefit but for the good of the organization or society. The person exercising power in the positive sense attempts to clarify the goals the group should achieve and then help the group's members gain the confidence to achieve them. Rather than inspiring submission, this type of power inspires a greater sense of unity; rather than powerlessness, it produces a feeling that the group and individual followers are powerful and can accomplish things on their own. Such power is social rather than personal.

One reason for the frequent misperception of power is that successful managers balance between personal dominance and a more socialized type of leadership.[11] Managers must take initiative—but not too much. They must take counsel—but not to the point of appearing weak.

Power can be used either directly or indirectly. In the case at the beginning of the chapter, none of the managers interviewed mentioned that squealing on the boss might cause the loss of his job or other negative consequences. The president of the company did not have to use his power in such a direct fashion as to threaten these negative consequences; yet, unmistakably, that message was communicated.

Power and Politics   The effective manager gains additional power through judicious use of **politics**—that is, the tactical use of resources, both physical and human, to increase power over others.[12] Although *politics* is another word that has negative connotations, both power and politics are essential to the functioning of organizations. Organizations are political structures: "People will readily admit that governments are organizations. The converse—that organizations are governments—is equally true but rarely considered."[13]

What are some of the political techniques by which managers gain and use power? Biographies of leaders such as Alexander the Great and Franklin D. Roosevelt and interviews with successful managers reveal some political tactics practiced by those whose success rests on the ability to control and direct the actions of others. These tactics include alliances, taking counsel, maneuverability, communication, compromise, proper timing, self-dramatization, confidence, and awareness of position.[14]

Taking counsel
Confidence   Alliances
Maneuverability

Political Tactics

Communication
Self-dramatization
Proper timing
Compromise

Alliances   The effective manager is able to form political relationships with others. Few organizations are ruled by a single person, so power coalitions are necessary to implement decisions. Even fewer organizations are pure democracies in which the majority rules. Most organizations require strong and skillful coalitions to bring about coordinated action. Without them, power is fractionalized and actions are divisive. Lyndon Johnson got more programs through Congress than did John F. Kennedy. One reason for this is that, as a senator, Johnson had developed better political alliances than had Kennedy.

Taking Counsel   The capable manager asks for advice only when necessary. Involving others in too many decisions can be seen as a sign of weakness. The effective manager also knows when advice is necessary and whom to ask. The right person can be extremely helpful in advising when an idea should be advanced and when it should be postponed or reworked.

Many decisions are made in committee meetings. A certain politically astute manager makes a point of never bringing up a recommendation before a group until he has sounded out its more influential members and received the go-ahead from them.

Maneuverability   Capable managers provide themselves several escape routes from potential problematic situations. Thus they do not become trapped in insoluble difficulties. And since situations keep changing, managers must maintain flexibility. Inflexible managers cannot adapt to changing circumstances.

Communication   The smart manager sometimes holds back on information or carefully times its release. This is particularly appropriate for plans for the future, which often are tentative and may need to be changed when new information comes in or when the situation changes.

As the nerve center of the unit, the manager must continually scan the environment to collect information. The effective manager designs a personal communications system that is largely informal and largely oral. The manager then pieces together all the incoming information into a mental image or model of the unit and its interaction with the external environment or with other units of the organization.

Information is power and should be treated as such. Rather than thinking only of increasing the information flow to subordinates, the capable manager considers who should know what, when, and for what purpose and what information should be withheld.

Compromise   Politics is the art of the possible. The capable manager accepts compromise when necessary while keeping in mind clearly defined goals. One politically astute manager makes a practice of never speaking at the beginning of a meeting. When she has specific ideas, she waits until a number of people have offered theirs. She has noticed that the first few suggestions often are not accepted, since others also have ideas that they want to explain. As a result, she does not make her suggestions until she can weave them in with others', thereby picking up their support.

Proper Timing   Managers are frequently urged to take immediate action, but sometimes immediate action is unwise. Indeed, sometimes managers should appear to be in the process of doing something even though it never quite gets done.

Self-Dramatization   Successful actors are able to influence audiences by both verbal and nonverbal communications. Successful managers sometimes use self-dramatization to deliver their messages. The first step in this process is observing successful portrayals by others. Formal classes in speech and drama can be helpful in learning better communications skills. The effective manager should have a well-trained and well-disciplined voice and body so that messages will be convincing.

Confidence   Successful managers need to look and act confident, especially when a decision has been made. If a manager lacks confidence about a decision, perhaps it should be delayed. In any case, the manager who maintains an attitude of confidence and certainty is simultaneously using power and increasing it.

Awareness of Position   Managers should get along well with subordinates; this adds to their referent (charismatic) power. At the same time, they should not get so involved with subordinates that their personal feelings become a basis for either positive or negative action.

These political tactics have no inherent moral value. They take on moral qualities only in the way they are used. Power can be used for either good or bad, but those with power have a moral obligation to use it responsibly. Good managers have the wisdom, knowledge, and skill to use power well.

THE IMPORTANCE OF ETHICS

One of the most important managerial attributes is a good sense of ethics. Unfortunately, almost daily disclosures of illegal political contributions, juggled books, overseas payoffs, wiretapping, and similar activities suggest a lack of ethics among all types of leaders in our society.[15] Consider the following events reported in the news media:

1. Abscam.
2. Marvin Mandel former governor of Maryland, was convicted in 1977 on seventeen counts of mail fraud and one count of racketeering.
3. Southwestern Bell Telephone lost a $1 million suit to a Southwestern Bell manager whose telephone it illegally tapped.
4. Gulf Oil admitted paying over $12 million to national and international political figures—including $4 million to the party backing President Park Chung Hee of Korea.
5. United Brands (Chiquita Banana) admitted spending $4 million to bribe government officials and others in Honduras to lower taxes on bananas.
6. Congressman Diggs of Detroit was convicted for using congressional funds to pad payrolls.
7. In 1976 the Air Line Pilots Association suspended Frontier Airlines

pilots after the pilots had agreed to fly Frontier's twin-engined Boeing 137s with only two men in the cockpit intead of three, although a similar aircraft, the DC-9, is flown with two.

The preceding list contains only those items newsworthy enough to make headlines or national television news. But ethical and legal issues do not always involve top corporate or government officials and large sums of money. What about the college student who passes the word to a friend about an upcoming exam? Or the manager who hires an engineer from a company that has just developed a technical breakthrough? Or the purchasing agent who buys from a particular vendor and receives a case of bourbon? Or the salesman who pads the expense account to buy a toy for his child? Or the manager who has long, three-martini lunches? Or the worker who stretches out the job? Or the salesclerk who waits on a friend before a stranger? Or the politician who shows favoritism in employment?

What is ethical or unethical behavior? How does it differ from legal or illegal behavior? Many instances of ethical as well as unethical behavior do not make headlines. Consider the purchasing agent who repeatedly refuses gifts of any kind from suppliers and the manager who always charges personal calls made from the office to his home number. A large number of managers turn in scrupulously honest expense accounts. And many managers believe that acting only in the interest of shareholders, without considering employees and consumers, is unethical behavior.

The term *ethics* is a slippery one. For example, an early study on ethics found that all the people in the study believed they were behaving

"Granted the public has a <u>right</u> to know what's in a hot dog, but does the public really <u>want</u> to know what's in a hot dog?"

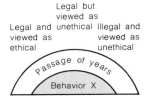

Legal and viewed as ethical   Legal but viewed as unethical   Illegal and viewed as unethical

Behavior X

Some of society's ideas about ethical behavior change, and then its laws change correspondingly.

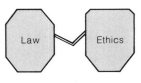

Law   Ethics

Law and ethics are related but not identical

ethically, according to their own standards.[16] Furthermore, society's ideas about laws and ethics keep changing. Almost everyone would agree that child labor in factories is not only illegal but unethical. Yet when the U.S. Congress passed the Child Labor Act in 1937, the act was bitterly contested and was not upheld as constitutional by the Supreme Court until 1941.

Laws and ethics are related but not identical. **Illegal behavior** is behavior that violates a law in a particular jurisdiction or area. For example, political contributions by corporations are illegal in the United States but legal in Canada and Italy. Ethical behavior stems from values and gives rise to laws. Thus behavior can be legal but unethical. Lavish entertainment of and gifts to customers is an accepted business practice in the United States. At what point, however, does the practice remain legal but become unethical?

While values influence a person's beliefs and behavior, ethics is concerned with moral rights and wrongs and with the individual's moral obligations to society. From the viewpoint of the manager, **ethics** is "the rules or standards governing the moral conduct of the organization management profession."[17] In simple terms, ethical behavior is behavior that society considers right. But determining specific rights and wrongs is complicated, since moral concepts, like other ideas, change over time. A minimal guide to ethics is the recommendation made by the chairman of the board of a large organization: "Possibly the best test—for a person with a family—might be to think whether you would be happy to tell your spouse and children the details of the action you are contemplating or whether you would be willing to appear on television and to explain your actions in detail."[18]

Under this definition, disclosure is the key to whether behavior is ethical. Thus a reasonable and practical standard is whether the behavior, if disclosed, would be embarrassing to the individual, the person's family, or the organization.

To talk of corporate ethics is to talk of the ethics of individual men and women, since it is not the organization that acts ethically or unethically but the individuals within that organization. Bob Dorsey, the chief executive of Gulf Oil, was the individual who gave $3 million to S. K. Kim, the Korean fund raiser, for the 1971 Korean election. In the case at the beginning of the chapter the president and the vice-president of finance were the two individuals who sent the distorted reports to the parent company.

Ethics is a set of guiding principles that help individuals retain their self-respect while behaving justly toward others. Ethics, then, is a personal responsibility for each individual.

Influences on Ethics   The many surveys and reports on ethics generally agree on the following:

1. Managers at all levels face ethical problems daily.
2. A majority of managers believe strongly that organizations should be more ethical.

On the Job

ETHICS: PLAIN AND SIMPLE

I am somewhat distressed by the article "Corporate Codes of Ethics: A Key to Economic Freedom" in your September 1980 issue. My major concern is the implication that a printed code of ethics will in some fashion substitute for federal regulations. I am certainly no fan of the tremendous and nonproductive proliferation of the federal regulations, but neither am I in favor of a printed code of ethics. Thus my dilemma.

First, I think we must all agree that minds greater than ours have been studying the formulation of a code of ethics for at least 4,000 or 5,000 years of recorded history. Some of them were rather straightforward and simple (for example, the Ten Commandments), while others were more sophisticated and subtle (Jesus' statements and parables in the *New Testament*). What skills, indeed, what right, do we have to suddenly tackle this complex and possibly unsolvable problem?

Carrying the above logic one step further, why can there possibly be more than one code of ethics for every corporation? The logical *reductio ad absurdum* would be for the federal government to print a code of ethics that we all would only need to adopt.

My second objection to a printed code of ethics is that it simply provides the framework for exceptions that the devious employee will hunt for if this is what he or she wants to do. Anyone can always find a crack left unpapered. Isn't it better to simply make it clear to your employees that you expect them to be ethical?

In our company there has been only one discussion of a code of ethics, to my knowledge. It was quickly laid to rest by a senior executive when he stated that a printed code of ethics would be an insult to our people. I completely agree.

GEORGE W. MEAD
Chairman of the Board
Consolidated Papers, Inc.
Wisconsin Rapids, Wisconsin

Source: "Ethics: Plain and Simple," *Management Review,* February 1981 (New York: AMACOM, a division of American Management Associations, 1981), p. 41.

3. Most managers want to be honest and ethical, but a majority of them (in both business and government) feel that they are under pressure to lower their personal ethical standards in order to achieve organizational goals. The pressure is felt more strongly by lower- and middle-level managers than by upper-level ones.

4. Managers are aware of a number of commonly accepted practices that they consider unethical—practices such as bribery and gift giving, price discrimination, dishonest or misleading advertising, dishonesty, or shadiness in making or keeping contracts, unfair credit practices, unfairness to employees, and prejudice in hiring.[19]

There is also evidence that many people employ a *double ethic*; that is, they use one standard with friends and another with strangers. A librarian may charge one person but not another a fine for overdue books. Managers with inside information about a stock may tell their friends but not their stockbrokers.

> Managers:
>
> • Face ethical problems daily
> • Believe organizations should be ethical
> • Want to be honest
> • Know of unethical practice

> Ethical problems influence all levels of managers—but especially low- and middle-level managers.

A series of questions intended to determine the causes of ethical behavior were asked of 1,700 managers. As Figure 20.2 shows, each manager's personal code of ethics is the main determinant of that person's ethical behavior. The behavior of immediate supervisors and formal company policy are the next strongest influences. When the influence is negative—that is, toward unethical behavior—the behavior of immediate supervisors is strongest.[20]

In one study (mentioned in Chapter 13) applicants for supervisory positions at a juvenile corrections institution completed an anonymous questionnaire. Their responses showed that they all considered punitive attitudes toward delinquency and delinquents unethical.[21] Some of the applicants were hired. After working several months, they again completed the same questionnaire. These newly hired workers had changed their opinions to conform with the views of the institutions's other personnel. Now they saw punitive and negative behavior toward the care and handling of delinquents as ethically acceptable. (One manager has said that the best advice for a young person entering an organization is to find a good boss. There is evidence that someone who wants to act ethically should work for an ethical boss.)

Similar results were found in a study that compared the responses of business and government managers to a series of questions on ethics. For example, 64 percent of business managers and 60 percent of government managers reported feeling pressure to achieve organizational goals. The pressure was strongest at the low- and middle-management levels.

As 78 percent of business and 76 percent of public sector (government) managers reported in this study, pressure from superiors sometimes caused people farther down the line to behave unethically, even when the organizational policies on the matter concerned were ethical. Indeed, top management may not know that subordinates are acting

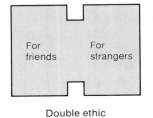

For friends   For strangers

Double ethic

FIGURE 20.2 Influences on managerial behavior

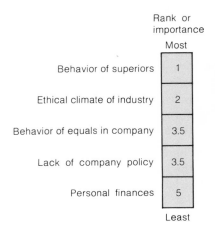

What influences an executive to make ethical decisions?

	Rank or importance
	Most
Personal code of ethics	1
Behavior of superiors	2.5
Formal company policy	2.5
Ethical climate of industry	4
Behavior of equals in company	5
	Least

What influences an executive to make unethical decisions?

	Rank or importance
	Most
Behavior of superiors	1
Ethical climate of industry	2
Behavior of equals in company	3.5
Lack of company policy	3.5
Personal finances	5
	Least

unethically out of loyalty to or fear of their immediate superiors. One of the questions asked in the study had to do with whether young managers in business would show their loyalty by behaving like the junior members of the Nixon reelection committee. The responses are shown in Table 20.1. Approximately 72 percent of the managers in government and 60 percent of the managers in the private sector felt that younger managers in business would behave unethically out of loyalty to their supervisors.[22] Apparently, the managers at Quasar Stellar were not unusual in being loyal to their boss.

Encouraging Ethical Behavior   To assume that a way can be devised to ensure that everyone in an organization behaves ethically and legally all the time is unrealistic. Nevertheless, there are a number of ways in which business ethics can be improved. A good starting point is for top management to examine such management practices as reward systems, managerial style, and decision-making processes. In some organizations the reward system promotes unethical behavior by creating the pressure to achieve organizational goals at almost any cost.

In one situation two general foremen were in charge of producing and shipping two almost identical products. Foreman A had ordered a railroad car and planned to load the product on the car at the beginning of the next workday. Foreman B had forgotten to order a railroad car and was going to have to wait several days to ship the product. Rather than wait, he took his crew out and, under cover of darkness, physically moved the railroad car ordered by Foreman A to his own area and loaded the product immediately. The next morning, Foreman A had no car and could not ship his product. In the prevailing climate of the organization, Foreman B was seen as resourceful and shrewd, and Foreman A was seen as having been caught unprepared. What sort of ethical message was management communicating in this organization?

Boards of directors and top management should regularly conduct internal audits to ensure that business is being conducted ethically. For example, the success of the Nixon Committee to Reelect the President was due in part to finding organizations that had slush funds. These organizations may have already been acting unethically when they were approached by the committee.

How an organization can encourage ethical behavior:

- Ensure that reward system and other management policies do not create pressure for unethical behavior
- Have top management set a good example and establish a code of ethics
- Conduct internal audits
- Enforce laws more thoroughly

Ethical conduct of managers and employees is strongly influenced by top-management's policies.

TABLE 20.1   The Influence of Loyalty

RESPONSE	PRIVATE SECTOR	PUBLIC SECTOR
Agree	59.3%	72.3%
Disagree	40.7	11.0
Undecided	—	16.7

Source: Adapted from James S. Bowman, "Managerial Ethics in Business and Government," *Business Horizons* 19 (October 1976): 52. Copyright, 1976, by the Foundation for the School of Business at Indiana University. Reprinted by permission.

Clearly, top management must set a good example. Development and enforcement of a code of ethics is one way for management to do this. However, such codes are often something like overall organization objectives in that they are written by a blue-ribbon panel and then ignored.

The importance of enforcing the company's code of ethics is gaining attention. Increasingly, managers are being held responsible for preventing or correcting violations when they have the necessary power and responsibility to do so. Furthermore, a number of organizations are being sued by stockholders or other organizations for acting illegally.

In the last analysis, ethical behavior results from personal decisions. Reducing the pressure from the top, establishing codes of ethics, conducting internal audits, and enforcing laws more thoroughly may be conducive to ethical behavior, but the individual manager must still make a personal decision to act ethically. The junior manager who is working for an unethical supervisor may need to change jobs or bosses in order to perform the job in an ethical manner.

In speaking about ethics to subordinates, the manager may find an indirect approach more effective. That is, the manager may want to express ethical ideas in a way that points out how ethical behavior contributes to the long-term good of the organization.

SUMMARY

The effective manager is aware that decisions are made not only on the basis of facts but because of personal values as well. Personal value systems influence both behavior and how people see the world. The effective manager is aware of both self-values and the values of others.

Many people think the term *power* is a dirty word. Yet, whether they admit it or not, good managers are those who know how to gain and use power effectively. They understand that there are two sides or faces of power, and they use each of them appropriately.

Politics is the art of gaining and using power. Effective managers have no choice but to be effective politicians. They must choose among political tactics in order to effectively wield their power.

But power and politics need to be used ethically. Few managers are unethical as a matter of policy. Yet at some point they all share the problem of determining what is ethical or unethical for dealing with a dilemma. In many organizations there is constant pressure to behave in unethical ways. Evidence exists that the pressure is greater at lower levels of the organization than at higher levels. Evidence also exists that the higher levels of management may be unaware of the pressures that lower-level managers endure. While ethics is a personal responsibility, it is heavily influenced by the actions of higher management. The effective manager must fight daily battles with regard to ethical standards. Winning these battles is essential if individuals and organizations are to survive and be respected.

STUDY QUESTIONS

1. How can values cause problems with people?

2. How does a value system affect behavior?

3. What is behavior channeling? How does it affect behavior?

4. What is perceptual screening? How does it affect behavior?

5. What is power? List some sources of power.

6. How do the two faces of power differ? Explain.

7. What is politics? List ways in which managers use politics to gain power.

8. What is ethics? What is one suggested criterion for ethical behavior?

9. What are some major influences on ethical behavior?

10. How can ethical behavior be encouraged?

11. What is your value system? List three or four terms that describe your value system.

12. What evidence of behavior channeling and perceptual screening stemming from individual values have you seen in other people?

13. How do you use power? Describe your observations of how others obtain and use power.

14. Does the case at the beginning of the chapter relate to anything in your own experience? Explain.

15. Interview managers about business practices that they feel are unethical. Ask them to explain why the practices are unethical.

16. Interview a physician, a lawyer, a psychologist, or a similar person in the professions. How much influence do you think ethical codes have on the behavior of such people? Explain.

17. What are the nine political tactics of obtaining power ethical? Explain.

Case for Discussion

JUST A FEW VOTES MORE

Weeks after the results have been announced, you learn that the alumni board election was rigged by your alumni director. What do you do?

She was gone now, but he would not soon forget her parting words.

"Frankly, I don't know what I'll do," she had said. "I just don't know if I can accept the presidency of the alumni association after this—this incident."

He had calmed her, promising a swift resolution of the problem.

"Tomorrow morning—" he had said. "I'll talk to Peters and Graves and get back to you tomorrow morning."

Now he was alone, staring out the window at the quad below, watching the students as they crisscrossed the lawn on their way to classes. President Mathews glanced at his watch, then called his secretary into the room.

"Doris, get John Peters and Bill Graves on the phone; tell them to be here at two o'clock without fail."

"Yes, sir. Can I tell them what the meeting is about?"

"Oh, I think they'll know, Doris."

"All right." She turned and left the room, pulling the door shut behind her.

Yes, he thought, I'm sure they'll know.

President Mathews talked with Peters first. John Peters had been hired just two years before on the recommendation of Graves, the vice president for institutional advancement. Peters was a personable young man, bright, eager, full of energy. Even Mathews had to admit that the alumni director was one of the best he had ever worked with—which made this particular conversation all the more difficult.

"John," he began, "I've just had a talk with Mary Chambers about certain irregularities in the alumni board election. She claims you tampered with the election results. Is that true?"

The blood seemed to drain from Peters' face, and when he began to speak, his lips trembled.

"Well," he said, "I wouldn't exactly call it *tampering.*"

"No? What would you call it then? She says you changed votes, John."

Peters squirmed in his chair, shifting his weight from one hip to the other.

"Yes, but I explained that to her. It was only a few votes out of thousands, and some of them were ambiguous anyway. Besides, we ended up with a new board that's more representative of the alumni constituency—geographically, by class, by sex, you name it."

He paused, hoping for some positive sign from Mathews, but the president just stared down at him, forcing him to avert his eyes.

"Look," he continued, "I did it for the good of the college."

Mathews grunted and shook his head.

"Oh, come now, John," he said. "For the good of the college?" The sarcasm was not lost on Peters.

"All right," said Peters, "I may have made an error in judgment. I told her that, I guess I was just too eager to have a board that represented the real interests of the alumni for once. And it was so close; I didn't see what harm it would do."

"No harm? John, what you did was wrong. And now we're sitting on a powder keg. Chambers has threatened to resign."

Peters looked up, startled.

"But—"

"And I'm not going to let that happen, John, not if I can help it. Do you understand?"

"Yes, but—"

"That's all for now, John, I'll talk to you again about this tomorrow." He turned and walked to the window, his back to Peters.

Peters got up and started for the door.

"And Peters—"

"Yes, sir?"

"Ask Bill Graves to come in."

Peters nodded and left the room. Moments later, Bill Graves, Peters' supervisor, came in. Mathews motioned him to sit down.

"Bill, we have a big problem."

"Yes, by the look on John's face just now, I thought we did. Is it the Chambers thing?"

"Yes, she's upset—and rightly so—about the alumni board election. But you know all about that, don't you, Bill? She says she talked to you about it."

"Yes, this morning. Stormed into my office—quite upset."

Mathews stood up, walked around to the front of the desk, and looked down at Graves.

"She claims you were aware of Peters' actions, and condoned them. Is that true?"

"After the fact, yes, but the point is—"

"The point is we've tampered with a free election, and we've got to rectify that situation, Bill." He leaned back against the desk, folding his arms across his chest.

Graves shook his head. "But I don't see how," he said. "The election results have already been announced to all the candidates; appointment letters have gone out. And, really, when you think about it, what harm has been done?"

Mathews thrust his hands into his pockets and began pacing back and forth in front of the desk.

"Not you, too, Bill? We did it *for the good of the college,* is that what you're going to say?"

"I'm only saying there's nothing we *can* do now. And Peters is such a good man—surely we can't risk losing him over a small matter like this. The best thing we can do is just forget it."

"You may forget it, Bill, and Peters may forget it, but Mary Chambers isn't going to forget it—she's threatened to resign over this, did you know that?—and I certainly can't forget it, either."

"But what choice do you have? You can't let the board or the alumni or the public get wind of this. And firing Peters would be cutting off your nose to spite your face. So I would—."

Mathews cut him off in mid-sentence.

"I know what you're saying. You're saying *be practical, ignore the moral questions just this once.* Well, I'm not so sure I can do that, or that I have to."

"What will you do, then?"

Mathews walked back to his chair and sat down.

"I told Chambers I'd get back to her tomorrow morning. I'll think it over tonight and let you all know tomorrow."

Next morning, President Mathews met with Mary Chambers.

"I've given this matter a great deal of thought," he began, "and I hope you'll agree with the decision I've come to. Here's what I propose to do. . . ."

What would you do? Why?

Source: "Just a Few Votes More," *Educational Record*, Winter 1981, pp. 71–73. © 1981 by American Council on Education, Washington, D.C. Used by permission.

1. What should Mathews do? Is he to blame for this situation? Explain.
2. Did Peters really make just an error in judgment, or was this action more serious than that? Explain.
3. Because Bill Graves is Peters' supervisor, should he be considered responsible for Peters' behavior in this case? If Mathews dismisses Peters, should he also have to dismiss Graves? Explain.
4. What errors in good management did Mathews make? Did he handle this situation effectively? Explain.
5. Under what conditions would Peters' behavior have been justified? For example, would his behavior have been justified if it meant increasing alumni contributions by a million dollars?

FOR YOUR CAREER

1. You can use power in organizations to benefit yourself or to benefit the organization. Which will you choose?
2. Your effectiveness and success in an organization often depends on how well you "play politics."
3. Playing politics is neither good nor bad in itself, but it is often a necessary aspect of life in organizations. Are you ready to play?
4. Illegal behavior and unethical behavior are sometimes different. Illegal behavior is subject to legal punishment whereas not all unethical behavior is. When no legal punishment exists for unethical behavior, does any other type of punishment ever occur?
5. As a manager, you play a critical role in determining the behavior of your employees. If you engage in unethical behavior, they may follow.
6. What will you tell your boss if he or she asks you to engage in unethical behavior?
7. Your code of ethics can be as important as rewards and punishment in determining your behavior.

FOOTNOTES

1. Adapted by permission from John J. Fendrock, "Crisis in Conscience at Quasar," *Harvard Business Review* 46 (March–April 1968): 112–120. Copyright © 1968 by the President and Fellows of Harvard College; all rights reserved.
2. R. Nader, P. Petkas, and K. Blackwell, eds., *Whistle Blowing: The Report of the Conference on Professional Responsibility* (New York: Grossman Publishers, 1972).
3. G. England, "Personal Value Systems of American Managers," *Journal of the Academy of Management* 10 (March 1967): 53–68; W. Guth and R. Tagiuri, "Personal Values and Corporate Strategy," *Harvard Business Review* 43 (September–October 1965): 123–132; and H. Bunke, "Heroes, Values and the Organization," *Business Horizons* 19 (October 1976): 33–41.
4. R. McMurray, "Conflicts in Human Values," *Harvard Business Review* 41 (May–June 1963): 130–145.
5. England, "Personal Value Systems of American Managers."
6. H. Singer, "Human Values and Leadership," *Business Horizons* 18 (August 1975): 85–88.
7. England, "Personal Value Systems of American Managers."
8. M. Zald, "Political Economy: A Framework for Com-

parative Analysis," in *Power in Organizations,* ed. M. Zald (Nashville, Tenn.: Vanderbilt University Press, 1970), p. 238.

9. C. Burck, "The Intricate 'Politics' of the Corporation," *Fortune,* April 1975, p. 109; R. Goodwin, "The Art of Assuming Power," *New York Times Magazine,* December 26, 1976, p. 7; G. Kelley, "Seducing the Elites: The Politics of Decision Making and Innovation in Organizational Networks," *Academy of Management Review* 1 (July 1976): 66–73; D. Mechanic, "Sources of Power of Lower Participants in Complex Organizations," *Administrative Science Quarterly* 7 (June 1962): 349–364; and A. Zaleznick, "Power and Politics in Organizational Life," *Harvard Business Review* 48 (May–June 1970): 47–60.

10. N. Long, "The Local Community as a Project of Games," *American Journal of Sociology* 64 (November 1958): 110.

11. D. McClelland and D. Burnham, "Power Is the Great Motivator," *Harvard Business Review* 54 (March–April 1976): 100–110. See also D. McClelland, "The Dynamics of Power and Affiliation Motivation," in *Organizational Psychology: A Book of Readings,* ed. D. Kolb, I. Rubin, and J. McIntyre (Englewood Cliffs, N.J.: Prentice-Hall, 1971), pp. 141–154.

12. McClelland, "The Dynamics of Power and Affiliation Motivation," p. 150.

13. T. Burns, "Micropolitics: Mechanisms of Institutional Change," *Administrative Science Quarterly* 6 (September 1961): 259.

14. N. Martin and J. Simms, "Approaches to Power," *Harvard Business Review* 34 (November–December 1956): p. 25.

15. M. Korda, *Success* (New York: Random House, 1977).

16. J. McCloy, "John J. McCloy on Corporate Pay-offs,"

Harvard Business Review 54 (July–August 1976): p. 45; "Payoff Is Not 'Accepted Practice,'" *Fortune,* August 1975, p. 123; J. Kaikati, "The Phenomenon of International Bribery," *Business Horizons* 20 (February 1977): 25–37; A. Carr, "Can an Executive Afford a Conscience?" *Harvard Business Review* 48 (July–August 1970): 48–64; W. Robertson, "The Directors Woke Up Too Late at Gulf," *Fortune,* June 1976, p. 121; R. Bauer and D. Fend, Jr., "What Is a Corporate Social Audit?" *Harvard Business Review* 51 (January–February 1973): 37–49; and S. Sethi, *Up Against the Corporate Wall,* 2d ed. (Englewood Cliffs, N.J.: Prentice-Hall, 1974).

17. M. Hurley, "Ethical Problems of the Association Executive," *Study Guide for Institutes of Organization Management* (Washington, D.C.: Chamber of Commerce of the United States, 1972), p. 8.

18. C. Walton, ed., *The Ethics of Corporate Conduct* (Englewood Cliffs, N.J.: Prentice-Hall, 1977), p. 5.

19. R. Baumhart, "How Ethical Are Businessmen?" *Harvard Business Review* 39 (July–August 1961): p. 6; R. Baumhart, *Ethics in Business* (New York: Holt, Rinehart and Winston, 1968); J. Bowman, "Managerial Ethics in Business and Government," *Business Horizons* 19 (October 1976): 48–54; A. Carroll, "Managerial Ethics: A Post-Watergate View," *Business Horizons* 18 (April 1975): 75–80; and W. Blumenthal, "Rx for Reducing the Occasion of 'Corporate Sin,'" *SAM Advanced Management Journal* 42 (Winter 1977): 4–13.

20. Baumhart, "How Ethical Are Businessmen?"

21. C. Perrow, *Organizational Analysis: A Sociological Veiw* (Belmont, Calif.: Brooks/Cole Publishing, 1970), p. 4.

22. Bowman, "Managerial Ethics in Business and Government."

Managing Conflict and Stress

CHAPTER 21

CONTENTS

THE PRESIDENT'S DECISION

On April 17, 1961, a brigade of about fourteen hundred Cuban exiles, helped by the United States Navy, Air Force, and CIA, invaded Cuba at the Bay of Pigs. The intent was to overthrow Fidel Castro's government. By the third day the battle was over, and most of the invaders were captured. The captives were later ransomed for $53 million in food and drugs. The Bay of Pigs invasion is generally considered a fiasco.

On October 16, 1962 CIA photo interpreters discovered recently finished buildings for ballistic missiles in Cuba. Intelligence estimates were that the installations would represent about one-third of the Soviet Union's current atomic warhead potential. On October 24, after the United States blockaded Cuba, Soviet cargo ships turned away from the country. The crisis was over on October 28, when the Soviets agreed to remove the missiles already there. The decisions leading to the solution of the Cuban missile crisis are generally regarded as excellent.[1]

What made the difference? Both decisions involved President John F. Kennedy and many of the same advisers—including some of the most capable and intelligent people ever to participate in government. It has been suggested that in the first case those taking part in the decisions were victims of groupthink, a form of decision making that occurs when "the members' strivings for unanimity override their motivation to realistically appraise alternative courses of action."[2] In the second case active disagreement was deliberately encouraged before the final alternatives were decided upon, and groupthink was thereby avoided.

Planning for a possible invasion of Cuba began before Kennedy took office. He was first briefed on the proposed invasion two days after his inauguration, in January 1961. The plan was discussed for the next eighty days and finally approved with only a few modifications. It was based on a large number of wrong assumptions, any of which could easily have been checked out. One assumption was that the invasion would be widely supported by the Cuban people. Actually, an overwhelming majority of Cubans supported Castro. Another assumption was that a brigade of fourteen hundred men could defeat Castro's army, which was perceived as poorly trained and ill-equipped. Actually, the brigade had no possibility of defeating Castro's well-trained army of two hundred thousand people.

Because of groupthink, these and other assumptions were never checked out. A desire for group cohesiveness and unanimity caused the adivsers to ignore conflicting evidence and to act without first calling in experts. Doubts were quickly squelched rather than being explored.

Exactly the opposite approach was taken in the Cuban-Russian missile crisis. Kennedy and basically the same set of advisers were able to avoid groupthink by accepting internal conflict as the norm. Outside experts were pulled into the discussion, and the group accepted information from all sources. On occasion, Kennedy left the room to allow fuller discussion. Moral issues were explicitly discussed, and reversals of judgment were common. A wide variety of plans and possible results were examined. The final decision involved contingency plans that utilized all possible information, including predictions of how other nations might act.

This case raises several critical questions, which you should be able to answer after reading this chapter. The questions include:

1. How and when can conflict help groups and organizations? How and when can conflict hinder groups and organizations?
2. What are some of the causes of conflict in organizations?
3. How can conflict be reduced or at least managed when it is hindering groups from working together?
4. How do you react when conflicting or ambiguous demands are made on you?

Using the opening case as a base, this chapter will examine the nature and importance of **conflict**—a struggle between two opposing forces, usually because of mutually exclusive impulses, desires, or activities. The chapter will trace changes in how conflict is viewed and will distinguish between competitive and constructive resolution of conflict. It will then deal with how the effective manager can reduce conflict in cooperative ways and stimulate constructive conflict when appropriate. Finally, the chapter will examine conflict within the individual that results from either too many conflicting demands on the person or from ambiguous demands and expectations.

CHANGING PHILOSOPHIES ABOUT CONFLICT

Over the years, three philosophies that reflect different managerial attitudes toward conflict have been developed. They can arbitrarily be called traditional, behavioral, and interactionist philosophies. Each emerged from a prevailing culture that had a different view of management than the other two cultures.[3]

The traditional, or classical, approach is a simplistic one. It sees any kind of conflict as destructive and deserving elimination. This philosophy posits management error as the only cause of conflict in an organization and management action as its only resolution. It assumes that conflict will not occur if sound management principles are applied in designing and directing the organization and if subordinates clearly understand the common interests holding management and employees together. It further assumes that if conflict occurs, it can be quickly and easily resolved through the management hierarchy. As a proponent of this approach, Henri Fayol, said, "From the instant that agreement ceases or there is no approval from supervisors direct contact comes [immediately] to an end and the scalar chain [vertical chain of command] is straightaway resumed."[4] Thus the traditional philosophy designates the supervisor as the final arbitrator of the conflict and requires that the solution to the problems causing the conflict be imposed from the top. This philosophy dominated management literature until about the middle 1940s. The problem with the approach, of course, is that it tends to ignore human feelings and the consequences in terms of those feelings among lower-level employees of a solution being imposed from above.

Later the behavioral philosophy of conflict emerged. It suggests that conflict is inevitably present in all organizations and thus cannot always be attributed to a specific failing on the part of management. The underlying rationale of this theory is that complex organizations by their very nature have built-in conflicts: disagreements over goals; departmental competition for prestige, status, and scarce resources; sectional competition for recognition; group competition for increased boundaries; and a constant competition by everyone for power. The behavioral view suggests that conflict can be functional at times, since it can identify problems and sometimes lead to good solutions. However, it assumes

Groupthink: Desire for unanimity prevents evaluation of alternatives.

Philosophies about conflict:

- Traditional
- Behavioral
- Interactionist

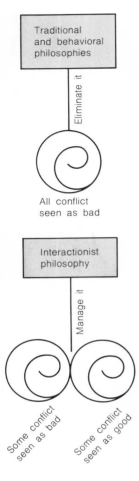

Traditional and behavioral philosophies

Eliminate it

All conflict seen as bad

Interactionist philosophy

Manage it

Some conflict seen as bad

Some conflict seen as good

that usually conflict is harmful and stresses the importance of eliminating or at least reducing it whenever possible. This philosophy still prevails today in most organizations.

The interactionist view, which has emerged recently, points out that organizational conflict is not only inevitable but sometimes desirable. It suggests that effective management includes stimulation of conflict as well as its resolution. It sees conflict as dysfunctional when it harms individuals or hinders the attainment of organizational goals but as functional when it leads to the search for better solutions, thereby bringing about innovation. Established groups can develop more and better decisions when there is conflict among the members, so long as the conflict is properly handled. The conflicting opinions should be viewed as additional information rather than as threats to other group members.[5] Because most conflict situations have functional as well as dysfunctional components the interactionist view of conflict is adopted for the remainder of this chapter. This philosophy makes the management of conflict a large area of responsibility for all administrators.

Organizations must change and adapt if they are to survive and prosper; those that stimulate constructive conflict are likely to examine the need for change. When the level of conflict is too low, the probability of stagnant thinking and inadequate decision making is increased, and the result is groupthink. An example of the effects of avoiding conflict is the bankruptcy of the Penn Central Railroad. There is evidence that the bankruptcy stemmed from two basic problems: mismanagement and the failure of the board of directors to question management's decisions and actions. The board, which consisted of directors from outside the company, met monthly to review the railroad's operations. Although a number of board members privately questioned the wisdom of many major decisions made by operating management, their desire to avoid conflict led them into the error of groupthink and the poor decisions went unquestioned. Had the board brought conflict into the open and forced management to justify key decisions, the bankruptcy might never have occurred.[6]

As Table 21.1 shows, conflict can have two contrasting outcomes. Constructive conflict is helpful to the organization; destructive conflict

TABLE 21.1   Constructive Versus Destructive Conflict

CONSTRUCTIVE CONFLICT	DESTRUCTIVE CONFLICT
Groupthink is avoided	Cooperation is discouraged
Organizational apathy is reduced	Individuals or groups work for individual goals
Creativity is encouraged	Unnecessary stress is created
Problems are identified and clarified	Effort is spent trying to win rather than working toward common goals
Effort on the part of individuals and groups is stimulated	Deviant or "oddball" thinking is discouraged

is harmful. The effective manager is able to diagnose the nature and type of conflict, resolve conflict cooperatively, and increase or decrease the level of constructive conflict as appropriate. The manager's goal is to manage conflict so as to attain objectives rather than to strive for continual harmony.

CONFLICT, COMPETITION, AND COOPERATION

Conflict occurs "whenever incompatible activities occur."[7] An activity that is incompatible with another one obstructs, prevents, or interferes with it in a way that makes the other less probable or less effective. Incompatible activities can involve one or more persons and can exist within and among groups or within and among organizations. This chapter will focus primarily on conflict among units or groups within the organization. For example, a company's sales department may want to get a particular customer's order out ahead of schedule, while its manufacturing department may want to reduce costs by holding to the established schedule.

Although the terms *conflict* and *competition* are often used interchangeably, they are not quite the same. Competition produces conflict, but not all conflict reflects competition. Indeed, **competition** "involves actions taken by one person to attain his or her most preferred outcome while simultaneously blocking attainment of the counterpart's most preferred outcome."[8] In other words, in competition there is an opposition in the goals of the interdependent parties so that the possibility of goal attainment for one party increases as it decreases for the other.

Cooperation involves two or more parties working together to attain mutual goals. It is possible for cooperation and conflict to exist at the same time. For example, two groups may agree on goals but strongly disagree on how the goals are to be reached. The distinctions among conflict, competition, and cooperation are important, since the context of conflict—whether it is cooperative or competitive—determines how it can be managed, as illustrated in Figure 21.1. When conflict can be resolved cooperatively, both parties gain, and the results are usually constructive. But when it is resolved competitively, a win-lose situation may be credited, and the resolution may leave one or both parties dissatisfied.

Sometimes organizational win-lose conflicts are constructive. For

Cooperation

Competition

Conflict

Conflict
- Resolved cooperatively (outcome constructive)
- Resolved competitively (can become win-lose situation—outcome destructive)

FIGURE 21.1 Cooperative and competitive outcomes of conflict

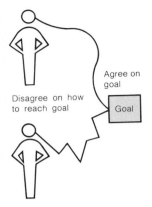

Disagree on how
to reach goal

Agree on
goal

Goal

Cooperation and conflict
can exist at the same time.

Sources of organizational
conflict:

- Differences in goals
- Allocation of scarce
resources
- Differences in values or
perceptions
- Work flow
- Organizational design
and structure

example, if each restaurant in a chain of restaurants (such as Mc-Donald's) competes for a bonus based on a percentage of sales, only one restaurant wins, but sales will probably increase throughout the chain, benefiting all parties. More frequently, though, win-lose conflicts reach the point where the parties involved lose sight of organizational goals and work primarily to destroy each other. In one situation, such conflict escalated until one manager sat behind a locked door while another manager beat and kicked on the door, screaming obscenities at the one within. Obviously, this kind of win-lose conflict is destructive to the organization and the individuals.

SOME SOURCES OF ORGANIZATIONAL CONFLICT

Conflict can arise from many sources. Some that will be described here are differences in goals and in values or perceptions, allocation of scarce resources, work flow, and organizational design and structure.[9] Most of these sources involve intergroup conflict; however, they can also involve conflict among individuals and between an individual and a group.

Differences in Goals   Chapters 9 and 10 described how organizational subsystems become differentiated or specialized in order to work on different tasks and problems. The differentiation frequently leads to a conflict of priorities or interests, even when the parties to the conflict agree on the organization's overall goals. The marketing department, for example, may want low prices and a variety of products in order to attract more customers. The production department may want fewer products at a higher price in order to show a greater profit in manufacturing. The finance department may want a relatively low inventory of parts so the money not used for inventory can be invested in something else, such as new machinery. And the purchasing department may want to order materials in large quantities to get a discount on them. The differentiation among subsystems may be healthy for the organization, but it may lead to conflict because of differing goals and points of view.

Allocation of Scarce Resources   Groups can function more smoothly and accomplish goals more easily when resources of money, people, materials, equipment, and space are plentiful. But in most organizations these resources are limited. As a result, conflict may arise over their allocation. There may be agreement on objectives but disagreement on how resources should be used to attain them. For example, a hospital's nursing department and radiology department may agree that improving patient care is a primary objective. But the nursing department may want to spend money on in-service training for nurses and on hiring nursing specialists, whereas the radiology department may want to purchase an expensive piece of equipment. Generally, the hospital cannot afford both.

Differences in Values or Perceptions Each individual sees the world differently and acts according to those personal perceptions. Groups often do the same, since those who work closely together tend to have common perceptions. Indeed, a frequent source of disagreement between one group and another is the tendency of each to value its own goals and ideas more highly than those of the other. This also occurs within a group when perceptual differences arise among the members because of the tendency of individuals to evaluate things in terms of their own experiences. Since the members of any organization have different backgrounds, experiences, training, and education, they cannot help but perceive many problems and their causes differently.[10]

Work Flow Conflict can develop because of the work flow within an organization. When work is interdependent (that is, two or more organizational units must depend on each other to complete their individual tasks), the potential for either conflict or cooperation exists. Conflict can occur when the groups involved are given too much to do or when the work is unevenly distributed. There is also a potential for conflict when the work is sequential—that is, when one group is unable to begin work until the other finishes its task.

Another cause of conflict is status. If it appears that individuals from a low-status unit are giving orders to those from a high-status unit, resistance and then conflict may develop. The higher-status group may find it difficult to take orders directly from lower-status people or from people whose status is unclear. Studies of the restaurant industry have shown that problems arise when waiters or waitresses (low status) give orders to chefs (high status).[11] It is for this reason that most restaurants use written orders or other indirect approaches for the orders coming to the chef.

Organization Structure As Chapters 9 and 10 have suggested, the structure of the organization can affect the amount of conflict generated. An organization or unit with a structure that does not fit its technology and environment will experience more dysfunctional conflict than one that is properly designed. Moreover, a good structure allows the development of constructive conflict that helps the organization attain its goals.

Organizations or units existing in a relatively certain environment with a stable technology are best organized along bureaucratic lines, with clear chains of command and specific rules and regulations; that is, they should have a mechanistic structure. Those existing in an uncertain environment with quickly changing technology are best designed along relatively open lines; that is, they should have an organic structure.

Structure can also produce conflict because it frequently results in the creation of line and staff positions.[12] In theory, line managers are part of a direct chain of command; they hold positions such as manufacturing manager, store manager, and area manager, and they make decisions. Staff specialists (who may also be managers) are supposed to provide advice and counsel to line managers to help their units accomplish orga-

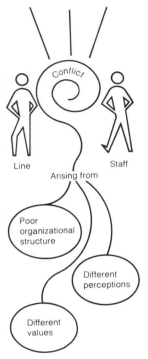

nizational objectives; they hold positions in marketing research, the personnel department, and the computer department, and they help line managers with their decisions.

The actual or potential conflict between line and staff personnel, either as groups or individuals, derives from more than one source of conflict. For example, the objective of the staff manager may be to bring about improvements; however, the line manager may be prepared to resist any advice from a person in the staff manager's position. A line manager in an outlying plant once said to a specialist attempting to install a company-wide job evaluation program. "Whatever you're selling, if you're from the home office, I don't want to buy."

Strong perceptual differences may exist between line and staff employees, growing out of age and social differences. The staff specialist may be a college graduate, whereas the production manager may have little formal education and may have come up through the ranks. The staff person may have primary loyalty to a particular profession, such as research or law, while the line manager may have primary loyalty to the organization.

There may also be status differences between line and staff. The staff manager may be short on experience but have the confidence of the president, and this may place the line manager in a lower-status position. A line manager with a great deal of status may resent receiving suggestions from a staff person who is viewed as lower in the hierarchy.

MANAGING TO REDUCE CONFLICT

Managing to reduce conflict:

- Dominance and forcing
- Smoothing
- Compromise
- Integrative problem solving

Trying to completely eliminate all conflict is futile. However, when conflict becomes destructive, the manager must take steps to reduce it. A number of basic approaches are available to managers for reducing conflict organizations.[13] The four major types are dominance or forcing, smoothing, compromise, and integrative problem solving. These approaches differ greatly in the type of resolution they accomplish (cooperative versus competitive) and in the conditions and processes they establish for later reduction of conflict situations.

The three approaches deal primarily with interpersonal or process mechanisms, ignoring the structural/task/resource mechanisms that can also be used to resolve or reduce conflict. (Chapter 10 described a number of these structural approaches.)

Dominance and Forcing   **Dominance** and forcing occur when a solution to conflict is imposed or dictated. The imposing can be done by (1) the most powerful person or group in the conflict, (2) a common supervisor or other individuals within the organization who have the power and authority to enforce decisions, and (3) a neutral umpire or arbitrator. Dominance and forcing methods do not usually resolve the conflict, however. Instead they repress the conflict, forcing it underground; and they tend to establish win-lose situations in which the loser, who must give in to higher authority, ends up disappointed and hostile. The dominance-forcing solutions to conflict have two obvious problems:

1. There is no guarantee that the winning side will make a decision that is best for the organization. The decision generally is in the best interests of the winning side.
2. The losing side generally remains unconvinced and frustrated and looks for opportunities to win at some other time.

Classical theorists unanimously agreed that the best way to eliminate conflict was for the common supervisor of the two parties in conflict to arbitrate between them.[14] In practice, of course, this solution does not always work. In one situation, for example, three managers who worked together reported to different upper-level managers. The conflict among the three was particularly destructive. After a company reorganization, these managers were directed to report to a single individual. When their new boss found out about the conflict, he called the managers together and announced to them that from that day forward they would cooperate closely with each other. All three nodded their heads. What they meant was, "Yes, boss, we hear you—but we don't agree with you." The conflict was thus driven underground and emerged in more subtle ways than before.

Majority rule is the attempt to resolve group conflict by a majority vote. This approach can be satisfactory if the process is seen as fair by participants in the conflict; however, if one party consistently outvotes the other, the losing side tends to feel dominated or forced.

Dominance and forcing do succeed in eliminating many types of conflict, at least in the short run. Clearly, there are times when dominance is the only practical approach—when the boss has to make a decision for opposing groups. However, the primary weakness of the approach is that it usually deals with symptoms rather than with the root of the problem.

Smoothing Smoothing is a subtle and diplomatic kind of dominance. Instead of dealing openly with conflict, it denies or hides it. Common interests are emphasized, and known areas of disagreement are avoided. Problems are ignored in the hope that they will go away.

Smoothing was apparent in President Kennedy's approach to the Bay of Pigs fiasco. People were polite to the extent that conflicting views were not mentioned, and groupthink prevailed. Smoothing was also obvious in the actions of the Penn Central's board of directors before the railroad went bankrupt. Rather than permit conflict, the directors avoided questioning management about its actions.

Compromise Compromise is the attempt to obtain agreement through mutual concessions—each party modifying its point of view to achieve a workable solution. It is the attempt to find a middle ground among two or more positions. The compromise approach is less likely to generate hostility than the dominance and forcing approaches. However, from the

On the Job

TEACHING HOW TO COPE WITH WORKPLACE CONFLICTS

It is nothing if not comical: Sixteen middle-aged executives, divided into teams, race against the clock—and each other—to build a device out of assorted junk that will catch raw eggs gently enough to keep them from breaking. They get the junk from an auctioneer who "sells" such things as metal strips and pieces of string, for which each team can bid up to $55,000. In the background a videotape machine quietly records the sights and sounds of the competition.

Later, the executives watch themselves in action. To their distress, they see themselves mocking their teammates, throwing out authoritarian orders, and showing impatience. Although their goal was to beat the other teams, they discover that most of their conflicts were with persons on their side.

The egg drop exercise, developed by Vector Management Systems Inc., of New York, to open a three-day course on managing conflict, is one of a growing number of techniques offered by consultants who teach managers to recognize and deal with on-the-job conflicts. The techniques may be as simple as self-administered and self-scored questionnaires, such as those offered by Houston-based Teleometrics International Inc. to let managers analyze their own styles of dealing with conflicts.

But they also include psychologist-scored surveys that allow subordinates and peers to rate managers on their ability to handle conflicts, as well as courses that run as long as nine days. The disparate methods have one thing in common—a belief that conflict, when properly recognized, is not debilitating to job effectiveness and can actually enhance it.

"There's a lot of energy wasted because many people work toward eliminating conflict," says Kenneth Sole, a psychologist who runs conflict seminars at NTL Institute for Applied Behavioral Science in Bethel, Me. "My goal is not to have fewer conflicts, but to make conflicts productive."

Charles Reiner, Vector's president, notes that there are five ways to deal with conflicts: compromise, competition, avoidance, collaboration, and accommodation. "As psychologists we've worked studiously to suspend value judgments about the five styles," he says. "We try to give course participants an ability to use all of them, and by the end of our seminar their bias against or for any one style is considerably reduced."

Increasing tension. The proliferation of conflict seminars comes at a time of increasing tension in the workplace. The in-

flux of women and minorities into the work force has caused problems that can rarely be resolved by fiat. The growing popularity of avant-garde management structures such as matrix management, in which many corporate employees wind up reporting to two bosses, has reduced many executives' authority to issue orders, making their interpersonal skills far more important. And in general, corporate management over the last decade has become far more amenable to judging managers by their behavior patterns as well as by bottom-line performance and has shown an increasing willingness to spend time and money on behaviorally oriented programs.

John W. Humphrey, president of Forum Corp., a Boston behavioral consulting firm, calls the trend an evolution from resolving conflict to managing conflict to working with conflict. "We've gone," he says, "from something that says, 'Get it out!' to something that says, 'Learn how to use it.'"

Acting it out. The techniques of teaching managers how to use conflict vary as much as the consultants who develop them. Vector, for example, includes a commercial movie, *Twelve Angry Men,* in its course because the jury members in the film use a variety of styles to resolve their conflicts. After each showing, the course participants analyze the conflicts and how to resolve them.

Other consultants rely more heavily on role-playing. In one exercise, Forum Corp. sets up groups of three people and gives them a hypothetical problem. One participant might play the part of a research manager, another a product manager, and a third an engineering department head. They have to figure out how to allocate scarce resources for each department. Situation Management Systems Inc., of Boston, offers courses on "Positive Power and Influence" and "Negotiating Skills" that deal heavily with resolving conflicts. They wind up with each trainee playing himself or herself, and a fellow participant acting as the trainee's boss or subordinate.

Not surprisingly, such methods have their detractors. One of them, Kenneth R. Hammond, director of the University of Colorado's Center for Research on Judgment & Policy, has been a conflict troubleshooter for such disparate organizations as the Denver Police Dept. and an international pharmaceutical company. He pays little attention to behavioral styles, concentrating instead on separating facts from values. "People assume that if they solve the emotional problems, the cognitive aspect will

solve itself, but then nobody focuses on issues," he maintains.

By focusing on issues, Hammond says, he resolved a two-year conflict between the Denver Police Dept., which wanted a new bullet with greater stopping power, and community leaders, who saw the request as bloodthirsty and possibly racist. He got the warring parties to rank in importance such values as stopping power, injury, and threat to bystanders. He discovered that the community as a whole would accept a bullet that had increased stopping effectiveness without increasing injury. Within six weeks, the police settled on ammunition that would flatten out and knock a person over on impact. As Hammond saw it, the solution had been elusive because of emotions. "When they couldn't agree," he says, "they attributed it to unpleasant motives, such as 'You hate blacks' or 'You want a lawless society.'"

To NTL's Sole, such real-life issues are the stuff of which conflict courses must be made. He also eschews role-playing and artificially created situations and arranges to have an equal distribution of warring factions in his workshops, allowing conflicts to arise naturally. He tries to have the same number of men and women, for instance, and to include a large smattering of minorities. With the participant dis-

tribution forming a built-in powder keg, he lets simple issues—such as whether or not to allow smoking—form the conflicts that will be analyzed. "We get a participant pool that guarantees differences but also guarantees pools of support," he explains. "My workshops are kind of a social microcosm, and the issues that emerge mirror issues in society."

Racism and sexism. In contrast to comprehensive efforts such as Sole's nine-day workshop, a number of corporations are putting in less sweeping programs of their own. More often than not, they are designed to resolve specific conflict problems within an organization. Northwestern Bell Telephone Co., for instance, has a program to combat racism and sexism. "We teach women and minorities to develop support systems and to confront people who use sexist or racist language," Larry L. Waller, staff manager for awareness training, explains.

At Sperry Vickers, a Troy (Mich.) division of Sperry Corp., a switch to matrix management, with its dual ladder of authority, dramatically increased conflict two years ago. B. Richard Templeton, manager of human resources and organization development, has since distributed conflict analysis questionnaires to

On the Job

TEACHING HOW TO COPE WITH WORKPLACE CONFLICTS (Continued)

managers and their subordinates and has been holding informal self-assessment meetings to help them understand how their behavior is perceived by their colleagues.

Templeton grants that the matrix system still causes clashes, but he says that his program is helping resolve the conflicts at an early stage. "It's like setting a course for the moon," he says. "The best place to make a course correction is as early as possible, before you're hopelessly off track."

Tailor-made seminars. Conflict consultants sometimes develop seminars to a company's specifications. Union Carbide Corp., for one, has sent nearly 200 managers through a tailor-made Vector course over the last two years. Stephen J. Wall, Carbide's manager of corporate management development, reports that informal feedback has been very positive. "The thread that runs through the comments is that people are startled to discover their own patterns of response to

conflicts," he says. "Now they say they can see what's coming and actually plan strategies to deal with it." Wall, who took the course before he bought it for Carbide, says he discovered that he had a tendency to be an accommodator and used to give in to unreasonable requests. "Now whenever I feel I'm about to give in, I roll it around in my head first," he says.

It is almost impossible to put a dollars-and-cents value on such behavioral awareness, but every conflict course graduate with whom BUSINESS WEEK spoke insisted that the course was worth the few hundred dollars it typically cost. Marilyn Loden, an organization development specialist at New York Telephone Co. and a graduate of Sole's program, noted that she had just had a conversation with a recalcitrant employee; it was difficult for her, but it cleared the air in the office. "A year ago I would have been stewing about the fact that he wasn't working out, but I would have said nothing,"

she says.

Raymond A. Murphy, a Carbide manager of systems software, and Leicia Marlow, a Carbide data processing applications manager, liked the Vector course so much that they have assigned several of their own employees to attend it. "Watching my people at staff meetings now, I see more conscious attempts to understand where the other guy is coming from," Murphy notes. "We've had people who were overassertive before who are now curbing their responses, while others who had sat back and watched have learned to be assertive."

The ability to choose among several styles as the situation requires is probably the most important result of all the courses. Marlow, who concedes that she needed help in becoming more assertive, insists that the course was far more complete than standard assertiveness training. As she sums it up: "It wasn't necessarily altering behavior; it was broadening it."

viewpoint of the organization, compromise is not a highly effective method of conflict resolution, since it does not necessarily aim for the best solution for achieving organizational goals. Rather, it tries for a solution that is satisfactory—even if it is only minimally satisfactory—to all parties to the conflict.

Integrative Problem Solving **Integrative problem solving** is the open, complete, and rapid sharing of information concerning the problem and a joint search through the shared information to arrive at a decision that best accomplishes organizational goals. The term *confrontation* has also been used for this approach.[15] All the relevant facts are brought into the open, and conflicting viewpoints and opposition are encouraged. Integrative problem solving was the method of conflict resolution used in the Cuban-Russian missile crisis discussed earlier.

Managers almost unanimously see this kind of problem solving as the most desirable mode of conflict resolution. Yet, according to sociologists Paul Lawrence and Jay Lorsch, "it is used much less than it is recommended."[16] One reason confrontation is seldom used is that most people instinctively avoid highlighting differences. Dominance, smoothing, and compromise are more comfortable techniques than confrontation. Also, confrontation tends to be more time-consuming, and it requires that the people involved trust each other and not feel alienated from the organization. It also requires skilled leadership and a willingness to accept additional stress while the problem is being worked through. Finally, it encourages unusual ideas.

In one factory the quality of manufactured parts was poor. Dominance, smoothing, and compromise had been tried without success. A number of groups were involved, and each was in conflict with the others. Finally, the manager suggested a weekly meeting to explore the reasons for poor quality. The thrust of these meetings was toward integrative problem solving and confrontation rather than defensiveness. The success of this approach was manifested when, over a period of six months, quality improved by 62 percent, for an annual savings of approximately $100,000.[17]

Integrative problem solving, which is usually superior to the other approaches to conflict resolution, is most effective when parties can meet face to face. The approach can also involve examining and changing the organization's structure, as described in Chapter 10. Actually, both structural and interpersonal approaches are sometimes necessary for conflict resolution.

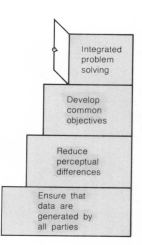

Integrated problem solving

Develop common objectives

Reduce perceptual differences

Ensure that data are generated by all parties

Three specific steps for integrated problem solving are ensuring that data for problem solving are generated in common, reducing perceptual differences, and developing a common set of objectives.

Ensuring That Data Are Generated in Common Many organizational problems involve more than one subsystem or group. If only one develops the solution to a problem, the odds are that the others will reject it. From a systems point of view, no single group has all the information. In addition, a solution developed by one group may be excellent from its point of view but may be less satisfactory from the others' viewpoints. When representatives of the different groups involved are brought together to study a problem and jointly develop a solution, all relevant information can be pooled, and the problem is likely to be solved in a way that reduces conflict.

Integrated problem-solving methods:

- Use common data
- Reduce perceptual differences
- Develop common goals

More and more, organizations are using task forces to solve problems that affect several groups and the organization as a whole. To be successful, the task force generally has to include representatives from each group involved with the problem. For example, one organization was having difficulty moving new products through the development, manufacturing, and marketing stages. The managers involved decided to appoint a task force of representatives from research and development, marketing, production, and purchasing. The task force met to integrate the work of the units and departments. It referred policy questions to higher management, but it thrashed out operating problems within the group—through confrontation. All the relevant facts were brought out as each issue was openly debated. Finally, a decision was reached on each of the problems. Conflicting viewpoints and opposition were encouraged. As a result, new products were designed, developed, and manufactured much more quickly and effectively than before.[18]

Reducing Perceptual Differences Earlier in the chapter perceptual differences were described as a source of conflict. To reduce conflict from this source, the parties involved can be brought together so they can share their perceptions, clear up misunderstandings, and understand one another's objectives. Sometimes, a single meeting can do much to clear the air, and follow-up meetings can be used to iron out persistent differences.

This is the method usually used to reduce conflict between union and management prior to bargaining. In its formal version it entails each group writing down its self-perceptions and its perceptions of the other group and then discussing these perceptions. Frequently, the process demonstrates that the perceptions are incorrect but that they have nonetheless influenced behavior.[19]

Developing a Common Set of Objectives Because subsystems within any organization frequently have different goals (as indicated in Chapter 3), conflict among these subsystems can develop. Many managers are rewarded on the basis of their success in attaining the goals of their particular subsystems. Sometimes these goals are achieved at the expense of other groups, and competitive conflict is generated.

The organization confrontation meeting is one method of encouraging groups to establish and work toward common objectives. The method consists of several steps. First, groups of ten to fifteen people are formed. Each group is a representative sample of the organization; its members are drawn from functional areas and hierarchical levels of the organization. The groups are assembled in one place and told that their task is to identify problems that affect individuals or the entire organization. Each group meets separately to determine the problems and then returns to the common meeting place to report on them. The problems are then categorized, and new groups are formed to begin working on their solution. The individual groups meet periodically either with the manager or with the larger group to report their progress.[20]

This approach has been used with engineers, managers, nurses, clerical staffs, and entire organizations. In one unionized plant of about three hundred employees, the approach involved everyone in the plant, including guards, janitors, secretaries, engineers, and managers. As Figure 21.2 shows, the program was started in manufacturing period 7. By the last period indicated, manufacturing costs had been reduced by about 45 percent, for a savings of more than $1 million per year. Productivity also climbed sharply, and morale and job satisfaction increased.[21]

STIMULATING CONSTRUCTIVE CONFLICT

As explained at the beginning of the chapter, conflict is not always negative; indeed, constructive conflict contributes to the organization's goals. Rather than always trying to minimize conflict, the effective manager diagnoses each situation to determine the most effective level of constructive conflict for the organization or subsystem.

Although writers often discuss ways of reducing conflict, relatively few write about ways of stimulating it.[22] Many organizations do not have enough functional, purposeful, constructive conflict; and the effective manager must therefore create such conflict. The easiest way to do this is to refrain from applying any of the conflict reduction techniques already described. For example, the manager may choose not to mediate or not to have each group develop solutions that can be discussed by all the groups. When conflict is not mediated, it escalates. Other approaches to stimulating conflict include communicating that conflict is acceptable, changing communications channels, redistributing power, and increasing or maintaining perceptual differences.

Stimulating constructive conflict:

- Communicating that conflict is acceptable
- Changing communications channels
- Redistributing power
- Increasing or maintaining perceptual differences

Communicating That Conflict Is Acceptable In many organizations conflict is unequivocally viewed as unacceptable. Such organizations want peace and harmony and see no role for conflict. Employees respond to the message by downplaying their differences of opinion, especially to their supervisors.

The single most effective way of stimulating manageable conflict is to let subordinates know that constructive disagreement has its legitimate place. One way of doing this is for the manager to show subordinates that problem identification is valued and that original thinking will be rewarded. The effective manager allows all ideas to be challenged and encourages the expression of different opinions.

To illustrate: A number of groups were asked to analyze a problem and develop a solution. Some of the groups contained a person who challenged the group's analyses and solutions; other groups did not. Those with the challenging person were better able to handle conflict and developed better analyses and solutions.[23]

Changing Communications Channels Once the message that constructive conflict is acceptable has been communicated, another method

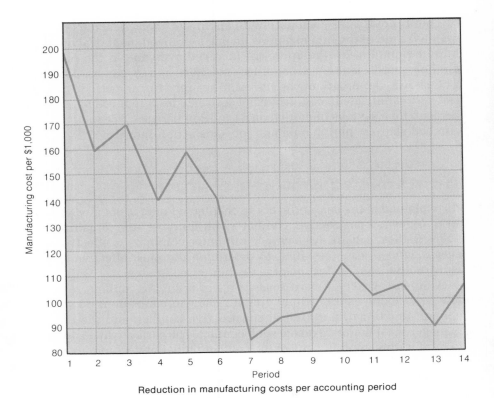

Reduction in manufacturing costs per accounting period

Productivity dollars per work hour

FIGURE 21.2 Reduction in costs and increased productivity using the organization confrontation approach

of stimulating conflict can be employed—changing the communications process. A basic way of changing the process is to alter the formal channels of communication. For example, a manager who regularly sends information to certain individuals or groups may discontinue that practice. Or a manager who normally does not send information to certain groups or individuals may begin doing so. An excellent way to create tension and conflict is to send a memorandum to the usual people but to omit one or two from the list. The omission will bring about reexamination of the situation.

On the informal level, a manager may carefully select which messages should go through the grapevine and who should get them. Changes in the traditional channels redistribute knowledge inside the organization. Since knowledge represents power, changing communication channels shifts the balance of power.

In addition, a manager seeking to stimulate conflict can send out ambiguous information. Suppose a memorandum has some implicit contradictions. Subordinates and others receiving it will question it, seek out more information, and take other actions to reduce the ambiguity.

Redistributing Power   Those who possess power can bring about constructive conflict by redistributing delegated power among the organization's members. Power is obtained from the activities that take place in an organization, and a reshuffling of responsibility for such activities stimulates the kind of conflict that leads to desired change.

Often, new managers entering an organization bring in subordinates with whom they have worked in the past. This kind of redistribution of power brings about a careful examination of present and past practices. Those who have become apathetic frequently regain their energy when the power is redistributed.

Maintaining or Increasing Perceptual Differences   In the Electronic Products Division Case described in Chapter 10, top management initially diagnosed a conflict situation as arising from poor intergroup relations. The division's general manager determined that there were many internal conflicts among the various functional groups, and he felt that these conflicts were severely hampering product development efforts. He decided at first to attempt to reduce the perceptual differences among the groups.

Further study of the problem, however, suggested that reducing perceptual differences was not the answer. The organization existed in a turbulent and uncertain environment and actually required a high degree of differentiation or perceptual variation in the areas of formality of structure, interpersonal orientation, and goal and time orientation. Under the circumstances, it was appropriate for the scientists to see the world differently than the assembly managers did. Reducing these perceptual differences would have ill served the organization. Instead, the company reorganized the groups into project teams, thereby maintaining the perceptual differences but lessening conflict. In cases such as this, managers must strive to maintain or even increase perceptual differences.

STRESS IN ORGANIZATIONS[24]

John R. is a thirty-eight-year-old middle-level sales manager in a large corporation. He is considered hard-working, dependable, loyal, and productive by his superiors, who nevertheless feel that he does not have potential for a top executive position. This belief was formalized eight months ago when a key promotion was given to one of John's subordinates instead of to John. Since then his on-the-job behavior has gradually changed. His attention to detail has slipped. He has become withdrawn and seems to have lost enthusiasm in his relationships with his superiors, who view his changed behavior as confirmation of their decision not to promote him.[25]

John R.'s unfortunate situation is an example of only one type of midcareer stress. Table 21.2 shows other common types. Stress in organizations and ways of managing it have been gaining attention. This text will discuss only the most obvious sources of such stress and some major strategies for its reduction.

Conditions Associated with Employee Stress   There are many conditions associated with employee stress. Some of the most pervasive are

TABLE 21.2   Organizational Stresses

Roles in the organization	*Job qualities*
Role ambiguity	Quantitative overload/underload
Role conflict	Qualitative overload/underload
Too little management support	Time pressures
Holding a middle-management position	Responsibility for things/people
	Work pace
Relationships	*Organizational structure*
With supervisors	Lack of participation
With subordinates	No sense of belonging
With colleagues	Poor communications
Inability to delegate	Restrictions on behavior
	Lack of opportunity
Physical environment	Inequity in pay and performance evaluation
Temperature, noise, lights	Hours of work
Spatial arrangements	
Crowding	*Career development*
Privacy	Status incongruity
	Underpromotion
Change	Overpromotion
Organizational	Midcareer
Individual	Obsolesence

Source: Adapted from Cary L. Cooper and Judi Marshall, "Occupational Sources of Stress: A Review of the Literature Relating to Coronary Heart Disease and Mental Ill Health," *Journal of Occupational Psychology* 49 (March 1976): 12.

those linked with the roles we play in organizations, such as role ambiguity and conflict.

Role Ambiguity   Insufficient information about the level of authority and amount of responsibility resident in one's position in the organization results in **role ambiguity.** It leaves a person unsure of what is expected in performance and how that performance will be evaluated. This ambiguity constrains an employee from performing well enough to gain recognition, to obtain a sense of achievement and responsibility, and to be a productive member of the organization. It produces tremendous stress. The more role ambiguity people perceive in their jobs, the less satisfied they are and the worse they perform.[26]

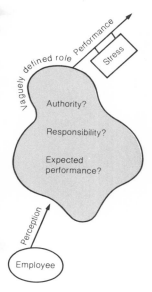

Role ambiguity produces stress, prevents best performance.

Role Conflict   Several forms of **role conflict** exist. They include *intra-sender* conflict, a situation in which a supervisor asks a subordinate to perform a job that requires more time and assistance than is provided. An employee's response to intra-sender conflict is often withdrawal and lessened concern for performing well.

An increasingly common type of role conflict is *inter-role* conflict, something experienced by many career-oriented women who have mother and wife roles. Each of these roles produces demands that sometimes need to be met at the same time. If the demands of one are fully met, the demands of the others cannot be fully met. The question "Which demand do I meet?" expresses the conflict involved.

When conflict ensues from the combination of an employee's non-work roles with the work role and the work role is relatively nonstressful by itself, the organization must decide whether it will take any responsibility for reducing the stress arising from that conflict. Organizations that have responded with concern have offered employees more flexibility in when and how long they work. Programs such as flexitime, split shifts, and four-day workweeks are examples of such responses.

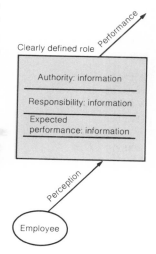

Providing more information about role removes ambiguity, allows better performance without stress.

Work Overload   There are two types of **work overload.** In *quantitative overload* the person does not have enough time to complete the work assigned. In *qualitative overload* the person does not have enough ability. Both conditions generate stress, particularly when they involve responsibility for the welfare of other people. The air traffic controllers at busy airports face extreme quantitative overload involving responsibility for people. The results are predictable: ulcers, high blood pressure, arthritis, headaches, allergies, upset stomachs, alcoholism, depression, and acute anxiety. The severity of the controller's job prompted this fictitious ad:

HELP WANTED: World's busiest airport seeks radar jockies for unusually stimulating, high-intensity environment. Must be able to direct at least 12 aircraft at one time and make instant decisions affecting the safety of thousands. No degree required, but prior experience as traffic cop, seeing-eye dog, or God helpful. Severe stress will jeopardize sanity and result in early termination from job, but employer will absorb cost of medical and psychiatric care.[27]

Work Underload   Although it is obvious that too much work produces stress, it is equally true, though less obvious, that too little work produces stress. This situation, called **work underload,** can take the form of *quantitative underload*, where not enough work is provided to fill the employee's on-the-job time, or *qualitative underload*, where the job does not require enough of the employee's ability. The result is boredom and stress. For many, the only way to combat this stress is to psychologically withdraw and thus become alienated. Some organizations fail to provide sufficient activities or challenge in many of their jobs and consequently have many apathetic workers.

Work Pace   Another source of potential stress in organizations is the work pace. The pace may be set by a machine or some other control besides the individual doing the work (called *machine pacing*), or it may be set by that individual (called *employee pacing*). Machine pacing prevents the individual from satisfying a crucial need for control. It has been reported that workers on machine-paced jobs feel exhausted at the end of the shift and are unable to relax soon after work because of increased adrenaline secretion—a physiological response to stress—during work. In a study of twenty-three white- and blue-collar occupations the assembly-line workers reported the most severe symptoms of stress.

Three classes of stress symptoms:

- Physiological (individual)
- Psychological (individual)
- Behavioral (organization and individual)

Symptoms of Stress   There are three major classes of symptoms associated with stress. Two are relevant to the individual—physiological and psychological symptoms. The other is relevant to the organization as well—behavioral symptoms.

Physiological Symptoms   Short-term physiological symptoms of stress are increased heart rate and respiration and frequent headaches. Long-term symptoms are ulcers, increased blood pressure (hypertension), and increased likelihood of coronary heart disease.[28]

Psychological Symptoms   Psychological symptoms are apathy, withdrawal, satisfaction and dissatisfaction, irritability, procrastination, forgetfulness, tunnel vision, increased tendency to misjudge people and inability to organize activities. All people have experienced some of these symptoms, since all have experienced stress. How can both satisfaction and dissatisfaction be symptoms of stress? Stress is a dynamic condition associated with favorable as well as unfavorable events. Satisfaction is the most likely response to a favorable event (an opportunity), and dissatisfaction is the most likely response to an unfavorable one (a constraint).

Behavioral Symptoms The third class of symptoms is organizational behavior consequences. Consistent with the positive and negative conditions of stress, organizational consequences associated with negative stress conditions are increased absenteeism, turnover, and accident proneness, plus overall poor performance (low quantity and quality). Associated with positive stress conditions are decreased absenteeism, turnover, and accident proneness, plus overall good performance. The stress associated with an uncertain opportunity stimulates increased adrenaline and blood sugar production, which provide extra energy. If the stress condition is a positive one, the energy is directed to performing well in that condition. If the condition becomes too complex, however, the performance-directed energy can actually impede successful performance, since excessive energy may lead to inappropriate haste.

Although most of the literature on stress in organizations focuses on the unfavorable results of stress, this text has demonstrated that not all the results of stress are unfavorable. To the extent that the energy produced by stress can be utilized effectively, the stress condition is reduced as a favorable outcome is created. If the stress condition cannot be reduced, the outcome is usually unfavorable. Fortunately several strategies exist for organizations to help employees reduce stress and for individuals to employ themselves. Each will be briefly described.

An Organizational Strategy One strategy that an organization can use to help reduce the stress for its employees is effective performance planning.[29] This strategy, which can be implemented through a management by objectives program, reduces stress by clarifying job responsibilities. In one organization it was used successfully to reduce role conflict, role ambiguity, and absenteeism. This planning strategy was part of a management by objectives program and included a training program for managers. Since the management by objectives program included the identification, specification, and assignment of work goals, the employees' performance was evaluated on six goal-oriented job dimensions before institution of the program and then five months after the managers received their training. Comparison of results before and after showed significant improvements in all six dimensions. The dimensions were difficulty of work goals, clarity of work goals, quality of performance feedback from the supervisor, amount of performance feedback from the supervisor, employee participation in setting work goals, and peer competition for work goal accomplishment.[30] It was through improvements in these dimensions that role conflict and role ambiguity were reduced and absenteeism decreased.

The results in this case illustrate the impact of just one personnel activity for reducing stress. The results also indicate that organizations should pay particular attention to their system of performance appraisal, especially to avert the phenomenon of the *vanishing performance appraisal,* in which this function gradually ceases because of decreasing care in its proper implementation.

Absenteeism can be a symptom of stress.

On the Job

HOW "BURNOUT" AFFECTS CORPORATE MANAGERS AND THEIR PERFORMANCE

It was a classic case of executive burnout.

John Nelson's enthusiasm for his job as employe-relations director for Robertson Factories in Taunton, Mass., began to cool. He had worked hard to boost morale and reduce high absenteeism at an Oklahoma plant of the maker of curtains, drapes and bedspreads. But although he had improved a health plan that employes there had complained about, absenteeism remained high.

"I just felt like a failure. I began to think all the work wasn't worth it," Mr. Nelson says. After that, "I removed myself from dealing with what was my job—people. I became more interested in writing policy manuals." And his job performance declined.

A growing number of corporate managers are experiencing the feelings of frustration, cynicism and helplessness known as executive burnout, experts say. And most of these managers aren't likely to talk about their problems. "It's a career version of a death wish," says James Gallagher, the chairman of Career Management Associates, an executive-counseling firm in New York. "They don't really want to be in the job any longer, but they won't blow the whistle on themselves."

More Seeking Help But increasingly, burned-out managers are seeking help. Mr. Nelson, for example, rekindled enthusiasm for his work after obtaining outside job counseling. And some companies are starting to provide counseling as more managers make their problems known.

"It's become socially acceptable, even chic, to say you're burnt out," says Donald Miller, a New York management consultant. Mr. Miller, like others, believes that burnout always has been a problem in stressful business situations, "but now that it has a name, more people are willing to talk about it." He sees this as a positive development that could prevent the "retiring on the job" that he says is common at some companies.

Job burnout emerged as a recognized syndrome about 10 years ago. But until recently, nearly all the attention was focused on the "helping" professions, such as teaching, social work and nursing. Herbert Freudenberger, a New York psychologist who claims credit for the term, says job burnout "is a depletion of energy" experienced by these professionals when they feel overwhelmed by others' problems. This, he says, is followed by a cynical attitude of "Why bother? It doesn't matter anyhow."

Evidence of the syndrome is showing up among corporate managers, experts say. James Manuso, the chief psychologist for Equitable Life Assurance Society of the U.S., estimates that "10% of the overall executive population exhibits the cynicism that could be a harbinger of burnout." And Opinion Research Corp., a Princeton, N.J., firm that has periodically surveyed employe attitudes at 188 companies for nearly 30 years, reports that last year managers' ratings of their job satisfaction fell to an all-time low.

Changed Environment Experts cite several reasons executive burnout appears to be on the rise. "There's a new psychology of entitlement out there. People now expect more from their jobs than just a paycheck," Mr. Manuso says.

Abraham Korman, a professor of psychology at New York's Baruch College, adds: "The traumas from the 1960s have filtered up. There's the loss of authority and a growing 'What's in it for me?' attitude." Others say rapidly changing technology and the turbulent economy have created conditions conducive to executive burnout.

Psychologists say burnout is different from mid-life crises. Burnout is related specifically to job stress rather than broader personal problems. Frequently, it is found in executives who deal directly with employe problems.

Burnout also is different from job boredom. "Almost everyone gets a spasm of boredom. But burnout is chronic and gets worse if it isn't treated," says Richard Issel, a clinical psychologist who says about one-fifth of his private patients exhibit the burnout syndrome.

Often the early symptoms of executive burnout go undetected, says Nathan Kline, a New York psychiatrist. He says these symptoms include difficulty concentrating and making decisions, chronic fatigue, failure of short-term memory, increased irritability and general feelings of guilt. Ultimately, he adds, burnout produces depression.

"Self-Fulfilling Prophecy" "To a certain extent, it is a self-fulfilling prophecy," he says. "Job performance deteriorates, the executive begins to feel incompetent and pretty soon he does become less competent."

Often, the executives who burn out are the ones that had the most sparkle. Lowell Cohn, for example, was a rising star in the early 1970s at Cunningham & Walsh, a big New York advertising agency. Mr. Cohn's creative talents helped him move quickly up the corporate ladder to a job paying more than $100,000 a year. But he discov-

ered that the more managerial responsibility he got, "the less I could do the things I liked and could do well. I had become a supervisor."

Soon, Mr. Cohn felt overwhelmed by personnel problems. "We had a high official who was a real bully. Dealing with him became finding ways to play games to protect the people I was in charge of," he recalls. Mr. Cohn wasted time devising strategies to thwart the other executive. "At meetings, I'd always try to sit behind him on the windowsill. It interrupted his train of thought when he was picking on people."

Burdened and distracted, Mr. Cohn says he soon became cynical about his dealings with clients, too. "I stopped doing my best and began giving them what they wanted to hear. The game became 'Feed the dog whatever he wants to eat.' I began to feel like the most expensive hooker in the city of New York.

"I knew my performance was really lousy. All I wanted to do was run out of that place every day at five o'clock," Mr. Cohn adds. Finally, after several warnings, the company's executive committee asked him to resign. Currently, Mr. Cohn heads the Biofeedback Study Center in New York. The center, he says deals in "stress management."

He says his own experience made him realize "that this problem is extremely widespread, but it isn't widely recognized yet."

Unlike Mr. Cohn, many executives who seek treatment for burnout are revitalized quickly and remain at their jobs. Often, treatment consists of helping the manager to appraise the job situation. For instance, Mr. Nelson is once more energetically involved in the problems of workers at Robertson Factories.

He remembers his discouragement when he first spoke to the job counselor, who is a friend. "I told him, 'Sounds like I ought to look around for something else.' But he convinced me that escaping into another line of work wouldn't solve the problem."

So Mr. Nelson spent about six months in weekly sessions with the counselor. "What he got me to do was make sure that every day I sat down with a real person and talked about a real problem, instead of pushing paper around. Pretty soon, I began to get some good feedback. I began to feel positive about my job again," he says.

Some Innovations Help Recently, for example, Mr. Nelson began offering employes assistance in filling out income-tax forms. He also started working with a federal jobs program to

On the Job

HOW "BURNOUT" AFFECTS CORPORATE MANAGERS AND THEIR PERFORMANCE (Continued)

train new workers for his company. He says his boss is pleased with his initiative and with the fact that the federal government is sharing the training costs.

Mr. Nelson says burnout often is ignored at many concerns. "Most companies are afraid to ask you to go to get help from somebody. They'd rather deal with a minimum-functioning employe. If it gets to be a real problem, they fire you. Or they just slide you into a slot where you'll be less productive, less critical to the operation."

A handful of companies, though, are beginning to provide help for executives on the way to burning out. Joseph Yeager, a clinical psychologist who specializes in treating burnout, works regularly with employes at such companies as Pfizer Corp. and American Can Co. "They don't

have formal burnout programs the way they have, say, alcohol programs. But, in effect, I'm their burnout program," he says.

Mr. Yeager estimates that nearly half the "performance problems" that he is asked to deal with involve executive burnout. "There are a lot of executives out there that get swamped because they can't deal with the people problems," Mr. Yeager says. He adds that burnout often surfaces about two years after an executive promotion.

Practical Treatment Mr. Yeager says executives generally respond well to treatment that is practical, short-term and goal-oriented. "It's a question of reconditioning their responses to situations," he says.

For example, Jean, a designer for a small knitwear firm, had

been ready to quit her job last December. She had been complaining to her boss about noisy working conditions. "I was being paid to create, and I wasn't given the right environment to do it in," she says. When the conditions weren't changed, her work deteriorated.

"Instead of reworking a pattern that I wasn't satisfied with," she adds, "I began to think that if it doesn't mean anything to them, it doesn't mean anything to me." A friend suggested that Jean see Mr. Yeager.

"He's shown me how to turn around my anger and make it work for me. I'm more vocal about dealing with the situation now, and my complaints are being listened to." Jean says she is again fully involved in her career. And she has learned how to get answers from her boss.

Source: Robert S. Greenberger, "How 'Burnout' Affects Corporate Managers and Their Performance," *Wall Street Journal,* April 23, 1981, pp. 1, 22. Reprinted by permission of The Wall Street Journal, © Dow Jones & Company, Inc. 1981. All rights reserved.

An Individual Strategy How often have you said "I wish I had more time; there are so many things I want to do," or "If I only had the time," or even "I just don't have the time"? If you have said these words frequently, you are in the company of millions. But for you and those millions, there may be a way to solve some of your time shortage problems. And by dealing with your time shortage problems you will not only accomplish more but also reduce stress.

Time management is a technique for increasing control over personal time and stress.[31] The essence of time management is:

1. Define goals (short-term and long-term), job and nonjob and assign

priorities to them. This is more difficult than it sounds and will require careful thought.

2. Determine measures and standards by which to evaluate progress in attaining your goals.

3. Identify personal strengths and weaknesses that will help or hinder attainment of the goals. Then identify strategies by which the weaknesses can be eliminated.

4. Solicit feedback from others who know you well or who will be involved in your goal attainment. Colleagues and friends often see us differently than we see ourselves and can help us identify strengths and weaknesses and even help formulate strategies for overcoming weaknesses.

5. Take the following steps to enhance the likelihood of attaining goals:
   a. Break large goals into smaller, more readily attainable goals.
   b. Make sure goals and standards are clearly stated.
   c. Establish goals with moderate levels of difficulty.
   d. Make a commitment to others and yourself to attain the goals.

6. Continually ask, in light of the prioritized goals, "What is the best use of my time right now?" Then act on your answer.

The technique of time management can help people attain the goals that reflect their important needs and values. By gaining better control of time, people also control the stress they experience. This technique is most helpful for those who have never clearly identified their important goals. Not clearly identifying goals and their importance often results in spending time doing things that are not very important, simply because they are often quick and easy to do and therefore make us believe we are getting a lot done.

SUMMARY

Conflict in organizations is unavoidable. It stems from a number of sources—people and their differences, jobs, interacting groups, and the inevitability of organizational change, among others. The effective manager understands the interactionist philosophy about conflict and distinguishes between conflict that is helpful to the organization and conflict that is not.[32]

As a part of managing conflict, the effective manager first examines his or her personal style of working with others. Is that style such that conflict can develop when appropriate? If not, the style needs to be changed. When conflict arises, the effective manager first diagnoses its nature and source and then decides whether the objectives of the organization would be best served by either increasing or decreasing the particular conflict in question.

When conflict must be reduced, the effective manager uses forcing or dominance if necessary but strives for integrative problem solving for cooperative rather than competitive solutions. Steps to integrative problem-solving include ensuring that the data for solving the problem are generated in common, that perceptual differences are reduced, and that a common set of goals and objectives is developed. The manager also reviews the structure of the organization, since it can contribute to conflict. Also, any process changes made to resolve conflict usually necessitate structural changes as well if the resolution is to be carried out cooperatively and constructively.

Stress resulting from role conflict, role ambiguity, work overload and work under-load occurs frequently in organizations. The effective manager can use problem-solving techniques to reduce both role conflict and role ambiguity and will be watchful to prevent work overload or underload.[33]

STUDY QUESTIONS

1. Explain how the thinking about conflict has changed over the years.
2. Compare and contrast the classical and inter-actionist views of conflict.
3. What are the differences among conflict, co-operation, and competition?
4. Identify and describe five sources of organizational conflict.
5. What are the conditions under which these types of conflict might emerge?
6. What are some consequences of a low conflict level in an organization?
7. Describe how managers can stimulate conflict.
8. What are the major types of conflict resolution?
9. Rank the different types of conflict resolution in order of their long-term effectiveness.
10. How does role conflict differ from role ambiguity?
11. Is role conflict necessarily bad? How about role ambiguity? Explain.
12. If you were a manager, how would you feel about deliberately increasing the level of conflict within or among groups?
13. By your own verbal and nonverbal communications, do you usually indicate that conflict is acceptable or unacceptable? Does this vary with the circumstances?
14. What is your personal response to role conflict? Is yours the best reaction? Explain.
15. How can organizational design affect conflict, conflict resolution, and stress?
16. What is the best way for you to deal with your stress?

Case for Discussion

THE E. F. HOWARD COMPANY

Richard Wise, corporate quality control manager for the E. F. Howard Company, hung up the phone and stared blankly out the window, thinking about his alternatives. The phone call had been from Art Johnson, a Howard vice-president and Wise's boss, and he had offered reassurance but no practical help. Wise was happy to know that he had his boss's support for whichever alternative he chose for solving the present problem, but he was unhappy with the available alternatives and would have appreciated some advice.

The E. F. Howard Company is a small manufacturer, established in 1920; annual sales are approximately $40 million. The company employs approximately four hundred people. Its two plants are located in small midwestern towns, and its corporate headquarters is in Denver. Wise has been corporate quality manager for one year. The position is a relatively new one. Until two years ago, the quality control staff reported directly to the production manager. Now, all plant quality control people report to the plant quality control manager, who in turn reports to Wise. The man who held the position before Wise had been on the job about a year, until he was fired by the president for being unqualified for the job.

The president of Howard had said to Wise, "Put in a tough quality control program. Don't worry about stepping on toes. I want you to make certain that our products are of the highest quality." Keeping that direction in mind, Wise had carefully scrutinized the quality control staff of several plants. He concluded that the quality control manager of the Drysdale plant was not effective. Wise realized that the small town location of the plant might be contributing to the slow pace of the plant personnel. He also appreciated the plant personnel manager's desire to keep the plant nonunion. But Wise was convinced that the quality control program in the plant could be vastly improved.

When a Drysdale quality control technician retired, Wise hired a competent young woman, Lois Carroll, to take his place. Carroll's dedication to a career in quality control impressed Wise and created a strong bond between them. Carroll reported to Wise by phone on a daily basis to keep him aware of impending problems. After six months with Howard, she was producing more work than Ralph Burgess, the quality control manager, and all the other technicians combined. She was never absent, she worked many hours of overtime, and she had changed a number of procedures, which substantially increased efficiency and quality.

Wise, delighted with Carroll's progress, was finally becoming optimistic about developing the "tough" quality control program the president had requested. The minor complaints he heard about Carroll's strained relationships with other members of the department and with production personnel were, he felt, based on their own lack of initiative and on envy of her superior performance.

When Wise received a request for a conference call, he had no idea what the topic of discussion might be. The call included Bill Lewis, the plant manager; Ralph Burgess, the plant quality control manager, and Marilyn Franklin, the plant personnel manager. Burgess told Wise that Franklin had received a serious complaint about Lois Carroll from one of the other technicians. Carroll was accused of intentionally disrupting the other technicians' work by giving them instructions and claiming she had Wise's permission to do so. The technicians believed this was an attempt by Carroll to undermine Lewis's authority. They also believed that Carroll, as the junior member of the department, was challenging the authority they had earned by virtue of their longer tenure with the company. The production people agreed and demanded that Carroll be fired because she was a disruptive force interfering with the work of two departments.

Burgess told Wise that he, Franklin, and Lewis all agreed that Carroll should be fired. Not to do so would cause trouble in the plant and might bring about unionization (which the president had told them to avoid at any cost), the ill will of several long-term employees, and the interruption of the smooth production flow. The three felt that Carroll, who had been with the company only six months, was certainly less valuable than the long-term employees in the quality control department. Burgess told Wise that he expected suitable action to be taken by the end of the week.

Stunned by this telephone conversation, Wise immediately called Art Johnson, who promised his support but offered no advice.

1. What seems to be the problem at the Howard Company?
2. How did it develop?
3. What recommendations do you have for Richard Wise?

FOR YOUR CAREER

1. Conflict in organizations is inevitable. To be an effective manager you must be able to manage and resolve it.
2. Everyone can win when conflict is dealt with in a problem-solving, collaborative manner.
3. Lack of trust among employees in an organization seriously hinders problem solving.

4. Managers usually have to deal with role ambiguity. Because ambiguity is stressful, if you are able to reduce it, you'll not only be a more effective manager but also a healthier one.

5. Stress is a complex phenomenon. You should continually identify sources of your stress in order to control the level of stress.

6. As a manager you can be a key source of stress for your employees.

7. Some managers manage by creating stress for their employees. How effective do you think this strategy is? Explain.

FOOTNOTES

1. This case is adapted with permission from I. Janis, *Victims of Groupthink* (Boston: Houghton Mifflin, 1972).

2. Ibid., p. 9.

3. S. Robbins, *Managing Organizational Conflict: A Nontraditional Approach* (Englewood Cliffs, N.J.: Prentice-Hall, 1974).

4. H. Fayol, *General and Industrial Management,* trans. C. Storrs (London: Pitman Publishing, 1949), p. 35.

5. J. Hall and M. Williams, "A Comparison of Decision-Making Performances in Established and Ad Hoc Groups," *Journal of Personality and Social Psychology* 3 (February 1966): 217.

6. P. Binxen and J. Daughen, *Wreck of the Penn Central* (Boston: Little, Brown, 1971).

7. M. Deutsch, *The Resolution of Conflict* (New Haven, Conn.: Yale University Press, 1973), p. 19.

8. R. Cosier and G. Rose, "Cognitive Conflict and Goal Conflict Effects on Task Performance," *Organizational Behavior and Human Performance* 19 (August 1977): 379.

9. J. Harvey, "The Abilene Paradox: The Management of Agreement," *Organizational Dynamics* 3 (Summer 1974): 63–80; A. Negandhi, ed., *Conflict and Power in Complex Organizations: An Interinstitutional Perspective* (Kent, Ohio: Kent State University Press, 1972); G. Strauss, "Tactics of Lateral Relationship," *Administrative Science Quarterly* 7 (September 1962): 161–186; R. Walton and R. McKersie, *A Behavioral Theory of Labor Negotiations* (New York: McGraw-Hill, 1965); and C. Argyris, "Human Problems with Budgets," *Harvard Business Review* 31 (January–February 1953): 1–14.

10. D. Dearborn and H. Simon, "Selective Perception: A Note on the Departmental Identification of Executives," *Sociometry* 21 (June 1958): 140–144.

11. W. Whyte, *Human Relations in the Restaurant Industry* (New York: Harper & Bros., 1948).

12. J. Belasco and J. Alutto, "Line and Staff Conflicts: Some Empirical Insights," *Academy of Management Journal* 12 (January 1969): 469–477; and M. Dalton, *Men Who Manage* (New York: Wiley, 1959).

13. R. Blake and J. Mouton, *The Managerial Grid* (Houston: Gulf Publishing, 1964); P. Lawrence and J. Lorsch, *Organization and Environment* (Homewood, Ill.: Richard D. Irwin, 1967); and R. Walton and J. Dutton, "The Management of Interdepartmental Conflict: A Model and Review," *Administrative Science Quarterly* 14 (March 1969): 73–84.

14. F. Taylor, *Principles of Scientific Management* (New York: Harper & Bros., 1911); and L. Urwick, *The Elements of Administration* (New York: Harper & Bros., 1943).

15. Lawrence and Lorsch, *Organization and Environment,* p. 220.

16. Ibid., p. 222.

17. E. Huse, "The Behavioral Scientist in the Shop," *Personnel* 42 (May–June 1965): 50–57.

18. E. Huse and M. Beer, "Eclectic Approach to Organizational Development," *Harvard Business Review* 49 (September–October 1971): 103–112.

19. R. Blake, H. Shepard, and J. Mouton, *Managing Intergroup Conflict in Industry* (Houston: Gulf Publishing, 1974).

20. R. Beckhard, *Organization Development: Strategies and Models* (Reading, Mass.: Addison-Wesley, 1969); and E. Huse, *Organization Development and Change* (St. Paul, Minn.: West Publishing, 1975).

21. E. Huse and J. Bowditch, *Behavior in Organizations: A Systems Approach to Managing,* rev. ed. (Reading, Mass.: Addison-Wesley, 1977), pp. 451–455; Huse, *Organization Development and Change,* pp. 140–142; and C. Barebo, personal communication.

22. R. Dubin, "Theory Building in Applied Areas," in *Handbook of Industrial and Organizational Psychology,* ed. M. Dunette (Chicago: Rand-McNally, 1975), pp. 17–39; S. Robbins, G. Salanick, and J. Pfeffer, "Who Gets Power—and How They Hold onto It: A Strategic-Contingency Model of Power," *Organizational Dynamics* 5 (Winter 1977): 3–21; D. Nightengale, "Conflict and Conflict Resolution," in *Organizational Behavior: Research and Issues,* ed. G. Strauss (Belmont, Calif.: Wadsworth Publishing, 1976); and A. Zaleznik, "Power and Politics in Organizational Life," *Harvard Business Review* 48 (May–June 1970): 47–60.

23. R. Kahn and E. Boulding, *Power and Conflict in Organizations* (New York: Basic Books, 1964).

24. This section was contributed by R. S. Schuler, in part from *Personnel and Human Resource Management* (St. Paul, Minn.: West Publishing, 1981), pp. 475–476, with permission.

25. Benami Blau, "Understanding Mid-Career Stress," *Management Review* August 1978, (New York: AMACOM, a division of American Management Associations, 1978), p. 57.

26. M. Van Sell, A. P. Brief, and R. S. Schuler, "Role Conflict and Ambiguity in Work Organizations: A Review of the Literature," *Human Relations* 34 (January 1981): 43–71; and A. A. Abdel-Halim, "Effects of Person-Job Compatibility on Managerial Reactions to Role Ambiguity," *Organizational Behavior and Human Performance* 26 (October 1980): 193–211.

27. R. Martindale, "Sweaty Palms in the Air Control Tower," *Psychology Today,* February 1977, p. 71. Reprinted from Psychology Today Magazine copyright 1977 Ziff Davis Publishing Co.

28. T. Cox, *Stress* (London: Macmillan, 1978); C. L. Cooper and J. Marshall, "Occupational Sources of Stress: A Review of the Literature Relating to Coronary Heart Disease and Mental Ill Health," *Journal of Occupational Psychology* 49 (March 1976): 11–28; A. P. Brief, R. S. Schuler, and M. V. Sell, *Managing Job Stress* (Boston: Little, Brown, 1981); and T. A. Beehr and J. E. Newman, "Job Stress, Employee Health and Organizational Effectiveness: A Facet Analysis, Model and Literature Review," *Personnel Psychology* 31 (Winter 1978): 665–699.

29. W. C. Duemer, N. F. Walker, and J. C. Quick, "Improving Work Life through Effective Performance Planning," *Personnel Administrator* 23 (July 1978): 23–26.

30. Ibid.

31. R. S. Schuler, "Time Management: A Stress Management Technique," *Personnel Journal* 58 (December 1979): 851–855.

32. H. M. Lacey, "Psychological Conflict and Human Nature: The Case of Behaviorism and Cognition," *Journal of the Theory of Social Behavior* 10 (October 1980): 131–156; J. E. Kelly and N. Nicholson, "The Causation of Strikes—A Review of Theoretical Approaches and the Potential Contribution of Social Psychology," *Human Relations* 33 (December 1980): 853–883; and D. Lebell, "Managing Professionals—The Quiet Conflict," *Personnel Journal* 59 (July 1980): 566–572.

33. For more details on stress and stress management strategies, see J. M. Ivancevich and M. T. Matteson, "Optimizing Human Resources: A Case for Preventive Health and Stress Management," *Organizational Dynamics* 9 (Autumn 1980): 5–25; J. C. Latack, "Person/Role Conflict: Holand's Model Extended to Role-Stress Research, Stress Management, and Career Development," *Academy of Management Review* 6 (January 1981): 89–104; R. S. Schuler, "Definition and Conceptualization of Stress in Organizations," *Organizational Behavior and Human Performance* 25 (April 1980): 184–215; R. J. Burke and T. Weir, "The Type A Experience: Occupational and Life Demands, Satisfaction and Well-being," *Journal of Human Stress* 6 (December 1980): 28–38; S. Parasuraman and J. A. Alutto, "An Examination of the Organizational Antecedents of Stressors at Work," *Academy of Management Journal* 24 (March 1981): 48–67; H. Benson and R. L. Allen, "How Much Stress Is Too Much?" *Harvard Business Review* 58 (September–October 1980): 86–92; and B. S. Lawrence, "The Myth of the Midlife Crisis," *Sloan Management Review* 21 (Summer 1980): 35–49.

Managing Change

CHAPTER 22

CONTENTS

THE INSTRUMENT DEPARTMENT

The Medford Company makes a variety of medical testing equipment. Its instrument department assembles electronic instruments for performing blood tests and other tests in hospitals and doctors' offices. Some of the instruments are highly complex, costing up to a hundred thousand dollars. About thirty men and women work in the department.

When the supervisor of the instrument department was promoted, Lou Barnes, an engineering technician, took over the job. It was his first supervisory job; in fact, he had not yet finished the work on his bachelor's degree in management and was attending night school to do so. Several of Barnes's courses had covered areas such as motivation, group dynamics, and the management of change; and working with one of his professors, Barnes decided to try out some of the ideas he had learned.

He began by being frank and open with his people in explaining why schedule and other changes were necessary. Holding team meetings, he involved his subordinates in the planning process by discussing with them how schedules could be met. When he took over the job, each assembler was performing limited tasks based on detailed, written instructions. Barnes encouraged workers to exchange tasks and to help each other out.

As the workers became more skilled and versatile, he allowed single workers to assemble the less complex instruments; and as the workers gained confidence in their abilities, he kept expanding their jobs. Within a year, individuals were undertaking the complete assembly of complex instrument systems. For the most complex instruments, Barnes had groups of workers do the assembly, but the workers themselves decided who would perform which tasks. Since everyone in the department knew the schedule, the workers could shift from one set of instruments to another if there were parts shortages or other complications.

During the next year four new instruments were introduced into the department for assembly. Each time, the drop in productivity was slight, in contrast to the large drop that had always occurred when new products had entered the traditional assembly line process.

Because of delays and other problems, one major instrument was brought into the department without any instructions or drawings. Using an instrument that had been built in the development department as a guide, the workers were told, "Make it like this one," and they succeeded.

To determine the effectiveness of Barnes's approach, the plant accountant studied the costs of several instruments that had been in production for at least two years before Barnes's entry into the department. The average productivity for the eight months preceding the change was used as a base. The accountant found that during Barnes's tenure, productivity had risen by 17 percent, or approximately $1,500 per year per worker. Quality also had improved; the number of rejects had decreased from an average of 25 percent to an average of 13 percent, an increase in quality of about 50 percent. Absenteeism had been reduced from 8.5 percent to 3.4 percent, a reduction of about 50 percent.[1]

This case raises several key questions that you should be able to answer after reading the chapter. The questions include:

1. Can all organizations be as successful as the Medford Company by simply changing the jobs of employees and giving them more participation?
2. Under what conditions will employees accept change? Under what conditions will they resist it?
3. How can organizations tell when they could be performing better than they are?
4. What are the ways in which organizations can improve? Which of these ways is the best one to use?

This case describes a situation of planned change. Although the instrument department's productivity had been satisfactory when Barnes took over, he was able to substantially improve both productivity and employee morale.

This chapter will examine the need for planned change in organizations that comes in part from the accelerated pace of change throughout the world. Sometimes organizational change is necessitated by the passage of new laws, or because the competition develops a better product, or because the organization is involved in a merger. Other times changes arise from within the organization. A new building must be built; a new machine is purchased; conflict among groups becomes destructive.

Change is indeed the norm for most organizations. The effective manager is able to manage change rather than simply reacting to it. This chapter therefore explores a number of ways in which managers can manage and even bring about change.

THE ACCELERATING PACE OF CHANGE

Change is accelerating in our society; revolutions are occurring in technological, communications, political, scientific, and institutional areas. Because changes are occurring more rapidly than before, better methods are needed for dealing with them. In the past twenty-five years, the amount of technological change has been greater than in the past two hundred thousand years. Moreover, both cultural and technological changes appear to be irreversible.

At least five areas of accelerating change are having an impact on today's organizations. They are the knowledge explosion, rapid product obsolescence, the changing composition of the labor force, the growing concern over personal and social issues, and the increasing internationalization of business.

Characteristics of change in society:

- Accelerating pace of change
- Knowledge explosion
- Rapid product obsolescence
- Changing composition of labor force
- Growing concern over personal and social issues
- Increasing internationalization of business

The Knowledge Explosion It has been said that more than 90 percent of all the scientists that have ever lived are still living. Particularly since World War II we have seen a tremendous explosion in the development of knowledge. For thousands of years the wheel was the most advanced invention in transportation, and relatively little improvement was made on it. It underwent only one major change—from being solid to having spokes. Only recently was the tubeless rubber tire invented. Yet, in about eighty years, transportation progressed from buggies to automobiles and then to rockets to the moon and probes to Mars and Venus. The rapid growth of knowledge that characterizes this present age brings with it rapid obsolescence of knowledge—and of organizations.

Rapid Product Obsolescence Obsolescence of knowledge means obsolescence of products. The vacuum tube was replaced by the transistor, which was replaced even more rapidly by chip technology, in which entire circuits can be viewed with only the aid of a microscope. This step ushered in the development of the modern computers. Product obsolescence is most evident in the medical instrumentation field, where new, complex instruments are continually being replaced by better instruments at lower cost.

The Changing Composition of the Labor Force A dramatic shift in the labor force is occurring in the United States as the country becomes increasingly urbanized. The educational level of the population is steadily rising. More than 60 percent of the urban population is involved in some form of education beyond high school. Another major change is the decrease in the median age of the work force. Managers are now dealing with better-educated and younger workers who do not readily accept outmoded styles of management.

Finally, the proportion of laborers and semiskilled workers (so-called blue-collar workers) in the work force is decreasing. There are many more managerial, professional, sales, and clerical workers (white-collar workers). In 1956 white-collar workers outnumbered blue-collar workers for the first time, and the trend is increasing. Agricultural and manufacturing jobs are decreasing, while jobs in government, service, and health care are increasing.

Growing Concern over Personal and Social Issues The younger, more mobile, more highly-educated labor force has shown an increasing desire to "do its own thing." Many workers are less interested in money as such and more concerned about the quality of work life. The rising educational levels and younger age of workers have also raised the level of worker discontent. An absenteeism rate of 40 percent is not uncommon in automobile plants where the traditional assembly line has remained relatively unchanged.

New college graduates expect to be able to use and apply their training in their first jobs, but they often are told not to rock the boat. Discouraged, they quit. According to consultant Richard Beckhard, "Over 70 percent of the masters graduates of the Sloan School of Management [Massachusetts Institute of Technology] are in their second companies within two years . . . and this statistic is not exclusive to our school. It's pretty expensive recruiting."[2]

The same kinds of dissatisfaction are being seen in middle and top management. One large consumer products company had openings for regional marketing managers. These jobs, which paid over $40,000 and included other incentives, were offered to two of the company's best men. Both refused, even though the job would have included a pay increase of at least $8,000 per year. Neither man wanted to move and disrupt his family.[3]

Increasing Internationalization of Business The increasing internationalization of business is demonstrated by the headlines of almost any newspaper. The expanding relationship between U.S. and Japanese auto makers and the dependence of the United States on outside energy are only two examples of this interdependence and growing internationalization. One report suggests that "60 percent of all the world's business will eventually be done by international firms."[4]

That change occurs is clearly observable to everyone. It is part of personal experience and organizational life. In a span of only about three years, more than sixty of the hundred largest industrial companies in the United States publicly reported organizational changes; and this was only the tip of the proverbial iceberg.[5] Organizations that are not flexible enough to change quickly become obsolete.

Immediately after Prohibition, there were more than 700 breweries. That number was reduced to 118 in 1965 and to 47 in 1977. By 1985 there may be only about 15. The message is clear. The breweries that did not adapt to change either disappeared or were taken over by more progressive ones.

In order to stay healthily flexible, organizations must be competent. The **competent organization** is both effective and efficient.[6] **Organizational effectiveness** is the degree to which a specific organization attains its objectives. **Organizational efficiency** is the amount of resources used by an organization to produce a unit of output. An organization may be efficient in attaining its goal of making high-quality buggy whips, but if no one wants buggy whips, the organization is not effective. On the other hand, goals can be well-chosen, yet the organization can be inefficient in reaching them. For example, it may go out of business because

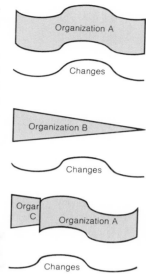

Organizations that do not adapt to change either disappear or are taken over by those that do adapt.

"I CAN REMEMBER WHEN ALL WE NEEDED WAS SOMEONE WHO COULD CARVE AND SOMEONE WHO COULD SEW."

Source: © 1979 Sidney Harris/*Wall Street Journal.*

its products are too costly and it cannot meet the competition's prices. Many breweries went out of business simply because they were inefficient.

STRUCTURAL AND PROCESS CHANGE

There are two overlapping and related ways of bringing about change. One is the **structural approach to change,** in which various activities are changed. At the strategic top level this may involve changing objectives, redesigning the organization, or purchasing another company. At the managerial level structural change may mean shifting lines of authority or communications or altering policies and procedures. At the operations level it may involve purchasing new machinery or developing new products. At all three levels, some formal aspect of the organization is modified to bring about improved organizational effectiveness and efficiency.

The **process approach to change** focuses on how things are done rather than on what is done. It is concerned with interpersonal interactions, group dynamics, and the attitudes of workers to their machines. Whereas the structural approach to change may lead to the purchase of a new machine, the process approach may focus on making a job more interesting and challenging. The structural approach may involve firing or transferring people who are quarreling; the process approach would require an attempt to determine the reason for the conflict.

Structural Change The structural approach has its roots in classical management theory, with its emphasis on worker efficiency. The process approach stems from the behavioral sciences, with their concern for both personal and interpersonal attitudes. In the structural approach the question is not whether workers will like the new machine but whether the machine will improve productivity. In the process approach the question is how well workers will adapt to the new machine and how it will affect their work experience. Although a philosophical distinction can be made between these two approaches, they do overlap, as Figure 22.1 shows.

Both structure and process need to be considered in managing change, since each affects the other. Structural change affects the process of people working together. For example, the acquisition of another organization may affect many managers. The purchase of a new machine may affect group and interpersonal relationships. Similarly, the process type of change affects structure. A shift in interpersonal or group relationships may affect the basic structure of an organization. In the case at the beginning of the chapter, the first actions Lou Barnes took—holding group meetings and increasing worker involvement in planning—were process changes. Later changes were structural, entailing changes in the design of the jobs.

The two approaches are practically inseparable, since changing the

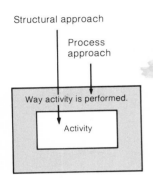

Structural approach

Process approach

Way activity is performed.

Activity

Two approaches to change

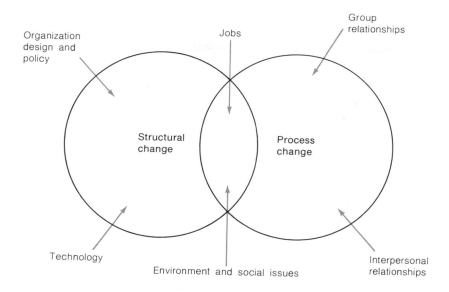

FIGURE 22.1 The interdependence of structure and process

organization eventually means changing the behavior of people as they work together to accomplish the organization's goals. Efforts at change can take many different forms. "In the final analysis, however, all organizational change efforts, regardless of initial focus, must take account of the fact that *people are called on to do things differently*."[7] Properly managing people in the change process is one of the most important tasks a manager can perform.

Change as a Process Although managers can discuss the idea of process in the abstract, they cannot work directly upon a process. Rather, they must work with specific individuals and groups to change the behaviors that created the ineffective processes. Unless they are highly motivated, most people do not significantly change their work behavior overnight. It takes time for them to recognize that their current work behavior is ineffective or inappropriate and that alternatives are possible. Then they can begin to change. Thus change can be considered a process that involves individuals or groups and their behavior.

Kurt Lewin, a sociologist, has developed a process model for change that consists of three basic steps—unfreezing, changing or moving, and refreezing.[8]

Unfreezing occurs when old values, attitudes, or behaviors are weakened by the realization that they are no longer effective or are somehow inadequate to the demands of a particular situation. This understanding is necessary before people become willing to change their behavior. Unfreezing is a disturbance of equilibrium that makes people receptive to the idea of new behaviors.

Changing, or moving, is the bringing about of specific changes through the development of new values, attitudes, or behaviors.

Basic change steps:

- Unfreezing
- Changing
- Refreezing

Unfreezing creates a vacuum unless realistic, known, and possible alternatives are available.

Refreezing is a stabilization after change—the establishment of a new state of equilibrium. New values, attitudes, and behaviors have been accepted. A person may experiment with new behaviors, see that they are better than the old ones, and adopt them permanently, at which point refreezing occurs.

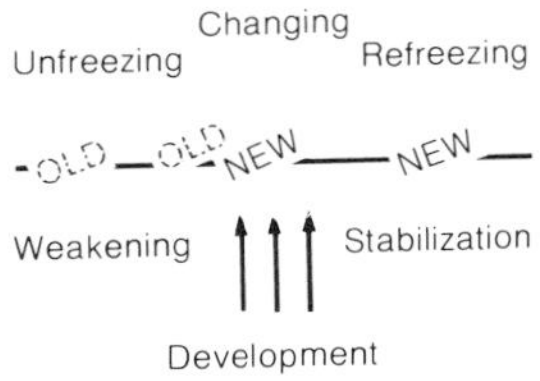

A review of eighteen studies of change in large organizations found that the more successful change attempts involved six major phases: pressure and arousal, intervention and reorientation, diagnosis and recognition, intervention and commitment, experimentation and search, and reinforcement and acceptance.[9] Thus the process of unfreezing, changing, and refreezing is a continuum rather than a series of discrete steps (as shown in Figure 22.2).

Pressure and arousal. A need for change is felt as a result of stress. The stress can come from internal forces in the organization, such as interdepartmental conflict, decreased productivity, or a strike, or from external forces, such as stockholder discontent or a technological breakthrough by a competitor. The need for change in present behavior is consequently felt by many in the organization, including the managers.

Intervention and reorientation. An influential and respected person, frequently a newcomer, acts as a change agent. Newcomers often have a more objective viewpoint. This enables them to help managers change their thinking by getting them to reexamine current practices. Often, what the manager perceives as the problem is only a symptom. Reexamination, prompted by the fresh outlook of a newcomer, may reveal the root cause of the symptom.

Diagnosis and recognition. The change agent or manager induces several people in the organization to examine past and present policies and practices overall in order to identify problems and their causes. This activity is more successful when it is shared than when it is unilateral or delegated.

Intervention and commitment. Using a participative approach to obtain full commitment, effective solutions are sought. To reach this phase requires an intensive search for innovative ideas involving many people working together. Without this step, attempts at change sometimes create so much resistance that they cannot be effectively applied.

Experimentation and search. Successful change also involves experi-

Changing

Unfreezing   Refreezing

–OLD— –OLD—NEW——NEW—

Weakening   ↑↑↑   Stabilization

Development

Continuum of behavior

FIGURE 22.2 The change process

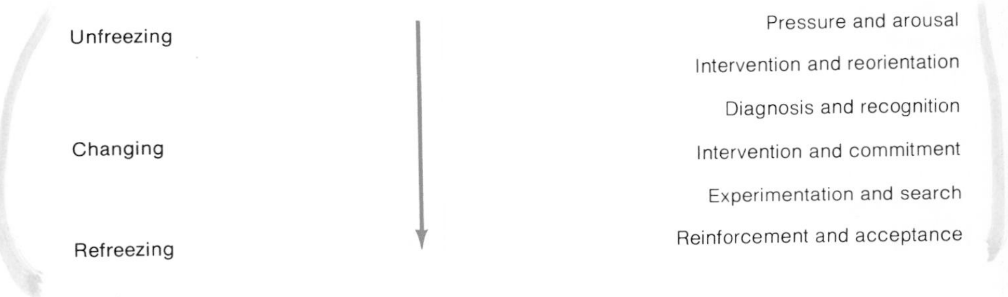

Unfreezing

Changing

Refreezing

Pressure and arousal

Intervention and reorientation

Diagnosis and recognition

Intervention and commitment

Experimentation and search

Reinforcement and acceptance

mentation with proposed solutions and innovations on a small scale before making any large-scale changes. The results of these tentative solutions are checked with personnel at different levels to discover flaws. This sharing of power ensures that poor decisions will be rescinded in time.

Reinforcement and acceptance. The success of small, tentative changes establishes a climate for further change—a support for change at all levels of the organization. An increasing number of people begin to see their personal interests as being served by the organizational change. This reinforces the impact of the change and rewards people for experimenting.

Thus Lewin's model and others suggest that successful organizational changes require four positive notions:

1. Managers must assume that change is not only for those below them in the hierarchy. Change can also come from the bottom up.
2. The idea that organizational change consists of a master blueprint designed and executed from the top down by an expert manager or consultant must be exposed as a myth.
3. Change is more successful when many people participate than when it is unilateral or delegated.
4. Those involved in the change must be encouraged to develop a broad perspective and become less parochial in their approach to change.[10]

Change should involve:

- All levels in the organization
- Top-down and bottom-up concerns
- Ownership by those changing
- Broad perspectives

CHANGE AND ORGANIZATIONAL DEVELOPMENT

In one sense, almost every chapter in this book deals with change. The process of motivating and working with groups involves change. Decision making and establishing or modifying organizational objectives involves change. Planning and establishing or reestablishing control systems to accomplish organizational goals involves change. Organizing and dealing with the staffing process involves change. One of the basic purposes of communications is to ensure that proper change is accomplished. Creativity and the management of conflict certainly involve change.

In this chapter the primary focus is on managing change through **organizational development(OD)**—the application of behavioral science knowledge in a long-range effort to improve an organization's ability to cope with changes in its external environment and increase its internal problem-solving capabilities.[11] Several parts of this definition need to be explored in order to distinguish OD from a change such as the purchase of a new machine. The application of behavioral science knowledge implies that the primary focus is on integrating the needs of individual employees for involvement, growth, and development on the job with the goals of the organization. OD tends to be a long-range effort; planned change comes about gradually. It is essentially an effort to improve an organization's ability to cope with change by improving the problem-solving capabilities of the people in the organization.

Assumptions in Organizational Development   The OD approach to change is based on humanistic values. Its thrust is to improve both the organization's competence and the quality of people's work life. OD makes the following assumptions:

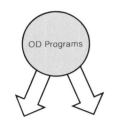

OD Programs

Health and growth of organization

Health and growth of individual

1. Most people want and need opportunities for growth and achievement.
2. When the basic needs have been satisfied, most people will respond to opportunities for responsibility, challenge, and interesting work.
3. Organizational effectiveness and efficiency are increased when work is organized to meet individual needs for responsibility, challenge, and interesting work.
4. Personal growth and the accomplishment of organizational goals are better attained by shifting the emphasis of conflict resolution from smoothing to open confrontation.
5. The design of individual jobs, group tasks, and organizational structure can be modified to more effectively satisfy the needs of the organization, the group, and the individual.
6. People hold many false assumptions about individuals, groups, and organizations that could be rectified through open confrontation.
7. Many so-called personality clashes result from problems of incorrect organizational design.

The basic difference between OD programs and other planned change programs is that OD programs are directed toward both the health and growth of the organization and the health and growth of the individual, whereas other planned change programs focus on either the individual or the organization.

The Need for Proper Diagnosis   A wide variety of OD techniques have been developed; many of them are highly effective, at least for some situations. Proper diagnosis of the situation requiring change is of prime importance, since some OD techniques are effective in one set of circumstances but totally ineffective in another.

Although a large number of OD tools are currently available, some OD practitioners cherish a particular tool and use it exclusively without considering whether it is right for the situation. For example, one large organization has a group of internal consultants who use the OD tool of attitude surveys in all situations. After they survey the workers, each work group discusses the results and develops plans for corrective action. By now, the organization has used attitude surveys at least three times for every work group. Indeed, one consultant commented, "We now know which managers will become defensive and will not really use the results of the survey." But he did not question whether the survey approach should continue to be used with these managers or whether there were more appropriate techniques for different situations.

MANAGING CHANGE THROUGH ORGANIZATIONAL DEVELOPMENT (OD)

OD approaches are classified in a number of ways.[12] One way is to view them as being directed toward organizational structure, intergroup relationships, group relationships, and interpersonal relationships, as shown in Table 22.1. From a systems point of view these four broad classifications are interrelated and interdependent, but they will be discussed separately.

Organizational Structure Structural change focuses on the functions of the organization. It involves identifying overall organizational problems and then changing either organizational design or the job assignments of individuals and groups.

Organizations or units in an uncertain, quickly changing environment need to be designed differently from those in a stable, known environment. Individuals can be highly motivated and have feelings of achievement, accomplishment, and competence when there is a good fit between the organization design and the environment, even when the organization is highly bureaucratic in nature.

Another structural design is **job enrichment**—a way of making jobs more satisfying by providing workers with more opportunity for meaningful achievement, responsibility, growth, and challenge.[13] Once the terms *job enrichment* and *job enlargement* were used almost interchangeably. Today most people use *job enlargement* to refer to job rotation (so that each worker learns more than one job) or activities added to a job (such as putting on both the front and rear wheels of a car rather than just one wheel). Recent research indicates that this approach to raising job satisfaction can instead have a negative effect on workers.[14] *Job enrichment*, on the other hand, refers to adding both horizontal and

Three basic elements of a job:

- Planning
- Doing
- Evaluating

TABLE 22.1 Different Approaches to Planned Change

Modifying organizational structure
  Contingency approaches to organization design
  Job enrichment
  Sociotechnical systems

Improving intergroup relationships
  The organizational confrontation meeting
  Changing intergroup perceptions

Improving group relationships
  Process consultation
  Team building

Improving interpersonal relationships
  Laboratory training
  Life- and career-planning interventions
  Management by objectives

On the Job

JED AND THE BEST JOB

While working for a paper products company one summer, I noticed that one person, Jed, had what seemd to be the most boring job in the plant. He sat on a stool, guided a piece of aluminum into an opening, and then repeatedly stamped on a peddle with his foot. The peddle action caused the machine, with resounding bangs, to press out circular metal rings that were later attached to the lips of paper containers for liquids such as milk, juice, and soft drinks. Once the strip of metal was inserted, it did not need much guiding, as it was automatically drawn forward into the machine with each stamp of the foot. After about two hundred stamps, a new strip had to be inserted.

A conversation with Jed revealed, much to my surprise, that he did not consider his job

boring. In fact, he told me that he had the best job in the plant. All he had to do was sit there and stamp his foot all day long—hardly any work at all. He explained it this way:

"When I need more metal strips, I just call out to Joe, 'Bring me some more strips,' and he brings me a new load. When the ring box is almost full, I call out to Jim to bring me a new empty box. He takes the full one away and brings me an empty. If I want to take a smoke or go to the rest room, I don't have to ask someone to take my place the way they do. [Jed pointed to the workers on an assembly line.] I just go. If someone comes by and wants to talk, I can talk and keep right on stamping out rings. If I want to take a longer lunch break or make a phone call, I do it. No

one bothers me as long as I make my quota, and I always do that. I usually make about 30 percent bonus each week. [The workers in this plant were paid a bonus for exceeding the production quota; the bonus was a percentage increase in pay equal to the percentage that production exceeded the quota.]

"I keep my machine in good shape, but if it needs repairs, Pete [the mechanic] fixes it quick. But it doesn't bother me if the machine is down a few hours like it does them [pointing to the workers on the assembly line again], because I know I can make up the work without too much trouble just by working my foot a little faster and maybe cutting down on my break time. Yes, sir! I've got the best job in the place!"

---

vertical activities to a job, thereby providing the whole person with a whole job. Adding horizontal activities means expanding the amount of the "doing" activities of the job. Adding vertical activities means adding "planning" and "evaluating" activities to the existing "doing" activities.

There are three basic elements in a whole job: (1) planning—deciding how it is to be done; (2) doing—actually performing the task; and (3) evaluating—obtaining feedback and taking appropriate actions. Many clerical and blue-collar jobs involve only the *doing* aspects.

The study of job enrichment has taken two separate but overlapping paths. The first focuses on the individual. It stems from Herzberg's stress on the growth factors of recognition, achievement, and responsibility (described in Chapter 15). The second focuses on the job and job tasks.[15]

A Job Diagnostic Survey (JDS) has been developed to measure the levels of jobs according to five core dimensions that reveal their amount of job enrichment.[16] Some individuals have strong growth needs and may respond more positively to enriched jobs, but others have weak growth needs and may not react as positively.

The five core dimensions of work tie into the second approach to job enrichment and lead to three critical psychological states. These in turn have personal and work outcomes, such as internal work motivation, work performance, work satisfaction and low absenteeism and turnover (see Figure 22.3). The **core job dimensions** are:

1. *Skill variety*—the greater the number of different skills involved, the more the potential for a meaningful job.
2. *Task identity*—the extent to which the job allows for a whole piece of work that is clear to the worker. Assembling an entire toaster is more meaningful than only attaching the electric cord to it.
3. *Task significance*—having a perceivable impact on others. A nurse working in an intensive care unit sees the impact of the work on others. A person who fills small boxes with paperclips does not.
4. *Autonomy*—the degree to which the job requires the worker's own discretion in scheduling and carrying out the task. Greater autonomy leads to a greater sense of responsibility while providing a greater sense of freedom and independence.

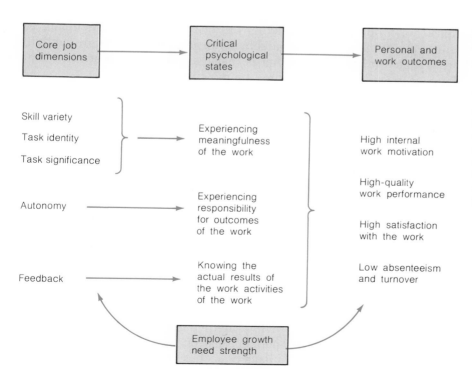

FIGURE 22.3 The relationships among the core job dimensions, the critical psychological states, and on-the-job outcomes

Source: James Hackman and Greg Oldham, "Development of the Job Diagnostic Survey," *Journal of Applied Psychology* 60 (April 1975): 161. Copyright 1975 by the American Psychological Association. Reprinted by permission.

5. *Feedback*—the amount of information that a worker is able to obtain about the effectiveness, quality, and quantity of the work performed. The best feedback comes directly from the work itself rather than from other sources.

The JDS is used basically to diagnose existing jobs on the core dimensions and to determine the effects of job changes on employees. Generally, a job must be high on all five core dimensions for the worker to be motivated by the job itself.

The instrument department case at the beginning of the chapter illustrates a successful job enrichment program for both individuals and groups. Skill variety was increased by allowing individual workers to assemble entire instruments themselves or to work as a group on more complex instruments. Task identity was increased by the workers doing a whole piece of work. Task significance was increased because the workers were able to visualize the impact of their work more clearly. Autonomy was increased by the workers' greater opportunity to plan and organize their jobs. Feedback was increased by the immediate testing of each instrument, so the workers knew at once whether it worked.

There are many positive reports on job enrichment. One book summarizes more than thirty studies showing increased productivity and job satisfaction.[17] Job enrichment also has been criticized, however. One criticism is that most job enrichment programs have not used scientific controls. Another is that job enrichment is used in a faddish way or as a tool for management to manipulate workers. For example, many union officials are opposed to it on the ground that it is only another way to speed up production. Yet another criticism is that job enrichment reduces the number of jobs available because it elicits more productivity from each worker. Still another is that the increased variety and challenge it provides are not desired by most workers.[18]

All these criticisms can be disputed. There is abundant evidence that job enrichment is effective under appropriate conditions. As the JDS is further developed, it may become an extremely useful tool for determining the proper conditions for job enrichment and for identifying these individuals who will respond positively to it.[19]

Intergroup Relationships Chapter 21 pointed out that conflict among groups can sometimes be positive, although often it is destructive. At times, conflict becomes so great that groups try to destroy each other—at least in a symbolic way. Each views the other as the enemy. The long and bitter coal strike in 1977 and 1978 is an example of groups locked in conflict.

Steps can be taken to improve such adversary relationships. Chapter 21 described organizational confrontation meetings, where groups are brought together to identify and work on organizational problems. Another basic strategy for improving interdepartmental or intergroup relationships is to change the perceptions (or, more accurately, the misperceptions) that the groups have of each other. A formal approach for

Job enrichment is not attractive to all employees.

Job simplification is preferred by some employees.

accomplishing this change consists of a six-step procedure. The steps are:

1. The managers of the conflicting groups choose a neutral third party, often a consultant, to assist them in improving the intergroup relationships. Without a third party the groups usually become deadlocked and the conflict escalates.

2. The groups meet together. The managers and the third party describe the purpose of the meeting—to develop better understanding and improved relationships. They ask the groups to consider questions such as the following: What qualities best fit our group? What qualities best fit the other group? How do we think the other group will describe us?

3. The groups go to separate rooms and write down their answers to these questions. The third party works with them to help them become more open and develop lists that accurately reflect their perceptions of both their own image and that of the other group.

4. The groups are brought together again after completing their lists. A representative from each group presents the written perceptions. Only the representatives are allowed to speak, since the primary objective is to insure that the perceptions, attitudes, and images are presented as accurately as possible. Arguments, hostility, and defensiveness might arise if the groups were allowed to argue with each other. Although arguments are prevented, questions are allowed in order to make certain that the groups clearly understand the written lists. At this stage each group learns how it is perceived by the other.

5. Once the lists have been presented and clearly understood, the groups again separate. Now each group's task is to analyze and review the reasons for the differing perceptions. The emphasis is not on whether the perceptions are right or wrong but on how they arose. The basic question for each group is: How have we contributed to these perceptions?

6. The next step is a joint meeting to share the identified reasons for differences and the approaches that will be taken to work on the problems represented by those reasons. The primary focus is on developing specific plans to solve present problems and improve future relationships. A follow-up meeting is scheduled so the two groups can report on actions, identify further problems that have emerged, and formulate additional action plans.[20]

This approach was first used with a union and management that were having frequent and bitter conflicts resulting in many strikes. Its success in that situation led to its subsequent use in a variety of situations. The approach is not always employed as formally as described in the preceding six steps. For example, on one occasion, the first-level supervisors of a manufacturing plant and the members of the engineering department were brought together. One of the biggest perceptual differences identified was that the engineers felt that the supervisors were stupid and could not solve problems. The supervisors, on the other hand, felt that the engineers were lazy and had nothing to do.

Over time, these perceptions had become exaggerated by the behavior of both groups. Believing that the engineers had nothing to do, the first-level supervisors had begun sending them problems that they could have solved themselves. This contributed to the engineers' belief that the supervisors were stupid and could not solve problems. They in turn put off working on some of the supervisors' requests in order to concentrate on what they perceived as more pressing problems. Getting little response, to their requests, the supervisors sent still more requests, and the cycle continued. After an intergroup meeting, the engineers and first-level supervisors gained a better understanding of their dynamics. The supervisors began solving more of their own problems, and the engineers became more responsive to the problems that the supervisors really could not solve.

Improving Group Relationships   Although managers spend much of their time in meetings, they frequently feel dissatisfied with the quality of these meetings. Ways exist of making groups more effective and improving working relationships among individuals and groups so that time spent in meetings is more productive. These methods attempt to improve communication and collaboration and include the stimulation or reduction of present and future conflicts as deemed appropriate. A typical method of this type is **team building**—helping a work group become more effective in accomplishing its tasks and in satisfying the needs of group members.

Many work groups distinguish among group task activities, group building activities, and self-serving activities (as described in Chapter 16). Group task activities are those directed at helping the group accomplish its goals. Group building activities are those that allow the group to maintain itself by helping to satisfy members' needs and by fostering cooperation among group members. Self-serving activities satisfy other individual needs.

Team building is a deliberate attempt to help groups become more productive by achieving the proper mix of these three activities. Among the many variations of team building is *process consultation*, which examines how groups go about their work (usually through actual observation) and then helps the groups understand, diagnose, and improve their behavior.[21] For example, a manager may ask someone skilled in group dynamics to sit in and observe regular staff meetings. The process observer pays much more attention to how the meeting is being conducted than to what is being discussed. During the meeting or later, the observer relates these observations to the group in order to help the group see its actions more clearly so that it can ultimately make its own diagnosis of its problems.

In one situation, a manager held meetings in order to obtain ideas from his subordinates. But without realizing what he was doing, he consistently interrupted others when they tried to speak. During an hour

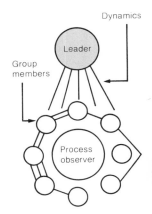

Dynamics

Leader

Group members

Process observer

A process observer first observes group dynamics, then reveals them to the group.

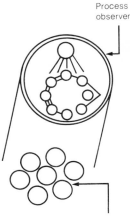

Process observer

Group seeing its own dynamics

and a half meeting, no one else was allowed to speak for more than thirty-five seconds without being interrupted, and the average time allowed was about eighteen seconds. The observer simply kept a time log in which she recorded who spoke, when, and how long. During the feedback session the manager was astonished to discover that his own actions were cutting him off from the ideas he was trying to get.

After process consultation, most groups become better able to use their own resources to identify and solve the interpersonal problems that cause their work problems. In the case just described, the manager was made aware of his habit of interrupting others and began to control it. At the same time, the other group members began to point out when they were being interrupted.

To be at their most effective, groups must pay close attention to group task and building roles. These roles enable them to improve communication and become more open to dissenting points of view.

Improving Intrapersonal Relationships The manager is the center of a series of communications networks involving superiors, subordinates, and people outside the work unit. Approximately a third to a half of the manager's time is spent with subordinates, and about 10 percent of the time is spent with supervisors. Most of the work day is spent with peers and others outside the actual work unit. The average manager may be in daily contact with twenty-five to fifty individuals or groups. At the lower levels the contact may be for a period of seconds; at the higher levels it may be somewhat longer. For chief executives, half the daily activities are completed in less than nine minutes, and only a tenth of them take more than an hour. Thus managers at all levels are in almost constant contact with others.[22]

Because of these fleeting and frequent contacts, the effective manager must use time effectively; and this requires an understanding of personal style and how it affects others. The manager described in the last section did not realize at first that he was constantly cutting others off, thereby reducing his effectiveness in bringing about change.

Management by objectives (MBO), described in Chapter 5, is a way of involving subordinates in formulating performance objectives and evaluating how well they are attained. The effective manager uses MBO to improve intrapersonal relationships and bring about change.

Sensitivity training is a way to increase managers' sensitivity to their effect on others. Managers learn by interacting with other members of their group. (Other terms describing *sensitivity training* are *laboratory training* and *T-group*.)[23] A typical sensitivity training group consists of ten to twelve members and a professional trainer. The group meets periodically for two days to two weeks. At the beginning of the first session the trainer tells the group that his or her role is to serve as a resource. Then, after a brief introduction, the trainer lapses into silence. Since the trainer has not taken on a leadership role, the group must work out its own methods of proceeding. Individual members usually try out different roles or approaches, many of which are unsuccessful. In one training

On the Job

THE BENEFITS OF WORKING WITH THE BEST WORKERS

Too many businessmen I work with want to be "messianic" managers. They feel it is their job to save people or situations. They want to spend their time changing people for the better or solving problems and improving processes in order to achieve results. What's wrong with the idea of managing those people or processes that are already working well? That is the area of management that produces the most results consistently. Why must managers constantly work in areas of low percentage returns, trying to turn situations around?

Can you as a manager change people? Yes, you can but rarely enough to justify your time investment.

"But," you say, "my job is to solve problems and change people. Not only that, I am pretty good at it. Take Mary Ellen over there—she used to come in late, leave early and do substandard work. I brought her around and now she is one of our most productive managers."

Of course. But why should the people who fail to perform or who cause trouble draw all your management time? Why not instead take already productive people and give them some attention, a little support, additional help and, above all, take the time to listen to them? I guarantee you, they will increase their

contributions considerably. Unfortunately, one of the penalties of doing a job well in an organization is that you are usually ignored.

The concept of working with only the most productive people was demonstrated to me quite by accident several years ago. A vice president of sales didn't like the part of his job that required him to listen to all the excuses and defensive reports that came in from his "also rans." On the other hand, he reveled in the stories of his winners.

Gradually he found less and less time for his "problem children" and more and more time for his heavy hitters. The results were outstanding. Sales grew at an accelerated rate. The most productive became even more productive and those on the bottom rungs left. Those in the middle were not happy with the lack of attention, but they soon found out that if they wanted to be noticed they had to perform.

In effect, the vice president divided the people he was managing into three groups. He spent 80% of his management time with the top third. He listened to them, asked the details of their successes, compensated them well, gave them extra help and, above all, tremendous recognition and visibility. They responded by doubling their efforts. And they kept at it for years.

He spent 15% of his management time with the bottom third. This was mostly invested in recruiting and selecting replacements. The best source seemed to be referrals from the top third. The key here was the constant budgeting of time to do a complete job of replacing those who were not productive. Training became a self-development challenge with some help in a buddy system from the top half and the middle group. Under no circumstances were people in the top third used in either training or temporary management assignments.

Finally, he spent only 5% of his management time with the middle third. They constantly screamed for attention, but the only acknowledgement they ever received was when they had results to contribute.

Strict adherence to this discipline opened up the time for the top group and made the strategy work. As an aside, our vice president arrived at the office each day at 8:30 and left promptly at 5:00. He never took work home with him, he never worked weekends and he visited only with his top producers (and eventually only his best managers) in the field.

In some cases, of course, messianic management may be necessary. Perhaps a supervisor of airline pilots, for example, had best spend his time with the bottom third-in the interests of safety. In some assignments a turnaround is required and solving problems is all that can be done. But in most business activities, it is a tremendous waste of resources not to cultivate the strengths of those responsible for the highest productivity.

If it works, make it better. Fine tune it. Add to it. If a person has a strength, find it and build on it. If weaknesses exist, and everyone has them and they are easy to find, don't try to correct them.

Ignore them if possible and work around them.

Besides, that top one-third is a great group to know. When you finish this article, say hello to some of them. Many of them haven't seen a manager in years.

Source: Jack Falvey, "The Benefits of Working with the Best Workers," *Wall Street Journal,* May 11, 1981, p. 26. Reprinted by permission of The Wall Street Journal, © Dow Jones & Company, Inc. 1981. All rights reserved.

group a member made a number of direct, forceful, and unsuccessful attempts to take over the leadership role. Finally, he conspicuously withdrew from the group and began to work a crossword puzzle. This person had two basic styles of working with others—dominance and withdrawal. He had never learned to collaborate.

When appropriate, the trainer will intervene or comment on the proceedings. Usually, the trainer encourages individuals to understand the group's activities, their own feelings, and the impact of their behavior on themselves and others. The primary emphasis is on the present experience rather than on past experiences.

Learning from a sensitivity training group is different for each member, but it is usually described as learning more about oneself as a person, learning to be more competent in interpersonal relationships, learning how others react to managers' behavior, and learning about the dynamics of group formation, norms, and growth.

Sensitivity training is being used less often as other techniques are developed, but it can be useful for personal growth and development. The technique has been criticized as being potentially dangerous to the participants' emotional health. But if the trainers are carefully selected and the participants thoroughly briefed on what to expect, the danger can be minimized.

This section has provided an overview of a number of approaches to managing change or preparing managers for it. No attempt has been made to describe all the OD techniques currently available; instead, a representative sample has been provided. Each of these techniques has had both positive and negative effects, depending on the circumstances in which they have been used. None should be applied before careful diagnosis of a situation.

Is this a problem
or a symptom?

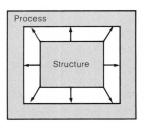

Separating process from
structure can help answer
that question.

Effective managers
constantly ask this
question.

Problems with managing
change:

● Reluctance to use
power
● People's resistance to
change
● Consequences of
change in one subsystem
for other subsystems
● Political nature of organizations
● Change possibly hurt-
ing some
● Change being uncer-
tainty

SOME PROBLEMS WITH MANAGING CHANGE

Earlier in the chapter some conditions that improve the chances of planned and managed change were listed. When these conditions are violated, the potential success of the planned change is reduced, and additional problems can occur. One problem is the failure of many OD practitioners to deal with the concept of power. Indeed, many of them deliberately ignore the problem of power and the politics of change.

Organizations are essentially political in nature. To expect openness and trust in an autocratic organization is to be unrealistic. To expect managers to give up power willingly is also unrealistic. In some circumstances the best way for the effective manager to bring about change is through the strategic use of power.

Another major problem arises in people's reactions to change. Change in an organization may challenge deeply rooted assumptions regarding the nature of managerial and worker responsibilities and skills. However, people do not resist change that they see as having a positive effect. They resist change that they believe will be negative or threatening. Sometimes their beliefs are based on false assumptions, but other times they may be correct in viewing a certain change as harmful. Thus resistance to change should not be seen as necessarily bad. Often it is a sign that something is going wrong.[24] Resistance can also indicate a need for more effective communications or for better approaches to implementing change. Moreover, on occasion, the lack of overt resistance to change can be a sign that something is wrong; it may indicate the presence of fear and suspicion.

Sometimes change will be harmful to an individual but must be implemented anyway. For example, it may be necessary to fire an incompetent worker. When such occasions occur, the manager must make the best decision possible under the circumstances, explain the reasoning, and implement the decision.

A final problem with change is that it may occur in a system that has complex, interrelated subsystems. A change in one subsystem can cause both intended and unintended consequences for the others. It may, for example, upset established norms and values elsewhere in the organization. Giving workers more responsibility may create bureaucratic barriers regarding pay or other factors. Numerous approval channels may be involved. Top management, staff groups, supervisors, unions, and the workers themselves are all related, so opposition from any of these may cause a program to fail. In one situation autonomous work groups had developed considerably higher productivity than other work groups; but the corporate wage and salary administration group ended the program rather than change their traditional pay system to reflect the increased responsibility to a group operating without a supervisor.

SUMMARY

Most managers know that change, like conflict, is both necessary and inevitable. Effective managers attempt to strike the best possible balance between maintaining the status quo and bring about, or responding to, change. This requires that they be both good diagnosticians and good change agents. Also they must constantly shift between the entrepreneurial and disturbance handling roles.

Perhaps the most important aspect of planned change is diagnosis. Managers should constantly ask, "Is this a problem or a symptom?" Clearly, separating structure from process can help in such diagnosis.

The people in an organization can either help or hinder the change process. Therefore, effective managers bring about necessary change in ways that satisfy both organizational and individual needs. Proper organizational development (OD) requires the diagnosis and identification of problems, then the selection of the best OD tools for solving those problems. For example, a good manager would not try to install a job enrichment program in an organization or unit that had a hostile and bitter union. Such an approach would be addressing a symptom rather than the basic problem of developing better union-management relations.[25]

Finally, effective managers recognize that there are problems with managing change and do not expect its quick and easy implementation. When resistance to change occurs, managers must explore the reasons for it. Using a systems approach, for example, they may find that a change in one subsystem has had an impact on others. Effective managers endeavor to anticipate the broad implications of any planned or unplanned change.

STUDY QUESTIONS

1. List and give examples of some major forces that are accelerating the pace of change in organizations.
2. Define and give examples of *structural change.*
3. Define and give examples of *process change.*
4. In what ways are structural and process change related?
5. What are the characteristics of a competent organization?
6. What are the assumptions underlying organizational development? Explain.
7. What are the major steps or phases in successful change attempts?
8. In your opinion, what is the key factor in the six phases of successful planned change programs? Defend your position.
9. Elaborate on the importance of proper diagnosis.
10. What is job enrichment? How does it relate to the assumptions regarding organizational development?
11. Under what circumstances might team building be helpful? Not helpful?
12. Under what circumstances might team building be helpful? Not helpful?
13. What are some major problems associated with planned change?
14. Interview several managers. What are their assumptions about people? About change? How might their assumptions affect their behavior?
15. From your own experience or from other sources, describe a failure of an attempt at planned change. What do you think caused the failure?
16. If you have held a job, give suggestions as to how that job could be enriched.

Case for Discussion

A NEW APPROACH TO MAKING PET FOOD

In the late 1960s the pet food division of a large corporation was facing serious trouble. Its manufacturing plant had low productivity, high absenteeism, and negative employee attitudes. Acts of sabotage and violence were occurring.

To combat these problems the organization decided to build a new plant that would combine improved technology with behavioral science knowledge. Four managers and their supervisor worked with a behavioral science consultant, visited other plants, and came up with an innovative plan that was designed to balance the needs of people with the needs of the business. The new plant opened in the early 1970s with workers assuming many of the responsibilities that were traditionally management's. They made job assignments, interviewed prospective employees, and even decided on pay raises.

The new plant eliminated layers of management and supervisory personnel. Its self-managing teams had three areas of responsibility: processing, packaging and shipping, and office work. Each shift had teams of seven to fourteen members who shared the responsibility for tasks in their area. For example, the processing team not only manufactured the pet food but was also responsible for unloading raw material and maintaining equipment and quality. The team was large enough to perform highly interdependent tasks and small enough to allow for effective face-to-face meetings to make joint decisions. Each team had a team leader rather than a supervisor, and this person acted more as a guide than a boss.

What were the results? Engineers had estimated that at least 110 employees would be needed to run the plant. But using teams, the plant was able to operate with only 70 people—40 fewer than anticipated. After eighteen months a reduction in manufacturing costs and low absenteeism had resulted in savings of approximately $1 million a year when compared to the traditional factory system. Morale appeared to be high, and managers, team leaders, and operators all

seemed deeply involved in their work. The plant's safety record was outstanding.

However, some difficulties began to emerge. There were reports that the system was working so efficiently that some management and staff people believed their long-term positions were threatened. They were not the only members of the organization who lacked enthusiasm for the new ideas. Fearing possible negative reactions from the National Labor Relations Board, company lawyers opposed the idea of having team members vote on pay raises. Personnel managers opposed having team members make hiring decisions. Engineers resented the idea of workers doing their own engineering work. Accountants did not like the idea of workers keeping records. To quiet some of these complaints, the plant eventually added seven management positions, including a plant engineering manager, a controller, and a manufacturing services manager.

Pay became a sticky issue. Besides the lawyers' opposition to team members voting on pay increases for fellow employees, such decisions were inherently difficult. Workers also began to feel that they should share in the plant's financial success, but a bonus system at one plant could cause problems elsewhere.

There were more subtle problems too. A vendor was surprised and disappointed to find herself talking with a worker rather than with a manager. At a corporation-wide meeting of safety officials, nearly all the participants were managers. The only nonmanager was the representative from the new plant, and his presence was at least potentially threatening to the status of the other participants.

Although the corporation has officially announced that the program is a success, there is evidence that the new practices are slowly being eroded. Several of the original managers have quit. One of them said: "They saw we had created something the company couldn't handle, so they put their boys in. By being involved, I ruined my career with the company."

Sources: R. Walton, "How to Counter Alienation in the Plant," *Harvard Business Review* 50 (November–December 1972): 70–81; and "Stonewalling Plant Democracy," *Business Week,* March 28, 1977, pp. 78–82.

1. What evidence would you need in order to determine whether the new plant was successful?
2. What assumptions and practices of organizational development were used in the design and operation of the plant?
3. What factors might cause the plant to be successful? Unsuccessful?
4. Could some of the problems have been predicted from what you know about the systems framework (Chapter 3)? Explain.

FOR YOUR CAREER

1. Change in your life and career is inevitable. It pays to "think change" and always be ready to react to it.
2. Organizations must change to survive and prosper. So must individuals.
3. Change can bring uncertainty, and uncertainty brings stress. Dealing effectively with uncertainty when it arises helps prevent stress.
4. Before changing, people often need to be dissatisfied with their current position.
5. You can get others to change by making the changed condition more rewarding to them than the present condition.
6. There are many ways to effect change in organizations. Before deciding which to use, it is important to diagnose the problem necessitating the change.
7. Not all employees like enriched jobs, but until a job enrichment program is tried, it is impossible to ascertain which employees will or will not respond to it.
8. Your career will be full of changes. It is better to perceive them as challenges than as threats.

FOOTNOTES

1. M. Beer and E. Huse, "A Systems Approach to Organization Development," *Journal of Applied Behavioral Science* 8 (January–February 1972): 79–101; E. Huse and M. Beer, "Eclectic Approach to Organizational Development," *Harvard Business Review* 49 (September–October 1971): 103–112; and L. Marcarelli, personal communication.
2. R. Beckhard, "The New Pressures on the Corporation," paper presented to Innovation Group, 3rd Conference, Harrison House, October 3, 1971, p. 3.
3. Ibid.
4. B. Bass, "Panel: Implications of the Behavioral Sciences on Management Practices in the Year 2000," in *Management 2000* (New York: American Foundation for Management Research, American Management Association, 1969), p. 10.
5. A. Toffler, *Future Shock* (New York: Random House, 1970).
6. A. Etzioni, *Modern Organizations* (Englewood Cliffs,

N.J.: Prentice-Hall, 1964); E. Huse and J. Bowditch, *Behavior in Organizations: A Systems Approach to Managing,* 2d ed. (Reading, Mass.: Addison-Wesley, 1977); and E. Schein, *Organizational Psychology,* 2d ed. (Englewood Cliffs, N.J.: Prentice-Hall, 1970).
7. N. Margulies and J. Wallace, *Organizational Change—Techniques and Applications* (Glenview, Ill.: Scott, Foresman, 1973), p. 2.
8. K. Lewin, *Field Theory in Social Science* (New York: Harper & Bros., 1951).
9. L. Greiner, "Patterns of Organizational Change," *Harvard Business Review* 45 (May–June 1967): 119–130.
10. W. Dinn and F. Swierczek, "Planned Organizational Change: Toward Grounded Theory," *Journal of Applied Behavioral Science* 13 (June 1977): 135–157; T. Qvale, "A Norwegian Strategy for Democratization of Industry," *Human Relations* 29 (May 1976): 543–469; and R. Golembiewski, K. Billingsley, and

S. Yeager, "Measuring Change and Persistence in Human Affairs: Types of Change Generated by OD Designs," *Journal of Applied Behavioral Science* 12 (June 1976): 133–157.

11. E. Huse, "Organization Development," *American Personnel and Guidance Journal* 56 (March 1978): 403–407; E. Huse, *Organization Development and Change* (St. Paul, Minn.: West Publishing, 1975).

12. W. Bennis, *Organization Development: Its Nature, Origins, and Prospects* (Reading, Mass.: Addison-Wesley, 1969); W. French and C. Bell, Jr., *Organization Development: Behavioral Science Interventions for Organization Improvement,* 2d ed. (Englewood Cliffs, N.J.: Prentice-Hall, 1978); and R. Harrison, "Choosing the Depth of Organizational Intervention," *Journal of Applied Behavioral Science* 6 (March–April 1970): 181–202.

13. L. Davis and J. Taylor, eds., *Design of Jobs: Selected Readings* (New York: Penguin, 1973); R. Ford, *Motivation through the Work Itself* (New York: American Management Association, 1969); and M. Myers, *Every Employee a Manager* (New York: McGraw-Hill, 1970).

14. S. Orelius, University of Gothenburg, Sweden, personal communication.

15. A. Turner and P. Lawrence, *Industrial Jobs and the Worker* (Boston: Harvard University Graduate School of Business Administration, Division of Research, 1965); J. Hackman et al., *A New Strategy for Job Enrichment,* Technical Report No. 3 (New Haven, Conn.: Yale University, Department of Administrative Sciences, May 1974); and J. Hackman and G. Oldham, "Development of the Job Diagnostic Survey," *Journal of Applied Psychology* 60 (April 1975): 159–165.

16. Hackman et al., *A New Strategy for Job Enrichment.*

17. *Work in America: The Report of a Special Task Force to the Secretary of Health, Education and Welfare* (Cambridge, Mass.: MIT Press, 1972); Huse and Beer, "Eclectic Approach to Organizational Development"; W. Paul, K. Robertson, and F. Herzberg, "Job Enrichment Pays Off," *Harvard Business Review* 41 (March–April 1969): 61–78; and W. Roche and N. McKinnon, "Motivating People with Meaningful Work," *Harvard Business Review* 48 (May–June 1970): 97–110.

18. C. Hulin and M. Blood, "Job Enlargement, Individual Differences, and Worker Responses," *Psychological Bulletin* 69 (January 1968): 41–51; M. Fein, "Job Enrichment: A Reevaluation," *Sloan Management Review* 15 (Winter 1974): 69–88; and F. Luthans and W. Reif, "Job Enrichment: Long on Theory, Short on

Practice," *Organizational Dynamics* 2 (Winter 1974): 30–38.

19. J. Pierce and R. Dunham, "Task Design: A Literature Review," *Academy of Management Review* 1 (October 1976): 83–97.

20. R. Blake, H. Shepard, and J. Mouton, *Managing Intergroup Conflict in Industry* (Houston: Gulf Publishing, 1954); Huse, *Organization Development and Change;* and R. Beckhard, *Organization Development: Strategies and Models* (Reading, Mass.: Addison-Wesley, 1969).

21. E. Schein, *Process Consultation: Its Role in Organization Development* (Reading, Mass.: Addison-Wesley, 1969); C. Argyris, *Intervention Theory and Method* (Reading, Mass.: Addison-Wesley, 1970); and R. Walton, *Interpersonal Peacemaking: Confrontations and Third-Party Consultation* (Reading, Mass.: Addison-Wesley, 1969).

22. H. Mintzberg, *The Nature of Managerial Work* (New York: Harper & Row, 1973); and R. Guest, "Of Time and the Foreman," *Personnel* 32 (May 1956): 478–486.

23. L. Bradford, J. Gibb, and K. Benne, *T-Group Theory and Laboratory Methods* (New York: Wiley, 1964); R. House, "T-Group Education and Leadership Effectiveness: A Review of the Empiric Literature and a Critical Evaluation," *Personnel Psychology* 20 (Spring 1967): 1–33; J. Campdell and M. Dunette, "Effectiveness of T-Group Experiences in Managerial Training and Development," *Psychological Bulletin* 70 (August 1969): 73–104; and G. Cooper, "How Psychologically Dangerous Are T-Groups and Encounter Groups?" *Human Relations* 28 (June 1975): 255–268.

24. P. Lawrence, "How to Deal with Resistance to Change," *Harvard Business Review* 32 (May–June 1954): 50–61.

25. For example, many organizations are implementing programs to change the type of work schedules on hours employees work as well as to change the nature of the work itself. For further discussion of what a manager can select and should consider, see C. A. Carnell, "The Evaluation of Work Organization Change," *Human Relations* 33 (December 1980): 885–916; C. Handy, "The Changing Shape of Work," *Organizational Dynamics* 9 (Autumn 1980): 26–34; R. E. Hill and E. L. Miller, "Job Change and the Middle Seasons of a Man's Life," *Academy of Management Journal* 24 (March 1981): 114–127; A. T. Cobb and N. Margulies, "Organizational Development," *Academy of Management Review* 6 (January 1981): 49–60; S. Ronen and S. B. Primps, "The Com-

pressed Work Week as Organizational Change: Behavioral and Attitudinal Outcomes," *Academy of Management Review* 6 (January 1981): 61–74; S. Ronen and S. B. Primps, "The Impact of Flexitime on Performance and Attitudes in 25 Public Agencies," *Public Personnel Management* 9 (June–July 1980): 201–207; J. L. Welch and P. Gordon, "Assessing the Impact of Flexitime on Productivity," *Business Horizons* 23 (November–December 1980): 61–65; and F. Friedlander, "The Facilitation of Change in Organizations," *Professional Psychology* 11 (June 1980): 520–530.

Social Responsibility and the Environment

Chapter 23

CONTENTS

THE ALASKAN PIPELINE

In 1969 the Standard Oil Company of Ohio (SOHIO) and six other large oil companies, which would later form the ALYESKA Pipeline Service Company, began what eventually became the largest business venture ever undertaken by private enterprise. The eight-hundred-mile pipeline was designed to carry 1.2 million barrels of crude oil a day from Alaska's North Slope to the Port of Valdex on its south coast. The original plan called for the oil to be transported by tanker to the California coast, where it would be unloaded and either refined or moved through a pipeline system to refineries lying east of the Rocky Mountains. These refineries have the greatest shortage of crude oil and represent 65 percent of the industry's total refining capacity.

SOHIO executives originally estimated that the Trans-Alaska Pipeline System (TAPS) would be completed by 1973 and would cost approximately $900 million. By mid-1977 TAPS was finally completed at a cost of more than $9 billion, ten times the original estimate. There were many reasons for the increased cost. Because of environmental and other concerns, construction of the pipeline was delayed until it was specifically authorized by Congress in 1973, after the Arab oil embargo. Because of increased equipment costs, the size of the line was doubled. Other delays resulted from hassles with regulatory bodies, weather problems, technical foul-ups, and accidents. An important cost factor was the need to protect the fragile Arctic environment—including the caribou and moose migration patterns and the fish streams.

Financing was hard to get, partly because of the uncertainties of the project and partly because it was not clear where the oil would actually go. A number of major institutional investors chose not to participate in the TAPS financing. Some feared that the government would not permit Alaskan crude oil to compete with world oil in the marketplace and thus would limit the rate of return the oil companies could pay to their investors.[1]

When the pipeline finally opened in 1977, the destination of the oil it would carry was still uncertain. There was a glut of oil on the West Coast, and permits to build a new terminal and connecting links to existing pipelines were still not available. Alternatives were to sell the oil to Japan or ship it to the Gulf Coast by tanker through the Panama Canal, which would be more expensive than a pipeline.

From Alaska came reports that appeared to justify many environmental concerns. ALYESKA had frequently violated state and federal environmental rules agreed to when the right-of-way lease agreement was signed in 1974. Those in charge apparently gave priority to the pipeline over the environment. For example, nearly 40 percent of the moose and caribou crossings built in 1975 were reported to be too low or wrongly located. Reports of environmental damage detailed erosion of tundra, water pollution resulting from improperly run sewage treatment plants, massive oil spills at construction sites, damage to fish spawning beds, and blocked fish streams. Some problems had been corrected, but it was too early to assess the overall environmental impact, especially on wildlife and fish.[2]

This opening case raises several key questions that you should be able to answer after reading the chapter. The questions include:

1. How do organizations influence the environment in which they operate? Should they be financially responsible for this influence?
2. What are some state and federal rules, regulations, and laws that influence organizations?
3. How can organizations influence state and federal rules, regulations, and laws?
4. Should lobbying by organizations be allowed? Who lobbies for your interests?

The Trans-Alaska Pipeline System is a vivid example of the complex interplay of the forces that surround organizations. This chapter will examine the interfaces between organizations and their environments. Many management texts have not recognized the impact that groups both within the organization and outside it have on managerial decision making. Although it is top management that makes the decisions relating to political issues, managers at all levels affect and are affected by such issues. Among the issues are affirmative action, pollution abatement, and federal and state laws, rules, and regulations.

THE CORPORATE DILEMMA

At the beginning of the century it was possible for a company president to state that business executives were "Christian men to whom God in his infinite wisdom has given control of the property interests of the country."[3] Although William Vanderbilt, the president of the New York Central Railroad, may or may not have said "the public be damned" (in about 1883), historians have confirmed that his father, responding to the possibility that he had acted illegally, exploded, "Law? What do I care about the law? Ain't I got the power?"[4]

In contrast, Daniel McNaughton, the chairman and chief executive officer of the Prudential Insurance Company of America, recently wrote, "Business belongs to the people. Business has, in effect, a franchise granted to it by society, and the franchise will be continued only as long as society is satisfied with the way it is handled."[5] He went on to say that business needed to be responsive to a wide variety of constituencies—for example, suppliers, consumers, employees, stockholders, and the general public—rather than to only one or two.

These remarks point up two extreme viewpoints—one longstanding, the other recent—both with their followers.[6] One extreme insists that business exists only to maximize long-run profit and that no other decision-making criteria are to be used. Thus economist Milton Friedman contends that the only business of business is profits and that even corporate gifts to charitable organizations such as the Community Fund or the Girl Scouts are wrong. Friedman says, "If the corporation makes a contribution, it prevents the individual stockholder from himself deciding how he should dispose of his funds. . . . There is no justification for permitting deductions for contributions to charitable and educational institutions."[7] Those who take this position argue forcefully that the role of government should be strictly limited to the major functions of preserving law and order, enforcing private contracts, and fostering competitive markets.

Others argue, just as forcefully, that as corporations become larger, they must be controlled in ways that make them more responsive to the needs of society. Their point is that business and industry have been insensitive to such needs in the past, and as a result, "public anger at corporations is beginning to well up at a frightening rate, bringing with

Corporations not willing to engage in self-control invite government control.

it a dizzying variety of protest movements.''[8] The protests center on air and water pollution, misleading advertising, low product quality, and meaningless warranties.

The Committee for Economic Development, a leading business group, has strongly urged management to involve itself in a wide variety of social issues, such as urban renewal, job opportunities for minorities and women, aid to education, and trianing of the disadvantaged.[9] They argue that the traditional economic model of business has worked well and business does not need to apologize for its important role in bringing economic plenty to much of the world, but that there have been so many significant changes in the world that the traditional business model must now be modified to more closely fit today's social environment and meet society's expectations.[10]

Organizations exist in a highly interdependent society.

The result of these conflicting viewpoints is what has become known as the ''corporate dilemma.''[11] The dilemma is how to determine the proper balance between long-run profits and social responsibility. Clearly, businesses must be responsive to the larger society. But individual corporations cannot sacrifice a large portion of their profits in order to take an active role in every area of social and economic life. Neither exclusive concentration on profits nor full response to every societal demand is possible.

In the case of SOHIO, environmental concerns and hassles with regulatory agencies contributed to the high cost of the pipeline. This chapter will discuss the issues involved in this kind of situation. It will attempt to answer the following questions: What were the responsibilities of the regulatory agencies and environmentalists in protecting the Arctic environment? What was SOHIO's responsibility in tapping the Alaskan North Slope oil reserves to bring needed oil to the United States? What was SOHIO's responsibility to its stockholders and to the environment?

One extreme viewpoint is that SOHIO should have remained within the law but done nothing more to protect the environment. The other extreme is that SOHIO should have protected the environment even at the expense of its survival as a company. Rather than debate the merits of the two extremes, this chapter will first briefly examine the origins of the economic system in the United States to determine how the opposing schools of thought emerged and then describe how forces in the environment external to the organization can significantly affect the success of business and industrial organizations.

CHANGING CONCEPTS OF THE ECONOMIC SYSTEM

The suggestion has been made that laws, regulations, and concepts regarding businesses' social involvement have gone through at least three phases: profit-maximizing management, trusteeship management, and quality-of-life management.[12]

Profit-Maximizing Management The industrial revolution swept through the United States in the nineteenth century, bringing with it new attitudes toward business. **Profit-maximizing management** emerged at the same time. It had but a single objective—to maximize profits. The only constraints observed were legal ones, and even these were frequently ignored.

In the nineteenth century and in the first third of the twentieth century U.S. society had a lot of room to expand, but at the same time it experienced economic scarcity. Its primary national goals were economic growth and the accumulation of wealth. Giant corporations began to dominate the economy. By the end of the nineteenth century the two hundred largest manufacturing organizations had added more to the gross national product than had the hundred thousand next largest.

Massive trusts with immense power developed. Their power was evident in such practices as lockouts of labor, manipulation of commodity prices, discriminatory pricing, kickbacks, and a lack of concern for employees and customers. In the cigar manufacturing industry almost three-fourths of all employees became ill after six months on the job. In the food industry milk was commonly preserved with formaldehyde. *Caveat emptor* (let the buyer beware) characterized decisions and actions in dealing with customers. These practices led to the development of federal antitrust legislation, railroad rate regulation, and fair trade laws. For example, Standard Oil, DuPont, and American Tobacco were divided into smaller companies.

Profit-maximizing values were based on Calvinist philosophy, which stressed the morality of hard work and the accumulation of wealth. Thus managers adhering to that philosophy believed that self-interest was an absolute good.

During the 1920s relations between business and government were amicable. As Secretary of Commerce, Herbert Hoover was so strongly pro business that he intervened to prevent an inquiry about the antitrust consequences of a proposed acquisition.[13]

Then came the crash of 1929, when the bottom fell out of the stock market. By 1932 a quarter of all U.S. workers were unemployed. In effect, U.S. business was "offered the choice between rugged individualism and business autonomy of economic security. The generation raised on the gospel of wealth gladly forfeited the former."[14] Franklin Roosevelt defeated Herbert Hoover for president in 1932, and the age of profit-maximizing management was ushered out.

Trusteeship Management Trustee management emerged from trends in society and in the structure of business organizations. The idea of **trustee management** is that the corporate manager is responsible not only for profits but also for maintaining a proper balance among the competing claims of stockholders, employees, suppliers, customers, and the broader community.

A structural change largely responsible for this concept of management was the increasingly broad ownership of U.S. corporations. A soci-

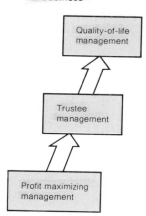

Social involvement
of business

etal change was increased pluralism. By the early 1930s the largest stockholders in corporations such as U.S. Steel, the Pennsylvania Railroad, and American Telephone & Telegraph owned less than 1 percent of the total outstanding shares. Although many large organizations were still closely controlled by the stockholders, others had such diversified ownership that management was firmly in control of them and could maintain that control through the use of voting proxies (a procedure allowing top management to vote the shares of many stockholders).

A *pluralistic society* is "one which has many semi-autonomous and autonomous groups through which power is diffused. No one group has overwhelming power over all others, and each has direct or indirect impact on all others."[15] Since the depression and the resulting legal and social changes, corporations have been increasingly expected to fulfill certain social obligations to a pluralistic society. The government has defined the responsibility of business toward a variety of groups through such actions as collective bargaining and minimum wage laws and regulations, laws requiring disclosure of corporation information, laws protecting civil rights and fair employment practice, and the establishment of agencies to promote nondestructive competition. In the 1930s the major pressure groups were the labor unions and the government. Now the list includes numerous environmental, minority, and consumer groups. Thus the task of the modern manager is to balance the claims of all these groups and still make a profit for the business.

The values of trusteeship managers have changed. The new generation of corporate managers includes many who are college-educated and heavily influenced by liberal arts humanism. These new managers recognize that self-interest is important but that it must be balanced against the interests of the many groups involved with and affected by the organization. Rather than resisting government regulations, they willingly cooperate with them.

Quality-of-Life Management Around the turn of the century and later, society assumed that business would indefinitely continue to produce increasing amounts of goods and services and thus increasingly raise the standard of living for its citizens. As the United States became an affluent society, however, other issues arose. There is now increasing concern about air and water pollution, the persistence of pockets of poverty, and urban blight. A new set of national priorities seems to be emerging, one that stresses the overall quality of life. Some believe that business should assume broader responsibilities—that its financial resources and technological and managerial skills should be directed more specifically toward the solution of society's major problems. John F. Kennedy said in his inaugural speech, "Ask not what your country can do for you; ask what you can do for your country."

Under the trusteeship management developed in the 1930s a relatively harmonious accord existed between government and business. In the late 1960s and the 1970s, however, the accord was disturbed. There was an increasing emphasis on consumerism, environmentalism, and

Pluralistic society

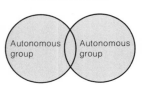

Past

Present

QL management concerns:

- Organizations
- Society
- Employees
- Environment

similar issues. Government began to impose new responsibilities on business, including consumer protection measures such as truth in advertising, truth in finance, and product assurance standards; environmental legislation to protect water and air quality; and campaign financing legislation to reveal the magnitude of corporate political contributions. From all these changes emerged a new kind of management—**quality-of-life management.** In quality-of-life management, managers are responsible for promoting the well-being of both the organization and the society while protecting the environment, and enhancing the dignity of employees.

Quality-of-life managers believe that society's interests are important, that although profits are essential to the organization's survival, they are not the only objective of the organization. They believe that people are more important than money and therefore that employment of minorities and the handicapped is essential. They believe that each employee has worth beyond an expensive machine.

Such managers also see that the environment must be preserved, since an adequate environment is essential to a high-quality life. Overall, they believe they are accountable to the organization's owners, to the others who contribute to the organization, and to society as a whole. They believe that government and politicians are necessary contributors to society and to the quality of life and that business and government need to cooperate in solving society's problems.

The growing feeling that a change has occurred in the social contract organizations have with society—and that when the social purpose changes, so do the activities of corporations—is expressed by Fletcher Byrom, chairman of the board of Koppers Company, a large manufacturing corporation: "You can't continue a business without profit, but profits are not the be-all and end-all of the corporation. . . . If it does not at the same time serve the needs of society, then the corporation as an instrumentality of accomplishment will surely perish, and deserves to perish."[16]

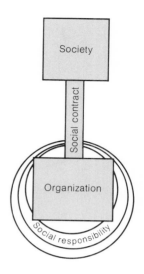

A change in the social contract between society and the organization has evoked greater social responsibility from the organization.

THE INTERPENETRATING SYSTEMS MODEL

The debate among proponents of each of the models—profit-maximizing, trusteeship, and quality-of-life—has been extensive and heated. Rather than further discuss the merits of any of the positions, however, this section of the chapter will describe how organizations exist in, influence, and are influenced by society and many subsystems within its environment.

Organizations and the society are inextricably interrelated. The scope of managerial responsibility extends to activities beyond those mediated by market contacts. **Social involvement** is the interaction of the organization, as a system, with other organizations and individuals and with society as a whole.[17] It is a neutral term; the degree of any organiza-

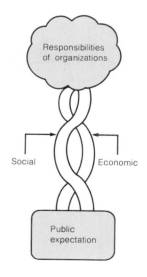

Because of public expectations, social and economic responsibilities of organizations have become inextricably interwoven.

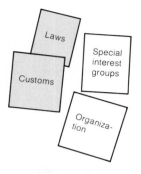

Customs affect laws,

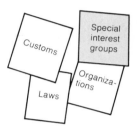

which affect special
interest groups,

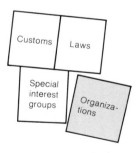

which affect organizations.

FIGURE 23.1　Interpenetrating systems

tion's involvement can be large or small, specific or general, benign or harmful.

Interpenetrating systems are two or more systems, neither of which totally contains or is contained by the other, that are involved in particular events or processes. Figure 23.1 shows how the federal government's efforts to raise the mandatory retirement age from sixty-five to seventy made the government act as an interpenetrating system with each organization affected. The event (passing the law) penetrated the organization (which had to create new retirement policies, change pension plans, and the like).

In the interpenetrating systems model the organization is viewed both as a micro unit of the larger society and as a system separate from the society. Thus organizations and society neither completely control nor are completely controlled by the broad social environment. The model provides the possibility "which has, in fact, become a necessity—of considering the potential differences, conflicts, and compatabilities among the goals of micro-organizations and those of society at large."[18] A vice-president of General Electric has commented, "The social and economic responsibilities of the corporation have been so broadened and interwoven in the public's expectations . . . that it no longer makes sense, if indeed it ever did, to talk as if they could be separated."[19]

Some of the other systems the organization must interact with and, in many cases, compete with or try to influence are shown in Figure 23.2. They include customers, bankers, suppliers, stockholders, employees, and government.

The diagram is misleading in that it does not show the complex interrelationships of the various influences on the organization. For example, laws are affected by customs and in turn affect special interest groups. A change in laws may affect a special interest group, which may in turn allow a minority person to sue an organization. Civil rights and other movements profoundly affect legislation and government regulations. As stockholders become more active in the affairs of an enterprise, their activity may influence employees, customers, unions, and special interest groups.

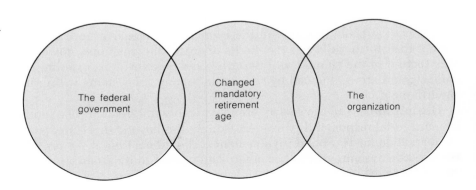

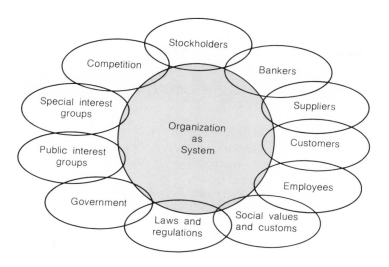

FIGURE 23.2 The many influences on the organizational system

Special Interest Groups Managers are constantly barraged by many **special interest groups**—groups that attempt to exert influence over someone in order to benefit one or a few specific causes that are important to them. Their decision making must therefore take into account not only the organization itself but the many and varied competitors for its scarce resources.

Although Figure 23.2 shows a number of influences on the organization, the text will discuss only a few—minorities, environmentalists, consumerists, shareholders, boards of directors, and lobbyists.

Minorities and Women Pressure from minority groups and women on businesses, especially in regard to discrimination in employment and promotion, has been steadily increasing. State and federal antidiscrimination laws (some of which were briefly described in Chapter 8) are now more strictly enforced than before. In 1973, for example, AT&T agreed to upgrade the jobs of approximately 50,000 women and 7,000 minority group members and to employ approximately 4,000 men to fill positions that had been traditionally held by women (such as telephone operators and clerks). The company also agreed to pay approximately $15 million to women and minority members who had not been given equal pay for their work. In 1978 the Supreme Court essentially upheld the lower court decision that had forced AT&T to change its policies by refusing to hear the company's appeal.

A number of organizations have taken antidiscriminatory steps beyond those required by law; among them are Atlantic Richfield, General Electric, and Standard Oil of Indiana.[20] Standard Oil, for example, has affirmative action programs to increase the number of minority members employed in construction jobs. Kaiser Aluminum established an affirmative Action Training Program that resulted in the *Weber* case decided by the Supreme Court.

Special interest groups and the manager

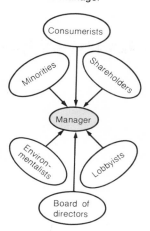

On the Job

DO SPECIAL INTEREST GROUPS HAVE MUCH CLOUT?

Friends of the Earth. Gray Panthers Project Fund. Common Cause. Center for New Corporate Priorities. Union of Concerned Scientists. National People's Action. Environmentalists for Full Employment. Council for a Livable World. Worldwatch Institute.

All the above are single issue or special issue groups whose activities, scope, purpose, methods of operation, funding and future agenda are closely watched by the Public Affairs Council (PAC) and its affiliate, The Foundation for Public Affairs.

The single issue groups listed are among the 1500 such organizations which PAC, a Washington, D.C.-headquartered organization of about 500 corporate public affairs executives, keeps an eye on.

Every two years the foundation publishes detailed profiles of 100 of these groups in a manner one corporate relations vice president described as "a scorecard for the ballgame—giving you the facts and figures, names and numbers of all the players."

The value of these profiles is obvious to the public affairs officers who belong to PAC. They realize the single issue groups are here to stay and during the '80s and '90s will be pulling ever strongly at the levers of power.

It's important for PAC members to know the answers to questions such as these: Who's on the board of the Environmental Defense Fund? What's the budget of the Pacific Legal Foundation? What's the goal of the Women's Action Alliance?

"As the power and influence of public interest groups grow," says the Foundation, "the need for more information on their activities, funding, leadership, and the basics of how to contact them, will persist."

Notes Richard A. Armstrong, president of PAC, "Back in the 1960s and early 1970s, the trend on the part of corporate management was to ignore these single issue groups and hope they would go away.

"That's not true today," he adds, "business leaders recognize that public policy is increasingly being set by these groups. These advocacy organizations are not just a bunch of wild-eyed kids up in a loft with a mimeograph machine.

"They're well financed, able to raise substantial funds quickly through direct mail and similar methods, and have almost instant access to the media. The more outrageous their demands, the more bizarre their demonstrations, the easier it is for them to get an audience."

However, Mr. Armstrong indicates it's still possible, at times, to effect working relationships, alliances and even coalitions between business companies and less than hard-core single issue groups. And he sees that as a trend which will increase as the 1980s advance.

Just how far the single issue groups have progressed into the world of business they are supposedly fighting is indicated by several incidents related by Mr. Armstrong. One single issue group has set up a pension plan for its members. At another advocacy group, one of its factions became dissatisfied with the way funds were being allocated in terms of crusades and issues. These dissident parts of a dissident whole, formed a labor union and picketed their "management."

Source: Paul Cathey, "Special Issue Groups Will Change Management in '80s," *Iron Age,* February 23, 1981, p. 57. Reprinted by West Publishing Co. from *Iron Age,* February 23, 1981; Chilton Company.

On the Job

THE WEBER CASE

Brian Weber was a white employee at the Kaiser Aluminum factory in a small Louisiana town. After five years at the plant Weber applied for a position in a training program for skilled workers. He was turned down even though he had more seniority (i.e., more years of experience) than some of those selected.

He was not selected because Kaiser Aluminum had started an affirmative action program designed to increase the number of blacks in skilled positions. To do this Kaiser and the local labor union had agreed to give 50% of the training positions to blacks and 50% to whites. The company felt this was necessary because while nearly 40% of the local work force was black, fewer than 2% of their skilled employees were blacks.

Weber felt that this plan was unfair and that it discriminated against him because of his race. Weber sued the company, relying on Title VII of the Civil Rights Act of 1964 which makes it illegal for employers to discriminate on the basis of race.

Source: Lee P. Arbetman, Edward McMahon, and Edward O'Brien, *Street Law,* 2d ed. (St. Paul, Minn.: West Publishing, 1980), p. 311.

Environmentalists **Environmentalists** are special interest groups concerned with the physical environment and the changes people have made in it. For many years only a few seemed to worry about the environment; now almost every day there are headlines about oil tanker spills, pollution of air and water, and danger from pesticides. According to the National Institute for Occupational Safety and Health, about 20,000 manufactured products need to be federally regulated because they contain toxic substances; more than 400 of these products contain cancer-causing agents.

Sometimes special interest groups become frustrated by inaction and seek to dramatize their concern. A few years ago, a mystery person called "The Fox" won the approval of many people when he stopped up the drainpipes and smokestacks of companies that he thought were polluting the environment. On one occasion he left a dead fish and sludge on the ivory-colored rug of a steel company executive. In 1977 more than 1,400 protestors were arrested and jailed for attempting to stop the building of a nuclear power plant in Seabrook, New Hampshire. In 1978 more than 8,000 farmers and students destroyed the control tower and other facilities of the new $4 billion Tokyo International Airport the day before it was to be opened (five years late). When the airport finally opened officially, it did so under extreme emergency conditions, with a security force of 14,000 guarding it.[21]

Consumerists **Consumerists** are special interest groups concerned with the safety and quality of products bought by consumers. Although there have always been consumer groups, consumerism first made headlines with the publicity that Ralph Nader generated with his book, *Unsafe at Any Speed,* and his head-on confrontation with General Motors regarding automotive safety. Perhaps the confrontation would have been less publicized if General Motors had not hired a private detective to investigate Nader. Eventually the president of GM had to appear before Congress and apologize to Nader. Congress has since passed a number of laws regarding the safety, reliability, side effects, and prices of products. Today, we accept automobile call-backs as a matter of course; but before the rise of consumerism, such an action would have shocked people.

Nader's case is only one illustration of how government and the environment interact. Another is the landmark case of 1978, in which the Supreme Court upheld the Federal Trade Commission's order for the makers of Listerine (Warner-Lambert) to pay for $10 million in advertising to correct false claims that Listerine was effective against colds and sore throats. The court fight had lasted almost seven years. The American Advertising Federation strongly objected to the decision, calling it "drastic" and "probably the most far-reaching advertising order ever issued by the commission."[22]

On the positive side many organizations have avoided government attention by voluntarily policing their own advertising. Lees Carpets has run advertisements that provide truly useful information to people thinking about buying carpets. Hunt-Wesson Foods has decided to avoid discussing relatively unimportant product differences in its advertising. Many other national advertisers are becoming interested in conducting educational campaigns and using more informative, specific copy than they were using a few years ago.[23]

Shareholders Shareholders are people who become part owners of businesses by buying shares of stocks issued by corporations. Some organizations have only a few owners of their stock; others have many. General Motors, for instance, has approximately 1.5 million individual shareholders. Traditionally, the chief executive of an organization has directed its affairs so as to please the major group of stockholders—the people who own large blocks of stock and the members of the board of directors. And for a long time the primary concern has been whether the price of the stock or the dividend is high enough. If it is, management has little to worry about. For example, the majority of the stockholders of General Motors do not influence or bear much responsibility for the company, so their sole concern is the price of the stock and the rate of return on their investments.

As a result, the annual stockholders' meeting for most large corporations is usually a relatively sedate and quiet affair. In recent years, however, these meetings have been stirred by confrontations between environmentalists and other interest groups. Questions have been raised and protests have been made by shareholders about such social issues as discrimination, pricing policies, pollution, and hiring practices in South Africa. More and more resolutions have been filed to influence social, political, and environmental decisions. Activist groups have involved such diverse shareholders as universities, churches, and labor unions (including the United Auto Workers). These organizations have put pressure on many large companies, including Johnson & Johnson, Coca-Cola, and Eastman Kodak.

Managers are reacting differently to shareholder questions and concerns than they were a few years ago. In the past, questions were seen as disruptive and impertinent. Now, managers carefully prepare for meetings and treat questions respectfully. John Bunting, chairman and chief executive officer of the First Pennsylvania Corporation, says, "Now there is greater recognition that the shareholder has the right to know." Another chief executive points out that "shareholders are becoming less lethargic about what they can do. They are making it clear that they will not put up with any nonsense during meetings."[24]

Boards of Directors Social involvement is also affecting boards of directors.[25] Membership on a board of directors used to be far more comfortable than it is now. Under state laws of incorporation, boards of directors are charged with protecting the interests of the companies' owners. For a long time this meant taking a relatively narrow view of stockholder interests. Now, however, critics are suggesting, or demanding, that directors take a wider view. In addition, boards are being asked to take more responsibility for the operation of the organizations. For example, the Securities and Exchange Commission (SEC) recently criticized the outside directors of National Telephone, a telephone equipment supplier that went bankrupt. The SEC charged that the directors did not sufficiently question the overly optimistic statements of the organization's managers.

Often boards of directors are composed primarily of insiders—those who were already employees of the company when they joined the board. A trend exists, however, toward the use of outside directors—people who are not members of management and who do not have strong ties to management. This trend began with a recent New York Stock Exchange ruling that all companies listed on the exchange must have audit committees and that the members of these committees must be outside directors. Of course, audit committees were used before the NYSE's ruling, partly because of scandals involving political payoffs in the early 1970s. In fact, many organizations have had audit committees for years. General Motors has had one since the late 1930s.

More and more organizations are establishing other active committees in such areas as wages, benefits, and other kinds of compensation; public affairs; and ethics. Furthermore, since they have become increasingly subject to lawsuits and other harassments, board members are taking their responsibilities more seriously than they did before. Some noted people have recently turned down appointments because they felt they did not have the time to properly handle the job of director.

Lobbying Lobbying involves actions taken by individuals or organizations to influence government agencies and federal, state, or local legislation. The term *lobbyist* need not have a negative connotation. Indeed, in most political systems, lobbyists and lobbies are essential for providing legislators with needed information. Government works better when it receives a variety of information. The Sierra Club may lobby for more environmental protection. The National Association for the Advancement of Colored People (NAACP) may lobby for more civil rights legislation or enforcement of such legislation. The local Parent-Teachers Association may lobby for or against a new school building. Unions may lobby for a higher minimum wage.

The squeaky wheel gets the grease.

Lobbying is a critical function for organizations, since management must present clear and accurate information to government bodies in order to get favorable legislation or rulings. Organizations that fail to lobby or that do it ineffectively are almost always hurt in a political system that has many competitive and diverse interests. Sometimes industrial lobbyists work in league with other special interest groups; other times they lobby intensively on opposite sides of an issue.

Organizations usually have a trade association (such as the American Bankers Association or the National Association of Realtors) to lobby for their special causes. Most large firms, such as General Electric and General Motors, also have their own representatives in Washington and the state capitals to lobby for their interests. Smaller firms frequently hire an organization that specializes in lobbying, usually a law firm. Other organizations may send their own members to directly approach regulatory agencies, local members of Congress, or state legislators.

Board members are often from companies on which the organization depends.

Top management may lobby directly to get favorable action. For example, J. Paul Austin, former head of Coca-Cola, spent at least half his time traveling from one country to another lobbying to open up new markets for his company.[26] Other heads of business firms are also becoming more involved in direct lobbying. In 1972 the Business Roundtable, an organization of about two hundred of the chief executives of the country's major corporations, was formed. The primary purpose of the Roundtable is to give business more political clout. As issues arise, members are organized into task forces that analyze them, take specific positions, and then argue these positions with regulatory agencies, the White House, or Congress.

The Roundtable was formed as a direct result of increased government regulation and taxation and the growth of special interest groups in the late 1960s and early 1970s. Ralph Nader has been an effective lobbyist because he and his organization provide Congress and government officials with lists of facts. The Roundtable now does the same thing. The proposal in earlier 1977 to create a federal agency for consumer protection was sponsored by Nader; but when the Roundtable mustered its own facts, the proposal was defeated by Congress.[27]

CORPORATE SOCIAL RESPONSIBILITY AND THE SOCIAL AUDIT

The previous section showed how organizations and the larger environment act as interpenetrating systesm. In addition to this involvement, organizations are assuming more social responsibility, mostly because of some changing values of society. The issues arising from these changing values have led to government programs such as Medicare, the Occupational Safety and Health Act, and the many laws and regulations affecting air, water, and other pollution—all of which have caused organizations to increase their social responsibility. Because an organization's legitimacy depends on its acceptance by the public, many managers believe in heeding the public's attitudes on important issues. It is thus that social responsibility and the social audit have come about.

Social Responsibility **Social responsibility** is behavior taken by organizations for society's good beyond what the law or common custom demand. For example, a certain amount of pollution control is required by law. When a firm takes steps to reduce pollution even further, it is demonstrating social responsibility. The U.S. Chamber of Commerce suggests that voluntary social action can be viewed at four levels, as shown in Figure 23.3.

The first level is conformity to legal requirements in fulfilling the economic function of the business. A profit-maximizing manager would probably follow this course. The second level is going beyond legal requirements to meet public expectations of social responsibility, a position the trusteeship manager might take. The third level is anticipating new social demands and preparing in advance to meet them, a position the quality-of-life manager would take. The fourth level is serving as a leader in setting new standards of business social performance.[28]

In order to show how the organization is fulfilling its social responsibilities, more and more organizations and authorities are contemplating the use of social audits. A **social audit** is generally an ongoing evaluation of performance measured against established goals in selected areas of social responsibility. For example, ABT Associates, a social research and consulting firm, includes in its annual report a listing, in dollar terms, of its social assets and liabilities.

Levels of social responsibility:

- Conformity
- Meeting expectations
- Anticipating new demands
- Setting new standards

A social audit serves to measure an organization's progress in meeting social responsibilities.

FIGURE 23.3 Levels of corporate social action

To successfully develop and implement a social audit or social measurement of some kind, a firm must evaluate the environment in which it
functions, establish objectives for improvement, make resource allocations to fill identified needs, and measure and evaluate its progress on an
ongoing basis. Although most annual reports touch on the subject of
social responsibility, few do so in financial terms. Reporting on progress
in this area tends to be sketchy and sporadic. But for the benefit of outsiders looking in, of company insiders, and of society as a whole, a comprehensive form of social accounting is needed.[29]

Most reporting on company social performance has been in response
to pressures from outside groups such as product safety and environmental protection agencies. Some of it has been simply a form of advertising
aimed at preventing outside interference in company policy making.
Much reporting has been confined to progress made in meeting legal
requirements in areas such as minority hiring and product safety. These
haphazard reporting efforts often miss large areas of both good and bad
performance by the organization that are relevant to overall social responsibility.

Because there is a significant investment today in social overhead—
from automobile safety to pollution to day care centers—a more rational
management of this investment is needed, both within and outside the
organization. A study of 185 firms from *Fortune*'s lists of the top 500 and
second 500 largest U.S. corporations indicated that only about half the
organizations had established objectives in the area of external affairs.
Those that had established even broad objectives, however, saw themselves as reaping more success from their social investments in such
areas as environmental affairs, stockholder relations, and good citizenship than organizations that set no objectives.[30]

Without clearly stated objectives, the returns of one social investment
cannot be accurately compared against the returns of another. Such comparison is valuable, since it enables an organization to replace less efficient investments with more efficient ones. An optimum mix of social
programs that will either give maximum benefits for a fixed cost or that
will cost the minimum amount for some fixed level of responsibility
needs to be achieved.

What constitutes an optimum mix is not always obvious. For example, in 1974 approximately $1 billion was spent to develop and install a
complex interlock system of seat belts for automobiles. The car would
not start unless the belts were connected. The belt system irritated drivers and passengers, and Congress eventually withdrew the requirement
for it. Perhaps all the money spent on this project could have been better
spent on developing good road signs, intensive driver training, more
thorough vehicle inspections, or other safety approaches.[31] The cost of
any social responsibility action must be carefully considered in light of
its possible ramifications both within and outside the organization.

Social Measurement and the Social Audit   The social audit must
answer two opposing desires on the part of the organization: the desire

to see evidence of responses to the demands of outside pressure groups and the desire to accurately assess its social performance. Consequently, the social audit may take one of two forms. It may be an internal management report used to determine the company's strengths and weaknesses in the area of social responsibility. Or it may be an external audit, in which case it may suffer from the organization's desire to make itself look good. The resulting inaccuracies may lead to an unwise use of resources for further social programs.

Four general approaches exist for reporting the results of a social audit. The first is a *straight inventory approach,* where a company lists all its social activities. The second is a *cost approach;* in addition to listing social activities, the company indicates the amount spent on each. The third is *program management;* here, cost information is given along with a statement about whether the organization has met its objectives for each activity. The fourth is a *cost-benefit* approach; it includes the cost information and the real worth or benefits of each expenditure.[32]

Clearly, the inventory approach is the simplest and easiest method, since it lists only what is being done to meet social responsibilities. The most difficult is the cost-benefit approach, which will show up many inefficiencies produced by an undersupply of social program services or an oversupply of services that are not strongly demanded. For example, an organization may support a bowling league even though relatively few employees like to bowl. At the same time, it may have a large population of working mothers but no day care center.

A major problem in reporting on social responsibility is definition. Business and social planners sharply disagree on what constitutes social responsibility. Another major problem is how to measure social costs and benefits. Out-of-pocket costs are relatively easy to establish for many activities. But the true costs—such as managerial time spent on a project—may be impossible to determine. Indeed, social benefits are nearly impossible to measure. A case in point is the benefit to society from pollution control. Although it is possible to measure the reduction in the amount of pollutants in the air, this reduction cannot be quantified in dollar terms. Still, there are a number of quantitative and qualitative approaches to measuring social performance. For example, one can count the number of minority group members hired, and this gives an indication of the organization's efforts at combating discrimination.

At present there is little agreement on what a social audit is, who should do it, or how it should be undertaken. The only point of agreement is that standards are needed. Without knowing the standards for acceptable social performance, managers are understandably reluctant to discuss what their organization has done and what its plans are. Standards are also needed for the way the audit should be performed. Without such guidelines, credibility becomes a problem. If the report is conducted primarily by an internal company group, there can be doubt as to how much negative performance is being reported. Even if outside auditors prepare the report, they must rely on internal sources to generate much of the data regarding the organization's social performance.

Four approaches for reporting social audit results:

- Straight inventory approach
- Cost approach
- Program management approach
- Cost-benefit approach

Some advances have been made in the area of social measurement. For example, the American Institute of Certified Public Accountants has established a committee on social accounting, and the American Accounting Association has set up a committee on measurement of social costs. The National Association of Accountants has organized a task force to establish goals for the accounting profession in setting forth principles of social accounting and improving the social performance of the business community. The Securities and Exchange Commission offered guidelines in late 1975 on how organizations should report their environmental performance to investors. Although the SEC declined to make suggestions for reporting in other social performance areas, the guidelines are at least a beginning. All in all, it appears that the next few years will bring a growing awareness of social responsibility and more effective techniques for measuring how well organizations are meeting their social responsibilities.

SUMMARY

The manager of today faces a dilemma. As the culture and values of society have changed through the years, so also have the manager's responsibilities. Under profit-maximizing management, the responsibility was clear—to make a profit. Now, however, the larger society is looking to organizations, particularly the larger corporations, to assume a larger responsibility for social goals. Many managers still believe in profit maximization, but many others reject this idea as simplistic.

Therein lies the dilemma. With rapidly shifting cultural values, what is the real responsibility of the manager to the organization, to the stockholders, and to the larger community? Should the manager adopt a trusteeship style and attempt to balance the conflicting interests of varied groups, or should the manager take up a quality-of-life approach and become a leader?

One piece of knowledge has emerged. If managers can organize with other businesses or special interest groups, their lobbying attempts stand a good chance of success. The unanswered question is: What is the proper balance?

Another point made in this discussion is that anyone hoping to successfully operate a business must be aware of the influences and interests of a wide range of special interest groups. Through the phenomenon of interpenetrating systems, these special interest groups are able to influence many business organizations. Thus consideration of issues ranging from racial discrimination in the job market to environmental pollution or corporate contributions to the arts is vital to today's corporate managers.

Social changes involve organizations of all types. Particularly in the past twenty years, a number of federal, state, and local laws and regulations have had a large impact on organizations. Simply obeying the law today is much more complicated than it was around the turn of the century.

Although many people, including some economists, would disagree, it appears that trusteeship management is taking the place of profit-maximizing management. The concept of interpenetrating systems shows why this must occur. For example, the change in the mandatory retirement age from sixty-five to seventy has forced managers to rethink their position on many related issues, such as performance appraisal and pension plans.

More and more organizations are moving

beyond simple social involvement and toward acceptance of social responsibility and the social audit. However, the thinking in this area is as yet relatively unsystematic. Some organizations have moved a long way in this direction. Others have ignored the whole idea of social responsibility.

The suggestion that an organization's legitimacy depends ultimately on its acceptance by the public has merit. Thus many managers have found it worthwhile to pay attention to the public's attitudes on important issues and to conscientiously evaluate the organization's performance in those areas.

STUDY QUESTIONS

1. Describe the changing concepts of the economic system held by organizations. How has the larger environment influenced their thinking?
2. Is *social involvement* a more neutral term than *social responsibility*? Explain.
3. What does the interpenetrating systems model show about current influences on organizations?
4. What is the corporate dilemma, and what are some of its causes?
5. How would you now answer the question, "Do organizations affect state and federal agencies?"
6. Visit a local or other regulatory agency, such as a board of zoning appeals or a liquor licensing commission. Interview the chairperson or a member of the commission to learn that individual's views about the purpose of the agency. Then write these views in a report to share with the rest of the class.
7. Interview several local business managers. Describe their opinions about regulatory agencies.
8. Compare and contrast the answers you get from the regulatory agencies and business managers. If there are differences, explain what causes them.
9. Suggest some ways in which organizations can or should take action regarding social responsibility. What is *your* social responsibility?

Case for Discussion

THE CHEVYMOBILE

A Chicago man took his new 1977 Oldsmobile back to his dealer to replace the fan belt on the engine. The dealer did not have the proper belt in stock; and when the owner looked at the engine, he discovered that the new Oldsmobile did not have an Oldsmobile engine. Instead it had a less expensive engine made by Chevrolet. The owner demanded a "pure Oldsmobile" and was turned down. At this point he took his case to the Illinois attorney general.

As the case unfolded, it became known that General Motors had put Chevrolet engines not only into other 1977 Oldsmobiles but also into 1977 Buicks and Pontiacs. As a result, GM became the target of about 250 private and state lawsuits.

In late December 1977 the company settled out of court with forty-four states that had banded together to sue for all "Chevymobile" owners in their states. (Six states—California, Iowa, Kentucky, Louisiana, New York, and Tennessee—did not join in the settlement.)

Under the terms of the settlement, all 75,000 owners in the forty-four states would receive a $200 cash rebate—about $120 more than the estimated difference between the value of the Chevrolet engine and the other engines. In addition, each owner would receive a transferable three-year or 36,000-mile warranty estimated to be worth about

$200 per car. If all the owners of the "Chevy-mobiles" in all fifty states were to agree to those terms, the total dollar cost to GM would be about $37 million, not including the costs of the lawsuits, the damage to the company's reputation, and other intangibles.

In making the announcement that the company had agreed to settle the dispute out of court to save the cost of many lawsuits, GM denied any wrongdoing or liability. The chairman of the board said:

> The interdivisional usage of engines is not new with General Motors or the automobile industry generally. General Motors used V-8 engines produced in a plant operated by its Chevrolet Motor Division in Buick, Oldsmobile and Pontiac cars because it sought to satisfy consumer demand for V-8 engines in its 1977 cars. Those engines were part of the General Motors family of engines and offer quality per-formance and durability. General Motors stands proudly behind those engines and all of its products.

He pointed out that car buyers who paid for a 350-cubic-inch, 170 horsepower engine got exactly that. However, some owners have experienced delays in getting their cars repaired because parts from Buick, Oldsmobile, and Pontiac engines do not always fit the Chevrolet engine. GM now warns buyers in its advertising that its automobiles may come equipped with equivalent components produced in GM plants.

Two notable features of the GM case are that the settlement was one of the largest awards ever in a consumer protection case and that this was the first time so many state attorneys general had banded together to fight for consumers against a single company. In effect, a national public service law firm was formed.

Sources: "End of the Great Engine Flap," *Time,* January 2, 1978, p. 66; "GM Settles Engine Cases in 44 States," *Boston Globe,* December 20, 1977; and "Costly Auto Troubles," *Business Week,* January 9, 1978, p. 30.

1. Do you believe that the Chicago owner had a right to demand a "pure Oldsmobile"?
2. Do you believe the statement of the chairman of the board of GM that the switch in engines was to satisfy consumer demand?
3. What are the legal, moral, and social responsibilities of GM in this case?
4. What are the implications of this case for the future?

FOR YOUR CAREER

1. As a manager, you have to be responsive to several different components of the environment at the same time.
2. Managers are increasingly concerned about what is best for the society and the employees as well as for the organization itself.
3. Interest groups are a potent force in our society and in the decision-making processes of organizations.
4. The relationship between business and government is generally conceived to be one of independence. In reality, the relationship is anything but independent.
5. Organizations and their managers can perceive the environment as a constraint or a challenge; they can also ignore it or take advantage of it.
6. Managers may find it in their best interests to work more closely and cooperatively with government if the society is to become more productive.
7. Organizations should evaluate managers on how well they deal with the environment.

FOOTNOTES

1. "Testimony during Hearings on Alaskan North Slope Pricing, Entitlement Issues before the Federal Energy Administration," March 21, 1977. (Statement of Avid P. Goodman, managing director of Morgan Stanley & Co., Inc.)

2. Information about the pipeline is from the following sources: A. Morner, "For SOHIO, It Was Alaskan Oil—Or Bust," *Fortune,* August 1977, pp. 173–184; "Pipeline to Mid-America," *The Sohioan,* February 1977, p. 10; R. James, "Alaska Pipeline Opens on Time, but Shortcuts Scar the Environment," *Wall Street Journal,* June 20, 1977, p. 1; and H. Ellis, "Alaska Oil May Be a 'Mixed Blessing,'" *Christian Science Monitor,* June 21, 1977, p. 1.

3. L. Canfield, *The United States in the Making* (Boston: Houghton Mifflin, 1949), p. 552.

4. N. Eberstadt, "What History Tells Us about Corporate Responsibilities," in *Managing Corporate Social Responsibility,* ed. A. Carroll (Boston: Little, Brown, 1977), p. 21.

5. D. MacNaughton, "Managing Social Responsiveness," *Business Horizons* 19 (December 1976): 19.

6. B. Nanus, "The Future-Oriented Corporation," *Business Horizons* 18 (February 1975): 5–12; and C. Burck, "The Intricate 'Politics' of the Corporation," *Fortune,* April 1975, pp. 109–112.

7. M. Friedman, *Capitalism and Freedom* (Chicago: University of Chicago Press, 1962), p. 135.

8. D. Ewing, "The Corporation as Public Enemy No. 1," *Saturday Review,* January 21, 1978, p. 12.

9. *Social Responsibility of Business Corporations* (New York: Committee for Economic Development, 1971).

10. K. Davis, "Social Responsibility Is Inevitable," *California Management Review* 19 (Fall 1976): 14–20.

11. D. Votaw and S. Sethi, *The Corporate Dilemma* (Englewood Cliffs, N.J.: Prentice-Hall, 1973).

12. R. Hay and E. Gray, "Social Responsibilities of Business Managers," *Academy of Management Journal* 18 (March 1974): 135–143.

13. F. Sturdivant, *Business and Society* (Homewood, Ill.: Richard D. Irwin, 1977), p. 67.

14. Eberstadt, "What History Tells Us about Corporate Responsibilities," p. 22.

15. G. Steiner, *Business and Society* (New York: Random House, 1971), pp. 70–71.

16. F. Byrom, *Koppers Foundation* (Pittsburgh, Pa.: Koppers Company, n.d.), p. 2.

17. L. Preston and J. Post, *Private Management and Public Policy* (Englewood Cliffs, N.J.: Prentice-Hall, 1975).

18. Ibid., p. 26.

19. V. Day, "Management and Society: An Insider's View," *Management and Public Policy,* proceedings of the Conference, School of Management, State University of New York at Buffalo, September 1971, p. 157.

20. C. Stabler, "For Many Corporations, Social Responsibility Is Now a Major Concern," *Wall Street Journal,* October 26, 1971, p. 1.

21. "Tokyo Airport Opens after Years of Strife," *Boston Globe,* May 20, 1978; and E. and P. MacInnis, "Showdown at Narita," *Boston Globe,* May 20, 1978.

22. R. McLean, "Gargle Go-Round Has Ad Industry Gagging," *Boston Globe,* April 9, 1978.

23. D. Aker and G. Day, "Corporate Responses to Consumerism Pressures," *Harvard Business Review* 50 (November–December 1972): 110–121.

24. Y. Ibrahim, "The Metamorphosis of the Shareholders' Meeting," *New York Times,* April 9, 1978, sec. 3, p. 9.

25. L. Smith, "The Boardroom Is Becoming a Different Scene," *Fortune,* May 8, 1978, p. 151.

26. M. Jensen, "A Market Thirst Never Quenched," *New York Times,* April 8, 1978, sec. 3.

27. W. Guzzardi, Jr., "Business Is Learning How to Win In Washington," *Fortune,* March 27, 1978, pp. 53–58.

28. Chamber of Commerce of the United States, Council on Trends and Perspective, *The Corporation in Transition* (Washington, D.C.: Chamber of Commerce of the United States, 1971).

29. D. Linowes, *The Corporate Conscience* (New York: Hawthorne Books, 1974); J. Paluszek, *Business and Society: 1976–2000* (New York: American Management Association, 1976); and A. Carroll, ed., *Managing Corporate Social Responsibility* (Boston: Little, Brown, 1977).

30. W. Hegarty, J. Aplin, and R. Cosier, "Achieving Corporate Success in External Affairs: A Management Challenge," *Business Horizons* 21 (October 1978).

31. M. Weidenbaum, "The High Cost of Government Regulation," *Business Horizons* 18 (August 1975): 43–51.

32. D. Fetyko, "The Company Social Audit," *Management Accounting* 10 (April 1975): 135–148.

The International Environment

CHAPTER 24

CONTENTS

THE COCA-COLA COMPANY

The Coca-Cola Company has been in business for about ninety years. It has annual sales of over $3 billion and operates in about 150 countries. In 1976 some 55 percent of its profits came from foreign operations. Much of the company's growth is due to its secret formula for producing Coke; the formula is the basis for a syrup that is sold to wholesalers and bottlers.

Coca-Cola also has many other products besides Coke. For example, it owns Taylor and Great Western wines, Tab, Fresca, and Sprite. It produces orange juice and instant coffee and tea products, including the brands Minute Maid and Butter-Nut. One of its wholly owned subsidiaries is Aqua-Chem, a company that designs and manufactures equipment for desalting sea water and other related equipment.

For Coca-Cola the world is divided into three parts, with an executive vice-president in charge of each. One part involves operations in the United States and Central and South America. Another involves Europe, Africa, Southeast Asia, and the Indian subcontinent. The third involves Canada, the Pacific, and the Far East.

Dealing in the multinational market requires decisions and strategies considerably different from those appropriate for organizations operating in only one country. For example, when Coca-Cola gave an Israeli firm a franchise to bottle and sell Coke in Israel in 1967, Coke was promptly boycotted in the Arab countries. However, Coca-Cola has technology and know-how that the Arab countries need. Aqua-Chem, for example, is an expert in water desalination, and Saudi Arabia alone is planning to spend billions of dollars in desalting over the next few years. Coca-Cola's foods division has expertise in agriculture, and the Arabs are interested in developing their agricultural know-how. Consequently, the company has reason to hope that this expertise will reopen the door to selling Coke to the Arab world.

Another multinational market decision made by Coca-Cola involved India. The Indian government insists that all multinationals transfer some of their knowledge and ownership to Indian nationals. Coca-Cola refused to make its secret formula known and has thus lost the lucrative Indian market. Management decided that disclosure of the secret formula would be even more adverse to the company's interests than losing India's business.

Even if Coca-Cola had no foreign sales or production facilities, its operations would still be greatly affected by the international environment. Imports are essential for two of the company's major products—soft drinks and coffee. Almost all coffee must be imported, and about half the sugar used in soft drinks comes from foreign sources.[1]

This case raises several key questions that you should be able to answer after reading the chapter. The questions include:

1. Should the U.S. government encourage corporations such as Coca-Cola to trade with and establish relationships with communist countries such as China and the Soviet Union?
2. Are multinational corporations good or bad for the United States?
3. How is your life affected by other nations?
4. What are the differences between international and multinational organizations?

24

The Coca-Cola case shows the increasing effect of the international environment on companies involved with both imports and exports. The importance of the international environment to U.S. businesses is further demonstrated by the fact that approximately one-third of U.S. corporate profits now come from foreign operations of U.S. firms. Moreover, projections indicate that by the turn of the century the United States will be completely dependent on foreign suppliers for such scarce resources as aluminum, manganese, tin, cobalt, and tungsten.[2] Conditions such as rising wages in the United States and the rise and fall of the dollar are other illustrations of how the U.S. economy is linked to an international economy. The Coca-Cola case also shows the conflicts of interest between companies and nations. The decision to franchise in Israel led to the boycott in the Arab countries. India's desire to help its nationals become knowledgeable resulted in Coca-Cola's withdrawal from that country.

This chapter will explore the reasons for international and multinational involvement, the different forms of such involvement, management practices in various countries, and environmental constraints on international management. Organizations become multinational in order to expand the alternatives open to them, to obtain scarce resources, or to compete more effectively with other organizations. Dealing in the international arena requires managerial strategies considerably different from those used by organizations operating in only one country.

INTERNATIONAL AND MULTINATIONAL FIRMS

A continuum exists from the domestic company to the international company to the multinational company. As Figure 24.1 shows, a **domestic organization** limits its purchases and sales to a single country. An **international organization** has interests that cut across national boundaries; it imports or exports goods, services, or products. Examples of such organizations are firms that buy uncut diamonds from Amsterdam or that import Oriental rugs from Iraq or India. Even a small U.S. bakery located close to the Canadian border that sells some of its bread in Canada is considered an international organization. The term *multinational firm*, which did not appear in any dictionary until the 1970s, has been defined several ways in both textbooks and common usage.[3] As will be

Domestic	International	Multinational
Purchases and sales only within one country.	Direct purchases and/or sales in home country and one or more host countries	Usually, one or more subsidiaries in host countries

FIGURE 24.1 Domestic, international, and multinational operations

International organization

Multinational organization

Domestic organization

seen later, a **multinational organization** usually is a company that has one or more subsidiaries abroad and that is willing to go anyplace in the world to secure resources and to make sales. This chapter will pay more attention to multinational than to international organizations, since multinationals often set their objectives on a global rather than a national basis.

There has been no worldwide census to determine the exact sizes and characteristics of international companies; however, the many fragments of information available indicate that they are a large and growing influence.[4] Nearly all large companies headquartered in the free world today are either international or multinational. The only general exceptions are utility companies and certain transportation firms; most countries simply do not allow foreign ownership of such industries.

Not all international companies are large; in fact, some companies with yearly sales of less than $1 million have acquired international status. However, the large firms receive most of the publicity because of the enormous power they wield. One startling fact is that if the hundred largest world organizations were ranked in terms of output, forty-nine of the top hundred would be nations (as measured by their gross national product), and the other fifty-one would be international companies (as measured by their yearly sales).

Today, most people will at some time work for an international company, unless they are employed throughout their careers by government agencies or nonprofit organizations. This means that many people will have to make decisions about operations in countries that have different operating environments and conditions than those of the United States. Some of these decisions may mean weighing what is best for the company as a whole against what is best for either the company's U.S. operations or the economic, political, and social objectives of the United States.

U.S. citizens working in the United States for foreign-owned companies may come to question some operating and management practices imported from abroad. They may also question whether they can realistically aspire to top-level management positions or whether these will be reserved to citizens of the country that has set up operations in the United States.

Multinationals differ considerably in the degree to which they are known as foreign entities in their overseas operating locales. At one extreme are companies such as Volkswagen and Honda, which were well-known as being German and Japanese long before they announced that they were setting up manufacturing facilities in the United States. Many other companies, however, have developed such a local profile that most people are unaware of their foreign ownership. Few people in the United States, for example, realize that Nescafé is a Swiss firm, Norelco a Dutch firm, and Bic a French firm—all with manufacturing facilities in the United States. Likewise, Hoover, Heinz, and Woolworth are so deeply entrenched in England that they are generally thought of as British rather than American. It is even common in England for people to say that a carpet has been Hoovered rather than vacuumed.

Reasons for International and Multinational Operations   Foreign operations provide opportunities not available to domestic companies. Since markets abroad imply additional people and income, the company can expect greater sales. It is also presented with greater market opportunities and can effect various internal economies by being able to cover fixed costs more readily and to recoup research and development expenditures before competitors have an opportunity to emulate advancements in the market.

Costs can be reduced through foreign operations in many other ways. One method is to acquire cheaper inputs to production in the form of labor, raw materials, power, or capital. The French firm, Pechiney, for example, mines bauxite in New Caledonia but processes it in the northwestern part of the United States, where electric power is relatively cheap. Another method is to develop risk aversion strategies by acquiring scarce resources or buying existing sales outlets abroad so that competitors are prevented from gaining control over essential supplies or markets. Since business cycles vary among countries, the dependence on multiple rather than one-country markets may help stabilize a company's earnings as well.[5]

Forms of International Involvement   Companies that use international markets usually employ multiple strategies for their operations. Some of these strategies are unique to international operations and require personnel with specialized knowledge. For example, exporting goods from one country to another involves special transportation, packaging, documentation, and financing, as well as knowledge of the laws and customs of the host country. There are six general methods of exporting: individual sale, exclusive sale, independent agent, branch office, subsidiary company, and joint export.

> Methods of conducting international exports:
>
> - Individual sale
> - Exclusive sale
> - Independent agent
> - Branch office
> - Subsidiary company
> - Joint export

Individual Sales   The first step in exporting is often individual sales to host company buyers. However, this approach may encounter difficulty in collecting payment, and it does not usually secure a steady flow of export orders. Usually, intensive exports can be achieved only if a permanent sales organization is established in the host country to create and maintain a demand for the goods and to provide the home organization with firsthand information on the special requirements of the market and the actions of the competition. Thus establishing a permanent sales organization is highly desirable, and a company that wants to export on a permanent basis usually takes one or more of the other five actions listed here as well.[6]

Exclusive Sales Agreements   Under exclusive sales agreements the exporter or seller grants the buyer in the host country sole rights to handle specific goods, products, or services in a particular geographical area.

The buyer agrees to rely on the seller as the sole source of supply from the home country. The contract usually states the general terms by which individual sales will be made. For example, suppose a typewriter manufacturer in the United States signs an exclusive sales contract with an importer in India. The agreement may prohibit the U.S. manufacturer from selling typewriters to other firms in India and the Indian purchaser from purchasing typewriters made by other firms in the United States.

Independent Agents Independent agents sell goods or services in the host country and receive commissions on the sales. They frequently have the authority to give credit and to receive direct payments for the goods. Companies that use independent agents must rely heavily on their judgment and so must choose the agents carefully.

Branch Offices In some cases exporters establish branch offices abroad and staff them with their own employees. Many organizations prefer this arrangement because it gives them direct control over the company's foreign market activities. This arrangement requires sufficient sales volume to warrant the expense of having employees in host companies. Furthermore, if the employees are of the same nationality as the exporter, two sets of laws must be followed—those of the home country and those of the host country. Of course, if the employees are residents of the host country, the exporters usually must comply only with the local employment laws.

Subsidiary Companies The most favored form of modern export trading is the establishment of a subsidiary company in the country into which the exports are directed. The **subsidiary** is wholly owned by the parent company but is incorporated under the laws of the host country. It possesses separate and independent legal rights and has the same status in the host country as any other firm in that country. The subsidiary is controlled by the parent firm, which may hold a majority of its shares. In some countries (such as Nigeria) foreign companies can carry on business only through the incorporation of a domestic company.[7] By establishing one or more subsidiaries abroad, a parent company becomes a multinational enterprise—"a combination of companies of different nationality, connected by means of shareholdings, managerial control, or contract and constituting an economic unit."[8]

There are a number of legal and other problems involving multinational organizations. For example, the interests of the host country in which the subsidiary is formed may conflict with those of the home country of the multinational. In such cases the laws and public policies of the host country prevail over those of the home country. As another example, in the European Community (also known as the European Common Market) the various subsidiaries of a multinational are treated as a single unit, even when they are in different countries of the Common Market.

Joint selling organizations are formed by groups of companies to operate outside the United States.

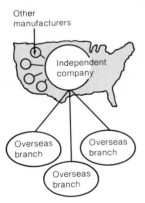

Joint selling organizations are formed by independent companies with overseas branches acting as the selling manufacturer for a limited number of manufacturers.

Joint Export Organization Increasing attention is being paid in modern export trade to combined exporting. The basic characteristics of this method are that a number of economically independent manufacturers or merchants set up a joint organization in order to coordinate their exports, but they keep their freedom of action in other respects. The cooperation may be tight or loose. The two most important forms of cooperative exporting are joint selling and consortium selling.

Joint selling organizations can take many forms. In one, a group of manufacturers or other companies form a marketing company to operate in a particular foreign territory; the expenses are shared by the members in some agreed-on way. Another involves an independent company with overseas branches that acts as the selling organization for a limited number of manufacturers. The manufacturers contribute as a group to the overhead expenses of the sales organization and are charged individually with any costs that are unique to an individual company.[9]

Consortium A **consortium** is an organization created when two or more companies cooperate so as to act as a single entity for a specific and usually limited purpose. For example, the Society of Lloyds, better-known as Lloyds of London, is a group of insurance underwriters who join together to cover certain insurance risks that are too great for any individual underwriter.

Other forms of international involvement include *international licensing*—the sale to an organization in a host country of the right to use patents, trademarks, or other intangible assets. For these transactions, it is especially important to have personnel with specialized legal knowledge, since each country treats these assets and their transfer differently. Another form of involvement abroad is the *management contract,* in which foreign management is provided a facility in a host country for a fee. Finally, in what is known as a *turnkey operation,* an organization or a consortium can build facilities in a host country for a local organization to eventually own and run. In theory, all the host country has to do after the preliminary agreements is to "turn the key" to start the facility. Automobile, cement, and fertilizer plants are the most common types of turnkey operations. Management contracts and turnkey operations have been increasing, because countries such as Iran, Saudi Arabia, and the Soviet Union wish to use Western management and technological expertise while maintaining ownership for themselves.

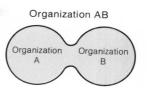

Organization AB

A consortium is created when two or more companies act as a single entity.

COMPARATIVE MANAGEMENT VERSUS INTERNATIONAL MANAGEMENT

Comparative management is the study of differences among management practices in various countries, usually with an attempt to determine which environmental conditions have been responsible for the different norms of managerial behavior. **International management** focuses on practices at the worldwide corporate level, since it is at this level that the activities in each of the countries where the multinational company operates must be coordinated. Both comparative and international management are obviously of immense importance to multinational companies.

Comparative Management Adjustments Comparative management helps identify the areas in which a firm needs to alter its operating methods for a particular country. When management practices in a given foreign country are observably different from those at home, the firm prepares for the possibility of adapting its operations to fit the local norm. Of course, it is not always desirable to operate exactly the same as local firms. Indeed, an important advantage of a multinational may be its efficient management techniques, not employed by competitors. However, to assume on entering a host country that one can always act exactly as at home is folly. Legal, political, or cultural obstacles may abound.

How do multinational companies react to comparative management differences? Over the past decade a large number of studies have confirmed what has long been suspected—that management and personnel practices vary substantially from country to country. Some of these studies describe practices on a country to country basis, and some compare attitudes of managers from different countries.[10] Studies of multinationals' reactions to the differences indicate an overall attempt to infuse into foreign operations many of the multinationals' home practices.

Many managers believe they are reducing the risk of failure by managing their foreign operations in a manner similar to their home operations. Many others believe that differences from country to country are so inconsequential that they can make their home country practices work anywhere. For example, U.S. firms (more so than Japanese or French ones) tend to use capital-intensive operating methods in place of labor wherever possible because of the cost and scarcity of labor in the United States. When these companies use the same methods in less-developed countries with abundant labor, they can be justly criticized for using inappropriate technology.

Organizations that do implement home country practices in foreign countries rarely transfer all their practices intact to the host country. Rather, most operations tend to be hybrids of home country practices and local ones. This is true for multinational companies from other countries as well as the United States. There are a number of reasons for this. One is that until the late 1960s many of the developed nations revered U.S. management practices. Now more and more managers in host countries have graduate degrees in management and are as well-versed in good management practices as U.S. managers. In some countries—such as West Germany, France, Sweden, and Japan—managers are somewhat critical of U.S. managerial practices.

A second reason for hybridization is that when a firm establishes a subsidiary in a host country, the parent organization frequently sends a whole battery of personnel. But as time goes on, these people are replaced with more and more citizens of the host country, especially in countries requiring work permits. Even when U.S. managers remain in foreign operations, they tend to alter their management styles to conform to local styles.

Evidence exists that the larger and more experienced multinational firms can use similar management techniques in all countries because of their size or the oligopolistic nature of their worldwide markets.[11] For example, a large U.S. automobile manufacturer wanted to construct a new plant in England. Because of the favorable impact the plant would have on England's economy, the company was able to get the government to modify a number of rules, regulations, and policies to allow the foreign subsidiary to operate with U.S. management techniques. Thus large multinationals can influence host countries, particularly if these countries are relatively small ones.

International Management Adjustments From a corporate standpoint, the operations in foreign countries have to be coordinated and controlled. Although constraints are placed on management because of the diverse country-to-country environments in which their companies operate, the parent firm still has to determine which decisions will be made by managers in the foreign country and which by managers at some regional or corporate headquarters. The corporate organization must thus establish the location of decision making, communications flow, and integration of activities.

Management policies and practices should be looked at from the corporate viewpoint as well as the country-by-country one because many decisions that are optimal for a given subsidiary are not optimal for overall corporate objectives. Corporate management is therefore particularly prone to control decision making that will affect more than one operating unit or that will minimize profits for a subsidiary in order to maximize profits for the corporation itself. Suppose a company is manufacturing the same product in both Canada and England. Corporate management may dictate that the two operations either can or cannot export the product to the other's market. Only at the corporate level can the overall repercussions of the decision be seen.

International management therefore includes the study of the transfer of resources (including managers) among entities in different countries where the companies are operating, organizational structures to cover multinational activities, and strategy development in a global context. Multinational companies need to study management from both a comparative and an international perspective. Comparative studies help them learn how to operate better in the countries where they have facilities. International management helps them learn how to coordinate and control the activities among these countries.

Environmental constraints

ENVIRONMENTAL CONSTRAINTS

Constraints are restrictions on managerial actions. The environmental conditions of a country provide certain constraints that are one reason management practices differ from country to country. Although every aspect of business operations—including marketing, finance, and accounting—can be affected by various constraints, the following discussion will center on those that affect overall policy and interpersonal relationships. The number of environmental constraints is so great that this discussion must be representative rather than conclusive.

Legal Constraints   Each country has its own set of laws, and these laws are a combination of formalized and traditional practices. It is often difficult for multinational companies to recognize that all countries have certain laws that are either not enforced or are enforced unevenly and certain practices that, although not specified in the written law, are nevertheless so customary that all companies are expected to follow them. Multinationals are apt to face more difficulties than domestic companies because their managers may lack the experience necessary to recognize the subtle differences between law and practice. Furthermore, multinationals may receive a great deal more criticism than domestic companies for not following the letter of the law. For example, in many countries the tax law is routinely circumvented whenever possible by the citizens. Yet if multinationals circumvent it to the same extent, a public outcry may ensue, and the multinationals may even be expelled from the country.

Countries also vary greatly in their hiring practices and laws. In the United States the law specifies nondiscrimination by sex, religion, race, and national origin. In South Africa the law specifies by race who can legally take which job. As another example, at the same time that the retirement age in the United States has been moved up to seventy, in Japan it has been forced down to fifty-five—a radical departure from decades of Japanese practice under which older people were revered and kept in positions until they reached a very advanced age. Most Western European countries have also been moving toward a lower mandated retirement age.

Most countries do not recognize the practice of laying off workers during slack periods. Instead, if a company wishes to reduce the work force, it must fire people and pay them settlement sums required by law. A number of countries actually prohibit the firing of employees after they have worked a specified period of time. In these countries the only way a company can fire people is by declaring bankruptcy, and then the employees have priority over creditors or stockholders to the assets of the business. In these sorts of situations management is pressured to stabilize production output.

Another area of marked contrast to U.S. practice is the policy of codetermination now followed in most Western European countries and being introduced in parts of Latin America. Under this policy, labor representatives are included in management or on boards of directors. The inclusion ensures not only that workers gain information that normally is kept from them but also that they share in policy-making decisions. Some of the countries that include workers on boards are Sweden, Norway, and West Germany. The concept has also been proposed in Great Britain.

Political Constraints Multinational companies usually must receive permission from political authorities in the country where they plan to operate before setting up facilities. In order to get the permission, they may have to agree in advance to follow certain practices. Recent negotiations with foreign governments have dealt with such issues as what a firm will do about pollution, whose ships will carry its merchandise, how much of its earnings will be reinvested, and who will serve in its management and on its board of directors. Once these issues are resolved, the multinationals may find themselves operating under a political system very different from their own. Today companies operate in communist as well as capitalist countries and in dictatorial as well as democratic ones.

Because of the large size of multinational companies in relation to the small size of some host countries, their operations often are scrutinized by the highest level of that country's government. Even in the Soviet Union corporate leaders such as Armand Hammer of Occidental Petroleum or Henry Ford II of Ford Motor Company talk directly to top-level officials at the Kremlin. This has some disadvantages for the company. It often forces managers to deal directly with systems with which they do not agree personally, and the close connections with foreign government leaders often creates adverse public opinion at home about the firm's foreign operations. Increasingly, problems are arising from joint operations between U.S. companies and foreign governments. Standard Oil of Indiana, for example, shares ownership of fertilizer plants with the government of India. The objectives of such a government may be the maximization of employment or minimization of prices, and these objectives must take precedence over the maximization of profits.

Economic Constraints Economic and social conditions vary for each country. For example, small countries often are plagued by low levels of education, poor social services, inadequate transportation facilities and utilities, high levels of unemployment, and small markets. These conditions dictate certain differences in the production process. For example, a high unemployment rate inclines a government to push for both low wage rates and absorption of as many people as possible into the work force. The result is that companies may have to use labor-intensive types of production instead of the machine-oriented production common to industrialized countries.[12] Further complications may then arise because of low levels of education, which may necessitate additional training and supervision.

Quality control and product uniformity are potential problems whenever people are used instead of machines. In Costa Rica, McDonald's is using people rather than machines to cut up the potatoes used for french fries and the potatoes are, of course, less uniform. This creates no problem, since they are sold only within Costa Rica; but if a company is trying to export and compete in world markets, quality control and consistency assume greater importance.

The economic system of a country may also prohibit many of the practices that keep firms competitive on the world market. In the Soviet Union, for example, multinational companies are prohibited from owning production facilities and from promoting their products as they do at home. Some U.S. steel producers have argued that the very close connection between Japanese firms and their government makes it almost impossible to export products into that market because locally owned firms are favored regardless of price. In other countries certain funtions are heavily controlled by government agencies. Pharmaceuticals, for example, may be sold almost entirely through government agencies as part of a national health plan.

By controlling the economy, governments also exert considerable control on the decision making of individual companies. If, for example, a company is prohibited from remitting home most of its profits from an overseas operation, its funds must be reinvested abroad to a great extent. This can lead the company to engage in new endeavors in order to use up the funds and, in the process, to shift the location of decision making elsewhere.

Government

controls

Economy

influences

Company's decision making

Cultural Constraints   Norms, or standards of behavior, vary from country to country. They are difficult to assess and thus are one of the more subtle environmental contraints facing companies as they expand abroad. There is growing evidence that a certain few behavioral variables, described in the following list, are most decisive:

Cultural differences exist regarding:

- Prestige of work
- Managerial reactions
- Compensation preferences
- Group identification
- Social mobility

1. *The prestige of work and of particular occupations within the society.* Some societies hold the pursuit of leisure in much higher esteem than do other socieites. Thus the axiom that some people live to work and others work to live has considerable validity for international comparisons. Also, certain types of occupations have higher prestige in some countries than in others. Since business and management are held in fairly high esteem in the United States, many highly qualified people seek business careers, whereas in, say, Argentina, many qualified people shirk business in favor of other professions.

2. *How managers react on the job.* Studies comparing managers from different countries have revealed significant differences in willingness to take personal responsibility for solving problems, in setting achievement goals, in taking calculated risks, and in requesting concrete feedback about performance.

3. *The preference for individual versus group oriented compensation.* In societies where individual achievement is emphasized more than group achievement, the work force tends to be mobile in terms of

changing employers and locations. The workers also tend to prefer monetary compensation as a direct form of feedback on their perceived worth. In other societies, such as Japan and parts of Latin America, fringe benefits may substantially exceed the amount of direct compensation given to employees. These benefits often include transportation to and from work, lunches at work, bonuses at Christmas, time off for the funerals of even distant relatives, and gifts to employees' children when they are married or graduate from school. This attitude extends to the method of decision making in that both workers and managers in such group oriented societies frown on individual decision making, preferring group consensus.

4. *The identification of individuals with certain groups.* The group affiliations are based on such things as sex, family, age, caste, religion, political preference, membership in associations, ethnic background, race, and occupation. Membership in the various groups often reflects the degree of access to economic resources, prestige, social relations, and power. If a company does not understand the subtle or overt meanings of these group affiliations, it may hire people who will be unacceptable to their peers and subordinates.

5. *Social mobility.* The more open or mobile the society, the more likely it is that a person can obtain a job strictly on the basis of his or her qualifications. Of course, even in the extremely mobile society of the United States, certain occupations have opened to certain groups only in the last few years. Nurses, elementary school teachers, and secretaries are almost always women; airline pilots, religious ministers, and trash collectors are almost always men. Certainly no innate male or female ability makes one person more qualified than another for these occupations. It is simply that tradition or culture has dictated certain occupational norms. Other countries deviate from the U.S. norm in many areas, including occupation.

These are but a few examples of the many cultural differences that affect foreign business operations. They indicate the caution appropriate for any multinational company operating abroad. Before introducing a change into the environment of another country, an organization should determine if the benefits of that change are worth the costs that will be incurred. Then, if the change is still deemed wise, the company should ensure that local persons participate in the decision making and in the rewards of that change. Those in charge of implementing the change should watch for obstacles arising from the host society's fears that social structures may be upset. Sometimes the time is simply not right for modifying practices or implementing new ones.

FOREIGN MANAGEMENT ASSIGNMENTS

When a multinational company sets up operating facilities, management contracts, or turnkey operations abroad, a major task is staffing the foreign operation. Most positions are usually filled by nationals of the host country. This is done for many reasons, among them:

1. It is usually less expensive to hire local people than to bring in people from the outside.
2. Governments often prohibit the hiring of foreigners.
3. Local people are familiar with the environment in which the business is to be conducted.

Besides using local people, multinational companies also transfer large numbers of U.S. citizens from one country to another. It is estimated that there are as many as a hundred thousand U.S. employees working for multinational companies outside the United States. Most of them are managers who have been transferred to foreign operations in order to implement certain management practices abroad or to ensure that corporate policy is followed. Those who are not managers are largely engineers and technicians who have been hired to work on turnkey projects in remote areas of the world.

Two other types of expatriate management are becoming popular with multinational companies. One is transferring a foreign national in a foreign operation to another foreign country (for example, transferring a British manager to an Australian operation because that person may know the culture better than a U.S. manager would). The other is transferring a foreign manager at a foreign operation to U.S. corporate headquarters. IBM and Mobil Oil, for example, now have non-U.S. managers of proven ability filling some of their top-level positions in the United States.

Regardless of the type of foreign assignment, the expatriate and his or her family face substantial adjustments. If they do not adjust, the manager's ability to manage may be hampered.[13] Since it is costly to move a manager with family to a foreign assignment, the company should take whatever steps it can to assure that the transplanted manager will be accepted by other employees and to ease the manager's family into comfortable living conditions. Such companies agree that an important attribute for someone being considered for a foreign assignment is the technical mastery of the job, because this proficiency can help the person become accepted by other employees. Of course, the expatriate manager may still face problems on the job, not only because of the changed operating environment but also because the distance from the home office makes it difficult to get staff assistance.

In terms of living conditions, spouses are sometimes prevented by local regulations from accepting any type of employment, which can make foreign assignments unattractive to husbands and wives who both want careers. Children may have to go to very different types of schools. Housing is usually difficult to find and expensive, and managers are usually forced to rent rather than purchase a home. Changes in language and eating habits may necessitate further adjustments. It is generally agreed that these adjustments in living conditions make it difficult for managers to perform their tasks successfully. There is little consensus, however, on how to cope with the adjustment problem.

On the Job

EXECUTIVES SUFFER KIDNAPPING ANXIETIES

NEW YORK, Feb. 10 (UPI)—The nation's top executives fear kidnapping and arson—crimes common to the corporate milieu—more than the general public does and spend hundreds of millions of dollars annually to combat them, according to a report released today.

The kidnapping and arson anxieties are especially strong among executives whose companies have links to countries subject to terrorist attacks, the survey found.

Moreover, the corporate leaders support fast punitive measures to fight crime, with 92 percent favoring the death penalty for murder compared with 66 percent among the general public, according to the survey.

The findings, based on responses from 30 percent of the top executives of the Fortune 1,000 companies, were contained in "The Figgie Report, Part II: The Corporate Response to Fear of Crime." The report

was published by A-T-O Inc., a New York-based diversified international corporation. Part I of the study covered attitudes toward crime among the general public.

Thirty-nine percent of the businessmen polled feared they, a family member or a business associate will be kidnapped, according to the report.

However, among the 43 percent of the Fortune 1,000 companies with links in countries where executives already were victimized, more than half the respondents said they face kidnapping fears on a daily basis. Only a quarter of executives in firms without such ties admitted to this fear.

Nearly 39 percent of the respondents also feared arson. Of these, 61 percent have extensive company security programs, compared with only 35 percent among the respondents unworried about arson.

The responses reflected the

fact that senior executives and their dependents in host countries are targets in more than 50 percent of all kidnapping attempts, the report said. In the past decade, businesses paid an estimated $250 million in ransoms.

Kidnapping concerns are much higher among the largest corporations. Those that feared kidnapping included 57 percent of executives with firms having annual sales of at least $1 billion, 38 percent of those in firms with sales of $301 million to $999 million and 24 percent in firms with $300 million or less in sales.

To combat crime, 53 percent of the executives polled secure their homes with burglar alarms, fire alarms and other safety devices. More than 25 percent have unlisted numbers and confidential addresses; more than 33 percent vary their daily routes to work and, when traveling, more than 25 percent check their hotel rooms for possible intruders.

Source: "Executives Suffer Kidnapping Anxieties," *Washington Post,* February 11, 1981, p. E3. Reprinted by permission of United Press International.

SUMMARY

International and multinational firms are becoming increasingly important to the world's economy. Organizations expand to multinationals in order to increase their opportunities, to obtain scarce resources, or to deal more effectively with competition. Coca-Cola, one

of the largest multinationals, operates in about 150 different countries.

International and multinational organizations can use a number of management strategies. For example, they can sell or purchase directly, have exclusive sales agreements, deal with independent agents, or establish branch offices in host countries. They can establish subsidiary companies controlled by the parent company but subject to the laws and regulations of the host country. They can use joint export organizations for large projects. (The Organization of Petroleum Exporting Countries has had a tremendous influence on the Western world, and this influence may well increase.) They can provide technical advice and services—for example, building a facility such as a cement or fertilizer plant that will be operated by the host country. In theory, all the other country has to do is begin operations. In the majority of cases, however, local managers and workers have to be trained before they an take over operation.

Management practices vary widely from country to country, usually because of legal, political, economic, and cultural constraints. But some similarities exist too. The effective manager is sensitive to the constraints but also knows when home country practices are more effective. A U.S. manager working for a Japanese or German company that operates in the United States must also be aware of the different norms and values of that organization.[14]

Because of differing laws and customs and other variables, the manager who wants to become involved in international or multinational operations must become thoroughly familiar with the specific host country. Operations management in the international environment is complex.

STUDY QUESTIONS

1. Discuss the reasons for the growth of multinational firms. Do you think this growth will continue? Explain.
2. Discuss the differences among domestic, interntional, and multinational forms of operation.
3. Identify and give examples of six basic forms of international involvement.
4. What types of legal, political, economic, and cultural constraints might affect international or multinational operations?
5. Reread the Radio Shack case in Chapter 6. What suggestions do you have for the management of Radio Shack?
6. What is the difference between a subsidiary and a consortium?

7. Several examples of foreign-owned organizations with manufacturing operations in the United States are given in the chapter. Using personal experience, the library, or any other source, list at least five more of these organizations.
8. List five foreign countries. In what ways might managing in these countries be the same as managing in the United States? In what ways might it be different?
9. Interview a manager working for a multinational company (for example, a foreign car dealer). What advantages and disadvantages does the manager see in working for a multinational?

Case for Discussion

JAPANESE IN THE UNITED STATES

MEMPHIS, Tenn.—At Japan's Sharp of America plant here in Memphis, the Japanese work ethic is meeting the American union ethic. Head-on.

On the Japanese side, there's *Saacho-san,* or "Mr. President," 51-year-old Sharp executive Paul Hagusa, from Osaka. "Harmony is power," Mr.

Hagusa preaches. "Trust each other for a united effort. Courage is the source of a meaningful life. Tackle difficulties with a positive attitude"—and, incidentally, don't join the union.

On the other side, there's Grady Parks, 48, from Little Rock, Ark., a professional representative, or organizer, for the AFL-CIO's International Brotherhood of Electrical Workers. "There's a big difference between a company handbook and a (union) contract," he says.

Tomorrow, Sharp employes will get a second chance to vote on representation by the IBEW. In an election last year, 68% voted against union representation. Sharp officials acknowledge that the new vote may be "too close to call." Although there's some evidence that the company message is still honored, Mr. Hagusa and Mr. Parks are campaigning energetically, engaging in some oratory notable even in a city well-known for its fire-breathing Gospel preachers.

Selling Loyalty Mr. Hagusa sells togetherness and loyalty. All new employes at the Sharp color television assembly plant complete an 18-hour course covering such topics as "Sharp Philosophy and History" and "Employe Cooperation." They learn some slogans, too, such as "Sharp people make sharp products." Mr. Hagusa meets each new class of workers. "Sincerity is the most fundamental of human ethics," he tells them, invoking the thoughts of the founder, Tokuji Harakawa.

Then, on the company's 62-acre property here, they go to work on streets called Sincere, Courage, and Trust. Assembly lines compete for trophies given to those who produce the most sets with the fewest defects. The attention paid to quality is "mostly a matter of pride," says Ben Kemker, an assembly-line worker. Mr. Kemker studies electronics engineering at night school, for which Sharp pays the tuition.

After 17 months of operation in Memphis, Sharp bought a series of double-page advertisements in Southern newspapers asserting that the quality of its Memphis output "is as good as anything we've done anywhere in the world."

The company clearly credits dedication and loyalty. "The workers don't stand up and sing the company song every morning," says Robert Wing,

a company spokesman, "but Sharp tries almost everything else to sell togetherness."

That gives the IBEW's Mr. Parks some misgivings. Mr. Parks has experience with Japanese employers; he helped win employes of a Toshiba Corp. television plant in Tennessee to the IBEW. "We're confident that we can win this time," he says of the new Sharp election. He says the company's contention that it can take care of its "family" better than a union is a "bunch of propaganda." IBEW regional vice president M.A. Williams says of Sharp. "That approach can't work. Americans just don't think like the Japanese."

The IBEW is the only union on the ballot. It has spent several hundred thousand dollars to try to organize Sharp, union officials say.

The second election was called by the National Labor Relations Board after the IBEW charged that Sharp violated labor law by offering workers a 40-cent-an-hour raise just a few days before the first election. Sharp denies that the raise was an unfair labor practice.

Although wages at Sharp fall a bit below the area industrial average of $6.87 an hour, generous fringes make the company's package "just as good if not better than what other electronics firms in the area offer," says Yuji Kimura, an administrator. Sharp gives 11 paid holidays and 10 days of sick leave a year, paid medical and life insurance, a minimum of four hours of pay for any time worked beyond a regular shift, and premium pay for night shifts. A pension plan goes into effect on April 1. "Our philosophy is to pay within our means at the start and share more of our profits as the company grows," Mr. Hagusa says.

Federations Are Okay In principle, Sharp is unopposed to unions. Like other big industrial concerns in Japan, it hasn't prevented employes from joining blue-collar federations, but those generally seem less militant than many hard-driving American unions. The company fears that such a union could divide employes' loyalties and undermine corporate goals.

Sharp got a great deal of friendly attention when it decided to produce in Memphis. More than 40,000 people applied for the plant's 880 jobs, thus permitting Sharp to skim the cream of the Memphis labor force. Memphis leaders went out of their way to welcome the company. When building trades unions tried to disrupt construction of the Sharp plant, the Chamber of Commerce managed to persuade union members that Sharp's contractor would hire only local labor and services.

Construction started in December 1978 and was completed in 11 months.

"We tried our best to make our Japanese friends feel right at home," says James McGehee, president of McGehee Mortgage Co. and former chief of the Chamber of Commerce. "We taught Paul (Hagusa) to drink Jack Daniel's and eat grits."

Source: Eduardo Lachica, "Japanese Work Ethic and Unionism Clash at Sharp of America's Memphis Factory," *Wall Street Journal,* February 26, 1981, p. 29. Reprinted by permission of The Wall Street Journal, © Dow Jones & Company, Inc. 1981. All rights reserved.

1. What are the constraints operating in this case?
2. How does the Japanese work ethic clash with the union ethic?
3. How might the American work ethic clash with the Japanese work ethic?
4. For companies to be effective in other nations, to what degree do you think they have to adapt to the cultural norms of their host nations?
5. What problems might U.S. companies face in attempting to operate in Japan?

FOR YOUR CAREER

1. Managers must become increasingly skilled in dealing with other nations. The world is clearly the marketplace for many organizations.
2. Although the United States is the most productive nation in the world, its rate of productivity increase is far from the highest. In addition, several nations have a higher standard of living than the United States. They include Sweden, Switzerland, and Kuwait.
3. The relationship between business and government varies dramatically from country to country.
4. Working in countries like Japan, China, West Germany, or Russia requires a thorough knowledge of and keen sensitivity to the culture of the countries. Knowing the language of one of these nations almost guarantees one a good job.
5. To be a successful manager in a multinational company, you need to be aware of the legal constraints in both the United States and other countries.
6. Getting a managerial assignment to another nation may be critical to your career success.

FOOTNOTES

1. *Moody's OTC Industrial Manual* (New York: Moody's Investors Services, 1977); "The Graying of the Soft-Drink Company," *Business Week,* May 23, 1977, pp. 68–72; "Coca-Cola Co. Seeking Access to Soviet Union, China and Middle East," *Wall Street Journal,* November 8, 1977, p. 21; M. Jensen, "The American Corporate Presence in South Africa," *New York Times,* December 4, 1977, p. D1; and K. Rangan, "Give Up Knowhow or Leave Country," *New York Times,* August 9, 1977. p. 45.

2. C. Bergstein and W. Cline, "Increasing International Interdependence," *American Economic Review* 66 (May 1976): 155–162.

3. J. Behrman, *Some Patterns in the Rise of the Multinational Enterprise* (Chapel Hill, N.C.: University of North Carolina Press, 1969).

4. Department of Economic and Social Affairs of the United Nations, *Multinational Corporations in World Development* (New York: United Nations, 1973).

5. E. Daniels, E. Ogram, Jr., and L. Radebaugh, *Inter-*

national Business: Environments and Operations (Reading, Mass.: Addison-Wesley, 1976), chaps. 3 and 25.

6. C. Schmitthoff, *The Export Trade: The Law and Practice of International Trade,* 6th ed. (London: Stevens and Sons, 1975); and I. Brownlie, *Principles of Public International Law,* 2d ed. (Oxford, England: Oxford University Press, 1973).

7. Nigerian Decree No. 51 of 1968.

8. Schmitthoff, *The Export Trade,* p. 169.

9. G. MacEwan, *Overseas Trade and Export Practice* (London: Macdonald and Evans, 1938).

10. N. Farmer and B. Richman, *Comparative Management and Economic Progress,* rev. ed. (Bloomington, Ind.: Cedarwood Publishing, 1970).

11. J. D. Daniels and J. Arpan, "Comparative Home Country Influences on Management Practices Abroad," *Academy of Management Journal* 15 (Fall 1972): 305–315.

12. L. F. Wells, Jr., "Don't Overautomate Your Foreign Plant," *Harvard Business Review* 52 (January–February 1974): 111–118.

13. C. Arensberg and A. Niehoff, *Introducing Social Change: A Manual for Americans Overseas* (Chicago: Aldine Publishing, 1964).

14. For an excellent overview of some of these similarities and differences see G. Hofstede, *Culture's Consequences: International Differences in Work-Related Values* (Beverly Hills, Calif.: Sage Publications, 1980); G. Hofstede, "Motivation, Leadership, and Organization: Do American Theories Apply Abroad?" *Organizational Dynamics,* Summer 1980, pp. 42–63; D. A. Wren, "Scientific Management in the U.S.S.R., with Particular Reference to the Contribution of Walter N. Polakov," *Academy of Management Review* 5 (January 1980): 1–12; T. Phelps and K. Asum, "Determinants of Administration Control: A Test of a Theory with Japanese Factories," *American Sociological Review* 41 (February 1976): 80–94; D. V. Nightingale and J. M. Tarlonge, "Values, Structure, Process, and Reactions/Adjustments: A Comparison of French- and English-Canadian Industrial Organization," *Canadian Journal of Behavioral Science* 9 (January 1977): 37–48; J. F. Springer and R. W. Gable, "Dimensions and Sources of Administration Climate in Development Programs of Four Asian Nations," *Administrative Science Quarterly* 25 (December 1980): 671–688; R. E. Cole, "Learning from the Japanese: Prospects and Pitfalls," *Management Review* 69 (September 1980): 22–28, 38–42; E. Page and A. Midwinter, "Remoteness, Efficiency, Cost and the Reorganization of Scottish Local Government," *Public Administration* 58 (Winter 1980): 439–464; G. D. Wilson and S. Iwawaki, "Social Attitudes in Japan," *Journal of Social Psychology,* 112 (Summer 1980): 175–180; and L. Kelley and R. Worthley, "The Role of Culture in Comparative Management: A Cross-Cultural Perspective," *Academy of Management Journal* 24 (March 1981): 164–173.

A Conclusion and a Beginning PART VII

Effective Managing— A Comparison and a Summary

CONTENTS

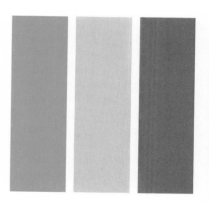

THE BUREAU OF VITAL STATISTICS

A bureau of vital statistics in the health department of a large city had three major tasks to perform: (1) the receiving, recording, and issuing of birth certificates; (2) the receiving, recording, and issuing of death certificates; and (3) the maintenance of vital statistics dealing with births, deaths, hospital admissions, gunshot wounds, child abuse, and the like.

A new director was appalled to learn that it took three months for the bureau to issue either a birth certificate or a death certificate. The bureau also received harsh criticism from state and federal agencies because of its six-month delay in reporting the city's vital statistics. It prompted complaints from parents each fall because of its delay in issuing birth certificates for children's admission to kindergarten. And it provoked further complaints from those who needed death certificates in order to collect survivor benefits from Social Security. The twelve clerks in the bureau were constantly being berated by unhappy citizens, and they felt themselves to be in a constant state of crisis.

The director first asked for funds to hire three more clerks to reduce the backlog. When the funds were denied (because of a lack of money in the budget), she discussed the problem with the personnel director. Together, they decided to see if they could simplify the bureau's work by studying tasks to see if any could be eliminated and if any could be combined to make the work flow easier.

At a meeting with the clerks it was decided to analyze the receiving and issuing of birth certificates, since this task caused the most problems. The clerks were enthusiastic about the possibility of reducing the pressure they all felt. Since there was no time for studying and analyzing the tasks during the day, the group decided to work extra hours two afternoons a week. Provided with forms and procedures, they began to analyze the work flow process. Since the process had evolved over the years, many overlaps, duplications, and unnecessary procedures were found and eliminated. Elated with their success, the group went on to study all the bureau's tasks.

Six months later the bureau looked very different. The work was caught up, and it was common for a request for a birth or death certificate to be honored the same day it was received. The number of employees in the bureau had dropped from twelve to ten (two clerks had transferred to other departments), and the group knew that the bureau could actually manage with one person less. Three months later an opportunity for a promotion occurred, and the total staff of the bureau was reduced to nine clerks and the director.

This case raises several key questions that you should be able to answer after reading the chapter. The questions include:

1. Would you rather work in a private organization or a public organization?
2. What are the differences in managing organizations in the three organizational sectors?
3. What are the differences between large and small organizations?
4. What impact does the profit motive have on managing an organization? What takes the place of this motive in public organizations?

25

This case illustrates the dilemma faced by almost all managers—how to plan, organize, and control the work with available resources. Although the problem concerned a large municipality, the approaches used to solve it can be applied to almost any type of organization. The case also shows that managers do not exist only in manufacturing firms. As Chapter 1 pointed out, only 14 percent of all managers work in manufacturing, while about 20 percent work in public administration.

This chapter has two major purposes: (1) to examine some of the similarities and differences in managing different but related types of organizations—the private sector, the public sector, and the third sector; and (2) to highlight some basic functions that managers perform in formal organizations of all kinds.

THREE ORGANIZATIONAL SECTORS

The **private sector** consists basically of profit-making organizations. The **public sector** consists of federal, state, and local government bodies. The **third sector** includes voluntary, semi-public, and semi-private organizations (such as private colleges, the Girl Scouts, the Postal Service, Amtrak, and voting leagues).

MANAGING BUSINESS ORGANIZATIONS (THE PRIVATE SECTOR)

Business firms come in numerous sizes and types. Because national and multinational firms are written about so often, we frequently think of them as the predominant kind of business firm. Actually, as Chapter 1 pointed out, 98 percent of all U.S. firms employ fewer than fifty people. Some of the advantages and disadvantages of small and large firms will be discussed before similarities and differences in managing them are dealt with.

No single definition of *small business* is completely satisfactory. However, for loan purposes, the Small Business Administration (SBA) defines a *small business* as one that is independently owned and operated, is not dominant in its field, and has the following characteristics:

- Manufacturing—250 or fewer employees
- Retailing and service—$1 million or less annual sales
- Wholesaling—5 million or less annual sales.[1]

Even the SBA-developed guidelines for distinguishing between large and small businesses often fail in their purpose (as was pointed out in Chapter 10). Nevertheless, the guidelines can be helpful in understanding some of the reasons for the existence of large and small businesses.[2]

Why Large Businesses Exist Organizations have many advantages in being large and complex. For example, General Motors and General

Types of organizations

Private sector
Profit-making organizations

Public sector
Federal, state, and local government bodies

Third sector
Voluntary, semi-public, and semi-private organizations

Electric can spend an enormous amount of money on research and development and are probably more financially stable than most small organizations. Of course, the temporary bankruptcy of Lockheed and the failure of the Penn Central railroad indicate that these advantages do not always hold.

Technology. Mass production of automobiles is a good example of the effect of technology on size. In order to reach economy of scale, an organization must invest millions of dollars in highly specialized equipment. The cost would be prohibitively high for a small organization. In the same fashion, a modern oil refinery requires millions of dollars in capital equipment.

Competitive edge. The economy of scale in manufacturing or purchasing frequently gives larger companies an edge over smaller competitors. For example, a large food or grocery chain can usually buy its products more cheaply than can a small grocery store, since discounts are usually given for purchases over a given amount.

Financial strength. In many cases large firms have greater financial strength and stability than smaller ones. For example, Westinghouse makes a large variety of products. Even if there is a reduced demand for one product, demand for others will probably take up the slack in overall profits. Sears, Roebuck can afford to take a loss on some of its merchandise while it makes a profit on other merchandise. A smaller firm might not be able to continue in business if demand for its products declined.

Why Small Businesses Exist   There are many reasons for some organizations remaining small. They include greater flexibility, an ability to offer more personalized or specialized service, and limited demand for that company's products. For example, a local garage can be much more effective than a large automobile company at customizing automobiles.

Greater flexibility. Large firms have much more of a management hierarchy and many more checks and balances than do small ones. As a result, smaller firms can shift to new products or services more easily. The suggestion has been made that had the originator of Pet Rocks been affiliated with a large firm, the product would never have been developed.

More personalized service. Many small firms, such as barber and beauty shops, are local. Their owners get to know the customers and can give personalized service. A local butcher shop or record shop will often better understand the needs and wants of customers than will a large organization servicing many cities.

Limited demand. Some products are not needed on a large scale. A demand does exist for tailor-made suits and dresses for which people are willing to pay extra, but it is a limited demand. The gourmet or health food store is another example of a specialty firm that provides products unavailable elsewhere.

Managing in Different-Sized Organizations   Although the distinction so far has been between large and small organizations, this is an

---

Reasons for large businesses:

- Technology
- Competitive edge
- Financial strength

Reasons for small businesses:

- Greater flexibility
- More personalized service
- Limited demand

oversimplification. Clearly, there exists a range of organizations from the very small (such as the corner grocery store) to the very large (such as General Motors). In addition, some organizations begin small and then grow. Of course, not all organizations grow, and not all continue growing. Nevertheless, management approaches and management problems are somewhat different at different levels of growth or size, as shown in Table 25.1. Organizations grow in stages, and each stage needs to be managed differently.[3]

Assume that an individual is starting a new business as an

TABLE 25.1 Managing in Different-sized Organizations

	CHARACTERISTICS OF COMPANY GROWTH		
OEGANIZATIONAL CHARACTERISTIC	PATTERNS OF THE FIRST STAGE	PATTERNS OF THE SECOND STAGE	PATTERNS OF THE THIRD STAGE
Core problem	Survival	Management of growth	Managerial control and allocation of resources
Central function	Fusion of diverse talents and purposes into a unified company	Fission of general authority into specialized functions	Fusion of independent units into an interdependent union of companies
Control systems	Personal (inside); survival in marketplace (outside)	Cost centers and policy formulation (inside); growth potential (outside)	Profit centers and abstract performance criteria (inside); capital expansion potential (outside)
Reward and motivation	Ownership, membership in the family	Salary, opportunities and problems of growth	Salary, performance bonus, stock options, peer prestige
Management style	Individualistic; direct management	Integrating specialists; collaborative management	Integrating generalists; collective management
	ORGANIZATION		
Structure	Informal	Functional specialists	Division organizations
CEO's primary task	Direct supervision of employees	Managing specialized managers	Managing generalist managers
Levels of management	Two	At least three	At least four

entrepreneur—a person who organizes and manages a business, taking a risk for the possibility of making a profit.

In Stage 1 the first task of the manager is to determine the specific niche that the organization is to fill in terms of products or services. If this is done properly, the organization will survive. The next and most central function is to bring together people with different talents and purposes and get them to work together. Control systems in Stage 1 organizations are relatively simple and usually personal, and the managerial style is individualistic and direct, since all the employees are working for the chief executive officer—the person who has started the business. The structure of the organization is relatively informal, with few written rules and procedures. In the absence of formal policies, many decisions are made on an ad hoc basis. For example, how much sick leave an individual should get may be clearly stated in a larger organization, but in a Stage 1 organization it will probably be determined on a personalized basis.

Stage 2 requires a different managerial approach. At this stage the organization usually has a steadily growing and perhaps diversified product line and a growing market for the products. Managing for survival is replaced by managing for growth.

The increasing size and complexity of the organization leads to increasing specialization. Second-level management is involved in such specialized activities or departments as marketing, finance, engineering production, and personnel. Authority is split among the different functions.

The chief operating officer can no longer maintain an intimate knowledge of all the details of the organization. Therefore, the management style is more collaborative. The top manager works with specialists in a cooperative fashion, since one of the primary tasks is integrating their work. Moreover, the manager needs their expert help to aid in decision making. The control function also changes, operating through the development of cost centers and the formal establishment of policies rather than being personally executed by the top manager.

At this stage the top manager usually no longer knows the names of all the employees. Formal personnel policies, such as those involving vacations, sick leave, salary, and fringe benefits, begin to emerge. Time clocks may be installed for hourly workers.

Planning changes from being immediate and ad hoc to a more formal process. Longer-range plans need to be developed and implemented throughout the organization. This implementation is done through the management hierarchy, and it requires more formalized rules and procedures.

At Stage 3, as shown in Table 25.1, the core problem shifts again. Now it is one of overall control and allocation of resources throughout the organization—which consists of at least four levels.

The structure of the organization at this stage may be vastly different from the structure in the first and second stages. Different product lines may have become different divisions or subsidiary companies. If the or-

Entrepreneur

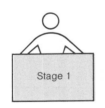

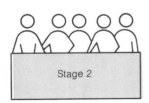

For a Stage 2 organization the manager needs the aid of specialists.

ganization has become multinational, the divisions may be on an area basis as well (for example, North America, Latin America, Europe, and the Middle East).

The organization may have general managers in the main office and in decentralized units or divisions. These managers work with other general managers and with functional specialists.

The control function shifts as well. At the first stage control can be directly exercised by the individual manager. At the second stage it requires the separation of general authority into specialized functions. At the third stage it requires further coordination through such approaches as profit centers (for example, the Chevrolet division versus the Cadillac division of General Motors).

Planning is now highly formalized, with planning units set up at different levels of the organization to assist both top management and division management. Policies and procedures are established for certain practices among the various departments and divisions.

The task of the top manager is now that of managing general managers. It requires the ability to integrate the work of managers who are themselves generalists but who are managing such specialized functions as marketing, finance, production, engineering, and personnel.

Of course, as Chapter 10 pointed out, size is a relative factor. A consulting firm with 500 employees may be large in comparison with most other such firms. American Motors, on the other hand, has more than 29,000 employees but is actually close to being too small a firm to efficiently produce automobiles. Largely because of its size, its automotive operations were losing about $90 million a year in 1978 and it was seriously considering merging with other organizations.[4] Shortly after this, American Motors established a retail agreement with Renault to sell its cars through American Motors dealerships.

The franchise business is another one where the distinction between large and small firms becomes blurred. The franchiser is a company that licenses others to sell its services or products. Some examples are McDonald's, Midas Muffler, Holiday Inn, Dunkin Donuts, and Pizza Hut. Two advantages of franchising are instant name recognition and standardized operation. For example, a Midas Muffler shop in New York City is similar in appearance, operation, and product to one in Denver, Colorado. Another advantage of franchising is that the individual franchisee is in a sense his or her own boss, managing a small business. A disadvantage is that the individual may be too tightly controlled by the parent corporation.

McDonald's is a large corporation in terms of total sales, but the manager of the local McDonald's is actually a small business person of a sort. McDonald's gives the individual franchisee the exclusive right to sell its products in a specified location. Each franchisee pays an initial fee and yearly sums for the right to use the trade name and to get managerial and financial help. Franchisees can be sure of getting a standardized product from the parent corporation. For example, the production of McDonald's hamburgers is computerized to make certain that each 4¾-inch ham-

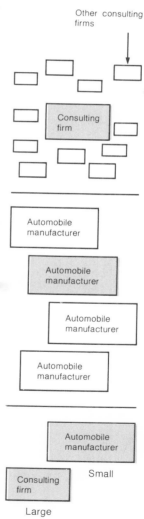

Other consulting firms

Consulting firm

Automobile manufacturer

Automobile manufacturer

Automobile manufacturer

Automobile manufacturer

Automobile manufacturer

Consulting firm

Small

Large

Size is a relative factor for organizations.

burger patty contains precisely 65 percent moisture, 17 percent protein, and 18 percent fat. When cooked, the hamburger patty slips precisely into the standardized 4-inch bun.[5]

Among the fastest growing franchise businesses are computer stores.[6] They sell microcomputers not only to hobbyists but also to small business people, who find them powerful, effective tools. Business people can purchase components that fit their individual businesses, such as small insurance offices and retail stores. In one instance, a Franciscan order of priests bought a microcomputer to keep track of its nine hundred brothers around the world. Computer stores are expanding by chains as well as by franchises. Industrial giants such as IBM, Xerox, and Digital are now opening their own stores across the country.

MANAGING PUBLIC SECTOR ORGANIZATIONS

As mentioned earlier, the *public sector* refers to government bodies. These bodies incorporate at least five levels of government: commissions and boards, municipalities (cities or towns), counties, states (in Canada, provinces), and the federal government.[7] Since there are so many different types of public organizations, primary emphasis in this section will be on the federal government; but other levels will be used to illustrate specific points.

Until recently the government sector was a growth industry. Between 1961 and 1976 the number of government workers increased from 8.7 million to more than 15 million. Today, however, the number of government employees is actually declining—at all levels of government.[8] It appears at this time that the employment situation in government will be stagnant at best.

Over the years there has also been a steady increase in interaction between the public and private sectors, with the two becoming interdependent. For example, the U.S. Department of Defense depends on private enterprise for the development, design, and manufacture of weapons. In turn, many private organizations depend on the Department of Defense for much of their business.

Despite increasing interdependence, major differences still exist between the two sectors. These differences are largely the result of organizations in the private sector having different reasons for existence than those organizations in the public sector.

Reasons for organizations in the public sector:

- Laws, rules, and regulations
- Protection of resources
- Problem of indivisibility
- Provision of special aid

Reasons for the Existence of Organizations in the Public Sector

Some of the reasons for the existence of government organizations follow.

Laws, rules, and regulations. Laws are often unclear or ambiguous. Therefore, many federal, state, and municipal organizations exist to interpret and enforce them for the public welfare through rules and regulations. The Interstate Commerce Commission regulates all commerce across state lines. The Federal Communications Commission oversees the activities of radio and television companies. The local school committee ensures that children get a proper education.

Protection of resources. A major function of many government agencies is the protection of life, property, and resources. Local fire and police departments offer protection from fire and theft. The National Park Service and the Environmental Protection Agency both protect the nation's resources.

The problem of indivisibility. Many problems cannot be divided into pieces that can be handled by individuals or individual profit-making organizations. National defense, for example, cannot be provided by individuals or individual firms, although individual firms can make products required for defense purposes. Building streets and highways is another activity that requires funding and coordination by a government organization. Although an individual firm can contract to plow snow or clean streets, the decision of whether to use the service cannot be left to individuals.

Providing special aid. Help often is needed by the elderly, the young, the sick, and the unemployed. Medicare, Medicaid, welfare, and aid to dependent children are examples of special aid to individuals and groups. The Small Business Administration provides loans, assistance, and advice to small businesses.

Problems in comparing profit-making and government organizations:

- The problem of objectives
- The problem of benefits
- The problem of politics

Managing in Profit-Making and Government Organizations—A Comparative Approach

Relatively little solid research has been done on the similarities and differences between managing in the private sector and managing in the public sector. Opinions have been expressed but not backed by evidence. Thus a respected professor at Harvard University argues that public management is different from corporate management in both degree and quality.[9] At the same time and in the same journal the chief administrative and management officer of the former Department of Health, Education, and Welfare (HEW) argues just as strongly that the differences in the approaches to management are heavily outweighed by the similarities.[10] This text, will not attempt to settle the argument but will simply demonstrate ways in which managements in the private and public sectors are both similar and different.

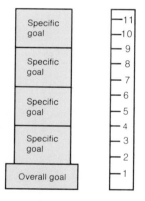

In the private sector organizations usually have clearly defined and easily measurable objectives.

The Problem of Objectives

In the private sector the primary objective, as defined by stockholders and boards of directors, has usually been to maximize return on investment. A number of separate goals are set to help reach the overall goal, or at least to be compatible with it. These separate goals include increasing the company's growth rate, developing new products, increasing market standing, and contributing to society. It is possible to translate both the primary objective and each separate goal into measurable units and to accurately measure them with sophisticated accounting tools.

Unfortunately, unanimously agreed-upon objectives and measurements do not exist so clearly in the public sector. Frequently little agreement exists between the public and the members of a government

In the public sector organizations usually have hard-to-measure goals stated in very general terms

agency on what the primary objective should be, and often there is even less agreement on the subobjectives, many of which are nebulously stated and difficult to measure.

Chevrolet Division of General Motors can easily count the number of automobiles it has manufactured and sold, which gives it a useful measurement of performance. However, the typical federal department is itself a conglomerate organization. For example, the Secretary of Health and Human Services (HHS) is responsible for directing such diverse programs as delivering hot meals to the elderly, determining eligibility for Medicaid benefits, and funding cancer research. Individual managers in the public sector thus rarely see a connection between their work effort and its results, and direct verification of these results is often unavailable.[11]

The Problem of Benefits   Measuring the ratio of costs to benefits in the public sector is more difficult than it is in the private sector. For example, although the dollar cost of teaching a disadvantaged child to read can be measured, the profitability of this service to society cannot. Furthermore, in the private sector the customer may refuse to buy the product; in the public sector the customer usually has no choice. No valid competitor exists for Medicare, the post office, or police and fire departments.

The Problem of Politics   The political climate of the two sectors is quite different. Private industry is affected by politics but not nearly as much as public agencies. The result is that the public sector has a shorter and more dynamic operating cycle than the private sector. Many appointed officials, for example, may be replaced after an election; and this leads to a higher rate of turnover among top-level, decision-making personnel in the government than in the private sector. Furthermore, objectives established by public sector managers in today's political setting may be changed to entirely different objectives in tomorrow's political climate. In addition, federal agencies are budgeted annually, and the budget may change with the political climate.[12]

Given these and many other difficulties, how do effective managers accomplish anything in the public sector? In effect, good managers learn to use the difficulties to their advantage. To show how this is accomplished, some common elements will be drawn from two examples: the reform of New York City's welfare program and the establishment of the U.S. Environmental Protection Agency (EPA). More attention will be paid to the reform of the welfare system, which in two years increased staff productivity by 16 percent, reduced the error rate by 50 percent, and resulted in a $200 million savings in welfare payments.[13]

Much of the success of a top government manager is determined by the first three months in office. The individual may be replaced in the next election, and whatever improvements that person wishes to make must be made before then, while resources are available. Furthermore, resources are more easily obtained at the beginning of an elected term than later. To be effective, the administrator must quickly develop well-defined targets and clear priorities. There is little time for studying problems in detail. Thus the administrator must concentrate on problems that are pressing and create programs that will show early results. For example, New York City's former welfare department director, Arthur Spiegel III, used two criteria for setting priorities—public expectations and simplicity of the problem. Three of his earliest projects were stopping welfare check fraud, establishing a central registry to identify and track down drug addicts, and issuing a photographic ID card to every welfare client. The latter reduced fraud and sharpened client scheduling skills. In another example, when the head of the EPA, William Ruckelshaus, had to bring together a collection of previously independent agencies, he chose air pollution as a primary issue because it was a "hot" item and everyone in the organization could identify with fighting it.

Often managers in the public sector simply do their best in the absence of tangible goals with no special emphasis on immediate versus long-range results. But in both situations just mentioned, the administrators established tight timetables and specific performance measures. For example, within sixty days after taking office, Ruckelshaus took steps to send out guidelines that would affect the entire U.S. auto industry. In New York Spiegel began by reducing six lines of command to one, instituting precise time-keeping and absenteeism records, and developing a set of productivity reports that provided a way of ranking the forty-five welfare centers.

The differences between most managers in private versus public organizations may be more apparent than real.

In both cases the press was used as an accountability tool. For example, Spiegel publicly issued agency-wide performance objectives and published regular reports on progress. Ruckelshaus kept the press fully informed in the same way in order to gain public support for actions and to make needed changes. He also enlisted the help of the environmental lobby (including the Sierra Club and the Audubon Society) in establishing goals and in determining the organization's position and measuring its accomplishments. This helped keep pressure on the agency and enabled it to obtain support for further efforts.

Gaining the support of civil servants was a problem for both the EPA and the New York City welfare department. Spiegel, for example, found that there was a great deal of untapped talent among New York's civil service employees, and he won their support on the basis of four factors: "proof of our [his immediate staff's] competence, the mayor's backing of our effort, our respect for their [civil service employees'] standard bureaucratic procedures, and insight into the mutuality of our objectives. Their support was not difficult to obtain." [14] Although he brought in a number of outsiders, they were carefully matched with people who had a thorough knowledge of standard agency problems and procedures. In one instance a revised procedure was not accepted by the civil service employees because it had been written by an outsider and was therefore not understood. A civil service supervisor rewrote it, referencing old procedures, and it was immediately implemented.

Rather than challenging the long-term civil service employees, both

Ruckelshaus and Spiegel were able to gain their support and thus make use of their rich experience and vast knowledge of procedures and regulations. Civil service workers are used to a constantly changing top management and constantly changing regulations. Thus they can be a force for continuity in the changing operations.

In the two situations being discussed here, the new top administrators were able to bring about change by using good management skills. Each was willing to lead, make decisions, and take responsibility; and each was able to turn difficulties into advantages. For example, the short time they had to establish themselves prompted the two administrators to set early, simple, and measurable goals that rallied the organization to a common cause and protected it politically. Private sector business managers avoid publicity. But in the open political arena, Spiegel and Ruckelshaus were able to use publicity to gain support for their programs. And rather than decrying the bureaucracy and criticizing the civil servants, both Spiegel and Ruckelshaus were able to find and use these people's potential.

MANAGING THIRD SECTOR ORGANIZATIONS

A large number of organizations are neither profit making (private sector) nor government bodies (public sector). Organizations in the public sector rely on *law* for their existence, and organizations in the private sector rely on *capital* for theirs. At one time writers on management and public administration largely ignored all organizations that did not fit into these two sectors of the economy. Lately these third sector organizations are attracting more attention, although the government reports cited earlier in this chapter do not yet identify the third sector as such.

Third sector organizations are developed to conduct both the social and the economic affairs of mature capitalism. "Some are created out of a mix of private business and governmental elements. Others take the form of voluntary organizations (e.g., Red Cross or League of Women Voters) and the non-profit corporations (e.g., the Ford Foundation)."[15]

Third sector organizations originally were voluntary organizations such as churches, community groups, and consumer groups. In recent years, however, the third sector has expanded and grown more political. Organizations such as Common Cause and the American Civil Liberties Union, for example, have "goals of either confronting large bureaucratic organizations in hope of making them more responsive, or of organizing around certain functions that established organizations will not or cannot perform."[16]

In addition, the differences between the public and private sectors are becoming blurred through greater cooperation between government and business. At least three broad areas of public and private sector cooperation have expanded the activities of third sector organizations beyond those of volunteer organizations. One area involves the government serving essentially as a partner with the private sector. For example, the

Types of third sector organizations:

- Voluntary
- Government edict
- Quasi-private

key to the effectiveness of the NASA Apollo project was the cooperation of a variety of organizations to achieve a specific function. The federal government has also asked U.S. physicians to set up professional standards review organizations (PSROs) to review and monitor the medical care given under federally supported programs. The PSROs are third sector organizations with authority over programs created by federal law. The physicians are not employed by the government but instead work with it to achieve certain goals.

The second form of third sector expansion occurs when the government establishes quasi-public corporations to handle certain functions. Amtrak and the U.S. Postal Service are examples of third sector organizations established by government edict. The theory of this action is that certain organizations can operate more effectively as private businesses free of government red tape. The efficacy of the resultant organizations is still unproved.

The third form of third sector expansion is represented by public organizations that are quasi-private. Examples are the Federal National Mortgage Association (FNMA—also known as Fannie Mae) and the Communication Satellite Corporation (COMSAT). These organizations are not truly private, but they issue stocks that are held by investors who exercise some of the rights shared by stockholders in other private corporations. Thus they differ from, say, the Postal Service and Amtrak, which do not issue any stock.

Fannie Mae, which was originally a government agency, is supposed to meet the public's need for housing by providing a secondary market for government-insured mortgages. It was made quasi-private in 1968, and its shares of stock were sold to the public. The people owning its stock can elect ten of the fifteen members of the board of directors. The other five are appointed by the Secretary of Housing and Urban Development. Fannie Mae is now one of the larger corporations in the United States.

COMSAT was created in 1962 through an act of Congress expressly to maintain communications satellites. It represents a unique blend of federal money and private technology. Federal funds were used in the development of the technology, and civilian participation was made possible by a corporation financed half by the U.S. government and half by commercial communications companies. The board of directors of COMSAT includes public officials, representatives of the communications industries, and directors appointed by the public.

Third sector organizations are as diverse in size and type as public and private sector organizations. Little research exists on the activities, responsibilities, and duties of managers in this sector, because they differ so from one organization to another.

Although the third sector is growing rapidly in the United States, it is growing even faster in other countries, particularly in the developing nations. Many of these nations refuse to leave development efforts totally in the hands of private enterprise. Instead they require interaction between the public and private sectors. In many highly industrialized

Third sector expansion:

• Partnership between public and private organizations
• Quasi-public private organizations
• Quasi-private public organizations

parts of the world, such as Scandinavia, public policy has such strong influence on the economic activities of organizations that the importance of third sector organizations is continually increasing.

MANAGING—SOME COMMON FUNCTIONS

Managers often claim that their organizations and their problems are unique. Although this claim has some validity, organizations also have a great deal in common, regardless of their sector.

Figure 25.1 shows the overlap of organizations in the private, public, and third sectors. The black area represents characteristics that formal organizations of all sectors share. For example, every formal organization exists as a system within an environment. Each has goals, objectives, structure, rules, people, and procedures for handling recurrent activities. Whereas some organizations have more rules and procedures than others, the chances of an organization having none are slim.

The striped areas represent areas in which organizations have some functions that are similar to each other and others that are unique to each. For example, consider two third sector organizations—the Postal

FIGURE 25.1 Similarities and differences among organizations

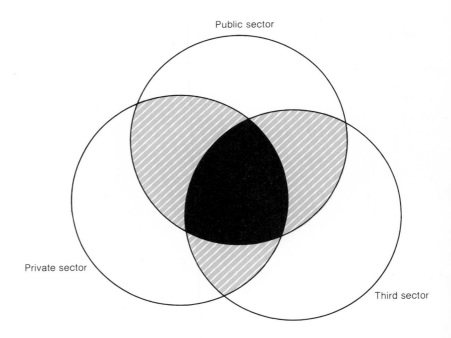

■ Area that organizations have in common with each other

▨ Areas in which some dimensions of organizations are similar to and others different from other organizations

□ Areas unique to particular organizations

Service and COMSAT. The Postal Service appears to have much more in common with the government than with private enterprise. COMSAT, on the other hand, appears to have more in common with private enterprise than with the public sector. Thus, while in the black area all dimensions overlap, in the striped area only some of them overlap.

The white areas are those unique to particular organizations. An organization may have a unique product, physical location, or history of development. It may even have a top manager with a personality different from that of top managers in other organizations. These and other differences create a combination of factors not found in any other organization.

The figure is intended to illustrate the relative importance of these three areas. If the white area predominates, then relatively few generalities can be stated about the organizations and their management. If the striped and black areas predominate, then some common functions of managing will cut across most, if not all, organizations in that category. Although no firm information exists on how these areas overlap among organizations, the best current evidence is that about 50 to 75 percent of the areas are common to most organizations. This percentage is shown by the combination of black and striped areas.[17]

EFFECTIVE MANAGING—A REVIEW AND A SUMMARY

This section will focus on some common tasks that managers face in all organizations and will point out how certain aspects of these tasks vary in different types of organizations. (Chapter 1 described specific working roles or activities that managers must engage in if the organization is to accomplish its objectives. A review of these roles may be helpful in understanding this section.) The basic roles are shown in Figure 25.2. In interpersonal roles the manager must deal with others at all levels of the organization. In informational roles the manager must obtain and distribute information to others. In decision-making roles the manager must act to improve the unit, to reduce disturbances, to allocate resources, and to negotiate for needed resources.

All three roles have functions that are common to organizations of any type. These functions involve determining the needs of the environment, establishing objectives, developing clear plans, dividing and coordinating the work, controlling, motivating, and decision making. Although the functions are the same from organization to organization, the way they are performed varies.

Determining the Needs of the Environment As systems, organizations take in raw materials, people, and other resources. They then transform the resources into outputs that fit the needs and wants of the receiving system. Thus managers must develop boundary spanning subsystems that tell them the needs and wants of the receiving system. Clearly, this

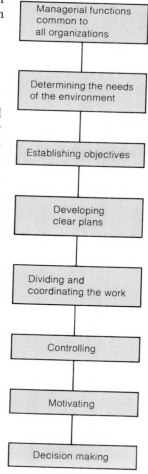

Managerial functions common to all organizations

Determining the needs of the environment

Establishing objectives

Developing clear plans

Dividing and coordinating the work

Controlling

Motivating

Decision making

approach is not one-way, since large organizations can also create needs through advertising and other methods.

In gathering information from the environment, managers must perform two related tasks—monitoring and disseminating information. In the monitor role, the manager uses a kind of radar to continually gather information of all kinds. In the disseminator role, the manager transmits that information to subordinates and others as necessary. Establishing the wants and needs of the environment may be easier in a private organization than in a public one. However, the classic failure of the Edsel (a project that cost Ford millions of dollars) shows the difficulty of getting an accurate reading on needs. The company spent enormous sums on market surveys and other kinds of information gathering that showed the need for the Edsel, but the public simply would not buy it.

Establishing Objectives The overall mission of any organization is to meet the needs and wants of the receiving system. One of the most common causes of organizational failure is the lack of clear-cut objectives. An effectively functioning organization must know what it is doing and why it exists.

In the leadership role the manager must establish adaptive subsystems to make certain that the organization's objectives are in line with the needs of the receiving subsystem. Since the organization's mission can change with changing environments, the manager needs to make

FIGURE 25.2 The interlocking and interrelated roles of the manager

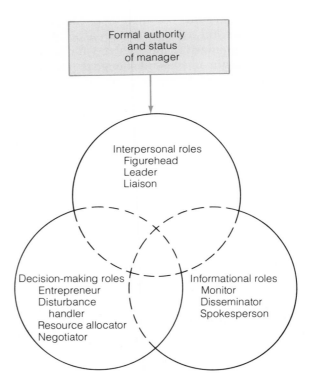

certain not only that the objectives are met but also that the objectives are changed when necessary.

The objectives of a private sector organization may be easier to define and put into operation than those of a public sector organization. The challenge to the manager as leader is to make them specific and tangible.

Developing Clear Plans   As discussed in Chapter 6, effective planning requires the clear statement of objectives, strategies, and policies as well as detailed plans that are clearly communicated, realistic, worthwhile, measurable (or at least verifiable), and adequately comprehensive. The manager as leader must develop and communicate these plans, modifying them as necessary. As entrepreneur the manager must ensure that the plans are designed to improve the performance of the unit. As disturbance handler the manager must control the planning process in order to be ready to implement unexpected changes in it when unexpected events so require. Because of laws, rules, and regulations, plans may have to be changed more quickly in a private enterprise than in a public one. In any organization such changes need to be accomplished efficiently.

Private organizations have to implement changes in plans more quickly than public organizations.

Structure—Dividing and Coordinating the Work   Since most organizations have many tasks, the work must be divided and coordinated. Structure refers to how work is specialized (differentiated) and coordinated (integrated). Thus no one type of structure is best for all organizations or their units. The proper structure depends on the size, the technology, and the environment of the organization.

Frequently, the structure of a public agency is determined at least in part by laws and regulations. For example, the reorganization of the executive office of the president can be disallowed by either house of Congress. Thus reorganization in any public agency may be more difficult and more time-consuming than reorganization in the private sector.

Controlling   Control ensures that activities are producing the desired results. The manager must continually evaluate how well activities are proceeding toward the desired outcomes and make adjustments when necessary. The basic purpose of control is positive in that it focuses on achieving organizational objectives. Controlling is usually easier in the private sector than in the public sector. It is easier to control the production of tangible goods than the provision of, say, mental health care. First, objectives can be more clearly defined, and measurements can be more specific. Second, human service delivery requires a relatively high proportion of professionals such as lawyers, physicians, teachers, and social workers. Often these people preserve their autonomy and the confidentiality of their relationships with the recipients of their care, whom they may think of as clients. This means that they are often unconcerned about what others in the system are doing. Thus, in an organization producing an intangible product, control may be directly related to the

On the Job

MATCHING MANAGERS TO A COMPANY'S LIFE CYCLE

Conventional management wisdom dictates that a competent executive with an in-depth knowledge of his industry can successfully run any company. But some management theorists insist that a manager's skills must be linked to the life-cycle stage of the product line he is managing. They claim that an entrepreneurial type who brings a product from, say, a 2% share of market to 20% in a few years is the wrong person to manage the line once it has become mature. At that point, someone whose forte is cutting costs and increasing productivity, rather than risk-taking and innovating, has to be moved in, while the entrepreneur should be placed in charge of another fledgling line.

That theory sheds light on the rapid fall from grace that Robert C. Hazard Jr. and Gerald W. Petitt experienced at Best Western International Inc., and their simultaneous welcome as saviors at competitor Quality Inns International Inc. Between 1974 and 1980, the two men brought the not-for-profit Best Western chain from 800 hotels to 2,597. They expanded into 18 countries, set up one of the most sophisticated computerized reservations systems extant—and were applauded every step of the way by affiliated hotels. But over the last year the hotel owners were ready to brake the growth, while Hazard and Petitt continued to push for full steam ahead. What had been a cooperative board of elected hotel operators became a confrontational board, and even those growth-oriented moves that the elected board approved wound up voted down by the increasingly restive affili-ates. Neither Hazard nor Petitt possessed the political skills that might have helped defuse the growing animosity.

Quality Inns, by contrast, emerged from several loss years into financial stability only three years ago. A recent merger further enhanced the company's cash position. When QI's president resigned last year, the company immediately went after Hazard. There were no "democratic" membership voting rules to worry about. But more important, the whole company saw itself as being in the early stages of its life cycle. Thus, the same entrepreneurial flair that made the Hazard-Petitt team sudden anathema at Best Western is making it welcomed with open arms by franchisees and directors at Quality Inns.

proper selection of professionals and the way in which they use their time.

Motivating Organizations of all types have employees. A significant function of managers in any organization is to establish the conditions under which both individuals and groups will be selected, trained, and motivated to accomplish the organization's objectives. Therefore, the effective manager knows and respects the basic principles of individual and group behavior and the ability to apply these principles in every area of structure and function.

Decision Making All the areas described above require decision making. A common denominator for managers in all types of organizations is the ability to make good decisions. Managers may make literally hundreds of decisions a week. Some will be minor, taking only a few seconds to make; others may be major, requiring a great deal of analysis. Because the work load is usually pressing, managers seldom try for the optimum decision. Instead they tend to *satisfice*—try for a solution that is satisfactory but not necessarily the best possible.

From a systems point of view, decision making is not an isolated process. Frequently, decisions affect other people in the organizational unit or in other units. As a result, the decision-making process is one of constant renegotiation. A number of analytical aids to decision making exist—among them linear programming, probability theory, queuing theory, PERT, and decision trees (see Chapter 14). They can be used most effectively when the decisions can be programmed. Other decisions require new, creative, and innovative processes.

Managers in private enterprise often have more freedom to make decisions than managers working in the public sector. For example, civil service rules and regulations that protect employees also reduce managers' freedom of action.

> The following functions are more easily performed in private as opposed to public organizations:
>
> • Identifying needs and wants of receiving system
> • Establishing clear objectives
> • Changing structure of organization or unit of it
> • Decision making (more freedom allowed manager).

SUMMARY

Although the basic functions of small and large organizations are essentially the same, the larger the organization, the greater its tendency to change structure and to formalize such functions as planning, control, and decision making.

Although more and more interaction between the public and private sectors is occurring, there remains disagreement as to whether the three sectors should be managed differently. Certainly their reasons for existence are different, but better comparative research is necessary to settle this question. Despite the differences, evidence does exist that organizations of all types have a large number of characteristics in common, and some valid generalizations are possible.

Although the emphasis may differ, managers in all organizations must hire, train, and motivate people. Organizational goals must be established and planning and controlling must be done carefully if the organization is to be effective. The internal climate and the external environment both affect and are affected by the manager.

Most people are in constant contact with a large variety of organizations, all of which need to be well managed in order to function effectively. Thus managing is an important, challenging, and exciting job that provides rewards such as achievement, recognition, and responsibility.

STUDY QUESTIONS

1. What are some reasons for the existence of large businesses? For the existence of small businesses?
2. How might managing in large and small businesses be similar? How might it be different?
3. Describe the stages in the growth of a small business to a large one.
4. Can you think of any managerial functions that

might be performed only in large organizations? Only in small ones?

5. Using the working roles of a manager as a guide (see Chapter 2 if necessary), give examples of organizations where one or more of these roles might be emphasized more than they are in other organizations.

6. List some basic reasons for the existence of public sector organizations.

7. Would the approaches to managing used by Spiegel and Ruckelshaus be appropriate for the private sector? Explain.

8. What are some functions common to most organizations?

9. List ways in which a particular organization might be unique.

10. Give examples of third sector organizations that are not mentioned in the text.

11. Is your contact with small firms as great as with large ones? Explain.

12. Visit at least two organizations. Interview or observe several managers. Describe how they spend their time. What are their roles?

Case for Discussion

THE COLLEGE PRESIDENT

Donald Kirk has arrived early at his book-lined office. As president of Jefferson College, a small, private, liberal arts college, he has spent the last two days with business executives in Chicago designing a capital funds campaign for a group of private colleges. He knows that a number of pressing matters await him even though his absence has been brief.

Jefferson College can pass as the ideal of a small midwestern college. It has modest but adequate facilities, a competent faculty, a dedicated staff, and a good suburban location. However, each year a smaller number of middle-income students can afford the high tuition and fees. Thus the full-time students are being drawn from two disparate socioeconomic classes. Extensive federal and state aid to students through scholarship grants, loans, and work-study programs has attracted students whose parents' incomes are low. These funds, along with internally generated scholarship funds, have permitted Jefferson to compete with state universities for such students. The other students came from affluent homes, where the parents are usually college-educated professionals.

Although the diversity of backgrounds does not create any unusual social problems, an extensive program of remedial teaching has been necessary

for many of the disadvantaged students, both black and white.

The complexity of the aid programs has required a full-time staff of three to handle all the paperwork. Additional admissions counselors have also been necessary for Jefferson College to compete for students who qualify for federal support.

Student fees pay for about 75 percent of the cost of running the college. The remainder comes from gifts or federal support programs (see Table 25.2). The college has been operating in the

TABLE 25.2 Report on Revenues and Gifts From All Sources, 1976–77

Student revenue	$5,150,000
Federal support grants	300,000
Annual fund (alumni/friends)	450,000
Endowment income	400,000
Church support	75,000
Foundations	400,000
Corporate support	55,000
Miscellaneous sources	45,000
Total revenue for operating purposes	$6,875,000
Capital support (consortium share)	$ 125,000
Gifts to endowment	100,000
Total revenue for capital/endowment purposes	$ 225,000

black, but any surplus generated in the short term quickly goes to cover unanticipated maintenance, utility, or personnel costs.

Kirk's concerns for the college's future are two-fold; he worries about the potential loss of students and increases in costs. Demographic studies have forecasted a decline (5 percent per year for the next four years) in the number of traditional prospective college students. Furthermore, increases in the cost of operating the college cannot be completely offset by raising tuition. Kirk feels that the college is being confronted by an elastic demand curve. If it raises the price of tuition, student enrollment will drop.

As Table 25.3 shows, in spite of the foreboding trends, Jefferson's enrollment has remained stable so far at 1,200 full-time equivalent students (FTEs). (FTEs are an accepted measure of students; two half-time students equal one FTE.) This stability has been effected by a number of programs to attract nontraditional students. Several years ago, Jefferson initiated an evening degree program for adults, and enrollment in that program has ex-

ceeded the college's expectations. Because of the way the program is priced, four part-time evening students are considered to equal one FTE. A new one-year program for teaching English to foreign (particularly Middle Eastern) students has also been instituted, but it has been less successful. Programs stressing vocational majors such as nursing and business have been expanded with apparent success. These programs alone attract one-third of the students as majors. A cooperative off-campus/on-campus work-study program has also been initiated with temporary government funding.

The college has other programs in the planning stages, but their diversity will create large additions to the nonteaching staff, increasing overhead, and some anguish on the part of senior faculty concerning the fundamental purpose of the college. Many of the programs are the result of development grants from government and foundations. Kirk is unsure whether these programs can even pay their own way after the external funding runs out. Along with three other presidents of local private colleges, he has just completed a grant application for funding a cooperative computer operation, and two other internally generated proposals await signature.

Kirk glances at his calendar for the rest of the month. It includes a trip to Russia with an alumni group, a meeting in Washington with HHS officials, a meeting with a generous benefactor, and two alumni club functions that will require more off-campus travel. He is scanning one of the documents on his desk when the intercom interrupts his reading: "Dr. Kirk, Roberta Myers [the business manager] is here with the proposal for the maintenance workers' union."

"Thanks, Betty. Ask her in," Kirk replies, as he muses on the fact that weeks have passed since he has confronted a problem concerning education of the students.[18]

TABLE 25.3 Jefferson College Enrollment

Full-time day students		1,065
Scholarship/grant equivalents	210	
Full-pay equivalents	855	
Special program students		465
Co-op work/study	30	
English for foreigners	15	
Adult evening program	420	
Other		15
Overseas semester	10	
Nondegree, special	5	
Total head-count enrollment[a]		1,545

[a] This is not the same as FTE enrollment because of part-time/partial tuition enrollments in the special program and other student categories.

Source: Case written by Gail Miller, Otterbein College. Reproduced by permission.

1. As manager of a third sector organization, does Kirk engage in activities significantly different from those of managers of profit-seeking or government organizations?
2. What roles must a college president such as Kirk assume?
3. What problems may arise from the expansion-by-grant strategy? What solutions can you recommend?
4. Are Kirk's activities concerned with educating students? Explain.

FOR YOUR CAREER

1. Being a manager in a small business is different from being a manager in a large business.

2. Being a manager in a public organization is different from being a manager in a private organization.

3. Just as different managers are needed to fit different organizational strategies, they are also needed to fit different types of organizations.

4. The abilities that make a manager successful at General Motors will not ensure success at Xerox or IBM.

5. Managers expect to manage growing organizations. They should also be prepared for the possibility of managing an organization that is stagnant or declining.

6. Under 15 million people are employed by the federal, state, and local governments in the United States. Over 80 million are employed elsewhere (in third sector and private sector organizations). Career opportunities are most abundant in the third and private sector organizations.

FOOTNOTES

1. U.S. Small Business Administration, *SBA Business Loans* (Washington, D.C.: Government Printing Office, February 1975), p. 3.

2. H. Mintzberg, *The Nature of Managerial Work* (New York: Harper & Row, 1973); R. Stewart, "Studies of Managerial Jobs," *International Studies of Management and Organization* 2 (Spring 1972): 7–37; A. Filley and R. House, *Managerial Process and Organizational Behavior* (Glenview, Ill.: Scott, Foresman, 1976); J. Carrington and L. Aurelio, "Survival Tactics for Small Business," *Business Horizons* 19 (February 1976): 13–24; L. Barnes and S. Hershon, "Transferring Power in the Family Business," *Harvard Business Review* 54 (July–August 1976): 105–114; and W. Copulsky and H. McNulty, "Finding and Keeping the Entrepreneur," *Management Review* 63 (April 1974): 5–11.

3. Barnes and Hershon, "Transferring Power in the Family Business."

4. J. Emshwiller, "AMC's Bid to Remain an Auto Maker Is Seen Linked to Non-Car Lines," *Wall Street Journal,* March 23, 1978, p. 1.

5. D. Anable, "Computerization of Hamburgers," *Christian Science Monitor,* July 6, 1977, p. 2.

6. G. Bylinsky, "The Computer Stores Have Arrived," *Fortune,* April 24, 1978, pp. 52–57.

7. M. Murray, "Comparing Public and Private Management: An Exploratory Essay," *Public Administration Review* 35 (July–August 1975): 364–371; N. Long, "Public Policy and Administration: The Goals of Rationality and Responsibility," *Public Administration Review* 14 (Winter 1954): 18–34; D. Pearlman, ed., *The Future of the American Government* (Boston:

Houghton Mifflin, 1968); D. Ink, "The President as Manager," *Public Administration Review* 36 (September–October 1976): 508–515; L. Lynn, Jr., and J. Siedl, "'Bottom-line' Management for Public Agencies," *Harvard Business Review* 55 (January–February 1955): 145–153; W. Turcotte, "Control Systems, Performance, and Satisfaction in Two State Agencies," *Administrative Science Quarterly* 19 (March 1974) 60–73; and R. Golembiewski and M. Cohen, eds., *People in Public Service* (Itaska, Ill.: F. E. Peacock, 1976).

8. U.S. Department of Labor, Bureau of Labor Statistics, *Handbook of Labor Statistics, 1977* (Washington, D.C.: Government Printing Office, 1978).

9. J. Bauer, "Effective Public Management," *Harvard Business Review* 55 (March–April 1977): 131–140.

10. R. Brady, "MBO Goes to Work in the Public Sector," *Harvard Business Review* 51 (March–April 1973): 65–74.

11. B. Buchanan II, "Government Managers, Business Executives, and Organizational Commitment," *Public Administration Review* 34 (July–August 1974): 339–347.

12. L. Goodstein, "Organization Development in Bureaucracies: Some Caveats and Cautions," paper presented to OD 78, a Conference on Current Theory and Practice in Organizational Development, University Associates, San Francisco, California, March 16–17, 1978.

13. Bauer, "Effective Public Management"; C. Grayson, Jr., "Management Science and Business Practice," *Harvard Business Review* 51 (July–August 1973):

41–49; and A. Spiegel III, "How Outsiders Overhauled a Public Agency," *Harvard Business Review* 53 (January–February 1975): 116–124.

14. Spiegel, "How Outsiders Overhauled a Public Agency," p. 120.

15. A. Etzioni, "The Third Sector and Domestic Missions," *Public Administration Review* 35 (July–August 1973): 315; T. Leavitt, The Third Sector (New York: AMACOM, 1973), pp. 28–29; M. McGill and

L. Wooten, "Management in the Third Sector," *Public Administration Review* 35 (September–October 1975): p. 445.

16. Etzioni, "The Third Sector and Domestic Missions," p. 315.

17. J. Galbraith, *Organization Design* (Reading, Mass.: Addison-Wesley, 1977); and G. Egan, "Model A: The Logic of Systems as OD Instrument," paper presented to OD 78.

GLOSSARY

Active listening Reflecting back to the other person not only what the person has said but also the perceived emotional tone of the message.

Activities Basic groupings of work, jobs, or tasks that are components of a project using PERT.

Actual objectives Shifting and uneasy compromises among the individuals within the organization and the changing demands made by the outside environment. They are the result of a continuing series of negotiations among constituencies.

Affirmative action Organizations must have a positive plan to reduce and/or eliminate internal minority imbalances or inequalities.

Alternatives The possible courses of action from which choices can be made. If there are no alternatives, there is no choice and, therefore, no decision.

Anticipatory socialization A process that involves the adoption of attitudes, values, and identity perceived to be associated with an anticipated role before ever entering it.

Apprentice A beginner or learner in an organization who works under the direction of others.

Authority The right to command and exact obedience from others. It comes from the organization and it allows the manager to use power.

Behavior channeling The idea that actual behavior is consistent with values. Behavior is channeled toward or away from particular actions as a result of the direct influence of values on behavior.

Body language An important part of nonverbal communications which involves the transmittal of thoughts, actions, and feelings through bodily movements and how other people "read" them.

Bottom-up approach An approach to strategy where the bottom of the organization pushes ideas to the top and strategy is then made.

Boundaries These are used in reference to organizations as systems and where the organization leaves off and the environment begins, i.e., the boundary of the organization.

Bounded rationality This is a technique that reduces the complexity of a problem to the level at which a manager can handle the possible alternatives. Bounded rationality is a natural limit on the human ability to handle complex situations.

Break-even analysis Break-even analysis is an analytical technique for examining the relationships among fixed costs, variable costs, and profits.

Budget Plans for a given future period that are stated in numerical (usually financial) terms. To some degree, budgets are a control device, since they govern a variety of different activities.

Budget control Organizations can be controlled by several methods; one is by giving the organization or part of the organization specific budgets or allocations of resources.

Career The sequence of behaviors and attitudes associated with past, present, and anticipated future work-related experiences and role activities as perceived by either the individual or some other observer. Thus a career is work-related and lifelong.

Career development A developing, progressing process whereby an individual proceeds from a point of having no career direction to that of attaining a career consistent with his or her interests, abilities, and aspirations.

Centralization Describes the organizational decision making where all the decisions are made by a small group, generally located at the top of the organization.

Charismatic power The power of attraction or devotion; the desire of one person to admire another.

Choice The opportunity to select among alternatives; if there is no choice, there is no decision to be made.

Closed system A system where the only major concern of management is the transformation of inputs to outputs and the environment is taken as a given.

Coercive power The ability to threaten or punish.

Command groups Formal groups that consist of managers and their direct subordinates.

Committee A formal group that is created to carry out specific organizational assignments or activities.

Communications The process by which information is exchanged and understood by two or more people, usually with the intent to motivate or influence behavior.

Communications channel Any way in which information reaches the receiver.

Compensation Direct or indirect, immediate or deferred rewards, some of which have a monetary value.

Competent organization An organization which is both effective and efficient.

Competition A process involving actions taken by one person to attain his or her most preferred outcome while simultaneously blocking attainment of the counterpart's most preferred outcome.

Completeness Refers to how broadly and inclusively the control system measures the behaviors involved.

Compromise An attempt to attain mutual concessions by having each party modify his or her point of view to achieve a workable solution.

Conditions of certainty Under such conditions, the manager has enough information to be able to closely predict the outcome of decisions. The alternatives are known and the decision can maximize the outcome desired by the manager.

Conditions of risk Under such conditions, the manager can develop alternatives and estimate the probability of their leading to the desired outcomes.

Conditions of uncertainty Under such conditions, the probabilities attached to the available alternatives are even less well known than those for risk.

Conflict Occurs whenever incompatible activities occur. An activity that is incompatible with another one obstructs, prevents, or interferes in a way that makes the other less probable or less effective.

Consideration Reflects the extent to which individuals are likely to have job relationships characterized by mutual trust, respect for subordinates' ideas, and consideration of subordinates' feelings.

Consortium An organization created when two or more companies cooperate so as to act as a single entity for a specific and usually limited purpose.

Constraints Restrictions or limitations on managerial actions.

Consumerists Special interest groups concerned with the safety and quality of products bought by consumers.

Content The subject of the meeting or of the task being performed.

Content models Motivation models that tend to focus primarily on the wants and needs that individuals are trying to satisfy within the situation.

Contingency approach This approach suggests that there is no single best way to design an organization, that the design instead depends on the situation.

Contingency models Descriptions of leader effectiveness based upon or dependent on a number of conditions such as the employee's task, skill level, and the supervisor's power.

Continuing objective An objective that is relatively unchangeable over time.

Continuous reinforcement The employee is reinforced every time the correct performance occurs.

Control The process that allows managers to determine whether activities conform to the plan and the objectives and to make adjustments when necessary.

Control graph A method of measuring the total control in an organization and plotting its relationship against things like performance.

Controllability Refers to the amount of influence (control) those being controlled have on the control system.

Cooperation A process involving two or more parties working together to attain mutual goals.

Coordinative planning Planning done at the middle level of management where the work of different units has to be coordinated.

Core job dimensions These are the five dimensions of work including skill variety, task identity, task significance, autonomy, and feedback.

Critical path The longest set of adjoining activities in a PERT network. Delays along this path cause delays in an entire project.

Culture The totality of socially transmitted ideas, beliefs, and values within a society.

Decentralization Describes the organizational decision making where the decisions are made by people scattered throughout the organization.

Decision A choice made from among alternative courses of action that are available. The purpose of making a decision is to establish and achieve organizational goals and objectives.

Decision making The process of generating alternative solutions to a problem and then selecting from among them.

Decision-making roles The manager makes decisions in four different roles: the entrepreneur role, the disturbance-handler role, the resource allocator role, and the negotiator role.

Decision tree A method of planning to achieve objectives by identifying and choosing among available alternatives. A decision tree is a relatively simple and understandable way of using probability.

Delegation Refers to the action whereby a supervisor passes along to a subordinate a task or duty to perform which is the responsibility of the supervisor to do but which enhances the task of the subordinate.

Delphi groups Sets of individuals who render expert opinions on issues, usually through questionnaires rather than face-to-face contact.

Departmentation The creation of a number of subunits, usually called departments.

Deviations Variations from a plan. Measurement of results against standards would allow deviations to be detected in time to make corrections.

Differentiation The difference in cognitive and emotional orientation among managers in different functional departments. High uncertainty leads to more differentiation and low uncertainty leads to less.

Dimensions of planning There are five dimensions of planning: organization, subject, elements, time, and characteristics.

Direct control The process of developing better managers to more skillfully use concepts, principles, and techniques to reduce the amount and degree of undesirable results.

Directing A task which includes leading, developing, training, and motivating subordinates.

Disseminator role Involves passing along special or privileged information that subordinates would not otherwise be able to obtain.

Disturbance handler A manager who takes corrective action in response to unforeseen problems which are beyond personal control.

Division of labor The specialization of workers, including management in accomplishing tasks.

Domestic organization A firm that limits its purchases and sales to a single country.

Dominance A state that occurs when a solution to conflict is imposed or dictated.

Dominant coalition Refers to the major top-level decision makers of an organization.

ERG Consists of three levels of core needs: existence, relatedness, and growth.

Emergent activities Informal actions beyond those required that result from changed sentiments.

Emergent interactions Informal interactions beyond those required resulting from changed activities and sentiments.

Emotional decisions Decisions based primarily on intuition with little real data to back them up. These decisions are made from an emotional state, such as fear, anger, or joy.

Empathy The development of a better understanding of other people's viewpoints.

Entrepreneur A person who organizes and manages a business, taking a risk for the possibility of making a profit.

Entrepreneur role The manager works to improve the unit, and bring about planned, voluntary, controlled change for the better.

Environmentalists Special interest groups concerned with the physical environment and the changes people have made in it.

Environmental variability Refers to the degree of change or uncertainty with which an organization or its subunits is involved.

Equifinality The concept that there are several equally good ways to get to the same end.

Ethics The rules or standards governing the moral conduct of the organization and management profession.

Events The activities in PERT which are circled to indicate they are completed.

Expanding-pie assumption The assumption that the amount of power or any resource held by people is not fixed but rather is expanding, and that all can gain.

Expectancy The belief, expressed as a subjective estimate or odds, that a particular act will or will not be successful.

Expectancy model A process model of motivation suggesting that people are motivated at work to choose among different behaviors or intensities of effort if they believe their efforts will be rewarded and if the rewards they expect to get are important to them.

Expense budget A plan for a future period detailing the projected costs or expenditures for a specific responsibility center.

Expense center A method of controlling an organizational unit by its expenses rather than other means such as a budget or revenues. It is a type of responsibility center.

Expert power The power of knowledge. It comes from specialized knowledge and skills that are important in getting the job done.

Extrinsic rewards Rewards given by the organization, such as pay, promotion, praise, tenure, and status symbols.

Feedback Feedback is information regarding the actual performance or the results of the activities of a system. In communications, looking for and using helpful responses from others. Feedback can improve self-awareness and thereby increase the ability to send clear and inoffensive messages.

Fiedler's contingency model The model suggests that a manager's effectiveness depends on two main factors: (1) the motivational system of the leader and (2) the extent that the situation is favorable or unfavorable to the leader.

Figurehead role All managerial jobs require some duties that are symbolic in nature. As head of the organization or organizational subunit, the manager represents the unit in formal matters, including ceremonies and symbolic activities.

Filtering A barrier to communication which occurs when the sender intentionally sifts or modifies the message so it will be seen more favorably by the receiver.

Fixed costs Expenses that remain unchanged regardless of the level of production.

Fixed-pie assumption The assumption that the amount of power or any resource held by people is fixed, and that one gains only at the expense of another.

Formal group A unit established by the organization to accomplish specific tasks. Individuals are usually assigned to formal groups.

Formal leader A manager or supervisor in an organization is a formal leader by virtue of the authority granted by the organization.

Formal organizational arrangements These are relationships between units in an organization, or between organizations, which are written down or set in policy.

Function One of the most common ways of creating departmentation or specialization is grouping activities according to similar functions, such as work, skills, knowledge, and technology.

Functional authority The authority to prescribe practices, procedures, policies, or other matters to units or groups not in the direct chain of command.

Game theory Used to develop a mathematical approach that is designed to maximize gains or minimize losses regardless of countermoves by competitors. Its purpose is to develop long- or short-term strategies that combine low costs with high gains.

Group Any number of people who: (1) have a common purpose or objective, (2) interact with each other to accomplish their objective, (3) are aware of one another, and (4) perceive themselves to be a part of the group.

Group building activities Those activities that allow the group to maintain itself by helping to satisfy members' needs and by fostering cooperation among members.

Group cohesiveness The degree to which group members are motivated to remain within the group and, in consequence, to behave in similar ways.

Hawthorne effect When workers' behavior changes and productivity increases because the workers are aware that persons important in their lives are taking an interest in them. (A myth.)

Hierarchy of objectives Various levels of objectives that correspond with the three broad managerial levels.

Horizontal coordination Refers to how the units or parts of the organization are integrated or held together.

Human resource planning Involves deciding who is needed where and when, and devising strategies to get people to fill the positions at the appropriate times.

Illegal behavior Behavior that violates a law in a particular jurisdiction or area.

Indirect control Traces the cause of an unsatisfactory result to the responsible person so that activities or practices can be corrected.

Influence group A set of individuals who actually influence a person in some way, e.g., in deciding what that person's opinion will be.

Informal group A group formed within the organizational structure by individuals rather than by management.

Informal leader One chosen by the group or an individual, regardless of the organization.

Information The knowledge or other data that are useful and pertinent to the individual or organizational unit.

Information overload A communications barrier which involves an excess of incoming information, to the point where it cannot be handled.

Informational roles The manager is the central focus for the receiving and sending of nonroutine information. As a nerve center, three roles characterize the manager: monitor, disseminator, and spokesperson. In these roles, information is received, transmitted, or recombined.

Initiating structure Reflects the extent to which individuals are likely to define and structure their roles and those of their subordinates toward goal attainment.

Inputs Human or other resources such as information, energy, and materials coming into the system or subsystem.

Inside-outside approach A strategy approach in which managers look first at the organization and then at the environment.

Integration The quality of the state of collaboration that exists among departments that are required to achieve unity of effort by the demands of the environment.

Integrative problem solving A process that involves the open, complete, and rapid sharing of information concerning the problem and a joint search through the shared information to arrive at a decision that best accomplishes organizational goals.

Interacting groups Refers to two or more groups that have relationships with each other.

International management Focuses on management practices at the worldwide corporate level including the study of the transfer of resources among entities in different countries where the companies are operating.

International organization A firm whose interests cut across national boundaries; it imports or exports goods, services, or products.

Interpenetrating system Two or more systems, neither of which totally contains or is contained by the other, that are involved in particular events or processes.

Interpersonal roles The manager has formal authority and status, from which the three interpersonal roles develop. They are the manager as figurehead, as leader, as liaison.

Intrinsic rewards Rewards that must originate and be felt within the person. Intrinsic rewards include feelings of accomplishment, achievement, and self-esteem.

Inventory control Concerned with making certain that the right amount of raw materials, work in progress, and finished goods are available.

Investment center A responsibility center in which the

manager is responsible for the use of assets as well as revenues and expenses.

Jargon Overly specialized or technical language.

Job enrichment A way of making jobs more satisfying by providing workers with more opportunity for meaningfulness, responsibility, growth, achievement, and challenge.

Key organizational processes These form the central elements in the systems diagnostic model of organizations. The elements are the processing of information and the transforming of energy or matter.

Leadership The ability to influence the behavior of others. The task of the leader is to help the group reach both organizational and personal goals.

Legitimate power The power that comes when the organization's authority is accepted. It is power that stems from either implicit or explicit rules.

Liaison role The manager makes contacts outside the vertical chain of command in an effort to bring information into the unit and gain favors from others. The role includes interacting in a network of contacts with peers and others in order to get that information.

Linear programming A mathematical technique for obtaining the optimal solution in situations where the relationships among variables can be expressed as directly proportional (linear) functions. Linearity means that a change in one variable must produce a proportionate change in another, the result being a straight line.

Line authority That relationship in which a supervisor directs a subordinate.

Lobbying A process involving actions taken by individuals or organizations to influence government agencies and federal, state, or local legislation.

Management audit A management audit is a systematic procedure for examining, analyzing, and appraising management's overall performance.

Management by exception Refers to the fact that management attention or control is only provided when something out of the ordinary, "the exception," happens.

Management by objectives (MBO) Management by objectives consists of periodic manager-subordinate meetings designed to accomplish organizational goals by mutual planning of the work, periodic review of accomplishments, and mutual solving of problems that arise in the course of getting the job done.

Management development Training or other processes to improve managers' knowledge and skills to improve managers' performance in present jobs and/or to prepare them for promotion.

Manager A person who works to accomplish the goals of the organization and directly supervises one or more people in a formal organization.

Managerial Grid The Managerial Grid suggests that each manager must be concerned about both production (structure) and people (consideration).

Managerial level Also called the administrative level. This is where the short-term, day-to-day decisions are made.

Matrix organization A device for integrating the activities of different specialists while maintaining specialized organizational units.

Mechanistic organization This type of organization is highly bureaucratic. Tasks are specialized and clearly defined. This type of organization is suitable when markets and technology are well established and show little change over time.

Mentor A person who in essence becomes a teacher, counselor, protector, and spokesperson for another, generally younger, person.

Models Representations of real situations, thoughts, or objects.

Monitor role An informational role in which the manager continually scans the environment to receive and collect information pertinent to the organization or unit he or she manages.

Motivation The conditions responsible for variation in the intensity, quality, and direction of ongoing behavior.

Motivation-hygiene model Describes factors in the work-place that dissatisfy people and factors that motivate them.

Multinational organization A firm having one or more subsidiaries abroad and willing to go worldwide to secure resources and to make sales.

Need hierarchy A model of motivation that describes a hierarchy of needs existing within people. The five need levels are psychological, safety, social, ego, and self-actualization.

Negotiator role The manager discusses and bargains with other units to obtain advantages for his or her own unit.

Noise Any factor that limits or distorts messages in the communications process.

Nominal groups Involves using a group of knowledgeable people who are aware of each other but who do not directly interact while they are working to improve creativity and make better decisions.

Nonverbal communications The transmission of ideas or messages without using words.

Novice phase The beginning stage of early adulthood when major choices are made in areas such as occupation, marriage, and style of living.

Objective probability The long-run frequency of occurrence that can be verified and predicted.

Objectivity Describes the process of collecting information in such a way that personal biases have minimum influence on what is collected.

Official objectives The "general purpose" of the organization. They are used in annual reports and other authoritative pronouncements.

Open systems Systems where the major concerns of management are the transformation of inputs to outputs *and* the environment of the organization.

Operating level This is the core of the organization where the functions are performed that really produce the organization's goods or services.

Operational planning Planning for the first level of the organization where coordination between different units is not necessary.

Operations The processes of transforming inputs into other forms.

Operations research (OR) An application of the scientific method to problems arising in the operations of a system which may be represented by means of a mathematical model and the solving of these problems by resolving the equations representing the system.

Operations technology Includes the tools, mechanical equipment, actions, knowledge, or material used in the production or distribution of a good or service.

Organic organization This type of organization is relatively flexible and relaxed. The organic style is most appropriate to unstable environmental conditions in which novel problems continually occur.

Organization An organization is composed of individuals and groups consisting of human, financial, and other resources existing over time to achieve common goals and objectives by operating as a complex system.

Organization chart A graphic model of a formal organization with two basic purposes: (1) it shows who is accountable to whom (the scalar principle), and (2) it shows, in abbreviated form, who does what in the organization.

Organization development (OD) The application of behavioral science knowledge in a long-range effort to improve an organization's ability to cope with changes in its external environment and increase its internal problem-solving capabilities.

Organizational authority The power to influence, which is granted or conferred on an individual by the organization because of the position he or she is in.

Organizational effectiveness The degree to which a specific organization attains its objectives and goals.

Organizational efficiency The amount of resources used by an organization to produce a unit of output.

Organizational goal An end or a state of affairs the organization seeks to reach.

Organizational norm A norm of the organization tells employees what is the proper way of behaving or the proper code of conduct.

Organizational socialization A process that involves learning not only the role requirements of the job but also the values and behavior norms considered important in the organization.

Organizational structure Refers to the way the parts of the organization are made and how they are connected in order to form a coordinated whole.

Outputs The results of what is transformed by the sys-

tem. Inputs that have been transformed represent outputs ready to leave the system or subsystem.

Outside-inside approach A strategy approach in which managers look first at the environment and then at the organization.

Partial reinforcement The employee is rewarded for correct behavior only part of the time the correct behavior occurs.

Path-goal model This contingency model of leadership defines the relationship between leader behavior and subordinate work attitudes and performance as situational. The essential ingredient of the path-goal model is that the leader smooths the path to work goals and provides rewards for achieving them.

Perceptual screening Personal values influence what the individual sees and hears.

Performance The behavior that a person selects on the job to meet or achieve personal goals.

Performance appraisal A formal written process for periodically evaluating managers' performance.

PERT (Program Evaluation and Review Technique) A way of providing management with an operational network that relates the activities of a project in a time frame, thereby allowing the identification of the project's critical and subcritical stages. PERT is a way to plan programs that have specific objectives and specific, measurable results.

Pivotal group norm A norm to which every member of the group must conform.

Plan Anything that involves selecting a course of action for the future.

Planning Developing in broad outline the things that need to be done and ways of doing them that will accomplish the objectives of the organization.

Politics The use of resources, both physical and human, to achieve more power over others. Politics deals with the methods, approaches, and tactics used to increase power and control.

Pooled interdependence Describes the relationships between units of an organization such that their separate products can be added together to form the total final product.

Positive reinforcement model A model of motivation that involves the use of positive rewards to increase the frequency or probability of the occurrence of the desired performance.

Post-action controls Those which compare results to a standard when the action or task is completed.

Power The ability of a person or group, for whatever reason, to affect another person's or group's ability to achieve its goals (personal or collective).

Power The exercising of influence over others.

Preferences The valuing of some rewards more highly than others and avoiding punishment.

Private sector Types of organizations that are oriented toward profit-making.

Probability theory The likelihood (or odds) of occurrence of uncertain events or environmental states.

Process How the content is handled or discussed by the group.

Process approach to change A focus on how things are done rather than on what is done. It is concerned with such areas as interpersonal interactions, group dynamics, and the relationships among workers and machines.

Process models Motivation models that focus on how managers can change the situation to better tie need satisfaction to performance.

Production control An activity concerned with the timing and routing of any product.

Profit budget A budget that includes expenses and revenue budgets in a single statement.

Profit center A responsibility center given the responsibility for earning a profit (income minus costs).

Profit-maximizing management A theory of business management based solely on the objective of profit maximization.

Programmable decisions Decisions that can be pre-planned because they relate to predictable events.

Promotion A move to another position, usually higher in the organization and usually with an increase in status and pay. Promotion is a reward for accomplishment.

Psychological contract The sum total of what the individual expects to get from the organization and of what the organization expects to get from the individual.

Public sector Types of organizations consisting of federal, state, and local government bodies.

Quality circle is an innovative, small group problem solving approach to management that helps contribute to productivity and quality of work life.

Quality control Concerned with controlling the quality of goods and services provided.

Quality-of-life management A type of management where managers are responsible for enhancing the organization, the society, the environment, and the dignity of employees.

Quality of work life (QWL) This refers to the extent to which the individual's needs and values are satisfied in the workplace. The more that are satisfied, the higher the QWL.

Queuing theory The study of waiting lines or queues to minimize total expected cost.

Ratio analysis An analysis that selects two significant figures from a financial statement and shows their relationship in terms of a ratio or percentage to assess performance of the organization.

Rational decisions Decisions are based primarily on facts and positive data or proof.

Reality shock A situation where the actuality does not agree with the expectations.

Reciprocal interdependence Describes the relationship between units of an organization such that the final

organization product represents the continuous and interactive efforts of the separate units.

Recruitment The process of attracting candidates from either inside or outside the organization who are qualified for and interested in the position.

Relevant group norm Not as central as a pivotal norm; following it is seen as not absolutely essential but considered as worthwhile and desirable.

Required activities The formally assigned tasks that a group must perform.

Required interaction Occurs when a person's activity follows or is influenced by the activity of another; interaction can be verbal or nonverbal.

Resource allocator role The manager decides who will get what resources in the unit. The resources can include time, money, material, equipment, people, and the unit's reputation.

Responsibility Refers to the phenomenon whereby one is given a duty to do and the *obligation* to do it. It is essentially then an obligation.

Responsibility center Denotes any organization or unit that is headed by a manager responsible for that unit.

Return on investment (ROI) A ratio of income over assets employed to produce the income. ROI is a ratio or fraction.

Revenue budget A plan for a future period detailing the projected income for a specific responsibility center.

Revenue center A responsibility center in which income or revenues are recorded.

Reverse discrimination The selection of minority persons or women for jobs or education in place of better qualified whites or men.

Reward power The present or potential ability to award something for worthy behavior.

Role conflict A result of the conflict between managerial expectations and managerial experiences with regard to performance of the role.

Rumor An unconfirmed message passed from person to person.

Satisficing Refers to the criterion of decision making which suggests that the decision made is okay: not the best, but okay.

Scalar principle This principle suggests that authority and responsibility should flow in an unbroken line from the top to the bottom of the organization.

Scenario A contingency plan based upon a specific set of assumptions about the future.

Science of management Observe the separate elements of each task performed. Carefully analyze and redefine the job to develop the "one best way" for all workers. Select and train the workers.

Selection The process of choosing the most qualified person from the available pool of candidates.

Selective perception The tendency to perceive only a part of a message, to screen out other information.

Self-actualization Development of the full potential of

the individual through self-development, creativity, and psychological health.

Self-serving activities Activities that satisfy individual needs at the expense of the group.

Semantics The study of meaning in language.

Sensitivity training A method of helping managers become more sensitive to their effect on others. Managers learn by interaction with other members of their group.

Sentiments The feelings or attitudes a person has about others such as like or dislike and approval or disapproval.

Sequential interdependence Describes the relationship between units of an organization such that the product of one is passed along to the next in order, after which the final product results.

Size The size of an organization usually is measured by the number of people working for the organization in a single location.

Smoothing Dealing with conflict by denying it or avoiding it.

Social responsibility Behavior for the social good beyond the law or common custom demanded.

Social system This is the fifth key element in the systems diagnostic model of organizations. Its two parts are the culture and the social structure.

Society The totality of social relationships among human beings.

Sociotechnical approach This approach is concerned with organizing and matching the technology (work flow and information flow) and the people.

Span of management Refers to the number of employees one supervisor must supervise.

Special interest group A group that attempts to exert influence for one or more specific issues important to its members.

Spokesperson role The manager speaks for the unit and represents it to others. A key concept of the spokesperson role is that of representation. The manager must act as an advocate for subordinates.

Stable environment Little or no unexpected or sudden change; that is, the few product or other changes that do occur generally can be predicted well in advance.

Staff The function of a staff is to do research for and to advise a line manager.

Staffing Identifying, assessing, placing, evaluating, and developing individuals at work by performing such actions as recruiting, selecting, appraising, and promoting individuals.

Standards The units of measurement that serve as reference points against which actual results can be compared.

Steering controls Controls in which results are predicted and corrective action is taken while the operation or task is being performed.

Strategic level Controls the managerial level and mediates between the organization and the broader community served by the organization.

Strategic planning A process that begins with goals and objectives and that creates strategies, policies, and detailed plans, and controls to achieve them.

Strategy Refers to management's actions in counteracting a competitor's strategy and in also deciding what broad goals and objectives the organization wants to attain.

Subjectives probabilities The frequency of occurrence of events which can only be estimated or guessed at.

Subsidiary A company established in a host country by an exporting organization. It is incorporated under the law of the host country.

Subsystem A part of a system. A change in any subsystem has an effect on the total system.

Suprasystem A series of interrelated and interdependent systems.

Synergism This essentially refers to the energy level or size of the end product upon combining two or more previously independent components. For example, $2 + 2 = 5$, if there is synergy between 2 and 2.

System A set of interdependent parts which together make up the whole because each contributes something and receives something from the whole, which in turn is interdependent with the larger environment.

Task accomplishment activities Activities aimed at helping the group accomplish its goals.

Task environment This represents the suppliers, competitors, regulators, and customers of an organization.

Task force A group established to solve a particular problem.

Team building The process of helping a work group become more effective in accomplishing its tasks and in satisfying the needs of group members.

Technology Refers to materials, procedures, and knowledge necessary to transform inputs to outputs.

Termination Action by the organization to remove an individual from the organization.

Theory X Typical Theory X managers believe that people dislike work and will avoid it whenever possible. Such managers feel they themselves are a small, elite group who want to lead and take responsibility but that the larger mass of people want to be directed and to avoid responsibility.

Theory Y Typical Theory Y managers usually assume that people will work hard and assume responsibility provided they can satisfy personal needs and organizational goals at the same time.

Third sector Types of organizations that include voluntary, semi-public, and semi-private organizations (such as private colleges, the Girl Scouts, railroads, voting leagues, and so on).

Tokenism A way of meeting the organization's obligations to affirmative action programs. The token person is usually put in a highly visible or specially created position but has little power or opportunity for advancement.

Top-down approach An approach to strategy where the major decisions are made at the top and transmitted to the bottom of the organization.

Transfer A move to another job, usually without an increase in either status or pay.

Trustee management Refers to the idea that managers

are responsible for/to the claims of stockholders, the broader community, employees, suppliers, and customers, in addition to being responsible for making a profit.

Turbulent environment Many sudden, rapid, and frequently unpredictable product or other changes.

Two faces of power (1) The negative face involves personal domination of others; (2) the positive face involves power being exercised not for personal advancement or benefit but for the good of the organization or society.

Types of departmentation Refers to how or on what basis groups or units in the organization can be divided or broken up.

Types of technology There are three types of technology which vary with the techniques and type of production. These are: (1) unit and small-batch production, (2) mass of large-batch production, and (3) continuous or process production.

Unity of command This principle suggests that no organization member should report to more than one supervisor for any single function.

Unprogrammable decisions Decisions that cannot be preplanned because they relate to unpredictable events.

Value judgment Statements or beliefs based on or reflecting the individual's personal or class values.

Values Relatively permanent ideals (or ideas) that influence and shape the general nature of people's behavior.

Variable costs Expenses that increase as the volume of production increases.

Vertical coordination Describes how the various levels of the organization are tied together or coordinated.

Wider environment This refers to aspects of the organization's environment outside the task environment.

Work overload Describes a situation where someone has too much to do (quantitative overload) or where someone does not have the necessary skills to perform the job (qualitative overload).

Work underload Describes a situation where someone has too little to do (quantitative underload) or where someone has many more skills than necessary to perform the job (qualitative underload).

Yes-no controls Controls that indicate that the work is either acceptable or unacceptable.

INDEX